ISBN 978-0-331-70626-0
PIBN 11062236

REPORT

OF THE

CHIEF QUARTERMASTER, DEPARTMENT OF CUPA,

PERTAINING TO

INSULAR AFFAIRS

FOR THE FISCAL YEAR ENDING JUNE 30th,

1901.

vol 7

HEADQUARTERS DEPARTMENT OF CUBA,

Havana, Cuba, June 30, 1901.

To the Adjutant General, Department of Cuba,

Havana.

SIR:

I have the honor to submit herewith my Annual Report, in connection with Insular Affairs under the supervision of this office for the fiscal year 1901, accompanied by various exhibits and enclosures as set forth herein.

I assumed the duties of this office upon July 24th, 1901, relieving Lt. Colonel Chas. F. Humphrey, Deputy Quartermaster General, United States Army, then under orders to proceed to take station as Chief Quartermaster of the China Relief Expedition.

The duties of this office in connection with Insular matters have been, briefly stated, as follows:

Disbursing Insular Funds:—In payment of Civilian Employees, for the Construction, Care and Illumination of Public Buildings in and about the city of Havana placed under the charge of the Chief Quartermaster, payment of Rentals for Quarters, and for Property occupied for sundry Military Purposes, and for various other objects as directed by the Military Governor.

The Receipt, Distribution and Accounting for School Furniture for the schools of the Island, throughout the Department of Cuba, and the settlement of the accounts of the various contractors, and for various expenses connected therewith.

The Receipt, Issue and Accountability for Insular Property placed under the supervision of the Chief Quartermaster of the Department.

The issuance of Insular Bills of Lading and Transportation Requests, upon due authority, for transporting passengers and freight; and the supervision of transportation matters connected with the administration of the Quartermaster's Department, pertaining to the Insular Establishment, throughout the Department of Cuba.

The operation of, and settlement of matters in connection with, the Triscornia Military Railway.

The supervision of the transfer of the Júcaro and San Fernando Railroad.

Leasing San Ambrosio Hospital, and receiving and accounting for the Revenues therefrom

The general work of construction, and maintenance in good repair of various public buildings in the city of Havana, placed under the supervision of this office.

The purchase and erection of the Ice Plant at Rowell Barracks, near Cienfuegos, Cuba.

The administration of:

Ice Plant, Municipal Hospital No. 1, Havana.

Electric Plant, do

Do Cuarteles de la Fuerza, Machine Shops and Marine Ways, Arsenal.

The drafting and execution of various deeds, contracts, and leases in connection with occupation of buildings and lands, and other matters of similar nature.

Financial Statement.

The Statements of Receipts and Expenditures herewith transmitted, include the operations of this office from the date of my assumption of duty, covering also the receipts and disbursements relating to the accountability of the late Major Geo. S. Cartwright, Acting Chief Quartermaster, Department of Cuba.

Receipts:

From Treasurer of Cuba	$ 318,642.77	
Transfers from Officers	1,293.48	
Collections:		
Repair Work, Arsenal	5,874.48	
Ice Plant, Municipal Hospital No. 1.	3,984 97	
Rental San Ambrosio Hospital	1,272.82	$ 331,068.52

Disbursements:

Public Buildings:			
Illumination	$ 6,002.46		
Repairs	21,717.94		
Construction	14,254.41	$ 41,974.81	
Triscornia Mil. Ry.			
Purchase of lands; rentals; construction, and fencing; ballasting; bridges, etc	96,713.14	$ 96,713.14	
Rentals:			
Quarters and lands for military purposes	15,653.08	15,653.08	
Civilian Employees	40,029.51	40,029.51	
Electric Light and Ice Plants:			
Mun. Hos. No. 1	7,193.62		
La Fuerza	7,420.81	14,614.43	
School Furniture:			
Purchase and h'dl'g		55,086.73	
Miscellaneous Purposes		21,487.52	
Deposited with Treasurer		30.299.70	
Encumbered Balances June 30, 1901		$ 15,209.60	$ 331,068.52

REPORT

SHOWING SCHOOL FURNITURE RECEIVED AND DISTRIBUTED THROUGHOUT THE DEPARTMENT OF CUBA AND THE DISBURSEMENT OF FUNDS EXPENDED IN PAYMENT THEREFOR AND IN SETTLEMENT OF INCIDENTAL EXPENSES CONNECTED WITH THE DISTRIBUTION.

The Report submitted herewith covers the period from January 3, 1900, up to and including June 30, 1901, no report having hitherto been rendered.

On February 19, 1900, a Board was convened in the Office of the Chief Quartermaster, Division of Cuba, for the purpose of opening and recommending award of contracts upon bids submitted to the Chief Quartermaster of the Division, in response to advertisement published in the Official Gazette of January 3, 1900, by General Adna R. Chaffee, Chief of Staff.

Upon the 26th of February, 1900, recommendations were submitted by the Board to the Adjutant General of the Division, for the acceptance of the following bids, which were subsequently approved by the Adjutant General of the Division:

CONTRACTOR	Amt. and Article.	Amt. of Each Article.	Total Amount.
Standard School Furniture Co	15,000 Desks		
	2,500 Rears		$ 58,979.00
J. T. Cavanagh	25,000 Desks		
	4,169 Rears		99,821.40
New Orleans Furniture Co	750 Bookcases		7,401.75
Ward & Huntington	1,500 Hand Bells	$ 780.48	
	750 Bookcases	7,989.40	
	6,000 Strips	1,083.58	9,853.46
G. M. Newhall Engr. Co	39,010 Strips		7,802.00
H. C. Swain	1,500 Chairs		1,825.31
W. F. MacLaughlin	750 Bookcases		8,197.50
B. S. Romero	1,000 Clocks		2,029.90
D. A. Tower	2,000 Clocks		4,500.00
Scarrit Comstock Furniture Co	500 Teachers' Desks		3,700.00
J. L. Hammett Co	700 Teachers' Desks	7,445.99	
	4,000 doz. Erasers	1,632.00	
	3,000 Maps	6,450.00	15,527.99
J. Wanamaker	3,000 Inkwells		487.50
A. H. Andrews Co	15,000 Desks		
	2,500 Rears		63,350.00
Sussdorf, Zaldo & Co.	30,000 Desks		
	5,000 Rears	122,350.00	
	14,990 Strips	3,389.75	
	750 Bookcases	8,687.75	
	1,500 Chairs	1,639.75	136,067.25
Champion & Pascual.	15,000 Desks		
	2,500 Rears		57,282.95
Merle & Heany	500 Teachers' Desks		4,474.00
		Total Awards	$481,300.01

Following this action, various shipments were made, all of which came through the port of New York, with the exception of shipments made by the New Orleans School Furniture Company, through the port of New Orleans, La. The major part of the furniture was distributed through the port of Havana. Other shipments, in more or less volume, were distributed through the ports of Santiago, Matanzas, Sagua la Grande, Cienfuegos, Gibara, Manzanillo, Guantánamo, Baracoa, Nuevitas, Caibarién and Cárdenas. Shipments upon arrival at ports were inspected by Quartermasters, and if in accordance with specifications, inspection certificates were issued in favor of the respective contractors, which were forwarded to the office of the

Chief Quartermaster at Havana, where the necessary vouchers were drawn, and, accompanied by the original bills and inspection certificates, were re-forwarded to the Adjutant General of the Department. Upon approval, checks were issued by the Treasurer of the Island, and all papers returned to the office of the Chief Quartermaster, through which channel checks were finally transmitted to the contractors.

After issuance of the necessary inspection certificates at various ports, the Quartermasters re-packed the furniture in the various quantities allotted to the different municipalities and effected shipment to the Mayors thereof. Receipts in triplicate were furnished each Mayor for signature, one copy being retained by the Quartermaster at the Post and two copies forwarded to the office of the Chief Quartermaster, whence upon proper record, the papers were finally forwarded to the office of the Adjutant General.

In the prosecution of this work, the question of School Furniture has been made a matter of separate record in this office. A proper accounting has been kept of all disbursements effected, whether through the simple transmission of checks or through the disbursement of funds by this office.

Up to and including June 30, 1901, 1,061 communications have been received upon the subject of School Furniture, and 1,393 letters sent.

A large number of the shipments were insecurely packed, causing numerous breakages, and loss of furniture parts, thereby necessitating additional shipments by the contractors. A further complication encountered has been the remoteness of a large number of the municipalities to which distributions were required, and the non-acquaintance of the persons to whom the furniture was delivered with the necessary requirements as to accomplishment of receipts and the verification of quantities, etc., all of which necessitated a large amount of correspondence, and was the cause of frequent unavoidable delays. Notwithstanding the numerous difficulties encountered, attention is invited to the fact that furniture of the total value of $481,300.01 has been distributed, at a total incidental expense of only $3,754.02; and the close of the fiscal year, as shown by the Schedules hereto attached, found all contractors paid, all furniture distributed, and receipts in hand for same, with one or two slight minor exceptions, as follows, to wit:

Shipment to Alcalde of Havana, Invoice No. 74, August 15, 1900. This office is now in correspondence with the Adjutant General upon the subject.

Shipment of one Bookcase to Alcalde of Moron, Puerto Príncipe, Invoice No. 179, April 12, 1901, delay caused by error of Transportation Company in forwarding Bookcase to Moron, Santiago Province.

30 dozen Erasers surplus in excess at Caibarién. Matter in course of adjustment.

The following Schedules are attached, showing in detail all information on this subject:

Schedule "A." Shows samples submitted by bidders and disposition thereof.

Schedule "B." Shows additional expenses incurred in the setting up, handling, storage and transporting of School Furniture.

Schedule "C." Shows the different ports of delivery, amount of articles shipped to different ports by the various contractors; excess in amount of allotment and disposition; excess in amount of contracts and disposition, and balance on hand.

Schedule "D." Shows the different contractors who supplied School Furniture to the Island of Cuba for use in Public Schools, through the Chief Quartermaster of the Department; the total amount and cost of each article; the total amount of contracts for each contractor; the amounts paid and the total award.

Schedule "E." Shows shipments made from surplus in amount of allotment.

Schedule "F." Shows amount of each kind of furniture delivered to the various Municipalities throughout the Island, as allotted by the Superintendent of Schools.

Schedule "G." Shows Miscellaneous School Supplies shipped by the Quartermaster's Department.

SCHEDULE OF SCHOOL FURNITURE ON HAND AT ARSENAL.

1 Bookcase .... (Sample).
1 Bookcase model. ,,
5 School Desks...... ,,
1 Chair .... ,,
1 Board Strip....... ,,
3 Teachers' Desks. ,,
2 Maps .... ,,
1 Eraser............... ,,
2 Clocks............... ,,
1 Inkwell Base..... ,,
1 Inkwell Glass.... ,,
Miscellaneous lot of Desk Parts.

TRANSPORTATION.

During the months of June, July and August, 1900, 1273 school teachers were sent upon U. S. Army Transports from various ports in the Island of Cuba, to the United States, en route to Harvard University, and were returned to their homes by the same means, without personal expense of any kind. The details of this work were arranged by the Quartermaster's Department.

Upon the return voyage of the "Sedgwick," several hundred female teachers were taken on board at Boston, and cared for while making side trips, en route to Havana. During this period, with table accommodations for only about eighty persons, it was necessary to work the Steward's Department of the "Sedgwick" for about twenty hours consecutively during every day of the trip. Not a single complaint of inattention to the wants of any of these teachers, nor a single instance of the loss of any of their effects appears recorded in connection with the entire excursion. The adaptability of the transport service, as then maintained, for meeting even this unique emergency, and the zeal and efficiency of its personnel, were fully equal to the requirements of this excursion, and I avail myself of the opportunity to place same upon record.

The transportation division of this office issues bills of lading for the school furniture delivered to this department by contractors, for such other freight as may be purchased by disbursing officers of Insular Funds, for Ordnance and Ordnance Stores invoiced to rural guards, and in other special instances. Passenger transportation upon insular requests is issued to all persons presenting orders therefor. The resources of this office have at all times been available, in an advisory capacity, to those handling the transportation branch of the office of the Treasurer of Cuba.

The Quartermaster's Department has frequently been called upon to perfect arrangements for receiving, shipping and distributing Insular property throughout the Island. Throughout the handling of vast quantities of Insular property and their re-shipments to remote points, notably with respect to school furniture, not a single instance of loss chargeable to the Quartermaster's Department, or any of its employees, has occurred.

During the fiscal year ending June 30, 1901, there was handled at this port by this office, exclusive of the quantities moved on Triscornia Military Railway, insular property and stores to the amount of 4,002,394 lbs.

Triscornia Military Railway:

The original purpose for which the Triscornia Military Railway was built was with a view to receiving troops from transports, and conveying them to camp grounds without involving their transit through the city of Havana, and to provide for the transmission of supplies and subsistence for these troops without transporting such materials through districts supposed to be infected with yellow fever. The road was built upon the recommendation of a Board of Officers which assembled in Havana late in 1898, of which Colonel J. G. C. Lee, U. S. A., was president. The cost of the road was great, but necessarily so from the standpoint of the Military necessities then existing. During the closing fiscal year all claims outstanding in connection with this property have been brought to an amicable adjustment, except parcel 13, papers in connection with which have been forwarded for action of the Military Governor, the owner refusing to entertain the offer recommended by a Board of Officers hitherto convened in this connection as being a fair valuation for his property. The terminal facilities afforded by the property are suitable. The property comprising the water front is at present under lease from Viuda de Carreras, with an option permitting purchase by the Government. The cost of maintaining the railroad has been defrayed by the Insular Government, while the expenses of operation have been a charge against the U. S. Quartermaster's Department. During the year the only freight moved over the road has been forage, wood, and materials for construction purposes.

On account of the reduced volume of freight now being transmitted it is recommended that the operation of the road by the Quartermaster's Department be abandoned, and that freight hitherto shipped via Triscornia be sent direct to the Arsenal for transfer to ultimate destination by means of wagon transportation, or local railway service. It is not believed that the reduced amount of traffic over the railway warrants the further continuance of its operation by the Quartermaster's Department.

Júcaro and San Fernando Railway:

On January 24th, 1901, by direction of the Military Governor this office entered into a lease with the Cuba Company whereby the said railway was leased for the term of three years, it being optional with the Government, however, to cancel said lease without previous notice and re-enter possession of the property and terminals immediately in case of any military necessity, or other emergency demanding, in the opinion of the Military Government, the resumption of the use and operation of the property by the authorities.

By the terms of this lease, the Cuba Company obligated itself to erect at Júcaro a wharf of the approximate valuation of $25,000, in accordance with certain agreed-upon specifications; said wharf to become the property of the Government upon the termination of three years' occupation of the property by the Cuba Company.

In further stipulation it was also agreed that all freight and passengers should be transported free of charge for account of the Government as required; that a satisfactory service and reasonable rates should be maintained, and that the entire property should be kept in as good a condition throughout as when received, and so delivered upon expiration or suspension of the agreement.

In turning the railway over, careful inventories were taken, showing all property of every description pertaining to the road, and such inventories, accompanied by sundry photographs, formed a part of the agreement; copies of said inventory being filed with the other papers in the office of the official notary.

An appendix is attached showing the operations of the Júcaro and San Fernando Railroad for the period July 1st, 1900, to January 31st, 1901, upon which date its operation by the Government ceased. (Exhibit "H.")

CARE OF PUBLIC BUILDINGS, GENERAL CONSTRUCTION, AND REPAIR AND RENTALS:

The buildings which have been placed under the charge of the Chief Quartermaster for maintenance and repair, are:

Governor General's Palace.
Palacio del Segundo Cabo.
Tacón No. 1.

Maestranza Building.
Castillo del Príncipe.
Arsenal:
Buildings (Quarters, etc.)
Shops.
Warehouses.
La Punta, Commissary Depot.
Headquarters Stables, Zulueta and La Punta.
Chief Quartermaster's Corral, Príncipe.
Quinta de los Molinos.
Electric Light Plant, La Fuerza.
Electric Light and Ice Plant, Municipal Hospital No. 1.

Other work of similar character has been carried out from time to time, as directed by the Military Governor.

During the fiscal year the buildings mentioned have received the necessary care as required; sundry sets of quarters for officers have been overhauled, repainted, whitewashed, and the necessary sanitary appliances placed in various buildings and quarters not hitherto so supplied. The two palace buildings have been entirely repainted within and without, at a moderate cost and in a creditable manner.

Practically no work of original construction was performed by this office during the year, with the exception of Observation Station, Morro Castle, upon which an expenditure of $352.02 was made, and the installation of a sanitary sewerage system and necessary baths and closets at Cabaña Barracks, which work is practically completed at the close of the year, at a total expenditure of $6,546.13, to date.

During the year the fencing of the right of way, and construction of engine house at Triscornia, in connection with the Triscornia Military Railway, were completed. This work was begun during the administration of my predecessor, Lt. Colonel Humphrey, under contract with the Manhattan Contracting Company.

The sum of $21,717.94 was expended during the fiscal year under the supervision of the Chief Quartermaster, for the purpose of repairs to public buildings, paid out under approval of the Military Governor, in the city of Havana.

The payments by this office during the past fiscal year for rentals of buildings and grounds, occupied for military and other Governmental purposes, were $69,856.86.

Under instructions of the Military Governor, this office leased to the R. B. Lyon Company for tobacco and general warehouse purposes, the ground floor of the public building known as San Ambrosio Hospital. The building was finally accepted by tenant, and the lease became effective in full, on April 23rd, 1901.

A list is attached hereto showing all premises owned, leased and occupied by the Government for Military and Civil purposes, placed under the supervision of the Quartermaster's Department, throughout the Department of Cuba. (Ex. I.)

Blue Prints are separately transmitted, showing premises occupied at the various posts and stations.

A list of formal contracts and civil leases executed under the supervision of this office during the year is attached hereto. (Exhibits J. and K.)

CONSTRUCTION OF ICE PLANT FOR ROWELL BARRACKS.

Under instructions from the Military Governor contained in endorsement dated October 10, 1900 (No. 5005, Civil File 1900, Headquarters Div. of Cuba), this office entered into a contract with the York Manufacturing Company, of York, Pa., and New York City, for the delivery on board vessel at New York City of one (1) three (3) ton ice plant complete, for Rowell Barracks, at a cost of $5,250.00; the said plant to be brought by transport to destination.

The plant was duly constructed and delivered on board the Transport "Rawlins," scheduled to sail from New York City on April 10th. The vessel, however, caught fire at the pier and was sunk to prevent total destruction. The machinery of the plant was consequently injured and had to be returned to the manufacturers for necessary repair on account of heat and submersion undergone.

The plant was re-shipped to New York, and finally loaded upon Transport "Sedgwick," departing May 10th, en route for Cienfuegos.

At the close of the fiscal year the erection of the plant is practically complete; the expenditures to date being $4,109.71, on account of construction work, installation, cost of labor, material, etc.

When in operation the plant should furnish for use of the troops stationed at Rowell Barracks, all the ice required, at reasonable cost.

ELECTRIC LIGHT AND ICE PLANT, MUNICIPAL HOSPITAL NO. 1.

During the fiscal year 1901, the operations of the Electric Light Plant and Ice Plants at Municipal Hospital No. 1 have been satisfactory in all respects. At the close of the fiscal year, both plants are in most excellent condition.

The operations of these plants are carried on under contract with Mr. F. Bennett, at the contract rate of $60 per day. This rate covers all expenses except material for installation purposes and light furnished during daylight hours.

According to contract rate, and as per payments for supplies, etc., made by this office, the statement for the year is as follows:

REVENUES.

Ice Plant.

The output of ice, July, 1900, to January, 1901, inclusive, was as follows:

July,	1900	462,710 lbs.
August,	,,	451,115 ,,

September,	1900	442,790	lbs.
October,	,,	496,200	,,
November,	,,	461,425	,,
December,	,,	386,625	,,
January,	1901	360,410	,,

A total of 3,061,265 lbs., at 30 cents per 100=$9,183.79.

On February 1, 1901, the matter of distribution and collection for ice was, by orders of the Military Governor, placed under supervision of this office, and the price was reduced to 25 cents per 100 lbs. The production since that date has been as follows:

February,	1901	326,300	lbs.
March,	,,	383,860	,,
April,	,,	422,650	,,
May,	,,	461,175	,,
June,	,,	529,478	,,

A total of 2,123,463 lbs., at 25 cents per 100=$5,308.66, showing a total output and revenue of 5,184,728 lbs., $14,492.45.

THE ELECTRIC LIGHT PLANT.

Furnished illumination for the Pirotecnia, Castillo del Príncipe and for Municipal Hospital No. 1, giving all-night service in order to afford all-night lighting where required, as follows, to wit:

MUNICIPAL HOSPITAL NO. 1.

10 Arc Lights, 1,000 C. P. each, and 950 Incandescent Lamps.

CASTILLO DEL PRINCIPE.

160 Incandescent Lamps.

PIROTECNIA MILITAR.

160 Incandescent Lamps.

A total of 1,270 Incandescent Lamps and 10 Arc Lights 1,000 C. P. each.

The Plant furnished during the year an average of 2,230 ampere hours in every twenty-four hours' lighting, of the commercial value, at regular rates of.................... $ 24,631.20

Less 5% reduction, allowed by Commercial Cos... 1,231.56

Net Commercial value of lighting...... .... $ 23,399.64

GENERAL STATEMENT.

The total actual revenue and value of services derived as above from the operations of the two Plants was as follows:

Ice Plant......	$ 14,492.45
Electric Light Plant	23,399.64
Total...	$ 37,892.09

The total expenses of operation were as follows:

F. Bennett, Contractor, 365 days at $60.00..........	$ 21,900.00	
For extra lights during day light hours	28.50	
For materials and supplies for installations and extensions.........	113.96	22,042.46
Balance, net savings......		$ 15,849.63

In addition to furnishing electric lights and ice, the Plant at Municipal Hospital No. 1 furnishes hot water required for Hospital purposes, and the necessary facilities for operation of the Hospital Laundry.

STATEMENT OF ELECTRIC PLANT CUARTELES DE LA FUERZA, FISCAL YEAR 1901.

This Plant was installed by the Department of Engineers. It was constructed from Insular Funds, and was turned over by direction of the Military Governor to the Quartermaster's Department, on September 1, 1900, to be operated in the electric lighting of the two Palaces, which were at first the only buildings lighted.

Subsequently, incandescent lights were installed throughout the Post Office Building, and in the Office of the Captain of the Port. Four arc lights were also installed on Caballeria Wharf, at the request of the Customs Department.

During the period since its installation, some alterations and betterments were found necessary, in order to put the plant in thorough running order.

The entire operating time is five months to June 30th.

The lights now furnished are as follows:

	Incandescent.	Arc.
Governor General's Palace....................................	695	......
Lieut. Governor's Palace......................................	378	......
Post Office Department, Post Office Building....	214	3
Post Office Building, 3rd Floor, Quarters................	64	......
Office Captain of the Port......................................	180	......
Caballeria Wharf...	1	4
A total of........................	1,532	7

FINANCIAL STATEMENT. REVENUE.

The value of service furnished on the basis of the average ampere hours per day of 24 hours, shows lighting furnished on the commercial value per month at regular rates of...	$ 1,721.40
Less 5% discount...	86.07
Net average value per month...............	$ 1,635.33

EXPENDITURES.

Operating:			
Civilian Employees..........	$3,806.67		
Coal..................................	1,335.75		
Oil, Waste, etc.................	530.14		
Total operating expense......		$5,672.56	
Maintenance:			
Electrical Supplies, Wire, Lamps, Sockets, etc......	$1,048.01		
Deduct supplies on hand unused...........................	663.48		
Total Maintenance......................		384.53	
Total expense Operating and Maintenance...			$6,057.09
Total Revenue, 5 mos. of actual operation..........	$8,607.00		
Total expenditure Sept. 1, 1900, to June 30, 1901: Operation & Maintennce.	6,057.09		
Net saving of service........	$2,549.91		
Permanent Improvements and Betterments:			
Installation Office Captain of Port and Post Office..	$ 301.23		
Tools, Machinery and Equipment.....................	839.76		
Purchased during period, not paid for, Tools, etc.	400.00		
Total permanent Betterments and new installation.........................		....	$1,540.99

Total Expenditure account Electric Light Plant La Fuerza, Sept. 1, 1900, to June 30, 1901....................	$7,598.08

Installation is now being effected in the Building Tacón No. 1, (175 Incandescent Lamps), and the same can be extended to other public buildings in the near neighborhood of the Plant with comparatively slight additions to the facilities at present provided.

STATEMENT OF WORK PERFORMED AT ARSENAL SHOPS, HAVANA, CUBA, FOR THE FISCAL YEAR 1901, FOR ACCOUNT OF THE INSULAR GOVERNMENT OF THE ISLAND OF CUBA, SHOWING BRIEFLY THE WORK DONE, THE COST OF LABOR AND MATERIALS, AND THE APPROXIMATE EXPENSE WHICH WOULD HAVE BEEN INCURRED BY THE INSULAR GOVERNMENT IF PAID FOR AT COMMERCIAL RATES.

	Value of Repairs Performed if paid for at Commercial Rates.
Immediately subsequent to the placing of the Arsenal Shops under the supervision of the Chief Quartermaster, the work of thoroughly overhauling all the various shops, including engines, boilers, smokestacks, all wood-working machinery, lathes, pulleys, belting, turntables, railway tracks, hoisting gear, etc., was performed, and all tools and machinery of every description were placed in thoroughly serviceable condition..........	$ 3,803.54
The Marine Railway and the Cradle, machinery and appurtenances have been repaired or entirely renewed during the year, representing a work of the value at commercial rates, including labor and material, of.......	$ 6,260.00

The regular force at the Arsenal Shops was found sufficient, with slight additional help, for the performance of the work of rehabilitating the Arsenal Shops and thoroughly repairing and renewing the Marine Railway, as above shown.

The following vessels pertaining to the Insular Service have been docked on the Marine Railway at the Arsenal, during the fiscal year, for the performance of the necessary repairs, in the order as noted, payment for which has been made from Insular Funds:

Launch	"Percy"..................	Immigration Bureau.
,,	"Fessenden"......	Marine Hospital Service.
	"Waldo".........	,, ,, ,,
,,	"Percy".....	Immigration Bureau.
,,	"No. 3"	Customs Service.
Tug	"Waban".........	U. S. Naval Station.
Launch	"No. 7"........................ ..	Customs Service.
,,	"No. 6".....	,,
Tug	"Percy"	Immigration Bureau.
Launch	"Swift"	Customs Service.
Revenue Cutter	"Alacran"...............	,,
Launch	"Evangelina"........	,,
Launch	"No. 6"........	Customs Service.
Revenue Cutter	"Baracoa"	,,
Launch	"No. 2"................	

Revenue Cutter	"Expreso Cubano".....	Customs Service.
Launch	"No. 7"	,,
,,	"Swift".....................	,,
,,	"Percy"	Immigration Bureau.
,,	"Josephine"	Post Office Department.
Revenue Cutter	"Alacran"	Customs Service.
Launch	"Percy"....	Immigration Bureau.
,,	"Evangelina"	Customs Service.
,,	"Swift.".........................	,,
,,	"No. 2."..	
,,	"No. 3."...........	
,,	"No. 6."...................	
,,	"No. 7."............................ ..	,,
,,	"No. 3."............................	,,
Tug	"Narciso Deulofeu."...........	Engineer Department.
Dredge	"Comercio."	,,
Scow	"A."	,,
,,	"B."	,,
Revenue Cutter	"Abeja."................	Customs Service.
Scow	"C."...........	Engineer Department.
,,	"D."............................. .	,,
Launch	"No. 6."....	Customs Service.

These vessels have been thoroughly overhauled and the necessary repairs furnished, in a number of instances involving the scraping and re-painting of the vessel and the entire renewal of portions of, and thorough overhauling of all the machinery.

In addition to the work above mentioned, various items of original and repair work have been performed, in connection with repairs to public buildings in the city of Havana; also certain work required at:

Cabaña Barracks,
Santa Clara Battery,
Ordnance Depot,
Signal Corps,
Principe Depot,

and sundry other items of general repair and mechanical work, insignificant as to separate items, but reaching a considerable aggregate volume, when considered for a year.

All work performed at the Arsenal Shops, for any of the branches of the Insular Service, has been charged for at the actual cost of material and labor, and the amount expended re-imbursed this office by the Department to which pertaining. The funds thus received have been covered into the Insular Treasury under the appropriations to which belonging in each case.

Respectfully submitted:

CHAUNCEY B. BAKER,

Major and Quartermaster, U. S. Vols.,

Chief Quartermaster, Dept. of Cuba.

LIST OF BLUE PRINTS

OF

POST MAPS, DEPARTMENT OF CUBA.

IN CONNECTION WITH ANNUAL REPORT OF CHAUNCEY B. BAKER, MAJOR AND QUARTERMASTER, U. S. V., CHIEF QUARTERMASTER, DEPARTMENT OF CUBA, JUNE 30TH, 1901, COMPRISING THE FOLLOWING POINTS:

Havana and vicinity:

Columbia Barracks, (2)
Artillery Headquarters, Vedado,
Batteries 3, 4, 5 and Santa Clara,
Pirotecnia Militar,
Artillery Corral, Vedado,
Morro Castle and Cabaña,
Cabaña Barracks,
Cabaña Hospital,

Cienfuegos, (3)
Rowell Barracks,
Manzanillo, (3)
Bayamo,
Cauto,
Santiago de Cuba, (7)
Morro Castle, Santiago,
Guantánamo,
Baracoa,
Holguín,
Gibara,
Nuevitas, (2)
Puerto Príncipe,
Camp R. S. Mackenzie, (2)
Ciego de Avila, (2)
Matanzas, (2)

And arranged in the following order on account of their size:

Cauto........................	Property occupied by Q. M. Dept.
Gibara............	Q. M. Warehouse.
Nuevitas....................	Offices.
,, ...	Q. M. Warehouse.
Guantánamo.........	Map of Post.
Baracoa	Barracks and Corral.
Pirotecnia Militar........	General Plan.
Manzanillo	Map of City.
,, ...	Q. M. Corral.
,, ...	Map of Post.
Bayamo..	Barracks, Hospital, Headquarters and Q. M. Corral.

Vedado	2nd Artillery Corral.
,, ...	Artillery Headquarters.
Ciego de Avila...........	City and property, small map.
,, ,, ,, ...	,, ,, ,, large ,,
Cabaña and Morro......	General Map.
Cabaña Barracks........	Hospital.
,, ,, ...	Map of Post.
Santiago de Cuba........	Warehouse at R. R. track.
,, ...	Administration Building.
....	Office of Ocean Transportation.
....	Warehouse No. 2.
....	Corral.
,, ...	Palace.
,, ...	Depot Q. M. Warehouse.
Morro Castle, Santiago.	Map of Roads, etc.
Puerto Príncipe..... ...	Leased Lands.
,, ...	District Headquarters.
,, ...	Disbursing Q. M. Office, etc.
,, ...	Q. M. Warehouse.
,, ...	Property "San Antonio."
,, ...	Cuban Warehouse.
Camp R. S. Mackenzie.	Map of Post (Agramonte.)
,, ..	,, ,, ,, (Capt. Flynn.)
Matanzas................	Military Reservation.
,, ...	Hamilton Barracks.
Cienfuegos	Forage Warehouse.
,, ...	Warehouse and dock.
,, ...	Proposed drill ground.
Rowell Barracks..	Map of Post and vicinity.
Holguín	Corrals, etc.
,, ...	Map of City, showing rented properties.
Battery No. 5...........	Officers' Quarters.
,, ,, 5...........	Map of Battery.
,, ,, 4...........	,, ,, ,,
,, ,, 3...........	,, ,, ,,
Santa Clara Battery....	,, ,, ,,
Columbia Barracks......	Small property map.
,, ...	Map of Post.

SCHEDULE "A."

SAMPLES SUBMITTED BY BIDDERS AND THE DISPOSITION THEREOF.

BIDDER.	Amount.	ARTICLE.	DISPOSITION.
W. F. McLaughlin	1	Bookcase	At Arsenal, Havana.
Ward & Huntington	1	Bookcase	To bidder.
Sussdorf, Zaldo & Co	1	Model bookcase	To bidder.
	1	School desk	To bidder.
	2	Chairs	To bidder.
	1	Board strip	At Arsenal, Havana.
Ward & Huntington	1	Hand bell	To bidder.
New Orleans Furniture Co	1	Model bookcase	At Arsenal, Havana.
J. L. Hammett Co	1	Teacher's desk	At Arsenal, Havana.
		Maps, world	At Arsenal, Havana.
		Blackboard eraser	At Arsenal, Havana.
Merle & Heaney		Teacher's desk	At Arsenal, Havana.
J. T. Cavanagh		School desks	To bidder.
Champion & Pascual		School desks	At Arsenal, Havana.
Standard School Furnishing Co.		School desk	At Arsenal, Havana.
A. H. Andrews Co		School desk	At Arsenal, Havana.
H. C. Swain		Chair	At Arsenal, Havana.
B. S. Romero		Clock	At Arsenal, Havana.
D. A. Tower		Clock	At Arsenal, Havana.
John Wanamaker		Inkstand base	At Arsenal, Havana.
Ward & Huntington		Inkwell glass	At Arsenal, Havana.
D. P. Elejalde		Teacher's desk	At Arsenal, Havana.
Ruiz Bros		Bell	To bidder.
		Inkstands	To bidder.
		Erasers	To bidder.
J. M. Sauder		School Desks	To Lt. E. C. Brooks.
		Chair seats	To Lt. E. C. Brooks.
Wright & Co		Bookcase	No record.
W. F. McLaughlin		Clocks	To bidder.
		School desk	To bidder.
		Rear seat	To bidder.
		Eraser	To bidder.
		Board strips	To bidder.
Rivorosa & Fernández		Samples	To bidder.
H. C. Swain		Samples	To bidder.
F. B. Benitez		Samples	To bidder.
Nieto & Co		Samples	To R. S. G. Gerente.
E. Hiller & Co		Samples	To R. S. G. Gerente.
G. M. Newhall		Bookcase	To bidder.
B. S. Romero		Clocks	To bidder.
		Map	To bidder.
		Eraser	To bidder.
		Model bookcase	To bidder.
Colton, Ohman & Co		Maps	To bidder.
Old Dominion Paper Co		Inkstands	No record.
		Erasers	No record.
Heywood Bros		Set Photos	To bidder.
Atwater & Small		Bell	No record.
		Inkstands	No record.
Manhattan Supply Co		Bookcase	To E. P. Elejalde & Co.
		Teacher's Desk	"
		School Desk	
		Rear seat	
		Chairs	
		Clocks	
		Bell	
		Inkstands	
		Erasers	
		Strip	

SCHEDULE "B."

Additional expenses incurred in storage, setting up, handling and transporting school furniture.

NAME.	PLACE.	PURPOSE.	Amount of bill and amount paid.
José Muñiz	Havana	Wharfage	$ 22.94
Planiol y Cagiga	Batabanó	Lumber	17.00
M. Requiera	Batabanó	Setting up	10.00
R. Requiera	Batabanó	Setting up	10.00
E. Menier	Batabanó	Setting up	10.00
L. Menier	Batabanó	Setting up	2.00
R. Ramírez	Batabanó	Setting up	10.00
C. Méndez	Cienfuegos	Lighterage	676.73
F. Soler y Pichas	Trinidad	Hauling	57.20
Jesús Arias	Manzanillo	Labor	32.00
M. Gutiérrez	Sancti Spíritus	Labor	391.00
M. Gutiérrez	Sancti Spíritus	Labor	138.00
M. Gutiérrez	Sancti Spíritus	Hauling	96.00
M. Gutiérrez	Sancti Spíritus	Hauling	9.00
J. Gurart	Matanzas	Storage	87.19
J. Vargas	Caibarién	Labor	1.15
M. García	Cienfuegos	Hauling	27.00
Wm. Iness	Sagua la Grande	Reimbursement	.91
Wm. Iness	Sagua la Grande	Reimbursement	3.72
A. Tabares	Sagua la Grande	Labor	9.00
J. Rodríguez	Sagua la Grande	Labor	5.00
J. Arias	Manzanillo	Setting up	54.00
V. Vía	Havana	Hauling	196.00
Wm. Iness	Havana	Subsistence, travel	35.50
F. M. Ruz	Havana	Subsistence, travel	35.00
F A. Hawker	Havana	Salary, Arsenal	75.00
L. Vega	Caibarién	Rent, storage	11.47
L. Vega	Caibarién	Rent, storage	3.04
Pay roll	Havana	Handling, Arsenal	86.50
V. Vía	Havana	Transportation	217.00
B. Cárdenas	Havana	Handling	1.20
Pay roll	Havana	Handling, Arsenal	60.00
V. Vía	Havana	Transportation	63.00
V. Vía	Havana	Transportation	98.00
Pay roll	Caibarién	Handling	66.00
Pay roll	Havana	Handling, Arsenal	135.00
Pay roll	Havana	Handling, Arsenal	64.20
Cuban Central R. R.	Cienfuegos	Switching	12.50
Martínez & Co	Caibarién	Storage	114.69
Sobrinos de Herrera	Caibarién	Storage	73.31
Beattie & Co	Manzanillo	Wharfage	3.25
Beattie & Co	Manzanillo	Handling, wharfage	3.12
Pay roll	Havana	Handling, Arsenal	110.00
Pay roll	Havana	Handling, Arsenal	13.50
Pay roll	Havana	Handling, Arsenal	22.30
Pay roll	Havana	Handling, Arsenal	29.90
W. D. Brown	Havana	Stamps, rubber	6.40
Pay roll	Havana	Handling, Arsenal	12.00
M. B. Stokes	Supt. Frye	Pilotage	14.00
Pay roll	Caibarién	Handling	61.00
Pay roll	Havana	Handling, Arsenal	8.80
Pay roll	Caibarién	Handling	104.50
V. Vía	Havana	Transportation	98.00
V. Vía	Havana	Cartage	7.00
V. Vía	Guayabal	Cartage	7.00
V. Vía	Havana	Cartage	7.00
E. Cenia	Caibarién	Storage	100.00
M. Cortina	Pinar del Rio	Transportation	109.00

Showing Ports,*s: excess in amount of allot*

Municipali *sition of same and Balance o*

PORT.	CO	ION.	BALANCE ON HAND.	REMA
Havana	J. L. Hi			
	"			
	"			
	B. S. R		296	At Arsenal.
	W. F.		296	At Arsenal.
	Merle &			
	G. M. N			
	New O		22	Shortage made up b
	Sussdo		111	At Arsenal.
			74	At Arsenal.
			Desk parts	At Arsenal.
	J. Wan		Rear parts	At Arsenal.
	Ward &	f Schools.		
	H. C. S			
	D. A. T			
	H. C. Sw			
	J. L. Ha			
	New Or			
	G. M. N			
	Merle &			
Guantánamo	W. F. M			
	J. L. Ha			
	Champ			
	H. C. S			
	D. A. T			
	Sussdo			
Gibara	Sussdo			
	Ward			
	D. A. T			
	J. T. C			
	J. L. H			
	Scarrit			
Caibarién	Standa			
	J. L. H		Parts	At Arsenal.
			Parts	At Arsenal.
	Sussdo			
	D. A. T			
	Ward			

SCHEDULE "D."

Showing Contractors, Articles and Amount of Articles and Total Amount of Contracts for Furnishing School Furniture and Supplies to the Island of Cuba as per contracts dated March 8th, 1900, with the Chief Quartermaster of the Division of Cuba, Havana, Cuba.

CONTRACTOR.	TOTAL AMOUNT.	ARTICLE.	Total Amount Each Article	Amount of Contracts and Paid
Standad School Furnishing Co.	17.500	School desks	$ 58,979.00	$ 58,979.00
J. T. Cavanagh	29,169	School desks	99,821.40	99,821.40
New Orleans Furniture Co	750	Bookcases	7,401.75	7,401.75
Ward & Huntington	1,500	Hand [illegible]ells	780.48	
	6,000	Board strips	1,083.58	
	750	Bookcases	7,989.40	9,853.46
Geo. M. Newhall Engineering Co.	39,010	Board strips	7,802.00	7,802.00
H. C. Swain & Son.	1,500	Office chairs	1,825.31	1,825.31
W. F. McLaughlin	750	Bookcases	8, 1?7.50	8,197.50
B. S. Romero	1,000	Clocks	2,029.90	2,029.90
D. A. Tower.	2, 00	Clocks	4,500.00	4,500.00
Scarritt Comstock Furniture Co.	500	Teachers' desks	3,700.00	3,700.00
J. L. Hammett Co.	1,000	Teachers' desks	7,445.99	
	4, 00	B. B. erasers	1,632.00	
	3, 00	Wall maps	6,450.00	15,527.99
John Wanamaker	3,000	Ink wells	487.50	487.50
A. H. Andrews Co.	17,500	[illegible]ol desks	63,350.00	63,350.00
Sussdorf, Zaldo & Co.	35, 00	School desks	122,350.00	
	1,500	Bentwood chairs	1,639.75	
	14,990	Board strips	3,389.75	
	750	Bookcases	8,687.75	136,067.25
Champion & Pascual	17,500	School desks	57, 282.95	57,282.95
Merle & Heaney	500	[illegible]hers' desks	4,474.00	4,474.00
		TOTAL AWARDS		$481,300.01
		Additional expenses (Schedule "B")		3,754.02
		TOTAL EXPENDITURE		$485,054.03

SCHEDULE "E."

Shipments made from Surplus in Amount of Allotment Distinct from Original Shipments.

SHIPPED TO	Book Cases.	Board Strips.	Clocks.	Maps.	Chairs, Wood.	Chairs, Cane.	Erasers, Dozens	REMARKS.
Mrs. Brooks, Guantánamo	2							
Anderson, Caibarién		2						
Commissioner of Schools	6		1	1				
Esperanza	1				12			
Perico	5			5				
Sabanilla	1				6			
San Nicolás	1				12			
Guanajay.	1				12			
Guanajay	1				6			
Puerto Príncipe	1				6			
Santa Clara	2				12			
Mariel	1							
Supt. of Schools	2							
Major Greble				11				
Unión de Reyes	1				8			
Matanzas					2			
Mantua	6		6	6	6			
Commissioner of Schools							60	Rec'd from Gibara.
Mantua	1				2			
Morón	1							
San Antonio de las Vegas	1							
Camajuaní	1				6			
Guanes	6				12			
Commissioner of Schools	1							
San Felipe	1							
Calabazar								8 No. 3 School Desks, made up from broken parts.
Supt. of Schools	1							
Santiago de las Vegas	2				12			
Regla	1				12			
Supt. of Schools	1				6			
Macagua	1				6			
Guanes	1							
Pinar del Río	6							
Ciego de Avila	20					24		
Consolación del Norte	6					5		
Guayabal	3				2			
Cabañas	5					5		
Morón	1							
Matanzas	2					12		
Ceja de Pablo	1					6		
Agramonte	2					12		
Matanzas	1							
Guayabal						6		
Havana	2					12		
San Antonio de los Baños	1					12		
Trinidad	1		1			6		

SHIPPED TO.		Board Strips.	Clocks.	Maps.	Chairs, Wood.	Chairs, Cane.	Erasers, Dozens.	REMARKS.
Bainoa	1					6		
Guanajay	1							
Bolondrón	1					9		
Santiago de las Vegas								Miscellaneous desk parts.
Macagua	1					3		
Commissioner of Schools							624	Surplus at Havana.
Campechuela	1							
Trinidad	2							
San Fernandode Camarones	4		4					
Alquízar	1					12		
Isl. Supt. of Schools	1							
Prov. Supt. of Schools	2							
Cifuentes	1					9		
Santo Domingo	1							
Bejucal	1					36		
Guamacaro			4					
Bayamo	2							
Nuevitas	2							
Abreus	6							
Guanabacoa	2							
Vereda Nueva	1							
Cifuentes			1					
San Luis	1					4		

SCHEDULE "F."

Showing Amount of each kind of furniture delivered to the various Municipalities as allotted by Superintendent of Schools, A. E. Frye.

PORT.	MUNICIPALITY.	School Desks. No. I.	School Desks. No. II.	School Desks. No. III.	Rear Seats. No. I.	Rear Seats. No. II.	Rear Seats. No. III.	Board Strips.	Teachers' Desks.	Bookcases.	Maps.	Clocks.	Chairs. Wood.	Chairs. Cane.	Erasers Doz.	Ink wells.	Hand Bells.
Matanzas	Bolondrón	100	200	200	20	30	30	300	15	15	15	15	15	......	15		
	Cabezas	70	130	130	10	25	20	198	......	9	9	9	9	......	9		
	Canasí	30	60	60	5	10	10	90	......	5	5	5	5	......	5		
	Jagüey Grande	130	295	295	25	50	45	432	18	18	18	18	18	......	18		
	Macurijes	180	360	360	30	60	60	540	19	19	19	19	19	......	19		
	Matanzas	1,250	2,475	2,475	205	405	420	3,720	140	153	153	153	153	......	153		
	Sabanilla	70	130	130	10	25	20	198	......	8	8	8	8	......	8		
	Santa Ana	40	80	80	5	15	15	120	......	5	5	5	5	......	5		
	Unión de Reyes	60	130	130	10	20	20	102	......	8	8	8	8	......	8		
Santiago	Caney	35	75	70	5	15	10	108	......	5	5	5	......	5	5		
	Cobre	25	50	55	5	10	10	78	......	4	4	4	......	4	4		
	Cristo	30	60	60	5	10	10	90	......	4	4	4	......	4	4		
	San Luis	120	240	240	20	40	40	360	15	15	15	15	......	15	15		
	Santiago	660	1,270	1,270	115	205	210	1,920	100	100	100	100	......	100	100		
	Songo	......	50	50	......	10	10	60	......	2	2	2	......	2	2		
Cienfuegos	Abreus	70	190	190	10	25	25	210	......	11	11	11	......	11	11		
	Cienfuegos	720	1,440	1,440	120	242	242	2,160	90	90	90	90	......	90	90		
	Cruces	160	320	320	25	55	50	480	20	20	20	20	......	20	20		
	Palmira	130	265	265	20	45	45	396	25	25	25	25	......	25	25		
	Ranchuelo	140	280	280	25	45	50	420	17	17	17	17	......	17	17		
	Rodas	200	365	375	35	70	65	612	40	40	40	40	......	40	40		

SCHEDULE "F."—(CONTINUED).

PORTS.	MUNICIPALITY.	School Desks. No. I.	School Desks. No. II.	School Desks. No. III.	Rear Seats. No. I.	Rear Seats. No. II.	Rear Seats. No. III.	Board Strips.	Teachers' Desks.	Bookcases.	Maps.	Clocks.	Chairs. Wood.	Chairs. Cane.	Erasers Doz.	Ink wells.	Hand Bells.
Cienfuegos (cont.)	San Juan de las Yeras	70	140	140	10	25	25	210	......	9	9	9	......	9	9		
	S. Fernando Camarones	90	175	175	15	30	30	276	......	13	13	13	......	13	13		
	Sancti Spíritus	400	800	800	60	135	135	1,200	70	70	70	70	......	70	70		
	Trinidad	290	560	550	50	90	95	840	57	57	57	57	......	57	57		
	Ciego de Avila	50	100	100	10	15	15	150	......	6	6	6	......	6	6		
	Moron	75	160	155	15	25	25	234	......	12	12	12	......	12	12		
	Santa Cruz del Sur	135	270	275	25	45	45	408	......	15	15	15	......	15	15		
Manzanillo	Bayamo	120	240	240	20	35	35	360	16	16	16	16	16	......	16		
	Campechuela	140	270	270	25	50	45	408	18	18	18	18	18	......	18		
	Jiguani	100	200	200	15	30	35	300	12	12	12	12	12	......	12		
	Manzanillo	520	1,040	1,040	90	175	175	1,560	54	54	54	54	54	......	54		
Cárdenas	Cardenas	600	1,200	1,200	105	195	200	1,800	60	70	70	70	70	......	70		
	Carlos Rojas	55	110	105	10	20	15	162	......	10	10	10	10	......	10		
	Colon	370	740	740	60	120	120	1,110	40	50	50	50	50	......	50		
	Jovellanos	140	280	280	20	50	50	420	16	16	16	16	16	......	16		
	Macagua	60	120	120	10	20	20	180	......	6	6	6	6	......	6		
	Martí	55	110	105	10	20	15	162	......	4	4	4	4	......	4		
	Maximo Gomez	70	130	130	10	25	20	198	......	8	8	8	8	......	8		
	Palmillas	160	310	330	25	55	55	480	24	24	24	24	24	......	24		
	Perico	60	120	120	10	20	20	180	......	6	6	6	6	......	6		
	Roque	70	140	140	10	20	25	210	......	8	8	8	8	......	8		
	San José de los Ramos	100	200	200	15	30	35	300	......	12	12	12	12	......	12		
	Esperanza	70	140	140	10	25	25	210	......	8	8	8	8	......	8		
	San Diego del Valle	40	90	90	5	15	15	132	......	10	10	10	10	......	10		
	Santa Clara	420	830	850	70	140	145	1,260	60	67	67	67	67	......	67		
	Mendez Capote	......	30	......	......	5	......	18	......	1	1	1	1	......	1		
Nuevitas	Nuevitas	110	220	220	20	35	35	330	15	15	15	15	......	15	15		

SCHEDULE "F"—CONTINUED.

PORTS	MUNICIPALITY	School Desks. No. I.	School Desks. No. II.	School Desks. No. III.	Rear Seats. No. I.	Rear Seats. No. II.	Rear Seats. No. III.	Board Strips.	Teachers Desks.	Bookcases.	Maps.	Clocks.	Chairs. Wood.	Chairs. Cane.	Erasers Doz.	Ink wells.	Hand Bells.
Nuevitas	Puerto Príncipe	970	1,940	1,940	160	325	325	2,910	120	170	170	170	......	170	170		
	Puerto Padre	30	60	60	5	10	10	90	......	5	5	5	......	5	5		
Guantánamo	Guantánamo	520	1,040	1,040	85	175	175	1,560	38	38	38	38	38	......	38		
	Niquero	50	95	95	10	15	15	144	7	7	7	7	7	......	7		
Baracoa	Baracoa	120	230	230	20	40	40	348	40	40	40	40	......	40	40		
Caibarien	Caibarién	110	220	220	20	35	35	330	16	16	16	16	......	16	16		
	Camajuaní	80	160	160	15	30	25	240	12	12	12	12	......	12	12		
	Placetas	110	210	210	15	35	40	318	18	18	18	18	......	18	18		
	Remedios	320	590	590	45	105	100	900	40	40	40	40	......	40	40		
	Vueltas	50	100	100	10	15	15	150	......	6	6	6	......	6	6		
	Yaguajay	80	160	160	15	25	30	240	......	8	8	8	......	8	8		
Sagua la Grande	Calabazar	140	290	300	25	45	50	438	19	19	19	19	19	......	19		
	Cifuentes	140	280	280	25	50	45	420	14	14	14	14	14	......	14		
	Quemado de Güines	80	160	160	15	30	25	240	......	9	9	9	9	......	9		
	Santa Isabel de las Lajas	150	300	300	25	50	50	450	16	16	16	16	16	......	16		
	Santo Domingo	130	260	250	20	40	40	384	15	15	15	15	15	......	15		
	Sagua la Grande	500	1,050	1,050	85	170	175	1,560	62	62	62	62	62	......	62		
Gibara	Gibara	110	225	225	20	35	35	336	14	14	14	14	......	14	14		
	Holguín	300	600	600	50	100	100	900	20	20	20	20	......	20	20		
	Mayarí	50	75	75	5	5	15	120	......	6	6	6	......	6	6		
Havana	Aguacate	60	130	130	10	20	20	192	......	10	10	10	10	......	10		
	Alquízar	80	160	160	15	25	25	240	......	8	8	8	8	......	8		
	Bainoa	60	100	100	10	20	15	156	......	7	7	7	7	......	7		
	Batabanó	200	400	400	30	70	70	600	22	22	22	22	22	......	22		
	Bauta	125	250	245	20	40	40	372	18	18	18	18	18	......	18		
	Bejucal	185	370	365	30	60	60	552	23	23	23	23	23	......	23		
	Cano	80	160	160	15	25	30	240	......	12	12	12	12	......	12		

SCHEDULE "F."—(CONTINUED).

PORT.	MUNICIPALITY.	School Desks. No. I.	School Desks. No. II.	School Desks. No. III.	Rear Seats. No. I.	Rear Seats. No. II.	Rear Seats. No. III.	Board Strips.	Teachers' Desks.	Bookcases.	Maps.	Clocks.	Chairs. Wood.	Chairs. Cane.	Erasers Doz.	Ink wells.	Hand Bells.
Havana	Catalina	70	145	145	10	25	25	216	......	16	16	16	16	......	16		
	Ceiba del Agua	80	160	160	15	25	30	240	......	6	6	6	6	......	6		
	Jibacoa	380	760	760	60	120	120	1,140	47	47	47	47	......	47	47		
	Guara	50	95	95	10	15	15	144	......	7	7	7	7	......	7		
	Güines	300	600	600	50	100	100	900	40	53	53	53	53	......	53		
	Güira de Melena	240	480	480	40	80	80	720	29	29	29	29	29	......	29		
	Habana	1,960	3,575	3,625	361	602	607	5,496	199	201	201	201	......	201	201	3,000	1,500
	Isla de Pinos	45	95	90	10	15	15	138	......	8	8	8	8	......	8		
	Jaruco	70	150	140	10	25	25	216	......	9	9	9	9	......	9		
	Madruga	150	300	300	25	50	50	450	21	21	21	21	21	......	21		
	Managua	30	85	85	5	15	15	120	......	5	5	5	5	......	5		
	Marianao	240	480	480	40	80	80	720	22	22	22	22	......	22	22		
	Melena del Sur	55	100	125	10	20	20	168	......	8	8	8	8	......	8		
	Nueva Paz	170	340	340	25	55	60	510	24	24	24	24	24	......	24		
	Quivicán	60	120	120	10	20	20	180	......	8	8	8	8	......	8		
	Regla	180	360	360	30	60	60	540	17	17	17	17	......	17	17		
	Salud	30	75	75	5	15	10	108	......	5	5	5	5	......	5		
	Santiago de las Vegas	200	400	400	30	65	65	600	26	26	26	26	26	......	26		
	San Antonio de los Baños	160	320	320	25	50	55	480	20	20	20	20	20	......	20		
	San Antonio de las Vegas	55	115	110	10	20	20	168	......	9	9	9	9	......	9		
	San Felipe	70	135	135	10	20	25	204	......	9	9	9	9	......	9		
	San José de las Lajas	160	300	300	25	50	50	456	......	17	17	17	17	......	17		
	Santa Cruz del Norte	30	95	95	5	15	15	132	......	6	6	6	6	......	6		
	Santa María del Rosario	70	140	140	10	25	25	210	......	8	8	8	8	......	8		
	San Nicolás	80	160	160	10	30	25	240	......	11	11	11	11	......	11		
	Tapaste	......	60	60	......	10	10	72	......	3	3	3	3	......	3		
	Artemisa	110	210	210	20	35	35	318	15	15	15	15	15	......	15		

SCHEDULE "F."—(CONTINUED).

PORT.	MUNICIPALITY.	School Desks. No. I.	School Desks. No. II.	School Desks. No. III.	Rear Seats. No. I.	Rear Seats. No. II.	Rear Seats. No. III.	Board Strips.	Teachers' Desks.	Bookcases.	Maps.	Clocks.	Chairs. Wood.	Chairs. Cane.	Erasers Doz.	Ink wells.	Hand Bells.
Havana	Bahía Honda	35	60	65	5	10	10	96	......	4	4	4	4	......	4		
	Cabañas	35	60	65	5	10	10	96	......	4	4	4	4	......	4		
	Candelaria	40	90	90	5	15	15	132	......	5	5	5	5	......	5		
	Consolación del Norte	30	55	55	5	10	10	84	......	4	4	4	4	......	4		
	Consolación del Sur	30	60	60	5	10	10	90	......	4	4	4	4	......	4		
	Guanajay	130	270	270	20	45	45	402	13	13	13	13	......	13	13		
	[illegible]	30	60	70	5	10	15	96	......	4	4	4	4	......	4		
	Mariel	40	110	100	5	20	15	150	......	6	6	6	6	......	6		
	Palacios	......	60	50	......	10	10	66	......	2	2	2	2	......	2		
	Pinar del Río	400	800	800	65	135	130	1,200	30	110	110	110	......	110	110		
	San Cristóbal	60	135	135	10	20	25	198	......	11	11	11	11	......	11		
	San Diego de los Baños	......	60	40	......	10	5	60	......	3	3	3	3	......	3		
	San Juan y Martínez	50	100	100	10	15	15	150	......	9	9	9	9	......	9		
	San Luis	120	240	240	20	40	40	360	20	20	20	20	20	......	20		
	Viñales	60	120	120	10	20	20	180	......	......	......	......	......	......	......		
	Alacranes	195	395	390	30	65	65	588	22	26	26	26	......	26	26		
	Cartagena	100	195	195	15	35	30	294	......	13	13	13	13	......	13		
	Ceja de Pablo	120	250	250	20	40	40	372	......	14	14	14	14	......	14		
	Rancho Veloz	80	160	160	15	25	25	240	......	12	12	12	12	......	12		
	Sagua de Tánamo	......	50	30	......	10	5	48	......	2	2	2	2	......	2		

SCHEDULE "G."

Shipments made by Chief Quartermaster at the Request of Lieutenant C. C. Carter, 2nd Artillery, Aide-de-camp, in Charge of State Property.

PLACE.	AMOUNT.	ARTICLE.	DATE SHIPPED.
Quemados de Güines	6 Boxes	School Supplies	October 3, 1900.
	20 Boxes	Ink	
Rancho Veloz	9 Boxes	School Supplies	October 3, 1900.
	20 Boxes	Ink	
Ceja de Pablo	6 Boxes	School Supplies	October 3, 1900.
	16 Boxes	Ink	
Cabañas	3 Boxes	School Supplies	October 20, 1900.
	12 Boxes	Ink	
Mariel	3 Boxes	School Supplies	October 10, 1900.
	16 Boxes	Ink	
Santa Cruz del Norte	3 Boxes	School Supplies	October 10, 1900.
	16 Boxes	Ink	
Canasí	4 Boxes	School Supplies	October 31, 1900.
	12 Boxes	Ink	

EXHIBIT "H"

JUCARO AND SAN FERNANDO RAIL ROAD.

OPERATING RESULTS.

EARNINGS FROM JULY 1st, 1900, TO JANUARY 31st, 1901.

FROM	July Dolls.	July Cts.	August Dolls.	August Cts.	September Dolls.	September Cts.	October Dolls.	October Cts.	November Dolls.	November Cts.	December Dolls.	December Cts.	January Dolls.	January Cts.	Total Dolls.	Total Cts.
Passenger Traffic	409	45	184	55	219	45	181	10	346	30	237	58	248	86	1,827	29
Freight Traffic	996	38	1,058	16	686	40	1,059	56	911	06	1,016	95	909	31	6,637	82
Wharfage Account	316	80	313	70	200	60	270	40	237	40	303	47	260	60	1,902	97
Lumber Account	575	52	354	90	362	52	413	62	119	06	321	46	599	04	2,746	12
Miscellaneous Account	25	93	12	15	1	03	11	95	25	93	28	45	30	48	135	92
Live Stock Account	......	......	......	......	......	......	......	......	2	00	39	35	1	35	42	70
Customs Appropriation	......	......	3,673	97	......	......	......	......	......	......	......	......	......	......	3,673	97
	2,324	08	5,597	43	1,470	00	1,936	63	1,641	75	1,947	26	2,049	64	16,966	79

EXPENSES FROM JULY 1st, 1900, TO JANUARY 31st, 1901.

FOR	July Dolls.	July Cts.	August Dolls.	August Cts.	September Dolls.	September Cts.	October Dolls.	October Cts.	November Dolls.	November Cts.	December Dolls.	December Cts.	January Dolls.	January Cts.	Total Dolls.	Total Cts.
Maint'nce of Way and Structures	666	84	306	80	740	34	405	95	1,147	62	414	40	370	72	4,052	67
Maintenance of Equipment	309	32	613	40	2,259	25	917	99	624	32	410	33	939	79	7,074	40
Conducting Transportation	724	95	776	19	781	01	673	55	725	94	684	18	1,350	46	5,716	28
General Expense	130	00	203	49	135	00	152	00	354	30	282	81	529	76	1,787	36
	1,831	11	1,899	88	3,915	60	2,149	49	2,852	18	1,791	72	3,190	73	17,630	71

RECAPITULATION.

	Dolls.	Cts.	Dolls.	Cts.
Cash Balance on hand July 1st, 1900	$ 1,152	06		
Gross Receipts	16,966	79		
Gross Expenditures	......	......	$ 17,630	71
Cash Balance on hand January 31st, 1901	......	......	488	14
	$ 18,118	85	$ 18,118	85

JUCARO AND SAN FERNANDO RAIL ROAD.

MILEAGE REPORT.

FROM JULY 1st, 1900, TO JAN. 31st, 1901.

CAR MILEAGE.	JULY.	AUGUST.	SEPTEMBER.	OCTOBER.	NOVEMBER.	DECEMBER.	JANUARY.	TOTAL.
Loaded Cars...........	224 Cars.	223 Cars.	154 Cars.	248 Cars.	204 Cars.	241 Cars.	254 Cars	1,548 Cars.
	Moved. 6,771 kils.	Moved. 5,608 kils.	Moved. 4,460 kils.	Moved. 6,678 kils.	Moved. 7,208 kils.	Moved. 6,625 kils.	Moved. 7,371 kils.	Moved. 44,721 kils.
Empty Cars...........	124 Cars.	122 Cars.	63 Cars.	158 Cars.	69 Cars.	102 Cars.	127 Cars.	765 Cars.
	Moved. 2,858½ kils.	Moved. 2,745 kils.	Moved. 2,280½ kils.	Moved. 3,043 kils.	Moved 1,596 kils	Moved. 2,256 kils.	Moved. 2,837 kils.	Moved. 17,616 kils.
Locomotive mileage....................	2,647 kils.	2,715 kils	2,386 kils.	2,668 kils.	2,612 kils.	3,432 kils.	3,408 kils.	19,868 kils.
Cost Engine Fuel per kil. traveled...	.0296	.0281	.0263	.0474	.025	.0191	.0237	*Average.* .02845
Cost Engine Oil per kil. traveled.....	.0044	.0024	.0032	.0027	.0031	.0119	.0144	.00601
Cost Engine Waste per kil. traveled	.0004	.0003	.0003	.0003	.0004	.0004	.0004	.00035
Cost Train Service per kil. traveled	.0744	.0731	.085	.0753	.0768	.071	.0634	.07411

JUCARO AND SAN FERNANDO RAIL ROAD.

PASSENGERS AND TONNAGE.

FROM JULY 1st, 1900, TO JAN. 31st, 1901.

	JULY	AUGUST	SEPTEMBER	OCTOBER	NOVEMBER	DECEMBER	JANUARY	TOTAL.
Number of Passengers carried......	625	198	273	139	294	195	203	1,927
Tons of Freight carried...............	236.9	250	159.9	281.9	226	325.19	243.86	1,723.75
Tons Wharfage.............	154.5	156.75	96.55	135.05	128.15	214.15	114.37	999.52
Feet of Timber Transported........	51,103	173,910	50,794	88,088	33,883	116,860	162,875	677,513
No. Tons Freight Transp'd 1 Kil. (Commercial)...........	5,000.25	5,475.85	6,593.55	7,988.45	4,691.25	8,780.13	4,221.21	42,750.69
No. Tons Freight Transp'd 1 Kil. (Military)..............	7,639.15	5,439.10	5,199.45	6,633.65	6,101.30	1,293.37	1,887.80	34,193.82
No. Feet Timber Transp'd 1 Kil. (Commercial)........................	973,053	1,396,171	800,586	1,806,297	386,646	1,404,741	2,566,842	9,336.336
No. Feet Timber Transp'd 1 Kil. (Military)	19,680	....	....	3,000	....	....	....	22,680
No. Passengers Transp'd 1 Kil. (Commercial).........................	12,828.5	3,996	5,306	5,129	7,510.5	4,787	4,920	44,477
No. Passengers Transp'd 1 Kil. (Military)	1,394	1,905	1,220	726	1,448	608	318	7,619

JUCARO AND SAN FERNANDO RAIL ROAD.

OPERATING RESULTS.

Material and Labor paid for from July 1st, 1900, to January 31st, 1901.

MONTH AND YEAR.	MATERIAL.		LABOR.		TOTAL.	
	DOLLARS.	CTS.	DOLLARS.	CTS.	DOLLARS.	CTS.
July 1900	101	05	1,730	06	1,831	11
August 1900	252	95	1,646	93	1,899	88
September 1900	2,312	97	1,602	63	3,915	60
October 1900	604	87	1,544	62	2,149	49
November 1900	1,291	47	1,560	71	2,852	18
December 1900	221	30	1,570	42	1,791	72
January 1901	197	90	2,992	83	3.190	73
TOTAL	4.982	51	12,648	20	17,630	71

RECAPITULATION.

DATE.		No. of Certificate of Deposit.	Dollars.	Cts.	Dollars.	Cts.
July 1st 1900 to January 31st 1901	Received from all sources as per statement				18,188	85
" " " " " " "	Total disbursements as per statement				17,630	71
January 31st 1901	Balance on hand				488	14
February 20th 1901	Transferred to Treasurer of Cuba	No. 005948	74	86		
" 20th 1901	" " " " "	" 005981	391	98		
March 6th 1901	" " " " "	" 006224	6	10		
" 6th 1901	" " " " "	" 006225	15	20	488	14
June 30th 1901	Balance on hand					

Ciego de Avila, June 30, 1901.

Respectfully submitted

(Signed) W. S. SCOTT,

Capt. and Q. M., U. S. A., In charge of J. and S. F. R. R.

EXHIBIT "I."

LIST SHOWING PREMISES OWNED, LEASED OR OCCUPIED FOR, OR IN CONNECTION WITH, MILITARY PURPOSES, IN THE DEPARTMENT OF CUBA UNDER THE SUPERVISION OF THE QUARTERMASTER'S DEPARTMENT.

HAVANA.

Governor General's Palace:

Occupied by Military Governor, Government Offices, and used for general Governmental purposes.	State Property.

Lieutenant Governor's Palace:

Occupied by the Offices of the Chief Quartermaster, Paymaster, U. S. A., and used for Offices and Quarters	State Property.

Arsenal and Navy-Yard:

Used for receiving Government property of every nature. Occupied by machine-shops, warerooms, storerooms and quarters	State Property.

Tacon Number 1:

Occupied by Government Offices and Quarters	State Property.

Commissary Buildings, La Punta:

Occupied by the Commissary, U. S. A., and used for offices and storerooms, Subsistence Department	State Property.

Maestranza de Artilleria:

Occupied by various Government Offices and used for Quarters	State Property.

Castillo del Principe:

Used as storage depot for Quartermaster's Department, for the receipt and issue of Q. M. property	State Property.

Electric Light Plant: adjoining Cuarteles de la Fuerza:

Supplies Electric Light to Government Buildings in immediate vicinity	State Property.

Cuarteles de la Fuerza:

Used for storage of old records	State Property.

Electric Light Plant, Municipal Hospital No. 1.

Supplies Electric Light to Pirotecnia Militar, Castillo del Principe, and Municipal Hospital	State Property.

Ice Plant, Municipal Hospital No 1:

Manufactures ice for sale to officers, Government offices and civilian employees...............................	State Property.

Zulueta Street Stables:

Used for shelter of carriages and horses attached to the Headquarters and used by Staff Officers.........	State Property.

Punta Stables:

Used for shelter of carriages and horses attached to the Headquarters and used by Staff Officers.........	State Property.

Depot Corral:

Containing about 33 acres. Rented at $119.00 per month. Used for shelter of animals and vehicles of the Quartermaster's Department, Quarters of civilian employees, and location of shops for repair of Army Transportation	Owned by Mercedes de la Torre, Ursulo J. Duval, atty.

San Ambrosio Hospital:

Fronting on Tallapiedra Wharf; 2-story building. 1st floor occupied by R. B. Lyon Co., under contract of rental with Q. M. Department; 2nd floor occupied by Insular Government for School purposes..	State Property.

No. 54 Calzada del Cerro:

Known as Parcel No. 1. Occupied by the Director of Posts; vacated Jan. 31, 1901; rentals paid up to date; $230.00 U. S. Currency per month. Rentals paid from July 1st, 1900. Public deed of lease executed December 17th, 1900. Authority, 160 Civ. Div. 1st Endorsement, Div. of Cuba, Sept. 13, 1900, being L. R. 24,005, O. C. Q. M. 1900, and 3rd Endorsement, Div. Cuba, Oct. 8, 1900, L. R. 24,720 O. C. Q. M...	Owned by and rented from Dolores Valcarcel de Echarte, 49 Manrique St., Havana, Cuba.

TRISCORNIA MILITARY RAILWAY.

	Price.	*From Whom Bought.*
Parcel No. 1. Comprising water front, wharves, etc.; area, 12.9 acres; leased at a monthly rental of $1,560 Currency, by authority of 5th Endorsement, October 2, 1900, upon L. R. 270, Division of Cuba, page 32 C. being L. R. 23,242 O. C. Q. M., and also 5th Endorsement, November 9, 1900, A. G. O., Havana, Cuba, upon L. R. 25,190, O. C. Q. M.; date of deed of lease, November 13, 1900, at which time there was paid back rental at said rate, from November 21, 1898, and also $5,150, damages for destruction of old buildings and wharves. Upon said water front the Government has constructed deep water piers and railway terminal facilities. Owner, Sra. Juana Pascual, Viuda de Carreras, and two grandchildren, of No. 116 Aguiar St., Havana..	$ 1,560 Ccy. monthly rental.................	Leased from Owner, Sra. Juana Pascual, viuda de Carreaas.

	Price.	From Whom Bought.
Parcel No. 2. Area 34.36 acres; comprises 26.53 acres Military Reservation; deed of conveyance dated February 20, 1900. Authority: 2nd Endorsement, December 18, 1899, and 3rd Endorsement, December 2, 1899, upon L. R. 5,034, Division of Cuba, being L. R. 15,235 and 14,710, O. C. Q. M............	$ 25,676.96...	The Oduardo heirs.
Parcel No. 3. Area, 3.8 acres; deed of conveyance signed on June 27, 1901, by authority of 5th Endorsement, January 22, 1901, upon L. R. 270, Division of Cuba, being L. R. 27,422, O. C. Q. M....	$ 1,420.00...	The heirs of Juan O'Naghten.
Parcel No. 4. Area, 6.94 acres; deed of conveyance dated July 5, 1900. Authority: 3rd Endorsement, May 9, 1900, upon L.R. 270, Division of Cuba, 1900, page 26, being L. R. 18,179, O. C. Q. M.	$ 979.00...	María de la Cruz Morales.
Parcel No. 5. Area, 3.34 acres; deed of conveyance dated June 14, 1900. Authority: 3rd Endorsement, April 6, 1900, upon L. R. 270, Division of Cuba, being L. R. 18,440, O. C. Q. M...........	$ 800.00...	María del Rosario de Castenada.
Parcel No. 6. Area, 5.1 acres; deed of conveyance executed May 3, 1900. Authority: 2nd Endorsement, March 12, 1900, upon L. R. 270, Division of Cuba, being L. R. 17,458, O. C. Q. M............	$ 1,289.52...	The heirs of Rafael Duran.
Parcel No. 7. Area, .56 acre; deed of conveyance dated February 10, 1900. Authority: 1st Endorsement, December 9, 1899, on L. R. 5,034, Div. of Cuba, being L. R. 14,953, O. C. Q. M............	$ 450.00...	Josefa Gutiérrez
Parcel No. 8. Area, 1.14 acres; deed of conveyance dated May 12, 1900. Authority: 3rd Endorsement, April 6, 1900, on L. R. 270, Division of Cuba, 1900, being L. R. 18,559, O. C. Q. M...	$ 400.00...	Hilario Alvarez
Parcel No. 9. Area, 1.65 acres: date of deed of conveyance, June 23rd, 1900. Authority: 3rd Endorsement, April 10, 1900, on L. R. 270, Division of Cuba, 1900, being L. R. 18,559, O. C. Q. M....	$ 465 00...	José Jesus Gonzalez.
Parcel No. 10. Area, 2.65 acres; date of deed of conveyance, August 25, 1900. Authority: 3rd Endorsement, May 9, 1900, on L. R. 270, Division of Cuba, 1900, page 53, being L. R. 19,645, O. C. Q. M..	$ 772 50...	Alberta Arcaya y Estalella.
Parcel No 11. Area, 1.49 acres; date of deed of conveyance, June 14, 1900. Authority: 3rd Endorsement, April 6, 1900, on L. R. 270, Division of Cuba, being L. R. 18,439, O. C. Q. M............	$ 250.00...	Hilario Alvarez

	Price.	From Whom Bought.
Parcel No. 12. Area, 4.23 acres; date of deed of conveyance, June 23, 1900. Authority; 3rd Endorsement, April 5, 1900, on L. R. 270, Division of Cuba, being L. R. 18,442, O. C. Q. M............	$ 500.00..........	Remigio Alvarez.
Parcel No. 13. Unfinished; no contract Owner asks $2,500, Spanish gold, for 3.38 acres. Board of officers appraised right of way at $608, U. S. currency. Owner, C. R. Aleman, of No. 32 Real St., Regla....................................	....	(Pending.)
Parcel No. 14. Area, 2.8 acres; date of deed of conveyance, February 23, 1901; purchase price, $609, plus $229.20 allowance made to the owners for clearing their title. Authority: 1st Endorsement, April 2, 1900, on L. R., 270, Division of Cuba, being L. R. 18,432 O. C. Q. M., and 2nd Endorsement, January 2, 1901, on L. R. 494, Department of Cuba, 1900, being L. R. 26,834 O. C. Q. M...	$ 838.20..........	The heirs of Francisco Maza Arredondo.
Parcel No. 15. Area, 1.74 acres; date of deed of conveyance, March 15, 1900. Authority: 1st Endorsement, December 27, 1899, on L. R. 5,034, Division of Cuba, being L. R 15,510, O. C. Q. M...	$ 200.00....	The heirs of Domingo Rodríguez.
Parcel No. 16. Area, 2.80 acres; date of deed of conveyance October 15, 1900. Price of conveyance includes the sum of $100 allowed to the owners for clearing the title. Authority; Endorsement, February 21, 1900, on L. R. 270, Division of Cuba, being L. R. 16,610 and 22,022, O. C. Q. M..	$ 400.00..........	The heirs of Felipe Mallorquín.
Parcel No. 17. Area, 1.94 acres; date of deed of conveyance, March 15, 1900. Authority: Endorsement, February 21, 1900, on L. R. 270, Division of Cuba, being L. R. 16,610, O. C. Q. M.............	$ 200.00..........	The heirs of Perdomo.
Parcel No. 18. Area, 3.14 acres; date of deed of conveyance, February 10, 1900. Authority: Endorsement, February 21, 1900, on L. R. 270, Division of Cuba, being L. R. 16,610, O. C. Q. M............	$ 500.00..........	Vicente Luis y Crespo.
Parcel No. 18, No. 2. Comprises a quarry, area, .7 acre, and also the pumping station, comprising .07 acre; date of deed of conveyance, May 12, 1900......	$ 200.00..........	Vicente Luis y Crespo.
Parcel No. 19. Area, 2.45 acres; date of deed of conveyance, June 14, 1900. Authority: 3rd Endorsement, March 12, 1900, on L. R. 270, Division of Cuba, being L. R. 17,459, O. C. Q. M............	$ 400.00..........	Justa González.

	Price.	From Whom Bought.
Parcel No. 20. Area, 1.64 acres; date of deed of conveyance, January 22, 1900. Authority: 1st Endorsement, December 2, 1899, on L. R. 5,034, Division of Cuba, being L. R. 14,729, O. C. Q. M.......	$ 150.00..........	Emilio Letamendi.
Parcel No. 21. Area, 4.21 acres; date of deed of conveyance, May 12, 1900. Authority: Endorsement, February 21, 1900, and April 17, 1900, on L. R. 270, Division of Cuba, being L. R. 16,110, O. C. Q. M..	$ 481.00..........	Lutgardo Gárciga.
Parcel No. 21½. Area, 1.19 acres; date of deed of conveyance September 1, 1900. Authority: 3rd Endorsement, April 10, 1900, on L. R. 270, Division of Cuba, page 29, being L. R. 18,560 O. C. Q. M.	$ 360.00.........	The heirs of Dolores Fernández.
Parcel No. 22. Area, 6.9 acres; date of deed of conveyance, May 3, 1900. Authority: 1st Endorsement, December 2, 1899, on L. R. 5,034, Division of Cuba, being L. R. 14,728, O. C. Q. M.............	$ 600.00..........	Ramón de Armas.

COLUMBIA BARRACKS.

	Monthly Rental	Lessor.
Parcel No. 1. Lands occupied by the Reservation; public deed of lease executed March 5, 1901. Authority: 1st Endorsement, February 5, 1901, upon L. R. 1,522, Dept. of Cuba, 1901, being L. R. 27,864. O. C. Q. M........................	$20. U. S. Cy....	Mrs. María de la Salud Guzmán de Benitez.
Parcel No. 2. Portion of Farm "Barreto;" public deed of lease executed March 8, 1901. Authority: 1st Endorsement, February 5, 1901, upon L. R. 1,522, Dept. of Cuba, 1901, being L. R. 27,864 O. C. Q. M	$17. U. S. Cy....	The heirs of Tomasa de Cárdenas.
Parcel No. 3. Portion of Farms "Maguelles" and "San Armas," property occupied under civil agreement. Authority: 1st Endorsement February 5, 1901, upon L. R. 1,522, Dept. of Cuba, 1901, being L. R. 27,864 O. C. Q. M..............	$30. U. S. Cy....	Rufino Otamendi.
Parcel No. 4. Portion of Farm "La Gomera;" occupied under civil agreement. Authority: 1st Endorsement, February 5, 1901, upon L. R. 1,522, Dept. of Cuba, 1901, being L. R, 27,864, O. C. Q. M..	$10. U. S. Cy....	Carlos Callejas.
Parcel No. 5. Portion of Farm "Buena Vista;" occupied under civil agreement. Authority: 1st Endorsement, February 5, 1901, upon L. R. 1,522, Dept. of Cuba, L. R. 27,864, O. C. Q. M	$40. U. S. Cy....	Frank Montros

	Monthly Rental	Lessor.
Parcel No. 6. Portion of Farm "El Recreo de las Tres Rosas;" Board of Officers appraised rentals at $105 per month; owners (the heirs of Manuel Nogueira) refuse to accept said rentals. Case unsettled..	....	(No lease.)
Parcel No. 7. Portion of Farm "Soledad;" occupied under civil agreement. Authority: 1st Endorsement, February 5, 1901, upon L. R. 1522, Dept. of Cuba, 1901, being L. R. 27,864, O. C. Q. M............	$20. U. S. Cy...	The Marianao and Havana R. R., Ltd.
Parcel No. 8. Portion of Farm 'La Serafina;" occupied under civil agreement. Authority: 1st Endorsement, February 5, 1901, upon L. R. 1522, Dept. of Cuba, 1901, being L. R. 27,864, O. C. Q. M..	$15. U. S. Cy..	José Domínguez Lemus.
Parcel No. 9. Portion of Farm "El Hipódromo;" occupied under verbal agreement. Authority: 1st Endorsement, February 5, 1901, upon L. R 1522, Dept of Cuba, 1901, being L. R. 27,864, O. C. Q. M..	$50. U. S. Cy..	Salvador Hernández.
Parcel No. 10. Portion of Farm "Jesús María;" property originally leased from Juan Guerra, a tenant, as per civil lease, approved by Gen. Lee, Quemados, December 12, 1899, at the rate of $45 U. S. Currency per month; subsequently Mr. Guerra has been dispossessed of the property, and Mr. Francisco Uribarri, of Mercadares No. 29, Havana, attorney for owner (Condesa del Val of Madrid) refuses to accept said rate of rentals..	....	(In dispute).
Parcel No. 11. Portion of Farm "Larrazabal;" public deed of lease executed April 20, 1901. Authority: 1st Endorsement, February 5, 1901, upon L. R. 1522, Dept. of Cuba, 1901, being L. R. 27,864, O. C. Q. M...............................	$17. Sp. Gold...	Joaquín Diego.
Parcel No. 12. Portion of Farm "Toscano;" claimed by Mr. Ramon O. Williams. Matter in course of investigation. No rental has been appraised as yet..	....	(Unsettled).
Parcel No. 13. Portion of Farm "Padre." Owner unknown..................................	....	....
Parcel No. 14. (See ' Cemetery")...........	....	....

	Monthly Rental.	*Lessor.*
Parcel No. 15. Building at No. 11 Adolfo Castillo St., Marianao, occupied as Headquarters Building, under civil lease dated April 20, 1900, for one year, and vacated on April 20, 1901. Authority: 1st Endorsement, February 28, 1901 upon L. R. 1522, Dept. of Cuba, 1901, or L. R. 28,416, O. C. Q. M. (authorizing C. Qr. Mr's Dept. to pay rentals thereon fron Jan. 1. 1901)........	$80. U. S. Cy..	Domingo Larrarte.
Parcel No. 16. Storehouse occupied under verbal agreement, and vacated January 31, 1901. Rentals paid by Post Quartermaster at Quemados, Cuba......	$40 U. S. Cy...	Emilio P. Bernat.
Parcel No. 17. Portion of Farm "La Conchita;" public deed of lease executed April 13, 1901. Authority: 1st Endorsement, February 28, 1901, upon L. R. 1522, Dept. of Cuba, 1901, being L. R. 28,416, O. C. Q. M........................	$35. U. S. Cy..	Mrs. Consuelo Boan de Suarez.
Parcel No. 18 House at No. 115 Real Street, Marianao, occupied under civil lease dated November 16, 1900, as Headquarters Building. In said lease the lessor is Francisco M. Durañona, represented by his attorney-in-fact, José Otermin of No. 4, Teniente Rey St., Havana, but Registrar's certificate shows that said Durañona is only part owner of said premises. No rental paid since January 1st, 1901. Authority for payment of rentals by Chief Quartermaster, commencing from Jan'y 1st, 1901. 1st Endorsement, Feb'y 5, 1901, upon L. R. 1522, Dept. of Cuba, 1901, being L. R. 27,864, O. C. Q M..............	$208.33U.S.Cy.	(In dispute).
Military Cemetery.		
Parcel No. 14. Portion of land near "La Playa de Marianao," occupied as Military Cemetery. Deed of Conveyance to the Government from Ramon González Socorro, signed before Notary Vidal, April 20, 1901. Price paid $300 U.S. Currency. Authority: 5th Endorsement, January 30th, 1901, upon L. R. 1400, Dept. of Cuba, 1901, being L. R. 27,732, O. C Q. M........................	....	Government property.
Pasture Ground.		
Two parcels of land for pasturing of animals; one parcel of about ¾ of a caballería, located on east side of private roadway, running from Columbia Barracks to beach at La Playa: the second parcel of about ¾ of a caballeria, located on west side of said roadway. L. R. 30,969, O. C. Q. M...........	$1. U. S. Cy. per head of the animals pastured.............	Rufino Otamendi.

Target Range.	*Monthly Rental.*	*Lessor.*
The land used for this purpose lies about two miles east of the Post and has been rented under contract	$130.00	Widow of Domingo Ortega.

PIROTECNIA MILITAR.

Occupied by:

Quartermaster's Post, Ordnance Department, Medical Supply Depot, and Various Officers comprising the Staff of the Military Governor	State Property. — (See Blue Print).

CABAÑA.

Cabaña Fortress, Morro Castle, Cabaña Reservation, occupied by detachment of Artillery Corps 30,812, 1901, O. C. Q. M.	State Property. — (See Blue Print.)

SANTA CLARA BATTERY.

Occupied by Detachment Artillery Corps	State Property. — (See Blue Print.)

HEADQUARTERS ARTILLERY DEFENSES OF HAVANA.

Batteries 3, 4 and 5, Occupied by detachments Artillery Corps	State Property.

2ND ARTILLERY CORRAL, VEDADO.

	Monthly Rental.	*Lessor.*
Parcel No. 1. Public deed of lease executed February 26, 1901, by authority of 5th Endorsement, Dept. of Cuba, Jan'y 10, 1901, upon L. R. 3786, Div. of Cuba, 1900, being L. R. 24,762, O. C. Q. M. Rentals paid from April 17, 1900	$80.00	Wm. H. Redding, 118 Prado, Havana...
Parcel No. 2. Public deed of lease executed April 13, 1901, by authority of 2nd Endorsement, Feb. 22, 1901, upon L. R. 1864, Dept. of Cuba, 1901, being L. R. 28,155, O. C. Q. M. Rentals paid from Dec. 15, 1900	$10.00	María de la Concepción Gascón, Peña Pobre 14, Havana
Parcel No. 3. Quarters (5 rooms), occupied by Colonel Haskin, 2nd Arty., 15 Baños St.; premises vacated April 22, 1901; rentals paid up to said date; civil agreement signed March 9, 1901..	$60.00	Concepción Hermosa, No. 15 Baños St., Vedado, Havana

	Monthly Rental.	Lessor.
Grounds and out-buildings complete, at No. 6 Second St., corner of 5th St., Vedado, Havana. Civil lease dated July 1st, 1900	$77.00	José Muniz Plá.
Building situated at No. 3 "G" St., Vedado, Havana. Civil lease dated July 1st, 1900	$51.00	Calixto López.
Building situated at No. 21 5th St., corner of "G" St., Vedado, Havana. Civil lease dated July 1st, 1900. Rental: From July 1st to December 31st, 1900; from Jan. 1st to June 30th, 1901. L. R. 31,261, O. C. Q. M.	$85.00 and $68.00	Eduardo Orduna.
Target range. Situated on the beach along the water front	None	(Owner unknown).

BATABANO.

Office of Quartermaster's Agent, 12x12x10. 30,266½, 1901, O. C. Q. M.	$5.62 U. S. Cy.	José Llano.

CIENFUEGOS.

Forage Warehouse rented from owner under verbal agreement; bounded on west by Sugar Warehouse belonging to Nicolás Castano	$150.00	García Capote.
Warehouse, property of Government, excepting ground and dock; no lease. Rental for ground and dock. 29,614, 1901, O. C. Q. M.	$60.00	(See Blue Print.)

ROWELL BARRACKS.

Parcel No. 1. Comprising Post of Rowell Barracks. Public deed of lease executed Feb'y 20, 1901, by authority of 10th Endorsement, A. G. O., Havana, Cuba, Jan'y 17, 1901, upon L. R. 806, Dept. of Cuba, 1900, being L. R. 26,831, O. C. Q. M. Rentals paid from Jan'y 1, 1901	$280.00	Antonio Porrua, Paseo de Vives 106, Cienfuegos.
Parcel No. 2. Comprising Post of Rowell Barracks. Public deed of lease executed Feb'y 28, 1901, by authority of 1st Endorsement, Havana, June 26, 1900, upon L. R. 976, Div. of Cuba, 1900, being L. R. 21,537, O. C. Q. M. Rentals paid from April 1, 1899.	$250.00	Owners represented by Pedro N. Entenza, 39 San Rafael St., Havana.
Parcel No. 3. Comprising Post of Rowell Barracks. Property occupied for the purpose of drilling and grazing of public animals Deed of lease executed June 24, 1901, by authority of 4th Endorsement, April 1, 1900, upon L. R. 1968, Dept. of Cuba, being L. R. 28,877, O. C. Q. M.	$100.00	Manuel Cabo of Cienfuegos, representing his wife, Clara Rodriguez. See Blue Print.

	Monthly Rental.	Lessor.
Target Range. The Target Range has been used since occupation here by the Second Infantry. Owners are now submitting a claim for the rent of the same since its occupation for a Target Range	(None).............	Owner: the heirs of Moreno.

(Rowell Barracks, July 11, 1901).

MANZANILLO.

East of red line on map of Military Post is rented, buildings on such lands having been erected by 10th Cavalry.........	$ 10.00..........	....
West of red line, former Spanish Hospital; now occupied as barracks by 10th Cavalry; no rent being paid except the "Gerona" property, rented as Officers' Quarters......................................	$ 50.00..........	The City of Manzanillo.
Buildings on Map of Quartermaster's Corral, formerly used by Spanish Government, are occupied without rent being paid..	(None).	....
Buildings shown in red on Map of City of Manzanillo are rented as Officers' Quarters, etc., and paid for by Civil Disbursing Officer..................	....	....
Dock (in red) was lately taken possession of by Civil Government in compliance with Order No. 73, Headquarters Department of Cuba............................	....	....
Near Southeast corner of Post is a one-half acre plot, rented as a burial plot....	$ 5.00..........	....
About ¾ mile Southeast of Post is a plot of about 6/8 acre, rented as a drill-ground..	$ 15.00..........	....
All rents paid by Disbursing Officer of Civil Funds..	....	(See Blue print.)

30,067, 1900. O. C. Q. M.

Target Range. At present (date of information, July 11, 1901), there is no Target Range at this Post. There was one in use until close of carbine firing. Rental was paid from civil funds. On complaint of people living in vicinity, the range was abandoned...........	$ 15.00	(Owner unknown.)

BAYAMO.

Quartermaster's Department occupies old Spanish Fort, built on private ground, as corrals and shops	(None).............	....

	Monthly Rental.	Lessor.
Headquarters Offices	$ 20.00	Porfirio Bonet.
Clothing Storeroom in part of Building with Commissary; rent paid from Island Funds by Disbursing Officer at Manzanillo	$ 50.00	S. Millones.
Hospital	$ 75.00	Mariano Castello.
(See sketches).		
Target Range. Was constructed by labor of troops on private, unused land, about 8 miles from town	(None)	(Owner unknown).

CAUTO.

Comprising one Warehouse and two Corrals, rented and paid by Disbursing Officer of Civil Funds at Manzanillo 30,578, 1901. O. C. Q. M	$ 75.00	Ramón Pastor. (See Blue print).

SANTIAGO.

Office Quartermaster in charge Ocean Transportation.

Frame Building and Wharf, shingle roof, built partly over water, on piles — Customs Dep. Property. See Blue print.

Quartermaster's Forage Warehouse No. 2.

Brick Building, tile roof, dirt floor and part plank. Roof in bad condition; used for forage warehouse. Rented at $75.00 per month with privilege of vacating at thirty days' notice — Rented from Pedro Viana. See Blue print.

Quartermaster's Warehouse at Railroad Track.

Frame Building, plank floors, corrugated iron roof, in good condition — Government Property. See Blue print.

Administration Building.

Occupied by Office Chief Paymaster, Chief Surgeon, Inspector General and Government Printing Office. Brick building, 2 stories high; tile roof, floor paved with marble; 2nd floor boards; yard paved with brick. In fair condition. Rented at $119.00 per month, with privilege of vacating on 15 days' notice — Rented from R. Mason. See Blue print.

Quartermaster's Corral.

Stables consist of frame buildings, dirt floors, board roof. Barracks and mess hall, frame buildings, rough board floors and board roof. Condition fair. Bath house of wood, cement floor and board roof, supplied with five showers and two lavatories in good condition. Frame building for latrines, board roof and floor and five latrine portable cans. Corral enclosed by barbed wire fence — Public Property.

Governor General's Palace.

Brick Building, marble floors, tile roof, 18 feet in height from floor to ceiling. Court and corridors paved with brick. In good condition. Rental price unknown. Used for various Governmental offices..........	State Property. See Blue print.

Depot Quartermaster's Warehouse.

Comprises several buildings of both stone and brick; tile roofs; Ice plant, Blacksmith shop, Stables..........	Government property.
Target Range. Comprises 200 yards by 1000 yards, situated 2½ miles from the reservation. Monthly rental: $25.00. ($300.00 per annum..)	(Owner unknown.)
Morro Castle. Reservation, including Barracks..	Government property. (See Blue print)

SAN LUIS.

The Post of San Luis consists of houses scattered over the town, and a map of the Post would be practically a map of the town. There is no Military Reservation, all land belonging to La Union Plantation. The houses rented—three sets Officer's Quarters, two sets Post N. C. Staff, and one set for Post Headquarters, are paid for from Customs Receipts of the Island. There is no sewer system, and water for use of troops is purchased from Insular Funds and brought from a small stream near town.

	Monthly Rental.	*Lessor.*
Quarters of Capt. H. F. Kendall, 8th Cav.; frame building, tile roof, hired under oral agreement..........	$ 17.00..........	Luisa Jiménez.
Post Headquarters; frame building; hired under verbal agreement..........	$ 22.00..........	Germán Muñiz.
Quarters of Lt. G. S. Norvell, 8th Cav.; frame building, tile roof; verbal agreement..........	$ 10.00..........	Pablo Rimban.
Quarters of A. A. Surgeon, I. P. Agostine. Frame building: tile roof; verbal agreement..........	$ 17.00..........	Joaquina Alayo de Ochoa.
Quarters of Post Commissary Sergeant, D. A. H. Kolster. Frame building, tile roof; verbal agreement..........	$ 12.00..........	Germán Muñiz.
Quarters of Post Quartermaster Sergeant F. L Fink. Frame building, tile roof; verbal agreement..........	$ 12.00..........	Ibañez y Aleclo.
Quartermaster and Commissary Storehouses. Frame building, tile roof; old Spanish buildings, formerly occupied by Spanish Troops..........	(None)..........	(Owner, Santiago Rousseau.)

	Monthly Rental.	*Lessor.*
Troop Quarters. This building supposed to have been built from Insular Funds, in March, 1900; but official records are lacking. Frame building, corrugated iron roof...........................	(None).............	(Owner, Santiago Rousseau.)
Post Hospital. Same remarks as foregoing paragraph................	....	....

28,126, 1901. O. C. Q. M.

Target Range. Ground occupied for this purpose, paid from Insular Funds........	(Unknown)	(Owner unknown.)

GUANTANAMO.

Buildings circled in red on plan, built and owned by Spanish Government. Other Buildings, from best information obtainable, built and material furnished by citizens of Guantánamo to be used as Hospitals for Spanish Troops. The land on which the latter buildings stand is property of Janay family of Guantánamo, and was loaned by them to Spanish Government..	....	(See Blue print.)

29,871, 1901, O. C. Q. M.

Target Range. Target practice has heretofore been had on vacant land, about 18 miles from Post, donated by citizens for temporary use...........................	(No Rental)......	(Private Property.)

BARACOA.

Barracks. Located in the centre of Baracoa, upon a hill..	State Property.
Water Supply. The water from the City supply-pipe is forced to the top of hill by means of a wind-mill.	....
Corral. Old Spanish Barracks located upon the sea front, were used by the 5th Infantry, mounted, as stables, and are suitable for this purpose. Stables large enough for 125 animals..................................	State Property.
The water is supplied from the City water system, through an inch pipe..	....

HOLGUIN.

	Monthly Rental.	Lessor.
State Lands transferred by Spanish upon evacuation to Alcalde, are: 1st, Site of Military Hospital-building, with patio, covering 2880 metres, an area of 600 sq. metres in addition being equally distributed East, West and South of Hospital; 2nd, Site of Barracks, whose boundaries are: North, Ce. de Quinta; East, Ce. de Maceo; South, Ce. de Cuba; West, Ce. de Máximo Gómez, making an area of 24,860 sq metres and 55 sq. centimetres; 3rd, Parque de Mantilla, or Maceo (new name), bounded by stone wall and including area of 12,000 sq. m.	....	(See Blue Print)
Thatched roof Q. M. Stable is in Ce. de la Quinta. The four thatched roof Cavalry Stables are not on State land. This is Municipal land, and contains an artesian well in construction	....	....
The Hacienda at Holguin is in possession of the documents, or certified copies of the same, by which this property was transferred to the Alcalde of Holguín, acting for the State, by the Spanish Military Commander. A survey has recently been made by the Municipal Surveyor under the direction of the Hacienda .... 29,151, 1901, O. C. Q M.	....	....
Target Range. 2000 x 400 yards; room for eight butts. Four butts are now built..	No Rental........	Owner, Municipality of Holguin.

DETAILED STATEMENT, SHOWING ALL BUILDINGS OCCUPIED BY AMERICAN GOVERNMENT.

	Size Front.	Depth.	Monthly Rental.
No. 1 No. 33 Peralta Street, occupied by Maj. Stedman	76'	96'	$ 25
No. 2 Nos. 7 and 9 Libertad, occupied by Capt. Bigelow..................................	76'	51'	20
No. 3 No. 12 Maceo Street, occupied by Capt. Watson..................................	38'	87'	12
No. 4 No. 32 Maceo Street, occupied by Cap. Paxton..................................	37'	156'	20
No. 5 No. 30 Maceo Street, occupied by Capt. Fleming..................................	37'	156'	20
No. 6 No. 27 Unión Street, occupied by Lt. Cavenaugh..................................	56'	96'	15
No. 7 No. 19 Maceo Street, occupied by Lt. Palmer..................................	103'	141'	20
No. 8 No. 25 Peralta Street, occupied by A. A. S. Harvey..................................	54'	63'	20

No.		Size Front.	Depth.	Monthly Rental.
No. 9	No. 11 Libertad Street, occupied by A. A. S. McMillan	30'	54'	$ 20
No. 10	No. 2 Martures Street, occupied by Vet. S. Service	31'	32'	8
No. 11	Nos. 3 and 5 Maceo Street, occupied by Post Lib. and School	71'	87'	10
No. 12	No. 21 Garayalde Steeet, occupied by Sgt. Maj. Conley	72'	49'	8
No. 13	Maceo Street, No. 7, occupied by 1 Com. Storehouse	45'	83'	20
No. 14	Maceo Street, No. 34, occupied by Headquarters	72'	156'	40
No. 15	No. 13 Libertad Street, occupied by 1 Q. M. Storehouse	45'	56'	8
No. 16	No. 25 Unión Street, occupied by 1 Q. M. Storehouse	72'	93'	25
No. 17	No. 23 Unión Street, occupied by 1 Q. M. Corral	43'	112'	15
No. 18	No. 64 Aria Street, occupied by 1 Q. M. Corral	86'	86'	14
No. 19	No. 33 Aria Street, occupied by 1 Q. M. Corral	75'	203'	8
No. 20	1 Q. M. Corral at No. 35 Aria Street	70'	203'	6
No. 21	No 37 M. Lemus Street, occupied by 1 Q. M. Corral	149'	156'	15
No. 22	No. 41 Libertad Street, occupied by Cmy. Sgt. Kidwell	38'	95'	8

All above premises are held under verbal agreement.

	Front.	Depth.	Monthly Rental.
Barracks. Situated at Maceo St	273'	254'	....
Park Independencia. Occupied by B. Troop, 10th Cavalry	225'	354'	State Property
Military Hospital. Llano Street	130'	235'	

L. R. 31,405, O. C. Q. M.

GIBARA.

(*Port of Holguin*)

	Monthly Rental	Lessor.
One Warehouse, private property, occupied by Quartermaster as granary. Rented and paid for by District Disbursing Officer under verbal agreement, to be given up on thirty days' notice by owner or renter. Rent paid to July 1st, 1901	$ 25.00	Carmen Marquina

CAMP R. S. MACKENZIE.

	Monthly Rental.	*Lessor.*
Agreement of April 6, 1901, between Capt C. J. Symmonds, for the U. S. Military Government, and the owner of lands known as "La Emelina" and "Guano Alto," located South of Puerto Príncipe and Nuevitas R. R. Kilometres 5, and consisting of 281 acres, 8 chains and 14 poles, as shown on map attached to lease, the term of which is from April 6 to June 30, 1901, renewable yearly. L. R. 28,061 O. C. Q. M.	$30.00	Sebastian Morán de la Vega.
The lands to the North and West of X-Y-V-W (See Blue print) belong to unknown owners. L. R. 28,061, O. C. Q. M.	None	Owner unknown.
Ground to the East will be leased, dating from March 1, 1901; same shown on separate tracing, and lease will be same as that of Mr. Moron de la Vega. (See Blue print No. 11). L. R. 30,195, O. C. Q. M.	$ 15.00	A. Santayana.

Water used is obtained: 1st, that for use of horses from springs on hill 300 yds. east of camp, which is good and abundant, and flows by gravity to troughs; 2nd, water used for all other purposes, which comes from a small stream flowing from hills several miles to S. E. of Camp, the stream being dammed about 1,000 yds. from Camp, water being pumped by steam to tank. The stream is small, and in drought decreases; but if necessary, other sources can be provided, water in vicinity being abundant. The pump used is an old, 2nd hand, 4 H. P. "Blake," very weak and requiring great care and nearly continual use to obtain sufficient water. Boiler is new and 15 H. P.

Pipe line is about 1,000 yds. in length, 2 in., wrought iron, old, 2nd-hand and poor, requiring considerable attention and use to keep in repair.

Tank is a wooden box, of about 5,000 gallons, leaks badly, and must soon be replaced. Shown on plan.

A 2-inch pipe leads from tank to mule trough, and four similar pipes lead from tank to bath-houses, operating 18 shower-baths for use of officers and enlisted men. All other distributions are effected by means of tanks drawn by mules and delivering water to barrels at desired points.

	Monthly Rental	Lessor.
Drainage and Sewer. Aside from a wooden. underground box, to carry waste from bath-houses, there is no sewer system. The Camp is situated upon a knoll and perfectly drained, naturally, on either side. All waste water, etc , is removed far beyond Camp by carts.		
28,061, 1901. O. C. Q. M.		
Target Range. Is distant from Camp about 3 miles, on waste land. No claim has ever been made for compensation for use of this land................................	None.................	Owner unknown.

PUERTO PRINCIPE

Building of 10 rooms used as offices of Disbursing Quartermaster. No lease....	$ 30.00...........	M. Valdez.
Buildings of five rooms and grounds of about ½ acre, used as Warehouse for Civil Disbursing officer. No lease. See tracing No. 3................	$ 75.00...........	B. S. Aden.
266 acres, used as pasture for U. S horses and mules. No lease...........................	$ 25.00.....	B. Arteaga.
Three buildings (one oven and nine rooms) and about one acre of ground. Warehouse and offices used by Q. M. Department. Pumping house used to supply water to public building. See tracing No. 4.........	None.................	State property.
One building (16 rooms) used as District Headquarters.....................	None...	State property.

NUEVITAS.

Warehouse at Nuevitas used by the Q M. Department is shown on Tracing V. 30,795, O. C. Q. M........	....	....
Office-rooms used are shown on Tracing VI. 30,795, O. C. Q. M......................	....	....
Two Rooms, 100×65, vacated August 17, 1900, no longer required; no lease. Owner B. S. Aden.....	$ 125 Sp. Gold.	B. S. Aden.
One Room used as store room for forage. Vacated August 17, 1900; no longer required; no lease	$ 100 .,	B. S. Aden.
Two Rooms, 75'×75.' Vacated Dec. 31, 1900; no longer required. Used by Q M. Department for storing means of transportation.	$ 55.................	Vicente Rodríguez and Co.

	Monthly Rental.	Lessor.
Two Rooms used as offices for Depot Q. M. Vacated Aug. 19, 1900, as offices were moved to more suitable place.......	$ 40......	...... Juan Bagés P.
Two Rooms, used as Quarters for Actg. Asst. Surgeon F. F. Mendoza, U. S. A., until October 31, 1900, when vacated; no longer required. No lease................	$ 12	Francisco Aguilera.
Two Rooms, rented by month since August 20, 1900, for offices for Civil Disbursing Officer and Q. M. Dept. Still rented	$ 40................	Henry Page.
Two Floors, five rooms, rented by month since April 1, 1901; no lease; used by Q. M. Dept. Still occupied....................	$ 50................	Carreras, Hno., and Co.
Two Rooms; no lease; rented by the month since Aug. 8th, 1900, at $150 per month. Used by Q. M. Dept., and still occupied. Rent reduced to $50 per month, after April 30, 1901, if retained. Will be vacated by May 31, 1901	....	Vicente Rodríguez and Co.
29,913, 1901. O. C. Q. M. 30,795, " "	....	(See two Blue prints.)

CIEGO DE AVILA.

Júcaro and San Fernando Railroad, leased to "The Cuba Company." Comprises line of Railroad from Júcaro to San Fernando, with all Stations, Roundhouses, Turntables, Storehouses, Engines, Cars, Trucks, and all Appurtenances	....	(See Blue prints)

MATANZAS.

RENTED QUARTERS.

12½ Isabel St., occupied by Col. H. E. Noyes, 2nd Cav., (including water)......	$ 60.00...........	Manuel Fabeada.
10 San Isidro St., occupied by Veterinarian W. V. Lusk, 2nd Cav.....................	$ 24.00...........	Antonio Ugarte.
12 San Isidro St., occupied by Capt. H. G. Trout, 2nd Cav., (including water)..	$ 24.00...........	Antonio Ugarte.
25 Isabel 1st St., occupied by Capts. C. B. Hoppin and T. J. Lewis, and Lieut. F. C. Johnson, 2nd Cav., (including water)...	$ 96.00...........	Alfredo Botet.
27 Isabel 1st St., occupied by Lieut. S. M. Kochersperger, 2nd Cav., (including water)	$ 24.00...........	M. Salgueiro.

	Monthly Rental.	Lessor.
5 Paseo de Martí, occupied by Lieut. E. J. Pike, 2nd Cav. (including water)	$ 19.00...........	City of Matanzas.
18 Navia St., Officers 2nd Cav. (including water). Vacated..........	$ 22.00..........	José Fernández.
14 Navia St., occupied by Contract Surgeon Burr, U. S. A. (including water)...	$ 24.00...........	Alejandro Maruri.
57 Navia St., occupied by Chief Musician Scully, 2nd Cav. (including water)	$ 12.00..........	Cecilia Delgado.
4 Santa Cristina St., Officers' Quarters (including water.) Vacated......	$ 22.00.........	Juan A. Zabala.
47 Navia St., Officers' Quarters (including water...	$ 36.00.........	Angel García.
35 Navia St., occupied by Post Q. M. Sergt. Flynn, U. S. A. (including water).	$ 12.00	Eduardo Cardounel.
10 Isabel 1st St., Officers' Quarters (including water)	$ 36.00...........	Antonio Molins.
97 Manzano St., occupied by Capt. J. H. Stone, Asst. Surgeon U. S A., (including water)..	$ 36.00...........	Rosa Olmo Serrate.
Paymaster's Office, No. 15 Santa Teresa St., (including water.) Vacated......	$ 25.00..........	Marcelino Díaz.
Forage warehouse, D. Q. M. Gelabert St., opposite City Wharf.......................	$ 300.00..	T. Bea and Co.
Storehouse, D. Q. M., No. 9, Comercio St.........	$ 100.00...........	Castaner, Rivas Co.
Corral, D. Q. M., Quarters for Civilian Employees, Q. M. D., and yard adjoining for wood-yard for general supplies..	$ 25.00...........	Caridad B. Vda. de R. Maribona.

L. R. 31,232, O. C. Q. M., 1901.

HAMILTON BARRACKS (Matanzas.)

	Monthly Rental.	Lessor.
Parcel No. 1, Matanzas. Target and Pistol Ranges. Civil lease signed April 20th, 1901. Authority: 3rd Endorsement, April 18, 1901, Department of Cuba, upon L. R. 29,095, O. C. Q. M.... Rental of Rifle Range.. .... ,, Pistol Range $25 per year, commencing from Jan. 1st, 1901	$ 20.00...........	José Trujillo, of No. 39 Consulado St., representing Francisco Viejo, in Spain.
Fort San Severino. Transferred by Spanish Government to Military authorities. Occupied by U. S. Troops.	....	State property.

	Monthly Rental	Lessor.
Land. East of Military Reservation, consisting of about 165 acres and four lots owned by Francisco Viejo Ysant, occupied by U. S. Troops as a drill and dump ground	$55 00	José Trujillo, attorney for owner.
Corral D. Q. M. Comprises lot No. 22; stables and wagon-yard have been built thereon by Disbursing Quartermaster, from Insular Funds. See proceedings of Board of Officers................................	(None)	(Owner unknown.)
Lots Nos. 16 and 17. East of above, stables and blacksmith shop for Troops "B," "E," "H," and Band 2nd Cav... The Hamilton Barracks Reservation comprises besides, sundry lots, numbered arbitrarily on map, 1, 2, 3, 4, 6, 7, 8, 9, 11, 12, 16, 17, the ownership of which is not clear. Board of Officers has recommended a rental of $5 for each lot per month, payable to owner on proving the title............ ...	(None)...........	(Owner unknown.)
On Lot No. 5. Two Hospital wards were built by the Disbursing Quartermaster, from Insular funds................................	(None)...........	(Owner unknown.)
U. S. Military Hospital. The Building on Lot No. 10, marked "Military Hospital," is owned by Manuel Michelena...	$25.00...........	Manuel Michelena.

NOTE:—As shown on plan, all stables and some of barrack buildings are built on Military Reservation; other buildings and parade ground on land of Sr. Cecilio Ayllon. The post is occupied by Troops "A," "C," "D," "F," and "G," 2nd Cav., and Pack Trains Nos. 24, 29, and 31.

(See proceedings Board of Officers. Also see Blue Prints.) L. R. 31,232, O. C. Q. M.

SANTA CRISTINA BARRACKS, MATANZAS.

The Santa Cristina Barracks were transferred to Military Authorities by the Spanish Government, and are occupied by Troops "B," "E," "H," and Headquarters 2nd Cavalry, Offices of Post Commissary, Depot Quartermaster, Disbursing Quartermaster, District Engineer Officer and City Sanitary Department, also Subsistence Storehouse	State property.
Band Quarters and Bakery. Adjoining Santa Cristina Barracks. Built by Disbursing Quartermaster from Insular Funds on public land transferred to Military Authorities by Spanish Government..............	State property.

L. R. 31,232, O. C. Q. M., 1901.

EXHIBIT "J."

LIST OF FORMAL CONTRACTS

MADE DURING THE FISCAL YEAR ENDING JUNE 30TH, 1901.

NAME OF CONTRACTING OFFICER.	NAME OF CONTRACTOR.	DATE OF CONTRACT.	NATURE OF CONTRACT.	CONSIDERATION.	CONTRACT, EXPIRATION OF
Chief Qr. Mr. Dept. of Cuba (Vendee)	María de la Cruz Morales	July 5, 1900	Conveyance of Right of Way	$979.00.	
Do.	Alberta Arcay y Estalella	Aug. 25th, 1900	Do.	$772.50.	
Do.	Heirs of Dolores Fernández	Sept. 1st, 1900	Do.	$360.00.	
Do.	Heirs of Felipe Mallorquín	Oct. 15th, 1900	Do.	$400.00.	
Maj. C. B. Baker, Chief Qr. Mr. (Lessor)	Juana Pascual, Vda. deCarreras	Nov. 13th, 1900	Lease of Right of Way	$1,560.00	Sept. 30, 1901.
Do.	Dolores Valcárcel de Echarte	Dec. 17th, 1900	Lease of house Director Gen'l of Posts	$230.00 per month	Vacated Jan. 31. 1901.
Maj. C. B. Baker, Chief Qr. Mr. (Grantee)	José Coto y Bello	Jan. 2nd, 1901	Release	$244.00.	
Maj. C. B. Baker, Chief Qr. Mr., (Lessor)	The Cuba Co	Jan. 24th, 1901	Lease of Júcaro and San Fernando R. R.	Free transportation of Govt. Freight and passengers and construction of a wharf value $24,000.00	Jan. 24th, 1904.
Maj. C. B. Baker, Chief Qr. Mr., (Lessee)	Antonio Porrua	Feb. 20, 1901	Lease of lands	$280.00 monthly	Feb. 20, 1902.
Maj. C. B. Baker, Chief Qr. Mr., (Vendee)	Heirs of Franc? Maza Arredondo	Feb. 23, 1901	Conveyance of Right of Way	$838.20.	

EXHIBIT "J."—CONTINUED.

NAME OF CONTRACTING OFFICER.	NAME OF CONTRACTOR.	DATE OF CONTRACT.	NATURE OF CONTRACT.	CONSIDERATION.	CONTRACT, EXPIRATION OF
Maj. C. B. Baker, Chief Qr. Mr., (Lessee)	William H. Redding	Feb. 26, 1901	Lease of lands	$80.00 per month	Feb. 26, 1902.
Do.	Pedro N. Entenza	Feb. 28, 1901	Lease of lands	$250.00 per month	Feb. 28, 1902.
Do.	María de la Salud Guzmán de Benítez	Mch. 5, 1901	Do.	$20.00 per month	March 5, 1902.
Do.	Heirs of Tomasa de Cárdenas	Mch. 8, 1901	Do.	$17.00 per month	March 8, 1902.
Maj. C. B. Baker, Chief Qr. Mr., (Lessor)	R. B. Lyon & Co	Apl. 13, 1901	Lease of San Ambrosio Hosp.	$11,500.00 per annum	March 8, 1903.
Maj. C. B. Baker, Chief Qr. Mr., (Lessee)	Mª de la Concepción Gascón.	Apl. 13, 1901	Lease of lands	$10 00 per month	April 13, 1902.
Do.	Consuelo Boan de Suárez	Apl. 13, 1901	Do.	$35.00 per month	April 13, 1902.
Do.	Joaquín Diago	Apl. 20, 1901	Do.	$17 Sp. Gd. per month	April 20, 1902.
Maj. C. B. Baker, Chief Qr. Mr., (Vendee)	Ramón González Socorro	Apl. 20, 1901	Conveyance Gov. Cemetery	$300.00.	
Do. (Lessee)	Manuel Cabe	Jun. 24, 1901	Lease of land	$100.00 per month	June 24, 1902.
Do. (Vendee)	Heirs of Juan O'Naghten	Jun. 27, 1901	Conveyance of Right of Way	$1,420.00.	

EXHIBIT "K."

LIST OF CIVIL LEASES

MADE DURING THE FISCAL YEAR ENDING JUNE 30, 1901.

Name of contracting officer.	*Name of Lessor.*	*Date of Lease.*	*Monthly Rental.*	*Term of Lease.*
Maj. C. B. Baker, Chief Quartermarter.	Concepción Hermosa	March 9, 1901	$60	Monthly.
do	José Trujillo	April 20, 1901	$20 (target range) $25 per annum (pistol range)	do.
do	Viuda de Illera	May 24, 1901	$12	do.
do	S. S. Friedlein	June 1, 1901	$12	do.
do	Ernesto Torro	June 1, 1901	$12	do.
do	Juan López	June 27, 1901	$5.62	do.

Fiscal Year ending June 30th, 1901.

		MILITARY DEPARTMENT.						COLLECTIONS.		TOTAL.	
ation.		Barracks and Quarters.		Administration.		Miscellaneous.		Miscellaneous Receipts.			
,976	40	$ 93,207	25	$ 65,273	68	$ 3,877	62	....	......	$ 318,642	77
....	......	1,293	48	....	......	....	......	....	......	1,293	48
....	......	....	......	....	......	....	......	$ 5,874	48	5,874	48
....	......	....	......	....	......	....	......	3,984	97	3,984	97
....	......	....	......	....	......	....	......	1,272	82	1,272	82
	40	$ 94,500	73	$ 65,273	68	$ 3,877	62	$ 11,132	27	$ 331,068	52
823	82	$ 85,804	21	$ 49,678	08	$ 3,731	95	....	......	$ 285,559	22
....	......	2,681	19	5,048	21	....	......	....	......	14,384	16
....	......	....	......	....	......	....	......	$ 11,132	27	11,132	27
13	75	942	71	2,125	08	145	67	....	......	4,783	27
138	83	5,072	62	8,422	31	....	......	....	......	15,209	60
76	40	$ 94,500	73	$ 65,273	68	$ 3,877	62	$ 11,132	27	$ 331,068	52

SCAL YEAR ENDING JUNE 30th, 1901.

ES.	MILITARY DEPARTMENT.			TOTAL
tion.	Barracks and Quarters.	Administration	Miscellaneous.	

INFORME

DEL

JEFE CUARTELMAESTRE DEL DEPARTAMENTO DE CUBA,

RESPECTO A

ASUNTOS INSULARES

EN EL AÑO FISCAL TERMINADO EN JUNIO 30

1901.

CUARTEL GENERAL, DEPARTAMENTO DE CUBA.

Habana, Cuba, Julio 30 de 1901.

Al Ayudante General del Departamento de Cuba,

Habana.

SEÑOR:

El que suscribe tiene el honor de remitir á Vd. su informe anual referente á los asuntos insulares sometidos á la supervisión de esta oficina, correspondiente al año económico de 1901, acompañando varios cuadros estadísticos, y otros documentos que se detallan en la presente memoria.

Entré á desempeñar mis funciones en esta oficina el 4 de Julio de 1901, relevando al Teniente Coronel Charles F. Humphrey, Jefe Auxiliar de la Administración Militar del Ejército de los Estados Unidos, entonces en expectación de embarque con objeto de hacerse cargo como Jefe de Administración Militar de la Expedición de Socorros á la China.

Las atribuciones de esta oficina con relación á los asuntos insulares, han sido brevemente detalladas, de la manera siguiente:

Desembolsar los fondos insulares para pagar los empleados Civiles por la construcción, cuidado y alumbrado de edificios públicos dentro y en los alrededores de la ciudad de la Habana, á cargo del Jefe de Administración Militar, pago de los alquileres de edificios destinados á oficinas y propiedades ocupadas por el Estado para diversos fines militares así como para varios otros fines, según disposiciones dictadas por el Gobernador Militar.

Recibir, distribuir y rendir cuentas del mueblaje de las escuelas de la Isla de Cuba, en todo el Departamento de la Isla, y liquidar las cuentas de los varios contratistas y de gastos varios en relación con los mismos.

Recibir, disponer y rendir cuenta de la propiedad insular que se halla bajo la inspección del Jefe de Administración Militar del Departamento.

Emitir conocimientos de embarques insulares y pasajes solicitados, con la debida autorización para la conducción de pasajeros y flete, y la supervisión del transporte de mercancías pertenecientes á la Administración del Departamento de Administración Militar, correspondientes á los Establecimientos Insulares en todo el Departamento de Cuba.

Del manejo del ferrocarril militar de Triscornia y de la decisión de los asuntos que con el mismo se relacionan.

De la supervisión del trasbordo al ferrocarril de Júcaro y San Fernando, contrata del Hospital de San Ambrosio, y del recibo y rendición de cuentas de las rentas derivadas del mismo.

El trabajo general de construcción y del mantenimiento en buenas condiciones de varios edificios públicos en la ciudad de la Habana, colocados bajo la inspección de esta oficina.

De la compra y construcción de la planta de hielo en el Cuartel Rowell, cerca de Cienfuegos, Cuba.

De la administración de:

Fábrica de Hielo, Hospital número 1, Habana.

Planta eléctrica ,,

,, en el Cuartel de la Fuerza, talleres de maquinaria y comunicaciones marítimas, Arsenal.

De la preparación y otorgamiento de varias escrituras públicas, contratos y arrendamientos relativos á la ocupación de edificios y terrenos, y otros asuntos de igual naturaleza.

Informe Financiero:

Las relaciones de las rentas y gastos que se acompañan, incluyendo, las operaciones de esta oficina desde que me hice cargo de sus funciones, que abarcan las rentas y gastos relacionados con la contabilidad del malogrado Comandante George S. Cartwright, Jefe de Administración interino del Departamento de Cuba.

Ingresos.

De la Tesorería general		$ 318,642.77	
Transferencias hechas por los empleados		1,293.48	
Recaudado:			
Reparaciones, Arsenal		5,874.48	
Fábrica de Hielo, Hospital Municipal Núm. 1		3,984.97	
Alquileres Hospital, San Ambrosio		1,272.82	$ 331,068.52

Egresos:

Edificios Públicos:			
Alumbrado	$ 6,002.46		
Reparaciones	21,717.94		
Construcciones	14,254.41	$ 41,974.81	
F. Carril Mr. de Triscornia:			
Compra de terrenos; arrendamientos; construcciones y cercados; balaustraje; puentes, etc	96,713.14	96,713.14	
Alquileres:			
Alojamientos y terrenos para servicio de guerra	15,653.08	15,653.08	
Empleados civiles	40,029.51	40,029.51	
Planta Eléctrica y Fábrica de Hielo:			
Hospital Municipal Núm. 1	7,193.62		
La Fuerza	7,420.81	14,614.43	
Muebles de escuela:			
Compra y colocación		55,086.73	
Conceptos varios		21,487.52	
Depositados en Tesorería		30,299.70	
Saldo á cuenta, Junio 30, 1901		15,209.60	$ 331,068.52

INFORME

DEMOSTRATIVO DEL MUEBLAJE DE LAS ESCUELAS RECIBIDOS Y DISTRIBUIDOS EN TODO EL DEPARTAMENTO DE CUBA, Y DEL DESEMBOLSO DE FONDOS HECHOS PARA PAGO DE DICHOS MUEBLAJES, ASÍ COMO PARA LA LIQUIDACIÓN DE GASTOS IMPREVISTOS QUE SE RELACIONEN CON LOS DESEMBOLSOS.

El informe que se acompaña comprende el período desde Enero 3 de 1900 hasta el 30 de Junio de 1901 inclusive, no habiéndose emitido anteriormente informe alguno.

El diez y nueve de Febrero de 1900 se convocó una Junta en las oficinas del Jefe de Administración Militar de la División de Cuba, con el objeto de abrir y recomendar la adjudicación de contratos, según ofertas hechas al Jefe de Administración Militar de la División en contestación á los anuncios publicados en la Gaceta Oficial de Enero 3 de 1900, por el General Adna R. Chaffee, Jefe de Estado Mayor.

El día 26 de Febrero de 1900 la Junta sometió al Ayudante General de la División recomendaciones para que se aceptasen las ofertas que después fueron aprobadas por el Ayudante General de la División:

CONTRATISTA.	Número de efectos.	Importe del efecto.	Importe Total.
Compañía "Standard School Furniture"	15,000 carpetas		$ 58,979.00
	2,500 reclinatorios		
J. T. Cavanagh	25,000 carpetas		
	4,169 reclinatorios		99,821.40
Compañía "New Orleans Furniture."	750 armarios		7,401.75
Ward y Huntington	1,500 campanillas	780.48	
	750 armarios	7,989.40	
	6,000 listones	1,083.58	9,853.46
Compª de grabados "G. M. Newhall"	39,010 listones		7,802.00
H. C. Swain	1,500 sillas		1,825.31
W. F. MacLaughlin	750 armarios		8,197.50
B. S. Romero	1,000 relojes		2,029.90
D. A. Tower	2,000 relojes		4,500.00
Compª de mueblaje "Scarrit Comstock"	500 pupitres		3,700.00
J. L. Hammett Cª	700 pupitres	7,445.69	
	4,000 dc. raspadores	1,632.00	
	3,000 mapas	6,450.00	15,527.99
J. Wanamaker	3,000 tinteros		487.50
A. H. Andrews y Cª	15,000 carpetas		
	2,500 reclinatorios		63,350.00
Sussdorf, Zaldo y Cª	30,000 carpetas		
	5,000 reclinatorios	122,350.00	
	14,990 listones	3,389.75	
	750 armarios	8,687.75	
	1,500 sillas	1,639.75	136,067.25
Champion y Pascual	15,000 carpetas		57,282.95
	2,500 reclinatorios		
Merle y Heany	500 pupitres		4,474.00
		Total adjudicado	$481.300.01

Después de esta acción, varios embarques se hicieron, todos los cuales vinieron del puerto de Nueva York con excepción de los embarques hechos por la "New Orleans School Furniture Company" por el puerto de Nueva Orleans, Louisiana. La mayor parte de los muebles fueron enviados á su destino del puerto de la Habana. Otros embarques en cantidad mayor ó menor fueron distribuídos por los puertos de Santiago, Matanzas, Sagua la Grande, Cienfuegos, Gibara, Manzanillo, Guantánamo, Baracoa, Nuevitas, Caibarién y Cárdenas.

A la llegada de los embarques á los puertos fueron inspeccionados por los Jefes de Administración, y si estaban de acuerdo con las especificaciones, certificados de inspección fueron emitidos á favor de los respectivos contratistas, siendo enviados á la oficina del Jefe de Administración Militar en la Habana donde se prepararon los comprobantes necesarios, y acompañados de las cuentas originales y certificados de inspección, devueltos al Ayudante General del Departamento. Al ser éstos aprobados, los cheques fueron emitidos por el Tesorero de la Isla, y todos los documentos devueltos á la oficina del Jefe de Administración Militar, por cuyo conducto los cheques fueron finalmente trasmitidos á los contratistas.

Después de haber sido emitidos los certificados de inspección en varios puertos, los administradores empaquetaron de nuevo los muebles en las diferentes cantidades señaladas á las Municipalidades respectivas, efectuándose el embarque á la consignación de los Alcaldes. A los Alcaldes les fueron presentados recibos en triplicado para que los firmaran, una copia, siendo conservada por el Jefe de Administración del lugar y las otras dos copias remitidas á la oficina del Jefe de Administración Militar, de donde los documentos fueron finalmente remitidos á la oficina del Ayudante General hechas las apuntaciones necesarias.

En la ejecución de este trabajo, el asunto de muebles escolares ha sido objeto de anotación especial en esta oficina. Se ha conservado cuenta debida de todos los pagos hechos, ya sea por la simple trasmisión de cheques ó por pagos en esta oficina.

Hasta el día 30 de Junio de 1901, inclusive, 1,061 comunicaciones fueron recibidas referentes á muebles escolares, mientras que 1,393 cartas fueron escritas.

Gran cantidad de los embarques fué remitida sin la seguridad necesaria, resultando en gran rotura y pérdida de partes de muebles, de lo que resultó que embarques adicionales se hiciesen necesarios, por los contratistas.

Otra de las complicaciones experimentadas fué la distancia de gran número de Municipalidades á donde fué preciso enviar muebles, y la inexperiencia de las personas á quienes los muebles fueron entregados con las instrucciones necesarias respecto á los recibos y la verificación de las cantidades, etc., todo lo cual exigió una larga correspondencia, ocasionando frecuentes dilaciones que no podían evitarse. A pesar del gran número de dificultades que se experimentaron, se llama la atención al hecho de que muebles cuyo valor total era de cuatrocientos ochenta y un mil trescientos pesos, un centavo ($481.300.1) fueron distribuídos con un gasto total incidental de sólo $3.754.2; y á la conclusión del año económico, según se demuestra por los cuadros que se acompañan, todos los contratistas habían sido pagados, todos los muebles distribuídos y los recibos ya obtenidos, con una ó dos pequeñas excepciones, á saber:

Embarque hecho al Alcalde de la Habana, según factura Nº 74 de Agosto 15, 1900. Esta oficina ahora sostiene una correspondencia con el Ayudante General, respecto á este asunto.

Embarque de una biblioteca al Alcalde de Morón, Puerto Príncipe, factura núm. 179, de Abril 12 de 1901, demora causada por equivocación de la Compañía de Trasporte, que remitió la biblioteca á Morón, Provincia de Santiago.

30 docenas de raspadores en demasía en Caibarién. Asunto que se halla en vía de arreglo.

Los siguientes cuadros Estadísticos se incluyen, en que detallanamente se dan informes relativos á este particular:

Cuadro "A." Contiene las muestras ofrecidas por los licitadores, y resultado.

Cuadro "B." Demuestra los gastos extraordinarios incurridos en la armazón, manejo, almacenaje y transporte de muebles escolares.

Cuadro "C." Contiene los diferentes puertos donde efectuaron entregas, la cantidad de artículos embarcados para los diferentes puertos por los contratistas respectivos; exceso en la cantidad prorateada y su distribución; exceso en la cantidad de contratos y el resultado, y la existencia restante.

Cuadro "D." Demuestra los diferentes contratistas que suministraron muebles para las escuelas de la Isla de Cuba por conducto del Jefe de Administración Militar del Departamento; la suma total y el costo de cada artículo; el número, la cantidad total de contratos de cada contratista; las cantidades pagadas y el total de lo concedido.

Cuadro "E." Demuestra los embarques hechos del sobrante en la cantidad del prorateo.

Cuadro "F." Demuestra la cantidad de cada clase de muebles entregada á la varias municipalidades de la Isla según fueron designadas por el Superintendente de Escuelas.

Cuadro "G." Contiene una miscelánea de material de escuelas embarcado por el Jefe de Administración Militar del Departamento.

ESTADÍSTICA DE LOS MUEBLES ESCOLARES EXISTENTES EN EL ARSENAL.

Una biblioteca	(Muestra.)
Un modelo de biblioteca	"
Cinco carpetas	"
Una silla	"
Un listón de pizarra	"
Tres carpetas de maestros	"
Dos mapas	"
Un raspador	"
Dos relojes	"
Una base de un tintero	"
Un tintero de cristal	"
Surtido de partes de carpetas	"

TRANSPORTE.

Dúrante los meses de Junio, Julio y Agosto de 1900, 1,273 maestros de escuela tomaron pasajes en transportes del Ejército de los Estados Unidos dirigiéndose á la Universidad de Harvard y regresaron á sus respectivos hogares de la misma manera, sin hacér gastos personales de ninguna clase. Los preparativos de este trabajo fueron hechos por el Departamento del Cuartelmaestre.

En el viaje de regreso del "Sedgwick," algunos centenares de maestras se embarcaron en Boston, y fueron atendidas en los puntos intermedios antes de llegar á la Habana.

Durante este período, y teniendo el vapor "Sedgwick," solamente ochenta cubiertos, se hizo necesario que la Mayordomía de dicho buque trabajase veinte horas consecutivas durante el viaje.

Ni una sola queja por falta de atención hacia las necesidades de dichas maestras, ni un solo caso de pérdida de nada de sus equipajes, aparece mencionada durante toda la excursión. La adaptabilidad del servicio de transportes, como entonces se sostenía, para hacer frente á esta apremiante necesidad, única en su clase y el celo y eficiencia del personal correspondieron á las necesidades de esta excursión, y aprovecho esta oportunidad para mencionar el hecho.

El Departamento de transportes de esta oficina expide los conocimientos para los muebles de las escuelas entregados á este Departamento por los contratistas, lo mismo que para cualquiera otra carga que sea comprada por los Oficiales Pagadores de fondos insulares por pertrechos de guerra facturados á la Guardia Rural, y en otros casos especiales. El transporte de pasajeros, á petición de las autoridades insulares se expiden á toda persona que presente órdenes para dicho transporte. Los recursos de esta oficina han sido en todo tiempo aprovechable por los que manejaban el ramo de transportes de la oficina del Tesorero de Cuba.

El Departamento del Cuartelmaestre, ha tenido bajo su cargo el embarque y distribución de propiedad insular por la Isla. Con respecto al total manejo de grandes cantidades de propiedades insulares, reembarque de las mismas á remotos puntos, especialmente en lo que se refiere á muebles para las escuelas no ha habido un solo caso de pérdida atribuída al Departamento del Cuartelmaestre, ni á ninguno de sus empleados.

Dúrante el año fiscal que terminó el treinta de Junio de 1901, el movimiento de la propiedad insular y de las provisiones efectuado en este puerto por conducto de esta oficina, con excepción de las transportadas por la línea ferrocarrilera militar de Triscornia, ascienden á libras. 4.002,394.

Ferrocarril Militar de Triscornia:

El objeto primordial para que fué construído el ferrocarril Militar de Triscornia fué para recibir las tropas que llegaban en transportes y conducirlos á los campamentos, sin que hubiera que pasarlas por la ciudad de la Habana, y para facilitar el envío de comestibles para estas tropas sin que fuera necesario hacer el envío de dichos comestibles desde los distritos que se suponían infestados por la fiebre amarilla El camino fué construído á propuesta de una Junta de oficiales que se reunieron en la Habana á fines de 1888, de la cual el Coronel J. G. C. Lee del Ejército de los Estados Unidos era Presidente. El costo de dicho camino fué considerable, pero absolutamente necesario por exigirlo así las necesidades militares entonces existentes. Al finalizar el año económico, todas las reclamaciones pendientes que se relacionaban con esta línea han sido amigablemente terminadas, con excepción del terreno marcado con el número 13, pues los documentos que al mismo se relacionan han sido remitidos al Gobernador Militar para que decida. El propietario rehusa aceptar la oferta propuesta por la Junta de Oficiales, hasta aquí constituída, con ese fin, la cual ha dado un precio justo á esa propiedad. Las comodidades que ofrece esta propiedad son aceptables. Dicha propiedad que á la orilla del mar está arrendada actualmente al Gobierno por la Sra. viuda de Carreras con opción á la compra de dicho terreno por el Gobierno. El costo del sostenimiento del ferrocarril ha sido pagado por el Gobierno Insular, y los gastos de su explotación corren por cuenta del Departamento del Cuartel maestre de los Estados Unidos. Durante el año la única carga transportada por esta vía ha sido forraje, maderas y materiales de construcción. En vista de la poca carga que ahora se recibe se recomienda que la explotación de la línea por el Departamento del Cuartel maestre cese y que la carga que hasta hoy se embarcaba por la línea de Triscornia sea remitida directamente al arsenal para su transportación definitiva por medio de carretones ó de ferrocarriles locales. No es de creerse que la reducida cantidad transportada por esta vía aconseje la continuación de la explotación por el Departamento del Cuartel maestre.

Ferrocarril de Júcaro y San Fernando.

El 24 de Enero de 1901, por orden del Gobernador Militar, esta oficina celebró un contrato de arrendamiento con la Cuba Company, en virtud del cual dicho ferrocarril fué arrendado por el término de tres años, quedando sin embargo, á elección del Gobierno cancelar dicho arrendamiento sin prévio aviso volviendo á tomar posesión de dicha propiedad y estaciones, inmediatamente en caso de surgir cualquier necesidad militar, ó cualquier otra emergencia, que exija, á juicio del Gobernador Militar, que las autoridades vuelvan á hacerse cargo del uso y explotación de dicha línea ferrocarrilera.

Según dicho contrato de arrendamiento, la "Cuba Company" se obligó á construir en Júcaro un muelle del valor aproximado de $25,000 de conformidad con ciertos detalles en que se convino; la cual propiedad pasará á ser del Estado después que la Cuba Company haya ocupado la misma durante tres años.

Además se convino que toda la carga y todos los pasajeros tenían que ser transportados gratis por cuenta del Gobierno, según fuese necesario; que un servicio satisfactorio y precios razonables debían prevalecer, y que la propiedad toda debía ser mantenida en buen estado, entregándose en este buen estado al vencimiento ó suspensión del contrato.

Al traspasar esta línea ferrocarrilera, hiciéronse inventarios minuciosos, en que se especificaron las propiedades de todas clases pertenecientes á la línea, y dichos inventarios, unidos con fotografías diversas, formaron parte del contrato, habiéndose archivado copias de dicho inventario, junto con los demás documentos, en las oficinas del Notario Oficial.

Se acompaña un apéndice en que se especifican las transacciones realizadas por el Ferrocarril de Júcaro y San Fernando, durante el período comprendido entre el primero de Julio de 1900 y el 31 de Enero de 1901, en la cual fecha el Gobierno cesó en la explotación del mismo. (Documento "H.")

DE LA CONSERVACION DE LOS EDIFICIOS PUBLICOS.

CONSTRUCCIONES GENERALES, REPARACIONES Y ALQUILERES.

Los edificios de que ha sido encargado el Comisario General para su sostenimiento y para atender á las reparaciones necesarias, son:

El Palacio del Gobernador General.
El del Segundo Cabo.
Tacón número 1.
Edificio de la Maestranza.
Castillo del Príncipe.
El Arsenal.
Edificios (Cuarteles, etc.)
Tiendas.
Almacenes.
La Punta, Depósito de la Comisaría.
Establos del Cuartel General, Zulueta y La Punta.
Corral del Comisario General (Chief Quartermaster) Príncipe.
Quinta de los Molinos.
Planta de la Luz Eléctrica, La Fuerza.
Fábrica de Hielo y la de la Luz Eléctrica, Hospital Municipal Número 1.

Otros trabajos de naturaleza semejante han sido realizados, de tiempo en tiempo, según lo dispuesto por el Gobernador Militar.

Durante el año económico de que se trata, los edificios mencionados han sido debidamente atendidos de acuerdo con lo dispuesto; varios alojamientos para oficiales han sido transformados, volviéndoseles á pintar, habiendo sido blanqueadas, y los aparatos de sanidad necesarios han sido colocados en varios edificios y departamentos hasta el presente no previsto de los mismos.

Los dos palacios han vuelto á ser completamente pintados por dentro y por fuera, satisfactoriamente, siendo el costo moderado.

En efecto, ninguna nueva construcción se llevó á cabo por esta oficina durante el año, exceptuando la estación de observaciones del Castillo del Morro que originó un gasto de $352,02, y la instalación de una cloaca de desagüe, baños é inodoros en los cuarteles de la Cabaña, obra de hecho terminada al cerrar el año, con un costo total de $6,546.13 hasta la fecha.

Se completó durante el año el cercado de la derecha y la construcción de una casa de máquina en Triscornia, para el servicio del camino militar de Triscornia. Esta obra fué comenzada durante la administración de mi predecesor el teniente coronel Humphrey, por contrata con la Compañía de Contratas de Manhattan.

Se invirtió la suma de $21,717.94, durante el ejercicio, bajo la dirección del Jefe de la Administración, para la reparación de los edificios públicos, pagada con aprobación del Gobernador Militar, en la ciudad de la Habana.

Los pagos hechos por esta oficina durante el pasado ejercicio por alquileres de casas y terrenos ocupados para atenciones militares y del Gobierno fueron $69,856.86.

Obedeciendo á instrucciones del Gobernador Militar, esta oficina arrendó á la Compañía R. B. Lyon, para almacenes generales y de tabaco, el piso bajo del edificio público conocido por el Hospital de San Ambrosio. El edificio fué, finalmente, aceptado por el inquilino, y el arrendamiento se hizo efectivo en todas sus partes, el 23 de Abril, 1901.

Una relación adjunta se acompaña expresiva de las casas que posee, que tiene arrendadas y están ocupadas por el Gobierno para atenciones del servicio Militar y Civil, bajo la inspección de la Aministración Militar en todo el Departamento de Cuba. (Documento I.)

En *estampado en azul* por separado, se consignan al casas que ocupan varios cuarteles y estaciones.

Se acompaña una relación de escrituras de contratas otorgadas bajo la dirección de esta oficina durante el año. (Documentos J. y K.)

Construcción de una planta para hielo en las barracas Rowell.

Obedeciendo á las instrucciones del Gobernador Militar, contenidas en su decreto de Octubre 10, 1900 (No. 5,005, colección Civil de 1900, Cuartel General de la División de Cuba), esta oficina celebró un contrato con la Compañía manufacturera de York, de Pensilvania y Nueva York, para la entrega á bordo, en el puerto de Nueva York, de una planta de hielo, de 3 toneladas para las barracas Rowell á un costo de $5,250.00; trayendo un transporte la planta á su destino.

Construyóse aquélla oportunamente y fué entregada á bordo del transporte "Rawlins," depachado para salir de Nueva York el día 10 de Abril. Pero el vapor se incendió en el muelle y se hechó á pique para evitar su destrucción por las llamas. La maquinaria de la planta quedó, en consecuencia, averiada, y hubo que devolverla á los fabricantes para las reparaciones necesarias que sobrevinieron á causa del calor y de haberla sumergido.

Reembarcose la planta para Nueva York y puesta á bordo del

transporte "Sedwick" salió el día 10 de Mayo con escala en Cienfuegos.

Al finalizar el año la planta está de hecho terminada; y es lo gastado á la fecha $4,109.71, en su construcción, instalación, mano de obra, material, etc.

Andando la planta surtirá á las tropas acuarteladas en las barracas de Rowell, de todo el hielo necesario, á un precio razonable.

LUZ ELECTRICA, PLANTA PARA HIELO, HOSPITAL MUNICIPAL NO. 1.

Durante el ejercicio de 1901, la Planta Eléctrica y la de Hielo en el Hospital No. 1, han funcionado á satisfacción. Al cerrar el año, las dos plantas se hallan en muy buen estado.

Estas plantas funcionan con sujección al contrato celebrado con Mr. F. Bennet, á razón del precio contratado de $60 al día. Este precio cubre los gastos todos menos los del material para la instalación y las luces suministradas durante las horas del día.

Según el precio de contrata y según pagos hechos en concepto de provisiones, etc., los realizados por esta oficina, dan el siguiente resultado durante el año.

ENTRADAS.

Planta para Hielo.

La existencia de hielo de Julio, 1900, á Enero, 1901, inclusive, fué como sigue:

Julio,	1900	462,710	libras.
Agosto,	,,	451,115	,,
Septiembre,	,,	442,790	,,
Octubre,	,,	496,200	,,
Noviembre,	,,	461,425	,,
Diciembre,	,,	386,625	,,
Enero,	1901	360,410	,,

un total de 3,061,265 á $0.30 por 100 -- $9,183.79.

En Febrero 1º, 1901, de la distribución y recaudación del producto del hielo se encargó esta oficina de fiscalizarla, por orden del Gobernador Militar, y se redujo el precio á 25 centavos las 100 libras. El producto desde entonces que rindió es el siguiente:

Febrero,	1901	326,300	libras
Marzo,	,,	383,860	,,
Abril,	,,	422,650	,,
Mayo,	,,	461,175	,,
Junio,	,,	529,478	,,

un total de 2,123,463 libras á $0.25 el 100 -- $5,308.66, resultando una existencia total y un producto de 5,184,728 libras, $14,492.45.

LA PLANTA ELECTRICA.

El alumbrado de la Pirotecnia, Castillo del Príncipe y Hospital Municipal No. 1, con el servicio de toda la noche para dar la luz á todas horas, fué como sigue:

HOSPITAL MUNICIPAL NO. 1.

10 luces de arco, 1,000 B. cada una y 950 lámparas incandescentes.

CASTILLO DEL PRINCIPE.

160 lámparas incandescentes.

PIROTECNIA MILITAR.

160 lámparas incandescentes.

Un total de 1,270 lámparas incandescentes y 10 luces de arco de á 1,000 B. cada una.

La planta suministró durante el año un promedio de 2,230.

Amperes cada veinticuatro horas de luz, valor comercial, precios corrientes......	$ 24,631.20
Menos 5% rebaja que hacen las Compañías.......	1,231.56
Valor líquido comercial de la luz......	$ 23,399.64

EXPOSICION GENERAL.

El producto efectivo total y valor del servicio, conforme al resultado de ambas Plantas, es el siguiente:

Planta para Hielo...........	$ 14,492.45
Planta Eléctrica......................	23,399.64
Total............	$ 37,892.00

El total de gastos fué el siguiente:

F. Bennet, contratista, 365 días á $60 uno.....	$ 21,900.00	
Luces extraordinarias durante el día.............	28.50	
Material y demás necesario para instalación y ensanche..............	113.96	$ 22.042.46
Saldo, economía, liquidación.		$ 15,849.63

Además de proporcionar luz eléctrica y hielo, la Planta en el Hospital No. 1, surte al Hospital del agua caliente necesaria, y de los recursos para que funcione el tren de lavado del Hospital.

ESTADO DE LA PLANTA ELÉCTRICA EN EL CUARTEL DE LA FUERZA, EJERCICIO DE 1901.

Esta Planta fué instalada por el Departamento de Ingenieros. Se levantó con cargo á los fondos de la Isla y se entregó por orden del Gobernador Militar á la Comisaría de Guerra en 1º de Septiembre de 1900 para dar luz eléctrica á los dos Palacios que fueron al principio los únicos edificios alumbrados.

Posteriormente, las luces incandescentes se instalaron en toda la casa de Correos y en la Capitanía del Puerto. Cuatro luces de arco se colocaron en el Muelle de Caballería á petición de la Jefatura de Aduanas.

Desde su instalación acá, se vió la necesidad de hacer algunas alteraciones y mejoras, con el objeto de que la Planta marchara con toda regularidad.

El tiempo que ha estado funcionando es de cinco meses hasta el 30 de Junio.

Las luces que actualmente suministra son las siguientes:

	Incandescente.	Arcos.
Palacio del Gobernador General	695	......
Palacio del 2º Cabo	378	......
Correos.—Casa Correos	214	3
Casa Correo, 3er. piso.—Cuartos	64	......
Capitanía del Puerto	180	......
Muelle de Caballería	1	4
Total	1,532	7

ESTADO DE CAUDALES.—ENTRADAS.

El precio del servicio prestado sobre la base del promedio de las horas de amperes al día de 24 horas, demuestra que el alumbrado al precio corriente de un mes, es al tipo de	$ 1,721.40
Menos 5% D	86.07
Promedio líquido, precio por mes	$ 1,635.33

GASTOS.

Trabajando.

Empleados civiles	$3,806.67	
Carbón	1,335.75	
Aceite desperdicios	530.14	
Gastos total trabajando		$5,672.56

Conservación:

Material eléctrico, alambre, lámparas, encajes, etc	$1,048.01	
A deducir, material existente intacto	663.48	
Conservación		$ 384.53

Total, gastos trabajando y de conservación, $6,057.09

Total entrada en 5 meses de trabajo	$8,607.00
Gasto total Sep. 1, 1900 á Junio 30, 1901:	
En operación y conservación	6,057.09
Economía liqdª del servicio	$2,549.91

Adelantos y mejoras permanentes:	
Instalación de la Capitanía del Puerto y de Correos.	$ 301.23
Utensilios, maquinaria y equipo	839.76
Comprado durante el período, no pagado, utensilios. etc	400.00

Total de las mejoras permanentes y nueva instalación	$1,540.99
Gasto total cuenta Planta Eléctrica en la Fuerza, Septiembre 1, 1900 á Junio 30, 1901	$7,598.08

Se está poniendo una instalación en el edificio Tacón núm. 1, (175 lámparas incandescentes) y la misma podría extenderse á otros edificios públicos en las cercanías de la Planta con un pequeño aumento relativamente, en los recursos que hoy se facilitan.

ESTADO de los trabajos realizados en los talleres del Arsenal de la Habana correspondiente al ejercicio de 1901, por cuenta del Gobierno Insular de Cuba, con breve expresión de lo realizado, costo de la mano de obra y materiales y el gasto aproximado en que se hubiera incurrido por el Gobierno Insular si se hubieran satisfecho con arreglo á los tipos corrientes.

	Costo de reparaciones con arreglo á tipos corrientes.
Seguidamente á la entrega de los talleres del Arsenal á la dirección del Jefe Comisario de Guerra, la tarea de reconocer tolos los talleres, incluso máquinas, pailas, chimeneas, sierras, correajes, poleas, serruchos, tornos, rieles, gruas, etc., fué llevada á cabo y todas las herramientas y las maquinarias de distintas clases fueron puestas en buenas condiciones para el servicio	$ 3,803.54
El ferrocarril marítimo y la armazón, la maquinaria y sus anexidades han sufrido reparaciones ó han sido renovados durante el año, representando un valor al tipo corriente, incluyendo material y mano de obra de	$ 6,260.00
La dotación de los talleres del Arsenal se vió que era suficiente, con un pequeño refuerzo para llevar á cabo la reconstrucción de los talleres y la reparación y renovación del ferrocarril marítimo como antes se ha expuesto.	

Los siguientes barcos pertenecientes al servicio Insular fueron metidos en dique sobre el ferrocarril marítimo del Arsenal durante el año, para hacerles las reparaciones necesarias en el orden que se expresa, y el pago á cargo de los fondos de la Isla.

Lancha "Percy"	Negociado de Inmigración.
,, "Fesseden"	Servicio Hospital de Marina.
,, "Waldo"	,, ,, ,, ,,
,, "Percy"	Negociado de Inmigración.
,, "Nº 3"	Servicio de Aduana.
Remolcador "Waban"	Estación Naval E. U.
Lancha "Nº 7"	Servicio de Aduana.
,, "Nº 6"	,, ,, ,,
Remolcador "Percy"	Negociado de Inmigración.
Lancha "Swift"	Servicio de Aduana.
Escampavía "Alacrán"	,, ,, ,,
Lancha "Evangelina"	,, ,, ,,
,, "Nº 6"	,, ,, ,,
Escampavía "Baracoa"	,, ,, ,,
Lancha "Nº 2"	,, ,, ,,
Escampavía "Expreso Cubano"	,, ,, ,,
Lancha "Nº 7"	,, ,, ,,
,, "Swift"	,, ,, ,,
,, "Percy"	Negociado de Inmigración.
,, "Josefina"	Departamento de Correos.
Escampavía "Alacrán"	Servicio de Aduana.
Lancha "Percy"	Negociado de Inmigración.
,, "Evangelina"	Servicio de Aduana.
,, "Swift"	,, ,, ,,
,, "Nº 2"	,, ,, ,,
,, "Nº 3"	,, ,, ,,
,, "Nº 6"	,, ,, ,,
,, "Nº 7"	,, ,, ,,
,, "Nº 3"	,, ,, ,,
Remolcador "Narciso Deulofeu"	Departamento de Ingenieros.
Draga "Comercio"	,, ,, ,,
Lanchón "A"	,, ,,
,, "B"	,, ,,
Escampavía "Abeja"	Servicio de Aduana.
Lanchón "C"	Departamento de Ingenieros.
,, "D"	,, ,, ,,
Lancha "Nº 6"	Servicio de Aduana.

Estas embarcaciones han sido examinadas por completo proporcionándoseles las reparaciones necesarias, que en muchos casos han sido calafateadas y renovada la pintura, con renovación de piezas y recorrido de la maquinaria.

Además de la obra antes mencionada, otra de nueva construcción y reparación se ha llevado á cabo al tratarse de refaccionar los edificios públicos en la ciudad de la Habana; también se hicieron obras en:

Las Barracas de la Cabaña.
Batería de Santa Clara,
Depósito de Artillería,
Cuerpo de Señales,
Depósito del Príncipe.

y varias obras de reparación general y de mecánica, insignificantes por sí solas, pero de mucho bulto en su totalidad tomándolas en cuenta dentro del año.

A todas las obras llevadas á cabo en los talleres del Arsenal en cualquiera de los ramos del servicio Insular, se les ha puesto precio con arreglo al valor efectivo del material y la mano de obra, y á esta oficina le ha sido abonada por la de su origen. Los fondos ingresados han sido cubiertos en la Tesorería Insular dentro de sus respectivos capítulos.

Respetuosamente comunicado:

El Comandante y Comisario V. E. U.,

Cuartelmaestre del Departamento de Cuba,

CHAUNCEY B. BAKER.

RELACION DE LO ESTAMPADO EN AZUL

EN LOS

PLANOS DE LOS CUARTELES DEL DEPARTAMENTO DE CUBA.

Con referencia al informe anual de Chauncey B. Baker, Comandante y Cuartelmaestre, V. E. U., Jefe del Ramo en el Departamento de Cuba, Junio 30, 1901, comprendiendo los lugares siguientes:

Habana y sus inmediaciones:
- Barracas de Columbia, (2)
- Cuartel de Artillería, Vedado,
- Baterias 3, 4, 5 y Santa Clara,
- Pirotecnia Militar,
- Vedado, Corrales de Artillería,
- Castillo del Morro y la Cabaña,
- Barracas de la Cabaña,
- Hospital de la Cabaña,

Cienfuegos, (3)
Barracas de Rowell,
Manzanillo, (3)
Bayamo,
Cauto,
Santiago de Cuba, (7)
Castillo del Morro Santiago,
Guantánamo,
Baracoa,
Holguín,
Gibara,
Nuevitas, (2)
Puerto Príncipe,
Campamento R. S. Mackenzie, (2)
Ciego de Avila, (2)
Matanzas, (2)

Conforme á dimensiones en el orden siguiente:

Cauto........................	Finca ocupada por la Administración.
Gibara..............	Almacén de la Administración.
Nuevitas....................	Oficinas.
,, ...	Almacén de la Administración.
Guantánamo.........	Plano del Cuartel.
Baracoa	Cuartel y Corral.
Pirotecnia Militar........	Plano general.
Manzanillo	Plano de la ciudad.
,, ...	Corral de la Administración.
,, ...	Plano del Cuartel.
Bayamo..	Barracas, hospital, cuartel y corrales de la Administración.

Vedado	Corral del 2º de Artillería.
,, ...	Cuartel de Artillería.
Ciego de Avila............	Mapa pequeño de la Ciudad y propiedades.
,, ,, ,, ...	Mapa grande la la Ciudad y propiedades.
Cabaña y Morro	Mapa general.
Barracas de la Cabaña...	Hospital.
,, ,, ,, ...	Mapa del Puesto.
Santiago de Cuba.........	Almacén cerca del Ferrocarril.
,, ...	Casa de la Administración.
,, ...	Oficina de Transportación Oceánica.
,, ...	Almacén No. 2.
,, ...	Corral.
....	Palacio.
,, ...	Almacén del Cuartelmaestre de depósito.
Castillo del Morro, Santiago..	Mapa de Caminos, etc.
Puerto Príncipe....	Terrenos alquilados.
,, ...	Cuartel General del Distrito.
....	Oficina del Cuartelmaestre Oficial Pagador.
....	Almacén del Cuartelmaestre.
,, ...	Propiedades "San Antonio."
,, ...	Almacén Cubano.
Campamento R. S. Mackenzie...	Mapa del Puesto (Agramonte.)
Campamento R. S. Mackenzie..	Mapa del Puesto (Capitán Flynn.)
Matanzas	Campo Militar.
,, ...	Barracas Hamilton.
Cienfuegos.............. ...	Almacén de Forrage.
,, ...	Almacén y muelles.
,, ...	Terreno propuesto para instrucción.
Barracas Rowell..	Mapa del puesto y vecindad.
Holguín	Corrales, etc.
,, ...	Mapa de la Ciudad y propiedades alquiladas.
Batería No. 5	Cuartel de Oficiales.
,, ,, 5	Mapa de la Batería.
,, ,, 4	,, ,, ,,
,, ,, 3	,, ,, ,,
Batería de Santa Clara..	,, ,, ,,
Barracas de Columbia...	Mapa pequeño de la propiedad.
,, ,, ...	Mapa del puesto.

Muestras presentadas por los postores y adjudicación de aquéllas.

POSTORES.	Nº	EFECTOS	ADJUDICATARIOS.
W. F. McLaughlin	1	Estante de libros	Arsenal, Habana.
Ward & Huntington	1	Idem	Postor.
Sussdorf, Zaldo & Co	1	Estante modelo	Postor.
	1	Carpeta de escuela	Postor.
	2	Sillas	Postor.
	1	Listón de pizarra	Arsenal, Habana.
Ward & Huntington	1	Campanilla	Postor.
New Orleans Furniture Co	1	Estante modelo	Arsenal, Habana.
J. L. Hammett Co	1	Pupitre de maestro	Arsenal, Habana.
	2	Mapa mundi	Arsenal, Habana.
	1	Esponja de pizarra	Arsenal, Habana.
Merle & Heaney	1	Pupitre de maestro	Arsenal, Habana.
J. T. Cavanagh	2	Carpeta de escuela	Postor.
Champion & Pascual	3	Idem	Arsenal, Habana.
Standard School FurnishingCo.	1	Idem	Arsenal, Habana.
A. H. Andrews Co	1	Idem	Arsenal, Habana.
H. C. Swain	1	Silla	Arsenal, Habana.
B. S. Romero	1	Reloj	Arsenal, Habana.
D. A. Tower	1	Reloj	Arsenal, Habana.
John Wanamaker	1	Pié de tintero	Arsenal, Habana.
Ward & Huntington	1	Tintero de vidrio	Arsenal, Habana.
D. P. Elejalde	1	Pupitre de maestro	Arsenal, Habana.
Ruiz Bros	1	Campanilla	Postor.
	3	Tinteros	Postor.
	2	Goma de borrar	Postor.
J. M. Sauder	3	Carpeta de escuela	Tte. E. C. Brooks.
	2	Sillas	Tte. E. C. Brooks.
Wright & Co	1	Estantes	No consta.
W. F. McLaughlin	4	Relojes	Postor.
	1	Carpeta de escuela	Postor.
	1	Reclinatorio	Postor.
	1	Goma de borrar	Postor.
	2	Listones de pizarras	Postor.
Rivorosa & Fernández		Muestras	Postor.
H. C. Swain		Idem	Postor.
F. B. Benitez		Idem	Postor.
Nieto & Co		Idem	R. S. Gerente.
E. Hiller & Co		Idem	R. S. Gerente.
G. M. Newhall	1	Estante	Postor.
B. S. Romero	8	Relojes	Postor.
	1	Mapa	Postor.
	1	Goma de borrar	Postor.
	1	Estante modelo	Postor.
Colton, Ohman & Co	2	Mapas	Postor.
Old Dominion Paper Co	2	Tinteros	No consta.
	3	Goma de borrar	No consta.
Heywood Bros	1	Colección de fotografías	Postor.
Atwater & Small	1	Campanilla	Postor.
	2	Tinteros	No consta.
Manhattan Supply Co	1	Estante	No consta.
	1	Pupitre de maestro	E. P. Elejalde & Co.
	1	Carpeta de escuela	,,
	1	Reclinatorio	
	2	Sillas	
	3	Relojes	
	1	Campanilla	
	4	Tinteros	
	4	Gomas de borrar	,,
	1	Correaje	,,
Chelsea Clock Co	1	Reloj	Admon. Militar

RELACION "B."

Gastos adicionales por almacenaje, armadura, acarreo y conducciones de menaje para las escuelas.

NOMBRE.	LUGAR.	OBJETO.	Importe de la cuenta y de lo pagado.
José Muñiz	Habana	Muellaje	$ 22.94
Planiol y Cagiga	Batabanó	Madera	17.00
M. Requiera	Batabanó	Armar	10.00
R. Requiera	Batabanó	Armar	10.00
E. Menier	Batabanó	Armar	10.00
L. Menier	Batabanó	Armar	2.00
R. Ramírez	Batabanó	Armar	10.00
C. Méndez	Cienfuegos	Lanchaje	676.73
F. Soler y Pachas	Trinidad	Retoque	57.20
Jesús Arias	Manzanillo	Mano de obra	32.00
M. Gutiérrez	Sancti Spíritus	Mano de obra	391.00
M. Gutiérrez	Sancti Spíritus	Mano de obra	138.00
M. Gutiérrez	Sancti Spíritus	Retoque	96.00
M. Gutiérrez	Sancti Spíritus	Retoque	9.00
J. Gurart	Matanzas	Almacenaje	87.19
J. Vargas	Caibarién	Mano de obra	1.15
M. García	Cienfuegos	Retoque	27.00
Wm. Iness	Sagua la Grande	Reintegro	.91
Wm. Iness	Sagua la Grande	Reintegro	3.72
A. Tabares	Sagua la Grande	Mano de obra	9.00
J. Rodríguez	Sagua la Grande	Mano de obra	5.00
J. Arias	Manzanillo	Armar	54.00
V. Vía	Habana	Retoque	196.00
Wm. Iness	Habana	Dietas	35.50
F. M. Ruz	Habana	Dietas	35.00
F. A. Hawker	Habana	Arsenal, jornales	75.00
L. Vega	Caibarién	Almacenaje	11.47
L. Vega	Caibarién	Almacenaje	3.04
Nómina	Habana	Arsenal, acarreo	86.50
V. Vía	Habana	Conducción	217.00
B. Cárdenas	Habana	Acarreo	1.20
Nómina	Habana	Arsenal, acarreo	60.00
V. Vía	Habana	Conducción	63.00
V. Vía	Habana	Conducción	98.00
Nómina	Caibarién	Acarreo	66.00
Nómina	Habana	Arsenal, acarreo	155.00
Nómina	Habana	Arsenal, acarreo	64.20
Cuban Central R. R.	Cienfuegos	Apartado, f. c	12.50
Martínez & Co	Caibarién	Almacenaje	114.69
Sobrinos de Herrera	Caibarién	Almacenaje	73.31
Beattie & Co	Manzanillo	Muellaje	3.25
Beattie & Co	Manzanillo	Acarreo, muellaje	3.12
Nómina	Habana	Arsenal, acarreo	110.00
Nómina	Habana	Arsenal, acarreo	13.50
Nómina	Habana	Arsenal, acarreo	22.30
Nómina	Habana	Arsenal, acarreo	29.90
W. D. Brown	Habana	Timbres de goma	6.40
Nómina	Habana	Arsenal, acarreo	12.00
M. B. Stokes	Supt. Frye	Pilotaje	14.00
Nómina	Caibarién	Acarreo	61.00
Nómina	Habana	Arsenal, acarreo	8.80
Nómina	Caibarién	Acarreo	104.50
V. Vía	Habana	Flete	98.00
V. Vía	Habana	Acarreo	7.00
V. Vía	Guayabal	Acarreo	7.00
V. Vía	Habana	Acarreo	7.00
E. Cenia	Caibarién	Almacenaje	100.00
M. Cortina	Pinar del Río	Flete	109.00
		TOTAL	$3,754.02

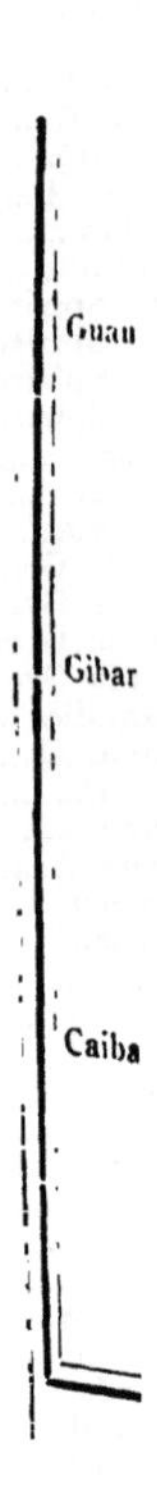
Guan
Gibar
Caiba

Expresiva de lo|s por los Contratistas; exces
consignado importe de los contratos y apl
del mismo

PUERTOS.	CON	EL EXCESO.	EXISTENCIA DISPONIBLE.	OBSERVA
Habana	J. L. H			
	"	....	296	Arsenal.
	"	....	296	Arsenal.
	B. S. R			
	W. F.			
	Merle &	....	22	Defecto compensado
	G. M.			
	D. A. To	a.		
	H. C. Sw	a.		
	J. L. Ha			
	New Or			
	G. M. N			
	Merle &			
Guantánamo	W. F. M			
	J. L. Ha			
	Champi			
	H. C. S			
	D. A. T			
	Sussdor			
Gibara	Sussdor			
	Ward &			
	D. A. T			
	J. T. Ca			
	J. L. Ha			
	Scarritt			
Caibarién	Standar			
	J. L. Ha	....	Partes	Arsenal.
		....	Partes	Arsenal.
	Sussdor			
	D. A. T			
	Ward &			

RELACION "D."

Expresiva de los contratistas, de los efectos y su cantidad y número total de los contratos para abastecer de muebles y otros efectos á las Escuelas de la Isla de Cuba, según los contratos de 8 de Marzo de 1900 celebrados con el Jefe Cuartelmaestre, de la División de Cuba en la Habana.

CONTRATISTA.	NUMERO TOTAL.	EFECTOS.	Precio del artículo.	Importe de lo pagado por contrata.
Compª Standard School Furnishing	17,500	[illegible]s	$ 58,979.00	$ 58,979.00
Compª J. T. Cavanagh	29,169	[illegible]s	99,821.40	99,821.40
Compª New Orleans Furniture	750	Estantes	7,401.75	7,401.75
Compª Ward & Huntington	1,500	[illegible]nillas	780.48	
	6,000	[illegible]s	1,083.58	
	750	Estantes	7,989.40	9,853.46
Compª Geo. M. Newhall Engineering	39,010	Listones	7,802.00	7,802.00
Compª H. C. Swain & Son	1,500	Sillas	1,825.31	1,825.31
Compª W. F. McLaughlin	750	Estantes	8,197.50	8,197.50
Compª B. S. Romero	1,000	Relojes	2,029.90	2,029.90
Campª D. A Tower	2,000	Relojes	4,500.00	4,500.00
Campª Scarritt Comstock Furniture	500	Pupitres	3,700.00	3,700.00
Campª J. L. Hammett	1,000	Pupitres	7,445.99	
	4,000	Raspadores	1,632.00	
	3,000	Mapas gr	6,450.00	15,527.99
Compª John Wanamaker	3,000	Tinteros	487.50	487.50
Compª A. H. Andrews	17,500	Carpetas	63,350.00	63,350.00
Compª Sussdorf, Zaldo	35,000	Carpetas	122,350.00	
	1,500	Sillas	1,639.75	
	14,990	Listones	3,389.75	
	750	Estantes	8,687.75	136,067.25
Compª Champion & Pascual	17,500	[illegible]s	57,282.95	57,282.95
Compª Merle & Heaney	500	Pupitres	4,474.00	4,474.00
			TOTAL DE ADJUDICACIONES	$481,300.01
			Gastos adicionales (Relación "B")	3,754.02
			TOTAL DE GASTOS	$485,054.03

RELACION "E."

Embarques procedentes de los sobrantes de consignación, á diferencia de los primeros embarques.

CONSIGNADOS A	Estantes.	Listones.	Relojes.	Mapas.	Sillas madera.	Sillas mimbre.	Docena de raspadores.	OBSERVACIONES.
Sra. Brooks, Guantánamo	2							
Anderson, Caibarién		2						
Comisionado de Escuelas	6		1	1				
Esperanza	1				12			
Perico	5			5				
Sabanilla	1				6			
San Nicolás	1				12			
Guanajay	1				12			
Guanajay	1				6			
Puerto Príncipe	1				6			
Santa Clara	2				12			
Mariel	1							
Superintendente de Escuelas	2							
Comandante Greble				11				
Unión de Reyes	1				8			
Matanzas					2			
Mantua	6		6	6	6			
Comisionado de Escuelas							60	Recibido de Gibara.
Mantua	1				2			
Morón	1							
San Antonio de las Vegas	1							
Camajuaní	1				6			
Guane	6				12			
Comisionado de Escuelas	1							
San Felipe	1							
Calabazar								8 carpetas del Nº 3, hechas de piezas averiadas.
Superintendente de Escuelas	1							
Santiago de las Vegas	2				12			
Regla	1				12			
Superintendente de Escuelas	1				6			
Macagua	1				6			
Guane	1							
Pinar del Río	6							
Ciego de Avila	20					24		
Consolación del Norte	6					5		
Guayabal	3				2			
Cabañas	5					5		
Morón	1							
Matanzas	2					12		
Ceja de Pablo	1					6		
Agramonte	2					12		
Matanzas	1							
Guayabal						6		
Habana	2					12		
San Antonio de los Baños	1					12		
Trinidad	1		1			6		

CONSIGNADOS Á	Estantes.	Listones.	Relojes.	Mapas.	Sillas de madera.	Sillas de mimbre.	Doc. raspadores.	OBSERVACIONES.
Bainoa	1					6		
Guanajay	1							
Bolondrón	1					9		
Santiago de las Vegas								Piezas sueltas de carpetas.
Macagua	1					3		
Commisionado de Escuelas							624	Sobrante en la Habana.
Campechuela	1							
Trinidad	2							
San Fernando de Camarones	4		4					
Alquízar	1					12		
Superintendente de Escuelas de la Isla	1							
Superintendente de Escuelas de la Provincia	2							
Cifuentes	1					9		
Santo Domingo	1							
Bejucal	1					36		
Guamacaro			4					
Bayamo	2							
Nuevitas	2							
Abreus	6							
Guanabacoa	2							
Vereda Nueva	1							
Cifuentes			1					
San Luis	1					4		

RELACION "F."

Expresiva del menaje de cada clase entregado á los varios Ayuntamientos, según lo asignado por el Superintendente de Escuelas A. E. Frye.

PUERTOS.	AYUNTAMIENTOS.	CARPETAS. No. I.	CARPETAS. No. II.	CARPETAS. No. III.	RECLINATORIOS. No. I.	RECLINATORIOS. No. II.	RECLINATORIOS. No. III.	Listones de pizarra.	Carpetas.	Estantes.	Mapas.	Relojes.	SILLAS. Madera.	SILLAS. Mimbre.	Doc. raspadores.	Tinteros.	Campanillas.
	Bolondrón	100	200	200	20	30	30	300	15	15	15	15	15	......	15		
	Cabezas	70	130	130	10	25	20	198	......	9	9	9	9	......	9		
	Canasí	30	60	60	5	10	10	90	......	5	5	5	5	......	5		
	Jagüey Grande	130	295	295	25	50	50	432	18	18	18	18	18	......	18		
Matanzas	Macurijes	180	360	360	30	60	60	540	19	19	19	19	19	......	19		
	Matanzas	1,250	2,475	2,475	205	405	405	4,720	140	153	153	153	153	......	153		
	Sabanilla	70	130	130	10	25	20	198	......	8	8	8	8	......	8		
	Santa Ana	40	80	80	5	15	15	120	......	5	5	5	5	......	5		
	Unión de Reyes	60	130	130	10	20	20	192	......	8	8	8	8	......	8		
	Caney	35	75	70	5	15	10	108	......	5	5	5	......	5	5		
	Cobre	25	50	55	5	10	10	78	......	4	4	4	......	4	4		
	Cristo	30	60	60	5	10	10	90	......	4	4	4	......	4	4		
Santiago	San Luis	120	240	240	20	40	40	360	15	15	15	15	......	15	15		
	Santiago	660	1,270	1,270	115	205	210	1,920	100	100	100	100	......	100	100		
	Songo	....	50	50	......	10	10	60	......	2	2	2	......	2	2		
	Abreus	70	190	190	10	25	25	210	......	11	11	11	......	11	11		
	Cienfuegos	720	1,440	1,440	120	242	242	2,160	90	90	90	90	......	90	90		
	Cruces	160	320	320	25	55	50	480	20	20	20	20	......	20	20		
Cienfuegos	Palmira	130	265	265	20	45	45	396	25	25	25	25	......	25	25		
	Ranchuelo	140	280	280	25	45	50	420	17	17	17	17	......	17	17		
	Rodas	200	365	375	35	70	65	612	40	40	40	40	......	40	40		

RELACIÓN "F."—(CONTINUACIÓN).

PUERTOS.	AYUNTAMIENTOS.	CARPETAS. No. I.	CARPETAS. No. II.	CARPETAS. No. III.	RECLINATORIOS. No. I.	RECLINATORIOS. No. II.	RECLINATORIOS. No. III.	Listones de pizarra.	Pupitres.	Estantes.	Mapas.	Relojes.	SILLAS. Madera.	SILLAS. Mimbre.	Doc. raspadores.	Tinteros.	Campanillas.
Cienfuegos	San Juan de las Yeras	70	140	140	10	25	25	210	....	9	9	9	....	9	9		
	S. Fernando Camarones	90	175	175	15	30	30	276	....	13	13	13	....	13	13		
	Sancti Spíritus	400	800	800	60	135	135	1,200	70	70	70	70	....	70	70		
	Trinidad	290	560	550	50	90	95	840	57	57	57	57	....	57	57		
	Ciego de Avila	50	100	100	10	15	15	150	....	6	6	6	....	6	6		
	Morón	75	160	155	15	25	25	234	....	12	12	12	....	12	12		
	Santa Cruz del Sur	135	270	275	25	45	45	408	....	15	15	15	....	15	15		
Manzanillo	Bayamo	120	240	240	20	35	35	360	16	16	16	16	16	....	16		
	Campechuela	140	270	270	25	50	45	408	18	18	18	18	18	....	18		
	Jiguaní	100	200	200	15	30	35	300	12	12	12	12	12	....	12		
	Manzanillo	520	1,040	1,040	90	175	175	1,560	54	54	54	54	54	....	54		
Cárdenas	Cárdenas	600	1,200	1,200	105	195	200	1,800	60	70	70	70	70	....	70		
	Carlos Rojas	55	110	105	10	20	15	162	....	10	10	10	10	....	10		
	Colón	370	740	740	60	120	120	1,110	40	50	50	50	50	....	50		
	Jovellanos	140	280	280	20	50	50	420	16	16	16	16	16	....	16		
	Macagua	60	120	120	10	20	20	180	....	6	6	6	6	....	6		
	Martí	55	110	105	10	20	15	162	....	4	4	4	4	....	4		
	Mo Gómez	70	130	130	10	25	20	198	....	8	8	8	8	....	8		
	Palmillas	160	310	330	25	55	55	480	24	24	24	24	24	....	24		
	Perico	60	120	120	10	20	25	180	....	6	6	6	6	....	6		
	Roque	70	140	140	10	20	25	210	....	8	8	8	8	....	8		
	San José de los Ramos	100	200	200	15	30	30	300	....	12	12	12	12	....	12		
	Esperanza	70	140	140	10	25	25	210	....	8	8	8	8	....	8		
	San Diego del Valle	40	90	90	5	15	15	132	....	10	67	10	10	....	10		
	Santa Clara	420	830	850	70	140	145	1,260	60	67	1	67	67	....	67		
	Mez Capote	....	30	....	....	5	....	18	....	1	....	1	1	....	1		
Nuevitas	[illegible]	110	220	220	20	35	35	330	15	15	15	15	....	15	15		

PUERTOS.	AYUNTAMIENTOS.	CARPETAS. No. I.	CARPETAS. No. II.	CARPETAS. No. III.	RECLINATORIOS. No. I.	RECLINATORIOS. No. II.	RECLINATORIOS. No. III.	Listones de pizarra.	Pupitres.	Estantes.	Mapas.	Relojes.	SILLAS. Madera.	SILLAS. Mimbre.	Doc. raspadores.	Tinteros.	Campanillas.
Nuevitas	Puerto Príncipe	970	1,940	1,940	160	325	325	2,910	120	170	170	170	......	170	170		
	Puerto Padre	30	60	60	5	10	10	90	......	5	5	5	......	5	5		
Guantánamo	Guantánamo	520	1,040	1,040	85	175	175	1,560	38	38	38	38	38	......	38		
	Niquero	30	95	95	10	15	15	144	7	7	7	7	7	......	7		
Baracoa	Baracoa	120	230	230	20	40	40	348	40	40	40	40	......	40	40		
Caibarién	Caibarién	110	220	220	20	35	35	330	16	16	16	16	......	16	16		
	Camajuaní	80	160	160	15	30	25	240	12	12	12	12	......	12	12		
	Placetas	110	210	210	15	35	40	318	18	18	18	18	......	18	18		
	Remedios	320	590	590	45	105	100	900	40	40	40	40	......	40	40		
	Vueltas	50	100	100	10	15	15	150	......	6	6	6	......	6	6		
	Yaguajay	80	160	160	15	25	30	240	......	8	8	8	......	8	8		
Sagua la Grande	Calabazar	140	290	300	25	45	50	438	19	19	19	19	19	......	19		
	Cifuentes	140	280	280	25	50	45	420	14	14	14	14	14	......	14		
	Quemado de Güines	80	160	160	15	30	25	240	......	9	9	9	9	......	9		
	Santa Isabel de las Lajas	150	300	300	25	50	50	450	16	16	16	16	16	......	16		
	Santo Domingo	130	260	250	20	40	40	384	15	15	15	15	15	......	15		
	Sagua la Grande	500	1,050	1,050	85	170	175	1,560	62	62	62	62	62	......	62		
Gibara	Gibara	110	225	225	20	35	35	336	14	14	14	14	......	14	14		
	Holguín	300	600	600	50	100	100	900	20	20	20	20	......	20	20		
	Mayarí	50	75	75	5	5	15	120	......	6	6	6	......	6	6		
Habana	Aguacate	60	130	130	10	20	20	192	......	16	10	10	10	......	10		
	Alquízar	80	160	160	15	25	25	240	......	8	8	8	8	......	8		
	Bainoa	60	100	100	10	20	15	156	......	7	7	7	7	......	7		
	Batabanó	200	400	400	30	70	70	600	22	22	22	22	22	......	22		
	Bauta	125	250	245	20	40	40	372	18	18	18	18	18	......	18		
	Bejucal	185	370	365	30	60	60	552	23	23	23	23	23	......	23		
	Cano	80	160	160	15	25	30	240	......	12	12	12	12	......	12		

RELACIÓN "F."—(CONTINUACIÓN).

PUERTOS.	AYUNTAMIENTOS.	CARPETAS.			RECLINATORIOS.			Listones de pizarra.	Pupitres.	Estantes.	Mapas.	Relojes.	SILLAS.		Doc. raspadores.	Tinteros.	Campanillas.
		No. I.	No. II.	No. III.	No. I.	No. II.	No. III.						Madera.	Mimbre.			
Habana	Catalina	70	145	145	10	25	25	216	......	16	16	16	16	......	16		
	Ceiba del Agua	80	160	160	15	25	30	240	......	6	6	6	6	......	6		
	Guanabacoa	380	750	760	60	120	120	1,140	47	47	47	47	......	47	47		
	Guara	50	95	95	10	15	15	144	......	7	7	7	7	......	7		
	Güines	300	600	600	50	100	100	900	40	53	53	53	53	......	53		
	Güira de Melena	240	480	480	40	80	80	720	29	29	29	29	29	......	29		
	HABANA	1,950	3,575	3,625	361	602	607	5,496	199	201	201	201	......	201	201	3,000	1,500
	Isla de Pinos	45	95	90	10	15	15	138	......	8	8	8	8	......	8		
	Jaruco	70	150	140	10	25	25	216	......	9	9	9	9	......	9		
	Madruga	150	300	300	25	50	50	450	21	21	21	21	21	......	21		
	Managua	30	85	85	5	15	15	120	......	5	5	5	5	......	5		
	Marianao	240	480	480	40	80	80	720	22	22	22	22	......	22	22		
	Melena del Sur	55	100	125	10	20	20	168	......	8	8	8	8	......	8		
	Nueva Paz	170	340	340	25	55	60	510	24	24	24	24	24	......	24		
	Quivicán	60	120	120	10	20	20	180	......	8	8	8	8	......	8		
	Regla	180	360	360	20	60	60	540	17	17	17	17	......	17	17		
	Salud	30	75	75	5	15	10	108	......	5	5	5	5	......	5		
	Santiago de las Vegas	200	400	400	30	65	65	600	26	26	26	26	26	......	26		
	San Antonio de los Baños	160	320	320	25	50	55	480	20	20	20	20	20	......	20		
	San Antonio de las Vegas	55	115	110	10	20	20	168	......	9	9	9	9	......	9		
	San Felipe	70	135	135	10	20	35	204	......	9	9	9	9	......	9		
	San José de las Lajas	160	300	300	25	50	50	456	......	17	17	17	17	......	17		
	Santa Cruz del Norte	30	95	95	5	15	15	132	......	6	6	6	6	......	6		
	Santa María del Rosario	70	140	140	10	25	25	210	......	8	8	8	8	......	8		
	San Nicolás	80	160	160	10	30	25	240	......	11	11	11	11	......	11		
	Tapaste	......	60	60	......	10	10	72	......	3	3	3	3	......	3		
	Artemisa	110	210	210	20	25	35	318	15	15	15	15	15	......	15		

RELACIÓN "F."—(CONTINUACIÓN).

PUERTOS.	AYUNTAMIENTOS.	CARPETAS.			RECLINATORIOS.			Listones de pizarra.	Pupitres.	Estantes.	Mapas.	Relojes.	SILLAS.		Doc. raspadores.	Tinteros.	Campanillas.
		No. I.	No. II.	No. III.	No. I.	No. II.	No. III.						Madera.	Mimbre.			
Habana.........	Bahía Honda................	35	60	65	5	10	10	96	....	4	4	4	4	....	4		
	Cabañas........................	35	60	65	5	10	10	96	....	4	4	4	4	....	4		
	[illegible] laria.....................	40	90	90	5	15	15	132	....	5	5	5	5	....	5		
	Consolación del Norte....	30	55	55	5	10	10	84	....	4	4	4	4	....	4		
	Consolación del Sur.......	30	60	60	5	10	10	90	....	4	4	4	4	....	4		
	Guanajay......................	130	270	270	20	45	45	402	13	13	13	13	....	13	13		
	Guayabal......................	30	60	70	5	10	15	96	....	4	4	4	4	....	4		
	Mariel...........................	40	110	100	5	20	15	150	....	6	6	6	6	....	6		
	Palacios........................	....	60	50	....	1 0	10	66	....	2	2	2	2	....	2		
	Pinar del Río............	400	800	800	65	135	130	1,200	30	110	110	110	....	110	110		
	San Cristóbal..................	60	135	135	10	20	25	198	....	11	11	11	11	....	11		
	San Diego de los Baños..	....	60	40	....	1 0	5	60	....	3	3	3	3	....	3		
	San Juan y Martínez......	50	100	100	10	15	15	150	....	9	9	9	9	....	9		
	San Luis.........................	120	240	240	20	40	40	360	20	20	20	20	20	....	20		
	Viñales..........................	60	120	120	10	20	20	180	....	....	....	....	....	....	....		
	Alacranes......................	195	395	390	30	65	65	588	22	26	26	26	....	26	26		
	Cartagena.....................	100	195	195	15	35	30	294	....	13	13	13	13	....	13		
	Ceja de Pablo................	120	250	250	20	40	40	372	....	14	14	14	14	....	14		
	Rancho Veloz................	80	160	160	15	25	25	240	....	12	12	12	12	....	2		
	Sagua de Tánamo..........	....	50	30	....	10	5	48	....	2	2	2	2	....	2		

RELACION "G."

Embarques hechos por el Jefe Cuartelmaestre á solicitud del Teniente C. C. Carter, del 2º de Artillería, Ayudante encargado de los Bienes del Estado.

DESTINO.	CANTIDAD.	EFECTOS.	FECHA DEL EMBARQUE.
[illegible]s de Güines	6 Cajas	[illegible] de escuela	Octubre 3, 1900.
	20 Caj[illegible]	Tinta	
Rancho [illegible]z	9 Cajas	Efectos de escuela	[illegible]tubre 3, 1900.
	20 Cajas	Tinta	
[illegible]a de [illegible]blo	6 Cajas	[illegible]s de escuela	Octubre 3, 9001
	16 Cajas	Tinta	
Cabañas	3 Cajas	Efectos de escuela	Octubre 20, 1900.
	12 Cajas	Tinta	
[illegible]el	3 Cajas	Ef[illegible]os de escuela	Octubre 10, 1900.
	16 Cajas	Ti[illegible]a	
[illegible]a Cruz del Norte	3 Cajas	Efectos de escuela	Octubre 10, 1900.
	16 Cajas	Tinta	
[illegible]	4 Cajas	[illegible]s de [illegible]cuela	Octubre 31, 1900.
	12 Cajas	Tinta	

FERROCARRIL DE JUCARO A SAN FERNANDO.

MOVIMIENTO DEL MISMO.

UTILIDADES DESDE 1º DE JULIO DE 1900, HASTA 31 DE ENERO DE 1901.

CONCEPTO	JULIO.		AGOSTO.		SEPTIEMBRE.		OCTUBRE.		NOVIEMBRE.		DICIEMBRE.		ENERO.		TOTAL.	
	Pesos.	Cts.	Pesos.	Cts.	Pesos.	Cts.	Pesos.	Cts.	Pesos.	Cts.	Pesos.	Cts.	Pesos.	Cts.	Pesos.	Cts.
Movimiento de pasajeros	409	45	184	55	219	45	181	10	346	30	237	58	248	86	1,827	29
Movimiento de mercancías	996	38	1,058	16	686	40	1,059	56	911	06	1,016	95	909	31	6,637	82
Cuenta de muelle	316	80	313	70	200	60	270	40	237	40	303	47	260	60	1,902	97
Cuenta de maderas	575	52	354	90	362	52	413	62	119	06	321	46	599	04	2,746	12
Miscelánea	25	93	12	15	1	03	11	95	25	93	28	45	30	48	135	92
Cuenta de ganado	......	......	......	......	......	......	......	......	2	00	39	35	1	35	42	70
Consignación de Aduanas	......	......	3,673	97	......	......	......	......	......	......	......	......	......	......	3,673	97
	2,324	08	5,597	43	1,470	00	1,936	63	1,641	75	1,947	26	2,049	64	16,966	79

GASTOS DESDE 1º DE JULIO DE 1900 HASTA ENERO 31, 1901.

INVERSION	JULIO.		AGOSTO.		SEPTIEMBRE.		OCTUBRE.		NOVIEMBRE.		DICIEMBRE.		ENERO.		TOTAL.	
	Pesos.	Cts.	Pesos.	Cts.	Pesos.	Cts.	Pesos.	Cts.	Pesos.	Cts.	Pesos.	Cts.	Pesos.	Cts.	Pesos.	Cts.
Conservación de la vía y construcciones	666	84	306	80	740	34	405	95	1,147	62	414	40	370	72	4,052	67
Conservación del material rodante	309	32	613	40	2,259	25	917	99	624	32	410	33	939	79	6,074	40
Conducción y transporte	724	95	776	19	781	01	673	55	725	94	684	18	1,350	46	5,716	28
Gastos generales	130	00	203	49	135	00	152	00	354	30	282	81	529	76	1,787	36
	1,831	11	1,899	88	3,915	60	2,149	49	2,852	18	1,791	72	3,190	73	17,630	71

RESUMEN.

Existencia efectivo 1º Julio, 1900	$ 1,152	06		
Ingresos totales	16,966	79		
Gastos totales	......	......	$ 17,630	71
Existencia en Efectivo Enero 31, 1901	......	......	488	14
	$ 18,118	85	$ 18,118	85

FERROCARRIL DE JUCARO A SAN FERNANDO.

VEHICULOS Y DISTANCIAS RECORRIDAS.

DE 1º DE JULIO DE 1900, A ENERO 31, 1901.

RECORRIDO DE CARROS.	JULIO.	AGOSTO.	SEPTIEMBRE.	OCTUBRE.	NOVIEMBRE.	DICIEMBRE.	ENERO.	TOTAL.
Carros cargados.......	224 Carros.	223 Carros.	154 Carros.	248 Carros.	204 Carros.	241 Carros.	254 Carros.	1,548 Carros.
	Recorrida. 6,771 kils.	Recorrida. 5,608 kils.	Recorrida. 4,460 kils.	Recorrida. 6,678 kils.	Recorrida. 7,208 kils.	Recorrida. 6,625 kils.	Recorrida. 7,371 kils.	Recorrida. 44,721 kils.
Carros vacíos............	124 Carros.	122 Carros.	63 Carros.	158 Carros.	69 Carros.	102 Carros.	127 Carros.	765 Carros.
	Recorrida. 2.858½ kils.	Recorrida. 2,745 kils.	Recorrida. 2,280½ kils.	Recorrida. 3,043 kils	Recorrida. 1,596 kils	Recorrida. 2,256 kils.	Recorrida. 2,837 kils.	Recorrida. 17,616 kils.
Recorrido de locomotoras............	2,647 kils.	2,715 kils.	2,386 kils.	2,668 kils.	2,612 kils	3,432 kils.	3,408 kils.	19,868 kils.
Costo de combustible por kilómetro............	.0296	.0281	.0263	.0474	.025	.0191	.0237	*Promedio.* .02.845
Costo del aceite por kilómetro.....	.0044	.0024	.0032	.0027	.0031	.0119	.0144	.00601
Desgaste de la máquina por kilómetro............	.0004	.0003	.0003	.0003	.0004	.0004	.0004	.00035
Costo del tren por kilómetro.......	.0744	.0731	.085	.0753	.0768	.071	.0634	.07,411

FERROCARRIL DE JUCARO A SAN FERNANDO.

PASAJEROS Y TONELADAS DE CARGA.

DE JULIO 1º DE 1900, A ENERO 31 DE 1901.

	JULIO	AGOSTO	SEPTIEMBRE	OCTUBRE	NOVIEMBRE	DICIEMBRE	ENERO	TOTAL.
Número de pasajeros	625	198	273	139	294	195	203	1,927
Toneladas de carga	236.9	250	159.9	281.9	226	325.19	243.86	1,723.75
Toneladas en muelle	154.5	156.75	96.55	135.05	128.15	214.15	114.37	999.52
Piés de madera de carga	51,103	173,910	50,794	88,088	33,883	116,860	162,875	677,513
Número de toneladas de carga por Kil. (Corriente)	5,000.25	5,475.85	6,593.55	7,988.45	4,691.26	8,780.13	4,221.21	42,750.69
Número de toneladas de carga por Kil. (Servicio militar)	7,639.15	5,439.10	5,199.45	6,633.65	6,101.30	1,293.37	1,887.80	34,193.82
Número de piés de madera de carga por Kil. (Ordinario)	973,053	1,396,171	800,586	1,806,297	386,646	1,404,471	2,566,842	9,336.336
Número de piés de madera por Kil. (Militar)	19,680	....	....	3,000	....	....	....	22,680
Número de pasajeros por Kil. (Pasaje ordinario)	12,828.5	3,996	5,306	5,129	7,510.5	4,787	4,920	44,477
Número de pasajeros por Kil. (Militares(	1,394	1,905	1,220	726	1,448	608	318	7,619

FERROCARRIL DE JUCARO Y SAN FERNANDO.

MOVIMIENTO DEL MISMO.

Material y Jornales pagados desde Julio 1º de 1900 á Enero 31 de 1901.

MES Y AÑO	MATERIAL.		JORNALES.		TOTAL.	
	PESOS.	CTS.	PESOS.	CTS.	PESOS.	CTS.
Julio 1900	101	05	1,730	06	1,831	11
Agosto 1900	252	95	1,646	93	1,899	88
Septiembre 1900	2,312	97	1,602	63	3,915	60
Octubre 1900	64	87	1,544	62	2,149	49
Noviembre 1900	1,291	47	1,590	71	2,852	18
Diciembre 1900	221	30	1,570	42	1,791	72
Enero 1901	197	90	2,992	83	3.190	73
TOTAL	4,982	51	12,648	20	17,630	71

RESUMEN.

FECHAS.		No. del Certificado de Depósito.	Pesos.	Cts.	Pesos.	Cts.
Julio 1º 1900 á Enero 31, 1901	Recibido de todos orígenes, según informe				18,118	85
" " " " " " "	Total pagado, según informe				17,630	71
Enero 31, 1901	Existencia				488	14
Febrero 20, 1901	Transferido al Tesorero de Cuba	No. 005948	74	86		
" 20, 1901	" " " " "	" 005981	391	98		
Marzo 6, 1901	" " " " "	" 006224	6	10		
" 6, 1901	" " " " "	" 006225	15	20	488	14
Junio 30, 1901	Existencia					

Ciego de Avila, Junio 30 1901

Respetuosamente se remite
Capt. y Cuartelmaestre del E. E. U., encargado del F. C. de J. á S. F.
(Firmado) W. S. SCOTT

ESTADO "I."

Relación demostrativa de los edificios propios, alquilados u ocupados para el servicio militar, ó en relación con el mismo, por el Departamento de Cuba, bajo la dirección de la Administración Militar

HABANA.

Palacio del Gobernador Militar:

Ocupado por el Gobernador militar, oficinas del Gobierno, y utilizado para las atenciones generales del mismo..........	Propiedad del Estado.

Palacio del Segundo Cabo:

Ocupado por las oficinas de la Administración Militar, Pagador del Ejército, y utilizado para escritorios y alojamientos..........	Propiedad del Estado.

Arsenal y Astillero:

Se utiliza para guardar las pertenencias del Gobierno de todas clases. Está ocupado por talleres de máquinas, almacenes, depósitos y alojamientos..........	Propiedad del Estado.

Tacón Nº 1:

Ocupado por oficinas y alojamientos pertenecientes al Gobierno..........	Propiedad del Estado.

Edificios de la Comisaría, La Punta:

Ocupado por la Comisaría del Ejército y utilizados para oficinas y almacenes, y depósito de provisiones..........	Propiedad del Estado.

Maestranza de Artillería:

Ocupada por varias oficinas del Gobierno y utilizada para alojamientos..........	Propiedad del Estado.

Castillo del Príncipe:

Usado para Depósito de la Administración Militar y para la entrada y salida de sus mercancías..........	Propiedad del Estado.

Planta Eléctrica, contigua al Cuartel de la Fuerza:

Surte de alumbrado eléctrico los edificios del Gobierno de las inmediaciones..........	Propiedad del Estado.

Cuartel de la Fuerza:

Utilizado para guardar el antiguo Archivo..........	Propiedad del Estado.

Planta Eléctrica, Hospital No. 1:

Surte de luz eléctrica á la Pirotecnia Militar, Castillo del Príncipe y Hospital Municipal..........	Propiedad del Estado.

Fábrica de Hielo, Hospital No. 1:

Produce y vende hielo á los oficiales, á las oficinas públicas y empleados civiles..........	Propiedad del Estado.

Caballerizas de la Calle de Zulueta:

Se utiliza para guardar los coches y caballos del Cuartel General que usan los oficiales de E. M..........	Propiedad del Estado.

Caballerizas de la Punta:

Se utiliza para guardar los coches y caballos del Cuartel General que usan los oficiales de E. M..........	Propiedad del Estado.

Corrales para el ganado:

Tienen como 33 *acres*. Alquilados en $119 mensuales. Sirven para guardar los animales y los vehículos de la Administración Militar, para alojamiento de empleados civiles y talleres de reparaciones de los carros del Ejército..........	Propiedad de Mercedes de la Torre, Ursulo J. Duval apoderado.

Hospital San Ambrosio:

Frente al muelle de Tallapiedra, casa de dos pisos. Ocupa el primer piso la compañía de R. B. Lyon, por contrato de arrendamiento con la Administración Militar, el segundo piso lo utiliza el Gobierno Insular para escuela.......	Propiedad del Estado.

Casa No. 54, Calzada del Cerro:

Conocida por Manzana Nº 1. Ocupada por el Director de Correos; desocupada Enero 31, 1901; alquileres pagados al corriente, $230, moneda de los E. U., al mes. Alquileres pagados desde 1º de Julio de 1900. Escritura de arrendamiento otorgada en Diciembre 17, 1900. Autorización 160, Sección Civil, Primer Decreto dorsal, División de Cuba, Septiembre 13, 1900, de Comunicaciones Recibidas Nº 24,005 en la oficina del Jefe Cuartelmaestre, 1900, y 3er. Decreto, División de Cuba, Octubre 8, 1900, Comunicaciones Recibidas Nº 24,720, oficina del Jefe Cuartel Maestre..........	Arrendada á su dueña Dolores Valcárcel de Echarte, calle Manrique Nº 49, Habana.

FERROCARRIL MILITAR DE TRISCORNIA.

	Precio.	*Vendedor.*
Manzana No. 1. Comprendiendo el frente al mar, muelles, etc, área 12,9 acres arrendada por $1,560 moneda E. U. al mes, autorización por Decreto Nº 5, Octubre 2, 1900, Comunicaciones Recibidas 270, División pág. 32 C, Comunicaciones Recibidas 23,242 en la oficina del Jefe Cuartelmaestre, también Decreto Nº 5, Noviembre 9, 1900. Despacho del Ayudante General, Habana, Cuba, Comunicaciones Recibidas 25,190 oficina del Jefe Cuartel Maestre; fecha de la escritura de arrendamiento, Nov. 13, 1900; en cuya fecha se pagaron alquileres atrasados desde Noviembre 21, 1898; también $5,150 por perjuicios del derribo de los antiguos edificios y muelles. Frente al mar el Gobierno ha construído muelles en el agua y lo necesario para la estación extrema del ferrocarril. Dueños: la senora Juana Pascual, viuda de Carreras y dos nietos, vecinos de Aguiar 116, Habana...........	$ 1,560 m. E. U. al mes.......	Arrendada á su dueña señora Juana Pascual viuda de Carreras.

	Precio.	Vendedor.
Manzana No. 2. Area, 34 36 acres; comprendiendo 26.53 acres para campo militar; escritura de traspaso fecha Febrero 20, 1900. Autorización, Decreto No. 2, Diciembre 18, 1899, y 3er. Decreto Diciembre 2, 1899; Comunicaciones Recibidas 5.034, División de Cuba, Com. Rec. 12,235 y 14,710 oficina del Jefe Cuartelmaestre............................	$ 25,676.96...	Herederos de Oduardo.
Manzana No. 3. Area, 3.8 acres; escritura de traspaso otorgada Junio 27, 1901, Autorización Decreto No. 5, Enero 22, 1901, Comunicaciones Recibidas 270, División de Cuba, Com. Rec. 27,422 oficina del Jefe Cuartelmaestre.............	$ 1;420.00...	Herederos de Juan O'Naghten................
Manzana No. 4. Area 6.94 acres; escritura de traspaso fecha Julio 5, 1900. Autorización Decreto No. 3, Mayo 9, 1900; Comunicaciones Recibidas 270, División de Cuba, 1900, pág. 26, Comunicaciones Recibidas 18,179 oficina del Jefe Cuartelmaestre........................	$ 979 00. .	María de la Cruz Morales.
Manzana No. 5. Area, 3.34 acres; escritura de traspaso fecha Junio 14, 1900. Autorización Decreto No. 3, Abril 6, 1900, Comunicaciones Recibidas, 270, División de Cuba, Comunicaciones Recibibas 18,440 oficina del Jefe Cuartelmaestre...	$ 800.00...	María del Rosario de Castenada.
Manzana No. 6. Area, 5.1 acres; escritura de traspaso otorgada Mayo 3, 1900, Autorización Decreto No. 2, Marzo 12, 1900, Comunicaciones Recibidas 270, División de Cuba, Comunicaciones Recibidas 17,458 oficina del Jefe Cuartelmaestre..	$ 1,289.52...	Herederos de Rafael Durán.
Manzana No. 7. Area, 5.6 acres; escritura de traspaso fecha Febrero 10, 1900. Autorización Decreto No. 1, Diciembre 9, 1899; Comunicaciones Recibidas 5,034, División de Cuba, Comunicaciones Recibidas 14,953 oficina del Jefe Cuartelmaestre.......	$ 450.00...	Josefa Gutiérrez
Manzana No. 8. Area, 1.15 acres; escritura de traspaso fecha Mayo 12, 1900. Autorización Decreto No. 3, Abril 6, 1900, C. R. 270 División de Cuba, 1900, C. R. 18.559, oficina del Jefe Cuartelmaestre..	$ 400.00...	Hilario Alvarez
Manzana No. 9. Area, 1.65 acres; fecha escritura traspaso Junio 23, 1900. Autorización, Decreto No. 3, Abril 10, 1900, C. R. 270, División de Cuba, 1900; C. R. 18,559, oficina del Jefe Cuartelmaestre......................................	$ 465.00...	José Jesús González.

	Precio.	Vendedor.
Manzana No. 10. Area, 2.65 acres; fecha de escritura Agosto 25, 1900. Autorización, Decreto No. 3, Mayo 9, 1900; C. R. 270, División de Cuba, 1900, página 53, C. R. 19,645, oficina del Jefe Cuartelmaestre	$772.50	Alberta Arcaya y Estalella.
Manzana No. 11. Area 1.49 acres; fecha de escritura Junio 14, 1900. Autorización, Decreto No. 3, Abril 5, 1900; C. R. 270, División de Cuba, C. R. 18,439, oficina del Jefe Cuartelmaestre	$250.00	Hilario Alvarez.
Manzana No. 12. Area, 4.23 acres; fecha de escritura Junio 23, 1900. Autorización, Decreto No. 3, Abril 5, 1900, C. R. 270, División de Cuba, C. R. 18,442, oficina del Jefe Cuartelmaestre	$500.00	Remigio Alvarez.
Manzana No. 13. Pendiente; no hay contrato. El dueño pide $2,500 oro español, por 3.38 acres. La Junta de Jefes tasó la servidumbre de tránsito en $608, moneda de los Estados Unidos. Dueño C. R. Alemán, núm. 32, Calle Real, Regla		Pendiente.
Manzana No. 14. Area, 2.8 acres; fecha de escritura Febrero 23, 1901; precio de venta $609, más 229.20 concedidos á los dueños para arreglar sus títulos. Autorización, Decreto No. 1, Abril 2, 1900, C. R. 270, División de Cuba, C. R. 432, oficina del Jefe Cuartelmaestre, y Decreto No. 2, Enero 2, 1901, C. R. Departamento de Cuba, 1900, C R. 26,834, oficina del Jefe Cuartelmaestre	$838.20	Herederos de Francisco Maza Arredondo.
Manzana No. 15. Area 1.74 acres; fecha de escritura Marzo 15,1900. Autorización Decreto 1, Diciembre 27, 1899; C. R. 5,034 División de Cuba, C. R 15,510, oficina del Jefe Cuartelmaestre		Herederos de Domingo Rodríguez.
Manzana No. 16. Area, 2.80 acres; fecha de escritura Octubre 15, 1900; incluidos en el precio $100 concedidos para depurar los títulos. Autorización, Decreto Febrero 21, 1900; C. R. 270, División de Cuba; C. R. 16,610 y 22,022, oficina del Jefe Cuartelmaestre	$400.00	Herederos de Felipe Mallorquín.
Manzana No. 17. Area 1.94 acres; fecha de escritura Marzo 15,1900. Autorización, Decreto Febrero 21, 1900: C. R. 270, División de Cuba; C. R. 16,610, Oficina del Jefe Cuartelmaestre	$200.00	Herederos de Perdomo
Manzana No. 18. Area 3.14 acres; fecha de escritura Febrero 10, 1900. Autorización, Decreto Febrero 21, 1900; C. R. 270, División de Cuba, C. R. 16,610, Oficina del Jefe Cuartelmaestre	$500.00	Vicente Luis y Crespo.

	Precio.	Vendedor.
Manzana No. 19. Area, 2.45 acres: fecha de escritura, Junio 14, 1900, Autorización, Decreto 3, Marzo 12, 1900. C. R. 270, División de Cuba, C. R. 17,459, Oficina del Jefe Cuartelmaestre.	$ 400.00....	Justa González.
Manzana No. 20. Area, 1.64 acres; fecha de escritura, Enero 22, 1900. Autorización, Decreto No. 1, Diciembre 2, 1899; C. R. 5,034, División de Cuba, C. R. 14,729, Oficina del Jefe Cuartelmaestre..................................	$ 150,00	Emilio Letamendi.
Manzana No. 21. Area, 4 21 acres; fecha de escritura, Mayo 12, 1900; Autorización, Decreto Febrero 21, 1900; y Abril 17, 1900; C. R. 270, División de Cuba, página 29; C. R. 18.500, Oficina del Jefe Cuartelmaestre..................................	$ 360,00..........	Herederos de Dolores Fernández.
Manzana No. 22. Area, 69 acres; fecha de escritura Mayo 3, 1900; Autorización, Decreto 1, Diciembre 2, 1900; C. R. 5.034, División de Cuba C. R. 14,728, Oficina del Jefe Cuartelmaestre............	$ 600.00.........	Ramón de Armas.

BARRACAS COLUMBIA.

	Alquiler mensual.	Arrendado.
Lote No. 1. Terrenos ocupados por el Campo Militar; escritura de arrendamiento Marzo 5, 1901; Autorización; Decreto núm. 1, Febrero 5, 1901; C. R. 1,522, Departamento de Cuba, 191, C. R. 27.864 Oficina del Jefe Cuartelmaestre..	$ 200.00 O. A...	María de la Salud Guzmán de Benítez.
Lote No. 2. Parte de la estancia "Barreto," escritura de arriendo, Marzo 8, 1901. Autorización, Decreto 1, Febrero 5, 1901; C. R. 1.522, Departamento de Cuba, 1901, C. R. 27.864, Oficina del Jefe Cuartelmaestre............................	$ 17.00 O. A...	Herederos de Tomasa de Cárdenas.
Lote No. 3. Parte de la estancia "Magüeyes" y "San Armas," propiedad ocupada por contrato Administrativo. Autorización, Decreto 1, Febrero 5, 1901; C. R. 1.522, Departamento de Cuba, 1901; C. R. 27,864, Oficina del Jefe Cuartelmaestre............................	$ 30.00 O. A...	Rufino Otamendi.
Lote No. 4. Parte de la Estancia "La Gomera" por contrato administrativo. Autorización, Decreto 1, Febrero 5 de 1901; C. R. 1.522, Departamento de Cuba 1901; 27,864, Oficina del Jefe Cuartelmaestre..................................	$ 10.00 O. A...	Carlos Callejas.
Lote No. 5. Parte de la Estancia Buena Vista por contrato administrativo. Autorización Decreto 1, Febrero 5, 1901; C. R. 1,522, Departamento de Cuba, C. R. 864 Oficina del Jefe Cuartelmaestre..	$ 40.00 O. A...	Frank Mont'ros

	Alquiler mensual.	*Arrendado*
Lote No. 6. Parte de la Estancia "Recreo de las Tres Rosas." La Junta de Jefes avaluó el alquiler en $105 al mes, los dueños (herederos de Manuel Nogueira) no convienen en ese precio. Pendiente	No hay arrendamiento.	
Lote No. 7. Parte de la Estancia "Soledad," con contrato administrativo. Autorización Decreto No. 1, Febrero 5, 1901; C. R. 1.522, Departamento de Cuba, 1,901 C. R. 27,864 oficina del Jefe Cuartelmaestre....................................	$20.00 O. A	Ferrocarril de Marianao.
Lote No. 8. Parte de la Estancia "La Serafina," contrato administrativo. Autorización Decreto No. 1, Febrero 5, 1901; C. R. 1,522 Departamento de Cuba; C. R. 27,864 oficina del Jefe Cuartelmaestre......	$15.00 O A......	José Domínguez Lemus...........
Lote No. 9. Parte de la Estancia "El Hipódromo," contrato verbal. Autorización Decreto No. 1, Febrero 5, 1901; C R. 1,522 Departamento de Cuba, 1901; C. R. 27,864 oficina del Jefe Cuartelmaestre....................................	$50.00 O. A......	Salvador Hernández.
Lote No. 10. Parte de la Estancia "Jesús María," arrendada primero á Juan Guerra, arrendatario por contrato administrativo, aprobado por el General Lee, Quemados, Diciembre 12, 1899, á razón de $45 oro americano; después Guerra fué deshauciado y Francisco Uribarri, de Mercaderes 29, Habana, apoderado de la condesa Val de Madrid, se negó á aceptar el precio del arrendamiento	....	En litigio.
Lote No. 11. Parte de la estancia "Larrazábal," escritura pública de arrendamiento Abril 20, 1901. Autorización, Decreto 1 Febrero 5, 1901; C. R. 1,522, Departamento de Cuba, 1901; C. R. 27,864 oficina del Jefe Cuartelmaestre..	$17 oro español	Joaquín Diago.
Lote No. 12. Parte de la estancia "Toscano" reclamada por Ramón O. Williams. En curso el expediente. No se le ha asignado alquiler...........	....	Pendiente.
Lote No. 13. Parte de la estancia "Padre." Dueño no conocido.......................	....	....
Lote No. 14. (Véase "Cementerio").......	....	....
Lote No. 15. La casa núm. 11 calle de Adolfo Castillo, Marianao, ocupada como pabellón del Cuartel General, contrato administrativo de Abril 20, 1900 por un año y desocupada Abril 20 1901. Autorización Decreto 1 Febrero 28 1901; C. R. 1,522, Departamento de Cuba, 1901; C. R. 28,416 oficina del Jefe Cuartelmaestre (autorizando á éste para pagar alquileres desde Enero 1º 1901.)..	$80 oro americ.º	Domingo Larrarte.

	Alquiler mensual.	*Arrendado.*
Lote No. 16. Almacén ocupado por contrato verbal y desocupado en Enero 31, 1901. Alquileres pagados por el Cuartelmaestre del Puesto en los Quemados, Cuba	$40. O. A..........	Emilio P. Bernal.
Lote No. 17. Parte de la estancia "La Conchita," escritura pública, Abril 13, 1901. Autorización, Decreto 1, Febrero 28, 1901; C. R. 1,522, Departamento de Cuba, 1901; C. R. 28,416, oficina del Jefe Cuartelmaestre..............................	$35. " ...	Consuelo Boan de Suárez.
Lote No. 18. Casa 115, calle Real, Marianao, contrato administrativo, Noviembre 16, 1900, para pabellón Cuartel General. El arrendador es Francisco M. Durañona, su apoderado José Otermín, Tte. Rey 4, Habana. Según el Registro Durañona es solo condueño. No se paga alquiler desde Enero 1º, 1901. Autorización para pago, del Jefe Cuartelmaestre desde Enero 1º, 1901, Decreto 1, Febrero 5, 1901; C. R. 1,522, Departamento de Cuba, 1901, C. R. 27,864, oficina del Jefe Cuartelmaestre.	$208.33 " ...	(Litigio),
Cementerio Militar:		
Lote No. 14. Porción de terreno cerca de la Playa de Marianao; sirve de cementerio militar. Escritura de traspaso al Gobierno, de Ramón González Socorro, ante el notario Vidal, Abril 20, 1901. Precio pagado $300, oro americano. Autorización, Decreto 5, Enero 30, 1901, C. R. 1400, Departamento de Cuba, 1901; C. R. 27,732, C. R. oficina del Jefe Cuartelmaestre.............	....	Propiedad del Estado.
Potrero:		
Dos lotes de terreno para apacentar el ganado; uno como de ¾ de caballería, sito en el lado E. de un camino vecinal, que se extiende desde el campamento de Columbia hasta La Playa misma; el otro de ¾ de caballería sito en el lado Oeste del mismo camino. C. R 30,969, oficina del Jefe Cuartelmaestre.	$1 oro americano por cabeza ganado á piso	Rufino Otamendi.
Tiro al Blanco:		
El terreno que sirve para este objeto está como á 2 millas del campamento, y está arrendado por contrato	$ 130.00..........	Viuda de Domingo Ortega.

PIROTECNIA MILITAR.

La ocupan:

El pabellón del Cuartelmaestre, oficinas de Artillería; Depósito de Sanidad, y varios oficiales incluso el E. M. del Gobernador Militar..	Bienes del Estdº — V. estampado azul.

LA CABAÑA.

La fortaleza de la Cabaña, castillo del Morro, campo militar de la Cabaña, ocupado por destacamentos de artillería........	Bienes del Estd? — V. estampado azul.

BATERIA DE SANTA CLARA.

La ocupa un destacamento de artillería........	Bienes del Estd? — V. estampado azul.

DIRECCION ARTILLERIA DEFENSAS DE LA HABANA.

Las baterías 3, 4 y 5 ocupadas por destacamentos de Artillería........	Bienes del Estd?

CORRAL 2? DE ARTILLERIA, VEDADO.

	Alquiler mensual.	*Arrendador.*
Lote No. 1. Escritura de Arrend? de Febrero 26, 1901, Autorización Decreto 5, Departamento Cuba, Enero 10 1901; C. R. 3.786, División Cuba, 1900; C. R. 24,762 oficina del Jefe Cuartelmaestre........	$ 80.00........	Wm. H. Reeding 118 Prado Habana.
Lote No. 2. Escritura pública de Abril 13, 1901. Autorización Decreto 2, Febrero 22, 1901; C. R. 1.864, Departamento Cuba, 1901; C. R. 28.165 oficina del Jefe Cuartelmaestre. Pagado alquiler desde Diciembre 15, 1900........	$ 10.00........	María de la Concepción Gascón, Peña Pobre 14 Habana
Lote No. 3. Habitaciones (5 cuartos) ocupados por el Coronel Haskin, 2? de Artillería, 15 calle de Baños; desocupada Abril 22, 1901, alquileres pagados hasta dicha fecha; contrato administrativo de Marzo 9, 1901........	$ 60.00........	Concepción Hermosa núm. 15 Baños, Vedado, Habana.
Terrenos y edificios completos, número 6, calle 2, esquina calle 5, Vedado, Habana. Arriendo, fecha Julio 1?, 1900........	$ 77.00........	José Muñiz Plá.
Edificio situado número 3 calle "G" Vedado, Habana. Arrend? Julio 1? 1900........	$ 51.00........	Calixto López.
Edificio situado número 21 calle 5?, esquina "G," Vedado, Habana; contrato Julio 1?, 1900. Alquiler de Julio 1? á Diciembre 31, 1900, de Enero 1? á Junio 30, 1901........	$ 68.00........	Eduardo Orduña.
Tiro al blanco. En la playa frente al mar........	Nada........	Dueño desconocido.

BATABANO.

	Alquiler mensual.	Arrendador.
Oficina; agente del Cuartelmaestre, 12×12×10, 30266½, 1901 oficina del Jefe Cuartelmaestre..............................	$ 5.62 oro am?	José Llano.

CIENFUEGOS.

Almacén de forrage, arrend? verbal con el dueño; lindando al O. con los Almacenes de Azúcares de Nicolás Castaño...	$150.00...........	García Capote.
Almacén, bienes del Estado, exceptuando el terreno y muelle; no hay contrato arrend? Alquiler del terreno y muelle...	$600.00...........	.... (V. Estampado azul.)

BARRACAS ROWELL.

Lote No. 1. Comprende el campamento Barracas de Rowell; contrato arrend? Febrero 20, 1901; autorización Decreto 10, Ayudantía General Habana, Enero 17, 1901; C. R. 806, Dep. Cuba, 1900; C. R. 26.831 oficina del Jefe Cuartelmaestre. Pagado alquiler desde Enero 1, 1901..	$280.00............	Antonio Porrúa Paseo de Vives, 106 Cienfuegos.
Lote No. 2. Comprende campamento Barracas Rowell. Escritura pública fecha Febrero 28, 1901; autorización Decreto 1, Habana, Julio 26, 1900; C. R. 976, División Cuba; C. R. 21.537 oficina del Jefe Cuartelmaestre. Alquileres pagados desde Abril 1, 1899................	$250.00............	Apoderado de los dueños Pedro N. Enteza, San Rafael 39, Habana.
Lote No. 3. Comprende campamento Barracas Rowell. Ocupado campo de ejercicios y pastos públicos. Escritura fecha Junio 24, 1901; autorización Decreto 4, Abril 1, 1900; C. R. 1968; Departamento Cuba; C. R. 28.877 oficina del Jefe Cuartelmaestre........................	$100.00............	Manuel Cabo, Cienfuegos, á nombre de su esposa Clara Rodríguez. (V. Estampado azul.)
Tiro al blanco. El tiro al blanco usado desde la ocupación por el 2? Infantería. Los dueños presentaron demanda por alquileres desde que se destinó al ejercicio de tiro..	Nada................	Dueños Herederos de Moreno

(Barracas Porwell, Julio 11, 1901.)

MANZANILLO.

Parte E, línea roja del mapa del campamento militar arrendada; los edificios fueron levantados por el 10? de Caballería..........	$10.00.............	....

	Alquiler mensual.	*Arrendador.*
Parte al O, línea roja, antiguo Hospital esp., actualmente cuartel del 10º Caballería; sin pagar renta excepto por la finca "Gerona", utilizada para habitaciones de Oficiales..............................	$50.00.......... ...	Ciudad de Manzanillo.
Los edificios en el mapa del Corral de la Administración utilizados antes por el Gobierno esp., están ocupados sin pagar alquiler.	Ninguno..........	....
Los edificios en línea roja en el plano de la ciudad de Manzanillo, alquilados para habits. de Oficiales, etc., y pagados por la ordenación de Pagos civiles.	....	....
El muelle (tinta roja) ocupado últimamente por el Gobierno Civil, según orden 73, Cuartel General de Cuba	....	....
Cerca del ángulo al S. E. del Cuartel hay lote de ½ acre, arrendado para camposanto	$5.00...............	....
Como á ¾ de milla al S. E. del Cuartel hay un lote de unos 6|8 de acre, arrendado para ejercicios militares.............	$15.00......	....
Todos los alquileres pagados por Ordenadores Civiles..	....	V. Est. azul.

30 067, O. del J. Cuartelmaestre.

Tiro al blanco. Actualmente (fecha del informe Julio 11, 1901) no hay tiro al blanco en este Puesto. Hubo uno hasta terminar el tiro de carabina. Alquileres se pagaban por las cajas de Administración Civil. Quejas del vecindario hicieron suspenderlo.............................	$15.00............	Dueño desconocido.

BAYAMO.

La Administración Militar ocupa el antiguo fuerte español, levantado en terreno particular como corrales y talleres.	Ninguno	....
Oficiales del General................................	$20.00............	Pofirio Bonet.
Depósito de ropas comparte con la Comisaría; alquileres pagados con fondos de la Isla por el Ordenador de Manzanillo	$50 00.............	S. Millones.
Hospital.	$15.00.............	Mariano Castelló.

(V. planos.)

Tiro al blanco. Construido por la tropa en terreno yermo, particular, como á 8 millas de la población...........................	Ninguno	Dueño desconocido.

CAUTO.

	Alquiler mensual.	*Arrendador.*
Comprende un almacén y dos corrales, alquilados y pagados por Ordenador de Administración Civil de Manzanillo	$75.00..............	Ramón Pastor. V. Est. azul.

SANTIAGO DE CUBA.

La Administración Militar encargada de transportes marítimos.

Armazón del edificio y muelle, techo de tejamaní, construído sobre el mar, pilotaje............	Pertenece á la Aduana. V. Est. azul.

Almacén de forrage número 2, de la Administración Militar.

Edificio de ladrillos, techo de tejas, piso estercolero, parte de tablones. Techos en mal estado, sirve de almacén de forrages. Arrendado á $75 por mes á condición de entregar mediante aviso de 30 días	Arrendado á Pedro Viana. V. E. azul.

Almacén de la Comisaría en el Ferrocarril.

Armazón del edificio, piso de tablones, techo de hierro encarrujado, en buen estado..	Bienes del Estado. V. Est. azul.

Edificio de la Administración.

Ocupado por la Pagaduría Principal, Cirujano Mayor, Inspector General, Imprenta oficial. Es de ladrillos, de dos pisos: techo de tejas; piso de mármol; segundo piso de madera; patio enladrillado. Buen estado. Arrendado por $119 al mes; á entregar mediante aviso previo de quince de días............................	Arrendado á R. Mazón.

Corrales de la Administración.

Los pesebres son construcciones de madera, piso estercolero, techos de tablas Las barracas y comedores armazones, pisos de madera ordinaria y techo de tablones. Buen estado. Casa de baños de madera, piso hormigón y techo tablas; tiene dos duchas y dos lavabos en buen estado. Armazón para letrinas, techo y piso de tablas y cinco vasijas portátiles para letrinas. El Corral está cercado de alambres..	Bienes del Estd°.

Palacio del Gobernador General.

Edificio de ladrillos piso de mármol, techo de tejas, 18 piés del suelo al cielo raso. Patio y corredores enladrillados. En buen estado. Precio en renta, se ignora. Ocupado por varias oficinas de Gobierno......................	Bienes del Estd°. V. Est. azul

Almacén de Depósitos de la Administración.

Comprende varios edificios de piedra y de ladrillo; techos de teja, herrería y pesebres.......................	Bienes del Est°.
Tiro al blanco. Mide 200×1.000 yardas, á 2½ millas del campo militar. Alquiler mensual $25.00 ($300 al año).	Dueño; se ignora
Castillo del Morro. Campo Militar, incluyendo las barreras	Bienes del Estd°. V. Est. azul.

SAN LUIS.

El campamento de San Luis consta de casas salteadas en la población, y un plano del cuartel sería de hecho un plano de aquellas. Las casas alquiladas, tres cuarterías pabellones para oficiales; dos para las clases, y una para el Cuartel General. Se pagan con los ingresos de Aduanas de la Isla. No hay cloacas, y el agua para la tropa se compra con los fondos de la Isla y se trae de un arroyo inmediato.

	Alquiler mensual.	*Arrendador.*
Pabellón del capitán H. P. Kendall, 8º de Caballería, construcción de madera, techo de tejas, por contrato verbal......	$ 17.00..........	Luisa Jiménez.
Pabellón de la Jefatura, construcción de madera; contrato verbal......................	$ 22.00..........	Germán Muñíz.
Pabellón del teniente G. S. Nowell, 8º de caballería, construcción de madera, techo de tejas; contrato verbal...............	$ 10.00..........	Pablo Rimbau.
Pabellón del cirujano J. P. Agustine, construcción de madera, contrato verbal..	$ 17.00...........	Joaquina Alayo de Ochoa.
Pabellón del Sargento Comisario del Puesto D. A. H. Kolster. Const. madera; techo tejas. Contrato verbal..........	$ 12.00..........	Germán Muñíz.
Pabellón del Sargento Cuartelmaestre F. L. Fink. Construcción madera; techo tejas. Contrato verbal...........	$ 12.00..........	Ibáñez y Alecio.
Depósitos de la Administración y Comisaría. Construcción madera; techo tejas; edificios españoles antiguos, fueron ocupados por fuerzas españolas..........	Ninguno..	Dueño, Santiago Rosseau.
Cuartel para la tropa. Se le supone construído con fondos de la Isla en Marzo de 1900; pero faltan datos oficiales. Es de madera con techo de hierro corrugado..	Ninguno..	Dueño, Santiago Rosseau.
Hospital del Campamento. Las mismas observaciones del párrafo anterior.......	....	......
28, 126, 1901. Oficina del J. Cuartel Maestre.		
Tiro al blanco. El terreno para ese objeto pagado con fondos de la Isla...........	Desconocido.....	Dueño, desconocido.

GUANTANAMO.

Los edificios estampados en carmín en el plano, construídos y poseídos por el Gobierno Español. Otros edificios, según los mejores informes, construídos y el material cedidos por vecinos de Guantánamo como hospitales para las tropas españolas. El terreno en que radican pertenece á la familia Janay de Guantánamo que lo facilitó al Gobierno Español..	....	V. Estampado azul.

29,871, 1901. Oficina del J. Cuartel Maestre.

El ejercicio de tiro hasta ahora estuvo en terreno yermo, como á 18 millas de lugar, cedido provisionalmente por los vecinos	Sin alquiler......	Bienes particulares.

BARACOA.

Barracas. Situadas en el centro de Baracoa sobre una cuesta	B. del Estado.
Provisión de agua. El agua de la cañería que surte la ciudad se eleva con un molino de viento	....
Corral. Antiguo Cuartel español que da frente al mar, fué utilizado por el quinto de Infantería, convertido en pesebre y útil para este objeto. Capacidad bastante para 125 animales	B. del Estado.

Se trae el agua de la cañería de la ciudad por una de una pulgada.

HOLGUIN.

Terreno del Estado traspasado por los españoles al Alcalde cuando la evacuación; son: 1º, sitio del Hospital Militar con patio, ocupa 2,880 metros un area de 600 metros cuadrados, distribuidos por iguales partes al Este, Oeste y Sur del Hospital; 2º, sitio de las Barracas con linderos, Norte calle de la Quinta al Este, calle de Maceo; al Sur, calle de Cuba al Oeste, calle de Máximo Gómez, con un área de 24,860 metros cuadrados y 55 centímetros; 3º Parque de Mantilla ahora Maceo lindando con una pared en una área de 12,000 metros cuadrados	.... V. est. azul.
Caballeriza de la administración, calle de la Quinta, techo de guano. Los cuatro pesebres de guano no están en terreno del Estado, es del Municipio y tiene un pozo artesiano en construcción	....
La Hacienda en Holguín tiene en su poder el documento ó testimonio de los mismos, según los cuales esta propiedad pasó al Alcalde de Holguín, en nombre del Estado, la recibió del jefe militar español. Ultimamente la ha medido el Arquitecto Municipal bajo la dirección de la Hacienda	....

29,151, 1901, oficina del Jefe Cuartelmaestre.

Tiro al blanco. 2,000+400 yardas lugar para ocho blancos. Actualmente hay 4 colocados	Sin alquiler......	Dueño el Ayuntamiento de Holguín.

RELACION DETALLADA DE TODOS LOS EDIFICIOS QUE OCUPA EL GOBIERNO AMERICANO.

		Medida Frente	Fondo	Alquiler mensual
1	Núm. 33, calle de Peralta, ocupada por el Comandante Stedman	76'	96'	$ 25
2	Núms. 7 y 9, calle de la Libertad, ocupada por el Capitán Bigelow	76'	51'	20
3	Núm. 12, calle de Maceo, ocupada por el Capitán Watson	38'	87'	12
4	Núm. 32, calle de Maceo, ocupada por el Capitán Paxton	37'	156'	20
5	Núm. 30, calle de Maceo, ocupada por el Capitán Fleming	37'	156'	20
6	Núm. 27, calle de la Unión, ocupada por el Teniente Cavanagh	56'	96'	15
7	Núm. 19, calle de Maceo, ocupada por el Teniente Palmer	103'	141'	20
8	Núm. 25, calle de Peralta, ocupada por A. A. S. Harvey	54'	63'	20
9	Núm. 11 calle de la Libertad, ocupada por A. A. S. Mc. Millian	30'	54'	20
10	Núm. 2, calle de Martures, ocupada por el servicio veterinario	31'	32'	8
11	Núms. 3 y 5, calle de Maceo, ocupada por la biblioteca y la escuela del Puesto	71'	87'	10
12	Núm. 21, calle de Garayalde, ocupada por el Sargento Mayor Conley	72'	49'	8
13	Núm. 7, calle de Maceo, ocupada por un almacén	45'	83'	20
14	Núm. 34, calle de Maceo, ocupada por la Jefatura	72'	156'	40
15	Núm. 13, calle de la Libertad, acupada por el almacén militar	45'	56'	8
16	Núm. 25, calle de Unión, ocupada por un almacén militar	72'	92'	25
17	Núm. 23, calle de la Unión, ocupada por un corral de la Comisaría	43'	112'	15
18	Núm. 54, calle de Aria, ocupada por un corral de la Administración	86'	86'	14
19	Núm. 33, calle de Aria, ocupada por idem	75'	203'	8
20	Un corral en el número 35, calle de Aria	70'	203'	6
21	Núm. 37, calle de M. Lemus, ocupada por un corral	149'	156'	15
22	Núm. 41, calle de la Libertad, ocupada por el Sargento Comisario Kidwell	38'	95'	8

Todas estas casas ocupadas por contratos vervales.

	Frente	Fondo	
Barracas. Situadas en la calle de Maceo	273'	254'	....
Plaza de la Independencia. Ocupado por el escuadrón de caballería B	225'	354'	Propiedad del Estado.
Hospital Militar. Calle de Llano	130'	235'	Propiedad del Estado.

C. R. 31,405 oficios del Jefe Cuartelmaestre.

GIBARA.

(Puerto de Holguín.)

	Alquiler mensual	*Arrendador*
Un almacén, propiedad particular, ocupado por el Cuartelmaestre como granero. Arrendado y abonado por el pagador del Distrito, según contrato verval, á entregarlo con aviso previo del dueño ó arrendatario de 15 días, pagado hasta Julio 1º de 1901......	$ 25 00............	Carmen Marquina.

CAMPAMENTO R. S. MACKENZIE.

Contrato de Abril 6 de 1901 entre el capitán C. J. Simmonds, por el Gobierno Militar y el dueño de los terrenos conocidos por La Emelina y Guano Alto, situados al Sur del F. C. de Puerto Príncipe á Nuevitas, 5 kilómetros consta de 281 acres 75½ piés conforme al plan anexo al contrato; comprende desde Abril 6 á Junio 30 de 1901 prorrogable por un año. C. R. 28,061 O. del J. Cuartel Maestre......	$ 30,00............	Sebastián Morán de la Vega.
Los terrenos al Oeste de X. Y. V. W. (Véase el estampado azul). Pertenecen á dueños desconocidos. C. R. 28,061, del J. Cuartel Maestre.....................	Ninguno............	Dueño desconocido.
Los terrenos al Este se arrendarán desde el 1º de Marzo de 1901; los mismos constan en trazado aparte y el arrendamiento será lo mismo que el del señor Morón de la Vega. (Véase en tinta azul número 11 C. R. 30,195 O. del J. Cuartel Maestre)................................	$ 15.00............	A. Santayana.

Surtido de agua: 1, la que usan los caballos, de manantial en las alturas á 300 yardas al Este del campamento, que es buena y abundante y viene por declive á la canoa; 2, agua para el demás servicio viene de un arrollo de lomas á varias millas al S. E. del campamento, el arroyo tiene represa como á mil yardas del campamento, llevándose el agua por medio de bombas de vapor al estanque. El arroyo es pequeño y en las sequías se achica; pero si es necesario pueden aprovecharse otros manantiales, pues el agua abunda en las inmediaciones. La bomba es usada, de segunda mano, de fuerza de cuatro caballos, es floja y exige mucho trabajo y contínuo darle para obtener agua suficiente. La paila es nueva, de 15 caballos de fuerza. La tubería es como de 1,000 yardas de largo, de 2 pulgadas, de hierro dulce, vieja, de segunda mano y mala; exije mucho cuidado para conservarla.

El estanque es de madera, como de 500 galones, se sale, y pronto se le deberá reemplazar. Consta en el plano.

Un tubo de 2 pulgadas une al tanque con la canoa, y 4 tubos con la misma clase van del tanque á las casas de baño, surtiendo 18 duchas para los Oficiales y tropas. La demás distribución se hace por medio de estanques trabajados por mulas, llenándose los barriles colocados en ciertos lugares.

Desagüe y Cloacas. Aparte de una parte de una caja de madera subterránea que se lleva el agua que desperdician los baños, no hay otra clase de cloacas El campameto está situado en una colina, naturalmente con desagüe á ambos lados. El agua sucia y demás se lleva fuera del campamento en carretas.

28,061, 1901, Oficina del Jefe Cuartelmaestre.

Tiro al blanco. Dista del Campamento como tres millas en terrenos yermos. No se ha presentado ninguna reclamación en pago del uso que de él se hace.	Ninguno..........		Dueño desconocido.

PUERTO PRINCIPE.

Edificio de diez cuartos para oficinas del Pagador Cuartelmaestre. No hay contrato.	$	30.00........	M. Valdés.
Edificio de cinco cuartos y terrenos de medio acre, usados como almacenes del Pagador administrativo. No hay contrato. Véase diseño Nº 3......	$	75.00........	B. S. Aden.
266 acres terrenos de pasto para caballos y mulos del Gobierno. No hay contrato....	$	25.00........	B. Arteaga.
Tres edificios (un horno y 9 cuartos) como de un acre de tierra. Almacén y oficinas ocupado por la Administración Militar. Una bomba surte de agua á los edificios públicos. Véase diseño número 4..................................	Ninguno		B. del Estado.
Un edificio (16 cuartos) Jefatura del Distrito..............	Ninguno...		B. del Estado.

NUEVITAS.

Almacén en Nuevitas utilizado por el ramo de Administración Militar, está en el diseño V........... .... C. R. Oficial del Cuartel Maestre............	....	....

Oficinas, véase diseño VI C. R. 30,795, del Cuartel Maestre............................	....	
Dos cuartos 100×65, desocupados Agosto 17, 1900, no se necesitan; sin contrato; dueño B. S. Aden........................	$125.00 o|e......	B. S. Aden.
Un cuarto, para almacén de forrage Desocupado Agosto 17, 1900; no se necesita, sin contrato....................	$100.00...........	B. S. Aden.
Dos cuartos 75'×75'. Desocupados Diciembre 31, 1900, no se necesitan. Utilizados por la Administración Militar para almacenes de trasportes..............	$55..................	Vicente Rodríguez y Cª.......
Dos cuartos utilizados como oficinas del Depósito de la Administración Militar. Desocupados Agosto 19, 1900, por mudanza de oficinas á sitio más adecuado.	$40..................	Juan Bagés P.
Dos cuartos, habitaciones para el Cirujano interino F. P. Mendoza, hasta Octubre 31, 1900, en que se desocupó; no se necesita. Sin contrato......................	$12..................	Francisco Aguilera.
Dos cuartos, alquilados por meses desde Agosto 20, 1900, para oficinas del Ordenador Civil y Administración Militar.	$40	Henry Page.
Dos pisos, 5 cuartos, alquilados por meses desde Abril 1º, 1901; sin contrato; utilizados por la Administración Militar	$50	Carreras, Hno. y Cª...............
Dos cuartos, sin contrato; alquilados por meses desde Agosto 8, 1900, á $150 m. Utilizados por la Administración Militar todavía. Alquiler rebajado $50 m. después de Abril 30, 1901, si siguen ocupadas. Se desocupará en Mayo 31, 1901.........................	....	Vicente Rodríguez y Cª.......
C. R. Oficina del Cuartelmaestre: 29,913 30,795	....	V. dos estampados en azul.

CIEGO DE AVILA.

F. C. de Júcaro á San Fernando, arrendado á la "Cuba Company." Comprende la línea de ferrocarril de Júcaro á San Fernando, con todos los paraderos, rotundas, tornos, almacenes, máquinas, carros, carriles y anexidades....	....	V. estampado azul.

MATANZAS.

HABITACIONES ALQUILADAS

12½ calle de Isabel, ocupada por el Corl. H. E. Noyes, 2º Cab. (agua inclusive) ..	$ 6.00..	Manuel Taboada.
10 calle San Isidro, ocupada por el veterinario W. V. Lusk, 2º Cab.........	$ 24.00..	Antonio Ugarte

12 calle San Isidro, ocupada por el Capitán H. G. Trout, 2º Cab. (agua inclusive)........	$ 24.00.........	Antonio Ugarte.
25 calle Isabel I, ocupada por los Capitanes C. B. Hoppin y T. J. Lewis y Teniente F. C. Johnson, 2º Cab. (incluyendo agua)........	$ 96.00.........	Alfredo Botet.
27 calle Isabel I, ocupada por el Teniente S. M. Kochersperger, 2º Cab. (incluyendo agua........	$ 24.00,.........	M. Salgueiro.
5 Paseo de Martí, ocupada por el Teniente E. J. Pike, 2º Cab. (incluyendo agua)........	$ 19.00.........	Ciudad de Matanzas.
18 calle de Navia, Oficiales del 2º Cab. (incluyendo agua) Desocupada........	$ 22.00.........	José Fernández.
14 calle de Navia, arrendada por contrato. El Cirujano Burr (incluyendo agua)	$ 24.00.........	Alejandro Maruri.
57 calle de Navia, ocupada por el Músico Mayor Scully, 2º Cabo (incluyendo agua)........	$ 12.00.........	Cecilia Delgado.
4 Sta. Cristina, Habitaciones de oficiales (incluyendo agua) Desocupada........	$ 22.00.........	Juan A. Zabala.
47 calle de Navia, Habitaciones de oficiales (incluyendo agua)........	$ 36.00.........	Angel García.
35 calle de Navia, Ocupada por el Sargento de Administración Fiyun (incluyendo agua)........	$ 12.00.........	Eduardo Cardounel.
10 calle Isabel 1ª Habitaciones de oficiales (incluyendo agua)........	$ 36.00.........	Antonio Molins
97 calle Manzano, Ocupada por el Capitán J. H. Stone, Cirujano (incluyendo agua)........	$ 36.00.........	Rosa Ulmo Serrate.
Oficina del Habilitado, núm. 15 Santa Teresa (incluyendo agua) Desocupada	$ 25.00.........	Marcelino Díaz.
Almacén de forrage de la Administración, calle de Gelabert, frente al muelle........	$300.00.........	F. Bea y Cª
Almacen de la Administración, número 9 calle del Comercio........	$100.00.........	Castañor Rivas y Cª
Corral de la Administración Militar, Habitaciones de empleados civiles, Departamento Sur y patio contiguo para depósito de maderas para uso general.	$ 25.00.........	Caridad B. viuda de R. Maribona.

C. R. del Jefe Cuartelmaestre 31.232, 1901.

BARRACAS HAMILTON (Matanzas).

Lote No. 1, Matanzas. Tiro de fusil y pistola. Contrato, fecha Abril 20, 1901. Autorización, Decreto núm. 3, Abril 18, 1901. Departamento de Cuba, C. R. 29,095, Oficina del Jefe Cuartelmaestre	$ 20.00.........	José Trujillo, nº 39, Consulado á nombre de Francisco Viejo, ausente en España.

Castillo San Severino. Traspaso del Gobierno Español á la Autoridad Militar. Ocupado por tropas de los E. U..........	....	B. del Estado.
Terrenos. E. del Campo Militar. Constan de 165 acres y 4 lotes, propios de Francisco Viejo Isaut, ocupados por tropas de los E. U. para campo de ejercicios..	$ 55.00..........	José Trujillo, apoderado del dueño.
Corral de la Administración Militar. Comprende el lote núm 22: pesebres y depósito de carros construídos por el Jefe Pagador de la Administración con fondos de la Isla. V. los expedientes de Juntas de Jefe..	Ninguno.........	Dueño desconocido.
Lote Nos. 16 y 17. Al E. del anterior; pesebre y herrería de los escuadrones "B," "E," "H," y charanga del 2º Cab. El Campo Militar de las barracas Hamilton comprende además, varios lotes, marcados arbitrariamente en el plano, 1, 2, 3, 4, 6, 7, 8, 9, 11, 12, 16, 17; sus dueños no constan. La Junta de Jefes ha propuesto un alquiler m. de $5 en cada uno pagadero al que resulte dueño	Ninguno.........	Dueño, se ignora.
En el lote No. 5. Se construyeron dos salas del Hospital por el Comisario Pagador con fondos de la isla......................	Ninguno.........	Dueño, se ignora.
Hospital Militar de los E. U. El edificio del lote nº 10 rotulado "Hospital Militar" es propio de Manuel Michelena....	$ 25.00..........	Manuel Michelena.

Nota.—Como consta en el plano, todos los pesebres y algunas barracas están construídos en el Campo Militar; otros y el Campo de Marte en terrenos de Cecilio Ayllon. El Cuartel, ocupado por los Escuadrones "A," "C," "D," "F," y "G," 2º de Caballería y trenes de bagajes Nos. 24, 29 y 31. (V. expedientes de la Junta de Jefes. También estampado azul) C. R. 31.232, O. del J. C.

BARRACAS DE SANTA CRISTINA, MATANZAS.

Las barracas de Santa Cristina, fueron entregadas á las autoridades militares por el Gobierno español y están ocupadas por los Escuadrones "B," "E," "H," y Jefatura del 2º Cabo, oficina del Comisario del Puerto, Depósito de la Administración, Pagador de Administración, oficial Ingeniero y Sanidad de la ciudad; también almacén de provisiones.............	Bienes del Estado.
Jefatura y Panadería, contiguas al Cuartel Santa Cristina, construídas por el Pagador; fondos de la Isla, en terrenos entregados á las autoridades militares por el Gobierno español................................	Bienes del Estado.

C. R. 31,232, oficina del Jefe Cuartelmaestre, 1901.

ESTADO "J."

RELACION DE LOS CONTRATOS

CELEBRADOS DURANTE EL EJERCICIO VENCIDO EN JUNIO 30, 1901.

NOMBRE DEL CONTRATANTE OFICIAL.	NOMBRE DEL CONTRATISTA.	FECHA DEL CONTRATO.	CLASE DE CONTRATO.	PRECIO DEL CONTRATO.	VENCIMIENTO.
El Jefe de la Admón. Militar de Cuba (adquirente)	María de la Cruz Morales	Julio 5, 1900	Cesión del derecho de tránsito	$979.00.	
Id.	Alberta Arcay y Estalella	Agosto 25, 1900	Id.	$772.50.	
Id.	Hreds. de Dolores Fernández	Sept. 1º, 1900	Id.	$360.00.	
Id.	Hreds. de Felipe Mallorquín	Octubre 15, 1900	Id.	$400.00.	
Comte C. B. Baker, Jefe de la Admón. Arrendatario	Juana Pascual, viuda de Carreras	Novbre. 13, 1900	Arrendamiento del derecho de tránsito	$1,560.00	Sept. 30, 1901.
Id.	Dolores Valcárcel de Echarte	Dicbre. 17, 1900	Id. de la Casa Dirección de Correos	$230.00. al mes	Desocupada Enero 31, 1901.
Comte. C. B. Baker, Jefe de la Administración (Concesionario)	José Coto y Bello	Enero 2, 1901	Subarrendado	$244.00.	
Comte. C. B. Baker, Jefe de la Admón. (Arrendatario)	La "Cuba Co."	Enero 24, 1901	Arrendº del F. C. de Júcaro á S. Fernando	Conducción grátis de mercancías del Gobierno y pasajeros y construcción de un muelle, valor $24.000	Enero 24, 1904.
Comte. C. B. Baker, Jefe de la Admón. (Arrendatario)	Antonio Porrua	Feb. 20, 1901	Arrendaminto de terrenos	$280.00 al mes	Feb. 20, 1902.
Comte. C. B. Baker, Jefe de la Admón. (Aquirente)	Herederos de Francisco Maza Arredondo	Feb. 23, 1901	Cesión del derecho de tránsito	$838.20.	

ESTADO "J."—CONTINUACIÓN.

NOMBRE DEL CONTRATANTE OFICIAL.	NOMBRE DEL CONTRATISTA.	FECHA DEL CONTRATO.	CLASE DE CONTRATO.	PRECIO DEL CONTRATO	VENCIMIENTO.
Comte. C. B. Baker, Jefe de la Admón. (Arrendatario)	William H. Redding	Febrero 26, 1901	Arrendº de terrenos	$80.00 al mes	Febrero 26, 1902.
Id.	Pedro N. Entenza	Febrero 28, 1901	Id.	$250.00 al mes	Febrero 28, 1902.
Id.	María de la Salud Guzmán de Benítez	Marzo 5, 1901	Id.	$20.00 al mes	Marzo 5, 1902.
Id.	Herederos de Tomasa de Cárdenas	Marzo 8, 1901	Id.	$17.00 al mes	Marzo 8, 1902.
Comte. C. B. Baker, Jefe de la Admón. (Arrendador)	R. B. Lyon y Cª	Abril 13, 1901	Arrendº del Hospital de San Ambrosio	$11,500.00 al año	Marzo 8, 1903.
Comte. C. B. Baker, Jefe de la Admón. (Arrendatario)	Mª de la Concepción Gascón	Abril 13, 1901	Arrendº de terrenos	$10.00 al mes	Abril 13, 1902.
Id.	Consuelo Boan de Suárez	Abril 13, 1901	Id.	$35.00 al mes	Abril 13, 1902.
Id.	Joaquín Diago	Abril 20, 1901	Id.	$17·00 oro esp. al mes	Abril 20, 1902.
Comte. C. B. Baker, Jefe de la Admón. (Adquirente	Ramón González Socorro	Abril 20, 1901	Cesión del Cementerio del Gobierno	$300.00 al mes	
Id. (Arrendador).	Manuel Cabe	Junio 24, 1901	Arrendº de terrenos	$100.00 al mes	Junio 24, 1902
Id. (Adquirente).	Heredrs. de Juan O'Naghten.	Junio 27, 1901	Cesión del derecho de transito	$1,420.00.	

ESTADO "K."

RELACION DE ESCRITURAS DE ARRENDAMIENTO PARA EL SERVICIO CIVIL,

OTORGADAS EN EL EJERECIO VENCIDO EN JUNIO 30, 1901.

Nombre del contratante oficial.	*Nombre del arrendador.*	*Fecha del contrato.*	*Alquiler mensual.*	*Plazos del contrato.*
Comandate C. B. Baker, Jefe de la Admón Militar.	Concepción Hermosa	Marzo 9, 1901	$60	Mensual.
id.	José Trujillo	Abril 20, 1901	$20 (tiro al blanco. $25 al año (tiro de pistola)	id.
id.	Viuda de Illera	Mayo 24, 1901	$12	id.
id.	S. S. Friedlein	Junio 1º, 1901	$12	id.
id.	Ernesto Torro	Junio 1º, 1901	$12	id.
id.	Juan López	Junio 27, 1901	$5.62	id.

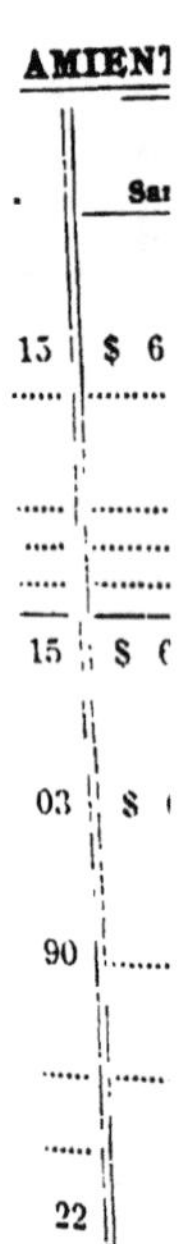

uba, dur

AMIENT

.	Sa
15	$ 6
......	....
......	....
.....	....
......	....
15	$ (
03	$ (
90	....
......	......
......	
22	
15	$

ıba, durante el eje

[TAMIENTOS.]				[1]
[..].	Sanidad.			Ba[...] y hab[...]
15	$ 6,976	40		$ 93,[...]
......	....	......		1,[...]
......	....	......		....
......	....	......		....
......	....	......		....
	$ 6,976	40		$ 94[...]
03	$ 6,823	82		$ 85,[...]
90	....	......		2,[...]
......	....	......		....
......	13	75		
22	138	83		5[...]
	$ 6,976	40		$ 94[...]

A.

VTE

UNTA

cion.

A.

TE EL EJE

UNTAMIENTOS.

ción.	Sanidad.
......	....

REPORT

OF THE

AUDITOR FOR CUBA

FOR THE

SIX MONTHS ENDED

JUNE 30, 1901.

OFFICE OF AUDITOR FOR CUBA,

Havana, Cuba, November 13, 1901.

The Adjutant General,
Department of Cuba,
Havana.

SIR:

I have the honor to forward herewith my report for the six months ended June 30th, 1901.

Very respectfully,

J. D. TERRILL,

Auditor for Cuba.

OFFICE OF THE AUDITOR FOR CUBA,

Havana, Cuba, November 8, 1901.

SIR:

Following the usual custom and in compliance with instructions of the Military Governor dated June 14, 1901, I have the honor to submit a report of the operations of the Office of the Auditor for Cuba for the six months ended June 30th, 1901, the previous and first six months of the fiscal year 1901 having been covered by a report rendered under date of March 12th last by my predecessor. This report would have been rendered more promptly but for the unusual press of work incident to an attempt to complete an audit of accounts pertaining to the fiscal year 1901 in order to meet the desires of the War Department.

In his last report my predecessor called attention to the unsatisfactory condition of the office, due in part to the independent spirit on the part of the Assistant Auditors arising out of the system first established under War Department instructions where each, however contrary to the intention of those instructions, was practically and in effect an independent auditor. This feeling, while it was gradually giving way to the demands of a better office system and discipline, was, nevertheless, at that time even, an obstacle in the way of thorough uniformity of action. He expressed the opinion that the offices of Assistant Auditors might be readily discontiued and that in their stead there be appointed a Deputy Auditor, upon whom would devolve duties similar to those devolving upon the deputies of the auditors for the several departments of the government at Washington, and who would be connected and identified with no particular branch of the work of the office. He recommended the creation of divisions, with chiefs of division, in order to better handle the various and natural classifications of accounting over which the office has jurisdiction.

He spoke at some length, too, of the uselessness of maintaining the distinction among Customs Receipts, Postal Receipts, Internal Revenue Receipts, and Miscellaneous Receipts after they have been covered into the Treasury. He maintained further that a sytem under which requisitions could be drawn bi-monthly would be preferable to the system then in force of making such requisitions once a month.

After considerable correspondence among the then Auditor, the War Department, and Department Headquarters, involving a discussion of the foregoing and other important measures and questions, the Secretary of War on March 13th, under authority of Executive Orders dated the day previous, published rules and instructions relative to the accounting system of the Military Government by the United States in Cuba. These instructions were published in Civil Orders No. 79, Headquarters Department of Cuba, dated Havana, March 22, 1901, appended hereto and marked Exhibit A. They incorporated the suggestions of the Auditor just referred to, as well as other important changes in the system previously in operation. They abolished the offices of Assistant Auditors and provided for a Deputy Auditor and Chief Clerk, and such divisions as the Auditor in his judgment deemed necessary for the greater expedition and more orderly disposition of the work, each of these divisions so established by the Auditor to be in charge of a chief of division. The instructions also provided that separate accounts of moneys arising from Customs Receipts, Postal Receipts, Internal Revenue Receipts, and Miscellaneous Receipts, should be kept, but that when such moneys were turned into the Treasury they should be covered into a general fund known as "Revenues of Cuba" and upon which fund all advances of moneys should be made. The instructions likewise provided for a bi-monthly system of requisitions.

The vacancy occurring by provision of Executive Orders of March 12, 1901, for a Deputy Auditor, was filled by the appointment on April 10th of Mr. Ernesto Fonts y Sterling, at that time the only remaining Assistant Auditor.

On April 15th Major E. C. Brooks, Q. M., U. S. Vols., and Auditor for Cuba, was granted leave of absence for thirty days, at the expiration of which time he was, at his own request, relieved from duty as Auditor for Cuba. During the interim, and until the time of the appointment of the present incumbent, Mr. Ernesto Fonts y Sterling, Deputy Auditor, acted as Auditor.

On May 17th, and under appointment of the Secretary of War, I assumed charge of the office of Auditor for Cuba.

Under authority of War Department instructions before cited, and on the advice of Major Brooks, whom I had met in Washington, and after consultation with those of the office who were best fitted to know its needs, I decided on a re-arrangement of the divisions and a re-distribution of the work of the office, and under date of May 23d, issued an office circular from which the following is an extract:

"For the greater expedition and more orderly disposition of the work of the office, there shall be established and maintained the following Divisions:

(1) Division of Disbursements.
(2) Division of Revenues.
(3) Postal Division.
(4) Property Returns Division.
(5) Division of Bookkeeping and Warrants.
(6) Mail and Record Division.

The following appointments and assignments are announced:

Mr. L. H. Mattingly, Chief Clerk.

Mr. H. J. Van der Beek, Chief of the Division of Disbursements.

Mr. W. H. Lancashire, Chief of the Division of Revenues.

Mr. A. J. Bowle, Chief of the Postal Division.

Mr. H. M. Wood, Chief of the Property Returns Division.

Mr. Nathaniel Nathan, Chief of the Division of Bookkeeping and Warrants.

.... Chief of the Mail and Record Division.

(This division to be under direct charge and supervision of the Chief Clerk.)"

The duties devolving on this office are of a varied character. It audits the accounts of collections of Collectors of Customs, Collectors of Internal Revenue, of Postmasters, and of all others who may receive moneys on behalf and on account of the Military Government. It examines and scrutinizes accounts of disbursements made by the officers and agents of the Government in all the branches of its service. It keeps an account of the appropriations made by the Military Governor and of the Warrants issued thereon. It keeps accounts of the funds in the hands of the Treasurer, and renders reports thereon from time to time at stated periods and whenever required. It is charged with the settlement of claims against and collection of debts due the Military Government. In general terms, the duties of the Auditor are defined in Section 45 of the War Department instructions of March 13, 1901, as follows:

"The Auditor for Cuba shall, except as herein otherwise provided, have like authority as that conferred by law upon the several Auditors of the United States and the Comptroller of the United States Treasury, and is authorized to communicate direct with any person or officer having claims before him for settlement, or with any officer or department having official relations with his office."

As an orderly arrangement of the comments to be made upon the events occurring during the period which this report is intended to cover, I shall take up, under the heading of the division charged with such subjects, the matters I wish to bring to your attention.

DIVISION OF DISBURSEMENTS.

(Mr. H. J. Van der Beek, Chief.)

Until April 1, the date on which the War Department instructions went into effect, accounts of disbursements had been kept against several funds, and were audited in the following divisions: Customs Division,—accounts of disbursements of all Collectors of Customs and Captains of the Port; Postal Division,—accounts of disbursements of the Disbursing Officer of the Department of Posts; Internal Revenue Division,—the disbursements against Internal Revenue funds; and Miscellaneous Division,—all other disbursements not audited by any of the aforenamed divisions.

On May 23, the date of the organization of the present division, the jurisdiction over all accounts of disbursements was transferred to it except the accounts of the Disbursing Officer of the Department of Posts, which were still retained in the Postal Division. This consolidation was prompted by the diversity of methods employed by the various divisions. It was thought that a consolidation in the audit of disbursing accounts would render more easy to accomplish the desired uniformity of action in this connection. It is believed that the results have in great measure justified the assumption.

The work of this division is less current than that of any other of the office, save the Property Returns Division. Nevertheless, considering the number and variety of the character of accounts audited, the showing made by the division is very creditable. Some of the accounts contain so many payments, even though some are small in amount, that they employ in their audit nearly a month of the time of the most capable auditing clerks. It will be understood that these clerks not only audit but prepare for rendition to the War Department, under its instructions, an itemized statement, by voucher, of every expenditure made on the Island, giving date and place of payment, name and address of payee, and amount and character of each disbursement under the proper heading and sub-heading of appropriation. All these statements are rendered in English and necessitate an immense amount of translation, as the greater portion of vouchers rendered are in Spanish.

Towards the latter part of April and during the months of May and June, 1900, several hundred transfers of funds were made from the accounts of regular disbursing officers to municipalities throughout the Island. These transfers were made to the respective alcaldes, to cover deficiencies of such municipalities, and to the directors of hospitals and charitable institutions, which, prior to that time, had received no support from the State. In most cases the officials to whom these transfers were made were unacquainted with the accounting system in force, and in fact in most instances failed to comprehend the instructions sent them from this office. These accounts then became the source of great vexation and annoyance, and it is only recently that any progress has been made in closing them. This has been accomplished through much correspondence, and in some instances by a statement of the account by this office, with the assistance of the Department of Charities, on vouchers secured personally by Inspectors of that Department. As a result of the foregoing experience this system of transfers has been largely discontinued, although at various times donations are still made to municipalities, for which, however, the receipt of the properly designated official to the regular disbursing officer of the State is considered a good and sufficient voucher. In other words, the transaction is considered as a gratuity, or simple donation to the municipalities.

In the audit of the March accounts of disbursements which were stated against either Customs, Postal, Internal Revenue, or Miscellaneous funds, those funds were credited with the balance which would ordinarily have been declared thereon, as being transferred to Revenue funds, and the accounts under those funds were thus closed. The April accounts of disbursing officers were then debited with the amounts transferred to Revenues and a new account under that head was thus opened.

From an experience gained in handling accounts in the United States, it soon became apparent to me that some changes were necessary in the stating of accounts, and in the manner of conducting audits. These changes were only instituted after the exercise of all possible caution to guard against confusion, and in most instances both the clerks of the office, and officers rendering accounts to it readily adapted themselves. They did, however, in some degree, occasion a slight delay in the work of auditing. However, as an auditing officer, I would much prefer to have a record for quality than for quantity of work. In an office of this kind it is easy to slight the examination of vouchers, and detection is difficult without a duplication of work. Every effort consistent with accuracy is being made for a prompt audit of accounts of disbursements as well as of all others.

There has been much work in connection with this division done in picking up the odds and ends which, owing to the press of business,—primarily the preparation of a report for the Senate,—had been neglected up to the time of my assumption of the duties of office. Prior to that little or no effort had been made looking to the collection of outstanding balances. This matter is now receiving attention and in the near future it is expected that many of the balances now outstanding, consisting largely of suspended items, will be settled. Those items which are now suspended and remain unexplained will be disallowed and the officers concerned called upon to refund the amount found due.

DIVISION OF REVENUES.

(Mr. W. H. Lacashire, Chief.)

This division is charged with the audit of collections of customs, Internal Revenue, and Miscellaneous Receipts. Its work involves the examination of all Custom House entries, ships' manifests, etc. In the examination of Custom House entries during the year 1901 nine hundred and sixty-five errors were discovered by this division, and, after allowing two hundred and forty-two on explanation of the Collectors, the net amount actually collected in respect to the remaining seven hundred and twenty-three, was $10,907.66. Collaterally, the salary list of this division amounts to $10,400 per annum. Aside from the well-known province and usefulness of a check on the collections of revenues of government, this division has unmistakably demonstrated its usefulness.

There are on the Island of Cuba and rendering accounts of collections, one port, Havana, and sixteen sub-ports as follows: On the north coast from west to east, Havana, Matanzas, Cárdenas, Sagua la Grande, Caibarién, Nuevitas, Gibara and Baracoa; and on the south coast from east to west, Guantánamo, Santiago de Cuba, Manzanillo, Santa Cruz del Sur, Júcaro, Tunas de Zaza, Trinidad, Cienfuegos, and Batabanó.

Collections arising from Internal Revenues are as follows: Inheritance and transfer taxes, industry and commercial taxes, forest proceeds, redemption of rent charges, interest on rent charges, interest on outstanding liabilities, rents of State properties, sale of State lands, sundry proceeds. and all other sources of revenue as are from time to time designated. Collections are made by Collectors of Internal Revenue for the Fiscal Zones of Cuba, which are eleven in number, as follows, from west to east as geographically situated: Pinar del Río, Guanajay, Havana, Matanzas, Cárdenas, Cienfuegos, Santa Clara, Puerto Príncipe, Manzanillo, Holguín, Santiago.

This division has also jurisdiction over the accounts of collections of Miscellaneous Receipts, probably a greater number of which are rendered by Captains of Ports. Each of the sixteen subports previously mentioned has a Captain of the Port, who is at the same time the Collector of Customs. The port of Havana has a Captain of the Port, whose duties are distinct from those of Collector of Customs at that port, and who has jurisdiction over all other Captains of Ports. The revenue collected by these officials results from the imposition of fines and penalties on shippers and vessels for infractions of harbor regulations, and very often for the issuance of maritime certificates.

To this division are also reported the proceeds of sales of public property and all other Miscellaneous Receipts. It has, in fact, jurisdiction over all collections except those arising from the Department of Posts. Its work is current, and will be kept so.

POSTAL DIVISION.

(Mr. A. J. Bowle, Chief.)

This division has jurisdiction over all accounts pertaining to collections and disbursements of the Department of Posts. It examines the accounts of postal receipts rendered by postmasters throughout the Island. It charges them with stamp stock received, and credits them with moneys turned in to the Treasury. At present there are about one hundred and seventy-five postmasters receiving stamps direct from the Department of Posts, collecting box rents, etc., and who render reports to this office of such collections and receipts. About seventy-five offices make reports of sales and cancellations only, and the stamps sold by these postmasters are purchased from the larger offices near at hand and are paid for from the private funds of the postmasters. About fifty-five authorized offices render no accounts whatever. Strong efforts are being made by the Director General of Posts and by this office to have the Bureau of Stamps and Supplies of the Department of Posts supply all postmasters throughout the Island their stamp stock, and to have the postmasters render a monthly report to this office, whether their offices have transactions or not. The salaries in the small offices are necessarily so small that postmasters deem the time engaged in the comprehension of the various and somewhat complex details of the postal system as not advantageously spent.

PROPERTY RETURNS DIVISION.

(Mr. H. M. Wood, Chief.)

As early as March 14, 1899, and in Civil Orders of Headquarters Division of Cuba bearing that date, the Military Governor provided for the rendition of property returns to the Auditor for the Island of Cuba, who had jurisdiction over all acounts of disbursements and funds obtained from the Customs Receipts of the Island except those which were then being rendered to the Auditor of the Customs Service. This Order also conferred concurrent jurisdiction on the Auditor of the Finance Department in connection with all accounts of moneys rendered him. It provided further, that accounts and returns should be rendered by native civilian officers of the Military Government, and that accounts and returns should be rendered from the first day of the Military Occupation, January 1, 1899. In this connection it is understood that returns of property were regularly rendered the Auditor of the Island, Major Ladd, Q. M., U. S. Vols., and settled by him. After the establishment of the present office of the Auditor on July 1, 1899, under authority of War Department instructions of May 11th of that year, it seems that but few property returns were rendered the Auditor and they were not made even the subject of acknowledgment by him. It is apparent from the records on file in the office that the Auditor did not consider that he was called upon, under his instructions, to audit such returns. The War Department, however, put a different construction upon the duties of the Auditor, and in a series of correspondence and upon his initiative, indicated to my predecessor, Major E. C. Brooks, that a complete and expeditious audit of the property accountability of the Fiscal Agents of the Government was greatly to be desired. In this opinion Major Brooks concurred, and in July of 1900, having secured the services of a War Department clerk, proceeded to organize a force for the examination of property returns then on file in the office and to institute the necessary measures for the securing of a proper accountability from officers who had heretofore neglected this detail.

While the division was in its early stages of organization an urgent call came from the War Department in connection with the Senate enquiry of May 26, 1900, and the work along property lines had to be for the time discontinued and the force that had been used in that connection was diverted towards the rendition of the required statements. This work on the Senate report was not completed until late in December, 1900, and a small portion of the force of the office was even employed thereon during the first month comprehended by this report.

Early in January last the Property Division was again put in process of organization, though little was accomplished during the first month or month and a half thereof, the time being taken up by the drill and instruction of the clerks engaged on the work and in its detail. It may be said that the effective work in this division really began about the middle of February last.

The money vouchers which had been in authorized use permitted the expenditure of property at the time of its purchase.

Attention has, heretofore, been repeatedly called to the fact that this system was greatly abused and all kinds of property unexpendable by its very nature was attempted to be expended on such vouchers. Further than this, officers had almost invariably failed to render abstracts of purchases; the latter difficulty, however, was partially overcome by the fact that it had been recognized and anticipated in the preparation of statements of property to the Senate, and at the time these statements were drawn a form, in the nature of an abstract of purchases, was compiled by this office in connection with each account current examined.

There has been in the past, and is still, an indiscriminate transfer of propery to irresponsible persons who, by the time we are enabled to reach them in an audit, no longer hold public positions and who are individually indifferent to calls of this office on them for an accounting. This matter has at various times been called to the attention of the Military Governor, and it is now respectfully recommended in this connection that every department of Government and public institution have some officer properly designated as accountable for all property pertaining to such department or institution. In some institutions and departments, disbursing but a comparatively small amount of money, there are a number of officials of such institutions and departments chargeable with the property thereof. If the foregoing recommendation is carried into effect this condition may be obviated, and with a single accountable officer the property of the institutions or departments may be issued out by that officer to others on memorandum receipts. In notable instances the heads of departments, where such conditions existed, have been requested to discontinue them by the designation of a property officer and the use of memorandum receipts as outlined above. Considerable difficulty has been met in this connection, through a misunderstanding of officials as to the status of officers concerned in the transfer of property on memorandum receipt and a misapprehension of the terms "responsibility" and "accountability" as applied to such a transaction. With mutual explanations and a better understanding there has been experienced no further difficulty and administrative officers have gladly acquiesced in our efforts to reduce the number of accountable officers. Just how far this may be done is not only a question of accounting, but is one that affects the administrative affairs of the departments and institutions concerned, and can only be effected with the hearty and intelligent cooperation of the executive officers of the several departments.

From March 14, 1899, the date of promulgation of Civil Orders affecting the accounting system of the Island, no specific provision for the accounting of property was made until the publication of War Department instructions of March 13, 1901, Sections 23, 24, and 25 thereof, providing as follows:

"SECTION 23. Disbursing officers and agents will be required to show the use and final dipposition of all property purchased by them, and all officers or agents of the Military Government of Cuba will be required to show such use and final disposition of all property in their possession and pertaining to such Government.

"SECTION 24. Returns of property will be rendered quarterly and will be transmitted to the Auditor within twenty days after the expiration of the quarter to which they pertain, accompanied by the proper abstracts and vouchers.

"SECTION 25. In case any officer or agent who is accountable for property pertaining to the Military Government of Cuba shall fail to render the required returns therefor to the Auditor, or to transmit the same within the period herein provided for, or shall neglect to render the same when requested to do so, it shall be the duty of the Auditor to report such case to the Military Governor for proper action."

During the six months ending June 30, 1901, there were received in the office seven hundred and twenty-five returns of property, of which number two hundred and sixty-one remain unexamined, and four hundred and sixty-four were examined, apportioned among the fiscal years as follows: Fifty-seven in 1901; three hundred and sixty-six in 1900; and forty-one in 1899. Of the accounts examined one hundred and ninety-eight were found to be correct, and settled. There were then remaining on hand at the close of this report five hundred and twenty-seven unsettled returns of property, of which two hundred and sixty-six had been examined, and the office was in correspondence with the officers concerned in connection with two hundred and twenty-one of the same at the time of the conclusion of the period covered by this report. During this period there were examined fourteen hundred and ninety-nine accounts current of disbursements pertaining to the fiscal year 1900, and one hundred and thirty-seven accounts pertaining to the fiscal year 1901. In the examination of these accounts current, as said before, as many abstracts of purchases were compiled by this Division.

From the foregoing it is calculated that at the conclusion of the fiscal year 1901 we had opened accounts of property with seven hundred and thirty-six officers, of which two hundred and thirty-three were army officers and five hundred and three civilians, and whose transactions aggregated nineteen hundred and six quarters, or returns of property. It will be seen, then, that the total number of returns received,—seven hundred and twenty-five,—is far short of that which should have been received; in fact, but little over one-third.

The work accomplished by this division during the period here covered was largely preparatory in its nature. Letters of exception to property returns have so far as possible been reduced to set forms, and every possible effort is being made to minimize the work.

The transactions scrutinized by this division are more varied in character, probably, than any accounting officers in the States will have to deal with. The returns comprehend medical supplies and subsistence for hospitals, returns of ordnance stores, engineering supplies, surveyors' supplies, machinery for arsenals and other public workshops, drafting instruments, etc. The audit of these various classes of accounts requires an amount of technical knowledge difficult to find among auditing clerks. The translation of these terms, necessitated by the general use of Spanish and English, has given rise to difficulties experienced by few other Auditors. To meet these conditions we have on hand all available Spanish dictionaries, though they are few in number, and frequently consult the catalogues of manufacturing houses in the United States which have been sent us on request.

The record system of this division has been established in connection with the general record system of the office,—the card system, or cross-reference system, and has grown as the work progressed, and developed as its needs became known. Ledgers of property, showing the varied accountability of officers extending over a period from the first day of Military Occupation until the present time, are now in use.

Great difficulty has been experienced in correspondence with officers affecting their property accountability. Their replies to specific enquiries from this office are many times of a general and inconsequent nature. While it is realized that the delay in calling on officers for an accounting has made it difficult in many instances for them to answer these enquiries, it seems that the proper effort is not being made by many accountable officers to adjust their accounts. In many instances the officers with whom we have to communicate, and especially officers of the army, have left the Island and it is months before a reply can be expected. When replies are received many of them do not go to the subject matter. but contain reasons why, in the opinion of the accountable officer, he should not render returns.

DIVISION OF BOOKKEEPING AND WARRANTS.

(Mr. Nathaniel Nathan, Chief.)

This division is charged with the duty of keeping accounts of general receipts and expenditures, as well as of all personal accounts. It issues all warrants and keeps a register of the same. It keeps a register of all bonds of the fiscal agents of the Military Government, and on requisition of the several Chiefs of Division, furnishes them with bookkeeper's certificates of the accounts of officers. It keeps a register of requisitions and estimates made by disbursing officers and of the appropriations of the Military Governor thereon under appropriate heads and sub-heads of appropriation. Requisitions and estimates for funds are received by this Division and verified before being sent to the Military Governor for his aproval. It is charged with the statement and audit of the accounts of the Treasurer of Cuba, and renders a semi-weekly statement to the Military Governor of the funds in the hands of the Treasurer and all unrealized advances against them. It renders at the conclusion of each month to the Secretary of War, a statement of moneys received by the Treasurer, giving in detail the names of officers from whom such moneys are received, as well as the sources from which they are derived; a statement of warrants drawn, under their several heads and sub-heads of appropriation; as well as a statement of warrants cashed by the Treasurer.

The warrants in present use and authorized by the Military Governor under date of April 17th, 1901, are in the form of a draft by the Military Governor on the Treasurer of Cuba in favor of the disbursing officer to whose credit it is desired the money shall be placed. These warrants, after countersignature and entry by the Auditor upon proper ledgers, are transmitted to the Treasurer of Cuba for payment. On these warrants the Treasurer draws a draft on his cashier or upon some duly authorized depository of public funds, for the amount, directing that it be there placed to the credit of the disbursing officer and subject to the latter's check. The warrant is then transmitted by the Treasurer to the officer in whose favor it is drawn, who returns it by endorsement, acknowledging to have received the money. This latter step is necessitated by the provisions of War Department instructions of March 13, 1901, as follows:

"Warrants paid by the Treasurer, with the proper evidence of payment, which shall be the proper endorsement of the payee thereon, shall constitute the vouchers upon which the Treasurer shall receive credit for payment made by him ...."

It will be readily seen that this provision and the necessary procedure thereunder is the occasion of no little delay to the Treasurer in the rendition of his accounts, for the Treasurer, having placed the moneys represented by a warrant to the credit of a disbursing officer, can no longer claim those funds to be in his possession, but until the return of the warrants properly endorsed, he can claim no credit for such disbursements, and as a consequence, and through no fault of his own, his accounts are invariably delayed. Occasionally these warrants are lost and it becomes necessary then for the Treasurer to file other and appropriate evidence, being primarily the acknowledgment of the officer concerned, of the receipt of the funds, as an evidence of payment upon which he may claim the necessary credit.

In my opinion it was intended that the warrant provided for under War Department instructions was to have served the purpose of a draft on the Treasurer, who, on its receipt, would have accepted the same and forwarded it to the officer in whose favor it was drawn, which officer then would have deposited the warrant with the bank endorsed in the manner necessitated by the usages of commercial practice. This procedure would have obviated the disadvantages pertaining under the present system save one, and that the difficulty attending either system in the lack of facility for communication with points removed from direct communication with Havana and the necessity for promptly placing funds at the disposition of disbursing officers.

On assuming charge of the office I found upon examination a great diversity in the manner of executing and filing bonds of fiscal agents. A number of them were filed with the Treasurer of Cuba, others with the Secretary of Finance, but probably a major portion were filed with the heads of executive departments in which the officers bonded were employed. The Auditor had no knowledge of these bonds and advances were being frequently made and countenanced by him to officers who were not under bond. Those who were bonded were often bonded in such a way as to fail to fully insure the Government in connection with the position and status in which they were receiving and disbursing moneys. I have called the attention of the Military Governor to this condition and he has remedied it by ordering that all bonds hereafter are to be filed with the Treasurer and forwarded that officer through the Auditor. This office then will extract from the bond so forwarded all necessary information and record the same in the register of bonds. Under these bonds all accounts will be stated, and the practice of carrying over balances from accounts rendered under one bond to accounts rendered under another, will be discontinued.

The forms of many bonds heretofore accepted by the Military Government are so unfavorable to the Military Government and impose such onerous conditions upon it that the attention of the Military Governor has been invited to the fact, and it is believed that in the not distant future some provision will be made for a new and more carefully drawn bond.

MAIL AND RECORD DIVISION.

(Under the supervision of the Chief Clerk.)

In his annual report for the fiscal year 1901 my predecessor called attention to the lack of a proper system of records, occasioning, as it did, lack of uniformity of action among those engaged in the audit of accounts. The condition failed to create a record of a line of precedents, and in consequence the record of the actions of my predecessors is incomplete and in many instances inharmonious. Major Brooks again dwelt on this subject in his report for the six months just preceding this, and to supply the want he adopted the mail and record system used by many of the governmental departments of Washington,—that of the card-record, or cross-reference system. It became necessary on the adoption of the system to gather together from the keeping of the various clerks of the office who had hitherto kept fragmentary records of an unsatisfactory character, all papers and arrange them with some little regard to order. The accounts themselves were numbered and the correspondence pertaining to them was collected, recorded, and filed with them. This work was accomplished by a small detail of those clerks who had been engaged in the preparation of statements in answer to the Senate enquiry of May 26, 1900. This work began about the latter part of last December, and by April 1st the greater bulk of all accounts and correspondence which had been received from July 1, 1899, to the time of the establishment of the Division, had been arranged under the new system.

From that time until now the division has handled current work and has been engaged from time to time, as occasion would allow, in completing the previous records of the office. From January 1, 1900, until the conclusion of this report, June 30, 1901, there were recorded on the files of this office fourteen thousand six hundred and twenty-one cases. These will include accounts, requisitions and estimates, and warrants thereon, Treasurer's Receipts in numbers from time to time as they are forwarded, property returns, and a considerable amount of general claims and correspondence. The institution of this division has resulted in the training of a number of clerks in record work and the relief of auditing clerks from the inconvenience of keeping their own records and searching for mislaid papers. As a means of preserving records and data for the easy reference of a large number of clerks, its utility has been sufficiently demonstrated elsewhere, and it is now from day to day growing more effective and of greater value to this office.

Most of the difficulties of the office and of officers rendering accounts to it have been found in the fact that the published orders and regulations affecting the accounting system in Cuba are at best but fragmentary. In order to meet this I ordered a compilation of the various principles underlying the accounting system in force in the United States. This compilation, however, I fear comes too late to be of practical value. It is realized that the time is not distant when this and other departments of the Military Government must be making preparations to turn over to their successors the work they have organized and instituted.

It shall be my object to complete and make permanent a record that will, if it is desired to follow it, establish for our successors a clear line of precedents based on justice and the principles of honest accounting. It has been my aim to require the accounts to be rendered so that there shall be such a record of official transactions as shall testify to present and future investigators exactly what has been done with the public funds and property. Nothing short of this will suffice to secure honesty and economy in public expenditures. That system of public accounting is nearest perfect which leaves no open doors for mistakes or fraud. Rigid accountability and constant publicity are among the foremost requisites in honesty and economy in governmental affairs. Close and constant supervision is necessary to secure this. No honest public officer has anything to conceal, nor does he make objection to showing in detail what he has done with the public funds and property; and I am gratified to be able to state that with few exceptions the officers who render accounts to this office are improving in their manner of rendering them, and if this improvement continues there is reason to believe that a fairly good system will be in force when the Military Government ceases its operations.

Respectfully submitted:

J. D. Terrill,

Auditor for Cuba.

The

Military Governor of Cuba,

Havana,

Cuba.

CIVIL ORDERS No. 79

HEADQUARTERS DEPARTMENT OF CUBA

DATED

HAVANA, MARCH 22, 1901.

CONTENTS.

War Department Orders, March 13, 1901, publishing Executive Orders, March 12, 1901, prefacing Rules and Instructions relative to the Accounting System of the Military Government by the United States in Cuba.

(REFERENCES ARE TO SECTIONS.)

HEADQUARTERS DEPARTMENT OF CUBA,

Havana, March 22, 1901.

By direction of the Secretary of War, the Military Governor of Cuba directs the publication of the following Order for the information and guidance of all concerned.

J. B. HICKEY,

Assistant Adjutant General.

WAR DEPARTMENT,

Washington, March 13th., 1901.

The following order of the President is published for the information and guidance of all concerned:

EXECUTIVE MANSION,

Washington, March 12, 1901.

The Executive Order of May 8, 1899, relating to the Island of Cuba, as promulgated by the Assistant Secretary of War, May 11, 1899, is hereby amended by substituting the following:

By virtue of the authority vested in me as the Commander-in-Chief of the Army and Navy of the United States, I hereby order and direct that during the maintenance of the Military Government by the United States in the Island of Cuba, there is hereby created and shall be maintained the office of the Auditor for Cuba, to be filled by appointment of the Secretary of War, whose duties shall be to receive and audit all accounts of the Island.

There is hereby created and shall be maintained the office of Deputy Auditor for Cuba, to be filled by appointment of the Secretary of War, whose duties shall be to sign in the name of the Auditor such official papers as the Auditor may designate, and perform such other duties as the Auditor may prescribe. He shall have charge of the bureau as Acting Auditor in case of the death, resignation, sickness, or other absence of the Auditor.

There is hereby created and shall be maintained in the office of the Auditor, the office of Chief Clerk, to be filled by appointment of the Auditor, and the Chief Clerk shall perform such duties as may be prescribed by the Auditor.

All rules and instructions necessary to carry into effect the provisions of Executive Orders relating to Cuba shall be issued by the Secretary of War, and such rules and instructions shall be in force until the same are amended or revoked by the Secretary of War.

WILLIAM McKINLEY.

The above order and the following rules and regulations will be duly proclaimed and enforced in Cuba, as therein provided, and shall take effect and be in force on and after April 1st, 1901, and all regulations and orders heretofore issued inconsistent therewith are hereby repealed.

ELIHU ROOT,

Secretary of War.

Rules and instructions relative to the accounting system of the Military Government by the United States in Cuba.

STATION OF OFFICERS.

SECTION 1.

The Military Governor of Cuba shall be stationed in the City of Havana, and the officers provided for in Executive Order of May 8, 1899, and its substitute of March 12, 1901, shall be stationed at and have their offices in said city.

THE AUDITOR OF CUBA.

SECTION 2.

The Auditor of Cuba, appointed under Executive Order of May 8, 1899, shall receive, examine and settle all accounts pertaining to the revenues and receipts derived from Cuba and expenditures paid therefrom, and certify the balances thereon to the Military Governor, and shall preserve the accounts and vouchers after settlement.

SECTION 3.

The Deputy Auditor shall sign, in the name of the Auditor, such official papers as the Auditor may designate, and perform such other duties as the Auditor may prescribe.

SECTION 4.

In the case of the death, resignation, absence or sickness of the Auditor, the Deputy Auditor shall act as Auditor and perform the duties of such Auditor until a successor is duly appointed and qualified, or such absence or sickness shall cease.

SECTION 5.

In the case of the death, resignation, absence or sickness of the Deputy Auditor, the Auditor may designate a clerk of the office of the Auditor who shall act as Deputy Auditor and perform the duties of such Deputy Auditor until a successor is duly appointed and qualified, or such absence or sickness shall cease.

SECTION 6.

There shall be maintained in the office of the Auditor such divisions as the Auditor may, in his judgment, deem to be required for the greater expedition and more orderly disposition of the work of the office, each of such divisions to be in charge of a Chief of Division to be appointed by the Auditor.

SECTION 7.

The Military Governor shall issue and sign all warrants for the payment of moneys by the Treasurer, which warrants shall be submitted to the Auditor to be countersigned by him. No warrants shall be drawn for the advance of moneys except upon requisition therefor made by the proper officer, approved by the Military Governor and allowed by the Auditor in conformity to appropriations made. No warrant shall be issued for the payment of the balance found due on any account, except upon the certificate of the Auditor, upon the settlement of such accounts.

SECTION 8.

Warrants drawn for making advances of moneys from funds in the Treasurer's hands shall be denominated "Accountable Warrants," and shall be numbered consecutively, a separate series being preserved.

SECTION 9.

Warrants drawn for the payment of balances due on accounts settled and certified by the Auditor shall be denominated "Settlement Warrants," and shall be numbered consecutively, in a separate series.

SECTION 10.

All receipts issued by the Treasurer for moneys paid to him shall be in duplicate and shall be countersigned by the Auditor. When so countersigned, one receipt, in every case, shall be retained in the office of the Auditor, and the other shall be delivered or transmitted by the Auditor to the person by whom the payment was made, after the same has been duly registered in all its particulars under its appropriate head.

SECTION 11.

The receipts retained by the Auditor will constitute the necessary check in his examination and settlement of the Treasurer's account of receipts, as the authority for charging the Treasurer with moneys received; and such receipts will be filed in the office of the Auditor with the accounts in which credit is taken.

SECTION 12.

Warrants paid by the Treasurer with the proper evidence of payment, which shall be the proper endorsement of the payee thereon, shall constitute the vouchers upon which the Treasurer shall receive credit for payment made by him, and after the settlement of his accounts by the Auditor, such warrants shall be filed therewith.

SECTION 13.

The certificates on the settlement of accounts made by the Auditor to the Military Governor shall be numbered consecutively and filed with the respective accounts and vouchers in the office of the Auditor, who shall preserve the same. A copy of each certificate of settlement shall be filed with the Military Governor to be retained by him.

SECTION 14.

The Auditor shall, with the approval of the Military Governor, prescribe the forms for keeping and rendering all accounts subject to his examination and settlement, which forms shall conform substantially with those used by officers rendering accounts to the Treasury Department of the United States, and issue all necessary instructions to the officers and agents rendering such accounts.

SECTION 15.

And in case any officer or agent whose duty it is to collect and receive moneys arising from the revenues of the Island of whatever kind, and to make disbursement of such moneys for any purpose, shall fail to render complete accounts of such receipts and disbursements to the Auditor, or to transmit the same within ten days after the expiration of the month to which they pertain, or shall neglect to render the same when requested to do so, it shall be the duty of the Auditor forthwith to report such case to the Military Governor for proper action.

SECTION 16.

There shall be in the office of the Auditor a Division of Bookkeeping, in which shall be kept proper books of entry and ledgers for recording the general accounts of receipts and expenditures pertaining to the revenues of Cuba, and the personal accounts of the agents and officers authorized to collect the same and to disburse moneys advanced by the Treasurer upon warrants as herein provided, and of all other accounts or claims allowed and certified by the Auditor, including accounts of appropriations.

ACCOUNTS OF GENERAL RECEIPTS AND EXPENDITURES.

SECTION 17.

The receipts issued by the Treasurer for moneys paid to him, before being countersigned by the Auditor, shall be entered in the proper ledgers of general receipts as funds arising from Customs Receipts, Postal Receipts, Internal Revenue Receipts and Miscellaneous Receipts, respectively, or as re-payments of such receipts, and in making such entries from the Treasurer's receipts the number and date of the receipt, and the name and official designation, if any, of the person by whom the payment or deposit was made shall be noted. These funds shall thereupon be transferred to one account as "Revenue," from which all appropriations from "moneys in the Treasury not otherwise appropriated" shall be made.

SECTION 18.

All warrants drawn by the Military Governor, after being countersigned by the Auditor, shall be charged against the revenue on account of the service and appropriation for which such warrant is drawn, and in making such debit entries, the number and date of the warrant and the person, with official designation, if any, to whom paid, shall be noted. The Auditor shall so keep his records as to be able to show, at any time, the amount of money disbursed on account of any appropriations, as shown by the accountable warrants issued and by the accounts as audited.

PERSONAL LEDGER ACCOUNTS.

SECTION 19.

In the ledgers for personal accounts all advances of money made upon requisitions and warrants to officers and agents authorized to disburse the same in accordance with appropriations, shall be charged to such officers, respectively, on account of the services and appropriation for which disbursement is to be made, at the time of issuing the warrants for such advances of money, the numbers and dates of the respective warrants being noted in making such debit entries; and for the disbursement made by such officers or agents, which may be allowed by the Auditor, in the settlement of accounts of such disbursements, proper credits shall be entered to the respective personal accounts from the certificates of the settlements made by the Auditor, the number and dates of the respective certificates being noted in making the credit entries.

SECTION 20.

In like manner the certificates of settlement of individual accounts of all kinds made by the Auditor shall be entered in the ledgers of personal accounts to the proper individual accounts, on account of the service and appropriation for which the account is rendered, the number and date of Auditor's certificate being noted; and all settlement warrants issued upon certificates of settlement of accounts made by the Auditor shall be charged to the proper individual account, under the appropriate head, in the ledgers of personal accounts, the number and date of the warrant being noted.

SECTION 21.

In making the settlement of each account, and before certifying the same, the Auditor shall require a statement from the Division of Bookkeeping in his office, setting forth the last certified balance on the particular account, and the debits or credits since entered thereon, in the personal ledgers, which statement or certificate shall be used as the basis of the Auditor's settlement of the account before him.

DISBURSING ACCOUNTS.

SECTION 22.

Accounts of disbursement shall be rendered monthly and transmitted to the Auditor within ten days after the expiration of the month to which they pertain, by the officers and agents authorized to make disbursements, in which such officers or agents shall charge themselves with all moneys advanced to them respectively, by the Treasurer, and take credit for the disbursements made by them, supported by proper vouchers. An abstract of the disbursements, accompanied by the vouchers thereior, consecutively numbered, shall be transmitted with each account.

SECTION 23.

Disbursing officers and agents will be required to show the use and final disposition ot all property purchased by them, and all officers or agents of the Military Government of Cuba will be required to show such use and final disposition of all property in their possession and pertaining to such Government.

SECTION 24.

Returns of property will be rendered quarterly and will be transmitted to the Auditor within twenty days atter the expiration of the quarter to which they pertain, accompanied by the proper abstracts and vouchers.

SECTION 25.

In case any officer or agent who is accountable for property pertaining to the Military Government of Cuba shall fail to render the required returns therefor to the Auditor, or to transmit the same within the period herein provided for, or shall neglect to render the same when requested to do so, it shall be the duty of the Auditor to report such case to the Military Governor for proper action.

REVENUE ACCOUNTS.

SECTION 26.

Officers or agents authorized to receive and collect money arising from the revenues of Cuba, of whatsoever kind, shall be required to pay the full amounts received and collected by them respectively, to the Treasurer of Cuba, and to render to the Auditor monthly accounts therefor within ten days after the expiration of the month to which they pertain, accompanied by properly itemized and certified statements and returns of the revenues collected, showing when, by whom and on what account paid.

SECTION 27.

In the rendition of such revenue accounts the officers or agents will charge themselves with all revenues received and collected during the period covered by the account, and take credit for the amounts paid to the Treasurer, as shown by the duplicate receipt in their possession and countersigned by the Auditor, the number and date of such receipts being noted in the entries of amounts paid to the Treasurer. These duplicate receipts will be retained by the officer or agent claiming credit therefor.

SECTION 28.

In the audit of such revenue accounts the Auditor shall compare and check the Treasurer's receipts on file in his office with the corresponding entries in the account of the office or agent as rendered.

SECTION 29.

All revenue accounts shall be rendered and kept separately under the appropriate funds or heads of account to which they respectively pertain;

that is, all revenues arising in the Department of Customs shall be entered and accounted for under the head of Customs Receipts; those arising in the Department of Post Offices under the head of Postal Receipts; all revenues arising from Internal Taxes and duties, as distinct from Customs Receipts and Postal Receipts, shall be entered under the head of Internal Revenue Receipts; and all revenues from other sources under the head of Miscellaneous Receipts.

REQUISITIONS.

SECTION 30.

Requisitions for advances from funds in the hands of the Treasurer for paying necessary and proper expenses chargeable to the revenues of Cuba shall be made bi-monthly by the respective officers or agents authorized to disburse the same, in such form as may be prescribed, pursuant to appropriations made, such requisitions to cover the periods beginning July 1, September 1, November 1, January 1, March 1 and May 1 of each fiscal year, and shall be accompanied by itemized estimates of the amounts required for disbursement during the two months, and no accountable warrant shall be drawn for an amount exceeding the requirements for that time.

SECTION 31.

Each requisition shall particularly state the items of appropriation under which the money is to be disbursed, and shall be forwarded to the Auditor, who shall cause to be endorsed thereon the balance due to or from the officer or agent making the requisition, as shown by the books of the Auditor's office, and the amount of credits shown by any unsettled accounts of such officer or agent remaining in the Auditor's office. Thereupon such requisition shall be transmitted to the Military Governor for his approval, and when his approval shall be endorsed thereon the requisition shall be returned to the Auditor for allowance, and when allowed by him and so endorsed upon the requisition, over his official signature, the proper warrant shall be issued for the amount allowed, to which the requisition shall be attached.

SECTION 32.

If at the time of the reference of a requisition to the Military Governor for his approval, or at any time before the warrant thereon shall have been issued, any facts shall come to the knowledge of the Auditor, which, in his judgment, afford sufficient grounds for disapproving the advance of money asked for, he shall forthwith communicate the same in writing to the Military Governor, whose decision shall be final, if the requisition is pursuant to appropriations made.

SECTION 33.

Claims of officers or agents whose duty it is to collect or account for public moneys, for losses of funds in transit, by fire, burglary or other unavoidable casualty, shall be submitted to the Auditor within one month after such loss occurs, with all the evidence in the case. If the Auditor shall find that the said funds were properly in the hands of such officer or agent, or properly remitted, or that the loss resulted through no fault of said officer or agent, he may, *with the written consent of the Military Governor*, credit the account of such officer with such loss. *Provided*, that in no case shall a credit in excess of one thousand dollars be given in this manner. Claims for losses in excess of one thousand dollars shall be submitted through the Auditor and Military Governor to the Secretary of War for relief.

SECTION 34.

The Auditor may, with the written consent of the Military Governor, mitigate, remit, remove, compromise, release or discharge any liability, in whole or in part, to the Military Government, in any matter before him, when in his judgment, the interests of the Government seem to require it, subject to such restrictions as may be provided by law.

SECTION 35.

The Auditor shall supervise the collection of all debts due the Military Government of Cuba through the usual civil or judicial channels, and institute all such measures as may be authorized by law to enforce the payment of such debts and the recovery of all amounts found to be due the said Military Government in connection with his settlement and adjustment of accounts.

SECTION 36.

Disbursing officers shall deposit funds placed in their hands for disbursement, pursuant to appropriations, only in such depositories as may be designated by the Military Governor. When a payment is made by check, its number shall be noted on the voucher to which it pertains. Such depositories shall report to the Auditor, at the close of each quarter, or oftener if he should require it, the balance to the credit of all disbursing officers, as shown by its records. In every case where after one year after the rendition and settlement of the final account of a disbursing officer there remains a balance in any depository to the credit of such disbursing officer, by reason of the non-presentation of checks or otherwise, the Auditor shall report said amount to the Military Governor, who shall require the said depository to deposit the said balance with the Treasurer of the Island to the credit of "Outstanding Liabilities." No disbursing officer's check shall be paid after one year from the last day of the month of its issue.

SECTION 37.

All claims arising on account of outstanding liabilities shall be filed with the Auditor, with the evidence pertaining thereto. If the Auditor shall find that such claim is valid and unpaid, he shall certify the amount to the Military Governor, who shall issue a settlement warrant on said certificate, which warrant shall be countersigned by the Auditor, and paid by the Treasurer out of the fund accruing on account of outstanding liabilities.

SECTION 38.

Transfers of funds from one disbursing officer to another shall be made only upon the authority of the Military Governor, notice of which authorization shall be given forthwith to the Auditor by the Military Governor. When there is a change in disbursing officers, the outgoing officer shall render an account in full, showing the disposition of his unexpended balance, whether transferred to his successor in accordance with the provisions herein contained, or deposited with the Treasurer of Cuba.

SECTION 39.

As soon after the close of each fiscal year as the accounts of said year may be settled and adjusted, the Auditor shall submit to the Military Governor and Secretary of War an anual report of the financial concerns of the Military Government, showing the receipts and disbursements of the various departments of the said Military Government, and make such other reports as may be required of him by the Military Governor or the Secretary of War.

SECTION 40.

The Auditor shall, at the time of settlement, send an official notification in writing to each person whose accounts have been settled in whole or in part in the Auditor's office, stating the balances found due thereon and certified, and the differences arising on such settlement by reason of disallowances or suspension made by the Auditor, or from other causes, which statement of differences shall be properly itemized. The reasons for a disallowance or suspension of credit shall in all cases be stated.

SECTION 41.

A true copy of all orders of the Military Government which may originate a claim, or in any manner affect the settlement of any account, shall be transmitted to the Auditor by the proper officer.

SECTION 42.

Every contract under which a payment may be made shall be submitted to the Auditor with the account to which such payment pertains.

MONEY ORDER ACCOUNTS.

SECTION 43.

The Auditor shall keep the accounts of the money order business separately, and in such manner as to show the number and amount of money orders issued at each post office, and the number and amount paid, and the fees received. The Auditor shall certify quarterly the receipts as fees from the sale of money orders and require the same to be deposited with the Treasurer of Cuba as Postal Receipts. Losses of money order funds in transit, by fire, larceny or other unavoidable casualty, for which credit may be given, shall be deducted from the fees collected before the quarterly transfer to the Treasurer of such fees, as Postal receipts.

SECTION 44.

Transfers of money from postal receipts to money order funds may be made by the Postmaster, under such regulations as the Auditor may prescribe, when his receipts from the sale of money orders are insufficient to pay the orders drawn upon his office. Credits for such transfer of postal funds to money order funds will be taken in the monthly postal account of the Postmaster. At the close of each quarter all such transfers of funds from postal to money order account, shall be deposited by the Director General of Posts with the Treasurer of Cuba, as revenues from the service of the Department of Posts, upon certification of the Auditor of the amount of such funds to be so deposited.

SECTION 45.

The jurisdiction of the Auditor of Cuba over accounts, and all vouchers pertaining thereto, shall be exclusive. His decisions shall be final and conclusive upon administrative branches of the Military Government, except that appeals therefrom may be taken by the party aggrieved or the head of the department concerned, within one year, in the manner prescribed in Section 72. The Auditor for Cuba shall, except as herein otherwise provided, have like authority as that conferred by law upon the several Auditors of the United States and the Comptroller of the United States Treasury, and is authorized to communicate direct with any person or officer having claims before him for settlement, or with any officer or department having official relations with his office.

SECTION 46.

The Auditor shall forward to the Secretary of War, not later than ten days after the expiration of each month, a full and complete report of all moneys received by the Treasurer during the preceding month, as shown by the entries made from the Treasurer's receipts retained in the Auditor's office; a statement of all advances of moneys made on warrants during the preceding month, and an itemized statement of all disbursements and expenditures audited during the preceding month.

Official Title of Auditor and Deputy Auditor.

Auditor's Seal.

SECTION 47.

The official title of the Auditor, to be affixed to his official signature, shall be "Auditor for Cuba," and the official title of the Deputy Auditor shall be "Deputy Auditor for Cuba "

SECTION 48.

The Auditor shall have and keep an official seal, upon which shall be engraved the following design: "Office Auditor, Cuba.—Official Seal." The Auditor shall affix his official seal to each warrant issued by the Military Governor, if the same shall be contersigned by him, and to all copies or transcripts of papers in his office which he may be required to certify officially.

TREASURER OF CUBA.

SECTION 49.

The Treasurer of Cuba shall receive and safely keep all moneys arising from the revenues of Cuba, from whatever source derived, and shall keep a properly detailed account thereof in permanent books of record in which such revenues and all receipts shall be entered under appropriate heads, with the name of the agents, officers and persons from whom received, and the dates of receipt.

SECTION 50.

All moneys received on account of the Department of Customs shall be credited to the account of Customs Receipts; all moneys received from the Department of Post-Offices shall be credited to the account of Postal Receipts; all moneys received from internal taxes and duties, as distinct from Customs Receipts and Postal Receipts, shall be credited to the account of Internal Revenue Receipts, and all moneys received from other sources shall be credited to the account of Miscellaneous Receipts.

SECTION 51.

The accounts of the Treasurer shall be kept in the money in which it is received and disbursed, but in all reports made to the Secretary of War the amounts therein shall be stated in the money of the United States at the authorized rate of conversion.

SECTION 52.

The Treasurer shall issue receipts in duplicate for all moneys received by him, which shall be numbered consecutively, and shall bear the date upon which deposit was actually made and show from whom, and on what account received, and the amounts in money of the United States; and also, when paid in any foreign coin or currency, the amounts and kind of foreign money in which payments were made shall be stated upon the receipts, and the rates at which the same are reduced to money of the United States.

SECTION 53.

All receipts, original and duplicate, issued by the Treasurer shall be registered and countersigned by the Auditor of Cuba, without which they shall be invalid, and for this purpose the Treasurer shall, immediately upon issuing each receipt in duplicate, transmit both receipts to the Auditor.

SECTION 54.

All moneys derived from the revenues of Cuba and receipts from all sources shall be paid to the Treasurer in full, without any deduction.

SECTION 55.

Needful advances from the moneys in the hands of the Treasurer shall be made bi-monthly, in accordance with appropriations, to the proper officers authorized to disburse the same, for the purpose of paying the necessary and proper expenses of collecting the revenues, auditing the accounts, and such other legitimate expenses connected with the Military Government of Cuba as are not specifically appropriated for by the Congress of the United States.

SECTION 56.

Such advances of moneys in the hands of the Treasurer shall be made upon warrants based upon requisitions showing under what appropriation the money is to be expended. Upon the approval of such requisitions by the Military Governor and the allowances of the same by the Auditor, the proper warrants thereon shall be issued by the Military Governor and countersigned by the Auditor.

SECTION 57.

No payment shall be made by the Treasurer except upon warrants issued by the Military Governor and countersigned by the Auditor, and such warrants, when paid and accompanied by the proper evidence of payment, which shall be the endorsement of the payee, shall be the vouchers upon which the Treasurer shall receive credit in the settlement of his accounts.

SECTION 58.

All warrants drawn by the Military Governor upon the Treasurer shall be debited on the books of the Treasurer to the moneys in his hands not otherwise appropriated, the service and appropriation for which the warrant is drawn to be entered in every case. No warrant shall be paid by the Treasurer until the same is countersigned by the Auditor.

SECTION 59.

The Treasurer shall render monthly accounts of the receipts and expenditures of his office, and submit the same to the Auditor for examination and settlement, not later than ten days after the expiration of each month. In rendering such accounts the Treasurer shall charge himself with all moneys received during the period covered by the account, under the appropriate funds or heads of account, and furnish therewith abstracts showing in detail the amounts received under each head, from whom received, and giving the numbers and dates of receipts issued therefor.

SECTION 60.

He shall credit himself with all moneys paid on account of the services for which such money is appropriated, and file with his account abstracts showing in detail the amounts paid under each head, to whom paid, and giving the numbers and dates of the warrants issued in payment, which warrants shall be filed with his account, submitted to the Auditor.

SECTION 61.

The Treasurer shall forward to the Secretary of War not later than ten days after the expiration of each month, a full and complete report, duly certified, of all moneys received by him, together with an itemized statement of all disbursements; and shall also transmit a duly certified copy of the same to the Military Governor.

OFFICIAL TITLE OF THE TREASURER.

SECTION 62.

The official title of the Treasurer, to be affixed to his official signature, shall be "Treasurer of Cuba."

Powers and Duties of the Military Governor in the Accounting System of Cuba.

EXAMINATION OF ACCOUNTS.

SECTION 63.

The Military Governor shall make quarterly, and oftener if deemed expedient, an examination of the books and accounts of the Auditor and Treasurer, and a comparison of the results shown by the same, and also an examination and count of the moneys in the hands of the Treasurer, and submit his report thereon to the Secretary of War.

APPROVAL OF REQUISITIONS.

SECTION 64.

All requisitions for the advances of money from funds in the hands of the Treasurer, to officers or agents authorized to disburse the same, shall be approved by the Military Governor, when submitted in proper form, and the advances of money asked for are in accordance with appropriations made.

SECTION 65.

Such requisitions shall be made pursuant to appropriations and shall cite the particular appropriation under which the requisition is made.

SECTION 66.

Such requisitions shall be forwarded by the officer or agent making the same to the Auditor, who shall endorse thereon the condition of the account of the officer or agent asking for the advance of money, as disclosed by the books of his office, and also the amount of credits shown by any account of such officer or agent remaining unsettled in the Auditor's office. The requisitions shall then be submitted to the Military Governor for approval.

WARRANTS.

SECTION 67.

The Military Governor shall issue and sign all warrants for the payment of moneys from the funds in the hands of the Treasurer, which warrants shall be drawn in accordance with requisitions as approved, or certificates of settlement, as the case may be, and no warrants shall be valid unless countersigned by the Auditor.

In case of the absence or disability of the Military Governor he may designate an officer of the Military Government to sign in his stead warrants drawn in conformity to approved requisitions or certificates of the Auditor.

SECTION 68.

The proper authority for the issue of an accountable warrant for the advance of moneys to authorized disbursing officers or agents, for the purpose of defraying necessary and legitimate expenses, shall be the requisition of such officer, in accordance with an appropriation already made, which requisition must, prior to the issuing of the warrant, be approved by the Military Governor and allowed by the Auditor.

SECTION 69.

The proper authority for the issue of a settlement warrant, in payment of a balance found due by the Auditor upon an account settled and certified by him, shall be the Auditor's certificate to the Military Governor of such settlement.

Section 70.

Wherever the term "appropriation" is used in these Rules and Instructions, the appropriations made by the Military Governor of Cuba are referred to.

TITLE TO BE OBSERVED IN THE RENDITION AND CERTIFICATION OF ACCOUNTS.

Section 71.

All accounts of the Treasurer of Cuba, and of the various officers and agents authorized to collect the revenues, receive money, and make disbursements, and all other accounts subject to examination and settlement by the Auditor, shall be with "The Military Government of Cuba," and all balances certified by the Auditor shall be certified as due to or from said Military Government, as the case may be.

APPEALS FROM THE ACTION OF THE AUDITOR.

Section 72.

Any person aggrieved by the action or decision of the Auditor in the settlement of his account or claim by that officer may within one year take an appeal in writing to the Military Governor, which shall specifically set forth the particular action of the Auditor to which exception is taken, with the reasons and authorities relied on for reversing such action. The decision of the Military Governor in such case shall be final and conclusive.

INFORME

DEL

INTERVENTOR GENERAL,

CORRESPONDIENTE AL SEMESTRE

VENCIDO EN

30 DE JUNIO DE 1901.

INTERVENCION GENERAL.

ISLA DE CUBA.

Habana, Noviembre 15, 1901.

Al Ayudante General,
Departamento de Cuba.

SEÑOR:

Tengo el honor de acompañar el informe de mi cargo, correspondiente al semestre vencido en 30 de Junio de 1901.

Atentamente de V.,

J. D. TERRILL,
Interventor General,
Isla de Cuba.

INTERVENCION GENERAL.

Habana, Noviembre 8, 1901.

SR:

Siguiendo la costumbre establecida y en cumplimiento de las instrucciones del Gobernador Militar de fecha 14 de Junio de 1901, tengo el honor de presentar un informe comprensivo de los trabajos realizados por la Intervención General de Cuba durante el semestre vencido en 30 de Junio de 1901, estando comprendidos los correspondientes al primer semestre anterior en el informe de fecha 12 de Marzo último que evacuó mi antecesor. Antes de ahora se hubiera éste ministrado, si no fuera por la desusada premura de otros trabajos al intentar la censura completa de las cuentas del año económico de 1901, para satisfacer los deseos del Departamento de la Guerra.

Mi antecesor en su último informe llamó la atención hácia el estado nada halagüeño de la oficina, causado en parte por el espíritu de independencia que prevalecía entre los Interventores Auxiliares, debido al sistema que primero se implantó por instrucciones del Departamento de la Guerra, por más que ello fuese contrario al espíritu de esas instrucciones, resultando en efecto que cada uno fuese un interventor independiente. Este criterio, al paso que gradualmente iba cediendo á las exigencias de un sistema mejor y de mejor disciplina, era en aquella época un obstáculo á la unidad de acción. Expresó su opinión de que podrían suprimirse de una vez las Intervenciones auxiliares, y en su lugar se nombrara un Interventor delegado, atribuyéndole facultades semejantes á las que corresponden á los Interventores Delegados de los varios Departamentos del Gobierno en Washington y que, no tuviesen relación, ni se identificasen con ninguna rama particular del servicio que corresponde á la oficina. Propuso la creación de secciones con Jefes de las mismas, para mejor despachar la calificación de las cuentas que fueran de la incumbencia de la oficina.

Se expresó con bastante latitud también acerca de la inutilidad de hacer distinción entre los ingresos de Aduanas, de Correos, de Rentas Interiores y de Conceptos Varios, después de realizado su ingreso en la Tesorería. Aun más, sostuvo que un sistema estableciendo que los pedidos se hicieran quincenalmente sería preferible al entonces vigente conforme al cual se hacían mensualmente.

Después de mucho cruce de correspondencia entre el entonces Interventor General, el Departamento de la Guerra y la Oficina del Cuartel General, producida la discusión de lo que antecede y de otras medidas y asuntos de importancia, el Secretario de la Guerra en Marzo 13, autorizado por órdenes del Ejecutivo del día anterior, publicó reglas é instrucciones referentes á la contabilidad del Gobierno Militar de los Estados Unidos en la Isla de Cuba. Se publicaron estas instrucciones comprendidas en Ordenes Civiles Nº 79, Cuartel General, Departamento de Cuba, fecha Habana, Marzo 22 de 1901, que se acompaña con el justificante rotulado A. En ellas fueron comprendidas las indicaciones del Interventor á que acabo de referirme, así como otras importantes alteraciones en el sistema que antes regía. Por ellas se suprimieron los puestos de los Interventores Auxiliares y se dispuso la creación de un Interventor Delegado y un Oficial Mayor Jefe del Despacho, y la de las Secciones que á su juicio creyera necesarias el Interventor General para el mejor servicio y para metodizar el trabajo, quedando cada una de estas secciones así creadas por el Interventor, á cargo de un Jefe de Sección. Igualmente disponían estas instruciones que se llevara cuenta por separado de los caudales procedentes de los ingresos de Aduanas, de los de Correo, de los de las Rentas Interiores y por Conceptos Varios; pero siempre que estos caudales ingresaran en la Tesorería, serían comprendidos en un fondo general con el nombre de Rentas de Cuba, sobre los cuales debían hacerse los anticipos de todas clases. También disponían las instrucciones que se observara un sistema de pedidos por bimestres.

La vacante ocurrida, por disposición de las órdenes de Marzo 12 de 1901, de un Interventor Delegado, se llenó con el nombramiento en 10 de Abril, del Sr. Ernesto Fonts y Sterling, único Interventor Auxiliar que por entonces quedaba.

El día 15 de Abril el Comandante E. C. Brooks, Cuartelmaestre, Voluntarios de los Estados Unidos, é Interventor de Cuba, obtuvo licencia de 30 días, al terminar la cual, á propia instancia, fué relevado del puesto de Interventor. Mientras tanto y hasta que se nombró al actual propietario, Ernesto Fonts y Sterling, Interventor Auxiliar, actuó como Interventor General.

El 17 de Mayo, por nombramiento del Secretario de la Guerra, me hice cargo de la Oficina de la Intervención General de Cuba.

Autorizado por las instrucciones del Departamento de la Guerra antes citadas, y por consejos del Comandante Brooks, á quién encontré en Washington, y después de consultar en la Oficina á los más á propósito para conocer las necesidades de la misma, resolví proceder á la reorganización de las secciones y á una nueva distribución de los trabajos de la oficina, y con fecha 23 de Mayo expedí una Circular, de la cual lo que sigue es un extracto.

"Para facilitar el despacho y más ordenadamente dar curso al trabajo de la oficina, se compondrá esta de las siguientes secciones.

1. Sección de Pagos.
2. Sección de Rentas.
3. Sección de Correos.
4. Sección de Cuentas de bienes y efectos del Estado.
5. Sección de Teneduría y Libramientos.
6. Sección de Registro y Correspondencia.

Se participan los siguientes nombramientos y destinos.

L. H. Mattingly, Oficial Mayor, Jefe del Despacho.

H. J. Vanderbeek, Jefe de la Sección de Pagos.

W. H. Lancashire, Jefe de la Sección de Rentas.

A. J. Bowle, Jefe de la Sección de Correos.

H. M. Wood, Jefe de la Sección de Cuentas de Bienes y efectos del Estado.

Nathaniel Nathan, Jefe de la Sección de Teneduría y Libramientos.

.........................., Jefe de la Correspondencia y Registro de la Sección.

Esta División estará directamente á cargo y dirección del Oficial Mayor, Jefe del Despacho.

Los deberes correspondientes á esta oficina son por su índole diversos. Censura las cuentas de recaudación de los Administradores de Aduanas, de los de las Rentas Generales, de los Administradores de Correos, y de todos los demás que perciban caudales á nombre y por cuenta del Gobierno Militar. Examina y fiscaliza las cuentas de pagos realizados por los empleados y agentes del Gobierno en todos los ramos del servicio que les atañen. Lleva cuenta de los créditos concedidos por el Gobernador Militar y de los libramientos que se expiden con cargo á los mismos. Lleva cuenta de los fondos que están en poder de la Tesorería, y acerca de ellos emite informes periódicamente y cuando se disponga. Tiene á su cargo liquidaciones y cobro de créditos pertenecientes al Gobierno Militar. En suma, los deberes del Interventor General están definidos en la Sección 45 de las Instrucciones del Departamento de la Guerra de Marzo 13 de 1901 de la manera siguiente:

"El Interventor General de Cuba, sin perjuicio de lo que en contrario por la presente se disponga, tiene la misma jurisdicción que la que la Ley confiere á los varios Interventores de los Estados Unidos y el Contador de la Tesorería de los Estados Unidos, y se le autoriza para que directamente se comunique con cualquiera persona ó funcionario que ante él tenga reclamaciones pendientes de liquidación, ó con cualquiera otro funcionario, ó Dependencia que con su oficina tenga relación."

Trataré de los particulares sobre que deseo llamar la atención de usted, en el capítulo respectivo dedicado á cada Sección, para expresar por su orden las observaciones que han de hacerse acerca de los mismos dentro del período que se propone abarque el presente informe.

SECCIÓN DE PAGOS.

(Jefe, H. J. Vander Beek.)

Hasta el 1º de Abril, fecha en que empezaron á regir las instrucciones del Departamento de la Guerra, se había llevado la cuenta de los pagos con cargo á ingresos por conceptos varios, y se fiscalizaban en las Secciones siguientes: Sección de Aduanas: Cuenta de los pagos realizados por los Administradores de Aduanas y Capitanes de Puerto. Sección de Correos: Cuenta de pagos realizados por el Ordenador del Departamento de Correos. Seccion de Rentas Interiores: la de los pagos con cargo á los ingresos por Rentas interiores; y la Sección de Asuntos Generales, la de los demás pagos no fiscalizados por las Secciones expresadas.

El 23 de Mayo, fecha en que se organizó la actual Sección, el despacho de todas las cuentas de pagos pasó á cargo de la misma, excepción hecha de las de la Ordenación del ramo de Correos, las cuales quedaron en la Sección de Correos. Esta unificación fué aconsejada por la diversidad de los métodos que seguían las diferentes Secciones. Creyóse que la unificación en la censura de las cuentas de pagos facilitaría la unidad del procedimiento á este respecto. Créese que los resultados en gran manera han justificado aquella presunción.

Los trabajos á cargo de esta Sección están menos al día que los de cualquiera otra, excepción hecha de la de Bienes y efectos del Estado. No obstante, si se tiene en cuenta el número y la variedad de las cuentas censuradas, el resultado que ofrece la Sección es muy plausible. Algunas de las cuentas abarcan tantos pagos, aún siendo muchos de menor cuantía, que en su censura invierten casi un mes los empleados más idóneos para el caso. Se comprenderá que éstos no sólo censuran las cuentas sino que redactan para rendirlas al Departamento de la Guerra, conforme á sus instrucciones, un estado minucioso, con sus justificantes, de todos los gastos efectuados en la Isla, con expresión de la fecha y lugar del pago, nombre y dirección del acreedor y de la cantidad y concepto del gasto, dentro del capítulo y artículo de su crédito. Todos estos estados van extendidos en inglés, lo que hace necesario que se hagan extensas traducciones, por venir la mayor parte de los justificantes en español.

Hácia últimos de Abril y durante los meses de Mayo y Junio de 1900, se efectuaron en las cuentas de las ordenaciones de pagos centenares de transferencias de caudales á los municipios de toda la Isla. Estos traspasos se hacían á los Alcaldes, para cubrir los déficits de los Municipios y á los directores de los hospitales y establecimientos de Beneficencia, los cuales hasta entonces no habían percibido recursos del Estado. La mayor parte de las veces, los empleados á quienes se hacían estas transferencias desconocían la contabilidad vigente, y en verdad que las más de las veces no llegaban á comprender las instrucciones que por esta Oficina se les comunicaban.

Estas cuentas por entonces llegaron á dar orígen á las mayores dificultades y disgustos; y recientemente es cuando se ha podido adelantar algo para terminarlas. Esto se ha logrado despues de escribir mucha correspondencia, y á veces porque esta Oficina confeccionó los estados de las cuentas con ayuda del Departamento de Beneficencia, calcándolos sobre los justificantes recabados personalmente por los Inspectores de aquel Departamento. Como resultado de la práctica mencionada, este sistema de transferencias se ha suprimido en gran parte, aunque en distintas ocasiones todavía se hagan donativos á los Municipios, respecto de los cuales, sin embargo, el recibo del funcionario designado al efecto otorgado al Ordenador de Pagos del Estado, se considera como un justificante válido y suficiente. En una palabra, estos actos considerânse como un regalo ó simple donativo á los Municipios.

En la censura de la cuenta de Pagos del mes de Marzo verificados con cargo á los conceptos de Aduanas, de Correos, Rentas interiores ó conceptos varios, esos caudales se abonaban en el Saldo que por lo común resultaba en las mismas, por traspaso á Rentas interiores, y las cuentas de esos fondos se cerraban de ese modo. A las cuentas de los ordenadores de pagos del mes de Abril se les cargaba la cantidad transferida á Rentas y se abría nueva cuenta bajo esa denominación.

Por la práctica adquirida en el manejo de cuentas en los Estados Unidos, pronto me la dí de que era necesario introducir algun cambio en la confección de las mismas y la manera de llevar á cabo la censura. Este cambio vino á efectuarse cuando ya se tomaron las precauciones posibles para evitar toda confusión, y las más de las veces, tanto los empleados de la oficina como los cuentadantes, se adaptaron á observarlas. Sin embargo, hasta cierto punto ocasionaron alguna demora en el procedimiento de la censura. Empero, como empleado fiscalizador, prefiero la calidad á la cantidad de trabajo. En una oficina de esta clase es cosa fácil la de pasársele á uno el examen de un justificante, y sin duplicar el trabajo, es difícil averiguarlo. Se pone todo empeño, compatible con la exactitud debida, en la pronta censura de las cuentas de pagos, así como en todas las demás.

Mucho que hacer ha habido en esta Sección recogiendo los cabos y puntos pendientes con motivo de la urgencia del despacho; antes que todo la redacción de un informe para el Senado; y los cuales se habian dado de la mano, cuando me hice cargo de los deberes de mi oficina. Antes de esto, poco ó ningún empeño se habia puesto en el cobro de los saldos que estaban pendientes.

Este particular es ahora objeto de atención, y es de esperarse que próximamente muchos de dichos saldos, procedentes en su mayor parte de conceptos que están en suspenso, serán liquidados. Esos conceptos que estan suspensos ahora y permanecen sin explicarse, serán desautorizados y los empleados á quienes se refieren serán requeridos para reintegrar las cantidades en descubierto.

SECCIÓN DE RENTAS.

(Jefe, W. H. Lancashier.)

Esta sección tiene á su cargo la recaudación de Aduanas, Rentas Interiores é Ing.esos Varios. Le corresponden el examen de todas las hojas de Aduanas durante el año 1901, la sección descubrió 964 reparos, y despues de pasar 242 para que los solventaran los Administradores, la cantidad liquidada efectiva que ingresó por lo restante, 723, fué la de $10,907.66. Incidentalmente diré que la nómina de personal de esta sección asciende á $10,400 al año. Aparte de lo que bien se sabe representa, y de la utilidad de un cheque girado sobre la recaudación de las rentas del Gobierno, esta sección ha demostrado su utilidad de una manera indubitable

Hay en la Isla de Cuba y rinden cuentas de recaudación un Puerto, el de la Habana, y 16 Puertos subalternos que son: en la costa Norte de Oeste á Este, la Habana, Matanzas, Cárdenas, Sagua la Grande, Caibarién, Nuevitas, Gibara y Baracoa; y en la costa Sur de Este á Oeste, Guantánamo, Santiago de Cuba, Manzanillo, Santa Cruz del Sur, Júcaro, Túnas de Zaza, Trinidad, Cienfuegos y Batabanó.

La recaudación procedente de las rentas interiores son las siguientes: derechos Reales y transmisiones de dominio, Industria y Comercio, aprovechamientos forestales, redención de censos, réditos de regulares,.réditos de fianzas, rentas de bienes del Estado, venta de terrenos del Estado, procedencias varias y de todos los demás conceptos que devengan periódicamente. La recaudación está á cargo de los Administradores de Contribuciones en las Zonas Fiscales de Cuba que son once, á contar del Este al Oeste geográficamente: Pinar del Río, Guanajay, Habana, Matanzas, Cárdenas, Cienfuegos, Santa Clara, Puerto Príncipe, Manzanillo, Holguín y Santiago.

Son de incumbencia de esta sección también las cuentas de la recaudación por ingresos varios, las que mayormente rinden casi siempre los Capitanes de Puerto. Cada uno de los 16 Puertos antes mencionados tiene un Capitán de Puerto que es al mismo tiempo Administrador de Aduana. El Puerto de la Habana tiene un Capitán de Puerto, cuyos deberes son distintos de los del Administrador de Aduana del Puerto, y que ejerce jurisdicción sobre los demás Capitanes de Puerto. La renta recaudada por estos empleados proviene de la imposición de multas y penas á los navieros y barcos, por infracción de las ordenanzas del Puerto y muy á menudo por el despacho de certificados marítimos.

A esta sección también se le dá cuenta de los productos de las ventas de los bienes del Estado y de otros ingresos generales. Efectivamente tiene jurisdicción sobre todas las recaudaciones, excepto las que proceden del Ramo de Correos. Sus trabajos están al día y así continuarán.

SECCIÓN DE CORREOS.

(Jefe A. J. Bowle.)

Esta sección tiene jurisdicción sobre las cuentas pertenecientes á la recaudación y pago del ramo de Correos. Examina los ingresos postales de que dan cuenta los Administradores de toda la Isla. Les carga la existencia de sellos que se reciben y les abona los caudales que traen al Tesoro. Actualmente hay como 175 Administradores que reciben los sellos directamente del Departamento de Correos, cobrando los derechos de apartados, etc., etc., y que dan cuenta á esta Oficina de lo recaudado y de lo ingresado. Como 75 Oficinas dan cuenta solamente de las ventas y cancelaciones, y los sellos que venden estos Administradores los compran á las Oficinas de más categoría que estén próximas y se pagan con los recursos particulares de los Administradores. Como 55 oficinas autorizadas no rinden cuenta alguna. Grande empeño se está tomando por el Director General de Correos y por esta Oficina á fin de que el Negociado de sellos y habilitaciones del Departamento de Correos, surta de sellos á todos los Administradores de la Isla y para que los Administradores rindan cuenta á esta Oficina mensualmente, haya habido ó no movimiento de despacho en sus Oficinas. Los haberes en las Administraciones pequeñas son necesariamente tan reducidos, que los Administradores juzgan que el tiempo empleado en estudiar los varios y hasta complejos detalles del sistema postal, no redunda en ningún provecho.

SECCION DE CUENTAS DE BIENES Y EFECTOS DEL ESTADO.

(Jefe H. M. Wood.)

Tan al principio como en Marzo 14 de 1899 y en Orden Civil del Cuartel General de la División de Cuba de esa fecha, el Gobernador Militar dictó disposiciones para la rendición de las cuentas de Bienes y Efectos del Estado, á la Intervención general de la Isla de Cuba, la cual ejercía jurisdicción sobre todas las cuentas de pagos y de los caudales procedentes del ingreso de las Aduanas de la Isla, exceptuando las que á la sazón se rendían al Interventor de las Oficinas de Aduanas. Esta Orden también confería igual jurisdicción al Interventor de Hacienda respecto de los caudales que á él venían. Se disponía, además, que rindieran sus cuentas los empleados civiles del Gobierno Militar, naturales del país, y que dataran desde el primer día de la ocupación militar, Enero 1º de 1899. Á este respecto se tiene entendido que de los productos de bienes del Estado se daba regularmente cuenta al Interventor de la Isla, Comandante Ladd, Cuartelmaestre, Voluntario de los Estados Unidos, y que él las liquidaba. Después de establecida la actual Oficina del Interventor, en 1º de Julio de 1899, con sujeción á las instrucciones del Departamento de la Guerra, de 11 de Mayo de dicho año, parece que sólo muy pocas cuentas de Bienes del Estado se remitieron al Interventor, y que ni aún fueron objeto por su parte de un acuse de recibo. Resulta de los antecedentes obrantes en la Oficina, que el Interventor no se consideraba obligado según sus instrucciones á fiscalizar tales cuentas. El Departamento de la Guerra, sin embargo, interpretó los deberes del Auditor de diferente manera, y en una continuada correspondencia, y por su iniciativa, indicó á mi antecesor, Comandante E. C. Brooks, que una fiscalización completa y breve de la responsabilidad por Bienes del Estado de los Agentes Fiscales del Gobierno, estaba en gran manera indicada. El Comandante Brooks estaba de acuerdo en este punto y en Julio de 1900, habiendo obtenido los servicios de un empleado del Departamento de la Guerra, procedió á la organización de personal para el examen de las cuentas de Bienes del Estado que habían tenido entrada en la Oficina y á dictar las medidas necesarias para exigir la responsabilidad consiguiente á los empleados que hasta entonces habían abandonado este servicio.

Mientras la Sección se hallaba en los comienzos de su organización, fué llamada con urgencia por el Departamento de la Guerra relativamente á la interpelación en el Senado, de Mayo 26 de 1900, y hubo mientras tanto que dar de mano á lo de Bienes del Estado, y el personal que se hubiera dedicado á aquel servicio, tuvo que dedicarse á la rendición de los datos que se pidieron. No se terminó este trabajo relativo á la interpelación del Senado hasta últimos de Diciembre de 1900, y una parte aunque pequeña, de los empleados de la Oficina pudo ocuparse en el asunto durante el primer mes comprendido en este informe.

Á principios del mes de Enero último, la Sección de Bienes del Estado volvió á pasar por una nueva organización, aunque poco se hizo durante el primer mes y medio, porque absorvieron el tiempo el ensayo é instrucción de los empleados destinados á esta obra y á llevarla á cabo minuciosamente. Puede decirse que el trabajo verdadero en esta Oficina realmente empezó como á mediados de Febrero último.

Las cartas de pago de uso autorizado, permitían la enagenación de efectos al comprador. Antes de ahora repetidamente se ha llamado la atención hácia el hecho de que este sistema traía el abuso en grande escala de que efectos que por su propia naturaleza no se inventariaban, se trataba de salir de ellos mediante dichas cartas de pago. Además de esto, casi sin excepción, los empleados habían omitido dar extractos de las compras, pero esta última dificultad en parte se allanó por el hecho de reconocerla y de preverla en la redacción de las relaciones de bienes y efectos del Estado, con destino al Senado, y cuando estas relaciones se hicieron, esta Oficina ideó un modelo de extracto de las compras realizadas, con vista de cada una de las cuentas corrientes examinadas.

En tiempos pasados y aun hoy, se llevan á cabo trasmisiones de bienes ó efectos sin distinción alguna, en favor de individuos irresponsables que en la época en que podemos entender en la censura de sus cuentas, ya no tienen posición oficial y que individualmente no responden á los emplazamientos de esta Oficina para rendirlas. Además de este punto, en distintas ocasiones se ha llamado la atención del Gobernador Militar; y ahora, salvo su mejor parecer, se propone que cada ramo del Gobierno y cada establecimiento público tenga algún funcionario debidamente designado como responsable de los bienes que respectivamente correspondan á los unos y los otros. En algunos establecimientos y Oficinas del Gobierno, para los gastos que no sean cantidades de muy pequeña cuantía se cuenta con un número de empleados adscritos, que se encargan de los bienes ó efectos que á aquellos establecimientos y oficinas corresponden. Si se acepta lo anteriormente propuesto, puede obviarse la dificultad y con un solo cuentadante responsable, los efectos de dichos establecimientos ú oficinas pueden facilitarse por dicho empleado á otras dependencias mediante recibos detallados. En muchos casos se ha solicitado de los Jefes de las dependencias, en donde tal cosa acontecía, que los suprimiera, designando un empleado encargado de esos efectos que adoptase los recibos antes referidos. Con muchas dificultades se ha tropezado á este respecto, por mala interpretación por parte de los funcionarios, en cuanto á la índole oficial de los empleados á quienes toca la trasmisión de efectos mediante esos recibos y á la despreocupación respecto de las palabras "responsabilidad" y "deberes del cuentadante" envueltas en acto semejante. Merced á explicaciones de una parte y otra y á una más clara interpretación, no se han tenido ulteriores dificultades, y los funcionarios administrativos han deferido á nuestro empeño de reducir el número de cuentadantes. Hasta donde exactamente puede llegarse acerca de este punto, no es ya solamente cuestión de contabilidad, sino que se roza con los asuntos administrativos de las dependencias y establecimientos públicos á que se refiere, y únicamente puede realizarse con la cooporación inteligente y sincera de los empleados que gobiernan las varias dependencias.

A contar desde el 14 de Marzo de 1899, fecha de la publicación de las órdenes civiles relativas á la contabilidad general de la Isla, no se dispuso nada en concreto sobre las cuentas de tales efectos ó bienes hasta que se publicaron las instrucciones de 13 de Marzo de 1901, que en sus secciones 23, 24 y 25 dispone lo siguiente:

"Art. 23. A los oficiales pagadores, así como á los agentes se les exigirá que demuestren el uso y destino final de todos los bienes comprados por ellos, y todos los funcionarios del Gobierno Militar de Cuba estarán obligados á demostrar cual ha sido dicho uso y destino final de los bienes todos en posesión de los mismos pertenecientes á dicho gobierno.

Art. 24. Se formarán trimestralmente estados de bienes que serán trasmitidos al Interventor dentro de veinte días después del vencimiento del trimestre á que correspondan, acompañados de los correspondientes resúmenes y comprobantes.

Art. 25. Siempre que cualquier funcionario ó agente que sea responsable de bienes pertenecientes al Gobierno Militar de Cuba dejare de formar los estados que sean necesarios de dichos bienes para el Interventor, ó dejare de trasmitir los mismos dentro del período aquí señalado, ó descuidare hacer y trasmitir los mismos cuando se solicite que así lo haga, será deber del Interventor dar cuenta del hecho al Gobernador Militar para la resolución que corresponda.''

Durante el semestre que venció en 30 de Junio de 1901, se recibieron en la oficina 725 relaciones de bienes y efectos, de cuyo número quedan 261 por censurar, habiéndose examinado 464 distribuídas por años económicos en la forma siguiente: 57 de 1901; 366 en 1900 y 41 en 1899. De las examinadas resultaron 198 sin reparos y saldadas. Quedaron entonces pendientes al cerrar este informe, 527 cuentas de bienes y efectos que no fueron saldadas, de las cuales se habían examinado 266; y la oficina está en comunicación con los empleados á quienes atañen 221 de las mismas al cerrar el período que abarca el presente informe. Durante este plazo se censuraron 1,499 cuentas corrientes de pagos, comprendidas en el año económico de 1900, y 137 cuentas del año 1901. En el examen de estas cuentas corrientes, como antes se ha dicho, otros tantos extractos de compras fueron obra de esta Sección.

De lo expuesto resulta el cálculo de que al finalizar el año económico de 1901, habíamos abierto cuentas de bienes y efectos á 736 empleados, de los cuales 233 eran oficiales del Ejército y 503 funcionarios civiles, cuyas operaciones comprendían 1,906 trimestres ó cuentas por el concepto de bienes ó efectos. Se verá, pues, que el número total de cuentas recibidas—275—es por mucho ménos de las que debieran recibirse, en efecto, algo más de la tercera parte.

Los trabajos llevados á cabo por esta Sección en el período de que se trata, fueron en gran parte preparatorios. Los pliegos de reparo á las cuentas de bienes ó efectos se han concretado en lo posible á los modelos impresos; y se toma el mayor empeño en simplificar este trabajo.

Las operaciones fiscalizadas por esta Sección, son de por sí de más variada índole que las que tienen que despachar las oficinas de contabilidad de los Estados Unidos. Las cuentas comprenden efectos sanitarios y para el mantenimiento de los hospitales; provisiones de Artillería; de las oficinas de Ingenieros; de las de los Inspectores de caminos; maquinaria para los Arsenales y otros talleres del Gobierno; estuches de dibujo etc., etc. La censura de estas cuentas diversas exige conocimientos técnicos difíciles de hallar entre los empleados que corren con aquella. La traducción de vocablos, que hace necesario el uso común del español y el inglés, ha dado márgen á dificultades que se han ofrecido á pocas oficinas interventoras. Para cohonestarlas tenemos á la mano toda clase de diccionarios españoles asequibles, aunque son pocos, y con frecuencia consultamos los catálogos de las fábricas de los Estados Unidos que han correspondido á nuestros deseos.

El sistema de registro de documentos de esta Sección se ha organizado eslàbonándolo con el que observa el registro general de la oficina,—el sistema de anotación extractada, que va de una mesa á otra, las cuales aumentan á medida que el trabajo adelanta, completándose según se va presentando la tramitación necesaria. Ahora se usan libros mayores con los asientos de bienes ó efectos que expresan las varias responsabilidades de los empleados, á contar desde el primer día de la ocupación militar hasta la fecha.

Gran dificultad ha ofrecido el cruce de comunicaciones con los empleados al tratar de su responsabilidad en las cuentas de bienes ó efectos. Sus contestaciones al solventar los reparos puestos por esta Oficina, muchas veces son generalidades ó divagaciones. Al paso que se comprende que la demora en emplazar á los cuentadantes les ha dificultado muchas veces el solventar esos reparos, parece que muchos de ellos no se han tomado empeño en liquidar sus cuentas. Muchas veces acontece que los empleados con quienes hemos de comunicarnos, especialmente los oficiales del Ejército, han salido de la Isla y pasan los meses antes de que sea de esperarse su contestación. Cuando ésta llega, no se refiere al punto cardinal del asunto, antes á una exposición de las razones que asisten al cuentadante para no creerse obligado á rendir cuentas.

SECCIÓN DE TENEDURIA Y LIBRAMIENTOS.

(Jefe, Mathaniel Nathan).

Esta Sección tiene á su cargo llevar las cuentas de los ingresos y gastos generales, así como las de carácter personal. Expide y lleva el registro de todos los libramientos. Lleva también el registro de todas las fianzas de los administradores fiscales del Gobierno Militar y á solicitud de los varios Jefes de Sección, les facilita certificados expedidos por Teneduría, de las cuentas de los empleados. Lleva registro de los pedidos y presupuestos que hacen los Ordenadores de Pagos, y de las consignaciones que hace el Gobernador Militar para los mismos, dentro del capítulo y artículo correspondientes. Los pedidos de fondos y su ascendencia vienen á esta Oficina y se comprueban antes de pasar á la aprobación del Gobernador Militar. Tiene á su cargo la extensión y censura de las cuentas de la Tesorería General, y bisemanalmente dá al Gobernador Militar el parte de los fondos que se hallan en poder de la Tesorería, y de los anticipos hechos con cargo á los mismos. A fin de cada mes dá el parte al Secretario de la Guerra de los caudales que entran en la Tesorería, con expresión al por menor del nombre de los empleados, y del concepto de su procedencia; una relación de los libramientos expedidos, consignando el capítulo y el artículo de la autorización; así como de los pagados por Tesorería.

Los libramientos que ahora se estilan, autorizados por el Gobierno Militar con fecha 17 de Abril de 1901, guardan la forma de un giro del Gobernador Militar á cargo de la Tesorería General á favor del empleado Pagador á cuya disposición se quiere poner el importe. Estos libramientos, después del Vto. Bno. y del asiento en el mayor correspondiente, que practica el Interventor, se pasan á Tesorería para su pago. La Tesorería gira sobre estos libramientos á cargo del cajero ó á cargo del depositario de fondos públicos, debidamente autorizado, por el importe, ordenando que se le abone á la cuenta del pagador para cubrir el cheque de éste. El libramiento pasa luego de la Tesorería al empleado á cuyo favor se expide y éste lo devuelve endosado, dando recibo del importe. Este último trámite es preciso para cumplir las disposiciones del Secretario de la Guerra de 13 de Marzo de 1901, á saber:

"Los libramientos pagados por la Tesorería, con la debida comprobación del pago que será el endoso del destinatario, constituirán los justificantes en que se ha de fundar para abonarle el importe del pago que haya hecho."

Desde luego se verá que esta disposición y los trámites que origina, causan no poca demora en la rendición de cuentas por la Tesorería, porque el Tesorero, una vez abonado el importe de un libramiento á un pagador, no puede partir de que esos fondos se hallen en su poder, sino después de la devolución de los libramientos debidamente endosados; no puede exijir que se le abonen tales pagos, y como una consecuencia y no por culpa suya, sus cuentas invariablemente se demoran. Alguna vez se extravían estos libramientos y se hace necesario entonces que el Tesorero haga constar otra prueba conducente, siendo la primera el recibo del empleado á quien atañe, de esos fondos como demostración del pago cuyo abono en su favor reclame como necesario.

A mi juicio, lo que se tuvo en miras fué que el libramiento dispuesto por el Departamento de la Guerra en sus instrucciones, sirviera de giro sobre el Tesoro, quien, al recibirlo, lo aceptaría y le daría curso dirigiéndolo al empleado á cuyo favor se girara, el cual empleado entonces depositaría el libramiento en el Banco, endosado en la forma que es de costumbre según las prácticas del comercio. Este procedimiento hubiera allanado los inconvenientes que ofrece el sistema actual, excepto uno, y evitaría que la dificultad que ofrece un sistema ó el otro, por la falta de facilidad para comunicarse con los lugares apartados del tránsito con la Habana, y la necesidad de situar con urgencia los fondos á disposición de los funcionarios pagadores.

Al hacerme cargo de la Oficina encontré que, estudiado el punto, existía una diversidad de formas en cuanto á la autorización y admisión de las fianzas prestadas por los administradores fiscales. Muchas tenían entrada en la Tesorería General, otras en la Secretaría de Hacienda, aunque probablemente la mayor parte la tenían en las oficinas del Gobierno en que estaban prestando sus servicios los empleados que por las mismas se afianzaban. El Interventor General no tenía conocimiento de estas fianzas y con frecuencia se hacían anticipos con su anuencia, á empleados que no habían prestado fianza. Los afianzados á menudo lo estaban de tal modo, que no garantizaban por completo al Gobierno el puesto y la condición en que se hallaban para percibir y pagar fondos. Llamé la atención del Gobierno Militar hácia esta circunstancia y le ha puesto remedio al mal disponiendo que en adelante todas las fiánzas deben ir á poder de la Tesorería General por conducto del Interventor General.

Esta oficina entonces extracta de la fianza que por este conducto ha recibido todos los datos necesarios y la consigna en el registro de fianzas. Con sujeción á estas fianzas se expresarán todas las cuentas, y la práctica de arrastrar los saldos de una fianza á las cuentas de otra, será suprimida.

La forma en que muchas de las fianzas han sido antes de ahora admitidas por el Gobierno Militar es tan inconveniente para el mismo y le impone tan onerosas condiciones, que se le ha llamado la atención acerca del particular, y es de creerse que en porvenir no lejano se dictará alguna disposición que determine una fórmula de fianza nueva y mejor redactada.

SECCIÓN DE CORRESPONDENCIA Y REGISTRO.

(Bajo la dirección del Oficial Mayor.)

En su informe anual correspondiente al año económico 1901, mi predecesor advirtió la falta de un método adecuado para llevar el registro, lo cual ocasisnaba en verdad falta de unidad de acción en los encargados de censurar las cuentas. De este modo de ser sobrevino la falta de precedentes consecutivos, y por decontado, el historial de los trámites dispuestos por mis predecesores es incompleto, y muchas veces desordenado.

El comandate Brooks volvió sobre el asunto en su informe correspondiente al semestre anterior inmediato á este, y para llenar ese vacío adoptó, el sistema de la correspondencia y del registo que se usan en muchas oficinas del Gobierno de Washington—el de la anotación extractada ó de una mesa á otra.—Fué necesario al adoptarlo reunir los datos sueltos que en su poder tenían hasta entonces los varios empleados de la ficina y los cuales no eran de suyo fehacientes, coleccionando los apuntes y arreglándolos con poca sujeción á un orden verdadero. Se numeraron las cuentas y la correspondencia referente á las mismas, fué acumulada, anotada y registrada con aquella. Para realizar esta tarea se destinó un grupo de empleados de los que habian tomado parte en la redacción de los estados que sirvieron para contestar la interpelación del Senado de 26 de mayo de 1900. Esta obra comenzó como á últimos del pasado Diciembre, y como para el 1º de Abril, la mayor parte de todas las cuentas y de la correspondencia que se habia recibido desde 1º de Julio de 1899 hasta la fecha en que se creó la Sección, se habia organizado conforne al nuevo sistema.

Desde entonces hasta ahora la Sección ha despachado lo corriente y de vez en cuando, llegada la ocasión, se ha ocupado en completar los datos anteriores de la oficina. De Enero de 1900 hasta la conclusión del informe, Junio 30, 1901, se habían registrado en esta oficina 14,621 expedientes. En estos se incluyen cuentas, pedidos y presupuestos, y libramientos sobre los mismos, ingresos de Tesorería, según periódicamente se efectúan; cuentas de bienes y efectos y una cantidad considerable de reclamaciones en general y la correspondencia. El establecimiento de esta Sección dió por resultado el adiestrar á un número de empleados en el trabajo del registro y en aliviar á los encargados del examen y censura con respecto á la dificultad de llevar ellos mismos sus registros y buscar los papeles extraviados. Como medio de conservar los registros y datos para consulta de un gran número de empleados, su utilidad se ha demostrado suficientemente en otro lugar y día por día se hace más patente y de mayor provecho para la oficina.

La mayor parte de las dificultades de la oficina y de los empleados cuentadantes ante la misma, se halló que consistía en el hecho de que las órdenes publicadas y los reglamentos vigentes para la contabilidad en Cuba cuando más son fragmentarios. Para salvar ésto, dispuse se hiciera una compilación de las distintas bases sobre que descansaba el sistema de contabilidad vigente en los Estados Unidos. Esta compilación, no obstante, me temo que llegue tarde para que sea de práctica utilidad. Se comprende que no está distante el día en que éste y demás Departamentos del Gobierno Militar se preparen para entregar á sus sucesores los trabajos que han organizado y planteado.

Es mi propósito completar y llevar á cabo un registro permanente, si se desea que se lleve, que ofrezca á nuestros sucesores una relación de antecedentes basados en la justicia y en los principios de una contabilidad honrada. Mi propósito ha sido exigir que las cuentas vengan de tal manera, que haya un historial de los asuntos oficiales que demuestre á los investigadores del presente y del porvenir lo que se ha hecho con los caudales públicos y los bienes y efectos del Estado. Nada menos que ésto se necesita para garantizar la honradez y la economía en los gastos públicos. Ese sistema de contabilidad es el que más se aproxima á la exactitud que no abre las puertas á los errores ni al fraude. Una contabilidad escrupulosa y una constante publicidad son los dos primeros requisitos para la honradez y la economía en los negocios del Gobierno. Se necesita una inspección exquisita y constante para asegurarlas. Ningún empleado público honrado tiene nada que ocultar, ni obstáculos que oponer para exhibir minuciosamente lo que ha hecho de los caudales y de los bienes públicos; y me complazco en poder decir que con pocas excepciones, los cuentadantes ante esta Oficina adelantan en la forma de rendir sus cuentas, y si por ese camino continúan, hay razón para creer que un sistema francamente bueno estará vigente cuando el Gobierno Militar cese en sus funciones.

Atentamente,

J. D. Terrill,
Interventor General de Cuba.

Al Gobernador Militar de Cuba,
Habana.

Cuartel General, Departamento de Cuba,

Habana, 22 de Marzo de 1901.

Por disposición del Secretario de la Guerra, el Gobernador Militar de Cuba ordena la publicación de la siguiente Orden para su conocimiento y efectos.

El Comandante de Estado Mayor,
J. B. HICKEY.

DEPARTAMENTO DE LA GUERRA,

Washington, 13 de Marzo de 1901.

Se publica la siguiente Orden del Presidente para general conocimiento.

RESIDENCIA DEL EJECUTIVO,

Washington, 12 de Marzo de 1901

La Orden del Ejecutivo de 8 de Mayo de 1899, referente á la Isla de Cuba, publicada por el Subsecretario de la Guerra en 11 de Mayo de 1899, queda por la presente modificada sustituyéndola con lo siguiente:

En virtud de las facultades de que me hallo investido como Jefe Supremo del Ejército y Armada de los Estados Unidos, por la presente ordeno y mando crear en la Isla de Cuba, para que funcione mientras rija el Gobierno Militar de los Estados Unidos en dicha Isla, la plaza de Interventor de Cuba, que será provista por nombramiento del Secretario de la Guerra, y cuyos deberes serán exigir é intervenir todas las cuentas de la Isla.

También se crea por la presente y se proveerá á la permanencia del empleo de Interventor Auxiliar de Cuba, quien será nombrado por el Secretario de la Guerra; y cuyos deberes serán firmar, á nombre del Interventor, los documentos oficiales que éste designe, y desempeñar las demás obligaciones que dicho Interventor le señale. En caso de muerte, renuncia, enfermedad ó ausencia del Interventor, por cualquier motivo, lo reemplazará aquél, quedando encargado de la Oficina.

También se crea por la presente y se proveerá á su permanencia en la Oficina del Interventor, el empleo de Jefe del Despacho, quien será nombrado por el Interventor, y dicho Jefe del Despacho desempeñará los deberes que el Interventor le imponga.

Todas las reglas é instrucciones necesarias á fin de llevar á efecto las disposiciones de las órdenes del Ejecutivo referentes á Cuba, serán dictadas por el Secretario de la Guerra, y dichas reglas é instrucciones quedarán en vigor hasta que las mismas sean modificadas ó derogadas por el Secretario de la Guerra.

WILLIAM MCKINLEY.

La precedente Orden y las siguientes reglas é instrucciones serán oportunamente publicadas y puestas en vigor en Cuba, según se dispone en la misma, y surtirán sus efettos y empezarán á regir desde el día primero de Abril de 1901 inclusive; y por la presente quedan derogadas todas las disposiciones y órdenes vigentes hasta la fecha, que sean contrarias á la presente.

Reglas é instrucciones relativas al sistema de contabilidad del Gobierno de los Estados Unidos en Cuba.

RESIDENCIA DE LOS FUNCIONARIOS.

ARTÍCULO 1.

El Gobernador Militar de Cuba residirá en la ciudad de la Habana y los funcionarios de que tratan la Orden del Ejecutivo de 8 de Mayo de 1899, y la que la sustituye de 12 de Marzo de 1901, residirán y tendrán sus oficinas en dicha ciudad.

EL INTERVENTOR DE CUBA.

ART. 2.

El Interventor de Cuba, nombrado por la Orden del Ejecutivo de 8 de Mayo de 1899, exigirá, examinará y aprobará todas las cuentas que pertenezcan á las rentas públicas é ingresos de Cuba, y á los gastos que se paguen con ambos, y certificará al Gobernador Militar el saldo de las mismas, conservando dichas cuentas y comprobantes después de finiquitadas.

ART. 3.

El Interventor Auxiliar firmará, á nombre del Interventor, los documentos oficiales que el segundo designe, y desempeñará los demás deberes que éste le señale.

ART. 4.

En caso de fallecimiento, renuncia, ausencia ó enfermedad del Interventor, el Interventor Auxiliar actuará como Interventor, y desempeñará los deberes de dicho Interventor hasta que se nombre y habilite en debida forma á su sucesor, ó hasta que cese la ausencia ó enfermedad.

ART. 5.

En caso de fallecimiento, renuncia, ausencia ó enfermedad del Interventor Auxiliar, el Interventor designará un funcionario de la Intervención, que actuará como Interventor Auxiliar, y desempeñará los deberes de éste hasta que se nombre y habilite en debida forma á quien le haya de sustituir ó hasta que cese dicha ausencia ó enfermedad.

ART. 6.

Habrá en la Intervención cuantas Secciones sean necesarias, á juicio del Interventor, para el mejor despacho y ordenada distribución del trabajo de la oficina; debiendo estar cada una de esas Secciones á cargo de un Jefe de Sección, que será nombrado por el Interventor.

ART. 7.

El Gobernador Militar expedirá y firmará todos los libramientos para el pago de cantidades por el Tesorero; los cuales libramientos se presentarán al Interventor para ser visados por éste. No se expedirá ningún libramiento para el anticipo de fondos, salvo cuando, con dicho objeto lo pida el funcionario correspondiente, y lo apruebe el Gobernador Militar, siempre que sea autorizado aquél por el Interventor, de conformidad con las asignaciones concedidas. No se expedirá ningún libramiento para pagar el saldo de ninguna cuenta, excepto en virtud de certificación del Interventor y después de liquidada la cuenta.

ART. 8.

Los libramientos expedidos para el anticipo de cantidades procedentes de fondos que estén en poder del Tesorero, se denominarán "Libramientos á justificar," y serán numerados consecutivamente, conservándose en serie aparte.

Art. 9.

Los libramientos expedidos para el pago de cuentas liquidadas y certificadas por el Interventor se denominarán "Libramientos en firme," y serán numerados consecutivamente en serie aparte.

Art. 10.

Todos los recibos expedidos por el Tesorero de cantidades á él pagadas, serán expedidas por duplicado y visados por el Interventor. Una vez así visados se conservará en cada caso un recibo en la Intervención, y el otro será entregado ó trasmitido por el Interventor á la persona por quien se hubiere hecho el pago, después que dicho recibo haya sido debidamente registrado con todos sus particulares bajo el epígrafe correspondiente.

Art. 11.

Los recibos que retenga el Interventor constituirán el comprobante necesario en el examen y liquidación que practique de la cuenta de ingresos del Tesorero y serán bastantes para cargar al Tesorero las cantidades recibidas, y dichos recibos serán archivados en la Intervención con las cuentas que sirven de abono.

Art. 12.

Los libramientos pagados por el Tesorero junto con el correspondiente comprobante de pago, que será el oportuno endoso del perceptor puesto en dichos libramientos, constituirán los comprobantes en virtud de los cuales al Tesorero se le abonarán en cuenta los pagos hechos por él, y después de la liquidación de sus cuentas por el Interventor, dichos libramientos serán archivados con estas cuentas.

Art. 13.

Los certificados de liquidaciones de cuentas extendidos por el Interventor para el Gobernador Militar serán numerados consecutivamente y archivados con las respectivas cuentas y comprobantes en la Oficina del Interventor, quien conservará los mismos. Un ejemplar de cada certificado de quidación será presentado al Gobernador Militar que lo conservará en su poder.

Art. 14.

El Interventor deberá, con la aprobación del Gobernador Militar, disponer los modelos conforme á los cuales han de llevarse y rendirse todas las cuentas sujetas á su censura y liquidación, y estos modelos deberán realmente ajustarse á los que usan los empleados oficiales que rinden cuentas al Departamento del Tesoro de los Estados Unidos, y dicho Interventor dará las instrucciones necesarias á los funcionarios y agentes llamados á rendir dichas cuentas.

Art. 15.

Siempre que cualquier funcionario ó agente, cuyo deber sea recaudar y percibir cantidades procedentes de las rentas públicas de la Isla, por cualquier concepto que sea, y dar salida á dichas cantidades cualquiera que sea su destino, dejare de rendir cuenta cabal de dichos ingresos y salidas al Interventor, ó de transmitir las mismas dentro del período de diez días, después de vencido el mes á que pertenezcan, ó descuidare rendir las mismas cuando se le pidan, será deber del Interventor comunicarlo inmediatamente al Gobernador Militar para la resolución que corresponda.

ART. 16.

Habrá en la Intervención una Sección de Teneduría de Libros donde se llevarán los correspondientes diarios y mayores para asentar las cuentas generales de ingresos y egresos, pertenecientes á las rentas públicas de Cuba, y las cuentas personales de los agentes y funcionarios autorizados para la recaudación de las mismas y para la salida de cantidades anticipadas por el Tesoro en virtud de libramientos, según se dispone en la presente, y todas las demás cuentas y descargos admitidos y certificados por el Interventor, incluso las cuentas de asignaciones de presupuestos.

CUENTAS DE INGRESOS Y GASTOS GENERALES.

ART. 17.

Los recibos, expedidos por el Tesoro, de las cantidades que perciba antes de ser visados por el Interventor, serán asentados en el Libro Mayor correspondiente de Ingresos Generales, como cantidades provenientes de los Ingresos de Aduanas, de Correos, Rentas Interiores y Varios, respectivamente, ó como pago de dichos recibos, y al hacer tales asientos de los recibos del Tesorero se hará constar el número y la fecha del recibo y el nombre y carácter oficial de la persona, si lo tuviere, por quien se hubiere hecho el pago ó depósito. Estos fondos se transferirán inmediatamente á una cuenta de "Rentas," á la cual se cargarán todas las asignaciones procedentes de "fondos en Tesorería destinados á otro fin."

ART. 18.

Todos los Libramientos expedidos por el Gobernador Militar, después de visados por el Interventor, se cargarán á las rentas por cuenta del servicio y asignación para los cuales dichos libramientos hubieren sido expedidos, y al hacer dichos asientos de cargo se anotará el número y fecha del libramiento y la persona, haciendo constar su carácter oficial si lo tuviere, á quién se hubiere pagado. El Interventor llevará sus libros Registros de tal modo que pueda exhibir á cualquier hora qué cantidad tuvo salida; á cargo de cuál crédito, tal como aparezca de los libramientos á justificar expedidos, y de las cuentas examinadas.

LIBRO MAYOR DE CUENTAS PERSONALES.

ART. 19.

En los Libros Mayores de cuentas personales todo anticipo de cantidades hecho en virtud de pedidos de fondos y de libramientos á funcionarios y agentes autorizados para el gasto, de acuerdo con los créditos asignados, se cargarán á dichos funcionarios respectivamente, con cargo al servicio y crédito, por los cuales se ha de hacer el pago al expedir los libramientos para dichos anticipos, y los números y las fechas de los respectivos libramientos se harán constar al hacer dichos asientos de cargo; y por los pagos hechos por dichos funcionarios ó agentes autorizados por el interventor en la liquidación de las cuentas de dichos pagos, los correspondientes créditos se asentarán en las respectivas cuentas personales, según resulte de los certificados de las liquidaciones hechas por el Interventor; haciéndose constar, al hacer los asientos de créditos, el número y las fechas de los respectivos certificados.

ART. 20.

Del propio modo los certificados de liquidaciones de cuentas particulares de todas clases, expedidos por el Interventor, serán asentados en los libros Mayores de cuentas personales en las correspondientes cuentas individuales con cargo al servicio y crédito por los cuales se rinde la cuenta; el número y la fecha del certificado del Interventor se hará constar asímismo y todos los libramientos de liquidaciones expedidos en virtud de certificados de liquidación de cuentas que lo sean por el Interventor, serán cargados á la correspondiente cuenta individual en la correspondiente partida en los Libros Mayores de cuentas personales, anotándose el número y la fecha del libramiento.

ART. 21.

Al hacer la liquidación de cada una de las cuentas y antes de certificar la misma, el Interventor exigirá una relación de la Sección de Contaduría de su Oficina, en que se hará constar el último saldo certificado de la cuenta particular, y los adeudos ó créditos subsecuentemente anotados en dicha cuenta en los libros mayores, cuya relación ó certificado servirá de base para la liquidación por el Interventor de la Cuenta que tenga puesta al despacho.

CUENTAS DE PAGOS.

ART. 22.

Las cuentas de pagos se rendirán mensualmente y se transmitirán al Interventor, dentro de diez días después del vencimiento del mes á que correspondan, por los funcionarios y agentes autorizados para hacer pagos, y en las cuales dichos funcionarios ó agentes se cargarán todas las cantidades que se les haya anticipado respectivamente, por el Tesorero y se abonarán los pagos que hayan hecho, justificados con la correspondiente documentación. Un resumen de los pagos acompañado de los comprobantes de los mismos, numerados en orden consecutivo, acompañará á cada cuenta.

ART. 23.

A los oficiales pagadores, así como á los agentes, se les exigirá que hagan constar el uso y destino final de todos los bienes y efectos que hayan comprado, y todos los funcionarios del Gobierno Militar de Cuba estarán obligados á demostrar cuál ha sido el uso y destino final ya dichos de los bienes todos en posesión de los mismos como pertenecientes al Gobierno.

ART. 24.

Se formarán trimestralmente estados de bienes y efectos, que serán trasmitidos al Interventor dentro de veinte días después del vencimiento del trimestre á que correspondan, acompañados de los correspondientes resúmenes y comprobantes.

ART. 25.

Siempre que cualquier funcionario ó agente responsable de bienes pertenecientes al Gobierno Militar de Cuba, dejare de formar para el mismo los estados que sean necesarios de dichos bienes, ó dejare de acompañar los mismos dentro del período aquí señalado, ó descuidare hacerlos y trasmitirlos cuando para ello se le requiera, será deber del Interventor dar cuenta del hecho al Gobernador Militar para la resolución que corresponda.

CUENTAS DE RENTAS PUBLICAS.

ART. 26.

Los funcionarios autorizados para percibir y recaudar cantidades procedentes de las rentas de Cuba, por cualquier concepto, estarán obligados á entregar las cantidades totales que hayan percibido y recaudado respectivamente, al Tesorero de Cuba, y á rendir al Interventor las cuentas mensuales de las mismas, dentro de diez días después de vencido el mes á que pertenecen, acompañando relaciones debidamente detalladas y certificadas y estados de las cuentas recaudadas, en los cuales se haga constar cuándo, por quién y por qué cuenta se pagaron,

ART. 27.

Al rendir dichas cuentas de rentas, los funcionarios ó agentes se cargarán todas las rentas percibidas y recaudadas durante el período comprendido en la cuenta, y se abonarán las sumas pagadas al Tesoro, según resulte de recibo por duplicado en su poder, visado por el Interventor, haciéndose constar el número y la fecha de dichos recibos en los asientos de las cantidades pagadas al Tesoro; estos recibos por duplicado los conservarán en su poder el funcionario ó el agente que gestionen la data de los mismos.

ART. 28.

Para la censura de dichas cuentas de rentas, el Interventor confrontará y comprobará los recibos del Tesorero obrantes en su oficina con los correspondientes asientos de la cuenta del funcionario ó agente, según se hubiere rendido aquella.

ART. 29.

Todas las cuentas de rentas serán rendidas y se llevarán separadamente con sujeción al crédito ó al epígrafe de cuentas á que respectivamente pertenezcan, es decir, todas las rentas que procedan del ramo de Aduanas se anotarán dentro del capítulo de Ingresos de Aduanas; las del ramo de Correos, dentro del capítulo de Ingresos Postales; todas las Rentas por concepto de contribuciones é impuestos interiores, distintas de los ingresos de Aduanas é Ingresos Postales, se anotarán dentro del capítulo de Ingresos de Rentas interiores; y todas las que surjan por otros conceptos dentro del capítulo de Ingresos Varios.

PEDIDOS DE FONDOS.

ART. 30.

Los pedidos de anticipo de fondos existentes en poder del Tesorero, para atender á gastos necesarios y procedentes, que deban cargarse á las rentas de Cuba, se harán cada dos meses por los respectivos funcionarios ó agentes autorizados para la inversión de dichos fondos, en la forma que se disponga, de conformidad con los créditos concedidos, y dichos pedidos se harán para atender á los periodos que empiezan los días primero de Julio, Septiembre, Noviembre, Enero, Marzo y Mayo de cada año fiscal é irán acompañados de presupuestos detallados de las cantidades que sea necesario invertir durante dichos meses, y ningún Libramiento á justificar se expedirá por una suma que exceda á la necesaria para cubrir las atenciones de dicho periodo.

ART. 31.

Cada pedido de fondos especificará los conceptos de la asignación en virtud de la cual se ha de invertir el dinero, y será remitido al Interventor, el cual hará que se anote en el mismo el saldo debido ó devengado por el funcionario ó agente que haga el pedido, según resulte de los libros de la Intervención y el montante de los créditos que resulte de cualesquiera cuentas ilíquidas de dicho funcionario ó agente que hayan quedado en la oficina del Interventor. Inmediatamente dicho pedido de fondos será presentado al Gobernador Militar para su aprobación, y cuando ésta se haya hecho constar en dicho pedido, éste será devuelto al Interventor para su autorización. Y una vez así autorizado por él y puesta la constancia sobre el pedido de fondos bajo su firma oficial, se expedirá el correspondiente libramiento por la suma autorizada acompañado del pedido de fondos.

ART. 32.

Si al darse cuenta de un pedido de fondos al Gobernador Militar para su aprobación, ó antes que el libramiento que se refiere al mismo hubiere sido expedido, cualesquiera hechos llegaren al conocimiento del Interventor, que á su juicio suministren suficientes fundamentos para desaprobar el anticipo de los fondos pedidos, comunicará inmediatamente esos hechos por escrito al Gobernador Militar, cuya decisión causará ejecutoria, si el pedido de fondos se hizo á consecuencia de créditos concedidos.

ART. 33.

Las reclamaciones de los funcionarios ó agentes que tienen el deber de recaudar ó dar cuenta de los caudales públicos, por pérdidas ocurridas en tránsito, á consecuencia de incendios, robos ú otro acontecimiento inevitable, serán sometidas al Interventor dentro de un mes después de haber ocurrido dichas pérdidas, con todas las pruebas del caso. Si el Interventor estimare que dichos fondos estaban legalmente en poder de dicho funcionario ó agente ó que fueron debidamente remitidos ó que la pérdida ocurrió sin culpa de dicho funcionario ó agente, podrá, *con el consentimiento escrito del Gobernador Militar* abonar en la cuenta de dicho funcionario la mencionada pérdida; *bien entendido* que ningun crédito que exceda de mil pesos se abonará de esta manera. Las reclamaciones por las pérdidas que excedan de mil pesos serán sometidas, por conducto del Interventor, y del Gobernador Militar, al Secretario de la Guerra, para descargo de los reclamantes.

ART. 34.

El Interventor podrá, con el consentimiento escrito del Gobernador Militar, disminuir, eximir, transigir, relevar ó sobreseer cuanto á cualquiera responsabilidad en todo ó en parte ante el Gobierno Militar, en todo asunto de que él conozca cuando, á su juicio, la conveniencia del Gobierno parezca hacerlo necesario con sujeción á las restricciones de la Ley.

ART. 35.

El Interventor inspeccionará la recaudación de todas las rentas que devengue el Gobierno Militar de Cuba, valiéndose de las vias civiles ó judiciales que se acostumbran, y adoptará todas las medidas que las leyes autoricen para hacer efectivos dichos adeudos y para cobrar todas las cantidades que resulten en deberse á dicho Gobierno Militar con referencia á su liquidación y saldo de las cuentas.

ART 36.

Los empleados oficiales pagadores depositarán los caudales de que se les haya dado posesión para su inversión en virtud de créditos asignados solamente en las depositarías que designe el Gobernador Militar. Cuando se haga un pago por medio de cheque, su número se anotará en el justificante á que pertenezca. Dichas depositarías darán cuenta al Interventor á la terminación de cada trimestre, ó más á menudo, si dicho Interventor así lo exigiere, de los saldos de los créditos de todos los Oficiales Pagadores, según lo que resulte de sus libros registros. En todos los casos en que después de la rendición y liquidación de la cuenta definitiva de un Oficial Pagador quedare algún saldo en cualquier depositaría al crédito de dicho Oficial Pagador, debido á la no presentación de cheques ó por otro motivo, el Interventor dará cuenta de dicha suma al Gobernador Militar, el cual exigirá de dicha depositaría que dicho saldo ingrese en la Tesorería de la Isla abonándolo á "Obligaciones pendientes." Ningún cheque de un Oficial Pagador será abonado después de transcurrido un año, á partir del último día del mes de su expedición.

ART. 37.

Todas las reclamaciones que surjan á consecuencia de obligaciones pendientes se presentarán ante el Interventor con las pruebas que correspondan á las mismas. Si el Interventor encontrare que dicha reclamación es válida, y que no está pagada, certificará su importe al Gobernador Militar, el cual expedirá un libramiento en firme, cuyo libramiento será visado por el Interventor y será pagado por el Tesorero, de los fondos existentes á consecuencia de obligaciones pendientes.

ART. 38.

Las transferencias de fondos de un Oficial pagador á otro se harán sólo en virtud de autorización del Gobernador Militar, dándole conocimiento inmediatamente de esta autorización, al Interventor, el Gobernador Militar. Cuando exista algún cambio de Oficiales pagadores, el saliente rendirá una cuenta completa expresando el destino del saldo subsistente, bien haya sido transferido á su sucesor, de acuerdo con las disposiciones contenidas en esta Orden, bien haya sido depositado en la Tesorería de Cuba.

ART. 39.

Tan pronto como quede cerrado el año económico y las cuentas de dicho año sean liquidadas y finiquitadas, el Interventor someterá al Gobernador Militar y al Secretario de la Guerra un informe anual tocante á la situación económica del Gobierno Militar, en la cual se harán constar los ingresos y pagos de los varios Departamentos de dicho Gobierno Militar, y dará los demás informes que le exija el Gobierno Militar ó el Secretario de la Guerra.

ART. 40.

El Interventor, hecha la liquidación, notificará oficialmente por escrito á toda persona cuya cuenta haya sido liquidada en todo ó en parte en su oficina, cuáles son los saldos que resulten debidos, con certificación de los mismos, y cuales las diferencias que arroje dicha liquidación por causa de reparos, ó por suspensión dispuesta por el Interventor, ó por otras causas, cuya relación de reparos se particularizará debidamente, las razones en que se funden los reparos ó las suspensiones de crédito se consignarán invariablemente.

ART. 41.

Una copia fiel de todas las órdenes del Gobierno Militar que puedan dar lugar á reclamaciones ó que de cualquier manera afecten la liquidación de cualquiera cuenta, será trasmitida al Interventor por el correspondiente funcionario.

ART. 42.

Todo contrato con arreglo al cual se pueda efectuar un pago, se presentará al Interventor junto con la cuenta á que dicho pago corresponda.

CUENTAS DE GIROS POSTALES.

ART. 43.

El Interventor llevará las cuentas de los giros postales separadamente, de manera que consten el número y la ascendencia de los giros postales expedidos en cada oficina de correos, y el número y ascendencia de los pagados, así como los derechos percibidos. El interventor certificará trimestralmente los ingresos de derechos procedentes de las ventas de Giros Postales y exigirá que los mismos sean depositados en la Tesorería de Cuba, como Ingresos de Correos. Las pérdidas de fondos de giros postales que vayan de tránsito, por fuego, hurto ú otros accidentes inevitables, los cuales puedan abonarse, se deducirán de los derechos recaudados antes de la transferencia trimestral de dichos derechos, al Tesorero, como Ingresos de Correos.

ART. 44.

Los traspasos de cantidades procedentes de Ingresos Postales á fondos de Giros Postales podrán hacerse por el Administrador de Correos de acuerdo con las Reglas que dicte el Interventor cuando sus ingresos procedentes de la venta de Giros Postales sean insuficientes para pagar los giros librados á cargo de su oficina. Los abonos en cuenta de dichas transferencias de fondos Postales á los fondos de Giros Postales se asentarán en la cuenta mensual de Correos del Administrrdor del ramo. Al vencimiento de cada trimestre todas dichas transferencias de fondos de cuentas de Correos á las de Giros Postales, serán depositadas por el Director General de Correos, en poder del Tesorero de Cuba, como Rentas destinadas al servicio del Departamento de Correos, en virtud de certificación del Interventor, de la ascendencia de los fondos que han de ser depositados de la manera antedicha.

ART. 45.

La jurisdicción del Interventor de Cuba sobre las cuentas y los justificantes pertenecientes á las mismas, será exclusivamente suya. Sus resoluciones serán definitivas y obligatorias para los departamentos administrativos del Gobierno Militar, excepto que se podrá interponer apelación contra dichas resoluciones por la parte perjudicada ó por el Jefe del Departamento interesado, dentro del término de un año, en la forma preceptuada en el art 72. El Interventor de Cuba tendrá, excepción hecha de los casos en que otra cosa se disponga en este reglamento, las mismas facultades que confiere la Ley á los distintos Contadores de las Tesorerías de los Estados Unidos, y se le autoriza para entenderse directamente con cualquiera persona ó funcionario que presente reclamaciones ante él para su resolución ó con cualquiera funcionario ó Departamento que tenga relaciones oficiales con su oficina.

ART. 46.

El Interventor remitirá al Secretario de la Guerra á más tardar dentro de los diez días después del vencimiento de cada mes, un in informe amplio y completo de todas las cantidades percibidas por el Tesorero durante el mes anterior, tal como resulte de los asientos de ingresos retenidos en la oficina del Interventor: una relación de todos los anticipos de fondos hechos en virtud de libramientos durante el mes precedente y una relación detallada de todos los pagos y gastos intervenidos durante el mes próximo anterior.

Título oficial del Interventor y del Interventor Auxiliar.

SELLO DEL INTERVENTOR.

ART. 47.

El título oficial del Interventor, que ha de usar en sus firmas oficiales será "Interventor de Cuba," y el título oficial del Interventor Auxiliar será 'Interventor Auxiliar de Cuba."

ART. 48.

El Interventor tendrá y guardará un sello que tendrá grabada la siguiente inscripción: "Office, Auditor, Cuba.—Official Seal." El Interventor pondrá su sello á cada libramiento expedido por el Gobernador Militar, siempre que dicho libramiento lleve su Visto Bueno, así como á todas las copias y atestados de documentos de su oficina, que deban ser certificados oficialmente por él.

EL TESORERO DE CUBA.

ART. 49.

El Tesorero de Cuba percibirá y guardará con la debida seguridad todos los caudales que procedan de las rentas de Cuba, sea cual fuere el concepto de su procedencia, llevando cuentas detalladas de los mismos en libros adecuados, donde anotará las entradas de los fondos bajo sus respectivos epígrafes, con el nombre de los agentes, empleados y personas de quienes los reciba, y las fechas de su ingreso.

ART. 50

Todos los caudales recibidos por cuenta del Departamento de Aduanas, serán abonados á la cuenta de ingresos de Aduanas; todos los caudales recibidos del Departamento de Corrreos, serán abonados á la cuenta de Correos; todos los caudales recibidos por contribuciones é impuestos interiores se abonarán á la cuenta de ingresos de Rentas Interiores; todos los caudales recibidos por otros conceptos se abonarán á la cuenta de Ingresos Varios.

ART. 51.

Las cuentas del Tesorero serán llevadas en la clase de moneda recibida y pagada; pero en todos los Informes que se hagan al Secretario de la Guerra.

todas las cantidades se anotarán en moneda de los Estados Unidos, al tipo de conversión oficial.

Art. 52.

El Tesorero expedirá recibos duplicados de todos los fondos que reciba (los que serán enumerados consecutivamente), haciendo constar la fecha en que se haya hecho el depósito y quién lo hizo, en qué cuenta se ha abonado, y la cantidad en moneda de los Estados Unidos; y cuando el ingreso se haga en otra moneda extranjera, también se harán constar las cantidades y clase de moneda recibidas, en los recibos, así como el tipo de su conversión á moneda de los Estados Unidos.

Art. 53.

El Interventor de Cuba tomará razón, y pondrá su Visto Bueno á todos los recibos, originales y duplicados, que expida el Tesorero, sin cuyos requisitos no tendrán valor alguno, y á este efecto el Tesorero, tan pronto como expida un recibo por duplicado, remitirá ambos ejemplares al Interventor.

Art. 54.

Todos los fondos que procedan de rentas de Cuba, y los ingresos de todas clases, se entregarán íntegros, al Tesorero, sin hacer deducción de ninguna clase.

Art. 55.

Los anticipos de fondos necesarios, que estén en poder del Tesorero, se harán cada 2 meses (con arreglo á las consignaciones) á los oficiales autorizados para su distribucion, con el objeto de pagar los gastos necesarios para la recaudación de los rentas, llevar las cuentas, y demás gastos legítimos relacionados con el Gobierno Militar de Cuba, cuando no estén expresamente consignados por el Congreso de los Estados Unidos.

Art. 56.

Estos anticipos de fondos existentes en poder del Tesorero, se harán mediante libramientos con arreglo á los pedidos de fondos, haciendo constar la aplicación que se dé á su importe. Después de aprobados dichos pedidos por el Gobernador Militar, y de concedidos por el Interventor, se expedirán los correspondientes libramientos por el Gobernador Militar, con el Visto Bueno del Interventor.

Art. 57.

El Tesorero no hará pago alguno sino mediante libramientos expedidos por el Gobernador Militar y visados por el Interventor; y dichos libramientos después de pagados, acompañados de la comprobación del pago (que será el recibo de la persona á quién éste se haya hecho) serán los documentos justificantes del abono que se hará el Tesorero al rendir sus cuentas.

Art. 58.

Todos los libramientos girados por el Gobernador Militar á cargo del Tesorero, se cargarán en los libros de Tesorería á fondos eventuales, y el objeto y el crédito á que se aplique el libramiento se hará siempre constar. El Tesorero no pagará ningún libramiento mientras no esté visado por el Interventor.

Art. 59.

El Tesorero rendirá mensualmente las cuentas de los ingresos y egresos de su oficina, y las someterá al Interventor para su exámen, dentro de los diez días siguientes al vencimiento de cada mes. Al rendir dichas cuentas, el Tesorero se cargará todas las cantidades recibidas durante el período de tiempo á que la cuenta se refiere, con expresión del crédito consignado y epígrafe de la cuenta y acompañará un extracto detallado de las cantidades recibidas bajo cada epígrafe, de quién se han recibido, expresando los números y fechas de los recibos expedidos.

Art. 60.

El Tesorero anotará en sus cuentas todas las cantidades que haya pagado y acompañará á las mismas extractos detallados expresivos de las cantidades pagadas bajo cada epígrafe, la persona á quién se hizo el pago, los números y fechas de los libramientos expedidos para los pagos, cuyos libramientos se acompañarán á las cuentas que presentará al Interventor.

Art. 61.

El Tesorero remitirá al Secretario de la Guerra, dentro de los diez días siguientes al vencimiento de cada mes, un informe completo, debidamente certificado, de todos los fondos por él recibidos, juntamente con un estado detallado de todos los pagos; igualmente remitirá una copia del mismo, debidamente certificada, al Gobernador Militar.

TITULO OFICIAL DEL TESORERO.

Art. 62.

El túlo oficial del Tesorero, que habrá de usar con su firma oficial, será el de "Tesorero de Cuba."

Facultades y deberes del Gobernador Militar, tocante á la contabilidad en Cuba.

EXAMEN DE LAS CUENTAS.

Art. 63.

El Gobernador Militar examinará cada trimestre, ó más á menudo si lo creyere conveniente, las cuentas y los libros del Interventor y Tesorero; hará una comparación del resultado que arrojen y un exámen y conteo de los fondos existentes en poder del Tesorero, y presentará su informe al Secretario de la Guerra.

APROBACION DE PEDIDOS DE FONDOS.

Art. 64.

Todos los pedidos de anticipos de fondos que estén en poder del Tesorero, para Oficiales autorizados para el pago de los mismos, serán aprobados por el Gobernador Militar, cuando se hagan en debida forma, y los pedidos estén de acuerdo con las consignaciones respectivas.

Art. 65.

Dichos pedidos se harán de conformidad con las consignaciones, determinando la consignación á que expresamente se refiere el pedido.

Art. 66.

Dichos pedidos se harán por el Oficial ó agente, al Interventor, quien hará constar el estado de la cuenta del Oficial ó agente que solicite el anticipo de fondos, según aparazca de los libros de su oficina, así como los créditos de dicho oficial ó agente que estén pendientes de liquidación en la oficina del Interventor. El pedido de fondos se someterá entonces á la aprobación del Gobernador Militar.

LIBRAMIENTOS.

ART. 67.

El Gobernador Militar expedirá y firmará todos los libramientos para pago de fondos existentes en Tesorería, cuyos libramientos se expedirán de acuerdo con los pedidos aprobados, ó certificaciones de liquidación, según el caso, y no será válido ninguno que no lleve el Visto Bueno del Interventor. En caso de ausencia ó imposibilidad del Gobernador Militar, éste designará un oficial del Gobierno Militar para firmar en su nombre los libramientos despachados de acuerdo con los pedidos aprobados ó las certificaciones del Interventor.

ART. 68.

Será suficiente para la expedición de un libramiento de anticipo de fondos á oficiales ó agentes autorizados para su distribución, con el objeto de pagar gastos legítimos y necesarios, el pedido de fondos por dicho Oficial ó agente, con arreglo á lo consignado con antelación, cuyo pedido deberá ser aprobado por el Gobernador Militar, con anuencia del Interventor, antes de expedirse el correspondiente libramiento.

ART. 69.

Bastará para autorizar la expedición de un libramiento en firme, en pago de un saldo que en contra del Interventor resulte de cuenta liquidada y que él certifique, el atestado de la liquidación que expida para el Gobernador Militar.

ART. 70.

Siempre que se emplee la palabra "asignación" de un crédito en estas reglas é instrucciones, se entenderá Consignación hecha por el Gobierno Militar de Cuba.

Título que habrá de emplearse para la rendición y certificación de las cuentas.

ART. 71.

Todas las cuentas del Tesoro de Cuba, y de los diversos oficiales y agentes autorizados para recaudar rentas, percibir fondos y hacer pagos; y todas las demás cuentas sujetas á examen y liquidación del Interventor, se llevarán con "El Gobierno Militar de Cuba", y todos los saldos que certifique el Interventor, serán certificados á favor ó en contra de dicho Gobierno Militar, según el caso.

Recurso contra las resoluciones del Interventor.

ART. 72.

Cualquiera persona que se crea perjudicada en la liquidación de su cuenta ó reclamación, por resolución del Interventor, podrá dentro del término de un año apelar por escrito para ante el Gobernador Militar, expresando concretamente el procedimiento del Interventor que motive su apelación, consignando las razones y disposiciones en que se pueda fundar para la revocación de la resolución. La decisión del Gobierno Miltar en tal caso será definitiva.

REPORT

OF

CARLOS ROLOFF,

TREASURER OF CUBA,

FOR THE LAST SIX MONTHS

OF THE

FISCAL YEAR 1901.

OFFICE OF THE TREASURER OF CUBA,

Havana, Cuba, July 25, 1901.

Adjutant General,
Department of Cuba,
Havana, Cuba.

SIR:

In compliance with instructions from your office of June 14th, 1901, I have the honor to report the operations of this office for the period from January 1st, 1901, to June 30th, 1901, under the same departments as treated by the Treasurer of Cuba in his Semi-Annual Report for the first six months of the fiscal year 1901, with the exception of the Auditing Department for the fiscal year 1899, the work of this department having been completed as reported by the late Treasurer in his Semi-Annual Report for the first six months of the fiscal year 1901, above referred to, viz.:

Treasury Department,
Disbursing Department,
Transportation Department.

Each of these departments will be separately treated of in brief.

In order to avoid any confusion in understanding the terms used in the following report, it is necessary to remember that when reference is made to the total receipts, net receipts or revenues received by the Treasurer during the fiscal year 1900, that both the receipts pertaining to the fiscal years 1899 and 1900 are entered, although received by the Treasurer of Cuba during the fiscal year 1900. Also in referring to the receipts or revenues received by the Treasurer during the fiscal year 1901, the receipts pertaining to the fiscal years 1899, 1900 and 1901 are included. To illustrate: All of the receipts received by the Treasurer during the fiscal year 1901 have been charged upon the books of this office under the proper fund headings, and also charged to the fiscal years to which they pertain, viz., 1899, 1900 and 1901.

The total sum of all deposits received by the Treasurer during the fiscal year 1901 (although including receipts properly pertaining and charged on the books to the fiscal years 1899, 1900 and 1901) will be the amount referred to as the total receipts of the fiscal year 1901. The net receipts referred to below consist of the total receipts for any fiscal year specified, less the repayments received during that year.

On December 31st, 1900, this Department had on hand a balance of...............	$ 1.847,452.28
as shown under the proper fund accounts in Exhibit "E." The cash receipts from January 1st to June 30th, 1901, as shown by same exhibit and under proper headings, have been	9.081,980.05
making a total of.......	$10.929,432.33
During the same period the payments were, as shown by same exhibit and under proper headings................	9.530,930.59
leaving a cash balance June 30th, 1901, revenues.	$ 1.398,501.74

On April 18th, 1901, in compliance with Order No. 79, Headquarters Department of Cuba, dated March 22d, 1901, this department discontinued the custom of recording the amounts paid on warrants and charged in the cash book and ledgers under the separate fund accounts, viz.:—Customs Receipts, Postal Receipts, Internal Revenue Receipts, and Miscellaneous Receipts, and in accordance with the above stated order, beginning with *April 18th*, all monies paid on warrants have been charged to revenue receipts alone and regardless of fiscal years.

A record of all Insular receipts, however, has continued to be kept as heretofore under the four above mentioned funds, and under the proper fiscal years to which they pertained, and are so shown in the exhibits attached to this report.

Therefore the balance above of $1,398,501.74 is shown only under the heading *Revenues*. The remaining part of Exhibit "E" shows the amount of United States currency, foreign gold and Spanish silver included in the balance, June 30th, 1901, of $1,398,501.74, as deposited to the credit of the Treasurer of Cuba, in the respective sums stated, with the North American Trust Company at New York, N. Y., Santiago, Cienfuegos, and Matanzas, Cuba, and on deposit with the Cashier of this department.

COMPARISON OF REVENUES RECEIVED DURING THE FISCAL YEARS 1900 AND 1901.

Of the total amount deposited with the Treasurer during any one fiscal year, a considerable portion consists of what is known as "Repayments." These repayments are monies allotted from Insular funds to the different disbursing officers of the Island of Cuba, on accountable warrants, but returned to the Treasury Department by the disbursing officers for various reasons. These sums not being revenues of the Island, it is necessary to deduct from the gross or total receipts of any fiscal year, these repayments, in order to ascertain the true net revenues. In the following statements, the net revenue referred to consists only of the total receipts, less the repayments:

Total receipts received during fiscal year 1900, as shown by Exhibit No. 11, Annual Report, fiscal year 1900		$19.276,394.07
Deduct repayments received during fiscal year 1900, as shown in Exhibits Nos. 5 and 6 of Report of fiscal year 1900	$ 1.430,580.82	
	606,140.33	2.036,721.15
True net revenues deposited with the Treasurer, during fiscal year 1900		$17.239,672.92
Total receipts, first half fiscal year 1901	$ 9.381,961.42	
Total Receipts second half fiscal year 1901	$ 9.081,980.05	
Total receipts, fiscal year 1901		$18,463,941.47
Repayments, first half fiscal Year 1901	$ 737,152.52	
Repayments, second half fiscal year 1901, as shown by Exhibit "A" of this report	$ 385,066.05	
Total repayments to be deducted		$ 1,122,218.57
True net revenues received during fiscal year 1901		$17,341,722.90
A gain in the actual net revenues as received by the Treasurer during fiscal year 1901 over the fiscal year 1900 of		$ 102,049.98

Exhibit "A" of this report shows the total cash receipts from January 1st, 1901, to June 30th, 1901, properly classified under proper funds, fiscal years, and months, as amounting to	$ 9,081,980.05
as compared with total receipts from July 1st to December 31st, 1900	$ 9,381,961.42
or a shortage in the gross receipts for the second half of the fiscal year 1901, of	$ 299,981.37

as compared with the first half of that period.

Making deductions from the total receipts of the repayments made during each of the above periods, as indicated heretofore, the following result is obtained:

True net revenues, first half fiscal year 1901	$ 8,644,808.90
True net revenues, second half fiscal year 1901	8,696,914.00
Net gain in revenues for the second half fiscal year 1901, of	$ 52,105.10

Exhibit "B" is practically the same as Exhibit "A," the only difference being that the collections are shown under proper fund headings in Exhibit "B," so that the total receipts can be ascertained in each month, while in Exhibit "A" the totals show the amounts collected for each of the six months under the proper funds specified.

Exhibit "C" shows the total amount of money paid out on warrants from January 1st to June 30th, 1901, and charged to the proper fund accounts for each month of this period. As after April 18th, 1901, all monies paid on warrants, as stated previously, have been charged to revenue fund, *the showing is incomplete.*

This exhibit shows the total amount allotted to disbursing officers during the second half of the fiscal year 1901	$ 9,530,930.59
as compared with the amount paid on warrants during first half of fiscal year 1901	10,236,562.89
a lesser amount by	$ 705,632.30

A comparison of the amounts paid on warrants for the fiscal years 1900 and 1901, is as follows:

Exhibit No. 12, of Treasurer's Report for the fiscal year 1900, shows total payments on warrants to have been		$16,574,340.32
As above shown, total payments on warrants,—		
First half fiscal year 1901	$10,236,562.89	
Second half fiscal year 1901	9,530,930 59	
Total payments, fiscal year 1901		$19,767,493.48
An increase of payments during the fiscal year 1901, over that of fiscal year 1900, of		$ 3,193,153.16

A recapitulation of the receipts and payments for the fiscal years 1900 and 1901, as above stated, gives the following results:

Total receipts for fiscal year 1900		$19,276,394.07
Total receipts for fiscal year 1901		18,463,941.47
Grand total receipts, fiscal years 1900 and 1901.		$37,740,335.54
Total payments, fiscal year 1900	$16,574,340.32	
Total payments, fiscal year 1901	19,767,493.48	
Grand total payments, fiscal years 1900 and 1901.		$36,341,833.80
Balance		$ 1,398,501.74

as shown by Exhibit "E" of this report, in hands of the Treasurer, and on deposit with the North American Trust Company, June 30th, 1901.

In order to arrive at an approximate estimate of the available cash assets of the United States Military Government of Cuba, June 30th, 1901, the following statement is submitted:

Cash balance as shown by Exhibit "E" of this report	$ 1,398,501.74
To the credit of disbursing officers with the North American Trust Company, as reported by the Bank, June 30th, 1901.	2,118,130.98
Estimated amount of revenues collected and in process of transmission to Treasurer	200,000.00
Total	$ 3,716,632.72

Exhibit "F" shows the amount of Revenues as reported by Collectors at the places stated, during the second half of the fiscal year 1901. These reports are made to the Treasurer of Cuba by telegram by the Collectors at the end of each month and are compiled and preserved in this office for statistical purposes, although not made a matter of official record.

The net revenues of the Island, as reported by the Treasurer, from January 1st to June 30th, 1901, are	$ 8,696,914.00
the revenues reported by Collectors, in this exhibit	8,676,027.12

which closely approximates the amount shown by the records of this office.

The two amounts can never be exactly the same, for the reason that the books of this office show the actual sums received by the Treasurer during the above named period, while the report of the Collectors shows the amounts actually collected by them during the same period; the time necessary in transmitting funds to this office, causing a difference at the end of each period of time.

Exhibit "G" is a comparison of the revenues of Cuba for the fiscal years 1900 and 1901, as reported by the Collectors of revenues and at the locations stated. It shows a falling off in the revenues of the fiscal year 1901, as compared with the fiscal year 1900, of $86.522.52. The total revenues as shown in this exhibit for both

the fiscal years 1900 and 1901, are	$34,671,780.00
The net revenues of the Island deposited with the Treasurer of Cuba, during these two years, as shown in above report, are	34,581,395.82
A difference of	$ 90,384.18

This difference is accounted for in the above explanation, it being obvious that the monies of the belated collections, made during the latter part of the fiscal year 1901, will appear on the books of the Treasurer in the fiscal year 1902, owing to delays in transmission of the same.

During the period from January 1st to March 31st, 1901, the

Treasurer of Cuba has paid to the North American Trust Company, commissions, $23,760.60; during the period from April 1st to June 30th, 1901, $14,567.80.

The expense of this office for the period January 1st to March 31st, 1901, has been as follows:

Salaries	$8,418.98
Rent, gas, ice, etc	1,348.46
Stationery and printing	1,204.13
Office furniture	45.00
Cab hire	89.54
*Incidentals	8,281.95

*Chief item of this expense—payment of vault, cages, etc.

The expense for the period, April 1st to June 30th, 1901, has been as follows:

Salaries	$ 7,304.13
Rent, gas, ice, etc	1,848.54
Stationery and printing	1,512.84
Office furniture	543.21
Cab hire	74.51
*Incidentals	1,359.38

*Chief item—premium on bonds.

DISBURSING DEPARTMENT.

The disbursements of this department during the period January 1st to March 31st, 1901, have been: account Treasurer's Office, $98,143.45; account Department of Cuba, $370,916.11; during the period April 1st to June 30th, 1901, account Treasurer's Office, $73,140.61; account Department of Cuba, $229,822.68.

The accounts of the Treasury Disbursing Clerk were inspected by the Inspector General's Department to include June 10th, 1901, and found correct.

The expense of this department for the period January 1st to March 31st, 1901, was:

Salaries	$ 1,401.00
Rent, gas, ice, etc	311.12
Stationery and printing	22.91
Incidentals	55.00

The expense for the period April 1st to June 30th, 1901, was:

Salaries	$ 1,596.50
Rent, gas, ice, etc	608.06
Stationery and printing	27.06
Incidentals	115.00
Cab hire	23.01

TRANSPORTATION DEPARTMENT.

During this period, January 1st to June 30th, 1901, this department has audited and settled 16,583 accounts, and has on hand for settlement 5,000 Transportation Requests and 1,500 Bills of Lading.

During the period January 1st to March 31st, 1901, Transportation accounts to the amount of $51,490.13 were paid; during the period April 1st to June 30th, 1901, to the amount of $41,881.60 were paid.

The expense of the department for the period January 1st to March 31st, 1901, was:

Salaries	$ 1,222.00
Rent, gas, ice, etc	117.34
Stationery and printing	330.47
Office furniture	45.00

The expense for the period, April 1st to June 30th, 1901, was:

Salaries	$ 1,152.16
Rent, gas, ice, etc	69.06
Stationery and printing	445.23
Cab hire	12.52

CURRENCY.

But little has been accomplished since my predecessor's last report to better the condition of this branch of the service; and although the United States currency is in fact the standard of the country for all Government transactions, it is also a fact that the Spanish and French monies still hold their own as the circulating medium for all commercial transactions; and as their value, especially that of silver, is subject to such a wide fluctuation, the demoralization caused thereby, influences to such an extent the revenues of the Island, that its effects are more practically and painfully evidenced by the Treasury Department than elsewhere.

It is a well known fact that the *modus vivendi* of Cuba depends entirely upon its sugar crops and that its income is largely increased during the sugar producing months, when money from the United States (its largest consumer) rushes into this market in great quantities, which money, following the rule of supply and demand, obtains then quite a low rate of exchange for Spanish and French money, which, as I have said before, is, if not the legal declared standard of the country, the circulating medium thereof. During this time of great affluence of United States currency into the Island, the Government revenues are well protected by the difference to its favor from the real value of the Spanish and French money to the fixed value given to it by Order No. 123, Headquarters Division of Cuba, July 28th, 1899.

While United States money can be obtained by tax payers and other contributors to the revenues of the Island for an amount in Spanish and French money less than the rate of exchange fixed by the aforesaid Order No. 123, it is naturally to be expected that all payments to the Government will be made in that specie, but when the sugar crop is gathered and sold and the importation of United States currency becomes rather nominal, and the exchange, on account of the small supply on hand, reaches its maximum rate, which exceeds always notably that fixed by the already mentioned Order No. 123' these payments, whenever feasible, are invariably effected to the Government in Spanish and French money, which enters into this Treasury at a fictitious value, and as the Government has prohibited by Order No. 229, Headquarters Division of Cuba, June 4th, 1900, that disbursements be made in foreign money, even at the ratio by which it is admitted, on exchanging that money into United States currency (the standard currency of the Island) at the market rate of value, which, as previously stated, is, at this time, greater than the rate fixed by the Government in the Order herein named, it becomes evident that the Government is the loser in the transaction by the difference between the value given to the foreign money as per Order No. 123, Division Headquarters, series of 1899, and the real value by which the purchases are actually made, and which can at present be estimated at somewhat over ½ of 1 per cent.

Several have been the suggestions offered by this Department in order to avoid this state of affairs, which is not only detrimental to the Government but to the Island at large, by reason of the fluctuations alluded to, and I now respectfully beg to submit herewith the following recommendation:

Inasmuch as the present financial condition of the Island would not permit it, for reasons well known to all those who have stopped to consider its economical standing, to issue its own currency in many years to come, and Cuba being, as it is, economically speaking, a dependency of the United States, and which condition will naturally become stronger in the future for motives of mutual interest, it is believed that its standard currency, even after its complete independence is obtained, would continue to be the currency of the United States. This principle being settled, and in order to save the future Government of the Island any discussion upon this point and to adjust in an advantageous manner its financial standing towards other nations, it is my opinion that orders should be issued by which all transactions relating to the Government, as well as private, be effected in United States currency, given a specified period (six months for instance) in which holders of foreign money may exchange it into the currency of the country. By this means the Spanish and French money now circulating in Cuba, which value is regulated by their value in Spain and France, would soon be demonetized by finding their way to their respective countries without serious loss or inconvenience to the holders.

While I firmly believe that the suggestions which I have the honor of hereby presenting will do away with the present uncomfortable and detrimental state of affairs, it is, of course, a matter of appreciation with the Government, which no doubt has the question under careful investigation and study, and which will, in its wisdom, solve the problem to the satisfaction of all concerned; my intervention in the matter being solely reduced to point out the facts as they appear to me from the position with which I have been honored.

I take pleasure in recommending to the favorable consideration of the Adjutant General of the Department the employees of this office for the honest, faithful and efficient services rendered by them. I have ever found them loyal to the interests of the Department and to the United States Military Government of Cuba. Each clerk in the Department is a competent representative for the position which he occupies.

Very respectfully,

CARLOS ROLOFF,

Treasurer of Cuba.

EXHIBITS

PERTAINING TO THE

REPORT

OF THE

TREASURER OF CUBA

JANUARY TO JUNE, 1901.

EXHIBIT "A."

CASH RECEIPTS FROM JANUARY 1, 1901, TO JUNE 30, 1901.

TOTAL BY FUNDS		Customs Dollars	Customs Cts.	Postal Dollars	Postal Cts.	Internal Revenue Dollars	Internal Revenue Cts.	Miscellaneous Dollars	Miscellaneous Cts.	Repayments Dollars	Repayments Cts	Total Dollars	Total Cts.
Fiscal year 1899.	January												
	February									216	06	216	06
	March										31		31
	April												
	May									1,027	04	1,027	04
	June									702	45	702	45
	TOTAL									1,945	86	1,945	86
Fiscal year 1900.	January	112	44							15,771	71	15,884	15
	February				32					6,179	60	6,179	92
	March			44	70			106	00	5,061	51	5,212	21
	April									6,959	38	6,959	38
	May									17,367	70	17,367	70
	June									270	13	270	13
	TOTAL	112	44	45	02			106	00	51,610	03	51,873	49
Fiscal year 1901.	January	1.259,170	40	38,411	94	45,429	73	40,406	29	54,218	26	1.437,636	62
	February	1.302,462	41	31,543	72	77,646	98	19,490	34	71,286	85	1.502,430	30
	March	1.477,298	83	31,559	66	59,587	55	20,837	39	41,537	54	1.630,820	97
	April	1.405,251	66	29,704	29	55,209	87	32,823	04	29,426	67	1.552,415	53
	May	1.285,086	37	28,749	23	60,771	56	22,851	16	75,526	08	1.472,984	40
	June	1.265,358	49	30,725	38	49,969	10	26,305	15	59,514	76	1.431,872	88
	TOTAL	7.994,628	16	190,694	22	348,614	79	162,713	37	331,510	16	9.028,160	70
	GRAND TOTAL	7.994,740	60	190,739	24	348,614	79	162,819	37	385,066	05	9.081,980	05

EXHIBIT "B."

CASH RECEIPTS FROM JANUARY 1, 1901, TO JUNE 30, 1901.

TOTAL BY MONTHS		JANUARY		FEBRUARY		MARCH		APRIL		MAY		JUNE		TOTAL	
		Dollars	Cts.	Dollars	Cts.	Dollars	Cts.	Dollars	Cts.	Dollars	Cts.	Dollars	Cts.	Dollars	Cts.
FISCAL YEAR 1899.	Customs	....	....	....	....	....	....	....	....	....	....	....	....	....	....
	Postal	....	....	....	....	....	....	....	....	....	....	....	....	....	....
	Internal Revenue	....	....	....	....	....	....	....	....	....	....	....	....	....	....
	Miscellaneous	....	....	....	....	....	....	....	....	....	....	....	....	....	....
	Repayments	....	....	216	06	....	31	....	....	1,027	04	702	45	1,945	86
	TOTAL	....	....	216	06	....	31	....	....	1,027	04	702	45	1,945	86
FISCAL YEAR 1900.	Customs	112	44	....	....	....	....	....	....	....	....	....	....	112	44
	Postal	....	....	....	32	44	70	....	....	....	....	....	....	45	02
	Internal Revenue	....	....	....	....	....	....	....	....	....	....	....	....	....	....
	Miscellaneous	....	....	....	....	106	00	....	....	....	....	....	....	106	00
	Repayments	15,771	71	6,179	60	5,061	51	6,959	38	17,367	70	270	13	51,610	03
	TOTAL	15,884	15	6,179	92	5,212	21	6,959	38	17,367	70	270	13	51,873	49
FISCAL YEAR 1901.	Customs	1.259,170	40	1.302.462	41	1.477,298	83	1.405,251	66	1.285,086	37	1.265,358	49	7.994,628	16
	Postal	38,411	94	31,543	72	31,559	66	29,704	29	28,749	23	30,725	38	190,694	22
	Internal Revenue	45,429	73	77,646	98	59,587	55	55,209	87	60.771	56	49,969	10	348.614	79
	Miscellaneous	40,406	29	19,490	34	20,837	39	32,823	04	22,851	16	26,305	15	162,713	37
	Repayments	54,218	26	71,286	85	41,537	54	29,426	67	75,526	08	59,514	76	331,510	16
	TOTAL	1.437,636	62	1.502,430	30	1.630,820	97	1.552,415	53	1.472,984	40	1.431,872	88	9.028,160	70
GRAND TOTAL		1.453,520	77	1.508,826	28	1.636,033	49	1.559,374	91	1.491,379	14	1.432,845	46	9.081,980	05

EXHIBIT "C."

WARRANTS PAID FROM JANUARY 1, 1901, TO JUNE 30, 1901.

TOTAL BY FUNDS	CUSTOMS		POSTAL		INTERNAL REVENUE		MISCELLANEOUS		REVENUES		TOTAL	
	Dollars	Cts.	Dollars	Cts.	Dollars	Cts.	Dollars	Cts.	Dollars	Cts.	Dollars	Cts.
January	836,513	27	46,669	28	475,032	08	5,239	58	....	....	1.363,454	21
February	747,625	97	37,146	70	616,623	03	4,936	62	....	....	1.406,332	32
March	665,339	51	33,819	05	1.212,601	26	729	59	....	....	1.912,489	41
April	26,470	03	....	....	260,048	64	....	....	1.075,090	45	1.361,609	12
May	....	....	....	....	....	....	....	....	1.264.305	73	1.264,305	73
June	....	....	....	....	....	....	....	....	2.222,739	80	2.222,739	80
TOTAL	2.275,948	78	117,635	03	2.564,305	01	10,905	79	4.562,135	98	9.530,930	59

EXHIBIT "D."

WARRANTS PAID FROM JANUARY 1, 1901, TO JUNE 30, 1901.

TOTAL BY MONTHS	JANUARY		FEBRUARY		MARCH		APRIL		MAY		JUNE		TOTAL	
	Dollars	Cts	Dollars	Cts	Dollars	Cts.	Dollars	Cts.	Dollars	Cts	Dollars	Cts	Dollars	Cts.
Customs	836,513	27	747,625	97	665,339	51	26,470	03	....	...	....	...	2.275,948	78
Postal	46,669	28	37,146	70	33,819	05	....	...	....	...	....	...	117,635	03
Internal Revenue	475,032	08	616,623	03	1.212,601	26	260,048	64	....	...	....	...	2.564,305	01
Miscellaneous	5,239	58	4,936	62	729	59	....	...	....	...	....	...	10,905	79
Revenues	....	...	....	...	....	...	1.075,090	45	1.264,305	73	2.222,739	80	4.562,135	98
TOTAL	1.363,454	21	1.406,332	32	1.912,489	41	1 361,609	12	1.264,305	73	2.222,739	80	9.530,930	59

EXHIBIT "E."

RECAPITULATION, SHOWING BALANCE JUNE 30, 1901.

	Customs		Postal		Int. Revenue		Miscellaneous		Revenues		TOTAL	
	Dollars	Cts.	Dollars	Cts.	Dollars	Cts.	Dollars	Cts.	Dollars	Cts.	Dollars	Cts.
Balance December 31, 1900	4.695,248	63	59,152	20	4.023,091	60	1.234,447	45	....	......	1.847,452	28
Receipts from Jan. 1, to June 30, 1901	7.994,740	60	190,739	24	348,614	79	547,885	42	....	......	9.081,980	05
Total Credits	12.689,989	23	131,587	04	3.674,476	81	1,782,332	87	....	......	10.929,432	33
Warrants paid from Jan. 1, to June 30, 1901	2.275,948	78	117,635	03	2.564,305	01	10,905	79	4.562,135	98	9.530,930	59
Balance, June 30, 1901.	....	......	....	......	....	......	....	......	....	......	1.398,501	74

DEPOSITED AS FOLLOWS:

	New York		Santiago		Cienfuegos		Matanzas		Cashier		TOTAL	
	Dollars	Cts.	Dollars	Cts.	Dollars	Cts.	Dollars	Cts.	Dollars	Cts.	Dollars	Cts.
U. S. Currency	48,247	15	126,041	83	35,734	78	22,524	21	902,356	96	1.134,904	93
Foreign Gold	....	......	5,064	06	9,730	49	67	48	243,607	57	258,469	60
Spanish Silver	....	......	77	20	35	86	542	36	4,471	79	5,127	21
Total	48,247	15	131,183	09	45,501	13	23,134	05	1.150,436	32	1.398,501	74

EXHIBIT "F."

REVENUES, AS REPORTED BY COLLECTORS, FROM JANUARY 1, 1901, TO JUNE 30, 1901.

		January		February		March		April		May		June		Total	
		Dollars	Cts.	Dollars	Cts.	Dollars	Cts.	Dollars	Cts.	Dollars	Cts.	Dollars	Cts.	Dollars	Cts.
Customs Receipts.	Baracoa	2,113	10	2,063	08	4,657	48	2,115	86	2,045	99	1,575	25	14,570	76
	Batabanó	171	89	377	15	163	12	128	71	290	16	161	14	1,292	17
	Caibarién	20,201	27	18,372	89	24,184	07	19,250	92	23,173	16	18,682	02	123,864	33
	Cárdenas	26,107	57	19,683	09	27,195	13	19,807	51	23,016	82	24,131	31	139,941	43
	Cienfuegos	99,230	13	108,564	66	138,588	44	140,864	56	107,815	74	92,325	56	687,389	09
	Gibara	28,464	72	25,396	35	25,800	14	25,950	45	24,485	10	28,018	21	158,114	97
	Guantánamo	17,984	89	14,036	95	17,225	11	9,150	87	8,972	45	9,588	46	76,958	73
	Havana	879,335	18	926,825	46	999,585	13	1.010,823	39	941,351	34	857,852	04	5,615,772	54
	Júcaro	....	...	....	...	....	...	....	...	....	...	4,860	49	4,860	49
	Manzanillo	12,811	32	21,777	40	20,039	22	26,027	73	30,641	18	21,495	66	132,792	51
	Matanzas	33,454	69	42,812	56	49,069	49	39,420	36	47,800	92	44,209	82	256,767	84
	Nuevitas	17,764	94	11,766	38	15,251	38	14,018	15	10,312	17	21,406	18	90,519	20
	Sagua la Grande	11,886	61	22,547	32	20,349	47	8,383	60	19,626	96	13,657	49	96,451	45
	Santa Cruz del Sur	573	43	316	12	717	12	682	19	1,044	13	103	17	3,436	16
	Santiago	106,985	64	71,036	75	97,199	43	104,801	81	92,357	14	82,235	56	554,616	33
	Trinidad	2,746	20	221	31	2,764	99	112	98	1,947	37	550	27	8,343	12
	Tunas de Zaza	709	05	129	12	6,013	33	2,414	81	3,002	81	346	90	12,616	02
	Total	1.260,830	63	1.285,926	59	1.448,803	05	1.423,953	90	1.337,883	33	1.221,209	53	7.978,307	14

EXHIBIT "F."

REVENUES, AS REPORTED BY COLLECTORS, FROM JANUARY 1, 1901, TO JUNE 30, 1901.—CONTINUED.

		January Dollars	January Cts.	February Dollars	February Cts.	March Dollars	March Cts.	April Dollars	April Cts.	May Dollars	May Cts.	June Dollars	June Cts.	Total Dollars	Total Cts.
Internal Revenue Receipts	Havana	31,796	75	64,406	20	36,133	45	35,856	55	32,693	04	27,449	05	228,335	04
	Pinar del Río	1,472	35	1,845	08	639	95	623	46	1,652	49	438	07	6.671	40
	Guanajay	281	86	615	64	1.027	67	329	18	1,264	64	309	23	3,828	22
	Matanzas	1,322	38	1,269	12	2,278	62	2,075	80	6,148	97	2,424	63	15,519	52
	Cárdenas	645	04	2,378	06	1,307	71	3,016	97	1,391	35	1,124	35	9,863	48
	Santa Clara	2,630	39	3,583	11	4,865	40	7,368	79	3,187	41	1,861	88	23,496	98
	Cienfuegos	1,502	83	2,420	56	3,059	68	5,168	79	2,204	72	2,729	11	17,085	69
	Puerto Príncipe	2,405	53	591	34	736	69	3,547	69	2,524	40	1,451	67	11,257	32
	Manzanillo	72	50	2,133	36	345	92	196	51	211	18	2,376	96	5,336	43
	Holguín	1,012	97	345	62	833	27	1,117	58	2,432	26	787	43	6,529	13
	Santiago	1,196	64	2,705	15	1,460	23	4,085	10	5,228	95	1,668	09	16,344	16
	Total	44,339	24	82,293	24	52,688	59	63,386	42	58,939	41	42,620	47	344,267	37
	Postal Receipts	38,411	94	31,544	04	31,604	36	29,704	29	28,749	23	30,725	38	190,739	24
Miscellaneous Receipts	Captains of the Port	60	00	507	82	134	58	297	88	107	00	110	00	1,217	28
	Telegraph Line	7,703	88	6,665	06	7,130	85	7,810	39	7,496	02	7,217	51	44,023	71
	Miscellaneous	32,642	41	12,317	46	13,571	96	24,714	77	15,248	14	18,977	64	117,472	38
	Grand Total	1.383,688	10	1.419,254	21	1.553,933	39	1.549,867	65	1.448.423	24	1.320,860	53	8.676,027	12

EXHIBIT "G."

COMPARISON OF REVENUES OF THE FISCAL YEARS 1900 AND 1901.

		Fiscal Year 1900.		Fiscal Year 1901.		+ Gain. — Loss.		
		Dollars.	Cts.	Dollars.	Cts.		Dollars.	Cts.
Customs Receipts	Baracoa	33,935	26	24,249	70	—	9,685	56
	Batabanó	2,743	89	2,367	24	—	376	65
	Caibarién	192,695	11	227,917	17	+	35,222	06
	Cárdenas	313,262	98	281,510	18	—	31,752	80
	Cienfuegos	1.158,417	36	1.297,179	81	+	138,762	45
	Gibara	186,454	98	311,654	62	+	125,199	64
	Guantánamo	126,030	64	147,253	80	+	21,223	16
	Havana	12.096.214	15	11.538,949	48	—	557,264	67
	Júcaro			4,860	49	+	4,860	49
	Manzanillo	173,741	51	231,643	49	+	57,901	98
	Matanzas	468,666	46	472,663	79	+	3,997	33
	Nuevitas	183,295	31	185,854	08	+	2,558	77
	Sagua la Grande	184,985	04	191,929	71	+	6,944	67
	Santa Cruz del Sur	3,117	71	5,337	29	+	2,219	58
	Santiago	999,950	12	1.038,429	15	+	38,479	03
	Trinidad	27,090	78	15,454	77	—	11,636	01
	Tunas de Zaza	3,289	32	16,163	17	+	12,873	85
Total		16.153,890	62	15.993,417	94	—	160,472	68

EXHIBIT "G."

REVENUES, AS REPORTED BY COLLECTORS, FROM JANUARY 1, 1901, TO JUNE 1, 1901.—CONTINUED.

		Fiscal Year 1900.		Fiscal Year 1901.		+ Gain. — Loss.		
		Dollars.	Cts.	Dollars.	Cts.		Dollars.	Cts.
Internal Revenue Receipts	Havana	547,887	63	447,211	79	—	100,675	84
	Pinar del Río	24,970	26	13,860	95	—	11,109	31
	Guanajay	....	....	8,889	79	+	8,889	79
	Matanzas	135,993	34	27,356	50	—	108,636	84
	Cárdenas	....	....	27,801	44	+	27,801	44
	Santa Clara	99,310	17	34,845	11	—	64,465	06
	Cienfuegos	....	....	29,019	97	+	29,019	97
	Puerto Príncipe	26,559	40	20,591	67	—	5,967	73
	Manzanillo	....	....	8,987	63	+	8,982	63
	Holguín	....	....	11,928	56	+	11,938	56
	Santiago	53,553	49	38,825	47	—	14,728	02
	TOTAL	888,274	29	669,318	88	—	218,955	41
Postal Receipts	Postal Receipts	235,854	26	376,263	43	+	140,409	17
Miscellaneous Receipts	Captains of the Port	....	....	....	....		....	....
	Telegraph Line	52,925	79	78,742	11	+	25,816	32
	Miscellaneous	48,206	30	174,886	38	+	126,680	08
	GRAND TOTAL	17.379,151	26	17.292,628	74	—	86,522	52

INFORME

DE

CARLOS ROLOFF,

TESORERO DE CUBA.

COMPRENDE EL SEGUNDO SEMESTRE

DEL

AÑO FISCAL DE 1901.

TESORERIA DE CUBA.

Habana, Cuba, Julio 25 de 1901.

Al Ayudante General,
Departamento de Cuba,
Habana, Cuba.

SEÑOR:

En cumplimiento de las instrucciones recibidas de ese Cuartel General, fecha Junio 14 de 1901, tengo el honor de elevar á sus manos el presente informe de las operaciones de esta Oficina durante el período comprendido del 1º de Enero al 30 de Junio de 1901, bajo los mismos departamentos en que fueron tratados por el Tesorero de Cuba en su primer informe semestral del año económico de 1901, exceptuando el Departamento de Contaduría, en el año económico de 1899, cuyo informe fué completado y presentado por mi antecesor en su primer Informe Semestral del Año Económico de 1901, según arriba se indica y el cual se subdivide como sigue:

Departamento de Tesorería,
Departamento de Pagaduría,
Departamento de Trasportes,

y de cuyos departamentos se tratará separadamente.

Para evitar toda confusión y ponerse al alcance de los términos usados en el presente informe, es de necesidad recordar que al hacer referencia al total de los ingresos, la recaudación líquida ó el importe de los ingresos recibidos por el Tesorero de Cuba durante el Año Económico de 1900, que ambos ingresos, pertenecientes á los Años Económicos de 1899 y 1900. han sido anotados, aunque recibidos por el Tesorero de Cuba durante el Año Económico de 1900. Así mismo, al hacer referencia á los ingresos ó rentas recibidas por el Tesorero durante el Año Económico de 1901, se han incluído los ingresos pertenecientes á los Años Económicos de 1899, 1900 y 1901. Por ejemplo: Todos los ingresos recibidos por el Tesorero durante el Año Económico de 1901 han sido entrados en los Libros de esta Oficina con cargo á los conceptos de sus respectivos fondos, así como también cargados á los años económicos correspondientes, es decir, 1899, 1900 y 1901.

La cantidad á que se hace referencia como el total de los ingresos del Año Económico de 1901, será la suma total de todos los depósitos recibidos por el Tesorero durante el Año económico de 1901, aunque en la misma se incluyan los ingresos pertenecientes y cargados debidamente á los Años económicos de 1899, 1900 y 1901. Los ingresos líquidos á que más abajo se hace referencia consisten en el total de los ingresos de cualquier año económico especificado, ménos los reembolsos recibidos durante ese año.

Con fecha Diciembre 31 de 1900, este Departamento tenía una existencia en Caja de..........	$ 1,847,452.28
según la correspondiente cuenta de fondos en el Estado "E." Efectivo recibido de Enero 1º á Junio 30 de 1901, según dicho Estado y anotado bajo sus correspondientes conceptos..........	9,081.980.05
que hacen un total de....................	$ 10,929,432.33
Durante dicho período de tiempo y según el referido Estado y bajo sus correspondientes conceptos, sumaron los egresos........................ ..	9,530,930.59
quedando un saldo en efectivo, en Junio 30 de 1901, rentas..................................	$ 1,398,501.74

Con fecha Abril 18 de 1901, en cumplimiento de la Orden Nº 79, del Cuartel General, Departamento de Cuba, de fecha Marzo 22 de 1901 se suprimió en este Departamento la costumbre de anotar las cantidades pagadas sobre Libramientos y cargadas en los Libros de Caja y Mayor, bajo las diferentes cuentas de fondos como sigue: Ingresos de Aduanas, Rentas Postales, Rentas Interiores ó Ingresos Miscelánea, y de acuerdo con dicha Orden, comenzando el día 18 de Abril todo el efectivo pagado por Libramientos ha sido cargado á Ingresos de Rentas recibidos solamente, sin tener en cuenta el año económico.

Se ha continuado, sinembargo, llevando un Registro, como hasta ahora bajo los cuatro arriba mencionados fondos y bajo sus correspondientes años económicos, según puede verse en los Estados que le son anexos á este Informe.

Por lo tanto, el saldo á que arriba se alude, de $1.390,501.74 es solamente mencionado bajo el concepto de Rentas. Lo restante del estado "E" demuestra la cantidad de dinero de los Estados Unidos, oro extranjero y plata española incluidos en el saldo de Junio 30 de 1901 de $1.398,501,74, como depósito al crédito del Tesorero de Cuba, en sus respectivas sumas designadas en el North American Trust & Co., de Nueva York, Santiago de Cuba, Cienfuegos y Matanzas y en las cajas de esta Tesorería.

COMPARACIÓN DE LAS RENTAS RECIBIDAS DURANTE LOS AÑOS ECONÓMICOS DE 1900 Y 1901.

Una parte considerable del total depositado en la Tesorería durante el año económico, consiste en los que se denomina

"Reembolsos." Estos reembolsos son consignaciones de fondos insulares hechos á los diferentes Tesoreros-Pagadores en la Isla, sobre libramientos á su favor, mas devueltos por razones varias por dichos Tesoreros á esta Tesorería. Como estas cantidades no pertenecen á Rentas de la Isla, es necesario deducir su importe del total de los ingresos del año económico, para averiguar de una manera cierta la renta líquida recibida. En los siguientes estados, la renta líquida á que se hace referencia consiste solamente del total de los ingresos, deduciendo estos reembolsos:

Total de Ingresos recibidos durante el Año Económico de 1900, según Estado número 11, Informe Anual de 1900............		$19.276,394.07
A deducir reembolsos recibidos durante el Año Económico de 1900, según Estados núms. 5 y 6 del Informe del Año Económico de 1900.	$ 1.430,580.82	
	606,140.33	$ 2.036,721.15
Rentas líquidas depositadas en Tesorería durante el año económico de 1900...............		$17.239,672.92
Total de ingresos primer semestre del año económico de 1901....	$ 9.381,961.42	
Total de ingresos segundo semestre del año económico de 1901	$ 9,081,980.05	
Total de ingresos del año económico de 1901		$18.463,941.47
Reembolsos, primer semestre del año económico de 1901.	$ 737,152.52	
Reembolsos, segundo semestre del año económico de 1901...... ..	$ 385,066.05	
Total de reembolsos á deducir..................		$ 1.122,118.57
Rentas líquidas recibidas en el año económico de 1901.		$17,341.722.90
Aumento en las Rentas según ingresos en Tesorería del año 1901 sobre las de 1900......		$ 102,049.98
El estado "A" de este informe demuestra el importe total en efectivo de los ingresos, de Enero 1º á Junio 30 de 1901, debidamente clasificados bajo sus respectivos fondos, años económicos y meses, los que ascienden á.		$ 9.081,980.05
Siendo el total de los ingresos de Julio 1º á Diciembre 31 de 1900, de...............		$ 9.381,961.42
ó sea una diferencia en contra de los ingresos en el segundo semestre de 1901, de......................		$ 299,981.37

Deduciendo del ingreso total los reembolsos hechos durante cada uno de los períodos arriba mencionados según se indica, se obtiene el siguiente resultado:

Rentas líquidas, 1er. semestre 1901.....	$ 8.644,808.90
Rentas líquidas, 2º semestre 1901..................	8.696,914.00
Aumento de la renta líquida durante el segundo semestre del año económico de 1901............	$ 52,105.10

Se puede decir que el estado "B" es igual al estado "A," con la sola diferencia que las recaudaciones insertas en el estado "B" por mensualidades, bajo sus correspondientes conceptos, mientras que el estado "A" sólo se refiere á las recaudaciones por semestres bajo sus respectivos fondos.

El Estado "C" comprende el total de las cantidades pagadas sobre Libramientos de Enero 1º á Junio 30 de 1901, y cargadas á las respectivas cuentas por cada mes de este período. Como después de Abril 18 de 1901 todo el efectivo pagado por Libramientos, según más arriba se menciona, ha sido cargado á Rentas, la demostración no se completa.

Este Estado comprende el total de las cantidades asignadas á los Tesoreros Pagadores, durante el 2º Semestre de 1901.....	$ 9,530,930.59
que comparadas con el importe pagado sobre libramientos en los primeros seis meses 1901........	10,236,562.89
Dan una diferencia de.....................................	$ 705,632.30

Al comparar las cantidades pagadas por Libramientos en los Años Económicos 1900 y 1901 vemos lo siguiente:

El Estado No. 12 del Informe de Tesorería del Año Económico 1900, demuestra que se pagaron Libramientos por valor de................................		$16,574,340,32
Según más arriba se indica el total de los pagos por Libramientos fueron:		
1er. Semestre Año Económico 1901.....	$10,236,562.89	
2º Semestre íd.	$ 9,530,930.59	
Total de Pagos durante el Año Económico de 1901..................		19,767,493.48
ó sea un aumento en los pagos durante el Año Económico de 1901 sobre los de 1900 de...........		$ 3,193,153.16

Haciendo una Recapitulación de los Ingresos

y Egresos de los Años Económicos de 1900 y 1901, según arriba se indica, obtendremos el siguiente resultado:

Total de Ingresos, 1900.....		$19,276,394.07
Total de Ingresos, 1901.....		19,463,941.47
Total de Ingresos durante los años 1900 y 1901		$37,740,335.54
Total de Egresos, 1900..	$16,574,340.32	
Total de Egresos, 1901..	19,767,493.48	36,341.833.80
y cuyo saldo de.....		$ 1,398,501.74

aparece en el Estado "E" de este Informe en poder del Tesorero de Cuba y en depósito en el North American Trust Co. en Junio 30 de 1901.

Para poder hacer un cálculo aproximado del efectivo disponible perteneciente al Gobierno Militar de los Estados Unidos en Cuba, en Junio 30 de 1901, se presenta la siguiente relación:

Efectivo según Estado "E" de este Informe...	$ 1,398,501.74
Cantidad al crédito de los Tesoreros-Pagadores en el North American Trust Co., según dicho Banco, en Junio 30 de 1901........................ ...	2,118,130.98
Cantidad aproximada de rentas recaudadas y en su tránsito á la Tesorería..........................	200,000.00
Total...........	$ 3,716,632,72

El Estado "F" demuestra el importe de las rentas recaudadas según relación de los Administradores de Aduanas en los lugares designados en el 2º Semestre del Año Económico de 1901. Estas relaciones son comunicadas por telégrafo al Tesorero por los Administradores de Aduanas al fin de cada mes y son compiladas y guardadas en esta Oficina para fines estadísticos, sin que se utilicen como estados oficiales.

La Renta líquida de la Isla, según Informe del Tesorero, de Enero 1º á Junio 30 de 1901, es de	$ 8,696,914.00
y los ingresos según Informes de los Administradores de Aduanas, en este Estado, es de.......	8,676,027.12

que se aproxima bastante á los datos obtenidos por esta Oficina.

Estas dos cantidades no pueden jamás ser iguales, puesto que los libros de esta Oficina contienen el importe verdadero recibido por el Tesorero durante el tiempo arriba especificado, mientras que los informes de los Administradores demuestran el importe recaudado por ellos durante ese mismo período de tiempo, existiendo, desde luego, la diferencia ocasionada por la transmisión de fondos á esta Oficina.

El Estado "G" es la comparación de las Rentas de Cuba en los Años Económicos de 1900 y 1901, según informes de los Administradores de Aduanas en sus respectivas localidades. En él se verá una disminución en dicha Renta durante el Año Económico de 1901, comparada con la del año Económico de 1900, por valor de $86,522.52.

El total de los ingresos según se demuestra en este Estado durante ambos Años Económicos de 1900 y 1901, es de	$ 34.671,780.00
La renta líquida de la Isla, depositada en Tesorería, durante estos dos años, según arriba se indica, es de	34.581,395.82
Resultando una diferencia de	$ 90,384.18

y cuya diferencia se concibe, según más arriba se hace notar, siendo evidente que las últmas recaudaciones hechas al finalizar el Año Económico de 1901, aparezcan en los Libros de esta Tesorería, en el Año Económico de 1902, debido á la demora en la transmision de las mismas.

Durante el período comprendido de Enero 1º á Marzo 31 de 1901, se ha pagado al North American Trust & Co. por concepto de comisiones $23,760.60 y de Abril 1º á Junio 30 de 1901, por el mismo concepto, $14,567.80.

Los gastos de esta Oficina desde Enero 1º á Marzo 31 de 1901, han sido los siguientes:

Sueldos	$ 8,418.98
Alquileres, Gas, Hielo, etc.	1,348.46
Efectos de Escritorio é Impresos	1,204.13
Muebles de Escritorio	45.00
Aquiler de Coches	89.54
*Imprevistos	8,281.95

*El gasto principal de este Capítulo ha sido Bóvedas y Cajas, etc.

Los gastos durante el período de Abril 1º á Junio 30 de 1901, han sido los siguientes:

Sueldos	$ 7,304.13
Alquileres, Gas, Hielo, etc.	1,848.54
Efectos Escritorio é Impresos	1,512.84
Muebles de Escritorio	543.21
Alquiler de Coches	74.51
*Imprevistos	1,359.38

*El gasto principal de este Capítulo es de premios sobre Fianzas.

DEPARTAMENTO DE PAGADURIA.

Los gastos de este Departamento durante el período de tiempo incluído de Enero 1º á Marzo 31 de 1901, ha sido: Por cuenta de la Oficina del Tesorero, $98,143.45; por cuenta del Dapartamento de Cuba, $370,916.11; y durante el período de Abril 1º á Junio 30 de 1901, por cuenta de la Oficina del Tesorero, $73,140.61, y por la del Departamento de Cuba, $220,822.68.

La contabilidad del Pagador de la Tesorería fué revisada por el Inspector General hasta el día 10 de Junio de 1901, inclusive, siendo encontrada en correcto estado.

El gasto de este Departamento durante Enero 1º á Marzo 31 de 1901, es el siguiente:

Sueldos	$ 1,401.00
Alquileres, Gas, Hielo, etc...........	311.12
Efectos de Escritorio é Impresos.	22.91
Imprevistos	25.00

El ocasionado desde Abril 1º á Junio 30 de 1901, es como sigue:

Sueldos	$ 1,596.50
Alquileres, Gas, Hielo, etc...	608.06
Efectos de Escritorio é Impresos.........	27.06
Imprevistos.............	115.00
Alquiler de Coches.	23.01

DEPARTAMENTO DE TRASPORTES.

Durante el período de Enero 1º á Junio 30 de 1901, este Departamento ha fiscalizado y liquidado 16,583 cuentas y tiene en existencia pendientes de liquidación 5,000 Peticiones de Pasages y 1,500 Conocimientos.

Durante el período de Enero 1º á Marzo 31 de 1901, se pagaron cuentas de trasportes por valor de $51,490.13, y durante Abril 1º á Junio 30 de 1901, el total de lo pagado ascendió á $41,881.60.

Los gastos de este Departamento desde Enero 1º á Marzo 31 de 1901, fueron como sigue:

Sueldos..........	$ 1,222.00
Alquileres, Gas, Hielo, etc................	117.34
Efectos de Escritorio é Impresos..... ...	330.47
Muebles de Escritorio........	45.00

Los gastos de Abril 1º á Junio 30 de 1901, fueron:

Sueldos......................................	$ 1,152.16
Alquileres, Gas, Hielo, etc................	69.06
Efectos de Escritorio é Impresos.........	445.23
Alquiler de Coches..............	12.52

MONEDA.

Muy poco se ha efectuado desde el último informe de mi predecesor, para mejorar el estado de este ramo del servicio y aunque la moneda de los Estados Unidos es de hecho la moneda legal para todas las transacciones gubernamentales, también es un hecho que la moneda española y francesa no ha sido derogada como el medio de circulación para todas las operaciones comerciales y como su valor, especialmente el de la plata, está sujeto á tan grandes fluctuaciones, la desmoralización que por esa causa se determina es de grave influencia para las Rentas del Estado y sus efectos se palpan mas claros en este Departamento que en ninguna otra parte.

Es de todos bien sabido que el *modus vivendi* de Cuba depende exclusivamente de sus azúcares y que su renta se aumenta considerablemente durante los meses de su zafra, cuando el dinero de los Estados Unidos (su consumidor en mayor escala) afluye á este mercado en grandes cantidades y cuyo dinero, siguiendo las leyes de Consumo y Demanda, se puede obtener en ese tiempo á un tipo inferior en su cambio por Oro español y francés, que según dejo dicho si no es considerado como la moneda legal del país, es sin embargo la de mayor circulación en el mismo. Durante el período de tiempo en que afluye gran cantidad de dinero americano, las rentas del Gobierno están bien protegidas por la diferencia á su favor del valor real de la moneda española y francesa contra el que se le estipula á la misma por la Orden No. 123 del Cuartel General, División de Cuba, fecha 28 de Julio de 1899.

Siempre que pueda obtenerse la moneda americana por un valor menor en su cambio por moneda española y francesa, que el que se la fijado por la referida Orden No. 123, claro está que todos los contribuyentes al Estado, harán sus pagos en dicha moneda, pero cuando se ha recogido y vendido la zafra y la importación de dinero de los Estados Unidos es casi nominal, y el cambio, en virtud de la poca existencia de dicha moneda, alcanza su tipo máximo, que siempre excede con mucho al que se le ha dado por la ya mencionada Orden No. 123, las recaudaciones, siempre que sea posible, serán efectuadas en moneda española y francesa, la que entra en Tesorería bajo un valor ficticio y como que el Gobierno tiene prohibido, según Orden No. 229, Cuartel General de la División de Cuba, fecha Junio 4 de 1900, de que los pagos que el Estado efectúe sean hechos en moneda extrangera aunque estos sean en proporción por la cual es admitida, al cambiar dicha moneda extrangera por moneda de los Estados Unidos, (que es la legal en la Isla,) al tipo de cambio en el mercado, que, como dije anteriormente, es, durante ese tiempo, mucho mayor que el fijado por la referida orden aquí mencionada, es evidente que el Gobierno es el que pierde en la transacción la diferencia entre el valor que se le dá al Oro extrangero por la referida Orden No. 123 y su valor real y efectivo al tipo que se hizo la compra y que al presente puede calcularse en algo mas que ½ de 1%.

Varias han sido las ideas sugeridas por este Departamento para evitar este estado de cosas, que no solo le es perjudicial al Gobierno sino también al país en general, con motivo de las graves fluctuaciones á que se hace referencia en este Informe, y en vista de lo cual respetuosamente tengo el honor de someter á su consideración la siguiente recomendación:

Como quiera que la actual situación financiera de la Isla no le permitirá por razones harto conocidas de aquellos que se hayan detenido á considerar su posición económica, emitir por muchos años aun, su propia moneda, y siendo Cuba, económicamente hablando, una dependencia de los Estados Unidos, y cuya condición acrecentará con mas fortaleza en lo sucesivo, por razones de mútuo interés, es de creer que su moneda oficial, aun después de obtener su completa independencia, continuará siendo la de los Estados Unidos. Sentado este principio y para ahorrar discusiones sobre este punto al futuro Gobierno de Cuba, así como para presentar de una manera ventajosa su posición financiera ante las demás potencias, es mi opinión que se debe decretar que todas las operaciones, tanto gubernamentales como las de carácter particular, sean precisamente efectuadas en moneda de los Estados Unidos, dando un tiempo determinado, (por ejemplo, seis meses) en el cual los tenedores de moneda extrangera puedan canjearla por la moneda legal del país. De este modo la moneda española y francesa que circula hoy en el país y cuyo valor está regularizado por su correspondiente valor en España y Francia, sería muy pronto demonetizada buscando su salida natural hácia sus respectivos países sin pérdida séria ni inconveniencia á sus tenedores.

A la par que creo firmemente que la proposición que tengo el honor de presentar concluiría con el presente perjudicial estado de cosas, es así mismo una cuestión de apreciación para con el Gobierno, quién sin duda alguna, tiene el asunto bajo una cuidadosa investigación y estudio, y el cual con su habitual sabiduría resolverá el problema, de la manera que mejor convenga á todos, quedando mi intervención en este caso solamente reducida á señalar los hechos tales como se me aparecen desde el puesto oficial con que he sido honrado.

Tengo grato placer en recomendar á la favorable consideración del Ayudante General del Departamento, los empleados de esta Oficina, por sus fieles y eficientes servicios. Siempre los he encontrado leales á los intereses del Departamento y al Gobierno Militar de los Estados Unidos en Cuba. Cada empleado del Departamento en sí, es un representante competente del puesto que ocupa.

Respetuosamente,

Carlos Roloff,

Tesorero de Cuba.

EXHIBITS

PERTAINING TO THE

SEMI ANNUAL REPORT

OF THE

TREASURER OF CUBA

COVERING THE PERIOD FROM

JULY 1, TO DECEMBER 31,

1901

OFFICE OF THE TREASURER OF CUBA,

Havana, Cuba, December 31st, 1901.

Adjutant General,

Department of Cuba.

Havana, Cuba.

SIR:

In obedience to instructions contained in your letter of November 9th, 1901, I have the honor to submit the following report covering the operations of this Department for the period from July 1st, 1901, to December 31st, 1901. In this report the Department will be treated of under the divisions, as has previously been the custom, viz.:

Treasury Department,
Disbursing Department,
Transportation Department.

Each of the Departments will be treated of in brief, noting the subdivisions as made by the Inspector General, Department of Cuba, in his recent inspection of the system and personnel of the office of the Treasurer of Cuba, reported under date of June 30th, 1901.

In order to arrive at the net revenues for the period above referred to, the same instructions will be observed as given in the preceding report of this office for the six months ended June 30th, 1901, viz:

When reference is made to the total receipts, net receipts or revenues received by the Treasurer of Cuba during the Fiscal Year 1902, that all the receipts pertaining to the Insular Government are included, regardless of the fiscal years to which the same pertain, but the same are taken up on the books of this office and charged to their respective fiscal years. The total deposits received by the Treasurer during the Fiscal Year 1902, although including the receipts pertaining to the Fiscal Years 1899, 1900, and 1901, will be the amount referred to as the total receipts for the Fiscal Year 1902, or so much thereof as is covered by this report, and the net receipts for the Fiscal Year 1902, or the portion thereof treated in this report, will be arrived at by deducting all repayments received during the period covered by this report.

On June 30th, 1901, this Department had on hand, Cash Balance		$ 1,398,501.74
as shown by Exhibit A of this report.		
The Cash Receipts for the period July 1st to December 31st, 1901, have been		9,546,106.64
as shown by same exhibit.		
Total		$10,944,608.38
During the same period the payments were	$9,826,813.59	
as shown by Exhibit A.		
The losses from sales of foreign gold	7,465.26	
as shown by same exhibit.		
Total		9,834,278.85
Leaving Cash Balance, close of business, December 31st, 1901		$ 1,110,329.53

As stated in Treasurer's previous report, for the period January 1st to June 30th, 1901, all disbursements of insular funds have been charged against "Revenues" and not to the several fúnds, Customs, Postal, Internal Revenue and Miscellaneous, but the Treasurer has continued to keep record of all receipts under the headings above referred to.

The remaining part of Exhibit A shows character of money in United States currency valuation, on deposit with the various depositories of insular funds and with the Cashier, Treasury Department of Cuba, which aggregated the balance of Revenues, close of business December 31st, 1901, $1,110,329.53.

COMPARISON OF REVENUES, CALENDAR YEARS 1900 AND 1901,

AS REPORTED BY COLLECTORS.

This report being taken from monthly reports received from collectors, showing actual revenues collected by them, no item of repayments will appear in this comparison.

Total Revenues, Calendar Year 1900	$17,405,393.11
as shown by Exhibit H of this report.	
Total Revenues, Calendar Year 1901	16,977,239,68
as shown by same exhibit.	
Decrease in Revenues, Calendar Year 1901, as compared with Calendar Year 1900 ....,...	$ 428,153.43

Exhibit H of this report, under proper fund accounts, shows decrease in Customs Receipts of.. $ 478,906.44
Internal Revenue Receipts show decrease of 104,758.86
Postal Receipts show a gain of................................ $ 37,531.02
Miscellaneous Receipts show a gain of.................... 117,990.85

Making a total loss of.....		$ 583,665.30
And a total gain of..........	$ 155,511.87	
Or a total decrease, as shown above, of...		428,153.43

COMPARISON OF CASH RECEIPTS

FOR THE FIRST SIX MONTHS OF THE FISCAL YEAR 1902,

WITH THE CASH RECEIPTS FOR THE SEMI-ANNUAL

PERIODS OF THE FISCAL YEAR 1901.

Cash Receipts, July 1st to December 31st, 1900.. $ 9,381,961.42
as shown by Exhibit 2a of Treasurer's report for said period.

Cash Receipts, July 1st to December 31st, 1901.. 9,546,106.54
as shown by Exhibit B of this report.

Increase in the Cash Receipts for the first half of the Fiscal Year 1902, as compared with the first half of the Fiscal Year 1901.. $ 164,145.22

COMPARISON, SECOND HALF FISCAL YEAR 1901.

Total Cash Receipts, January 1st to June 30th, 1901.. $ 9,081,980.05
as shown by Exhibit E of Treasurer's report for said period.

Cash Receipts, first half Fiscal Year 1902.... 9,546,106.64
as shown by Exhibit B of this report, showing an increase in the Cash Receipts, first half Fiscal Year 1902, as compared with last half Fiscal Year 1901, of.................... $ 464,126.59

COMPARISON OF NET RECEIPTS, FIRST SIX MONTHS FISCAL YEAR 1902, WITH SEMI-ANNUAL PERIODS OF THE FISCAL YEAR 1901.

Total Cash Receipts, July 1st to December 31st, 1900 as shown by Exhibit 2a, Treasurer's report for said period.	$9,381,961.42	
Repayments.................................. as shown by same exhibit.	737,147.52	
Net Receipts first half Fiscal Year 1901..		$ 7,644,813.90
Total Cash Receipts, first six months Fiscal Year 1902.................................. as shown by Exhibit C of this report.	$9.546,106.64	
Repayments.................................. as shown by same exhibit.	702.823.44	
Net Receipts, first half Fiscal Year 1902..		8,843,283.20
Gain in Net Receipts first half of the Fiscal Year 1902, as compared with first half of Fiscal Year 1901..................................		$ 198,469.30

COMPARISON LAST HALF FISCAL YEAR 1901.

Total Cash Receipts, January 1st to June 30th, 1901.................................. as shown by Exhibit E, Treasurer's report for said period.	$9,081,980.05	
Repayments.................................. as shown by same exhibit.	385,066.05	
Net Receipts for last half Fiscal Year 1901..................................		$ 8,696,914.00
Net Receipts, first half Fiscal Year 1902		8,843,283.20
Increase in Net Receipts for the first half of the Fiscal Year 1902, as compared with last half of Fiscal Year 1901..................................		$ 146,369.20

COMPARISON OF RECEIPTS AND PAYMENTS FOR THE CALENDER YEAR 1901.

Total Payments, Calendar Year 1901...... as shown by Exhibit F of this report.	$19,357,744.18
Total Receipts for Calendar Year 1901.... as shown by same Exhibit.	18,628,086.69
Showing expenditures during the Calendar Year 1901, in excess of Receipts, in the amount of..........	$ 729,657.49

COMPARISON OF EXPENDITURES FOR THE FIRST SIX MONTHS OF THE FISCAL YEAR 1902, WITH THE SEMI-ANNUAL PERIODS OF THE FISCAL YEAR 1901.

Total Payments, July 1st to December 31st, 1900.......... as shown by Exhibit 8 of Treasurer's report for said period.	$10,236,562.89
Total Payments, July 1st to December 31st, 1901.......... as shown by Exhibit D of this report.	$ 8,826,813.59
Decrease in Payments, first half Fiscal Year 1902, as compared with Payments first half Fiscal Year 1901..........	$ 409,749.30

COMPARISON OF THE LAST HALF FISCAL YEAR 1901.

Total Payments, January 1st to June 30th, 1901.......... as shown by Exhibit E of Treasurer's report for said period.	$ 9,530,930.59
Payments first half Fiscal Year 1902...... as shown above.	9,826,813.59
Increase in Payments first half of Fiscal Year 1902, as compared with Payments last half of Fiscal Year 1901..........	$ 295,883.00

Exhibit C of this report shows same information as Exhibit B, except that in Exhibit B total receipts are shown under fiscal years, headings and months, while in Exhibit C is shown the total amount collected under the respective headings for the period covered by this report, July 1st to December 31st, 1901.

Exhibit D shows the total amount paid out on accountable warrants and settlement warrants and charged to the respective accounts—Revenues, Money Order Fund and Disbursing Officers' Fund. A separate account is kept of the two latter funds deposited with the Treasurer of Cuba for specific purposes and do not figure in any way as available revenues. This Department practically assumes the status of a depository for the Post Office Department as relates to Money Order Fund account, this being money deposited with the Treasurer of Cuba for the payment of money orders; the same is true of Disbursing Officers' Fund account, this being money deposited with the Treasurer of Cuba to pay outstanding checks of the North American Trust Company, at close of business August 16th, 1901, at which time all funds to the credit of disbursing officers of insular funds (as well as funds to the credit of the Treasurer of Cuba) were ordered deposited with this Department.

Exhibit E shows dates of sales of foreign gold by this Department, during the period July 1st to December 31st, showing character of coin, United States currency valuation, and total valuation of each sale in United States currency. The losses sustained in said sales, as shown in this exhibit, aggregated $7,465.26. In regard to the loss sustained on the sale of foreign gold, it became apparent to the Treasurer of Cuba that some decided action should be taken as to the valuations fixed by Circular No. 2, Division of Customs and Insular Affairs, January 4th, 1899, fixing the values of the centen at $4.82 and the louis at $3.86, respectively. This foreign gold could not always be sold on the Havana market at the rate at which it was received in payment of taxes, customs, etc., 1.0995 for a centen and 1.0984 for a louis, and if shipped to the United States for recoinage would sustain a greater loss than if sold here. Order No. 229, Headquarters Division of Cuba, June 4th, 1900, requires all payments of insular indebtedness in United States currency; consequently it became necessary for the Treasurer to convert at different times a great portion of foreign gold into United States currency, in order to enable him to comply with said order. The question was of such importance that the Treasurer considered it devolving upon him to take such action in the matter as to protect the Government against the heavy loss sustained in the sale (shipment for recoinage) of the foreign gold above referred to, and after having thoroughly studied the situation, recommended to the Military Governor of Cuba a reduction in the values of the gold coins, centen and louis, as fixed in Circular No. 2, Division of Customs and Insular Affairs, January 4th, 1899, which recommendation was approved by the Military Governor of Cuba, and upon his recommendation, Executive Order of December 28th, 1898, promulgated by Circular No. 2, Division of Customs and Insular Affairs, series 1899, was modified by the President of the United States, as follows:

No. 193.

HEADQUARTERS DEPARTMENT OF CUBA,

Havana, August 21, 1901.

The following order of the President of the United States is, by direction of the Military Governor of Cuba, published for the information and guidance of all concerned:

Executive Mansion, August 19, 1901.

It is hereby ordered that so much of the Executive Order of December 28, 1898, as fixes the rates at which the Spanish alphonsino (centén) and the French louis shall be accepted in payment of customs, taxes public and postal dues in the Island of Cuba, is modified to read as follows:

Alphonsino (25 peseta piece)	$4.78
Louis (20 franc piece)..........	3.83

William McKinley.

H. L. Scott,
Adjutant General.

Since the promulgation of the above order, this Department has been enabled to make, when necessary, sales of foreign gold under the authority of the Military Governor of Cuba, so that all sales of this gold, collected at the new rate (with one exception) for the period from August 21st, 1901, to December 31st, 1901, have resulted in a gain.

During said period this Department has sold $1,105,283.98, the gain on which has been $1,123.41, for which Treasurer's Receipts in regular form have issued.

Exhibit F of this report shows total Receipts and Payments for the Calendar Year 1901. Receipts are shown by months under proper fund accounts, giving total monthly receipts from all sources for each of the months covered by this exhibit, and the total receipts for the entire period covered by this exhibit.

The showing is as follows:

Total Receipts are shown to be................	$18,628,086.69
Payments are shown by months to be......	19,357.744.18
And to be in excess of Receipts by............	$ 729.657.49

COMPARISON OF NET RECEIPTS RECEIVED BY THE TREASURER, FIRST HALF OF FISCAL YEAR 1902, WITH REVENUE COLLECTIONS REPORTED BY COLLECTORS FOR THE SEMI-ANNUAL PERIODS OF THE FISCAL YEAR 1901

Total Cash Receipts, July 1st to December 31st, 1900 as shown by Exhibit 2a of Treasurer's report for said period.	$9,381,961.42	
Repayments.................... as shown by same exhibit.	737,147.52	
Net Receipts, first half Fiscal Year 1901..		$ 8,644,813.90
Total Revenues reported by Collectors, July 1st to December 31st, 1901...............		$ 8,301,212.56
as shown by Exhibit G of this report, showing:		
Net Receipts, first half Fiscal Year 1901.. in excess of amount reported by collectors for the first half of the Fiscal Year 1902.		$ 343,601.34
Total Cash Receipts, January 1st to June 30th, 1901. as shown by Exhibit E of Treasurer's report for said period.	$9.081,980.05	
Deducting Repayments. . as shown by same exhibit.	385,066.05	
Net Receipts second half Fiscal Year 1901		$ 8,696.914.00
as compared with Revenues reported by Collectors for first half of Fiscal Year 1902......		8,301.212.56
shows Net Receipts last half of Fiscal Year 1901..		$ 395.701.44
in excess of amounts reported by collectors, first half of Fiscal Year 1902.		

COMPARISON OF REVENUES REPORTED BY COLLECTORS, FIRST HALF OF FISCAL YEAR 1902, WITH REVENUES REPORTED BY COLLECTOR FOR THE SEMI-ANNUAL PERIODS OF THE FISCAL YEAR 1901

Revenues reported by Collectors, July 1st to December 31st, 1900......................... as shown by Exhibit 11, Treasurer's report for said period.	$ 8,594,056.28
Revenues reported by collectors, July 1st to December 31st, 1901.............................. as shown by Exhibit G of this report.	$ 8,301,212.56
Decrease in Revenues during first half of Fiscal Year 1902, as compared with first half of Fiscal Year 1901..............................	$ 292,844.72

Revenues reported by Collectors, January 1st to June 30th, 1901 .... as shown by Exhibit F of Treasurer's report for said period.	$ 8,676,027.12
Deducting amount reported by collectors July 1st to December 31st, 1901	8,301,212.56
shows .... decrease in Revenues reported by Collectors first half Fiscal Year 1902, as compared with last half Fiscal Year 1901.	$ 374,814.56

RECAPITULATION OF THE RECEIPTS AND PAYMENTS FOR THE SEMI-ANNUAL PERIODS OF THE FISCAL YEAR 1901 AND FIRST HALF OF THE FISCAL YEAR 1902

Balance close of business June 30th, 1900.	$ 2,702,053.75
Receipts, July 1st, 1900, to December 31st, 1900	9,381,961.42
Receipts, January 1st, 1901, to June 30th, 1901	9,081,980.05
Receipts, July 1st, 1901, to December 31st, 1901	9,546,106.64
Total to be accounted for	$30,712,101.86

Payments, July 1st, 1900, to December 31st, 1900	$10,236,562.89
Payments, January 1st, 1901, to June 30th, 1901	9,530,930.59
Payments, July 1st, 1901, to December 31st, 1901	* 9,834,278.85
Total Disbursements	$29,601,772.33

Total to be accounted for, as above	$30,712,101.86
Total Disbursements	29,601,772.33
Balance, close of business December 31st, 1901	$ 1,110,329.53

* In this amount is included the losses on sales of foreign gold, as shown in Exhibit E of this report.

In order to arrive at an approximate estimate of the available cash assets of the United States Military Government of Cuba, December 31st, 1901, the following statement is submitted:

Cash Balance, as shown by Exhibit A of this report	$ 1,110,329.53
To the credit of disbursing officers with the Banco Nacional de Cuba, as reported by the respective branches of the Company, December 31st, 1901	$ 2,057,783.62
Estimated amount of Revenues collected and in process of transmission to the Treasurer	$ 200,000.00
Total	$ 3,368,113.15

Exhibit G of this report shows amount of Revenues as reported by Collectors at the various ports throughout the Island, during the first half of the Fiscal Year 1902. These reports are made to the Treasurer of Cuba by monthly statements and telegrams from the Collectors, at the end of each month, and are preserved in the office for statistical purposes, but not as a matter of official record.

The Net Receipts of the Island as reported by the Treasurer, July 1st to December 31st, 1901, are	$ 8,843,283.20
Revenues reported by collectors for same period, as shown in Exhibit G, have been....	$ 8,301,212.56

which closely approximates the amount shown by the records of this office. The difference in these reports is explained for the reason that the books of this office show the actual sums received by the Treasurer during the period covered by this report, while the reports from the collectors show the amount actually collected by them during same period, the time necessary in transmitting funds to this office causing a difference at the end of each period of time.

As previously stated in this report, this Department will be treated of under sub-divisions as noted by the Inspector General in his report of inspection, June 20th, 1901, viz.: General Record Department, Disbursing Department and Transportation Department.

GENERAL RECORD DEPARTMENT.

The General Record Department is composed of the following sections: Record Department, Cancelled Check Department. Each of these sub-departments, will be treated of in brief in order to show the entire system employed in the Treasury Department.

Record Department.—In this Department are kept the general records of the Office. The card system is employed; a complete index of both names and subjects is made, a copy taken of all communications passing through the office and all papers in Spanish are translated into English, an English copy being kept on file for reference and records.

Bookkeeping Department.—In this Department is kept the record of all moneys receipted for by the Treasurer and disbursed by him on warrants issued by the Governor General and countersigned by the Auditor for Cuba.

Cancelled Check Department.—Checks are issued to disbursing officers upon their request and charged to them, by numbers, in a book called "Record of cancelled checks." When the checks issued by disbursing officers are received from the depositories on which they are drawn, they are checked in this book, which shows at the end of each month the checks drawn prior thereto, that have not been cashed by the depositories, and those which the officer still has on hand and for which he is responsible. Disbursing officers upon being relieved either forward their unused checks to the Treasurer or transfer them on receipts to their successors. All checks cancelled by disbursing officers for any cause are returned to the Treasurer for record and file.

CASH DEPARTMENT.

The system in vogue respecting the cash is as follows: The Cashier checks it up at the end of each day's business, and balances with the books of the Treasurer of Cuba. At the end of each month the Treasurer, assisted by the Cashier, goes through the vaults and checks up the amounts by the tags on the bags or packages, but does not count the money. It is counted, however, by the Inspector General of the Department of Cuba, about every three months, during his inspections of the Office.

With respect to the safeguard and proper care of the moneys in the Treasury, all cash and bonds are deposited in the large steel vault with time locks, recently constructed. The old safe, formerly used for the storage of cash, is used for miscellaneous matters; and, in addition to this, there is a small safe, used for daily cash transactions. A strong guard is kept over the Treasury, day and night, composed of American soldiers from the Cavalry and Artillery and a detachment of Cuban Rural Guards. No employee of this Department is permitted to enter the cash room except during office hours.

The work of the Treasury Department has been greatly increased during the past six months owing to the North American Trust Company and its branches having been relieved by the War Department as fiscal agent of the United States Military Government of Cuba. This company was relieved in its capacity above referred to July 18th, 1901, and for a period of two or three weeks the entire system of the Government as related to the placing of funds at the disposal of disbursing officers was inoperative and the Treasurer was of necessity, as directed by the Military Governor of Cuba, caused additional labor and responsibility in the shipment of all funds allotted to disbursing officers outside the Province of Santiago, during the period from July 18th to August 30th, 1901. Excepting in that Province all funds were shipped either by registered mail or express to disbursing officers outside the City of Havana, who were directed to make disbursements in cash until the qualification of the Banco Nacional de Cuba as fiscal agent of the United States Military Government of Cuba, August 30th, 1901. There being no authorized depositories except in Santiago, the majority of collectors and disbursing officers forwarded all revenues direct to the Treasurer of Cuba, either by express or registered mail, devolving upon this Department the work of at least two branches of the Trust Company. but the Department has been ample to meet the exigencies of the service, and business during the perturbed period has progressed to the entire satisfaction of all officials and parties concerned. This is not applicable to disbursements in the Province of Santiago, that branch having qualified in accordance with the instructions of the North American Trust Company as fiscal agent of the Government in the amount of $ 485,000, in two per cent United States Consols of 1930. Upon the general qualification of the Banco Nacional de Cuba, August 30th, 1901, all disbursing officers were directed to make deposit of their balances of insular funds with the new institution, since which time the business in connection with this Department has proceeded in its usual manner with the exception of the extra labor in connection with the settlement of the outstanding checks against the North American Trust Company.

OUTSTANDING CHECKS

In accordance with instructions from this Office of August 3rd, 1901, all disbursing officers of insular funds were instructed (except in the Province of Santiago, where transfer to Banco Nacional de Cuba was ordered), to withdraw all funds from the North American Trust Company, excepting the amount to cover outstanding checks of each official. On August 16th the North American Trust Company and its branches were instructed to deposit with the Treasurer of Cuba all funds in their custody standing to the credit of disbursing officers, presumablly to cover the outstanding checks of those disbursing officers. Instructions were also issued directing the Trust Company to deposit with the Treasurer of Cuba at Havana (excepting in the Province of Santiago, where transfer was ordered), of all funds on deposit with them to his official credit. There was turned over by the North American Trust Company on account of checks outstanding the following:

On August 15th, Havana branch..........	$	82,072.41
August 16th, Santiago branch........		25,094.93
August 16th, Cienfuegos branch......		17,960.39
August 16th, Cienfuegos branch Treasurer's account....................		953.29
August 16th, Matanzas branch.......		12,369.65
October 12th, New York branch......		3.50
Total............................	$	138,454.17
There have been deposited with the Treasurer, on account of overdrafts, amounts aggregating................		429.49
Outstanding Liabilities............................		15.00
Repayments...		105.00
Total received................	$	139,003.66

Of the above amount deposited with the Treasurer, there has been allotted and placed to the credit of the Treasury Disbursing Clerk $138,537.27; there has also been transferred $114.17 from Finance, Central Office, making a total of $138,651.44, at the disposal of the Treasury Disbursing Clerk for the payment of outstanding checks.

Each officer having credit with the Bank at close of business August 15th and 16th, has been requested to furnish the Treasurer with an itemized list of his checks outstanding, showing number, date, name and amount of each check (officers on duty in Alaska, Porto Rico and the Philippines whose retained records are not at hand have not reported itemized lists of checks outstanding). These exceptions are few and do not aggregate amount in excess of $ 400. All of the accounts so itemized have been found correct or have been corrected by an additional deposit from the officials with the exception of the account of F. González Gari, Tesorero Pagador, Guanajay, in whose account there is a small difference between the amount turned in by the Bank and the amount of the list received regarding the account in question. Funds of the nature above referred to have been receipted for by the Treasurer not as Revenues, but under the heading of Disbursing Officer's Fund. The condition of the account against this at close of business December 31st, 1901, was as follows:

RECEIPTS

Various branches of the Bank	$	138,454.17
Deposited with the Treasurer, account overdrafts		429.49
Repayments		104.00
Outstanding liabilities		15.00
TOTAL RECEIVED by Treasurer	$	139,003.66

DISBURSEMENTS

Allotted Treasury Disbursing Clerk on Treasurer's estimates	$ 138.537,27		
Transferred Treasury Disbursing Clerk from Finance, Central Office to D. O. Fund.	$114.17		
Total received by Treasury Disbursing Clerk	$ 138,651.44		
Balance unallotted	466.39	$	139,117.83
Deducting transfer			114.17
TOTAL RECEIVED by Treasurer		$	139,003.66

Total allotted and transferred to the Treasury Disbursing Clerk, account D. O. Fund	$	138,651.44
Amount expended in payment of outstanding checks		129,832.32
Balance in hands of Disbursing Clerk	$	8,819.12

To cover the liability of the North American Trust Company regarding funds in their possession in connection with the settlement of outstanding checks, the Treasurer has in his possession as security two hundred and fifty second mortgage bonds of the City of Havana of $100 each, aggregating $25,000.

During the period from July 1st to December 31st, 1901, the Treasurer of Cuba has paid to the North American Trust Company, commission, $12,174.12; and for insurance on shipments of foreign gold to the United States Assay Office, New York City, for recoinage, $ 756.57.

The expenses of this Department for the period July 1st to December 31st, 1901, have been as follows:

Salaries	$ 15,202.08
Rent, ice, gas, etc	1,199.26
Stationery and Printing	1,565.94
Office Furniture	145.12
Cab hire	162.24
Premium on bonds, officials of this Department	100.00
Board of Treasury Guard	635.65

DISBURSING DEPARTMENT

The Treasury Disbursing Clerk pays all bills of this Department, including all bills of lading and transportation requests issued by officials of the insular goverment to the various companies doing business in the Island of Cuba. This Department also makes payments for the Military Governor and such other special bills as are referred to the Treasurer of Cuba for settlement.

The disbursements of this Department during the period July 1st to December 31st, 1901, have been, Account Treasurer's Office. $101,850.77; Account Department of Cuba, $790,648.61.

The accounts of the Treasury Disbursing Clerk were inspected by the Inspector General, Department of Cuba, to include December 23d, 1901, and found correct.

The expenses for this Department for the period July 1st to December 31st, 1901, were:

Salaries	$ 3,367.83
Rent, ice, gas, etc	762.04
Stationery and Printing	170.00
Cab hire	39.51

TRANSPORTATION DEPARTMENT

In this Department are received the bills of the various transportation companies for transportation of passengers and freight throughout the Island, which are accompanied by the original bills of lading in case of freight and by transportation requests in case of passengers. The bills are audited in this Department and record made thereof, after which they are certified to the Treasury Disbursing Clerk for payment.

During this period this Department has audited and settled 9,980 accounts and has on hand for settlement about 10,000 transportation requests and bills of lading.

During the period July 1st to December 31st, 1901, transportation accounts to the amount of $60,976,31 were paid.

The expenses of the Department for this period were:

Salaries	$ 3,130.97
Rent, ice, gas, etc	415.00
Stationery and Printing	928.60
Cab hire	7.53
Typewriter	112.00

The expenses of three Departments above, for the first half Fiscal Year 1902, as compared with the last half Fiscal Year 1901, show decrease in expenses of this office of $3,358.39.

BANCO NACIONAL DE CUBA

As has previously been stated, the Banco Nacional de Cuba, under authority of the Secretary of War of the United States of America, and by direction of the Military Governor of Cuba, was designated August 30th, 1901, as fiscal agent of the United States Military Government of the Island of Cuba, it having deposited with the Treasurer of Cuba collateral bond in the amount of $1,385,000 in mortgage bonds of the City of Havana and consols of the United States of America of 1930 for the faithful performance of said duty, as per temporary agreement of the date above referred to, August 30th, 1901. It has since deposited additional collateral security in the amount of $340,000, making a total collateral security on deposit with the Treasurer of Cuba of $1,725,000.

I have information that the Bank has recently increased its capital stock to $5,000,000. I consider the institution thoroughly reliable and highly beneficial to financial interests of the Island. It comes to supply the long felt need of an institution where loans can be obtained at low rates of interest secured by collaterals well worth the amount of the principal, a condition which has heretofore not existed in Cuba. It already has branches in four cities of the Island and will no doubt be further extended as the requirements may justify. It is my opinion that banking institutions of the kind of the Banco Nacional de Cuba, will exert great influence over the future of this country, provided its program can be carried out as proposed. I have no reason to doubt that it will be otherwise, as the Directors are well known to this community and their responsibility and credit, individually as well as jointly, are a sufficient guarantee that the success desired will be obtained.

As to the financial status of the Banco Nacional de Cuba, attention is invited to Statements and Certificate of Messrs. Haskins & Sells, Certified Public Accountants, New York City, showing the financial condition of the National Bank of Cuba under date of October 31st, 1901.

CONSOLIDATED BALANCE SHEET

National Bank of Cuba, Havana, Santiago, Cienfuegos, Matanzas, Cuba.

Assets.		United States Currency.
Cash		$1,215,013.05
Cash, in transit		3,746.12
Bonds:		
United States Government 2%	$813,735.82	
Havana 6%	923,751.15	
		1,737,486.97
Loans and Bills of Exchange		1,489,646.93
J. P. Morgan & Company		574,909.64
Other Banks		132,754.09
Furniture and Fixtures		35,423.10
Real Estate		39,652.74
Sundry Items		89,384.60
Total assets		$5,318,017.24

Liabilities

Due depositors and Banks	$3,791,363.90
Cashiers' and certified checks	419,973.98
Capital	1,000,000.00
Profit and Loss Accounts	106,679.36
Total Liabilities	$5,318,017.24

CURRENCY

In my report for the last six months of the Fiscal Year 1901, dated July 25th, 1901, under the heading of CURRENCY, I took up the matter, making recommendations as to the adoption of United States currency as the standard circulating medium for Cuba, which recommendations, had they been adopted, it is believed, would have unified all accounts, governmental and private, and materially bettered the conditions of the country generally from a financial standpoint, but that another six months have elapsed without any action having been taken in the matter, and as everything points to a prosperous future for Cuba as regards the development of the political issues of the Country, it would seem advisable that steps be taken as to the adoption of measures whereby the agricultural interests of Cuba, which is the source of all the progress and welfare which we possess and which we anticipate possessing, be encouraged, as Cuba eminently and entirely depends upon her agriculture. This being true, it is apparent that no step is more important than that of the Government in furthering to the highest degree the interests of those at present engaged in agricultural pursuits and every assistance offered by way of financial aid which will induce scores of the unemployed population of the various cities throughout the Island to return to tilling our fertile soil, which avocation, when sufficiently patronized, will afford more wealth, peace and happiness than the furtherance of any other one interest which I might mention.

It is a sorrowful fact that Cuba, with her wonderful soil, her superb geographical position, by which reason she is generally termed "Key of the New World," and despite the fact that millions upon millions of wealth have been accumulated from her agricultural resources, she has never, in the broadest sense, been able to boast of having had a real banking institution whose object it was to promote generally, the agricultural interests of the country, and to make richer and more fruitful its territorial resources.

I therefore have the honor to submit the following plan for your consideration, and if my suggestions are deemed worthy, respectfully request that the Government of Intervention take the necessary steps in the matter previous to its departture from our shores:

That one or more banks be permitted to be established on the same basis as the National Banks operated in the United States, viz.: Permitting them to issue a currency, which will be guaranteed by the Government, with whom they shall deposit collateral security in the amount of the currency issued by them, and that a decree be issued designating the rate of interest which they, as well as all other money lending institutions in Cuba, shall charge, or in other words establish a legal rate of interest, and that it be a violation of law to charge interest in excess of the authorized rate, thus protecting the interests of the needy as well as preventing the present calamitous speculators in the conduct of an illegitimate business, who, regardless of principle, have become a menace to the sound doctrines of legal business.

Had something of this kind been done by the late rulers of the Island, its present economical condition would have been quite different, but as its future was entirely left more to its own destiny than to any specific or reasonable conclusion, the afflicted present economical distress has made it compulsory, in order to eradicate this serious trouble, to appeal to the United States for a helping hand in this hour of our sorrow. Let us hope that this appeal be not made in vain, that the future Government of Cuba will reap the benefit of our past experience and that the adoption of such measures as outlined above will promote the agricultural interests of the Island in such a conclusive manner that the country will enter upon an age of progress and prosperity heretofore unparalleled in Cuba.

PERSONNEL

The personnel of the Department has remained practically intact since my last report and I again take pleasure in stating that each clerk in the Department has continued to perform the duties incident to his position honestly, faithfully and efficiently. Personal mention is not deemed necessary in this report, but I will gladly recommend individually each employee of this office for fidelity and efficiency in the position in which he is employed.

As regards the efforts on the part of the American employees now serving with the United States Military Government of Cuba, to further their services with the Government of the United States, when their duties have finished in Cuba, I have the honor to state that the majority of the clerks of this Department have been in continuous service in this office for over two years, some since the inception of the Office of the Treasurer of Cuba, and I respectfully request that they be recommended favorably to the President of the United States of America and to the Secretary of War for future service with the United States Government when their services are no longer required in Cuba.

Respectfully submitted,

CARLOS ROLOFF,
Treasurer of Cuba.

EXHIBIT "A."

RECAPITULATION SHOWING BALANCE CLOSE OF BUSINESS DECEMBER, 31, 1901

Dr. | Cr.

Dr.	Dollars	Cts	Cr.	Dollars	Cts
Warrants paid from July, 1, to Dec. 31 1901	9.826,813	59	Balance on hand June, 30, 1901	1.398,501	74
Losses sustained from sales of Foreign Gold	7,465	26	Cash Receipts from July, 1, to Dec. 31, 1901	9.546,106	64
Balance on hand December, 31, 1901	1.110,329	53		10.944,608	38
	10.944,608	38	Balance close of business December, 31, 1901	1.110,329	53

DEPOSITED AS FOLLOWS:

CHARACTER OF MONEY	SANTIAGO		CIENFUEGOS		MATANZAS		CASHIER		TOTAL	
U. S. Currency Valuation.	Dollars	Cts	Dollars	Cts	Dollars	Cts	Dollars	Cts	Dollars	Cts
United States Currency	97,558	91	74,225	30	46,611	49	851,138	79	1.069,534	49
Spanish and French Gold	5,716	35	3,165	86	27	73	30,712	61	39,622	55
Spanish Silver	600	.....	1	44	.....	17	570	88	1,172	49
TOTAL	103,875	26	77,392	60	46,639	39	882,422	28	1.110,329	53

EXHIBIT "B"

CASH RECEIPTS FROM JULY 1st TO DECEMBER, 31st 1901

TOTAL BY MONTHS FISCAL YEAR AND FUND		JULY Dollars	Cts	AUGUST Dollars	Cts	SEPTEMBER Dollars	Cts	OCTOBER Dollars	Cts	NOVEMBER Dollars	Cts	DECEMBER Dollars	Cts	TOTAL Dollars	Cts
FISCAL YEAR 1900.	Customs														
	Postals														
	Internal Revenue														
	Miscellaneous			122	49									122	49
	Repayments	7.553	46	353	24	13	97	80	56	175	49		50	8,177	22
	Money Order Funds														
	Disb. Officers Funds														
	TOTAL	7,553	46	475	73	13	97	80	56	175	49		50	8 299	71
FISCAL YEAR 1901.	Customs	110,518	85											110,518	85
	Postal	12.543	46	27		15	62	9	35					12,595	43
	Internal Revenue	3,853	47											3,853	47
	Miscellaneous	516		2,264	13					14				2,794	13
	Repayments	524,270	56	46.584	75	18,629	29	7,438	62	13,616	20	7.701	63	618,241	05
	Money Order Funds														
	Disb. Officers Funds														
	TOTAL	651,702	34	48,875	88	18,644	91	7,447	97	13,630	20	7,701	63	748,002	93
FISCAL YEAR 1902.	Customs	1.095.746	10	1.134,146	58	1.257,807	54	1.412.259	12	1.356,913	80	1.225,432	56	7.482,305	70
	Postal	12,417	03	28,070	96	32,606	23	27,753	88	30,738	98	35.874	30	167,461	38
	Internal Revenue	50,785	84	60,792	17	59.304	55	57,926	21	58,136	73	53.694	93	340,640	43
	Miscellaneous	11,902	11	10,237	26	12,278	50	16,998	21	23,428	57	27,411	06	102,255	71
	Repayments	472		2,481	59	11 849	12	8,425	87	16,640	01	36,536	58	76,405	17
	Money Order Funds			189,798	16	41.900	54	87,000		78,000		85,033	25	481,731	95
	Disb. Officers Funds			113,355	74	25,094	98	423	82	114	17	15		139 003	66
	TOTAL	1.171 323	08	1.538,882	46	1.440,841	41	1 610.787	11	1 563,972	26	1.463,997	68	8.789,804	
GRAND TOTAL		1 830,578	88	1.588,234	07	1.459.500	29	1 618,315	64	1.577.777	95	1.471.699	81	9.546.106	64

EXHIBIT "C."

CASH RECEIPTS FROM JULY, 1st., TO DECEMBER, 31st., 1901

TOTAL BY FUNDS		CUSTOMS		POSTAL		INTERNAL REVENUE		MISCELLANEOUS		REPAYMENTS		MONEY ORDER FUNDS		DISB. OFFICERS FUNDS		TOTAL	
FISCAL YEAR AND MONTH		Dollars	Cts	Dollars	Cts	Dollars	Cts	Dollars	Cts	Dollars	Cts	Dollars	Cts	Dollars	Cts	Dollars	Cts
Fiscal year 1900	July									7.553	46					7.553	46
	August							122	49	353	24					475	73
	September									13	97					13	97
	October									80	56					80	56
	November									175	49					175	49
	December										50						50
	TOTAL							122	49	8.177	22					8.299	71
Fiscal year 1901	July	110.518	85	12.543	46	3.853	47	516	00	524.270	56					651.702	34
	August			27	00			2.264	13	46 584	75					48.875	88
	September			15	62					18.629	29					18.644	91
	October			9	35					7.438	62					7.447	97
	November							14	00	13.616	20					13.630	20
	December									7.701	63					7.701	63
	TOTAL	110.518	85	12.595	43	3.853	47	2.794	13	618.241	05					748.002	93
Fiscal year 1902	July	1.095,746	10	12.417	03	50.785	84	11 902	11	472	00					1.171,323	08
	August	1.134.146	58	28.070	96	60.792	17	10.237	26	2.481	59	189.798	16	113.355	74	1.538,882	46
	September	1.257,807	54	32.606	23	59.304	55	12.278	50	11.849	12	41 900	54	25.094	93	1.440,841	41
	October	1.412,259	12	27.753	88	57.928	21	16 998	21	8.425	87	87.000	00	423	82	1.610,787	11
	November	1.356,913	80	30.738	98	58.136	73	23.428	57	16 640	01	78.000	00	114	17	1.563.972	26
	December	1.225,432	56	35.874	30	53.694	93	27.411	06	36.536	58	85.033	25	15	00	1.463,997	68
	TOTAL	7.482.305	70	167 461	38	340.640	43	102.255	71	76 405	17	481 731	95	139.003	66	8.789,804	00
GRAND TOTAL		7 592,824	55	180.056	81	344 493	90	105.172	33	702.823	44	481.731	95	139 003	66	9.546 106	64

EXHIBIT "D"

WARRANTS PAID FROM JULY 1st., TO DECEMBER 31st., 1901.

		July		August		September		October		November		December		TOTAL	
		Dollars	Cts.	Dollars	Cts.	Dollars	Cts.	Dollars	Cts.	Dollars	Cts.	Dollars	Cts.	Dollars	Cts.
Accountable and Settlement Warrants	Revenues	1.158,469	78	2.145,929	55	882,292	03	2.084,612	06	1.391,949	66	1.603,071	34	9.266,324	42
	Money order Funds	....	....	141,951	90	65,000	....	70,000	....	105,000	....	40,000	....	421,951	90
	Disb. Offic. Funds	....	....	50,000	. ..	50.000	....	37,916	62	620	65	....	....	138,537	27
	Total . . .	1.158,469	78	2.337,881	45	997,292	03	2.192,528	68	1.497,570	31	1.643,071	34	9.826,813	59

EXHIBIT "E"

LOSSES SUSTAINED FROM SALES OF FOREIGN GOLD

DATE OF SALE		CHARACTER AND U. S. CURRENCY VALUATION OF COINS						TOTAL VALUATION		RECEIVED IN EXCHANGE		LOSS	
Month	Day	Centenes	Dollars	Cts.	Luises	Dollars	Cts.	Dollars	Cts.	Dollars	Cts.	Dollars	Cts.
August.	10	20,849	4	82	½	3	86	100,494	11	99,998	94	495	17
,,	14	1,709	4	82	½	3	86	8,239	31	8,198	94	40	37
,,	14	4,167	4	82	½	3	86	20 086	87	19,999	72	87	15
,,	14	20,848	4	82	2	3	86	100,495	08	99,999	88	495	20
,,	15	......	......	......	13,030½	3	86	50.297	73	49,999	32	298	41
,,	16	3,126	4	82	1½	3	86	15 073	11	14,999	16	73	95
,,	17	20,849	4	82	......	......	......	100,492	18	99,999	70	492	48
,,	19	3,126	4	82	1½	3	86	15 073	11	14,999	16	73	95
,,	20	1,876	4	82	½	3	86	9,044	25	8,999	92	44	33
,,	21	1,042	4	82	½	3	86	5,024	37	4,999	72	24	65
,,	21	2,084	4	82	1	3	86	10 048	74	9,999	44	49	30
,,	22	6,884	4	82	1	3	86	33,184	74	32,999	44	185	30
TOTAL......	......	86,560	......	......	13,040	......	......	467,553	60	465,193	34	2,360	26
September.	3	14,000	4	78	}	......	......	100,159	72	99,999	80	159	92
,,	3	6,896	4	82									
,,	27	* 104,000	4	82	......	......	......	501.280	......	498,820	06	2,459	94
TOTAL......	......	124,896	......	......	......	......	......	601 439	72	598,819	86	2,619	86
October.	17	54,759	4	78	10,000½	3	83	300 049	93	299,999	83	50	10
,,	29	* 40,491	4	82	* 78,430	3	86	} 507,481	42	505,046	38	2,435	04
,,	29	......	......	......	* 2,500	3	83						
TOTAL......	......	95,250	......	......	90,930½	......	......	807,531	35	805,046	21	2,485	14
Grand Total.	......	306,706	......	......	103,970½	......	......	1.876 524	67	1.869,059	41	7,465	26

EXHIBIT "F"

RECEIPTS AND PAYMENTS FOR THE CALENDAR YEAR 1901.

	CUSTOMS		POSTAL		INTERNAL REVENUE		MISCELLANEOUS		REPAYMENTS		MONEY ORDER FUNDS		DISB OFFICERS FUNDS		TOTAL RECEIPTS		TOTAL PAYMENTS	
	Dollars	Cts	Dollars	Cts	Dollars	Cts	Dollars	Cts	Dollars	Cts	Dollars	Cts	Dollars	Cts	Dollars	Cts	Dollars	Cts
January	1.259,282	84	38,411	94	45,429	73	40,406	29	69,989	97	....	...	....	...	1 453,520	77	1.363,454	21
February	1.302,462	41	31,514	04	77,646	98	19,490	34	77,682	51	....	...	....	...	1.508,826	28	1.406,332	32
March	1 477,298	83	31,604	36	59 587	55	20,943	39	46,599	36	....	..	....	...	1.636 033	49	1.912,489	41
April	1.405,251	66	29,704	29	55,209	87	32,823	04	36,386	05	....	..	....	...	1.559,374	91	1.361,609	12
May	1.285,086	37	28,749	23	60,771	56	22,851	16	93,920	82	....	...	....	...	1.491,379	14	1.264,305	73
June	1.265 358	49	30.725	38	49.969	10	26,305	15	60,467	34	....	...	....	...	1.432,845	46	2.222,739	80
July	1.206,264	95	24,960	49	54,639	31	12,418	11	532,296	02	....	...	....	...	1.830,578	88	1.158,469	78
August	1.134,146	58	28 097	96	60,792	17	12,623	88	49,419	58	189.798	16	113.355	74	1.588,234	07	2 337,881	45
September	1.257,807	54	32.621	85	59,304	55	12 278	50	30,492	38	41,900	54	25,094	93	1.459,500	29	997,292	03
October	1.412,259	12	27,763	23	57,926	21	16,998	21	15,945	05	87 000	00	423	82	1 618.315	64	2.192,528	68
November	1.356,913	80	30,738	98	58,136	73	23,442	57	30,431	70	78,000	00	114	17	1.577,777	95	1.497,570	31
December	1 225.432	56	35.874	30	53,694	93	27,411	06	44.238	71	85,033	25	15	00	1.471.699	81	1.643,071	34
TOTAL	15.587,565	15	370,796	05	693.108	69	267,991	70	1.087,889	49	481.731	95	139,003	66	18.628,086	69	19.357,744	18

EXHIBIT "G"

REVENUES AS REPORTED BY COLLECTORS FROM JULY 1st., 1901 TO DECEMBER 31st. 1901.

Source.	Port or Zone	July Dollars	July Cts.	August Dollars	August Cts.	September Dollars	September Cts.	October Dollars	October Cts	November Dollars	November Cts.	December Dollars	December Cts	TOTAL Dollars	TOTAL Cts.
CUSTOMS RECEIPTS.	Baracoa	1,255	91	1,902	62	2,828	47	1,684	04	1,027	91	1,811	76	10,510	71
	Batabanó	175	75	146	78	161	08	82	95	83	21	107	67	757	39
	Caibarién	19,223	40	16,200	86	8,226	27	23,035	72	20 548	78	17,438	37	104,673	40
	Cárdenas	30,786	33	34,769	24	29,716	97	35,277	11	31 265	09	30,570	50	192.385	24
	Cienfuegos	110,161	39	97,451	42	97,864	54	124,224	68	132,292	12	130,395	50	692,389	65
	Gibara	40,151	70	38,386	28	24,135	42	33,162	39	18.900	96	33,800	20	188,536	95
	Guantánamo	12,724	23	13,904	24	8,302	30	9,519	62	12,635	38	12,469	50	69,555	27
	Havana	847,156	67	869.776	53	793,608	32	1 026,871	41	900,638	54	824,160	77	5 262,212	24
	Júcaro	5,218	04	2,092	98	2,531	80	55	05	5,307	45	11,031	91	26,237	23
	Manzanillo	16,634	60	38,034	45	24.101	87	26,983	24	19,720	36	14 224	19	139,698	71
	Matanzas	38,895	13	43,661	44	31,947	46	41,493	08	38,461	17	47,833	86	242,292	14
	Nuevitas	12,562	78	17.307	79	15,620	26	25,653	80	30,683	94	17.452	48	119,281	05
	Sagua la Grande	18,966	58	8,275	21	11,808	98	12,383	71	11,425	21	15,441	02	78,295	71
	Sta. Cruz del Sur.	54	35	2,883	09	173	05	11	09	155	78	436	18	3,713	54
	Santiago	92 582	27	84,249	76	84,646	35	77,370	70	84,185	35	108,143	32	581,177	75
	Trinidad	1,164	61	630	81	3,161	57	3,869	03	1,348	89	85	65	10,260	56
	Tunas de Zaza	654	01	1,168	32	2,434	32	51	35	2,806	11	218	05	7 332	16
	TOTAL	1 248 367	75	1.270,841	82	1.141,263	98	1.441,728	97	1,311,486	25	1,265,620	93	7.679,309	70
POSTAL RECEIPTS.	Postal Receipts	24 960	49	28,097	96	26,521	89	27,763	23	31,070	28	29,907	55	168 321	40
	TOTAL	24,960	49	28,097	96	26,521	89	27,763	23	31,070	28	29,907	55	168 321	40

EXHIBIT "G"

REVENUES AS REPORTED BY COLLECTORS FROM JULY, 1, 1901 TO DECEMBER 31, 1901.

Source	Port or Zone	July Dollars	July Cts	August Dollars	August Cts	September Dollars	September Cts.	October Dollars	October Cts	November Dollars	November Cts.	December Dollars	December Cts	TOTAL Dollars	TOTAL Cts.
INTERNAL REVENUE RECEIPTS.	Cárdenas	2,092	65	3,479	87	841	33	2 997	80	2,089	11	3,535	32	15,036	08
	Cienfuegos	1,529	31	2 432	80	15,170	64	3,115	80	1,761	01	1,416	08	25,425	64
	Guanajay	549	48	347	31	1,073	24	1,274	88	1,007	06	591	90	4.843	82
	Havana	38,705	23	38,964	36	21,234	66	34,190	29	36,549	99	38,923	96	208,568	49
	Holguín	1,039	88	3,610	04	3,576	18	311	15	1,056	35	819	32	10 412	92
	Manzanillo	685	93	1,279	87	287	30	444	77	519	09	503	55	3.720	51
	Matanzas	6,837	05	2,778	48	3,465	31	2,081	04	3,091	25	1,095	82	19,348	95
	Pinar del Río	1,289	60	1,700	04	1,817	67	2,280	57	783	29	689	18	8,560	35
	Puerto Príncipe	1,409	25	2,462	56	1,507	20	1,561	97	5,900	08	1,241	65	14,082	71
	Santa Clara	4,360	86	4,732	06	1,996	20	2,190	31	2 065	62	3,635	06	18,980	11
	Santiago	3,760	42	2,608	69	3,848	82	4,674	79	2 404	64	3,345	17	20,63 2	53
	TOTAL	62,259	61	64,391	08	54,813	55	55,123	37	57,227	49	55,797	01	349,612	11
MISCELLANEOUS RECEIPTS.	Captains of the Port	259	00	157	00	174	00	147	50	99	00	105	00	941	50
	Telegraph Line	6,990	89	6.867	13	6,506	68	7,225	29	3,039	64	8,177	37	38.807	00
	Other Sources	5,168	22	5,599	75	4.497	82	9,625	42	20,303	93	19,025	71	64,220	85
	TOTAL	12 418	11	12.623	88	11,178	50	16,998	21	23,442	57	27 308	08	103,969	35
	GRAND TOTAL	1,348,005	96	1.375,954	74	1.233,777	92	1,541,613	78	1,428,226	59	1,378,688	57	8.301,212	56

EXHIBIT "H"

COMPARISON OF REVENUES FOR THE CALENDAR YEARS 1900 AND 1901.

Source.	Port or Zone	Calendar Year 1900 — Jan. to June — Dollars	Cts.	July to Dec. — Dollars	Cts.	TOTAL — Dollars	Cts.	Calendar Year 1901 — Jan. to June — Dollars	Cts.	July to Dec. — Dollars	Cts.	TOTAL — Dollars	Cts.	Gain or Loss + — Dollars	Cts.
Customs Receipts.	Baracoa	18,023	87	9,678	94	27,707	81	14,570	76	10,510	71	25,081	47	— 2,626	34
	Batabanó	2,064	85	1,065	07	3,139	92	1 292	17	757	39	2,049	56	— 1,090	36
	Caibarién	97,545	69	104,052	84	201,598	53	123,864	33	104,673	40	228.537	73	+ 26,939	20
	Cárdenas	159,894	98	141,568	75	301,463	73	139,941	43	192,385	24	332.326	67	+ 30.862	94
	Cienfuegos	558,682	82	609,790	72	1.168,473	54	687,389	09	692,389	65	1 379,778	74	+ 211,305	20
	Gibara	84,177	16	153,539	65	237,716	81	158,114	97	188,536	95	346,651	92	+ 108,935	11
	Guantánamo	57,248	80	70,295	07	127,543	87	76,958	73	69,555	27	146,514	...	+ 18,970	13
	Havana	6.145,222	11	5.923,176	94	12.068,399	05	5.615,772	54	5.262,212	24	10.877,984	78	—11.90,414	27
	Júcaro	....	...	....	...	....	...	4,860	49	26,237	23	31,097	72	+ 31,097	72
	Manzanillo	76,890	07	98,850	98	175.741	05	132.792	51	139,698	71	272,491	22	+ 96 750	17
	Matanzas	241,027	35	215,895	95	456,923	30	256,767	84	242,292	14	499'059	98	+ 42,136	68
	Nuevitas	85,028	81	95,334	88	180,363	69	90,519	20	119,281	05	209,800	25	+ 29,436	56
	Sagua la Grande	109,139	27	95,478	26	204,617	53	96,451	45	78,295	71	174,747	16	— 29 870	37
	Santa Cruz del Sur	2,646	25	1,901	13	4,547	38	3,436	16	3,713	54	7,149	70	+ 2,602	32
	Santiago	468,102	..	483,812	82	951,914	82	554,616	33	531,177	75	1.085,794	08	+ 133,879	26
	Trinidad	15,016	35	7,111	65	22,128	...	8,343	12	10,260	56	18,603	68	— 3,524	32
	Tunas de Zaza	697	10	3,547	15	4,244	25	12,616	02	7,332	16	19,948	18	+ 15,703	93
	TOTAL	8.121,412	48	8.015.110	80	16 136.523	28	7.978 807	14	7.679,309	70	15 657 616	84	— 478,906	44
Postal Receipts.	Postal Receipts	136,015	43	185,524	19	321,539	62	190,789	24	168,321	40	359,060	64	+ 37,521	02
	TOTAL	136,015	43	185,524	19	321,539	62	190.739	24	168.321	40	359,060	64	+ 37,521	02

EXHIBIT "H"

Comparison of revenues for the Calendar Years 1900 and 1901.—Continued.

Source.	Por ot Zone	Calendar Year 1900 Jan. to June Dollars	Cts.	July to Dec. Dollars	Cts.	TOTAL Dollars	Cts.	Calendar Year 1901 Jan. to June Dollars	Cts.	July to Dec. Dollars	Cts.	TOTAL Dollars	Cts.	Gain or Loss — + Dollars	Cts.
Internal Revenue Receipts	Cárdenas	...	...	17,937	96	17,937	96	9,863	48	15,036	08	24,899	56	+ 6,961	60
	Cienfuegos	...	...	11,934	28	11,934	28	17,085	69	25,425	64	42,511	33	+ 30,577	05
	Guanajay	...	...	5,061	57	5,061	57	3,828	22	4,843	82	8,672	04	+ 3,610	47
	Havana	279,899	86	218,876	75	498,776	61	228,335	04	208,568	49	436,903	53	— 61,873	08
	Holguín	...	...	5,399	43	5,399	43	6,529	13	10,412	92	16,942	05	+ 11,542	62
	Manzanillo	...	...	3,651	20	3,651	20	5,336	43	3,720	51	9,056	94	+ 5,405	74
	Matanzas	79,727	87	11,836	98	91,564	85	15,519	52	19,348	95	34,868	47	— 56,696	38
	Pinar del Rio	15,133	22	7,189	55	22,322	77	6,671	40	8,560	35	15,231	75	— 7,091	02
	Puerto Príncipe	16,588	90	9,334	35	25,923	25	11,257	32	14,082	71	25,340	03	— 583	22
	Santa Clara	48,469	84	11,348	13	59,817	97	23,496	98	18,980	11	42,477	09	— 17.340	88
	Santiago	33,767	14	22,481	31	56,248	45	16.344	16	20,632	53	36,976	69	— 19,271	76
	Total	473,586	83	325,051	51	798,638	34	344,267	37	349,612	11	693,879	48	— 104,758	86
Miscellaneous Receipts	Captains of the Port	...	...	183	62	183	62	1,217	28	941	50	2,158	78	+ 1,975	16
	Telegraph Line	32,115	79	34,718	40	66,834	19	44,023	71	38,807	...	82,830	71	+ 15,996	52
	Other Sources	48,206	30	33,467	76	81,674	06	117.472	38	64,220	85	181,693	23	+ 100,019	17
	Total	80,322	09	68,369	78	148,691	87	162,713	37	103,969	35	266,682	72	+ 117,990	85
		8.811,336	83	8.594 056	28	17.405,393	11	8.676,027	12	8.301,212	56	16.977,239	68	— 428,153	43

JUSTIFICANTES

ADJUNTOS AL INFORME SEMESTRAL

DEL

TESORERO DE CUBA

QUE COMPRENDE DESDE

el 1º de Julio á 31 de Diciembre de 1901.

AÑO FISCAL DE 1902

TESORERIA DE CUBA

Habana, Cuba, Diciembre 31 de 1902.

Al Ayudante General del Departamento de Cuba.

Habana, Cuba.

Señor:

En cumplimiento de las instrucciones contenidas en su comunicación de Noviembre 9, tengo el honor de presentar este informe, relativo á las operaciones verificadas por este Departamento, desde el 1º de Julio de 1901 hasta el 31 de Diciembre de 1901.

En este Informe, según ha sido costumbre, se considera dividido el Departamento de Tesorería de Cuba en tres partes que son:

Departamento de Tesorería.
Departamento de Pagaduría,
y
Departamento de Trasportes.

Cada uno de estos Departamentos es tratado separadamente, distinguiendo las sub-divisiones según lo hizo el Inspector General del Departamento de Cuba, al dar cuenta en su Informe de 20 de Junio de 1901, de su última inspección, del sistema y del personal de esta Tesorería de Cuba.

Para obtener el montante exacto de las Rentas durante el período de referencia se observará igual sistema que en el precedente informe de esta Oficina, por el semestre que terminó el 30 de Junio de 1901, á saber:

Que cuando se hace referencia á las entradas totales y líquidas ó Rentas recibidas por el Tesorero de Cuba durante el Año Económico de 1902, se incluye todo lo ingresado perteneciente al Gobierno Insular, prescindiendo de los años económicos á que pertenecen, pero en los libros aparecen anotados á sus respectivos años económicos. El total de los depósitos recibidos en esta Tesorería durante el Año Económico de 1902, aunque incluye los ingresos pertenecientes á los años económicos de 1899, 1900 y 1901, será la suma de referencia como total recibido durante el Año Económico de 1902, en el tiempo que cubre este informe y la Renta líquida del Año Económico de 1902, en el período comprendido por este Informe se obtendrá deduciendo todos los reintegros recibidos durante el periodo á que este Informe se contrae.

El 30 de Junio de 1901 este Departamenro tenía en Caja un saldo efectivo de.........., según demuestra el Estado "A" de este Informe.		$ 1,398,501.74
El efectivo recibido desde Julio 1º á Diciembre 31 de 1901 ha sido de.....................		9,546,106.64
Total..		$10,944,608.38
Los egresos durante el mismo periodo fueron........ según demuestra el Estado "A."	$9.826,813.59	
Las pérdidas por venta de Oro Extranjero................. como demuestra el mismo Estado.	7,465.26	
Total..		$ 9,834,278.85
Dejando en Caja al cerrarse las operaciones el 31 de Diciembre de 1901 un saldo en efectivo de..		$ 1,110,329.53

Como se expresó en el precedente Informe del Tesorero, correspondiente al periodo de Enero 1º á Junio 30 de 1901, todos los desembolsos de Fondos Insulares han sido cargados á Rentas y no á los diversos fondos de "Aduanas," "Correos," "Rentas Interiores" y "Miscelánea," pero la Tesorería continúa anotando bajo tales denominaciones, todos los Ingresos.

La parte restante del Estado "A" demuestra reducido á moneda de los Estados Unidos la clase de moneda que queda en depósito en poder de los diversos depositaríos de Fondos Insulares, así como en poder del Cajero de este Departamento, cuyas sumas al cerrar las operaciones el 31 de Diciembre de 1901 daban un saldo en las Rentas de....	$ 1,110,329.53

ESTADO COMPARATIVO DE LAS RENTAS DURANTE LOS AÑOS COMUNES DE 1900 Y 1901, SEGUN LOS INFORMES DE LOS ADMINISTRADORES.

Como estos datos están tomados de los informes mensuales recibidos de los Administradores, dando cuenta de solo las Rentas por ellos recibidas, no aparecerá en esta comparación ningún reintegro.

Renta total del año común de 1900, según el Estado "H" de este Informe.............		$17,405,393.11
Renta total del año común de 1901, según el antedicho Estado............................		16,977,239.68
Disminución en la Renta en el Año Común de 1901, comparado con el Año Común de 1900..		$ 428,153.43
El Estado "H" de este Informe bajo su respectiva cuenta demuestra una disminución en los Ingresos de Aduana de.............		478,906.44
Las Rentas Interiores demuestran una disminución de...		104,758.86
Las Rentas Postales demuestran un aumento de	$ 37,521.02	
Los Ingresos por Miscelánea un aumento de..........	117,990.85	
Resulta un total de disminuciones de...		$ 583,665.30
y un total de aumento de	$ 155,511.87	
ó sea una disminución total en la renta de...		428,153.43

según más arriba se indica.

ESTADO COMPARATIVO DE LOS INGRESOS EN EFECTIVO DURANTE EL PRIMER SEMESTRE DEL AÑO ECONÓMICO DE 1902 CON IGUALES PERIODOS DEL AÑO ECONÓMICO DE 1901.

Efectivo recibido desde el 1º de Julio al 31 de Diciembre de 1900............................ según el Estado 2 "A" del Informe del Tesorero referente á tal periodo.	$ 9,381,961.42
Efectivo recibido desde el 1º de Julio al 31 de Diciembre de 1901, según el Estado "B" de este Informe..	9,546,106.64
Aumento en el efectivo recibido en el Primer Semestre del Año Económico de 1902, comparado con igual periodo del Año Económico de 1901..	$ 164,145.22

Comparacion del 2º semestre del año economico de 1901

Total en efectivo recibido del 1º de Enero al 30 de Junio de 1901.............................. según el Estado "E" del Informe del Tesorero por dicho periodo.	$ 9,081,980.05
Efectivo recibido en el primer semestre del Año Económico de 1902............................ según el Estado "B" de este informe.	9,546,106.64
Aumento en el efectivo recibido en el primer Semestre del Año Económico de 1902, comparado con el último Semestre del Año Económico de 1901......................................	$ 464,126.59

Estado comparativo de los ingresos liquidos durante el primer semestre del año económico de 1902 con los semestres del año económico de 1901.

Total efectivo recibido desde el 1º de Julio al 31 de Diciembre de 1900....... según demuestra el Estado 2 "A" del Informe del Tesorero en dicho período.	$ 9,381,961.42	
Reintegros.................... según el mismo Estado.	737,147.52	
Ingresos Líquidos del primer Semestre del Año Económico de 1901........................		$ 8,644,813.90
Total recibido en efectivo en el Primer Semestre del año Económico de 1902.............................. según el Estado "C" de este imforme.	$9.546,106.64	
Reintegros....................... como se demuestra en el mismo Estado.	702,823.44	
Ingresos líquidos del Primer Semestre del Año Económico de 1902............................		$ 8,843,283.20
Aumento en los ingresos líquidos del Primer Semestre del Año Económico de 1902 comparado con el Primer Semestre del Año Económico de 1901..		$ 198,469.30

COMPARACIÓN DEL ULTIMO SEMESTRE DEL AÑO ECONÓMICO DE 1901

Total recibido de Enero 1º á Junio 30 del Año de 1901..................... .... según el Estado "E" del informe del Tesorero por dicho periodo.	$9,081,980.05	
Reintegros........................	$ 385,066.05	
como se demuestra por el mismo Estado.		
Ingresos líquidos en el 2º Semestre del Año Económico de 1901....................................		$ 8,696,914.00
Ingresos líquidos en el Primer Semestre del Año Económico de 1902............................		8,843,283.20
Aumento en los Ingresos líquidos en el Primer Semestre del año económico de 1902, comparados con los del último Semestre del Año Económico de 1901............................		$ 146,369.20

ESTADO COMPARATIVO DE LOS INGRESOS Y EGRESOS DURANTE EL AÑO COMUN DE 1901.

Total de egresos en el Año Común de 1901, según el Estado "F" de este Informe.	$19,357,744.18
Total de Ingresos en el Año Común de 1901 según el mismo Estado......................	18,628,086.69
Los egresos han excedido á los ingresos durante el Año Común de 1901 en la suma de..	$ 729,657.49

ESTADO COMPARATIVO DE LOS EGRESOS EN EL PRIMER SEMESTRE DEL AÑO ECONÓMICO DE 1902 CON LOS SEMESTRES DE 1901.

Total de egresos desde el 1º de Julio al 30 de Diciembre de 1900.................................. según el Estado "3" del Informe del Tesorero por dicho período.	$10,236,562.89
Total de Egresos del 1º de Julio al 31 de Diciembre de 1901 según el Estado "D" de este Informe...........	9,826,813.59
Disminución en los Egresos durante el Primer Semestre del Año Económico de 1902, comparado con los Egresos del Primer Semestre del Año Económico de 1901..	$ 409,749.30

ESTADO COMPARATIVO DEL ULTIMO SEMESTRE DEL AÑO ECONÓMICO DE 1901.

Total de Egresos del 1º de Enero al 30 de Junio de 1901.. según el Estado "E" del informe del Tesorero por dicho período.	$ 9,530,930.59
Egresos durante el Primer Semestre del Año Económico de 1902 según arriba se indica..	9,826,813.59
Aumento en los egresos en el Primer Semestre del Año Económico de 1902, comparado con los egresos del último Semestre del Año Económico de 1901........................	$ 295,883.00

El Estado "C" de este Informe contiene los mismos datos que el Estado "B," con la diferencia de que en el Estado "B" los totales de los Ingresos se demuestran por años económicos por encabezamientos y meses, mientras que en el Estado "C" aparece el importe total de lo recaudado bajo sus respectivos encabezamientos por el período que comprende este Informe de Julio 1º á Diciembre 31 de 1901.

El Estado "D" demuestra el total de la suma pagada por Libramientos corrientes y de liquidación y cargados á sus respectivas cuentas. Rentas, Fondos de Giros Postales, y Fondos de Oficiales Pagadores. De estos fondos últimamente mencionados se lleva una cuenta separada por ser fondos depositados en Tesorería para fines especiales y no figuran bajo ningún concepto como rentas disponibles. Este Departamento prácticamente asume la posición de un depositario del Departamento de Correos en lo que se refiere á la cuenta de Fondos de Giros Postales cuyos fondos son depositados en esta Tesorería de Cuba para el pago de Giros Postales: sucediendo lo mismo con la cuenta de Fondos de Oficiales Pagadores, que consiste en un depósito efectuado en esta Tesorería para atender á los checks que quedaron pendientes de pago y girados contra la North American Truts Co. al cerrar las operaciones el 16 de Agosto de 1901, en cuya fecha se dispuso que todos los Fondos acreditados á Oficiales Pagadores de Fondos Insulares (así como todos los Fondos acreditados al Tesorero de Cuba) fueran depositados en este Departamento.

El Estado "E" demuestra las fechas de las ventas de Oro Extrangero efectuadas por este Departamento durante el período de Julio 1º á Diciembre 31 de 1901 significando la clase de moneda y su valor en moneda corriente de los Estados Unidos. Las pérdidas sufridas en dichas ventas según se demuestra en este Estado alcanzan á $7,465.26. Teniendo en cuenta esta pérdida sufrida por la venta de Oro

Extrangero, el Tesorero de Cuba vió claramente que se debía tomar una determinación referente á los valores fijados por la Circular Nº 2 de la División de Aduanas y Asuntos Insulares de fecha 4 de Enero de 1899, que fijaba el tipo oficial del centén en $4.82 y el del luis $3.86. Este oro extrangero no siempre podía ser vendido en plaza al tipo á que es recibido en pago de contribuciones, derechos de Aduanas, etc., 1.0995 por un centen y 1.0984 por un luis, y si se le remitía á los Estados Unidos para acuñarlo la pérdida resultaba mayor que vendiéndolo aquí. La Orden Nº 229 del Cuartel General de la División de Cuba fechada Junio 4 de 1900 dispone que todos los pagos de deudas insulares se verifiquen en moneda de los Estados Unidos, en consecuencia resulta necesario para el Tesorero en diferentes ocasiones, el convertir una gran cantidad de Oro Extrangero en moneda de los Estados Unidos, para poder cumplimentar dicha orden. El asunto era de tal importancia que el Tesorero consideró indispensable el tomar una determinación sobre el particular para proteger al Gobierno contra las grandes pérdidas sufridas en la venta ó embargo para la reacuñación del Oro Extrangero á que se hace referencia y después de haber estudiado debidamente el asunto, recomendó al Gobernador Militar de Cuba una reducción en el valor que á las piezas de oro, centén y luis se les marcaba en la Circular Nº 2 de la División de Aduanas y Asuntos Insulares de Enero 4 de 1899, cuya recomendación fué atendida por el Gobernador Militar de Cuba y á su solicitud fué modificada dicha Orden por el Presidente de los Estados Unidos, en la forma siguiente:

Nº 193:—Cuartel General del Departamento de Cuba, Habana, Agosto 21 de 1901.—Por disposición del Gobernador Militar de Cuba se publica para conocimiento y guía de los interesados la siguiente Orden del Presidente de los Estados Unidos—Palacio del Poder Ejecutivo, Agosto 19 de 1901. Por la presente se dispone que la orden del Poder Ejecutivo de Diciembre 28 de 1898 en la parte que fija el tipo al cual el alfonsino español (centén) y el luis francés, deben ser aceptados en pago de derechos de Aduanas, contribuciones é impuestos públicos y de correos en la Isla de Cuba, se modifica para que diga así:

Alfonsino (pieza de 25 pesetas)...	$ 4.78
Luis (pieza de 20 francos)...........	3.83

William McKinley,

H. L. Scott,

Ayudante General.

Desde la promulgación de esta Orden, este Departamento ha estado capacitado para hacer, cuando así lo ha creido oportuno, ventas de Oro Extrangero, con la autorización del Gobernador Militar de Cuba, de manera que las ventas de este Oro recibido al nuevo tipo (con una sola excepción) en el período de Agosto 21 de 1901 á Diciembre 31 de 1901 han resultado beneficiosas.

Durante dicho período este Departamento ha vendido $1,105,233.98 con una ganancia de $1,123.41 por los cuales el Tesorero ha expedido los correspondientes recibos en la forma regular.

El Estado "F" de este Informe demuestra el total de ingresos y egresos del año común de 1901. Los ingresos están demostrados por meses bajo sus respectivos encabezamientos dando el total mensual recibido de todas fuentes para cada uno de los meses comprendidos en este Estado y el ingreso total durante el período á que este Estado se contrae.

La demostración es como sigue:

El total de ingresos demuestra ser...............	$18,628,086.69
el de los Egresos mensuales demuestra ser...	19,357,744.18
cuyo exceso sobre los ingresos es de............	$ 729,657.49

ESTADO COMPARATIVO DE LOS INGRESOS LIQUIDOS RECIBIDOS POR EL TESORO EN EL PRIMER SEMESTRE DEL AÑO ECONÓMICO DE 1902 CON LA RECAUDACION DE RENTAS, SEGUN LOS INFORMES DE LOS ADMINISTRADORES DURANTE LOS SEMESTRES DEL AÑO ECONÓMICO DE 1901.

Total recibido en efectivo de Julio 1º á Diciembre 31 de 1900......................................	$ 9,381,961.42
según el Estado "2" A del Informe del Tesorero por dicho periodo.	
Reintegros..	737,147.52
según aparecen en dicho Estado.	
Ingresos Líquidos durante el Primer Semestre del Año Económico de 1901............	$ 8,644,813.90
Total de las Rentas según los informes de los Administradores de Julio 1º á Diciembre 31 de 1901, según el Estado "G" de este informe..	8.301,212.56
Lo cual demuestra que fueron mayores en..	$ 343,601.34

los ingresos líquidos en el Primer Semestre del Año Económico de 1901, que los avisados por los Administradores en el Primer Semestre del Año Económico de 1902.

Total efectivo recibido desde Enero 1º á Junio 30 de 1901, según el Estado "E" del

Informe del Tesorero que cubre dicho periodo................................ $ 9,081,980.05
Deduciendo los Reintegros................................ 385,066.05

Según se demuestra en el mismo Estado, queda

Líquido recibido en el Segundo Semestre del Año Económico de 1901........................ $ 8,696,914.00
comparado con las Rentas según los informes de los Administradores en el Primer Semestre del Año Económico de 1902............ 8,301,212.56
demuestra que los ingresos líquidos en el Segundo Semestre del Año Económico de 1901 fueron mayores en 395,701.44
que los avisados por los Administradores en el Primer Semestre del Año Económico de 1902.

Estado comparativo de la Recaudación de Rentas según los informes de los Administradores en el Primer Semestre del Año Económico de 1902, con las mismas durante los semestres del Año Económico de 1901.

Rentas según los informes de los Administradores de Julio 1º á Diciembre 31 de 1900 $ 8,594,056.28
según el Estado 11 del Tesorero por dicho periodo.
Rentas según los informes de los Administradores de Julio 1º á Diciembre 31 de 1901. 8,301,212.56

Disminución en las Rentas durante el Primer Semestre del Año Económico de 1902 comparado con igual periodo de 1901 292,844.72

Rentas según los informes de los Administradores del 1º de Enero al 30 de Junio de 1901.. $ 8,676,027.12
según el Estado "F" del Informe del Tesorero por dicho periodo.
Deduciendo la suma según los informes de los Administradores de Julio 1º á Diciembre 31 de 1901................ .... 8.301.212.56

Resulta una disminución en las Rentas de $ 374,814.56 según los informes de los Administradores en el Primer Semestre del Año Económico de 1902 comparado con el último Semestre del Año Económico de 1901.

Recapitulación de los Ingresos y Egresos durante los Semestres del Año Económico de 1901 y el Primer Semestre del Año Económico de 1902.

Saldo al cerrarse las operaciones el 30 de Junio de 1900	$ 2,702,053.75
Ingresos del 1º de Julio al 31 de Diciembre de 1900	9,381,961.42
Ingresos del 1º de Enero al 30 de Junio de 1901	9,081,980.05
Ingresos del 1º de Julio al 31 de Diciembre de 1901	9,546,106.64
Total de Ingresos	$30,712,101.86
Pagado de Julio 1º á Diciembre 31 de 1900	$10,236,562.89
Pagado de Enero 1º á Junio 30 de 1901	9,530,930.59
Pagado de Julio 1º á Diciembre 31 de 1901	9,834,278.85
Total de Egresos	$29,601,772.33
Total de Ingresos según la demostración que antecede	$30,712,101.86
Total de Egresos id. id. id.	29,601,772.33
Saldo al cerrarse las operaciones el 21 de Diciembre de 1901	$ 1,110,329.53

En esta suma están incluidas las pérdidas en las ventas de Oro Extrangero como lo demuestra el Estado "E" de este Informe.

Para llegar á un cálculo aproximado del efectivo disponible perteneciente al Gobierno Militar de los Estados Unidos en Cuba, el 31 de Diciembre de 1901, se presenta la siguiente relación:

Saldo en efectivo según el Estado "A" de este Informe	$ 1,110,329.53
Cantidad que aparece al crédito de los Oficiales Pagadores en el Banco Nacional de Cuba según los informes de las respectivas sucursales de la Compañía el 31 de Diciembre de 1901	2,057,783.62
Cálculo aproximado del montante de las Rentas recaudadas en proceso de transmisión al Tesoro	200,000.00
Total	$ 3,368,113.15

El Estado "C" de este Informe demuestra el montante de las Rentas según los informes de los Administradores en los diversos puertos de la Isla durante el Primer Semestre del Año Económico de 1902. Estos informes han sido remitidos al Tesorero de Cuba por Estados Mensuales y por Telegramas de los Administradores al final de cada mes y se conservan en esa Oficina para fines estadísticos pero no como comprobantes oficiales.

Los Ingresos Líquidos de las Rentas de la Isla según Informe del Tesorero de 1º de Julio á 31 Diciembre de 1901, fueron............. $ 8,843,283.20

Las Rentas según informes de los Administradores durante el mismo período, como se demuestra en el Estado "C," han sido.... 8,301,212.56

lo que se aproxima mucho á la suma que demuestran los registros de esta Oficina.

La diferencia en estos informes se explica por la razón que los libros de esta Oficina demuestran exactamente la suma recibida por el Tesorero durante el periodo que cubre este Informe, mientras que los Informes demuestran la suma realmente recaudada por ellos durante el mismo periodo. El tiempo necesario para trasmitir fondos á esta Oficina ocasiona una diferencia al final de cada periodo de tiempo.

Como se deja dicho en este Informe este Departamento será considerado bajo las sub-divisiones indicadas por el Inspector General en su Informe de Inspección de Junio 20 de 1901 á saber: Departamento del Registro General, Departamento de Caja, Departamento de Pagaduría y Departamento de Trasportes.

DEPARTAMENTO DE REGISTRO GENERAL.

Se divide en tres secciones como sigue: Archivo, Teneduría de Libros y Confronta de Checks. En párrafo aparte se tratará de cada uno de estos sub-departamentos por separado, para de esa manera demostrar el sistema empleado en esta Tesorería.

ARCHIVO.

En este Departamento se archiva toda la correspondencia de esta Oficina, usando para ello el sistema de tarjetas; se lleva un índice completo de nombres y conceptos, reteniendo copia de todas las comunicaciones que pasan por estas Oficinas y traduciendo al Inglés y archivando también todas aquellas que se reciben escritas en Español.

DEPARTAMENTO DE TENEDURIA DE LIBROS.

En este Departamento se lleva cuenta de los ingresos recibidos en el Tesoro así como de los desembolsos hechos por libramientos emitidos por el Gobernador General y visados por el Auditor de Cuba.

DEPARTAMENTO DE CONFRONTA DE CHECKS.

A los Oficiales Pagadores se les provee de checks, á su petición, ya numerados, y se lleva nota de los mismos en un libro llamado "Registro de checks cancelados." Cuando los checks emitidos por dichos Oficiales Pagadores son recibidos de los diferentes Bancos sobre los cuales se han girado, se confrontan con dicho libro, el cual demuestra al fin de cada mes los checks que anteriormente se han girado, y que no han sido hechos efectivo por los Bancos, y los que aún tiene en su poder el Oficial Pagador y por los cuales es responsable.

Al ser relevados los Oficiales Pagadores remiten á la Tesorería los checks que aún no han usado ó los transfieren á sus sucesores mediante el correspondiente recibo. Los checks que por cualquier causa han sido inutilizados por estos Oficiales Pagadores se devuelven á Tesorería donde se archivan para constancia.

DEPARTAMENTO DE CAJA.

El sistema en voga referente á este Departamento es el siguiente: El Cajero hace su corte diariamente después de las operaciones del día y las confronta con los libros de la Tesorería. Al fin de cada mes el Tesorero, auxiliado por el Cajero, examina las bóvedas y confronta el total por las etiquetas en los sacos y paquetes; pero no cuenta el efectivo. Cada tres meses, el Inspector General gira su visita de inspección y cuenta el dinero en Caja.

Referente á la seguridad y cuidado del efectivo y valores de la Tesorería, tengo que decir que el efectivo y las fianzas se depositan en una caja grande de acero con cerradura-reloj, últimamente construída. La caja antigua que se usaba para el dinero en efectivo, se usa para asuntos diversos, habiendo además de ésta una caja pequeña destinada á las transacciones diarias de Caja.

Existe una Guardia suficiente en la Tesorería, día y noche, compuesta de soldados americanos de caballería y artillería, y de un destacamento de la Guardia Rural Cubana. No se le permite á ningún empleado de este Departamento entrar en el cuarto de la Caja fuera de las horas de Oficina.

El trabajo de la Tesorería se aumentó considerablemente durante estos últimos seis meses, debido á que la North American Trust Co. y sus sucursales fueron relevadas por el Departamento de la Guerra como Agentes Fiscales del Gobierno Militar de los Estados Unidos en Cuba, con fecha de Julio 18 de 1901, y durante un periodo de tiempo de tres semanas se cambió por completo la forma de hacer depósitos á la disposición de Oficiales Pagadores, haciéndose necesario que el Tesorero, por disposición del Gobernador Militar, asumiese una labor extraordinaria y responsabilidad en el embarque de fondos destinados á los Oficiales Pagadores, fuera de la Provincia de Santiago de Cuba, desde Julio 18 á Agosto 30 de 1901, lo cual se efectuaba bien por correspondencia certificada ó por expreso directamente á los Oficiales Pagadores á quienes se les instruía hicieran sus pagos en efectivo hasta tanto el Banco Nacional de Cuba prestase la garantía suficiente para actuar como Agente Fiscal del Gobierno Militar de los Estados Unidos en Cuba, lo que sucedió en Agosto 30 de 1901. Como durante dicho periodo de tiempo, á excepción de la Provincia de Santiago de Cuba, no existía Banco alguno donde pudieran hacerse los depósitos, los Administradores de Aduanas y Rentas, así como los Oficiales Pagadores, hacían estos depósitos remitiendo directamente al Tesorero de Cuba, bien por expreso ó por correo certificado, recayendo sobre esta Tesorería por lo menos, el trabajo de dos de las sucursales del North American Trust Co. habiendo este Departamento cumplido las exigencias de ese nuevo servicio durante el periodo de referencia á entera satisfacción de los Oficiales Pagadores y demás interesados. Esto no se refiere á la Provincia de Santiago, cuya sucursal prestó desde un principio, de acuerdo con las instrucciones del Gobernador Militar, la fianza necesaria, inmediatamente después de la retirada del North American Trust Co., como Agente Fiscal del Gobierno Militar de los Estados Unidos en Cuba, por valor de $485,000 en bonos consolidados del 2% de los Estados Unidos de 1930.

Al prestar fianza el Banco Nacional de Cuba, con fecha de Agosto 30 de 1901, se les ordenó á todos los Oficiales Pagadores depositasen en dicha institución los saldos en su poder, procedentes de fondos insulares, desde cuya época este Departamento ha seguido la misma rutina en sus operaciones como anteriormente, menos en lo que se relaciona con la liquidación de checks pendientes de pago contra la North American Trust Co.

CHECKS PENDIENTES DE PAGO.

Según instrucciones de esta Oficina fecha Agosto 3 de 1901, se le ordenó á todos los Oficiales Pagadores de Fondos Insulares (excepción hecha de los de la Provincia de Santiago donde se autorizó la transferencia de fondos) retirasen sus fondos del North American Trust Co. exceptuando el importe necesario para cubrir sus checks aún no pagados. Con fecha 16 de Agosto se le dieron instrucciones al North American Trust Co. y sucursales para que depositasen en la Tesorería de Cuba todas las cantidades en su poder que apareciesen al crédito de los diferentes Oficiales Pagadores y que se suponía perteneciente á ckecks aún no pagados y girados por dichos Oficiales Pagadores. También se recomendó á dicha institución bancaria depositase en la Tesorería de Cuba en la Habana, (excepción hecha en la Provincia de Santiago, donde se autorizó la transferencia) todos los fondos que hubiese en depósito al crédito oficial del Tesorero de Cuba. Con este motivo fueron entregadas por el North American Trust Co. las siguientes cantidades:

En Agosto 15, Sucursal de la Habana......	$	82,072.41
En Agosto 16, Sucursal de Santiago........		25,094.93
Agosto 16, Sucursal de Cienfuegos...........		17,960.39
Agosto 16, Sucursal de Cienfuegos por cuenta del Tesorero................................		953,29
Agosto 16, Sucursal de Mantanzas...........		12,369.65
Octubre 12, Sucursal de New York............		3.50
Depositado en Tesorería por cuenta de sobre-giros..		429.49
Seguridades pendientes............................		15.00
Reintegros..		105.00
Total recibido............................	$	139,003.66

De esta cantidad depositada en Tesorería se han consignado y puesto á la disposición del Oficial Pagador de la Tesorería la suma de $138,537.27, habiéndose también transferido la suma de $114.17 de la Oficina Central de Hacienda, haciendo un total de $138,651.44 para que el Pagador de la Tesorería, atendiese al pago de los checks aún pendientes de pago.

A cada Oficial Pagador con cuenta abierta en dicho Banco en Agosto 15 de 1901, se le exigió enviase al Tesoro de Cuba, una lista detallada de sus cheks aun por pagar, dando cuenta del número, fecha, nombre y cantidad de cada check (los Oficiales Pagadores que actualmente se hallan en Alaska, Puerto Rico y Filipinas y cuyos activos no están á mano aún no han dado cuenta de sus checks pendientes de pago). Sin embargo son muy pocos los que se encuentran en este caso y el importe total no excede de unos $400,00. Todas estas listas detalladas han sido encontradas de conformidad ó han sido corregidas ingresándose en un depósito adicional por aquellos pagadores, con la única excepción de Francisco González Garí, Tesorero Pagador de la Zona Fiscal de Guanajay, en cuya cuenta existe una pequeña diferencia entre el importe entregado por el Banco y el importe de las listas recibidas referentes á la cuenta de que se trata. Estos fondos han sido recibidos por esta Tesorería no como ingresos de las Rentas sino bajo el encabezamiento de Fondos de Oficiales Pagadores cuya cuenta se encontraba en las siguientes condiciones con fecha 31 de Diciembre de 1901.

Ingresos

De varias sucursales del Banco	$	138,454.17
Depositado en la Tesorería, cuenta sobregirada		429.49
Reintegro		105.00
Seguridades pendientes		15.00
Total recibido	$	139,003.66

Egresos

Consignado al pagador de la Tesorería según presupuesto del Tesorero	$	138,537.27		
Transferido por el pagador de la Tesorería al fondo de Oficiales Pagadores de la Oficina Central, Depto. de Hacienda		114.17		
Total recibido por el pagador de la Tesorería	$	138,651.44		
Saldo no consignado		466.39		
				139,117.83
Deduciendo el traspaso				114.17
Total recibido en Tesorería			$	139,003.66

Total de lo consignado y traspasado al pagador de la Tesorería por cuenta de Fondos de Oficiales Pagadores	$	138,651.44
Importe empleado en pago de checks pendientes		129,832.32
Saldo en poder del Pagador de la Tesorería		8,819.12

Como garantía para responder á los fondos en poder del North American Trust Co., referentes á la liquidación de checks aún pendientes, el Tesorero de Cuba les ha exigido y tiene en su poder como fianza, 250 bonos de 2ª hipoteca del Ayuntamiento de la Habana, de $100 cada uno ó séase $25,000.00.

Esta Tesorería ha abonado desde Julio 1º de 1901 hasta Diciembre 31 del mismo año, á la North American Trust Co. por concepto de comisiones la suma de $12,174.12 y $756.57 por seguro marítimo sobre embarques de oro extrangero para ser acuñado, á la casa de moneda de los Estados Unidos.

Los gastos de este Departamento durante el período comprendido desde Julio 1º á Diciembre 31 de 1901, han sido los siguientes:

Sueldos	$	15,202.08
Alquileres, hielo, gas, etc		1,199.26
Impresos y efectos de Escritorio		1,565.94
Muebles de Oficina		145.12
Alquileres de coches		162.24
Premios sobre fianzas de empleados de este Departamento		100.00
Manutención de la Guardia de la Tesorería		635.65

PAGADURIA

El Pagador de la Tesorería paga todas las cuentas de este Departamento, incluyendo todas las cuentas de fletes y de trasportes emitidas por empleados del Gobierno Insular á las varias empresas establecidas en esta Isla. También esta Oficina hace los pagos pertenecientes á la Oficina del Gobierna Militar y á todas aquellas cuentas especiales remitidas para su liquidación á esta Tesorería.

Los pagos de este Departamento desde Julio 1º hasta Diciembre 31 de 1901 han sido por cuenta de la Tesorería de Cuba $101,850.77 y por cuenta del Departamento de Cuba $790,648.61.

Los libros del Pagador de la Tesorería fueron inspeccionados por el Inspector General del Departamento de Cuba con fecha Diciembre 23 de 1901 inclusive y sus cuentas fueron encontradas de conformidad.

Los gastos de este Departamento de Julio 1º á Diciembre 31 de 1901 fueron:

Sueldos	$	3,367.83
Alquileres, hielo, gas, etc		762.04
Impresos y efectos de escritorio		170.00
Alquileres de coches		39.51

DEPARTAMENTO DE TRASPORTES

En este Departamento se reciben las cuentas de las varias empresas de pasajeros y de carga de la Isla las que vienen acompañadas de los conocimientos originales en caso de flete y por peticiones de pasaje cuando á pasajeros se refieren. Las cuentas son examinadas en este Departamento y anotadas, después de lo cual son remitidas debidamente certificadas al Pagador de la Tesorería para su pago.

Durante el tiempo comprendido por este informe, este Departamento ha examinado y liquidado 9,880 cuentas y aún tiene en su poder 10,000 conocimientos y cuentas de trasportes por liquidar.

Desde Julio 1º á Diciembre 31 de 1901 se han pagado cuentas de trasportes por valor de $60.976,31.

Los gastos de esta Oficina han sido como sigue:

Sueldos	$	3,130.97
Alquileres, hielo, gas, etc		415.00
Impresos y efectos de escritorio		928.60
Alquileres de coches		7.53
Type-writer		112.00

Los gastos de estos tres Departamentos durante el primer semestre del Año Económico de 1902, han tenido una disminución de $3,358.39, comparado con el último semestre del Año Económico de 1901.

BANCO NACIONAL DE CUBA

Según ya se ha manifestado, el Banco Nacional de Cuba, por autorización del Secretario de la Guerra de los Estados Unidos y por orden del Gobernador Militar de Cuba, fué designado con fecha 30 de Agosto de 1901 Agente Fiscal del Gobierno Militar de los Estados Unidos en Cuba, habiendo con tal motivo depositado en esta Tesorería de Cuba, como garantía, fianza por la suma de $1.385,000 en bonos hipotecarios de la ciudad de la Habana y consolidados de 1930 de los Estados Unidos, para el fiel cumplimiento de sus deberes según convenio temporal fecha 30 de Agosto de 1901, ampliado desde entonces con la suma de $340,000 que hace un total en depósito en la Tesorería de Cuba de $1.725,000.

Según informe obtenido dicho Banco ha aumentado últimamente su capital en acciones á $5.000,000 y lo considero capaz y muy beneficioso para los intereses financieros de esta Isla. Viene á llenar la necesidad hace tiempo sentida de una institución donde pueden obtenerse préstamos á un tipo inferior de intereses asegurados por colaterales que bien valgan el importe del principal, cuya condición no había existido en Cuba. Al presente cuenta con sus sucursales en cuatro ciudades de la Isla y sin duda alguna se extenderá según lo justifiquen las exigencias. Soy de opinión que una institución de la índole del Banco Nacional de Cuba ejercerá gran influencia sobre los destinos del país, siempre que su programa sea llevado á efecto según se propone, y no dudo que sea llevado á efecto pues sus Directores son bien conocidos aquí donde todos nos conocemos y su responsabilidad y crédito, tanto individual como colectivamente, son una garantía suficiente para que el éxito corone sus esfuerzos.

Con referencia á la posición financiera que dicha institución ocupa, llamo la atención al informe y certificación emitidos por los Sres. Haskins & Selles, de la ciudad de New York en el cual aparece la condición monetaria del Banco Nacional de Cuba con fecha Octubre 31 de 1901.

BALANCE CONSOLIDADO

Banco Nacional de Cuba, Habana, Santiago, Cienfuegos, Matanzas, Cuba.

Activo

Efectivo		$ 1.215,013.05
Efectivo en tránsito		3,746.12
Bonos de 2% de los Estados Unidos	$ 813,735.82	
Habana 6%	923,751.15	
		1.737.486.97
Préstamos y pagarés		1.489,646 93
J. P. Morgan & Co		574,909.64
Otros Bancos		132,754.09
Muebles, etc		35,423.10
Propiedades inmuebles		39,652.74
Varios		89,384.60
Total activo		$ 5 318,017.24

Pasivo

Depósitos y Bancos	$ 3.791,363.90
Checks certificados del Cajero	419,973.98
Capital	1.000,000.00
Ganancias y pérdidas	106,679.36
Total pasivo	$ 5.318,017.24

MONEDA

En mi último informe semestral fechado Julio 25 de 1901, bajo este epígrafe, hice la recomendación de que se adoptara el signo fiduciario de los Estados Unidos como el patrón para la Isla de Cuba, cuya recomendación, es mi creencia, que si se hubiese aceptado, unificaría todas las clases de contabilidad, gubernamental así como particular, y hubiera financieramente mejorado la condición del país; pero ya que otro semestre ha transcurrido sin que se haya tomado acción alguna sobre el particular y como quiera que todo parece indicar un porvenir próspero para Cuba en lo que se refiere al programa político del país, creo prudente se den los pasos necesarios y se adopten medidas por las cuales los intereses agrícolas de Cuba que son la fuente de todo su progreso y bienestar, sean adelantados, pues Cuba es un país eminentemente agrícola, y su suerte depende por completo de su agricultura. Esto sentado, se infiere que el Gobierno no podría llevar á cabo acto más trascendental, que adelantar en todo lo posible los intereses de aquellos que actualmente se dedican á la Agricultura, siendo todas aquellas ventajas que se le puedan ofrecer desde un punto de vista financiero, al mejor ayuda para el éxito de sus empresas, lo cual induciría á muchos que están aún cruzados de brazos, á labrar el fértil suelo que al remunerar sus esfuerzos, derramaría riquezas, paz y bienandanza.

Es sensible tener que admitir, que Cuba, á pesar de su rico suelo y su magnífica posición geográfica, por cuya razón es generalmente conocida como la "Llave del Nuevo Mundo" y á despecho de los millones que su agricultura ha producido, no ha podido nunca, en la más lata extensión de la palabra, poseer una verdadera institución cuyo objeto haya sido ayudar de una manera franca sus intereses agrícolas de manera de hacer más ricos y más fructíferos sus recursos territoriales.

En virtud de lo expuesto tengo el honor de someter á su superior consideración el siguiente plan, que si es aceptado en principio, ruego respetuosamente al Gobierno Interventor dé los primeros pasos para llevarlo á efecto, antes de abandonar definitivamente nuestras playas.

Que se establezcan uno ó más Bancos bajo las bases en que operan los Bancos Nacionales de los Estados Unidos ó sea: Permitirles la emisión de moneda propia, la cual será garantizada por el Gobierno del país con quien se depositará una fianza igual á la cantidad emitida por ellos, que se decrete el tipo legal de interés bajo el cual deban hacerse las operaciones de préstamos en Cuba ó en otras palabras el establecimiento de un tipo legal de interés, excederse del cual será considerado como una violación de las leyes, todo lo cual protegerá los intereses del necesitado y pondrá coto á la avaricia de los especuladores que conducen negocios ilegítimos y sin prestar obediencia á ningún principio amenazan constantemente á las fuentes del comercio legal.

Si algo se hubiese hecho sobre este particular por los anteriores Gobernantes de Cuba, sería muy distinta su presente situación económica; pero como el porvenir del país más bien se dejaba á sus propios destinos que á una conclusión razonada y científica, ha resultado que el presente desastre económico ha hecho necesario, para poder eradicar esta terrible condición que se apele á los Estados Unidos en esta hora de angustia pidiéndoles amparo y protección. Esperemos que esta apelación no será en vano y que el futuro Gobierno de Cuba sabrá recojer los beneficios derivados de esta triste experiencia y que la adopción de las medidas más arriba indicadas, promuevan los intereses agrícolas de la Isla de una manera tan conclusiva que el país entre de lleno en una era de progreso y prosperidad como nunca se haya visto.

PERSONAL

Sin variación alguna se ha sostenido el personal de este Departamento desde mi último informe, y sírveme de placer el manifestar que cada empleado ha seguido desempeñando su cometido de la misma manera fiel y eficiente como hasta ahora. No se hace necesaria ninguna mención personal, pero tengo sumo gusto en recomendar individualmente á cada uno de los empleados de este Departamento por su fidelidad y eficiencia en sus respectivos cargos.

Referente á los esfuerzos efectuados por parte de los empleados americanos que actualmente desempeñan cargo en el Gobierno Militar de los Estados Unidos en Cuba, tengo el honor de manifestar que la mayoría de los empleados de esta Oficina han servido en la misma por más de dos años, y respetuosamente suplico que sean favorablemente recomendados al Presidente de los Estados Unidos y al Secretario de la Guerra para que se les dé empleo en el servicio del Gobierno de los Estados Unidos cuando ya sus servicios en Cuba no sean necesarios.

Respetuosamente,

CARLOS ROLOFF.

Tesorero de Cuba.

REPORT

OF THE

SECRETARY OF FINANCE.

1901.

OFFICE OF THE SECRETARY OF FINANCE.

Havana, August 19th, 1901.

Brigadier General Leonard Wood,

Military Governor of Cuba.

SIR:

I have the honor to submit the general summary of the services rendered by this Office and its dependencies, during the second half of the fiscal year that closed on the 30th of June last.

The receipts from Internal Revenues have had a slight increase during the second half, for they amounted to $344,271.77, against $326,781.64, collected in the first half, showing a balance of $17,490.13 in excess over the first one. This is but normal, in view of the fact that all transactions and acts that produce the conveyance revenues are more numerous during the sugar crop and the tobacco harvest than in the rest of the year; and, besides, the taxes paid by stock companies, whose business year generally expires with the calendar year, are settled and paid in the same period.

During all the fiscal year, or, namely, from July 1st, 1900, to June 30th, 1901, the receipts for the item of Internal Revenues amounted to $671,053.41, against $884,838.40 in the fiscal year of 1899 to 1900; which shows a difference of $213,784.99 against last year. Said decrease is due to the fact that the tax of 3 and 10 per cent, levied on passenger fares and freight rates, whose yield exceeded $300,000 in the previous year, was suppressed after July 1900. If we were to make the comparison between the products of the same taxes, it would be ascertained, on the contrary, that there results a favorable balance for last year.

Payments made during the half year by the Central Treasury and those of the Fiscal Zones, amounted to $4,546,244.81 and to $7,743,407.85 during the fiscal year, the result in favor of the second half being an excess of $1,349,081.77. The operations have been punctually performed, notwithstanding the bulk of the payments and the fact that they consisted in their greater part in small obligations like the salaries of the teachers, rentals of school houses, salaries of electoral clerks, accounts of office material, etc. The complaints of the creditors, never very numerous and seldom justified, have diminished in the measure that the entities and officials called to acknowledge the credits have become conversant with the proceedings established by the regulations for that kind of service.

In my judgment, the main contributor to that result was the division of the territory for the services of Finance in eleven fiscal zones in which the attempt was made to group together the regions that by their social, mercantile and postal relations formed a homogeneous whole.

A principal part of the powers of this Office is the inspection of municipal finances and the cognizance of the appeals of all kinds filed by the tax payers against the resolutions and acts of the local authorities, related with taxation. In the exercise of those powers, I have had cognizance of appeals proceeding from all parts of the Island and visits of inspection have been made to the Ayuntamientos and I have always had the honor to tender you reports of their result.

The inspections are generally fruitful, not only because they correct errors and retrieve the vices of municipal management, but also in that they raise the normal standard of local officials and inspire confidence to the people.

Discoursing upon this theme, Sr. Francisco López Leyva, Administrator of the Fiscal Zone of Santa Clara, writes me the following:

Acting upon your express power, I have made visits of inspection to the Ayuntamientos of San Juan de las Yeras, Santo Domingo, Cifuentes, Santa Clara, Calabazar, Camajuaní and Remedios.

As a general impression, I have acquired the conviction that these inspections are both necessary and useful. At the same time that they redress abuses and correct defects they serve as profitable teaching, when not as a stimulus to the popular corporations. I have received petitions from different Mayors begging me to go to inspect their accounts and treasuries; and I have answered them all saying that I did not act upon my own authority but upon powers conferred by that Superior Centre. Naturally, these petitions came after the results of the inspections in other districts were made known by the press, and when they had brought their books up to date and had corrected all the informalities that might be detected. The precept contained in Art. XXIX of Order No. 254 does not need better commendation than such petitions made by the interested parties themselves.

Speaking in general terms, Municipal Finance is on the verge of bankruptcy. If it had to meet all its proper and natural obligations, Instruction, Sanitation, Charity, Hygiene, and Embellishment, etc., etc., either bankruptcy would ensue or the services, even those that cannot be dispensed with in all civilized countries, would not be rendered by the Ayuntamientos. In my view, two factors concur to produce this disastrous situation; one of them is the creation of necessities that are superior to the taxable forces of the towns, and the other one that there are more municipalities than those really and positively needful. I cannot understand the reason why neither in San Diego del Valle, nor in Cifuentes, nor in Cartagena, nor in other places of this province such a costly municipal organization should be maintained. Those so-called Ayuntamientos do not meet any of the aims of collective life; they only serve to impoverish the proprietor, who is made to pay the municipal taxes, general and special, not to return it in the shape of bridges and roads, in schools and hospitals, but to distribute petty salaries among Secretaries, Mayors and other bureaucrats of lesser importance. It will be a patriotic task to do away with those small foci of passions and Byzantine discords, of spoliations to tax payers and of continuous petitions to the Military Government to which they are always extending a beseeching hand as if instead of being administrators of towns a congregation of mendicants were dealt with.

Those observations are well grounded and they could be made extensive to the whole Island. Not a few municipalities in the same case of those mentioned by Sr. López Leyva, are to be found in all the provinces of Cuba. The greater part of them lack competent personnel for the management of the local administration; and in those that regularly keep their accounts it is not seen that the money of the tax payers is laid out in services of public utility, but in the reward of personnel that usually receive salaries that exceed the rational proportion of the resources of the Municipal Treasury.

What occurred when the General Treasury of the Island ceased to pay the Municipal police is worthy of special mention. That purpose was announced since the first months of the year, commencing by the withdrawal of the twenty-five per cent of the monthly subvention, then another twenty-five, and, lastly, the whole amount. Now then, not a few, perhaps the majority of the Ayuntamientos, left the structure of their budgets intact; they kept up the same salary for their officials, commencing with the Mayor, and they continued including voluntary expenditures in the same. When the first of July arrived, they quietly abolished the service, or they left it so scantily allowed that the insufficiency of their police is evident and no other solution occurs to them than that of appealing to the Central Administration petitioning for posts of the Rural Guard, or for new imposts and special taxes.

The Central Administration had already paid heed to the necessity of strengthening Municipal Finance, directing, on September, 1900, that a general record of rural and urban estates should be made in all the Island, and providing, by Order No. 141, current series, that rural estates destroyed during the war that might be in a state of production should commence to contribute with the only reduction of thirty-three per cent on the regular quotas assigned by the orders in force. Well, then, the majority of the Ayuntamientos of all the Island hardly devoted any attention to the assessment and even now the municipalities that have progressed in its execution are but few.

The Administrators of the Fiscal Zones, who preside over the Superior Boards of Assessment of their territory, are of one accord to state that the conduct of the Ayuntamientos in this matter is deplorable. The Administrator of Pinar del Río tells me that the Municipal Boards of Assessments are carrying out their work with inexplicable tardiness; until the 10th of July he had only received the assessments of Mantua and San Juan y Martínez.

The same slowness is remarked in the Fiscal Zone of Guanajay, as only three of the eleven Municipal Boards existing in the same, or namely, those of Palma, Cabañas and Bahía Honda, have progressed in their work. In the zone of Havana, the delay of the records of this city is notorious and in the rest of the province only the Municipal Boards of Alquízar, Aguacate, Bainoa, Bejucal, San José de las Lajas, Madruga, Managua and the Isle of Pines had their records in an advanced condition on July 15th, date of the report of the Administrator. Only the

Municipality of Santa Ana, which is one of the least important of the zone of Matanzas, had forwarded its record to the Zone Board until July 19th. The same is observed in the other Fiscal Zones. The following observations, made by the Administrator of the Fiscal Zone of Santa Clara, are applicable to all of them:

The works of the assessment have had but relatively small progress in this Zone, notwithstanding the constant efforts made by the Board presided over by me.

Until now we have only been able to approve the drafts of the registers Nos. 3 and 4 of the following Ayuntamientos, with numerous corrections:

Santa Clara, Remedios, Calabazar, Santo Domingo, San Diego del Valle, San Juan de las Yeras, Vueltas, Ceja de Pablo, Cifuentes and Yaguajay.

Therefore, the Municipal Boards of Esperanza, Placetas, Caibarién, Rancho Veloz, Sagua, Quemado de Güines, Ranchuelo and Camajuaní have not forwarded any document.

And it is not only this, but that some of these districts have not even forwarded the duplicates of the statements, nor have even reported on the condition of the works.

Order No. 141, current series, dictated by the Military Government, upon the recommendation of that Office, will undoubtedly give an impetus to the formation of the Assessment because the Municipalities will have to avail themselves of the statements presented by the proprietors in order to levy the taxes, or cannot collect them if they have not finished the registers and records by certain dates. At all events, the work is being carried out with certain passive resistance, easily explained by the fact that the principal burdens of the towns being subventioned by the State, the scanty receipts obtained by the Ayuntamientos suffice to cover the attention of their personnel. Not having to meet pressing engagements, the municipalities have no hurry to make the records of property, as they have the Public Treasury as the principal payer for what is urgent and necessary.

As I have already said, the Zone Board has not neglected nor omitted to address to the municipal ones the instructions, elucidations and exhortations it has considered necessary to impress activity to the work. Different circulars have been sent to those corporations, and, above all, to those evincing the greatest tardiness, as I have duly had the honor to communicate to that Office; but as this Administration unfortunately has no coercive means at its disposal, the assessment advances very slowly and it is only due to the restrictions of Order No. 141 that they may be terminated, and not very satisfactorily at that.

As a proof that the Ayuntamientos are not able to outgrow the ancient practices and abuses, I can mention the fact that the Municipal Board of Calabazar, instead of personally and individually notifying the proprietors whose statements have been rectified, conformably to the provisions of Articles 29 and 32 of the Regulations, publishes an announcement in the Official Bulletin of the province calling all the tax payers in general who are in that case that they may resort to the town hall to be informed of the alterations; with the proviso that if fifteen days elapse without any complaint or claim being filed, the decisions of rectification shall be held as firm. In view of such an infraction of the regulations that notoriously injures the principles of justice upon which the former rest, I have called the attention of the Board of Calabazar and I have reported the matter to the Zone Board for the reestablishment of the sway of law.

Under such conditions, how can we listen to the solicitations of authority for new exactions on public wealth or consumption? Before all, the municipalities ought to diligently administer their present finance, as that is the only manner in which they can show that the resources at their disposal are insufficient.

On the other hand, circumstances are unpropitious to think of the increase of taxes. Our agriculture, that is almost the only source of our wealth, is traversing a difficult period, which has its exponent in commerce in general and in the custom revenues. In consequence of the terrible ravages of the war our mercantile estimate shows a balance of thirty-five million dollars against the country during two years and a half; the tobacco harvest, the hope of our rural middle classes and of the majority of the husbandmen in the province of Pinar del Río, Western Havana, Northeast Santa Clara and part of Santiago de Cuba, has been sold at ruinous prices when buyers were to be had, leaving retail commerce and the local industries in a distressed situation; the crops of garden products have been scantily remunerated in consequence of the strong competition of the producers in the United States, whose corn, potatoes and cereals are sold at prices that our products cannot resist; and the cane growers and sugar manufacturers see very low prices looming up in the perspective with the increase and cheapness of universal production.

A proportional reduction in the expenditures of life that rather increase than diminish in the urban centres and principally in Havana, Santiago de Cuba, Cienfuegos and other places, does not correspond as it should to the general fall of our fruits, perhaps owing to the lack of competition among merchants, who prefer to agree to keep up high prices, or to raise them, to contend for obtaining the greatest advantages in the market by attracting consumers.

It is my belief, therefore, that the orders published to this date in all matters pertaining to municipal finance should be maintained in force and that it would become efficient to general welfare to suppress those Ayuntamientos that do not really render any service, as has been said above.

***

I enclose separate statements of receipts and payments made in the Department.

In general, the officials of this Department have evinced zeal and the proper diligence in the performance of their duties. When the service was reorganized in June of the previous year of 1900, the actual tasks at the time were attended to. But in the course of the year great development has been attained by the operations of payment of the Treasuries and the collection of internal revenues, with that of the pensions of annuities and the promissory notes in behalf of the State, the collection of which was in suspense by virtue of the delays granted to debtors in different provisions not mentioned here, for they are but too well known; and, consequently, the personnel of the offices of the Fiscal Zones are at present insufficient. Hence, I had the honor to recommend some increase when drafting the project of a budget for the current fiscal year, and, if I do respect the reasons of necessary economy upon which the decision of the Military Government was grounded to not allow the requested increase at present, yet I will reiterate it as soon as circumstances are more favorable.

Your obedient servant,

LEOPOLDO CANCIO,

Secretary of Finance.

A

DEPARTMENT OF FINANCE.

BUREAU OF ACCOUNTS.—SECTION OF BOOK-KEEPING.

BALANCE OF OPERATIONS EFFECTED AT THE TREASURER'S DEPARTMENT DURING THE MONTHS OF JANUARY TO JUNE OF THE CURRENT YEAR.

Dr.	CASH.	SECURITIES	Cr.	CASH.	SECURITIES
ON HAND ON DECEMBER 31, 1900....	$ 128,262.24	$ 54.300.00	Paid during the half-year for Public Expenses as per enclosed Statements	$ 1.020,439.62	$ ....
Receipts for Bonds on Public Works.	236.00	....	Bonds on Public Works........	236.00	....
Receipts for Bonds on Finance.......	....	100,000.00	" " Justice	....	8,000.00
" " " " Justice......	1,000.00	....	Judicial Deposits........	2,260.76	....
" " " Judicial Deposits...	23.80	....	Provisional Deposits........	3,960.00	....
" " " Provisional Dep.....	2,760.00	....	Voluntary Deposits........	124.41	....
" " " Voluntary Deposits	124.41	....	Compulsory Deposits........	1,012.50	....
" " " Miscellaneous deposits	5,809.04	....	Miscellaneous Deposits........	2,805.00	....
Receipts for Bonds, compulsory deposits........	1,012.50	....	Municipal Poll dists........	424.00	....
Receipts for transfer of funds for payment of Poll lists at Santiago de Cuba and for Provincial Courts.	911.50	....	Remitted to the Treasurer's Department of the Island for settlement......	98,080.90	....
Remittances received from the Treasurer's Department........	1.001,236.41	....	ON HAND, JULY 1........	12,032.71	146,300.00
	$ 1.141,375.90	$154,300.00		$ 1.141,375.90	$154,300.00

E. & O. Exc.

Havana, July 1st, 1901.

SALVADOR FELIX,
Book-Keeper.

Countersigned:
MONTALVO,
Chief of Bureau.

DEPARTMENT OF FINANCE.

BUREAU OF ACCOUNTS.—BOOK-KEEPING.

PUBLIC EXPENSES.

Months from January to June 1901.

RESUMÉ OF PUBLIC EXPENSES paid during the current half year.

ITEMS.	By items.		TOTAL.	
DEPARTMENT OF STATE AND GOVERNMENT.				
Secretary and Subsecretary's Departments, Personnel..........	$ 28.957	47		
Secretary and Subsecretary's Departments, Material.....................	2.630	90		
Pan American Medical Congress......	4.655	78		
Centre of Vaccination, Personnel.	2.302	98		
,, ,, Material........	1.488	04		
Prisons of the Island, Personnel.......	27.464	59		
,, ,, ,, Material.........	19.017	91		
,, ,, ,, Maintenance..	24.043	08		
,, ,, ,, Special Credit.	960	00		
Women's Prison, Personnel	1.316	33		
,, ,, Material...............	1.271	93		
,, ,, Maintenance.........	884	25		
Printing matter for the Live Stock Register.........................	6.481	62		
General Archives of the Island, Personnel..	7.158	46		
General Archives of the Island, Material	297	60		
Constitutional Convention, Personnel and per diems.........................	56.065	88		
Constitutional Convention, Subaltern Personnel............................	18.907	06		
Constitutional Convention, Stenographers......................................	8.365	00		
Constitutional Convention, Material and expenses................................	2.588	53		
Constitutional Convention, House rents..	8.181	78		
Constitutional Convention, Diary of Sessions..	2.056	75		
Constitutional Convention, Installation Expenses................................	4.890	42		
Constitutional Convention, Journeying expenses..................................	103	70		
Insane Asylum................................	550	80		
Buffalo Exposition	254	00		
Extra expenses................................	110	50		
Special Commissions on Glanders, Indemnities.................	2.232	50		
Rural Guard..................	41	75		
Letters requisitorial Expenses.	51	00		
Special Commission on Glanders, Material..	1.887	20		
Special Commission on Glanders, Personnel	1.550	43		
Department of State and Government, Acquisition of Furniture......	2.976	42		
Const. Convention, Extra expenses..	172	00		
Carried forward......	$ 239.916	66	$ 239.916	66

E

RESUMÉ OF PUBLIC EXPENSES paid during the current half year.—CONTINUED.

ITEMS.	By items.		TOTAL.	
Brought forward.............	$ 140,814	89	$ 739.696	59
DEPARTMENT OF AGRICULTURE, COMMERCE AND INDUSTRY.				
Buffalo Exposition.	25.545	09		
Furniture and Extra Expenses.........	982	00		
Printing of Annual Report................	2.615	00		
	$ 169.956	98	$ 169 956	98
DEPARTMENT OF PUBLIC WORKS.				
Commission on Lighthouses, Personnel..........	$ 11.912	11		
Commission on Lighthouses, Material............	491	76		
Lighthouses, Light Keepers and Watchmen..........	19.610	74		
Lighthouses, Laundry and communicating service..........	5.099	57		
Lighthouses, Plant and projects.......	1.221	80		
,, Incidental expenses......	820	95		
,, oil, articles and transportation..........	2.655	86		
Lighthouses, Buoys and marks..... ...	37.493	57		
,, Visits of Inspection......	537	00		
Construction of the Lighthouse Punta de los Colorados................	544	25		
Painting of the Buoy mark of Cabeza de Arreola..........	4	05		
Lighthouses, and Cayo Jutía Punta de la Gobernadora..	30.368	82		
Light for Faro, Pasa Caballos.........	25	57		
	$ 110.786	05	$ 110.786	05
General total	....	.....	$1.020.439	62

RESUME.	Total for the Departments.	
Department of State and Government..........	$ 239.902	14
Department Justice..........................	87.042	54
,, Public Instruction.........	363.440	72
,, Finance..........................	49.311	19
,, Agriculture, Industry and Commerce..........................	169.955	98
Department Public Works................	110.786	05
Grand total....................	$1.020.439	62

Countersigned:

Havana, June 30th, 1901.

MONTALVO,

Auditor.

SALVADOR VELIZ,

Bookkeeper.

F

GENERAL STATEM~~~*scal Zones of the Island of Cuba, during the half year*

	Cienfuegos.	Holguín.	Manzanillo.	TOTALS.
Transference of propert	$16,459.69	$ 5,880.99	$ 5,288.47	$ 202,771.55
Mines' property...........	....	....	....	2,435.00
Industrial tax..............	....	244.67	....	66,971.61
Products of Public Woo	....	....	....	602.20
Redemption of annuities	....	....	....	2,918.49
Interest on annuities....	....	....	....	14,076.61
Interest on arrears........	295.75	79.28	6.07	2,141.13
Rentals of property......	....	140.00	....	3,257.23
Sale of lands...............	....	....	....	1,063.92
Miscellaneous products.	298.97	183.95	41.89	46,268.87
Surcharge 5%..............	131.27	....	....	1,437.81
Sale of waste articles....	....	....	....	27.35
	$17,085.69	$ 6,528.89	$ 5,336.43	$ 344,271.77

Havana, June 30th, 1901.

RAM

CARLOS CAVALLÉ,
Chief Accountant.

E

RESUMÉ OF PUBLIC EXPENSES paid during the current half year.—CONTINUED.

ITEMS.	By items.		TOTAL.	
Brought forward.............	$ 140,814	89	$ 739,696	59
DEPARTMENT OF AGRICULTURE, COMMERCE AND INDUSTRY.				
Buffalo Exposition.	25.545	09		
Furniture and Extra Expenses.........	982	00		
Printing of Annual Report...............	2.615	00		
	$ 169.956	98	$ 169.956	98
DEPARTMENT OF PUBLIC WORKS.				
Commission on Lighthouses, Personnel..........	$ 11.912	11		
Commission on Lighthouses, Material..	491	76		
Lighthouses, Light Keepers and Watchmen....................................	19.610	74		
Lighthouses, Laundry and communicating service........................	5.099	57		
Lighthouses, Plant and projects.......	1.221	80		
" Incidental expenses......	820	95		
" oil, articles and transportation......................................	2.655	86		
Lighthouses, Buoys and marks..... ...	37.493	57		
" Visits of Inspection......	537	00		
Construction of the Lighthouse Punta de los Colorados................	544	25		
Painting of the Buoy mark of Cabeza de Arreola................................	4	05		
Lighthouses, and Cayo Jutía Punta de la Gobernadora..	30.368	82		
Light for Faro, Pasa Caballos.........	25	57		
	$ 110.786	05	$ 110.786	05
General total....	....	.....	$1.020.439	62

RESUMÉ.	Total for the Departments.	
Department of State and Government..	$ 239.902	14
Department Justice............................	87.042	54
" Public Instruction.........	363.440	72
" Finance.........................	49.311	19
" Agriculture, Industry and Commerce..............................	169.955	98
Department Public Works.................	110.786	05
Grand total....................	$1.020.439	62

Countersigned:

MONTALVO,

Auditor.

Havana, June 30th, 1901.

SALVADOR VELIZ,

Bookkeeper.

E F

GENERAL STATEM[scal Zones of the Island of Cuba, during the

half year

	Cienfuegos.	Holguín.	Manzanillo.	TOTALS.
Transference of property	$16,459.69	$ 5,880.99	$ 5,288.47	$ 202,771.55
Mines' property	....	....	....	2,435.00
Industrial tax	....	244.67	....	66,971.61
Products of Public Wood	....	....	....	602.20
Redemption of annuities	....	....	....	2,918.49
Interest on annuities	....	....	....	14,076.61
Interest on arrears	295.75	79.28	6.07	2,141.13
Rentals of pro ert	....	140.00	....	3,257.23
Sale of lands..p....y	....	....	....	1,063.92
Miscellaneous products	298.97	183.95	41.89	46,268.87
Surcharge 5%	131.27	....	....	1,437.81
Sale of waste articles	....	....	....	27.35
	$17,085.69	$ 6,528.89	$ 5,336.43	$ 344,271.77

Havana, June 30th, 1901.

RAM

CARLOS CAVALLÉ,

Chief Accountant.

	fuegos.	Holguin.	Manzanillo.	TOTALS.
Transference of Property..	424.95	$ 950.24	$ 66.40	$ 26,250.03
Mines' property..............				328.00
Industrial tax..................				5,020.06
Products of Public Woods				400.20
Redemption of annuities..				793.42
Interest on annuities.......				3,911.04
Interest on arrears..........	21.88	4.03	10	241.42
Rentals of Property..........		40.00		448.76
Sale of lands....................				1,018.26
Miscellaneous products....	56.00	18.70	6.00	5,677.01
Surcharge 5%..................				255.68
	502.83	$ 1,012.97	$ 72.50	$ 44,343.88

	fuegos.	Holguin.	Manzanillo.	TOTALS.
Transference of Property.	364.34	$ 333.66	$ 2,132.66	$ 33,425.07
Mines' property........				
Industrial tax..................				37,922.81
Products of Public Wood				42.00
Redemption of annuities..				
Interest on annuities.......				3,970.31
Interest on arrears..........	20.51	5.96	70	225.29
Rentals of Property.........				418.45
Sale of lands....................				
Miscellaneous products...	30.85	6.00		5,999.38
Surcharge 5%.......	4.86			289.93
	420.56	$ 345.62	$ 2,133.36	$ 82,293.24

H

	Cienfuegos.	Holguín.	Manzanillo.	TOTALS.
Transference of Proper	$ 2,908.57	$ 808.16	$ 324.84	$ 39,273.83
Mines' property				209.00
Industrial tax				1,214.36
Products of Public Wo				1,702.13
Redemption of annuitie				3,070.04
Interest on annuities	92.18	3.12	.08	1,012.38
Interest on arrears		20.00		425.57
Rentals of Property				
Sale of lands				80.00
Miscellaneous products	14.25	1.75	21.00	5,312.36
Surcharge 5%	44 68			388.69
	$ 3,059.68	$ 833.03	$ 345 92	$ 52,688.35

	Cienfuegos.	Holguín.	Manzanillo.	TOTALS.
Transference of Propert	$ 4,971.71	$ 811.39	$ 193.40	$ 42,511.33
Mines' property				276.00
Industrial tax		134.20		11,503.26
Products of Public Wo				80.00
Redemption of annuitie				299.08
Interest on annuities				1,130.21
Interest on arrears	74.25	38.99	3.11	456.54
Rentals of Property		20.00		618.24
Sale of lands				
Miscellaneous products	54.40	113 00		6,263.55
Surcharge 5%	68.43			248.21
	$ 5,168.79	$ 1,117.58	$ 196.51	$ 63,386.42

		Cienfuegos.	Holguín.	Manzanillo.	TOTALS.
Transference of prope	6	$ 2,134.24	$ 2,390.15	$ 197.32	$ 32,244.04
Mines' property........					558.00
Industrial tax					10,921.73
Products of Public W					
Redemption of annuit					123.86
Interest on annuities.	6				1,215.20
Interest on arrears....	3	22.48	14.61	1.86	280.91
Rentals of property.			20.00		493.30
Sale of lands..........					45.66
Miscellaneous produc	7	42.88	7.50	12.00	12,920.17
Surcharge 5%	3	5.12			136.54
	5	$ 2,204.72	$ 2,432.26	$ 211.18	$ 58,939.41

		Cienfuegos.	Holguín	Manzanillo.	TOTALS.
Transference of prop	3	$ 2,655.88	$ 587.39	$ 2,373.85	$ 29,067.25
Mines' property........					1,064.00
Industrial tax..........			110.57		389.39
Produce of Public Wo					
Redemption of annuit					
Interest on annuities.	5				779.81
Interest on arrears....	8	64.44	12.57	.22	224.64
Rentals of property ..			40.00		852.91
Sale of lands					
Miscellaneous produc	0	.60	37.00	2.89	10,096.40
Surcharge 5%...........	9	8.18			118.76
Sale of waste articles.					27.35
	5	$ 2,729.11	$ 787.43	$ 2,376.96	$ 42,620.51

GENERAL RESUME *he half year from January 1 to June 30, 1901.*

	Cienfuegos.	Holguín.	Manzanillo.	TOTALS.
State and Government....	16,117.55	$ 3,264.00	$ 3,234.71	$ 556,394.11
Finance....	6,766.02	6,670.81	4,645 39	149,121.17
Justice....	14,657.20	10,301.93	7,106.85	416,630.66
Agriculture, Industry, and Commerce...	....	....	....	195,191.10
Public Instruction....	....	....	....	506,353.59
Public Works (Lighthouses)...	....	....	....	110,786.05
Municipalities....	243,851.72	116,814.69	91,913.91	2,059,609.92
Military Government.—Rural Guard...	....	....	....	17,924.84
Hospitals and Asylums...	83,859.93	14,298.75	14,687.02	534,233.37
	365,252.42	$151,350.18	$121,587.88	$ 4,546,244.81

1901.	Holguín.	Manzanillo.	TOTALS.
January	$ 433.70	$ 939.02	$ 50,096.95
February	354 40	243.60	86,104.24
March	575.80	383.85	107,952.69
April	600.60	540.30	87,470.52
May	516.00	262.50	81,888.72
June	783.50	865.44	142,880.99
	$ 3,264.00	$ 3,234.71	$ 556,394.11

1901.	Holguín.	Manzanillo.	TOTALS.
January	$ 2,201.42	$ 722.92	$ 18,188.63
February	753.05	236 90	19,643.55
March	1,570.98	1,339.00	32,115.58
April	.....	849.42	22,147.05
May	715.40	30.85	20,409.40
June	1,429.96	1,466.30	36,616.96
	$ 6,675.81	$ 4.645.39	$ 149,121.17

L

1901.	Cienfuegos.	Holguín.	Manzanillo	TOTALS.
January	$ 1,025.23	$ 403.13	$ 466.64	$ 31,793.50
February	780.81	3,163.66	1,745.98	47,037.30
March	2,714.40	696.28	968.28	73,692.10
April	2,706.60	1,528.76	1,446.62	83,984.85
May	2,560.36	1,323.91	499.98	60,315.47
June	4,869.80	3,186.19	1,979.35	119,807 44
	$ 14,657.20	$ 10,301.93	$ 7,106.85	$ 416,630.66

ERCE.

1901	Cienfuegos.	Holguín.	Manzanillo.	TOTALS.
January	......	......	......	$ 55,081.72
February	......	......	......	8,972.16
March	......	......	......	14,988.45
April	......	......	......	9,855.78
May	......	......	......	69,269.22
June	......	......	......	37,023.77
	......	......	......	$ 195,191.10

1901.	Cienfuegos.	Holguín.	Manzanillo.	TOTALS.
January				$ 23,061.97
February				47,428.36
March				87,278.76
April				87,388.87
May				65,280.78
June				195,914.85
				$ 506,353.59

1901.	Cienfuegos.	Holguín.	Manzanillo.	TOTALS.
January				$ 8,398.18
February				10,900.34
March				14,494.67
April				23.784.77
May				8,787.15
June				44,420.94
				$ 110,786.05

1901.	Cienfuegos.	Holguín.	Manzanillo.	Totals.
January	$ 44,425 85	$ 19,387.12	$ 17,301.68	$ 296,185.68
February	34,551.93	15,134 54	13,326.72	293,746.37
March	32,524.65	16,524.80	12,334.19	315,271.03
April	38,205.70	20,939.87	13,202.94	338,234.10
May	35,610.42	16,581.69	12,313.80	318,454.93
June	68,533.17	28,246.67	23,434 58	515,642.65
	$243,851.72	$116,814.69	$ 91,913.91	$ 2,077,534.76

1901.	Cienfuegos.	Holguín.	Manzanillo.	Totals.
January	$ 13,026.91	$ 1,057.15	$ 1,937.50	$ 65,894.36
February	11,873 10	2,022.60	2,042.23	88,797.79
March	12,209 00	3,293.40	1,015.00	72,287.12
April	11,702.17	1,986 90	1,414.35	80,496.03
May	12,398.67	1,813.33	2,467.15	73,601.62
June	22,650.68	4,125.37	5,810.79	153,156.45
	$ 83,859.93	$ 14,298.75	$ 14,687.02	$ 534,233.37

GENERAL RESUME a *from July 1, 1900, to June 30, 1901.*

	De	Cienfuegos.	Holguín.	Manzanillo.	TOTALS.
Revenue receipts..............	$....	29,020.03	$ 11,688.11	$ 8,984.63	$ 671,053.41
Funds received from the Treasurer of the Island for expenses..............	1.7	502,811.08	246,960.80	196,407.47	8.208,601.80
Transfers among Disbursing Officers....................		7,226.00	5,180.00	2,630.00	64,706.83
Disbursements for surplus from the expenses account......................		136.33	15.00	109.20	13,685.85
Deposits for mines...........	....	....	....	....	5,774.00
Promissory notes not due.	....	....	....	....	4,301.26
Deposits and bonds.........	2	8,512.42	3,580.03	886.58	1.093,844.70
	$1.9	547,705 86	$267,423 94	$209,017.88	$10.061,967.85

	De	Cienfuegos.	Holguín	Manzanillo.	TOTALS.
Public expenses...............	$1.5	579,985.39	$239,272.91	$190,762.66	$ 7.743,407.85
Remittances to the Treasurer of the Island for revenue receipts............	......	29,020.03	11,688.11	8,984.63	669,340.72
Transfers among disbursing officers..................		....	....	....	64,706.83
Reimbursements to the Treasurer of the Island for surplus from expenses		14,618.69	5,883.00	5,544.14	272,916.07
Deposits of mines...........	......	....	....	....	5,774.00
Deposits and bonds.........		3,327.24	1,171.20	....	659,188.65
BALANCE.........	1	20,754 51	9,408.72	3,726.45	646,633.73
	$1.9	547,705.86	$267,423.94	$209,017.88	$10.061,967.85

e, 1901.

		ıfuegos.	Holguín.	Manzanillo.	TOTALS.
Balance of revenue with the collectors...............	$...	....	$.................	$.................	$ 1,712.69
Cash on hand for expenses.........	.....	15,569.33	6,999.89	2,839.87	205,963.73
Promissory notes not due	..... .	....	....	....	4,301.26
Deposits and bonds.........		5,185.18	2,408.83	886.58	434,656.05
		),754.51	$ 9,408.72	$ 3,726.45	$ 646,633.73

INFORME

DEL

SECRETARIO DE HACIENDA.

1901.

SECRETARIA DE HACIENDA.

Habana, Agosto 19 de 1901.

Brigadier General Léonard Wood,

Gobernador Militar de Cuba.

SEÑOR:

Tengo el honor de presentarle un resumen general de los servicios prestados por esta Secretaría y sus dependencias durante el segundo semestre del año fiscal terminado el 30 de Junio último.

La recaudación de Rentas Interiores ha tenido un ligero aumento durante el segundo semestre, pues fué de $344,271.77 contra $326,781.64 recaudado en el primero, arrojando un saldo de más á favor del segundo, de $17,490.13; hecho normal, toda vez que las transacciones y actos que devengan el impuesto de derechos reales son más numerosas durante la zafra y recolección de la cosecha de tabaco que en el resto del año, y además en el mismo período se liquidan y pagan los impuestos que satisfacen las sociedades anónimas, cuyo año social vence generalmente con el año natural.

Durante todo el año fiscal ó sea de 1º de Julio de 1900 á 30 de Junio de 1901 la recaudación por dicho concepto de rentas interiores fué de $671,053.41 contra $884,838.40 en el año fiscal de 1899 á 1900; lo cual arroja una diferencia de $213,784.99 contra el año último. Consiste esa baja en que desapareció desde Julio de 1900 el impuesto de 3 y 10 por ciento sobre tarifas de viajeros y mercancías, cuyo rendimiento en el año anterior fué de más de 300 mil pesos. Si se hace la comparación entre el rendimiento de los mismos impuestos resulta, por el contrario, un saldo favorable al año último.

Los pagos hechos durante el semestre por la Tesorería Central y las de las Zonas fiscales ascendieron á $4.546,244.81 y durante el año á $7.743,407.85 resultando á favor del segundo semestre un exceso de $1.349.081.77. No obstante el volumen de los pagos, y el hecho de consistir en gran parte en pequeñas acreencias como sueldos de los maestros, alquileres de casas escuelas, haberes de escribientes electorales, cuentas de material de oficinas, etc., las operaciones se han hecho con puntualidad, disminuyendo las quejas de los acreedores nunca muy numerosas y pocas veces justificadas, á medida que las entidades y funcionarios llamados á reconocer los créditos se han ido familiarizando con las formas establecidas por los reglamentos de contabilidad para esa clase de servicios.

A ese resultado ha contribuido principalmente, á mi juicio, la división del territorio para los servicios de la Hacienda en once zonas fiscales, en que se procuró agrupar las regiones que por sus relaciones sociales, mercantiles y postales formaban un conjunto homogéneo.

***

Es parte muy principal de las atribuciones de esta Secretaría la inspección de la hacienda municipal y el conocimiento de los recursos de todas clases que establecen los contribuyentes contra las resoluciones y actos de las autoridades locales relacionados con la tributación. En ejercicio de estas atribuciones he conocido de recursos procedentes de todos los confines de la Isla, y se han girado visitas de inspección á los Ayuntamientos, cuyos resultados siempre he tenido el honor de comunicar á V.

Las visitas son generalmente provechosas, no sólo porque enmiendan errores y corrigen los vicios de la gestión municipal, sino porque elevan el nivel moral de los funcionarios locales é inspiran confianza al pueblo.

Discurriendo sobre este tema me dice el Sr. Francisco López Leyva, Administrador de la Zona Fiscal de Santa Clara lo siguiente:

"Por delegación expresa de Vd. he girado visitas de inspección á los Ayuntamientos de San Juan de las Yeras, Santo Domingo, Cifuentes, Santa Clara, Calabazar, Camajuaní y Remedios.

Como impresión general he adquirido el convencimiento de que estas visitas son necesarias á la vez que útiles, ya que se corrigen abusos, se subsanan defectos y á la vez sirven de provechosa enseñanza cuando no de estímulo á las Corporaciones populares. He recibido distintas peticiones de Alcaldes rogándome fuera á inspeccionarles sus cuentas y caudales; y á todas ellas he contestado que yo no procedía por autoridad propia, sino por delegación de ese Centro Superior. Naturalmente estas solicitudes vinieron después que la prensa dió á conocer los resultados de las visitas á otros términos y cuando se hubieron puesto al día los libros y arreglado todas las informalidades que pudieran encontrarse. No necesita el precepto contenido en el Artículo XXIX de la Orden núm. 254 mayor encomio que semejantes peticiones formuladas por los interesados mismos.

La Hacienda Municipal, en términos generales, está próxima á la bancarrota. Si tuviera que hacer frente á todas sus obligaciones propias y naturales, Instrucción, Sanidad, Beneficencia, Higiene y Ornato, etc., etc., ó bien sobrevendría la quiebra ó los servicios, aún los más imprescindibles en todo país civilizado, no se prestarían por los Ayuntamientos. A mi modo de ver, concurren dos factores á esta desastrosa situación: el uno es que se han creado necesidades superiores á las fuerzas contributivas de los pueblos; y el otro que existen más municipios de los que real y positivamente debieran existir. No se me alcanza la razón por la cual se sostiene una costosa organización municipal en San Diego del Valle, ni en Cifuentes, ni en Cartagena, ni en otros lugares de esta Provincia. Ningún fin de la vida colectiva llenan esos titulados ayuntamientos; sirven nada más que para esquilmar al propietario á quien se le hace pagar la contribución y los arbitrios municipales, no para devolverles su dinero en puentes y caminos, en escuelas y hospitales, sino para repartir unos mezquinos sueldos entre secretarios, alcaldes y otros burócratas de menor cuantía. Obra patriótica será acabar con todos esos pequeños focos de pasiones y de luchas bizantinas, de expoliaciones á los contribuyentes y de continuas peticiones al Gobierno Militar, hacia el cual tienen constantemente extendida la mano, como si en vez de ser administradores de los pueblos se tratara de una congregación de mendicantes."

Fundadas son esas observaciones, y se pueden haser extensivas á la Isla entera. En todas las provincias de Cuba se hallan no pocos municipios en el mismo caso de los mencionados por el Sr. López Leyva. La mayor parte de ellos carece de personal idóneo para dirigir la administración local, y en aquellos que llevan sus cuentas con regularidad no se vé que se invierta el dinero de los contribuyentes en servicios de utilidad pública, sino en la retribución del personal que suele cobrar sueldos que no están en proporción racional con los recursos del Tesoro Municipal.

Es digno de especial mención lo ocurrido al cesar el Tesoro general de la Isla en el pago de la policía municipal. Se anunció ese propósito desde los primeros meses del año, empezándose por retirar el veinte y cinco por ciento de la subvención mensual, luego otro veinte y cinco y por último la totalidad. Pues bien; no pocos, tal vez la mayoría de los Ayuntamientos dejó intacta la estructura de sus presupuestos, conservó el mismo salario á sus funcionarios empezando por el Alcalde, y siguió consignando en ellos gastos voluntarios; al llegar el primero de Julio abolieron tranquilamente el servicio, ó lo dejaron tan indotado que la insuficiencia de su policía es evidente, sin ocurrirles más solución que la de apelar á la Administración central en demanda de puestos de la guardia rural ó de nuevos impuestos y arbitrios.

Ya había atendido la administración central á la necesidad de reforzar la hacienda municipal, disponiendo desde Septiembre del pasado año de 1900 que se procediera á hacer en toda la Isla un padrón general de fincas rústicas y urbanas, y por la orden 141 de la serie de este año que empezasen á tributar las fincas rústicas destruidas durante la guerra que se hallaran en producción, con la sola rebaja de un treinta y tres por ciento de las cuotas ordinarias asignadas en las órdenes vigentes. Pues bien la mayoría de los Ayuntamientos de la Isla apenas si dedicó alguna atención al amillaramiento, y hoy todavía son contados los municipios que han adelantado en su ejecución.

Los Administradores de las zonas fiscales, que presiden las Juntas Superiores de Amillaramiento de su territorio, están contestes en que es deplorable la conducta de los Ayuntamientos en esta materia. El de Pinar del Río me dice que las Juntas de Amillaramiento vienen realizando sus trabajos con inexplicable morosidad; el 10 de Julio no había recibido más que los amillaramientos de Mantua y San Juan y Martínez.

En la zona fiscal de Guanajay se observa la misma lentitud, pues sólo tres de las once Juntas Municipales que en ella existen han adelantado en sus trabajos, á saber, las de Palma, Cabañas y Bahía Honda. En la zona de la Habana notorio es el atraso en que se halla el padrón de esta capital, y del resto de la provincia sólo las Juntas Municipales de Alquízar, Aguacate, Bainoa, Bejucal, San José de las Lajas, Madruga, Managua é Isla de Pinos tenían adelantados sus padrones el 15 de Julio, fecha del informe del Administrador. En la zona de Matanzas sólo el Municipio de Santa Ana, que es uno de los menos importantes de ella, había remitido á la Junta de la Zona su padrón hasta el 19 de Julio. Lo mismo se observa en las demás zonas fiscales.

A todas son aplicables las siguientes observaciones que hace en informe á esta Secretaría el Administrador de la Zona Fiscal de Santa Clara.

"Las trabajos del Amillaramiento en esta Zona han adelantado relativamente poco, á pesar de los constantes esfuerzos hechos por la Junta que presido.

Hasta hoy sólo se han podido aprobar, después de innumerables correcciones, los borradores de los Registros números 3 y 4 de los Ayuntamientos siguientes:

Santa Clara, Remedios, Calabazar, Santo Domingo, San Diego del Valle, San Juan de las Yeras, Vueltas, Ceja de Pablo, Cifuentes y Yaguajay.

No han remitido, pues, documento alguno, las Juntas Municipales de Esperanza, Placetas, Caibarién, Rancho Veloz, Sagua, Quemado de Güines, Ranchuelo y Camajuaní.

Y no es esto solamente, sino que muchos de estos Términos ni han remitido los duplicados de las planillas, ni siquiera han dado cuenta del estado de los trabajos.

La orden del Gobierno Militar nº 141, serie corriente, dictada á propuesta de esa Secretaría, impulsará á no dudarlo la formación del Amillaramiento, puesto que los Municipios tendrán que utilizar las planillas presentadas por los propietarios para cobrar las contribuciones ó no podrán hacerlas efectivas si para determinadas fechas no tienen terminados los Registros y Padrones. De todos modos, el trabajo se viene practicando con cierta resistencia pasiva, que me explico por el hecho de que subvencionando el Estado las principales cargas de los pueblos, la poca recaudación que obtienen los Ayuntamientos les basta para cubrir las atenciones de su personal. No teniendo compromisos apremiantes que llenar, los Municipios no se dan prisa en hacer el empadronamiento de la riqueza, puesto que para lo urgente y lo necesario tienen al Erario Público como principal pagador.

Como llevo dicho, la Junta de Zona no ha descuidado ni omitido dirigir á las de Municipio las instrucciones, aclaraciones y excitaciones que ha considerado necesarias para imprimir movimiento al trabajo. Distintas circulares se han enviado á esas Corporaciones, sobre todo á las que mayor morosidad han demostrado, conforme he participado á esa Secretaría en su oportunidad; pero como desgraciadamente, no dispone esta Administración de medios coercitivos suficientes, el Amillaramiento adelanta con lentitud suma, y sólo merced á las restricciones de la Orden 141, podrá terminarse y no muy satisfactoriamente que digamos.

Como prueba de que los Municipios no saben salir de las antiguas prácticas y corruptelas, puedo señalar el hecho de que la Junta Municipal de Calabazar en vez de notificar personalmente y uno por uno á los propietarios cuyas declaraciones se han rectificado, conforme previenen los artículos 29 y 32 del Reglamento, publica un aviso en el *Boletín Oficial* de la Provincia, llamando en conjunto á los contribuyentes que se encuentren en dicho caso para que acudan á la Casa Consistorial á enterarse de las alteraciones; apercibiéndoles que pasados quince días sin establecer queja ó reclamación, se darán por firmes los acuerdos de rectificación. Ante semejante infracción del Reglamento que perjudica notoriamente á los propietarios y ataca los principios justicieros en que aquél descansa, he llamado la atención de la Junta del Calabazar y he dado cuenta á la de Zona para que se restablezca el imperio de la Ley."

En tal situación ¿cómo dar oidos á la pretensión de que se autoricen nuevas exacciones á la riqueza pública ó al consumo? Antes deben los municipios administrar con diligencia su hacienda actual, pues sólo así podrán demostrar que son insuficientes los recursos de que disponen.

Por otra parte, muy poco propicias son las circunstancias para pensar en el aumento de los impuestos. Nuestra agricultura, que es casi la única fuente de nuestra riqueza, atraviesa momentos difíciles, que tienen su exponente en el comercio general y en

la renta de Aduanas. A consecuencia de los terribles estragos de la guerra, nuestra balanza mercantil arroja un saldo en contra del país de 35 millones de pesos durante dos años y medio; las cosechas de tabaco, esperanza de nuestra clase media rural y de la mayoría de los labradores de la provincia de Pinar del Río, O. de la Habana, N. E. de Santa Clara y parte de Santiago de Cuba se ha vendido á precios ruinosos cuando ha tenido compradores, dejando en apurada situación al pequeño comercio é industrias locales; las cosechas de frutos menores han sido poco remuneradas por la ruda competencia de los productores de los Estados Unidos, cuyo maíz, papas y cereales en general, se venden á precios que nuestros cultivos no pueden resistir; y los colonos y fabricantes de azúcar ven en perspectiva precios muy bajos ante el aumento y baratura de la producción universal.

A esa baja general de nuestros frutos no corresponde, como debiera, una reducción proporcional en los gastos de la vida, que en los centros urbanos, principalmente en la Habana y Santiago de Cuba, Cienfuegos y otros lugares mas bien aumenta que disminuye; quizás por falta de competencia entre los comerciantes, que prefieren concertarse para mantener altos ó elevar los precios á luchar por obtener las mayores ventajas en el mercado atrayendo á los consumidores.

Entiendo, pues, que en todo lo relativo á la hacienda municipal deben mantenerse en vigor las órdenes publicadas hasta la fecha, y que más eficaz para el bien general sería la supresión de aquellos Ayuntamientos que realmente no prestan ningún servicio, como he expresado mas arriba.

***

Acompaño por separado cuadros de los ingresos y pagos verificados en el Departamento.

En general, los funcionarios de este Departamento han demostrado celo y la debida diligencia en el cumplimiento de sus deberes. Cuando se reorganizó el servicio en Junio del pasado año de 1900 se atendió á las tareas efectivas en aquella sazón; pero en el curso del año han tenido extraordinario desarrollo las operaciones de pago de las tesorerías y la recaudación de rentas interiores con la exigibilidad de las pensiones de censos y los pagarés, á favor del Estado cuya cobranza estaba en suspenso por virtud de las moratorias concedidas á los deudores en diversas disposiciones, que no cito por ser demasiado conocidas; y de consiguiente, el personal de las oficinas de las zonas fiscales es insuficiente actualmente. De ahí que tuviera el honor de proponerle algún aumento al formular el proyecto de presupuesto para el año fiscal corriente, y, si bien respeto las razones de necesarias economías en que se ha fundado el acuerdo de ese Gobierno Militar para no conceder por ahora el aumento solicitado, he de volver sobre ello tan luego como sean más favorables las circunstancias.

De V. obediente servidor,

LEOPOLDO CANCIO,

Secretario de Hacienda.

A

SECRETARIA DE HACIENDA.

NEGOCIADO DE CONTADURIA.—TENEDURIA DE LIBROS.

BALANCE DE LA LAS OPERACIONES EFECTUADAS EN LA TESORERIA CENTRAL DURANTE LOS MESES DE ENERO Á JUNIO DEL AÑO ACTUAL.

Debe. **Haber.**

Debe	EFECTIVO.	VALORES.	Haber	EFECTIVO.	VALORES.
EXISTENCIA EN 31 DE DICIEMBRE 1900	$ 128,262.24	$ 54.300.00	Pagado en el semestre por atenciones de Gastos Públicos según relación adjunta.	$ 1.020,439.62	$ ....
Ingresos por Fianzas por Obras Públicas..	236.00	....	Pagado Fianzas por Obras Púbicas...	236.00	....
,, ,, ,, ,, Hacienda.	....	100,000.00	,, ,, ,, Justicia........	....	8,000.00
,, ,, ,, ,, Justicia....	1,000.00	....	,, Depósitos Judiciales........	2,260.76	....
,, ,, Depósitos Judiciales......	23.80	....	,, ,, Provisionales.......	3,960.00	....
,, ,, ,, Provisionales	2,760.00	....	,, ,, Voluntarios........	124.41	....
,, ,, ,, Voluntarios...	124.41	....	,, ,, Forzosos........	1,012.50	....
,, ,, ,, Varios........	5,809.04	....	,, ,, Varios	2,805.00	....
,, ,, ,, Forzosos.......	1,012.50	....	,, Municipios. — Elecciones. — Listas de Electores........	424.00	....
,, ,, transferencia de fondos.. para pago de listas de electores de Santiago de Cuba y Tribunales de Provincia	911.50	....	Remitido á la Tesorería de la Isla por Saldos	98,080.90	....
Remesas recibidas de la Tesorería de la Isla........	1.001,236.41	....	EXISTENCIA PARA 1º DE JULIO........	12,032.71	146,300.00
	$ 1.141,375.90	$154,300.00		$ 1.141.375.90	$154,300.00

S. E. ú O.

Vto. Bno.
El Contador,
MONTALVO.

Habana, Julio 1º de 1901.
El Tenedor de Libros,
SALVADOR FELIX.

B

SECRETARIA DE HACIENDA.

NEGOCIADO DE CONTADURIA. TENEDURIA DE LIBROS.

GASTOS PUBLICOS.

Meses de Enero á Junio de 1901.

RESUMEN DE GASTOS PUBLICOS pagados en el presente semestre.

CONCEPTOS.	Por conceptos.		TOTAL.	
SECRETARIA DE ESTADO Y GOBERNACION.				
Secretaría y Subsecretaría, Personal.	$ 28.957	47		
Secretaría y Subsecretaría, Material.	2.630	90		
Congreso Médico Pan Americano.....	4.655	78		
Centro de Vacuna, Personal............	2.302	98		
Centro de Vacuna, Material............	1.488	04		
Presidio de la Isla, Personal............	27.464	59		
Presidio de la Isla, Material............	19.017	91		
Presidio de la Isla, Manutención......	24.043	08		
Presidio de la Isla, Crédito especial..	960	00		
Casa de Recogidas, Personal...........	1.316	33		
Casa de Recogidas, Material...........	1.271	93		
Casa de Recogidas, Manutención......	884	25		
Impresos para el Registro Pecuario..	6.481	62		
Archivo General de la Isla, Personal.	7.158	46		
Archivo General de la Isla, Material	297	60		
Convención Constituyente, Personal y Dietas..	56.065	88		
Convención Constituyente, Personal subalterno..	18.907	06		
Convención Constituyente, Personal Taquígrafo..	8.365	00		
Convención Constituyente, Material y Gastos	2.588	53		
Convención Constituyente, Alquileres..	8.181	78		
Convención Constituyente, Diario de Sesiones...	2.056	75		
Convención Constituyente, Gastos instalación..	4.890	42		
Convención Constituyente, Gastos de viaje..	103	70		
Asilo de Enagenados, Reparaciones..	550	80		
Exposición de Buffalo, Estado y Gobernación..	254	00		
Gastos Extraordinarios....................	110	50		
Comisión Especial del Muermo, Indemnizaciones...............................	2.232	50		
Guardia Rural..................................	41	75		
Gastos de exhortos..........................	51	00		
Comisión Especial del Muermo, Material..	1.887	20		
Comisión Especial del Muermo, Personal..	1.550	43		
Secretaría de Estado y Gobernación Adquisición de muebles.................	2.976	42		
Convención Constituyente, Gastos Extraordinarios............................	172	00		
A la vuelta..............	$ 239.916	66	$ 239.916	66

C

RESUMEN DE GASTOS PUBLICOS pagados en el presente semestre.—Continuación.

CONCEPTOS.	Por conceptos.		TOTAL.	
De la vuelta			$ 239.916	66
SECRETARIA DE JUSTICIA.				
Secretaría y Subsecretaría, Personal.	$ 24.442	19		
Secretaría y Subsecretaría, Material.	913	50		
Tribunal Supremo y Fiscalía, Personal	47.608	98		
Tribunal Supremo y Fiscalía, Material	1.049	08		
Consejo Administrativo, Personal	533	28		
Consejo Administrativo, Material	101	08		
Tribunales de Provincias	1.237	50		
Comisión Investigadora de Bienes del Estado, Personal	1.288	33		
Comisión Investigadora de Bienes del Estado, Material	.....	.....		
Adquisición de Libros	249	74		
Inspección de Penales, Personal y Dietas	3.562	78		
Tribunal Supremo, Mobiliario	362	50		
Gastos Extraordinarios, Secretaría Justicia	5.629	46		
Derechos de Notario	49	60		
	$ 87.028	02	$ 87.028	02
SECRETARIA DE INSTRUCCION PUBLICA.				
Secretaría y Subsecretaría, Personal.	$ 9.219	84		
Secretaría y Subsecretaría, Material.	434	70		
Universidad, personal	105.949	96		
Universidad, Material	15.460	07		
Escuela de Pintura, Personal	5.299	86		
Escuela de Pintura, Material	387	79		
Escuela de Pintura, Material Artístico	500	02		
Escuela de Artes y Oficios, Personal.	9.982	87		
Escuela de Artes y Oficios, Material.	4.875	73		
Academia de Ciencias, Subvención	450	00		
Laboratorio Bacteriológico, Subvención	2.250	00		
Superintendencia de Escuelas, Personal	8.828	76		
Superintendencia de Escuelas, Material	706	68		
Oficina del Comisionado de Escuelas, Personal	11.688	15		
Oficina del Comisionado de Escuelas, Material	36.194	11		
Oficina del Comisionado de Escuelas, Alquileres	1.225	00		
Oficina del Comisionado de Escuelas, Gastos de distribución de libros	3.537	98		
Instrucción Pública.—Institutos	100	00		
Al frente	$ 217.091	52	$ 326.944	68

Resumen de gastos publicos pagados en el presente semestre.—*Continuación.*

CONCEPTOS.	Por conceptos.		TOTAL.	
Del frente	$ 217,091	52	$ 326,944	68
SECRETARIA DE INSTRUCCION PUBLICA				
Exposición de Buffalo.—Universidad.	$ 288	72		
Exposición de Buffalo.—Escuela de Pintura	250	00		
Exposición de Buffalo.—Escuela de Artes y Oficios	497	89		
Oficina del Comisionado de Escuelas. Gastos Extraordinarios	1.376	19		
Oficina del Comisionado de Escuelas Dietas	1.097	08		
Oficina del Comisionado de Escuelas. Compra de libros	113.328	92		
Universidad.—Material Científico.—Gastos Especiales	29.510	40		
	$ 363.440	72	$ 363.440	72
SECRETARIA DE HACIENDA.				
Secretaría y Tesorería, Personal	$ 40.886	46		
Secretaría y Tesorería, Material	2.662	67		
Impresos de carácter general	965	25		
Visitas Oficiales	1.693	14		
Comisión investigadora de la Deuda Municipal	102	00		
Comisión investigadora del Municipio de la Habana	1.197	50		
Comisión especial supervisora del Amillaramiento de la Habana	304	17		
Tasación de terrenos de la Iglesia	1.500	00		
	$ 49.311	19	$ 49.311	19
SECRETARIA DE AGRICULTURA, COMERCIO É INDUSTRIA.				
Secretaría y Subsecretaría, Personal.	$ 9.390	50		
Secretaría y Subsecretaría, Material.	443	92		
Sección de Agricultura, Comercio é Industria, Personal	9.769	41		
Sección de Agricultura, Comercio é Industria, Material	431	52		
Visitas Oficiales de Agricultura	6	00		
Fomento á la Agricultura	3.500	00		
Inspección Montes y Minas, Personal	5.064	79		
Inspección Montes y Minas, Material	208	75		
Agricultura Provincias.—Ganado para la Isla	112.000	00		
A la vuelta	$ 140,814	89	$ 739.696	59

E

RESUMEN DE GASTOS PUBLICOS pagados en el presente semestre.—Continuación.

CONCEPTOS.	Por conceptos.		TOTAL.	
De la vuelta.............	$ 140,814	89	$ 739,696	59
SECRETARIA DE AGRICULTURA, COMERCIO É INDUSTRIA.				
Exposición de Buffalo......................	25.545	09		
Mobiliario y gastos extraordinarios.	982	00		
Impresión de la memoria anual........	2.615	00		
	$ 169.956	98	$ 169.956	98
SECRETARIA DE OBRAS PUBLICAS.				
Comisión de Faros, Personal............	$ 11.912	11		
Comisión de Faros, Material.....	491	76		
Faros, Torreros y Vigías, Personal..	19.610	74		
Faros, Lavado de paños y servicio de comunicaciones.........................	5 099	57		
Faros, Estudios y Proyectos..............	1.221	80		
Faros, Gastos imprevistos................	820	95		
Faros, Aceite, efectos y su conducción	2.655	86		
Faros, Boyas y Valizas......................	37.493	57		
Faros, Visitas oficiales.	537	00		
Construcción del Faro, Punta de los Colorados.......................................	544	25		
Pintura á la valiza del Cabeza de Arreola	4	05		
Faros, Cayo Jutía y Punta de la Gobernadora.................................	30.368	82		
Luz del Faro Pasa Caballos.............	25	57		
	$ 110.786	05	$ 110.786	05
Total general	....	.....	$1.020.439	62

RESUMEN.	Total por Departamentos.	
Secretaría de Estado y Gobernación.	$ 239.902	14
Secretaría de Justicia.......................	87.042	54
Secretaría de Instrucción Pública......	363.440	72
Secretaría de Hacienda.	49.311	19
Secretaría de Agricultura, Industria y Comercio....................................	169.956	98
Secretaría de Obras Públicas	110.786	05
Total General....................	$1.020.439	62

Habana, 30 de Junio de 1901.

Vto. Bno.:

El Contador, *El Tenedor de Libros,*

MONTALVO. SALVADOR VELIZ.

F

ESTADO GENERAL ¦*s Fiscales de la Isla de Cuba, en el semestre comprendido*

	…nfuegos.	Holguín.	Manzanillo.	TOTALES.
Derechos reales	…5,459.69	$ 5,880.99	$ 5,288.47	$ 202,771.55
Pertenencias mineras	....	....	....	2,435.00
Subsidio Industrial	....	244.67	....	66,971.61
Productos forestales	....	....	....	602.20
Redención de censos	....	....	....	2,918.49
Réditos de censos	....	....	....	14,076.61
Intereses de demora	295.75	79.28	6.07	2,441.13
Alquileres de fincas	....	140.00	....	3,257.23
Venta de terrenos	....	....	....	1,063.92
Productos diversos	198.98	183.95	41.89	46,268.87
Recargo 5%	131.27	....	....	1,437.81
Venta de efectos inútiles	....	....	....	27.35
	…7,085.69	$ 6,528.89	$ 5,336.43	$ 344,271.77

C…a, 30 de Junio de 1901.

RAMON… CARLOS CAVALLÉ,

Jefe del Nego… Jefe de la Contabilidad.

G

	Cienfuegos.	Holguín.	Manzanillo.	TOTAL.
Derechos reales..............	$ 1,424.95	$ 950.24	$ 66.40	$ 26,250.03
Pertenencias mineras.....	....	....	....	328.00
Subsidio Industrial........	....	....	....	5,020.06
Productos forestales......	....	....	....	400.20
Redención de censos.......	....	....	....	793.42
Réditos de censos...........	....	....	....	3,911.04
Intereses de demora.......	21.88	4.03	10	241.42
Alquileres de fincas.........	....	40.00	....	448.76
Venta de terrenos...........	....	....	....	1,018.26
Productos diversos	56.00	18.70	6.00	5,677.01
Recargo 5%..................	....	....	....	255.68
	$ 1,502.83	$ 1,012.97	$ 72.50	$ 44,343.88

	Cienfuegos	Holguín.	Manzanillo.	TOTAL.
Derechos reales.............	$ 2,364.34	$ 333.66	$ 2,132.66	$ 33,425.07
Pertenencias mineras....	....	....	....	....
Subsidio Industrial.......	....	....	....	37,922.81
Productos forestales.....	....	....	....	42.00
Redención de censos.. ...	....	....	....	....
Réditos de censos...........	....	....	....	3,970.31
Intereses de demora.........	20 51	5.96	70	225.29
Alquileres de fincas............	....	....	....	418.45
Venta de terrenos...............	....	....	....	....
Productos diversos..............	[illegible].85	6 00	....	5,999.38
Recargo 5%........................	[illegible]6	....	....	289.93
	[illegible]	$ 345 62	$ 2,133.36	$ 82,293.24

	Cienfuegos.	Holguín.	Manzanillo.	TOTALES.
Derechos reales	$ 2,908.57	$ 808.16	$ 324.84	$ 39,273.83
Pertenencias mineras				209.00
Subsidio Industrial				1,214.36
Redención de censos				1,702.13
Réditos de censos				3,070.04
Intereses de demora	92.18	3.12	.08	1,012.37
Alquileres de fincas		20.00		425.57
Venta de terrenos				
Productos forestales				80.00
Productos diversos	14.25	1.75	21.00	5,312.36
Recargo 5%	44.68			388.69
	$ 3,059.68	$ 833.03	$ 345 92	$ 52,688.35

	Cienfuegos.	Holguín.	Manzanillo.	TOTALES.
Derechos reales	$ 4,971.71	$ 811.39	$ 193.40	$ 42,511.33
Pertenencias mineras				276.00
Subsidio Industrial		134.20		11,503.26
Productos forestales				80.00
Redención de censos				299.08
Réditos de censos				1,130.21
Intereses de demora	74.25	38.99	3.11	456.54
Alquileres de fincas		20.00		618.24
Venta de terrenos				
Productos diversos	54.40	113.00		6,263.55
Recargo 5%	68.43			248.21
	$ 5,168.79	$ 1,117.58	$ 196.51	$ 63,386.42

	.	Cienfuegos.	Holguín.	Manzanillo.	TOTAL.
Derechos reales.....	36	$ 2,134.24	$ 2,390.15	$ 197.32	$ 32,244.04
Pertenencias mineras..	....	....	....	....	558.00
Subsidio Industrial....	....	....	....	....	10,921.73
Productos forestales..	....	....	....	....	....
Redención de censos...	....	....	....	....	123.86
Réditos de censos.......	56	....	....	....	1,215.20
Intereses de demora...	43	22.48	14.61	1.86	280.91
Alquileres de fincas....	....	....	20.00	....	493.30
Venta de terrenos	....	....	....	....	45.66
Productos diversos....	27	42.88	7.50	12.00	12,920.17
Recargo 5%..............	33	5.12	....	....	136.54
	35	$ 2,204.72	$ 2,432.26	$ 211.18	$ 58,939.41

	s.	Cienfuegos.	Holguín.	Manzanillo.	TOTAL.
Derechos reales.........	43	$ 2,655.88	$ 587.39	$ 2,373.85	$ 29,067.25
Pertenencias mineras.	....	....	....	....	1,064.00
Subsidio Industrial...	....		110.47	....	389.39
Productos forestales..	....	....	....	....	....
Redención de censos...	....	....	....	....	....
Réditos de censos.......	75	....	....	....	779.81
Intereses de demora...	88	64.45	12.57	.22	224.64
Alquileres de fincas....	....	....	40.00	....	852.91
Venta de terrenos......	....	....	....	....	....
Productos diversos....	00	.60	37.00	2.89	10,096.40
Recargo 5%..............	29	8.18	....	....	118.76
Venta de efectos inúti	....	....	....	....	27.35
	35	$ 2,729.11	$ 787.43	$ 2,376.96	$ 42,620.51

J

RESUMEN GENER...nte el semestre comprendido de 1º de Enero á 30 de J...

	...ienfuegos.	Holguín.	Manzanillo.	TOTALES.
Estado y Gobernación	...16,117.55	$ 3,264.00	$ 3,234.71	$ 556,394.11
Hacienda	6,766.02	6,670.81	4,645 39	149,121.17
Justicia	...14,657.20	10,301.93	7,106.85	416,630.66
Agricultura, Industria, y Comercio				195,191.10
Instrucción Pública				506,353.59
Obras Públicas (Faros)				110,786.05
Municipalidades	...43,851.72	116,814.69	91,913.91	2,059,609.92
Gobierno Militar.—Guardia Rural				17,924.84
Hospitales y Asilos	...33,859.93	14,298.75	14,687.02	534,233.37
	...35,252.42	$151,350.18	$121,587.88	$ 4,546,244.81

K

1901.		Holguín.	Manzanillo.	TOTALES.
Enero	2,604.99	$ 433.70	$ 939.02	$ 50,096.95
Febrero	2,121.02	354.40	243.60	86,104.24
Marzo	1,932.47	575.80	383.85	107,952.69
Abril	2,268.31	600.60	540.30	87,470.52
Mayo	3,204.78	516.00	262.50	81,888.72
Junio	3,985.98	783.50	865.44	142,880.99
	,117.55	$ 3,264.00	$ 3,234.71	$ 556,394.11

1901.	egos.	Holguín.	Manzanillo.	TOTALES'
Enero	983.37	$ 2,201.42	$ 722.92	$ 18,188.63
Febrero	841.11	753.05	236.90	19,643.55
Marzo	1,020.28	1,570.98	1,339.00	32,115.58
Abril	929.26	....	849.42	22,147.05
Mayo	1,040.50	715.40	30.85	20,409.40
Junio	1,951.50	1,429.96	1,466.30	36,616.96
	,766.02	$ 6,670.81	$ 4.645.39	$ 149,121.17

L

1901.	uegos.	Holguín.	Manzanillo	TOTALES.
Enero	$ 1,025.23	$ 403.13	$ 466.64	$ 31,793.50
Febrero	780.81	3,163.66	1,745.98	47,037.30
Marzo	2,714.40	696.28	968.28	73,692.10
Abril	2,706.60	1,528.76	1,446.62	83,984.85
Mayo	2,560.36	1,323.91	499.98	60,315.47
Junio	4,869.80	3,186.19	1,979.35	119,807 44
	4,657.20	$ 10,301.93	$ 7,106.85	$ 416,630.66

1901	iegos.	Holguín.	Manzanillo.	TOTALES.
Enero				$ 55,081.72
Febrero				8,972.16
Marzo				14,988.45
Abril				9,855.78
Mayo				69,269.22
Junio				37,023.77
				$ 195,191.10

1901.	Teso Cent / Cienfuegos.	Holguín.	Manzanillo.	TOTALES.
Enero	$ 4,0			$ 23,061.97
Febrero	28,8			47,428.36
Marzo	64,7			87,278.76
Abril	65,1			87,388.87
Mayo	46,5			65,280.78
Junio	153,8			195,914.85
	$363,2			$ 506,353.59

1901.	Teso Cent / Cienfuegos.	Holguín.	Manzanillo.	TOTALES.
Enero	$ 8,3			$ 8,398.18
Febrero	10,9			10,900.34
Marzo	14,4			14,494.67
Abril	23,7			23.784.77
Mayo	8,7			8,787.15
Junio	44,4			44,420.94
	$110,7			$ 110.786.05

1901.	Teso Cent Cienfuegos.	Holguín.	Manzanillo.	TOTALES.
Enero	$ 4,0	....	....	$ 23,061.97
Febrero	28,8	....	....	47,428.36
Marzo	64,7	....	....	87,278.76
Abril	65,1	....	....	87,388.87
Mayo	46,5	....	....	65,280.78
Junio	153,8	....	....	195,914.85
	$363,2	....	....	$ 506,353.59

1901.	Teso Cent Cienfuegos.	Holguín.	Manzanillo.	TOTALES.
Enero	$ 8,3	....	....	$ 8,398.18
Febrero	10,9	....	....	10,900.34
Marzo	14,4	....	....	14,494.67
Abril	23,7	....	....	23,784.77
Mayo	8,7	....	....	8,787.15
Junio	44,4	....	....	44,420.94
	$110,7	....	....	$ 110,786.05

1901.	Tc C	Cienfuegos.	Holguín.	Manzanillo.	Totales.
Enero		$ 44,425.85	$ 19,387.12	$ 17,301.68	$ 296,185.68
Febrero		34,551.93	15,134 54	13,326.72	293,746.37
Marzo		32,524.65	16,524.80	12,334.19	315,271.03
Abril		38,205.70	20,939 87	13,202.94	338,234.10
Mayo		35,610.42	16,581.69	12,313.80	318,454.93
Junio		68,533.17	28,246.67	23,434 58	515,642.65
		$243,851.72	$116,814.69	$ 91,913.91	$ 2,077,534.76

1901.	T C	Cienfuegos.	Holguín.	Manzanillo.	Totales.
Enero		$ 13,026.91	$ 1,057.15	$ 1,937.50	$ 65,894.36
Febrero		11,873 10	2,022.60	2,042.23	88,797.79
Marzo		12,209 00	3,293.40	1,015.00	72,287.12
Abril		11,702.17	1,986 90	1,414.35	80,496.03
Mayo		12,398.67	1,813 33	2,467.15	73,601.62
Junio		22,650.08	4,125 37	5,810.79	153,156.45
		$ 83,859.93	$ 14,298.75	$ 14,687.02	$ 534,233.37

RESUMEN GEN…ulio de 1900 á 30 de Junio de 1901.

	T… …nfuegos.	Holguín.	Manzanillo.	TOTAL.
Rentas recaudadas..........	$ …9,020.03	$ 11,688.11	$ 8,984.63	$ 671,053.41
Fondos recibidos del Tesorero General para Gastos..........	1.7…2,811.08	246.960.80	196,407.47	8.208,601.80
Transferencias entre Oficiales Pagadores..........	7.226.00	5.180.00	2,630.00	64,706.83
Reintegros por sobrantes de la cuenta de Gastos.	136 33	15.00	109.20	13,685.85
Depósitos de Minas..........	......	....	....	5,774.00
Pagarés á vencer..........	......	....	....	4,301.26
Depósitos y Fianzas..........	2…3,512.42	3,580.03	886.58	1.093,844.70
	$1.9…7,705 86	$267,423 94	$209,017.88	$10.061,967.85

	T… …nfuegos.	Holguín	Manzanillo.	TOTAL.
Gastos Públicos..........	$1.5…9,985.39	$239,272.91	$190,762.66	$ 7.743,407.85
Remesas al Tesorero General por Rentas recaudadas..........	…,020.03	11,688.11	8,984.63	669,340.72
Transferencias entre Oficiales Pagadores..........	…........	....	....	64,706.83
Reintegros al Tesorero General por sobrantes de Gastos..........	…,618 69	5,883.00	5,544.14	272,916.07
Depósitos de Minas..........	......	....	....	5,774.00
Depósitos y Fianzas..........	…,327.24	1,171.20	....	659,188.65
BALANCE..........	1…,754.51	9,408.72	3,726.45	646,633.73
	$1.9…7,705.86	$267,423.94	$209,017.88	$10.061,967.85

…901.

	T… C…fuegos.	Holguín.	Manzanillo.	TOTAL.
Remanente de Rentas en manos de Colectores..........	$	$........	$........	$ 1,712.69
Efectivo disponible para Gastos..........	…,569.33	6,999.89	2,839.87	205,963.73
Pagarés á vencer..........	......	....	....	4,301.26
Depósitos y Fianzas..........	15…,185.18	2,408 83	886.58	434,656.05
	$ 15…,754.51	$ 9,408.72	$ 3,726.45	$ 646,633.73

REPORT

OF THE

SECRETARY OF FINANCE,

FOR THE PERIOD OF SIX MONTHS ENDING

DECEMBER 31, 1901.

DEPARTMENT OF FINANCE.

Havana, March 15, 1902.

Brigadier General Leonard Wood,
Military Governor of Cuba.

Sir:

I have the honor to report the operations of this office during the last half year without making any mention of the special commissions conferred on the undersigned, as being alien to the proper functions of this Department.

The first eleven statements enclosed comprise a general summary of the receipts and payments made during the calendar year of 1901 in the eleven zones in which the territory of the Island is divided for the fiscal service, and the twelfth contains the general summary of the payments made by the Treasury annexed to this office. It will thus be easy to make a comparison of the receipts and disbursements of public funds in the second half year to which this report refers with those of the first half year that have already been the object of a report forwarded to Headquarters.

The receipts of the second half year exceeded those of the first in Pinar del Río, Guanajay, Matanzas, Cárdenas, Cienfuegos, Puerto Príncipe, Santiago de Cuba and Holguín, and were less in Havana, Santa Clara and Manzanillo. It will be noticed that the increase in the former is principally due to the tax on the transfer of real estate and the receipts from interest on censos, owing no doubt to Order No. 139, of 1901, which as a general rule put an end to the extensions of time that had been granted since 1896 to debtors for certain kinds of dues on territorial property. The falling off in the receipts in the Zone of Havana is undoubtedly due to the fact that the tax on mercantile firms and Companies referred to in Order No. 463, of 1900. generally falls due in the first half of the year.

Statement No. 13 contains the total for the calendar years of 1900 and 1901. Comparing the one with the other there appears a difference of $73,380.35 in favor of 1901 in the receipts from taxes common to both years, it being noted that the tax on passenger fares and freight rates, which produced $178,731.65 in 1900, had been abolished in 1901.

The yield from what are now called internal revenues, and which were formerly called terrestrial taxes, is of scanty importance in relation to the State expenditures. Almost all the obligations of the State are borne by the customs revenues; but as the tariff will have to undergo alterations which will produce a falling off in the revenues if the reciprocity now being sought in Washington is obtained, it may be necessary to have recourse to new sources of income to compensate for the difference.

The danger entailed to the Public Treasury by its dependence on an almost exclusive source of income have never been discounted by the undersigned, but he has also been of the opinion that our economic condition lacked sufficient elasticity to bear new taxes at the end of a devastating war that ravaged our fields and destroyed or ruined our principal agricultural industries. A change in the tributary system of a country is never to be desired during a crisis, especially if the system already in force produces a plentiful income, as is the case with the one now in existence here since 1899, and it is hardly conceivable that any other system could have been devised which would have produced the sum of 20,000,000 dollars annually which has been collected from the customs, internal sources of revenue, the post office and municipalities during the period above mentioned. This is borne out by an approximate analysis of our production in general and also by the figures in connection with our mercantile transactions in the statistics of the Custom House, which are of course the best index as to the economic activity of a country which exports perhaps seventy-five per cent of what it produces and imports at present eighty per cent of what it consumes. Without doubt, the burden has been more bearable from the fact that it is in accordance with customary methods of taxation here, and any radical change would have been greatly felt, if indeed such a change had not proved intolerable.

In the same statements of the eleven fiscal zones and following the receipts, are to be seen the payments made by their respective Treasuries, these being lower in the second half of the calendar year of 1901 than in the first, for the reasons that when the fiscal year commenced the General Treasury stopped the payment of Municipal Police, the service of Hospitals and Charities was reorganized, Primary Instruction was regulated in all the Island, the charge to the State for Correctional Courts was limited to the deficits resulting from the insufficiency of their special receipts to meet the cost of the same, and a general increase in the burden to be borne by the municipalities, all of which charges caused a marked reduction in the expenditures from public funds.

Statement No. 2 that comprises payments made by the Treasury annexed to this Department shows the same spirit of ecomomy. $1,020,863.62 were paid in the first half of the calendar year and $717,073.18 in the second, or a difference of $303,790.44 in favor of the latter. Adding this sum to the $875,515.12 which was the reduction in the amount paid by the eleven fiscal zones, it is seen that the burden on the General Treasury was diminished by $1,179,303.56 in the services paid by this office and its dependencies during the second half of 1901 as compared with the first half of the same year. These differences appear in Statement No. 14.

It is a circumstance that I deem well worthy of noting that all these disbursements represent payments for services rendered in the country and the remuneration for which re-enters the channels of circulation through all the Island; and, for that reason, the present pressure of taxation is more bearable; just the opposite to what occurred under the former régime, in which the administration was an insatiable consumer that neglected local needs to attend to those of Sovereignty, and did not return the large amounts it collected to the circulation of the country but took them out of the Island to pay interest on the public debt, subventions, pensions, and salaries with the aggravating circumstance that even the greater part of the salaries that were paid went to employes whose families and interests were almost all located in the Metropolis.

I forward separately some statements. One of them contains the percentage of the total receipts of internal revenues that correspond to each fiscal zone and the other the proportion corresponding to each item of taxation. Another statement shows the proportion of public expenditures in each department with relation to the total amount of payments made by this Office and its dependencies. Finally, another statement contains the general summary of the account of deposits and guarantees.

Several statistical works of a general character are about to be published. One of them on the cattle slaughtered in municipal abbatoirs, with a note of the weight and price of the meat consumed and another on the Municipal budgets of 1900-1901 and the liquidation of the budgets of 1899-1900.

During the half year inspections have been made in a great number of Ayuntamientos, the results of which have been reported to Headquarters. As a general rule, but scanty care has been observed in the administration of Municipal finances and veritable incompetency has been observed in not a few of them. Cases of delinquency have not been lacking, which compelled this Office to forward the proceedings to the Fiscal of the Supreme Court, the most notable of these cases being that of the Ayuntamiento of San Luis, in the Province of Pinar del Río.

The result of these inspections is to show the propriety of the suppression of Ayuntamientos made by Order No. 23, current series. The inspections show that these rural Municipalities were without resources wherewith to fulfil their obligations and lacked a competent personnel for the management of public affairs. The same defects found in the suppressed Ayuntamientos are still observed in not a few of the existing ones.

A fact worthy of special mention is that the Ayuntamientos draft their budgets according to the requirements established by the legislation in force, balancing their expenditures and receipts within the prescribed regulations; but these are hardly put into practice when they commence to request authority for new expenditures, transfers of credits, creation of services, and above all of personnel; so that if said petitions were granted the approved budget would be virtually disfigured. This latter document contains provision for Public Works, repair of roads, lighting and other expenditures, which provision is not expended according to the amount estimated because the actual receipts hardly exceed what is consumed by the personnel, office material and other indispensable expenses. There are Ayuntamientos like

Santa María del Rosario that have annual receipts amounting to six thousand dollars, in which fifteen hundred are absorbed by the salary of the Mayor.

I forward separate statements showing the condition of the work of the assessment, directed by Order No. 335, series of 1900. It is seen that among the Ayuntamientos left standing after Order No. 23, a minority of 33 have finished their enrollments and in 49 they are still pending, it being worthy of attention that among the latter figure all the provincial capitals, with the exception of Santa Clara, and towns of such importance as Guanajay, Güines, San Antonio de los Baños, Santiago de las Vegas, Cárdenas, Sagua la Grande, Cienfuegos, Trinidad, Sancti Spiritus, Caibarién and Gibara.

I am preparing a more general and detailed report that will comprise all the year up to the coming change of régime, and I will then have the occasion to deal at length on the services of this Department.

Very respectfully,

LEOPOLDO CANCIO.

Secretary of Finance.

Besides the civil orders which the Secretary of Finance has proposed to the Military Governor, the following dispositions have been published in the Gazette during the second half of the year 1901.

Assessments. Circular dated September 26, 1901, instructing the Municipal Alcaldes to carry out what is laid down in Order 141 as to the completion of the assessments.

.... Circular dated October 22, 1901, establishing the manner in which rural properties are to be assessed when said properties belong to more than one municipal district and to the same proprietor.

Modification of Fiscal Zones. By an order dated October 21, 1901, it is decided that the Municipality of Sagua de Tánamo, which belongs to the zone of Holguín, shall in the future form part of the zone of Santiago.

Municipal Finances. Circular of October 24, 1901, to the Municipal Alcaldes, reminds them that they are prohibited to transfer credits without the authorization of the chief authority in the Island.

..........................Circulars of October 31, and November 26, 1901, instructing the zone administrators and Municipal Alcaldes that proceedings for enforcement of payment of taxes should not be allowed to stop during the electoral period.

.... Resolution of November 25, 1901, regarding the manner in which the taxes are to be collected in the suppressed Ayuntamiento of Regla.

Transfer Taxes. Circular of October 11, 1901, reproducing resolutions of the Secretary of Justice in order that the functionaries of the judicial department and Notaries carry out the orders in Regulations for the Fiscal tax on the transfer of property.

INFORME

DEL

SECRETARIO DE HACIENDA,

COMPRENDIENDO

EL SEMESTRE TERMINADO EN DICIEMBRE 31

DE 1901.

SECRETARIA DE HACIENDA.

Habana, Marzo 15 de 1902.

Al Brigadier General Leonard Wood,
Gobernador Militar de Cuba.

SEÑOR:

Tengo el honor de dar á Vd. cuenta de las operaciones de esta Secretaría durante el último semestre sin hacer mención de las comisiones especiales conferidas al que suscribe, extrañas á las funciones propias del Departamento.

Los once primeros cuadros adjuntos comprenden un resúmen general de los ingresos y pagos habidos durante el año natural de 1901 en las once Zonas en que está dividido el territorio de la Isla para los servicios fiscales y el duodécimo el resumen general de los pagos hechos por la Tesorería anexa á esta Secretaría. Así es fácil la comparación del movimiento de las cajas públicas del segundo semestre á que se contrae este informe con el primero que ya fué objeto de informe elevado á ese Cuartel General en su oportunidad.

La recaudación del segundo semestre superó á la del primero en Pinar del Río, Guanajay, Matanzas, Cárdenas, Cienfuegos, Puerto Príncipe, Santiago de Cuba y Holguín y fué inferior en la Habana, Santa Clara y Manzanillo, siendo de notar que el alza en las primeras procede principalmente del impuesto de transmisión de bienes ó derechos reales y del cobro de réditos de censos, sin duda por efecto de la orden número 139 de la serie de 1901, que puso término por regla general á las moratorias que desde 1896 venían concediéndose á los deudores de ciertas clases de créditos sobre la propiedad territorial. La diferencia en menos que se nota en la zona de la Habana es debida sin duda al hecho de que la contribución sobre las sociedades y empresas á que se contrae la orden número 463 de 1900 vence generalmente en el primer semestre.

El cuadro Nº 13 contiene la recaudación total de los años naturales de 1900 y 1901. Comparada una y otra resulta una diferencia en favor de 1901 de 73.380 pesos 35 centavos, en los conceptos que subsistían en el año último, pues había sido abolido el importe sobre tarifas de viajeros y fletes de mercancías que en 1900 produjo 178.731 pesos 65 centavos.

De poca monta es en relación con los gastos del Estado el rendimiento de las llamadas hoy rentas interiores, que antes se denominaban terrestres. Casi todas las obligaciones del Tesoro gravitan sobre la renta de Aduanas, pero como los aranceles han de sufrir alteraciones que producirán baja en la renta si se concierta la reciprocidad que se gestiona en Washington será forzoso acudir á nuevas fuentes de ingresos que compensen tales quebrantos.

No se ha ocultado nunca al que informa los peligros que entraña para el Tesoro público su dependencia de una fuente de ingresos casi exclusiva, pero también ha sido de parecer que nuestras fuerzas económicas no tenían elasticidad suficiente para sorportar nuevos tributos á raíz de la guerra asoladora que arrasó nuestros campos y dejó á nuestras principales industrias agrícolas destruídas ó arruinadas. Nunca es oportuna la alteración de un sistema tributario en momentos de crísis, sobre todo si el vijente asegura pingues rendimientos, como ha venido sucediendo desde 1899, pues apenas se concibe que en ninguna otra forma hubiera podido extraerse de la riqueza de Cuba en ese período la suma de 20.000.000 pesos anuales en moneda americana que han producido las aduanas, las rentas interiores, correos y rentas municipales. Así lo demostraría un cálculo, aproximado siquiera de nuestra producción en general y particularmente el estudio de nuestro movimiento mercantil en las estadísticas de Aduanas, que son el mejor exponente de la actividad económica en un país que exporta el setenta y cinco por ciento quizás de todo lo que produce é importa hoy el ochenta por ciento de todo lo que consume. La costumbre de tributar en la forma actual ha hecho, sin duda, llevadera la carga, que con cualquier cambio radical habría sido más sensible, si no imposible de sobrellevar.

En los mismos cuadros de las once zonas fiscales aparecen á continuación de los ingresos los pagos realizados en sus respectivas tesorerías, inferiores en el segundo semestre al primero del año natural de 1901, pues al empezar el año fiscal dejó de pagar el Tesoro General la Policía Municipal, se reorganizó el servicio de Hospitales y de Beneficencia, se regularizó en toda la Isla la Instrucción Primaria, se limitó la carga de los Juzgados Correccionales á los déficits resultantes de la insuficiencia de sus ingresos especiales y en general fueron castigados todos los presupuestos, haciéndose reducciones apreciables en los gastos públicos.

El Estado Nº 12 que comprende los pagos realizados por la caja anexa á esta Secretaría, demuestra el mismo espíritu de economía. En el primer semestre del año natural se pagaron $1.020,863.62 y en el segundo $717,073.18 ó sea una diferencia en menos de $303,790.44. Unida esta cifra á los $875,515.12 que se pagaron de menos en las once zonas fiscales, resulta que en los servicios pagados por esta Secretaría y sus dependencias la carga del Tesoro General durante el segundo semestre disminuyó en $1.179,305.56 comparada con la del primero del año 1901. Esas diferencias aparecen del cuadro número 13.

Es circunstancia que no me parece ocioso consignar la de que todos esos pagos representan servicios efectivos que se prestan en el país, y cuya remuneración entra de nuevo en los canales de la circulación por todo el ámbito de la Isla por lo cual también es más soportable la presión tributaria actual; al revés de lo que acontecía bajo el antiguo régimen en que la administración era un consumidor insaciable, y, dejando abandonados los servicios locales para atender á los de soberanía, no devolvía al torrente circulatorio las sumas cuantiosas que recaudaba, sino que tenían que sacarse de la Isla para pagar intereses de la deuda pública, subvenciones, pensiones y salarios, con el adimento de que aún la mayor parte de los sueldos que se pagaban aquí iban á manos de empleados cuyas familias é intereses radicaban casi todos en la Metrópoli.

Acompaño por separado cuadros que contienen uno el tanto por ciento de la total recaudación de rentas interiores que corresponde á cada zona fiscal, y el otro la proporción correspondiente á cada concepto contributivo. Otro cuadro expresa la proporción de los gastos públicos por cada departamento con relación á la totalidad de los pagos hechos por esta Secretaría y sus dependencias. Por último, otro cuadro contiene el resúmen general de la cuenta de depósitos y fianzas.

Están próximos á su publicación varios trabajos estadísticos de interés general. Uno sobre el ganado beneficiado en los mataderos municipales, con expresión del peso y el precio de las carnes puestas al consumo y otro de los presupuestos municipales de 1900 á 1901 y la liquidación de los presupuestos de 1899 á 1900.

Durante el semestre se han girado visita á gran número de Ayuntamientos, dando cuenta á usted del resultado. Por regla general se ha observado poca diligencia en la administración de hacienda municipal, y en no pocos municipios verdadera incompetencia. No han faltado tampoco casas de delincuencia, que han obligado á esta Secretaría á remitir el tanto de culpa al Fiscal del Tribunal Supremo de la Isla, siendo el más notable de todo el del Ayuntamiento de San Luis, provincia de Pinar del Río.

El resultado de tal inspección demuestra la coveniencia de la supresión de Ayuntamientos hecha por la Orden Nº 23 de la serie de este año; municipios rurales sin recursos para atender á los servicios propios de su institución, y en los cuales no se encuentra personal idóneo para la gestión de los interéses públicos, á juzgar por el resultado de las visitas. Todavía en no pocos Ayuntamientos de los que subsisten se observan los mismos defectos que en los suprimidos.

Es digno de especial mención que los Ayuntamientos preparan sus presupuestos, con los requisitos de forma que establece la legislación vijente, nivelando sus gastos é ingresos dentro de las prescripciones reglamentarias; pero apenas los ponen en ejecución empiezan á solicitar autorizaciones para nuevos gastos, transferencias de créditos, creación de servicios, sobre todo de personal; de tal suerte que de accederse á tales solicitudes quedaría virtualmente disfigurado en el presupuesto aprobado. En este aparecen obras públicas, reparaciones de caminos, alumbrado y otros gastos, que al cabo no se hacen en la cuantía con que se proyectan, porque lo recaudado efectivamente poco supera á lo que consume el personal, el material de oficinas y otras erogaciones indispensables. Hay Ayuntamientos como el de Santa María del Rosario en que de una recaudación de seis mil pesos anuales absorbe mil quinientos el sueldo del Alcalde Municipal.

Por separado acompaño cuadros que demuestran el estado de los trabajos del Amillaramiento ordenado por la Orden Nº 335 de la serie de 1900. Resulta que de los Ayuntamientos que subsisten después de la Orden 23 una minoría, 33 tienen terminados los padrones y 49 los tienen pendientes, llamando la atención que figuren entre estos últimos todas las capitales de provincia, con excepción de Santa Clara y poblaciones tan importantes como Guanajay, Güines, San Antonio de los Baños, Santiago de las Vegas, Cárdenas, Sagua la Grande, Cienfuegos, Trinidad, Sancti Spíritus, Caibarién y Gibara.

Preparo el informe más general y detallado que comprenderá todo el año hasta el cambio de régimen que se aproxima y entonces tendré ocasión de extenderme más sobre los servicios de este Departamento.

De usted respetuosamente.

LEOPOLDO CANCIO.

Secretario de Hacienda.

Además de las órdenes civiles que la Secretaría de Hacienda ha propuesto al Sr. Gobernador Militar, han sido publicados en la "Gaceta" durante el 2º semestre del año natural de 1901 las siguientes disposiciones:

Amillaramientos. Circular de 26 de Septiembre de 1901 á los Alcaldes Municipales para que cumplan lo dispuesto por la Orden 141 sobre terminación de los Amillaramientos.

.... Circular de 22 de Octubre de 1901 disponiendo la forma de amillarar las fincas rústicas cuyos terrenos pertenecen á más de un término municipal y á un mismo propietario.

Modificación de Zonas Fiscales. Por resolución de 21 de Octubre de 1901 se dispuso que el Municipio de Sagua de Tánamo que pertenecía á la Zona de Holguín pasara á formar parte de la de Santiago de Cuba.

Hacienda Municipal. Circular de 24 de Octubre de 1901 á los Alcaldes Municipales recordándoles estar prohibidas las transferencias de créditos sin la autorización de la Superior Autoridad de la Isla.

.... Circulares de 31 de Octubre y 26 de Noviembre de 1901 manifestando á los Administradores de Zona y Alcaldes Municipales no deben paralizarse los procedimientos de apremio durante el período electoral por contribuciones y derechos corrientes.

.... Resolución de 25 de Noviembre de 1901 respecto á la forma en que debe realizarse en el suprimido Ayuntamiento de Regla la cobranza de las contribuciones.

Derechos Reales. Circular de 11 de Octubre de 1901 reproduciendo resoluciones de la Secretaría de Justicia á fin de que los funcionarios del Orden judicial y Notarios cumplan los preceptos del Reglamento del Impuesto Fiscal de Derechos reales y trasmisión de bienes.

ADMINISTRACION DE RENTAS E IMPUESTOS DE LA ZONA FISCAL DE PINAR DEL RIO.

Resumen del año natural de 1901.

INGRESOS.

CONCEPTOS	1er. SEMESTRE	2º SEMESTRE	TOTAL
Derechos Reales.........	$ 3,709.45	$ 4,264.53	$ 7,973.98
Intereses de demora....	54.16	88.66	142.82
Réditos de Censos......	9.09	625.33	634.42
Redención de Censos....	123.86	....	123.86
Alquileres de fincas......	38.40	4.50	42.90
Productos forestales.....	42.00	160.00	202.00
Venta de efectos inútiles....................	....	260.37	260.37
Penales	59.50	116.25	175.75
Recargos	13.84	162.71	176.55
Productos diversos......	2,621.10	2,832.50	5,453.60
Totales.........	$ 6,671.40	$ 8,514.85	$ 15,186.25

PAGOS.

CONCEPTOS	1er. SEMESTRE	2º SEMESTRE	TOTAL
Estado y Gobernación..	$ 18,400.56	$ 11,102.77	$ 24,503.33
Hacienda	11,663.31	5,895.38	17,558.69
Justicia	30,936.42	27,356.36	58,292.78
Instrucción Pública......	18,024.27	14,568.64	32,592.91
Agricultura, Industria y Comercio	2,701.31	1,793.49	4,494.81
Municipalidades.........	100,395.11	65,834.82	166,229.93
Hospitales y Asilos......	5,834.63	6,120.40	11,955.03
Totales.........	$182,955.62	$132,671.86	$315,627.48

ADMINISTRACION DE RENTAS E IMPUESTOS DE LA ZONA FISCAL DE GUANAJAY.

Resumen del año natural de 1901.

INGRESOS.

CONCEPTOS.	1er. SEMESTRE	2º SEMESTRE	TOTAL
Derechos Reales.........	$ 2,492.75	$ 2,987.71	$ 5,480.46
Intereses de demora....	36.26	16.61	52.87
Réditos de Censos.......	509.86	1,077.10	1,586.96
Redención de Censos...	....	60.94	60.94
Penales..........................	....	44.40	44.40
Alquileres de fincas....	246.74	206.26	453.00
Pertenencias mineras..	209.00	....	209.00
Multas........................	37.00	....	37.00
Reintegros..................	48.00	360.81	408.81
Ingresos eventuales....	10.11	135.11	145.22
Productos diversos......	286.50	213.00	499.50
Totales........	$ 3,876.22	$ 5,101.94	$ 8,978.16

PAGOS.

CONCEPTOS.	1er. SEMESTRE	2º SEMESTRE	TOTAL
Estado y Gobernación.	$ 3,532.75	$ 5,406.28	8,939.03
Hacienda..................	4,991.99	5,841.87	10,833.86
Justicia......................	4,858.38	7,233.36	12,091.74
Municipalidades.........	78,670.35	54,766.26	133,436.61
Hospitales y Asilos.....	19,894.23	7,411.52	27.305.75
Totales.........	$ 111,947.70	$ 80,659.29	$ 192,606.99

ADMINISTRACION DE RENTAS E IMPUESTOS DE LA ZONA FISCAL DE LA HABANA.

Resumen del año natural de 1901.

INGRESOS.

CONCEPTOS.	1er. SEMESTRE	2º SEMESTRE	TOTAL
Derechos Reales	$116,706.68	$106,036.47	$ 222,743.15
Contribución Industrial	56,552.70	34,292.26	90,844.96
Alquileres de fincas	2,397.01	2,802.18	5,199.19
Réditos de censos	11,351.98	12,643.10	23,995.08
Venta de terrenos	1,018.26	11,143.21	12,161.47
Redención de censos	2,630.94	4,146.69	6,777.63
Venta de bienes vacantes	58.30	69.36	127.66
Venta de efectos inútiles	27.35	....	27.35
Pertenencias mineras	2,226.00	3,248.50	5,474.50
Productos diversos	32.855.06	28,249.56	61,104.62
Recargos	2,510.76	1,156.60	3,667.36
Intereses de demora	....	1,273.15	1,273.15
Penales	....	3,407.41	3,407.41
Reintegros	....	100.00	100.00
Totales	$228,335.04	$208,568.49	$ 436,903.53

PAGOS.

CONCEPTOS	1er. SEMESTRE	2º SEMESTRE	TOTAL
Estado y Gobernación	$156,475.76	$178,511.38	$ 334,987.14
Hacienda	16,301.93	20,103.14	36,405.07
Justicia	87,109.42	100,118.98	187,228.40
Instrucción Pública	33,882.03	31,842.29	65,724.32
Agricultura, Industria y Comercio	4,052.44	3,402.36	7,454.80
Municipalidades	549,192.15	414,336.22	963,528.37
Hospitales y Asilos	124,651.10	92,683.65	217,334.75
Departamento Militar	13,598.19	....	13,598.19
Totales	$985,263.02	$840,998.02	$1.826,261.04

ADMINISTRACION DE RENTAS É IMPUESTOS DE LA ZONA FISCAL DE MATANZAS.

Resumen del año natural de 1901.

INGRESOS.

CONCEPTOS.	1er. SEMESTRE	2º SEMESTRE.	TOTAL.
Derechos Reales.........	$ 9,025.08	$ 13,623.99	$ 22,649.07
Intereses de demora....	196.82	94.88	291.70
Réditos de censos........	591.50	5.19	596.69
Alquileres de fincas....	349.18	270.40	619.58
Subsidio Industrial.....	2,882.29	....	2,882.29
Venta de terrenos	....	124.86	124.86
Productos diversos......	2,474.65	5,229.63	7,704.28
Totales.........	$ 15,519.52	$ 19,348.95	$ 34,868.47

PAGOS.

CONCEPTOS.	1er. SEMESTRE	2º SEMESTRE.	TOTAL.
Estado y Gobernación.	$ 26,763.95	$ 23,209.33	$ 49,973.28
Hacienda..................	7,655.10	7,525.60	15,180.70
Justicia	39,045.40	37,470.76	76,516.16
Instrucción Pública....	26,666.59	25,175.00	51,841.59
Agricultura, Industria y Comercio	1,127.43	805.19	1,932.62
Municipalidades.........	179,143.85	129,764.27	308,908.12
Hospitales y Asilos.....	50,982.39	42,145.95	93,128.34
Totales.........	$331,384.71	$266,096.10	$ 597,480.81

ADMINISTRACION DE RENTAS É IMPUESTOS DE LA ZONA FISCAL DE CÁRDENAS.

Resumen del año natural de 1901.

INGRESOS.

CONCEPTOS.	1er. SEMESTRE	2º SEMESTRE.	TOTAL.
Derechos Reales.........	$ 9,214.03	$ 9,845.08	$ 19,059.11
Interéses de demora....	81.82	149.44	231.26
Réditos de censos.......	314.27	2,454.40	2,768.67
Redención de censos...	....	56.37	56.37
Venta de terrenos del Estado	....	327.28	327.28
Penales....................	18.25	65.90	84.15
Ingresos eventuales....	15.69	90.98	106.67
Productos diversos......	219.42	1,046.63	1,266.05
Totales............	$ 9,863.48	$ 14,036.08	$ 23,899.56

PAGOS.

CONCEPTOS.	1er. SEMESTRE	2º SEMESTRE	TOTAL.
Estado y Gobernación.	$ 10,856.10	$ 10,106.53	$ 20,962.63
Hacienda.................	6,680.69	4,515.41	11,196.10
Justicia..................	13,605.83	12,420.55	26,026.38
Municipalidades.........	166,042.78	125,288.68	291,331.46
Hospitales y Asilos.....	30,649.36	23,584.28	54,233.64
Totales............	$ 227,834.76	$ 175,915.45	$ 403,750.21

ADMINISTRACION DE RENTAS E IMPUESTOS DE LA ZONA FISCAL DE SANTA CLARA.

Resumen del año natural de 1901.

INGRESOS.

CONCEPTOS	1er. SEMESTRE	2º SEMESTRE	TOTAL
Derechos Reales	$ 19,212.74	$ 15,948.75	$ 35,161.49
Intereses de demora	289.27	139.74	429.01
Réditos de Censos	1,212.62	493.90	1,706.52
Alquileres de fincas	25.00	145.80	170.80
Productos forestales	560.20	57.50	617.70
Recargos de apremio	41.65	53.95	95.60
Pertenencias mineras	....	156.00	156.00
Productos diversos	2,155.50	1,984.47	4,139.97
Totales	$ 23,496.98	18,980.11	$ 42,477.09

PAGOS.

CONCEPTOS	1er. SEMESTRE	2º SEMESTRE	TOTAL
Estado y Gobernación	$ 39,670.17	$ 30,535.53	$ 70,205.70
Hacienda	9,162.99	6,928.68	16,091.67
Justicia	43,549.36	46,106.04	89,655.40
Instrucción Pública	21,625.56	16,574.73	38,200.29
Agricultura, Industria y Comercio	2,568.67	2,314.86	4,883.53
Municipalidades	260,475.59	177,482.25	437,957.84
Hospitales y Asilos	44,987.16	36,257.93	81,245.09
Totales	$422,039.50	$316,200.02	$ 738,239.52

ADMINISTRACION DE RENTAS É IMPUESTOS DE LA ZONA FISCAL DE CIENFUEGOS.

Resúmen dél año natural de 1901.

INGRESOS.

CONCEPTOS.	1er. SEMESTRE	2º SEMESTRE.	TOTAL.
Derechos Reales.........	$ 16,459.69	$ 24,774.52	$ 41,234.21
Intereses de demora....	295.75	128.77	424.52
Réditos de censos.......	....	50,38	50.38
Alquileres de fincas....	....	34.48	34.48
Penales	....	10.00	10.00
Recargos	131.27	92.62	223.89
Productos diversos......	198.98	334.87	533.85
Totales.........	$ 17,085.69	$ 25,425.64	$ 42,511.33

PAGOS.

CONCEPTOS.	1er. SEMESTRE	2º SEMESTRE.	TOTAL.
Estado y Gobernación.	$ 16,117.55	$ 13,334.70	$ 29,452.25
Hacienda.................	6,766.02	6,546.98	13,313.00
Justicia	14,657.20	13,287.19	27,944.39
Obras Públicas..........	....	96.22	96.22
Municipalidades.........	243,851.72	134,741.18	378,592.90
Hospitales y Asilos.....	83,859,93	50,938 52	134,798.45
Totales.........	$365,252.42	$218,944.79	$ 584,197.21

ADMINISTRACION DE RENTAS E IMPUESTOS DE LA ZONA FISCAL DE PUERTO PRINCIPE.

Resumen del año natural de 1901.

INGRESOS.

CONCEPTOS.	1er. SEMESTRE	2º SEMESTRE	TOTAL
Derechos Reales.........	$ 4,548.70	$ 6,514.05	$ 11,062.75
Interéses de demora ...	35.24	58.81	94.05
Réditos de censos........	87.27	13.52	100.79
Redención de censos...	163.69	463.02	626.71
Subsidio Industrial.....	4,504.84	2,848.01	7,352.85
Alquileres de fincas.....	54.60	347.04	401.64
Pertenencias mineras..	....	328.00	328.00
Bienes vacantes	....	110.91	110.91
Productos diversos......	1,825.93	3,116.84	4,942.77
Totales	$ 11,220.27	$ 13,800.20	$ 25,020.47

PAGOS.

CONCEPTOS.	1er. SEMESTRE	2º SEMESTRE	TOTAL
Estado y Gobernación.	$ 16,148.22	$ 12,705.91	$ 28,854.13
Hacienda..................	6,936.73	4,909.58	11,846.31
Justicia	28,597.93	27,577.76	56,175.69
Agricultura, Industria y Comercio	1,951.35	2,413.08	4,364.43
Instrucción Pública...	20,934.09	17,772.47	38,706.56
Municipalidades.........	107,905.22	71,413.98	179,319.20
Hospitales y Asilos....	41,188.94	28,080.90	69,269.84
Totales.........	$ 223,662.48	$ 164,873.68	$ 388,536.16

ADMINISTRACION DE RENTAS É IMPUESTOS DE LA ZONA FISCAL DE SANTIAGO DE CUBA.

Resumen del año natural de 1901.

INGRESOS.

CONCEPTOS	1er. SEMESTRE	2º SEMESTRE	TOTAL.
Derechos reales..........	$ 10,218.40	$ 9,713.75	$ 19,932.15
Subsidio Industrial.....	2,787.01	351.82	3,138.83
Intereses de demora....	44.25	69.92	114.17
Alquileres................	6.30	62.60	68.90
Venta de terrenos	45.66	1,091.82	1,137.48
Productos diversos......	3,242.54	5,900,62	9,143.16
Pertenencias mineras...	....	3,442.00	3,442.00
Totales.........	$ 16,344.16	$ 20,632.53	$ 36,976.69

PAGOS.

CONCEPTOS	1er. SEMESTRE	2º SEMESTRE	TOTAL.
Estado y Gobernación.	$ 31,975.40	$ 23,061.44	$ 55,036.84
Hacienda................	18,669.61	20,560.85	39,230.46
Justicia	49,837.56	40,790.09	90,627.65
Agricultura, Industria y Comercio............	12,932.91	8,143.54	21,076.45
Instrucción Pública....	21,996.49	18,790.45	40,786.94
Municipalidades.........	166,199.57	101,468.87	267,668.44
Hospitales y Asilos.....	95,401.83	66,532.27	161,934.10
Totales.........	$ 397,013.37	$ 279,347-51	$ 676,360.88

ADMINISTRACION DE RENTAS E IMPUESTOS DE LA ZONA FISCAL DE HOLGUIN.

Resúmen del año natural de 1901.

INGRESOS.

CONCEPTOS	1er. SEMESTRE	2º SEMESTRE	TOTAL
Derechos Reales..........	$ 5,881.69	$ 9,544.78	$ 15,426.47
Intereses de demora.....	79.28	53.14	132,42
Alquileres de fincas.....	140.00	125.00	265,00
Subsidio Industrial.....	244.67	....	244.67
Productos diversos......	183.25	690.00	873.25
Totales.........	$ 6,528.89	$ 10,412.92	$ 16,941.81

PAGOS.

CONCEPTOS	1er. SEMESTRE	2º SEMESTRE	TOTAL
Estado y Gobernación.	$ 3,264.00	$ 2,612.30	$ 5,876.30
Hacienda..................	6,670.81	5,566.28	12,237.09
Justicia	10,301.93	6,407.94	16,709.87
Municipalidades.........	116,799.69	63,098.75	179,898.44
Hospitales y Asilos......	14.298.75	7,382.11	21,680.86
Totales.........	$151,335.18	$ 85,067.38	$ 236,402.56

ADMINISTRACION DE RENTAS É IMPUESTOS DE LA ZONA FISCAL DE MANZANILLO.

Resúmen del año natural de 1901.

INGRESOS.

CONCEPTOS.	1er. SEMESTRE	2º SEMESTRE.	TOTAL.
Derechos Reales.........	$ 5,288.47	$ 3,394.66	$ 8,683.13
Interéses de demora...	6.07	39.78	45.85
Réditos de censos......	....	81.07	81.07
Productos diversos......	41.89	205.00	246.89
Totales	$ 5,336.43	$ 3,720·51	$ 9,056.94

PAGOS.

CONCEPTOS.	1er. SEMESTRE	2º SEMESTRE.	TOTAL.
Estado y Gobernación.	$ 3,234.71	$ 2,117.20	$ 5,351.91
Hacienda.................	4,645.39	4,336.24	8,981.63
Justicia....................	7,106.85	6,138.37	13,245.22
Obras Públicas..........	....	86.62	86.62
Municipalidades.........	91,913.91	61,118.68	153,032.59
Hospitales y asilos......	14,687.02	10,190.31	24,877.33
Totales.........	$121,587.88	$ 83,987.42	$205,575.30

PAGOS REALIZADOS POR LA CAJA DE LA TESORERIA CENTRAL DE HACIENDA.

Año natural de 1901.

CONCEPTOS	1er. SEMESTRE	2º SEMESTRE	TOTAL
Estado y Gobernación.	$ 239,902.14	$173,199.22	$ 413,101.36
Hacienda.................	49,311.19	85,718.72	135,029.91
Justicia....................	87,042.54	93,973.11	181,015.65
Instrucción Pública.....	363,440.72	221,826.36	585,267.08
Agricultura, Industria y Comercio............	169.956.98	83,707.64	253,664.62
Obras Públicas (Faros)	110,786.05	50,473.58	161,259.63
Municipalidades.........	424.00	8,174.55	8,598.55
Totales.........	$1.020,863.62	$717,073.18	$1.737,936.80

RECAUDACION TOTAL POR RENTAS INTERIORES EN LOS AÑOS NATURALES DE 1900 Y 1901.

CONCEPTOS	1900	1901	AUMENTO EN 1901	DISMINUCION EN 1901
Derechos Reales.	$370,017.96	$409,405.97	$39,388.01	
Subsidio Industrial..............	112,269.84	104,463.60	....	(1) $7,806.24
Productos diversos...............	86,771.79	95,907.94	9,136.15	
Réditos de censos	24,557.33	31,520.58	6,963.25	
Venta de terrenos................	8,915.90	13,751.09	4,835.19	
Pertenencias mineras.............	30.00	9,609.50	9,579.50	
Redención de censos..............	5,146.36	7,645.51	2,499.15	
Alquileres de fincas.............	5,483.83	7,255.49	1,771.66	
Recargos..........	....	4,163.40	4,163.40	
Penales..........	....	3,721.71	3,721.71	
Intereses de demora..............	2,990.37	3,231.82	241.45	
Productos forestales.............	1,192.60	819.70	....	372.90
Reintegros.........	256.30	508.81	252.51	
Venta de efectos inútiles........	1,807.67	287.72	....	1,519.95
Ingresos eventuales..............	....	251.89	251.89	
Venta de bienes vacantes.........	....	238.57	238.57	
Multas..........	....	37.00	37.00	
	$619,439.95	$692,820.30	$83,079.44	$9,699.09
Recargos 10 y 3 %	178,731.65	Abolido.	9,699.09	
Totales.....	$798,171.60	$692,820.30	$73,380.35	

(1) Por la orden 254 y otras disposiciones posteriores pasaron á los Ayuntamientos las contribuciones sobre ferrocarriles urbanos, sub-urbanos y empresas de alumbrado eléctrico, teléfonos, etc.

ESTADO COMPARATIVO DE LOS PAGOS VERIFICADOS EN EL AÑO NATURAL DE 1901:

CAJAS.	1er. SEMESTRE	2º SEMESTRE	DE MÉNOS EN EL 2º SEMESTRE
Tesorería Central	$1.020,863.62	$ 717,073.18	$ 303,790.44
Zona Fiscal de la Habana	985,263.02	840,998.02	144,265.00
,, ,, ,, Santa Clara	422,039.50	316,200.02	105,839.48
,, ,, ,, Santiago de Cuba	397,013.37	279,347.51	117,665.86
,, ,, ,, Matanzas	331,384.71	266,096.10	65,288.61
,, ,, ,, Cienfuegos	365,252.42	218,944.79	146,307.63
,, ,, ,, Cárdenas	227,834.76	175,915.45	51,919.31
,, ,, ,, Puerto Príncipe	223,662.48	164,873.68	58,788.80
,, ,, ,, Pinar del Rio	182,955.62	132,671.86	50,283.76
,, ,, ,, Holguin	151,335.18	85,067.38	66,267.80
,, ,, ,, Manzanillo	121,587.88	83,987.42	37,600.46
,, ,, ,, Guanajay	111,947.70	80,659.29	31,288.41
Totales	$4.541,140.26	$3.361,834.70	$1.179,305.56

RECAUDACION DE RENTAS INTERIORES POR ZONAS FISCALES Y TANTO POR CIENTO QUE REPRESENTA CADA ZONA.

Año natural de 1901.

ZONAS FISCALES.	RECAUDADO.	%
Habana	$ 436,903.53	63.06
Cienfuegos	42,511.33	6.14
Santa Clara	42,477.09	6.13
Santiago de Cuba	36,976.69	5.34
Matanzas	34,868.47	5.03
Puerto Príncipe	25,020.47	3.61
Cárdenas	23,899.56	3.44
Holguín	16,941.81	2.45
Pinar del Río	15,186.25	2.19
Manzanillo	9,056.94	1.31
Guanajay	8,978.16	1.30
Total	$ 692,820.30	100 %.

RECAUDACION DE RENTAS INTERIORES POR ZONAS FISCALES, Y TANTO POR CIENTO QUE REPRESENTA CADA PARTIDA CON RELACION AL TOTAL.

Año natural de 1901.

CONCEPTOS.	RECAUDADO.	%
Derechos Reales	$ 409,405.97	59.09
Subsidio Industrial	104,463.60	15.08
Productos diversos	95,907.94	13.84
Réditos de censos	31,520.58	4.55
Venta de terrenos	13,751.09	1.98
Pertenencias mineras	9,609.50	1.39
Redención de censos	7,645.51	1.10
Alquileres de fincas	7,255.49	1.05
Recargos	4,163.40	0.60
Penales	3,721.71	0.54
Interéses de demora	3,231.82	0.47
Productos forestales	819.70	0.12
Reintegros	508.81	0.07
Venta de efectos inútiles	287.72	0.04
Ingresos eventuales	251.89	0.04
Venta de bienes vacantes	238.57	0.03
Multas	37.00	0.01
Total	$ 692,820.30	100 %

RESUMEN GENERAL DE LOS PAGOS POR GASTOS PUBLICOS DE LA ISLA.

Año natural de 1901.

DEPARTAMENTOS.	PAGOS.	TANTO % SOBRE EL TOTAL.
Municipalidades	$ 3.468,502.45	43.89 %
Estado y Gobernación	1.047,243.90	13.25 ,,
Hospitales y Asilos	897,763.18	11.36 ,,
Instrucción Pública	853,119.69	10.80 ,,
Justicia	835,529.33	10.57 ,,
Hacienda	327,904.49	4.15 ,,
Agricultura, Industria y Comercio	297,871.26	3.77 ,,
Obras Públicas (Faros)	161,442.47	2.04 ,,
Departamento Militar	13,598.19	0.17 ,,
Totales	$ 7.902,974.96	100.00 %

MOVIMIENTO DE LA CUENTA DE DEPOSITOS Y FIANZAS

EN EL

Año natural de 1901.

CAJAS.	Existencias 1º en 1901.	Constituidos en 1901.	TOTAL.	Devueltos en 1901.	Existencia para 1902.
Tesorería Central	65,765.63	111,006.37	176,772.00	22,617.81	154,154.19
Zona de la Habana	200,330.81	382,897.83	583,228.64	407,034.56	176,194.08
Zona de Pinar del Río	5,602.37	2,524.09	8,126.46	4,317.98	3,808.48
Zona de Matanzas	9,109.14	9,177.74	18,286.88	7,846 35	10,440.53
Zona de Santa Clara	29,399.21	4,853.13	34,252.34	6,028.01	28,224.33
Zona de Puerto Príncipe	5,387.52	14,150.63	19,538.15	16,221.03	3,317.12
Zona de Santiago de Cuba	2,216.52	24,035.09	26,251.61	15,888.19	10,363 42
Zona de Guanajay	2,377.53	2,474.86	4,852.39	2,358.93	2,493.46
Zona de Cárdenas	4,322.41	13,295.99	17,618 40	8,452.55	9,165.85
Zona de Cienfuegos	3,221.08	10,149.96	13,371.04	6,620.09	6,750.95
Zona de Holguín	2,287.87	3,754.50	6,042.37	1,260.85	4,781.52
Zona de Manzanillo	527.14	647.99	1,175.13	100.00	1,075.13
Totales	330,547.23	578,968.18	909,515.41	498,746.35	410,769.06

AMILLARAMIENTOS.

Situación de los trabajos para la formación de los padrones para la riqueza rústica y urbana de la Isla.

ZONAS.	AMILLARAMIENTOS. TERMINADOS.	NUMS.	PENDIENTES.	NUMS.
Pinar del Río..	Mántua	...	San Luis	...
Idem	Guane	...	Consolación del Sur	...
Idem	S. Juan y Martínez..	...	Pinar del Río	...
Idem	Viñales	4		3
Guanajay	C. del Norte	...	San Cristóbal	...
Idem		...	Guanajay	...
Idem		...	Artemisa	...
Idem		...	Cabañas	4
Habana	Madruga	...	Habana	...
Idem	Isla de Pinos	...	Bauta	...
Idem	Aguacate	...	Guanabacoa	...
Idem	Sta. Mª del Rosario.	...	Jaruco	...
Idem	S. José de las Lajas.	...	S. Atnio. de los Baños..	...
Idem	Alquízar	...	Güira de Melena	...
Idem	Batabanó	...	Santiago de las Vegas..	...
Idem	Bejucal	...	Güines	...
Idem	Marianao	9	Nueva Paz	9
Matanzas		...	Matanzas	...
Idem		...	Alacranes	...
Idem		...	Bolondrón	...
Idem		00	Unión de Reyes	4
Cárdenas	Martí	...	Macurijes	...
Idem		...	Colón	...
Idem		...	Jagüey Grande	...
Idem		...	Cárdenas	...
Idem		...	Jovellanos	5
			Al frente	25

ZONAS.	AMILLARAMIENTOS. TERMINADOS.	NUMS.	PENDIENTES.	NUMS.
			Del frente..........	25
Santa Clara....	Santa Clara..........		Ranchuelo................	
Idem	Calabazar............		Sagua la Grande........	
Idem	Esperanza		Quemados de Güines..	
Idem	Rancho Veloz.......		Santo Domingo.........	
Idem	Vueltas		Caibarién	
Idem	Yaguajay............		Jiguaní..................	
Idem	Remedios............	7	Placetas..................	7
Cienfuegos	Palmira..............		Cienfuegos...............	
Idem	Sta. Isabel Lajas....		Rodas.....................	
Idem	Cruces		Trinidad	
Idem	Morón................		Sancti Spíritus..........	
Idem	....		Ciego de Avila..........	5
Prto. Príncipe	....	0	Puerto Príncipe.........	
Idem	....		Nuevitas.................	2
Stgo. de Cuba.	Guantánamo.........		Santiago de Cuba.......	
Idem	Palma Soriano		San Luis..................	
Idem	Cobre.................		Caney.....................	
Idem	....		Alto Songo	
Idem	....	0	Baracoa..................	
Idem	....		Sagua de Tánamo.......	6
Holguín	....		Holguín..................	
Idem	....		Puerto Padre............	
Idem	....		Gibara....................	
Idem	....	0	Mayarí...................	4
Manzanillo.....	Manzanillo..........		....	
Idem	Bayamo		....	
Idem	Jiguaní		....	0
Idem	Santa Cruz del Sur.	4	....	
	Total......	33	Total.........	49

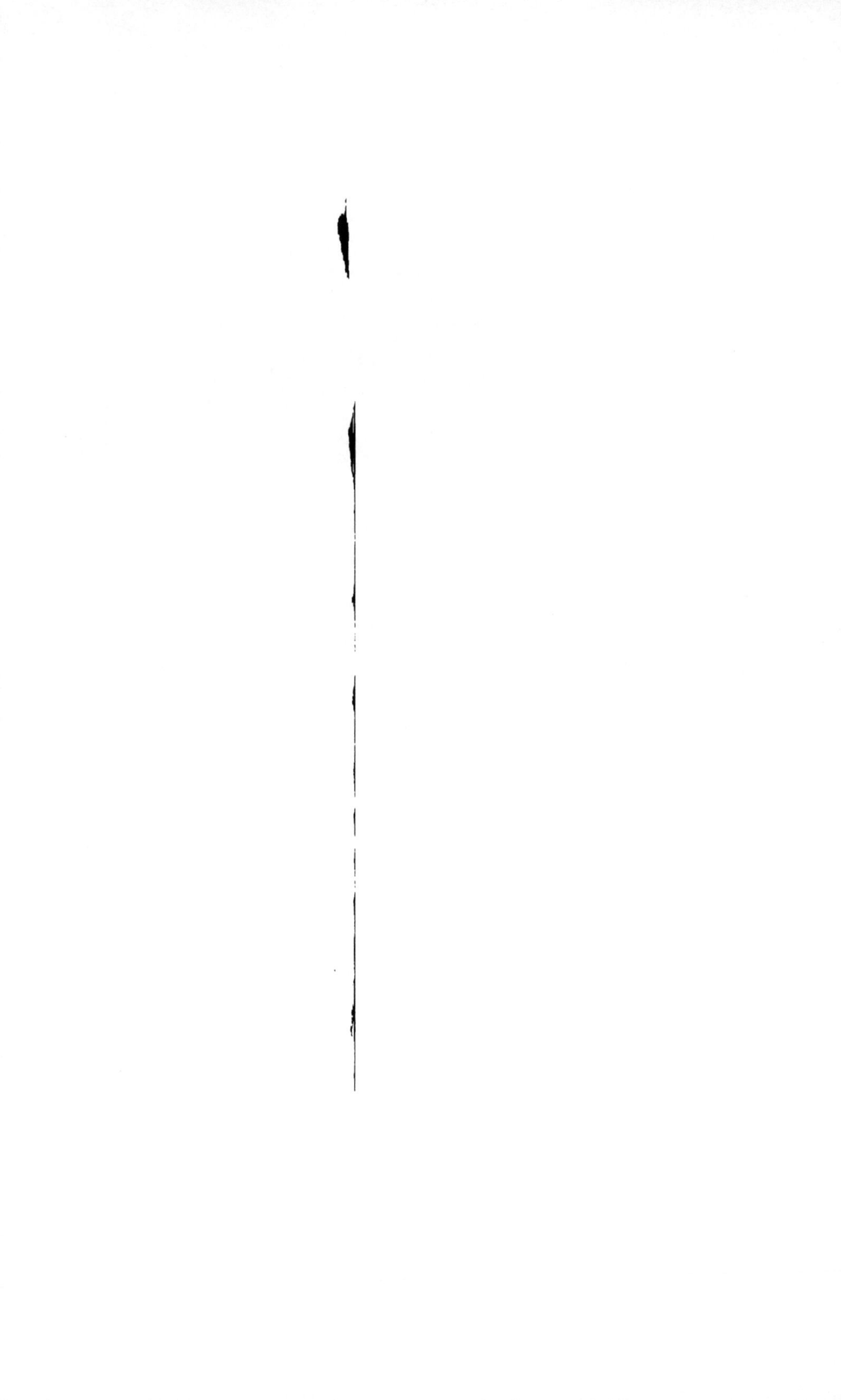

REPORT

OF THE

DEPARTMENT OF POSTS OF CUBA

FOR THE

FISCAL YEAR ENDED JUNE 30, 1901.

OFFICE OF THE DIRECTOR-GENERAL,

DEPARTMENT OF POSTS OF CUBA.

Havana, August 23, 1901.

SIR:

I have the honor to submit herewith the annual report of this department, covering in detail the transactions of its several bureaus, as well as those of a general nature in the management and control of this important branch of the public service on the island of Cuba.

Complying with instructions, I submitted to you, under date of February 12, 1901, a report covering the first six months of the fiscal year, which report was supplemental to my report for the fiscal year 1900. The present report is made to cover the whole year ending June 30, 1901, as the character of the work of the department is such that to get an intelligent understanding of the service it is necessary to include the full twelve months, treating the fiscal year as a unit. This will of necessity overlap the semi-annual report in the statistical parts, showing the transactions of the full year in the present general summary.

It is unnecessary to enlarge on the unfortunate circumstances under which the fiscal year opened for the department of posts, further than to regret that so much of the time and energy which should have been devoted to constructive work of administration, in a normal course of affairs, have been absorbed by the retroactive investigation in its numerous and complicated phases, including proceedings in the courts growing out of the same. Despite this heavy and constant burden, still upon us, I am pleased to be able to report that during the year the postal service has been improved in all its branches, the interest of officials has increased, with the result that they have shown marked improvement in their work; the revenues have kept well up with the expectations of the department; expenses have been very largely reduced, and the postal system of the island has been firmly reestablished on a basis which it is fair to believe will prove lasting, and of increasing benefit, as the years pass, to the people who are so vitally interested in having the best system of which the conditions will admit.

It has been the primary fixed purpose of the administration to provide a good service, next to keep expenses down to a reasonable minimum, and to carefully husband the revenues, looking forward to the time when the postal service of Cuba may become self-sustaining. The execution of this policy imposed the necessity of retrenchment, but of course no individual hardship was intended in any case. The policy has continued of retiring Americans as rapidly as could be, without detriment to the service, and placing Cubans for permanent tenure in the vacated positions. I am gratified with the result of the practical application of this policy, and glad to report that the Cuban officials as a rule have shown aptitude for the work, a commendable zeal in performance of duty, and have proven efficient and faithful to an encouraging degree. The policy has resulted in the retirement of all American acting postmasters on the island, with the exception of Santiago de Cuba. Peculiar conditions existing at that office have made it unwise thus far to attempt a change. At Havana, by far the largest and most important office in Cuba, Col. Charles Hernández has been placed in charge as acting postmaster. This action was taken May 1, 1901, upon the recall to the United States of Postoffice Inspector J. R. Harrison, who had served for nearly a year as acting postmaster. He had shown marked ability in the management of the office, had steadily reduced the force and the expenses, striving to approximate the same to the ratio of an office of the same size in the United States. Colonel Hernández has been actuated by the same desire, and while maintaining an efficient and satisfactory service, has effected further reduction of expenses, until they have finally been brought below $100,000 per annum, an aim which had been held in steady view.

In the department offices it has not been practicable to retire Americans to the extent that it has been done in postoffices. Necessarily, under present conditions, the business of the department in its relation to the Military Government of the island, and with the administration at Washington, has been conducted in the English language. With all postal officials on the island the correspondence is conducted in their own language, and in every way they are made to feel that they are a part of the service, and personally interested in its development and permanent improvement.

As previously stated, the great aim of the department has been to reduce expenses, increase the revenues, and at the same time better the service. While effort has been to decrease the expenses of every character, the most marked results in this direction have been in the item of salaries. After the great curtailment of expenses of this character by my immediate predecessor, Hon. Joseph L. Bristow, Fourth Assistant Postmaster-General, the total salary list stood on June 30, 1900, at $385,679. On June 30, 1901, the salary list was $314,773, showing a reduction during the fiscal year of $70,906. It is proper to say that at the present time changes are contemplated and practically decided upon which will make a further reduction of about $5,500. This will show a reduction in the salary list since June 30, 1900, of $76,000 in round figures. For the purpose of showing where these reductions occur, the following statement is of value:

ANNUAL EXPENDITURE FOR SALARIES.

	June 30, 1900.	June 30, 1901.
Department of Posts	$ 89,420	$ 58,280
Postmasters	89,400	90,302
Clerks in postoffices	109,234	75,110
Letter carriers	70,310	61.514
Mail messengers, janitors, etc	8,215	8,843
Railway postal clerks	19,100	20,724
Total	$ 385,679	$ 314,773
Decrease		$ 70,906

It will be observed that of this decrease, practically $31,000 was made in the department of posts force in Havana. Postmasters' salaries were increased about $1,000, salaries of clerks in postoffices decreased $34,000, in round numbers, letter carriers decreased $9,000, and railway postal clerks increased $1,000. A readjustment of salaries of postmasters was undertaken upon a basis of sales and cancellations, as nearly as such plan can be made to operate in a service so new as the present system. Inequalities in these salaries had existed, measured by the volume of business transacted at the various offices. Many readjustments have been made, and while some reductions occurred from the retirement of American acting postmasters, the general effect has been an increase in the salaries of Cuban postmasters. The great reduction in the salary list of clerks in postoffices occurred for the main part in the Havana postoffice, though the clerical force has been reduced in all offices where found consistent with good service. The reduction of salaries of letter carriers was occasioned by the discontinuance of free delivery at many of the smaller offices on the island. The increase in the salary list of railway postal clerks is because of deserved promotions, and to meet the increasing business of the department in the way of handling the mails on the island.

By the operations of the system of accounts described more in detail in my last report, stamped stock is furnished by the Postmaster-General of the United States, and charged to the director-general of posts. It passes immediately into the hands of the chief of the bureau of stamps and supplies, a bonded officer, who receipts to the director-general, and then becomes responsible for the same. This stock is furnished to postmasters upon requisitions. To bonded postmasters the stock is sent on credit, there being a safe margin between the limit of the amount of credit and the amount of the bond. To postmasters not under bond, the stamped stock is furnished upon the certificate of the Treasurer of the Island that the postmaster has deposited with him the amount of money to pay for stock represented in the requisition. I shall not further burden this report with the details of the audit of these accounts, and the system in operation by which the Auditor of the Island is kept informed of all transactions between the department and postmasters. This was touched upon in the semi-annual report, and suffice it to say the system works satisfactorily.

During the fiscal year there was received from the Postmaster-General, and issued to postmasters, the following amounts of stamped paper:

MONTH.		RECEIPTS.	ISSUES.
July,	1900	$ 50,000.00	$ 31,789.32
August,	,,		25,328.11
September,	,,	57,237.50	28,054.83
October,	,,	40,053.00	38,552.60
November,	,,	21,074.50	24,006.13
December,	,,	40,063.60	34,847.39
January,	1901	2,173.30	33,177.12
February,	,,	10.60	32,306.23
March,	,,	76,117.50	37,187.42
April,	,,	2,373.00	28,613 56
May,	,,	190.80	21,257.70
June,	,,	40,021.20	21,306.21
Total		$ 329,315.00	$ 356,426.62

There was a larger issue of stamped paper than the amount received, but the amount on hand June 30, 1900, was much larger than the amount on hand June 30, 1901.

The average monthly output of stamped paper was $29,702.21 for the fiscal year, and the daily average $976.51. This shows a slight decrease from the average monthly and daily output for the first six months of the year. But such decrease is readily accounted for by the reduction to domestic basis of the postage rates between Cuba and the United States, which became effective April 1, 1901. The following table shows the monthly sales of stamps and stamped paper for the first 9 months of the year, when the foreign postage rates were in force between Cuba and the United States, and separately for the last 3 months, under the reduced rates:

MONTH.		RECEIPTS.
July,	1900	$ 27,905.57
August,	,,	28,043.79
September,	,,	25,496.28
October,	,,	28,327.95
November,	,,	27,304.81
December,	,,	31,666.35
January,	1901	31,900.87
February,	,,	29,582.62
March,	,,	31,640.79
Total		$ 261,869.03
Monthly average		29,096 56
Daily average		955.73

For the months of April, May, and June, after the domestic rates had gone into effect, the receipts were as follows:

April,	1901	$ 26,845.15
May,	,,	27,016.97
June,	,,	25,056.97
Total		$ 78,919.09
Monthly average		26,306.36
Daily average		867.24

The average daily difference of $88.49 is equivalent to an annual total of $32,298.85. But the three last months fall in the season of light business, and it is fair to accept as demonstrated that the annual loss of revenue from this cause will come within the advance estimate of $30,000. And it is hoped that the incident increase of postal business will overcome this loss within the present year.

RECEIPTS.

The following table shows the total postal receipts from all sources during the fiscal year ended June 30, 1901:

MONTH.	Stamp Sales.	Box Rents.	M. O. Fees. (By Quarters.)	Miscl.	TOTAL.
July, 1900	$ 27,905.57	$ 3,065.00	....	$ .81	$ 30,971.38
August, ,,	28,043.79	128.45	....	.80	28,173.04
September, ,,	25,496.28	67.10	$ 3,362.22	1.44	28,927.04
October, ,,	28,327.95	3,073.50	....	1.68	31,403.13
November, ,,	27,304.81	116.87	....	3.30	27,424.98
December, ,,	31,666.35	101.30	3,345.65	1.81	35,115.11
January, 1901	31,900.87	3,188.50	....	32.56	35,121·93
February, ,,	29,582.62	93.07	....	11.33	29,687.02
March, ,,	31,640.79	112.96	3,203.64	17.20	34,974.59
April, ,,	26,845.15	3,220.50	....	10.61	30,076.26
May, ,,	27,016.97	132.42	....	135.57	27,284.96
June, ,,	25,056.97	159.30	3,232.50	26.29	28,475.06
Total......	$340,788.12	$13,458.97	$13,144.01	$ 243.40	$367,634.50
Total receipts from all sources					$367,634.50
Average monthly receipts					30,636.20
Average daily receipts					1,007.21

EXPENDITURES.

In the report of the disbursing officer of the department, will be found in detail the disbursements for the fiscal year. From that report I show here the following monthly totals:

MONTH.		DISBURSEMENTS. F. Y. 1901.
July,	1900	$ 16,160.14
August,	,,	42,809.54
Carried forward		....

MONTH.	DISBURSEMENTS. F. Y. 1901.
Brought forward	....
September, ,, ...	32,640.92
October, ,, ...	39,881.13
November, ,, ...	34,831.91
December, ,.	36,267.63
January, 1901........	42,619.98
February, ,, ...	37,760.79
March, ,, ...	35,458.55
April, ,, ...	37,934.47
May, ,, ...	37,872.89
June, ,, ...	34,793.82
July, ,, ...	22,406.12
Total........................	$ 451,437.89

This table shows the actual expenses of the department for the fiscal year covered by this report, so far as known up to July 31, 1901. The item of $22,406.12 disbursed in July of this year, as shown by the table, was for expenditures made previous to the first of July, and must be included to show the total expenditures for the fiscal year.

The total of revenues and expenditures for the fiscal year thus stand as follows:

Receipts..........	$ 367,634.50
Expenditures	451,437.89
Deficit.....	$ 83,803.39

APPOINTMENTS AND BONDS.

The director-general is empowered to make appointments to the postal service and all necessary changes, but, in harmony with an order of the Postmaster-General, appointments are certified to the Military Governor for his information and approval. On June 30 there were 300 postoffices in operation on the island, 31 of which are free-delivery offices. This shows an increase of 5 in the number of offices. During the year 19 offices were established, and 14 were discontinued. At the close of the fiscal year there were 726 employees in the postal service in all its branches. Of these, 300 were postmasters, 266 employees in postoffices, 43 employees in the department of posts, 43 railway postal clerks, and 74 star-route contractors and mail messengers. Of the 726 employees, 686 are Cubans and 40 are Americans. During the year allowances for miscellaneous purposes were made at 191 offices, amounting to $8,154.63. Stated annual allowances at 26 offices amount to $7,967.15. At 84 offices, stated allowances were discontinued, amounting to $5,101.75.

In the matter of bonds, the department has continually striven during the year to impress upon postmasters not bonded the importance of giving bond, and upon all bonded postmasters the advantages of personal bonds, as being something of an index of their standing in the community. On July 1, 1900, there were 209 employees under bond, the aggregate penalty on which bonds amounted to $521,000. During the year, 254 employees gave bond, the penalties on which amounted to $425,900, and bonds of 197 employees were cancelled, wherein the penalties amounted to $457,500. However, this does not mean that the new bonds represent new appointees, because many corporation bonds were cancelled, and the same employees gave personal bonds. The bonds in force on June 30, 1901, were 266 in number, and the penalties aggregated $489,400. Included in these are two schedule bonds, one, in the sum of $45,000, covering railway postal clerks, and the other, embracing employees in the Havana post-office, in the sum of $67,000.

TRANSPORTATION.

Attention is specially invited to the report from the bureau of transportation, which has charge of the letting of contracts for carrying the mails, including railroad, steamboat, and star-route contracts. On the island there are 118 mail routes of all kinds in operation, with a total mileage of 5,563.30, and operated at an annual expense of $77,478. To this expense for the transportation of mails must be added the salaries of railway postal clerks amounting to $20,724 for the fiscal year, making a total expense for the domestic service of $98,202.

The amount assessed against Cuba, under the Universal Postal Union regulations, for transportation of her mails to and by foreign administrations, called "maritime transit of mails, territorial transit, and extraordinary territorial transit," is $12,299.15 per annum. This amount added to that for domestic mail transportation makes $110,501.15, which represents the expense to the department of mail transportation. These expenses have been somewhat increased by the fact that the Ward Line Steamship Company now requires payment for carrying Cuban mails to the United States and Mexico, where heretofore no payments were made. In fact, payment has been demanded and made during the fiscal year covered by this report for past services of this character since the American occupation of Cuba began.

There has been but little change in the mail routes during the fiscal year. The service has improved as the postal clerks and other postal officials have become better acquainted with the present methods of handling the mails. I believe the island is being given the best service possible to give it under existing conditions.

SPECIAL AGENTS.

As the postal service on the island has settled down toward more normal conditions, and postmasters and clerks have become more familiar with their work, it has not been so necessary to make frequent investigations of postoffices, and complaints have tended to decrease. This has made it possible to reduce still more the number of special agents in the field, and correspondingly the office force. There are now but eight men employed in this branch of the service. The acting chief special agent is a United States postoffice inspector detailed here for service. In addition, there are three clerks employed in the office, and four agents in the field. With these, it is believed practicable to keep this important work properly in hand. There have been very few serious cases of violation of law during the year, and those have been handled so promptly and so thoroughly that the lessons have been salutary.

The special agents made during the year a very thorough investigation of all the offices on the island, and in connection with that work instructed postmasters in their duties, and in many ways have toned up the service in an appreciable degree.

One of the most annoying things in connection with the whole service has been the persistent effort on the part of many people to use cancelled stamps for postage on letters. Some seem to have done this through ignorance, but in the great majority of cases the violation of law appears to have been knowing and wilful. There have been numerous prosecutions and some convictions and fines imposed. The punishment provided in the postal code of the island is so severe, that it has been a hard matter in many instances to secure conviction, and an amendment of the Code has been recommended. However, the arrest of the offending parties and bringing them before the local magistrates, where they were publicly reprimanded, has undoubtedly had a restraining and wholesome effect, tending to reduce such offences in the particular locality where the arrests were made. This petty crime has discovered to the officials some peculiar traits in people, and a deplorable lack of integrity in little things among the unfortunately ignorant classes. The more detailed report of the acting chief special agent will show the number and character of the cases treated during the year, and the final disposition of those which have been closed.

REGISTRY SYSTEM.

I am pleased to report that the records of the service show a very decided increase in the use of the registry system for the dispatch of valuable mail matter, both domestic and foreign. There have been increased facilities during the year, and the public has taken advantage of the safe methods provided for handling valuable matter, with the result that the system has grown in favor, and the business has naturally increased. During the year 76,117 letters and 7,090 parcels for foreign destination were dispatched by registered mail, and 64,170 letters and 7,697 parcels by domestic mail, on which fees were paid, showing a total of 155,074 pieces of mail handled, resulting in revenues to the service. There were 31,444 pieces of mail matter registered free. The total number of all pieces handled was 186,518.

The total number of paid registered letters and parcels for the year shows an increase of 27,360 over the fiscal year of 1900, with an increase of the revenues amounting to $1,874.96. The service is to be congratulated on this showing, and the increasing confidence of the public in the service.

MONEY ORDERS.

The money-order business done on the island during the year is smaller in amount of money handled than it was for the previous year. This does not mean that there has been a decrease of business among the class of people for which the system was originally designed. The postal money-order service is not a banking business, but a general means of remittance for smaller sums of money, in the nature of an accommodation to the general public. Previously, government officials in transmitting money from one province to another, or from Havana to points on the island where large disbursements were to be made, used the money-order system. This practice was discontinued by official order, and a limit placed upon the amount which might be sent by officials. An order was also made by the Postmaster-General of the United States, during the fiscal year 1900, by which the number of orders which could be issued to one purchaser for one payee at the same office in the States was limited, and continued in force during the last fiscal year; all of which materially reduced the business as compared with that of the fiscal year 1900, and tended to confine it within a normal and legitimate scope.

I may say that the money-order business of Cuba for the fiscal year 1901 was conducted along lines contemplated by the order creating the service, that is, for the benefit of the general public in transmitting small sums of money safely and quickly. The total number of money orders, domestic and foreign, issued by the postmasters of Cuba during the year, was 83,107, representing in the aggregate $2,567,521.24. The total number of orders certified on the United States through the exchange office at Tampa was 36,544, representing in amount $911,509.44. The number of domestic orders paid on the island was 46,291, and the number of international orders paid was 5,460, representing respectively $1,688,347.55 and $150,657.68, or a total of 51,751 orders, and of $1,838,915.23 in amount. The number of international orders issued, payable in Porto Rico, as certified by the Havana exchange list, was 240, and the amount $4,057.03. The number issued in Porto Rico certified on Cuba by the San Juan exchange list was 213, representing the amount of $9,697.65. The number of money-order offices in operation on June 30, 1901, was 94, and the number of stations doing a money-order business was 10.

The fees collected for the money-order business transacted amounted to $13,144.01.

The matter of transmitting balances due the United States has been somewhat of a troublesome problem. The international money-order business as now working produces constantly balances in favor of the United States on money-order account. How to remit these funds has been the question. It has fortunately happened that army paymasters and the Quartermaster-General have at times wanted quite large sums of money, and I have given my official checks on the money-order fund to them, taking in return their official checks on the Sub Treasury in New York, which have been forwarded to the Postmaster-General payable to his order. This has proved a safe method of transferring the funds, and involved no expense.

During the year there was transmitted to the Postmaster-General the sum of $756,318.11, on account of money-order funds due the United States.

DEAD LETTERS.

Into the dead-letter bureau there came during the fiscal year 175,890 pieces of mail matter, on account of unclaimed letters, letters returned from foreign countries, held for postage, misdirected, refused, and for any reason undeliverable. As is well known, every letter or parcel which can not, for any reason, be handled by postal officials, finds its way into the dead-letter bureau, where effort is made to deliver. Failing in this, foreign matter is returned to the country of origin, and domestic matter is opened and returned to the writer, if the name can be ascertained. The methods of this branch of the service are so well known that more extended reference to them is unnecessary. There were returned during the year as undeliverable, 16,420 pieces of mail matter to the United States, and 12,114 to Spain. These represent the greater proportion of mail returned to foreign countries, although undeliverable mail matter was sent back to sixty-five foreign administrations.

This summary has been prepared under pressure for time, and is not so well digested as could be wished, yet I venture to believe it will show a satisfactory condition and progress of the Cuban postal service. And further detailed information may be found in the following reports from the several bureaus composing the department of posts.

Very respectfully,

M. C. Fosnes,

Director-General.

Brig. Gen. Leonard Wood,
Military Governor,
Havana.

REPORT

OF THE

BUREAU OF APPOINTMENTS, SALARIES AND ALLOWANCES,

DEPARTMENT OF POSTS.

DEPARTMENT OF POSTS OF CUBA

BUREAU OF APPOINTMENTS.

Havana, June 30 1901.

SIR:

I have the honor to submit herewith my report on the operations of the bureau of appointments for the fiscal year ending June 30, 1901.

NUMBER OF POSTOFFICES IN OPERATION.

Province.	*Number.*
Havana	62
Matanzas	50
Pinar del Río	40
Puerto Príncipe	10
Santa Clara	93
Santiago	45
Total	300

Of the number shown, thirty-one are free-delivery offices, employing one hundred and seventeen carriers.

Number of postoffices in operation June 30, 1900			295
Number of postoffices established July 1, 1900, to December 31, 1900		5	
Number of postoffices established January 1, 1901, to June 30, 1901		14	
Total established July 1, 1900, to June 30, 1901		19	
Number of postoffices discontinued July 1, 1900, to December 31, 1900	6		
Number of postoffices discontinued January 1, 1901, to June 30, 1901	8		
Total discontinued July 1, 1900, to June 30, 1901		14	
Net increase July 1, 1900, to June 30, 1901			5
Number of postoffices in operation June 30, 1901			300

NUMBER OF EMPLOYEES IN THE SERVICE.

Employed as	*Cubans.*	*Americans*	*TOTAL.*
Postmasters......	298	2	300
Employees (P. O.)................	253	13	266
Employees (D. P.).	18	25	43
Railway postal clerks......	43	....	43
Total	612	40	652

Postmasters, postoffice and department employees.....	652
By adding the number of employees serving under contract, we obtain the following result:	
Star-route contractors	64
Mail and transfer messengers........................	10
Grand total of all employees.................	726

ADDITIONS TO AND SEPARATIONS FROM THE SERVICE.

	Additions.		*Separations*	
July 1 to December 31, 1900.				
Departmental employees...	16		24	
Postmasters	63		64	
Other employees.........	43		76	
Total		122		164
January 1 to June 30, 1901.				
Departmental employees	3		28	
Postmasters	74		68	
Other employees...............	53		69	
Total		130		157
Total July 1, 1900, to June 30, 1901		252		321

ANNUAL EXPENDITURE FOR SALARIES.

On June 30, 1901.

Department of Posts.	$	58,280
Postmasters....................		90,302
Clerks in postoffices		75,110
Letter carriers		61,514
Messengers, janitors, etc.........		8,843
Railway postal clerks.........		20,724
Total......................	$	314,773

ALLOWANCES.

Miscellaneous Purposes.

	NUMBER.	AMOUNT.
July 1 to December 31, 1900	89	$ 3,281.96
January 1 to June 30, 1901	102	4,872.67
Total	191	$ 8,154.63

Stated Annual Allowances.

NUMBER OF OFFICES.	AMOUNT.
26	$ 7,967.15

Stated Annual Allowances Discontinued.

	NUMBER OF OFFICES.	AMOUNT.
July 1 to December 31, 1900.	57	$ 3,380.50
January 1 to June 30, 1901.	27	1,721.25
Total	84	$ 5,101.75

BONDS.

Bonds in force June 30, 1900:				
Department clerks	19	$ 75,000		
Postmasters and acting postmasters	81	255,000		
Postoffice employees	91	170,000		
Assistant postmasters	18	21,000		
Total			209	$521,000
Bonds issued July 1 to December 31, 1900:				
Department clerks	5	$ 25,000		
Postmasters and acting postmasters	91	108,700		
Postoffice employees	29	73,000		
Total			125	206,700
			334	$727,700

Bonds cancelled July 1 to December 31, 1900. (Including personal bonds invalidated.)

Department clerks..	10	$ 36,000		
Postmasters and acting postmasters	27	75,600		
Postoffice employees	30	98,500		
Assistant postmasters................	13	13,000		
Total			80	$223,100
			254	$504,600

Bonds in force December 31, 1900:

Department clerks....................	14	$ 64,000		
Postmasters and acting postmasters	145	288,100		
Postoffice employees	90	144,500		
Assistant postmasters	5	8,000		
Total...............			254	$ 504,600

Bonds issued January 1 to June 30, 1901:

Department clerks...	2	$ 21,000		
Postmasters and acting postmasters	73	135,200		
Postoffice employees	53	61,000		
Assistant postmasters	1	2,000		
Total............			129	$ 219,200
			383	$ 723,800

Bonds cancelled January 1 to June 30, 1901. (Including personal bonds invalidated):

Department clerks.	9	$ 40,000		
Postmasters and acting postmasters	43	116,400		
Postoffice employees	61	71,000		
Assistant postmasters	4	7,000		
Total......			117	$ 234,400
Total bonds in force June 30, 1901.			266	$ 489,400

RECAPITULATION.

Corporation bonds in force June 30, 1900			209	$ 521,000
Corporation bonds issued July 1, 1900, to June 30, 1901	125	$ 284,300		
Corporation bonds cancelled July 1, 1900, to June 30, 1901	180	446,600		
Decrease in corporation bonds July 1, 1900, to June 30, 1901			55	$ 162,300
Corporation bonds in effect June 30, 1901			154	$ 358,700
*Personal Bonds Executed:				
Personal bonds executed July 1, 1900, to June 30, 1901	129	141,600		
Personal bonds invalidated July 1, 1900, to June 30, 1901	17	10,900		
Increase in personal bonds July 1, 1900, to June 30, 1901			112	130,700
Total bonds in force June 30, 1901			266	$ 489,400

Of the 112 personal bonds in effect June 30, 1901, 36 cover postmasters in money-order offices.

*No personal bonds were executed prior to July 1, 1900.

SPECIAL AGENTS' REPORTS.

Considered and acted upon July 1 to December 31, 1900	275
Considered and acted upon January 1 to June 30, 1901	124
Total	399

CASES REFERRED TO BUREAU OF SPECIAL AGENTS FOR INVESTIGATION AND REPORT.

July 1 to December 31, 1900	113
January 1 to June 30, 1901	73
Total	186

APPLICATIONS FOR POSITIONS IN THE SERVICE.

	CUBANS.	AMERICANS.	TOTAL.
July 1 to December 31, 1900...	176	18	194
January 1 to June 30, 1901.....	113	9	122
Total..................	289	27	316

Very respectfully,

ALBERT J. XANTEN.

Chief, Bureau of Appointments.

MR. M. C. FOSNES,

Director-General.

REPORT

OF THE

BUREAU OF TRANSPORTATION,

DEPARTMENT OF POSTS.

DEPARTMENT OF POSTS OF CUBA

BUREAU OF TRANSPORTATION.

Havana, July 30, 1901.

SIR:

I have the honor to present herewith for your consideration, a statistical report, with a few explanatory remarks, of the affairs of the Cuban postal service that are looked after directly through this bureau, during the fiscal year ending June 30th, 1901.

Since June 30th, 1900, the changes in the facilities for transporting the Cuban mails have changed very little. There is shown an increase of nine mail carrying routes. But seven of these are mail-messenger routes, which service has not heretofore been shown in this bureau. Therefore, there is only, in comparing similar service with that of last year, a net increase of two routes. The only changes of consequence are shown in the star-route service. The steamboat and railroad services have practically remained the same.

Eight star routes have been established, and five discontinued, and two transferred to steamboat class. However, the statement shows an increase of only one star route over that of last year. The two foregoing remarks should be taken in connection one with the other.

The following is a general statement of service that comes under the direct supervision of the bureau of transportation:

TRANSPORTATION MAIL SERVICE IN GENERAL.

	Number.	LENGTH.	ANNUAL COST.
Star routes	64	1,366.74 miles	$ 27,634.00
Steamboat routes	13	3,087.25 ,,	38,610.00
Railroad routes	31	1,092.01 ,,	5,244.00
Wagon-transfer routes	3	14.64 ,,	4,950.00
Mail-messenger routes	7	2.66 ,,	1,040.00
Total routes	118	5,563.30 miles	$ 77,478.00
Railway postoffice lines	27	1,931.06 ,,	
Railway postal clerks	43		$ 20,724.00
Total for domestic service			$ 98,202.00
Foreign mail service			$ 12,299.15
Total per annum			$110,501.15

Thus it is seen that the cost of transporting the mails of Cuba and the pay of the employees necessary for proper distribution in transit, is $110,501,15 per annum.

Following is a table showing the actual cost per annum for carrying the mails by the various transportation facilities at the disposal of the department, and an analysis of this rate of pay:

SUMMARY OF ALL CLASSES OF MAIL ROUTES.

Number of routes, 118.
Length of all routes, 5,563.30 miles.
Annual rate of expenditure, $77,478.00
Number of miles traveled per annum, 1,776,112 miles.
Rate of cost per mile of length, $13.93.
Rate of cost per mile traveled, 4.36 cents.

As compared with the service operative on June 30th of last year, the following is shown:

COMPARISON WITH SERVICE IN OPERATION JUNE 30TH 1900.

Increase in number of routes, 9.
Decrease in length of routes, 54.25.
Increase in annual rate of expenditure, $16,237.00.
Increase in miles traveled per annum, 139,826 miles.
Increase in rate of cost per mile traveled, .66 of a cent.
Increase in cost per mile of length, $3.04.

It is observed that the total length of all routes has decreased 54.25 miles, while the annual expenditure has increased $16,237.00 per annum. This condition is accounted for in the following manner: The distances stated a year ago have been revised and corrected as far as possible. The revision caused a reduction in the stated mileage sufficient to account for the decrease as stated.

It is well known that last year there were several steamboat lines now receiving quite a large annual compensation, reported performing service without charge. The large percentage of increase in annual cost and rate of cost per mile is thus explained.

CONTRACTS.

The making of contracts for carrying the mails has been much simplified during the past year. The method has been better understood, and bidders have presented their propositions in good form, and the contracts have been executed with little trouble. In the star-route service there was much competitive bidding.

In the steamboat service this year there were no advertisements issued, as it seemed an unnecessary expenditure. The agreements were made with the companies by letters and interviews, after which the bonds and contracts were executed. The competition for business by the steamboat companies is not very great on the same routes, and all lines are engaged to carry the mails. It would, therefore, be useless to advertise the service.

The following is a statement of the contracts by class of service executed during the last fiscal year:

CONTRACTS MADE.

For steamboat service..	13
For star-route service	47
For wagon-transfer service	1
For railroad service	2
Total	63

Contracts on all star routes in the provinces of Havana and Matanzas expired June 30th, and some on routes in the other provinces, amounting in all to 22 contracts. These contracts were advertised in due form and let in continuance of the service July 1st. The sum of the former contracts was $8,794.00 per annum, and of the new, effective July 1st, 1901, $7,689.00 per annum, a reduction of $1,105.00. It is only fair to state, however, the greater part of this amount was caused by the reduction of service on the route from Ciego de Avila to Puerto Príncipe, formerly carried as two routes with service twice a week, to once a week service, and combining under one route. As this reduction in service was practically $900.00 per annum, the reduction in cost of the identical service as compared to that under the former contracts was $205.00.

FINES.

The following fines were made against mail contractors, on account of failure to perform service according to contract, for irregularities and failures:

Fines against steamboat contractors	$ 390.68	in 17	cases.
Fines against star-route contractors	81.48	,, 41	,,
Fines against wagon-service contractors...	5.00	,, 3	,,
Fines against mail messengers	2.50	,, 2	,,
Total	$ 479 66	,, 63	,,

The service is not so large but that many reported irregularities are known beforehand by the bureau, and mitigating circumstances being already understood no fines are assessed in many cases, unless it is quite certain that no sufficient excuse can be rendered. For this reason there are few remittances reported.

REMITTANCES OF FINES

Steamboat contractors................	Remitted	$ 4.25	1 case
Star-route contractors..................	,,	2.72	2 cases
Wagon-service contractors.	,,	......	
Mail messengers......	,,	......	
Total........................		$ 6.97	3 cases

In inspecting the steamboat service, consideration is taken of the fact that almost all vessels carrying the mails travel in the open sea. Great leniency is, therefore, exercised in requiring them to make their schedule time. As a matter of fact few fines have been imposed on this account. The fines against steamboat contractors have been more in the nature of reductions for not making trips, on account of the state of the weather not permitting vessels to go out with safety.

In the case of star routes, the fines have been imposed on account of many reasons, mostly in the cause of discipline.

It is believed that the carriers in this branch of the service deserve much commendation for their efforts to carry the mails on schedule time. At certain seasons of the year the hardships are unusually severe. Within a short time a road that is easily passable can become almost impassable, by reason of the rains that fall in this country. A stream that appears most harmless can soon become a dangerous torrent. Some of the cases called to attention show that the star-route carriers often risk these elements when they could just as easily have waited a more propitious time, in order not to have a delay charged to them. The knowledge of such interest has a tendency to cause one to believe the reasons of delay, when stated to be swollen streams and impassable roads. It is a pleasure to in this manner note the faithfulness and interest that is found in those who carry the mails over the star routes over the island.

FOREIGN MAILS.

About one-third of all mail matter originating in Cuba is addressed to foreign countries. The foreign mail service, therefore, is not of much less importance than the domestic.

A large portion of the foreign mail is for the United States. That country maintains a steamship line from Port Tampa, Fla., to Havana, which not only must carry mail to Cuba on its outward trips, but from Cuba to the United States on its homeward trips. As our part of maintaining the communication, a similar line has been under contract with this department to carry the mail in both directions between Havana and Miami, Florida. The two lines mentioned have provided very good interchange of service, four times a week in each direction. Communication is also maintained between New York and Havana twice a week. These facilities are also employed in dispatching correspondence to European and other countries via New York.

Dispatches are made direct to Spain on the 15th and 20th of each month from Havana by service maintained by Spain, and correspondence is received from that country three times a month. The Spanish mail service is maintained, however, from Spain by Havana to Mexico and the republics of Columbia and Venezuela, which permits dispatches to those countries from Havana. France also maintains a service from the port of San Nazaire by Santander, Spain, to Havana and on to Veracruz, Mexico, once a month in each direction. Both lines are used by the Cuban service.

There is also once a weekly exchange between Havana and Mexico by the New York and Cuba Mail Steamship Co.

As before mentioned, Cuba has a very large foreign mail, and is very dependent upon the facilities of other countries for its reaching its destination. Of course payment for these facilities is made subject to the Universal Postal Union regulations. Service is also paid for direct dispatches to foreign countries, under the same regulations, to the New York and Cuba Mail Steamship Co. This payment is made for dispatches by that line to Mexico and to New York.

STATEMENT OF THE RATE OF EXPENDITURES PER ANNUM FOR DISPATCHING FOREIGN MAIL.

Amount due under the Universal Postal Union regulations to foreign countries. For maritime transit	$	5,119.90
For territorial transit		5,473.69
Total	$	10,593.59
Amount paid for direct dispatches from Cuba to foreign countries	$	1,705.56
	$	12,299.15

Amount of mail dispatched to foreign countries, for which payment was made at the rate of 44 cents per lb. for letters and post-cards, and 4½ cents per lb. for other matter:

Letters and post cards, 3,008.20 lbs.	$	1,323.60
Other matter, 8,488.12 lbs.		381.96
Total	$	1,705.56

Besides the amount of $1,705.56 paid to the New York and Cuba Mail Steamship Co. for services during the fiscal year, that company called upon the department for settlement in full for services rendered since January 1st, 1899, the beginning of the American occupation of Cuba. A settlement was made on the above basis for carrying 3,794.52 pounds of letters and post-cards, and 12,189.30 pounds of other matter, amounting to $2,218.10, during the period from January 1st, 1899, to June 30th, 1900.

Communication with the islands of Santo Domingo and Porto Rico is maintained twice a month by the Herrera line, who will receive compensation under the Universal Postal Union rules hereafter. There are no regular recognized mail facilities between Cuba and the island of Jamaica, but dispatches are occasionally exchanged between Santiago de Cuba and Port Antonio, Jamaica.

SERVICE IN DETAIL.

STAR-ROUTE SERVICE.

Number of routes, 64.
Length of routes, miles, 1,366.74.
Annual travel, miles, 378,260.
Rate of annual expenditure, $27,634.00.
Average number of trips per week, 4.25.
Rate of cost per mile of length, $20.22.
Rate of cost per mile traveled, 7.31 cents.

COMPARISON WITH JUNE 30TH, 1900.

Increase in number of routes, 1.
Decrease in length of routes, miles, 16.76.
Increase in annual cost, $3,635.00.
Increase in annual travel, miles, 56,557.
Increase in cost per mile of length, $2.87.
Decrease in cost per mile traveled, .19 of a cent.
Increase in average number of trips per week, .75.

BY PROVINCES.

PROVINCES.	Number of Routes	Miles.	Annual Cost.	Cost Per Mile.	Annual Travel.	Cost per Mile Traveled.
Havana	9	104.87	$ 3,154.00	$ 30.07	54,470	5.79 Cents.
Pinar del Río	15	252.87	6,925.00	27.38	92,833	7.45 "
Matanzas	4	30.	940.00	31.33	10,400	9.00 "
Santa Clara	19	295.	6,615.00	22.42	119,704	5.52 "
Puerto Príncipe	4	212.	3,280.00	15.47	36,608	8.96 "
Santiago	13	472.	6,720.00	14.40	64,245	10.46 "
Total	64	1,366.74	$27,634.00	$ 20.22	378,260	7.31 Cents.

INCREASES, DECREASES AND CHANGES DURING THE FISCAL YEAR.

No. of new routes established		8	
No. of routes discontinued	5		
Transferred to S. S. service	2		
A net increase of		1	route.

Increased mileage, new routes...........		192	miles.
Mileage of discontinued routes..........	68		
Decrease caused by transfer, rearrangement and more accurate distances..	140.76		
A net decrease of...		16.76	miles.

Increased cost by new routes established..		$ 2,554.00
Increase by cost of new contracts executed at expiration of old...		1,136.00
Adding additional service on routes...		605.00
Decrease by discontinuance of routes...	$ 660.00	
Net increase in cost............		$ 3,635.00

SPECIAL SERVICE.

There are nine postoffices supplied by special service, at five of which it is incumbent upon their postmasters to carry the mails to the base of supply, and their salaries are fixed with that understanding. At two of them private railroads carry the mail, and at the remaining two, extraordinary facilities are employed, but without expense to the department.

STAR-ROUTE SERVICE IN OPERATION JULY 1ST, 1901.

Number of routes, 66.
Length of routes, miles, 1,462.74.
Rate of cost per annum, $27,513.00.
Increase in number of routes, 2.
Increase in mileage, 96.
Decrease in annual cost, $121.00.

Three new routes have been established and service began July 1st. The number of routes given, however, shows only an increase of two routes. This is explained by the fact that to take effect July 1st, two routes were consolidated into one.

The lettings of contracts under last advertisement, taking effect July 1st, as stated under the head "Contracts," shows a reduction in annual cost of $1,105.00. The cost of the three new routes is $984.00 per annum. There is, therefore, a net reduction of $121.00 in the annual cost of the service, beginning July 1st, 1901.

STEAMBOAT SERVICE.

The steamboat service, as far as the service actually rendered, is practically the same as last year. Every steamboat performing service around the island that can be of any practical utility in doing so is employed in carrying the mails. It is well known that up to June 30th, 1900, there were some lines that this year have received a large portion of the compensation paid under this head carried the mails without pay. For this reason a comparative basis of cost per mile of length or traveled would be of no value.

The tables given are, therefore, plain statements of the service regularly in operation.

STEAMBOAT SERVICE.

No. of routes, 13.
Length of routes, miles, 3,087.25.
Cost per annum, $38,610.00.
Cost per mile of length, $12.51.
Annual travel, miles, 327,505.
Cost per mile traveled, 11.78 cents.

COMPARISON WITH SERVICE OPERATIVE JUNE 30TH, 1900.

Increase in number of routes, 1.
Decrease in length of routes, 44.
Increase in cost per annum, $11,302.00.
Decrease in annual travel, miles, 11,950.

ITEMIZED STEAMBOAT SERVICE.

OPERATIVE FROM JULY 1. 1900, TO JUNE 30, 1901.

Route No.	TERMINI.	CONTRACTOR.	Annual Pay.	Length Miles.	Trips per week.
1	Havana to Santiago.	Sobrinos de Herrera	$ 12,000.00	840.	3 a month.
2	Batabanó to Santiago	Menéndez and Co	9,000.00	614.46	1 a week.
3	Batabanó to Nueva Gerona.	Angel G. Ceballos	600.00	92.	1 a week.
4	Santiago to Caimanera	Gallego–Messa and Co	1,000.00	45.	2 a week.
5	Havana to Nuevitas	Alonso Jauma and Co	300.00	409.	1 a week.
6	Cienfuegos to Tunas de Zaza	José Castro Monje	300.00	82.08	2 a week.
7	Havana to La Fé	A. del Collado and Co	1,200.00	227.49	4 a month.
10	Cienfuegos to Rodas	Boullon and Co	360.00	30.	7 a week.
11	Batabanó to Manzanillo	Alonso Jauma and Co	200.00	425.22	2 a month.
12	Mayarí to Port of Mayarí	Carlota Grau	600.00	15.	1 a week.
13	Manzanillo to Niquero	José Muñoz	1,200.00	51.	7 a week.
14	Miami., Fla. to Havana, Cuba	Pen. and Occ. S. S. Co	11,700.00	242.	1 a week.
15	Cienfuegos to Belmonte	E. Atkins and Co	150.00	14.	2 a week.
			$ 36,610.00	3087.25	

On July 1st, service by the Peninsular and Occidental S. S. Co. was relinquished, and explains the reduction of one route, and 242 miles, in the following statement:

STEAMBOAT SERVICE PROVIDED FOR AFTER JULY 1ST, 1901.

No. of routes, 12.
Length of routes, miles, 2,845.25.
Rate of cost per annum, $26.910.00.

COMPARISON WITH JUNE 30TH, 1901.

Decrease in number of routes, 1.
Decrease in mileage, 242.
Decrease in cost, $11,700.00.

RAILROAD SERVICE.

Number of railroad routes, 31.
Length of railroad routes, 1,092.01.
Annual travel, miles 942,089.80.
Annual pay, $5,244.00.

This service has not practically changed during the past year. The correction of an error in the estimate of distance shows a slight increase in the mileage reported, 3.85 miles.

Conditions existing regarding the railways of Cuba carrying the mails are well known and need not be reiterated here. Out of 1092.01 miles of railway on the island, there are only 188.88 miles that are compensated for carrying the mails, or 17 per cent.

The United Railways of Havana are paid at the rate of $32.00 per mile for 143.25 miles; $4,584 per annum (229.20 kilometers at $20.00 per kilometer). This company has 261 miles of track. There are, therefore, 117.25 miles for which they receive no compensation, being required by the Royal Decree of December 10, 1858, to carry the mails.

The Puerto Príncipe and Nuevitas railway is not obliged by its charter to carry the mails free. That company is paid at the rate of $14.46 per annum per mile for carrying the mails over its whole road, 45.63 miles, $660.00 73 kilometers at $9.04 per kilometer.

The railroad routes in operation are as follows:

Route No.	TERMINI.	NAME OF RY. Co.	Length Miles
101	San Felipe to Batabanó........	United Rys. of Havana......	9.38
102	Caibarién to Placetas...........	Cuban Central Ry. Ltd......	32.93
103	Caibarién to Placetas...........	Cuban Central Ry. Ltd......	22.31
104	Cárdenas to Esperanza.........	Cárdenas and Júcaro Ry....	96.47
105	Cárdenas to Yaguaramas.....	Cárdenas and Júcaro Ry....	71.16
106	Rodas to Cartagena.............	Rodas, Turquino and Cartagena Ry.......................	20.00
107	Cienfuegos to Santa Clara....	Cuban Central Rys. Ltd....	42.81
108	Palmira to Congojas............	Cuban Central Rys. Ltd....	15.63
109	Gibara to Holguín................	Gibara and Holguín Ry......	20.00
110	Havana to Alacranes............	United Rys. of Havana......	81.20
111	Regla to Guanabacoa..........	United Rys. of Havana......	3.00
112	Rincón to Guanajay..............	United Rys. of Havana......	21.26
113	Havana to Jovellanos...........	United Rys. of Havana......	88.70
114	Havana to Marianao...........	Marianao Ry....................	10.00
115	Havana to Pinar del Río......	Western Ry of Havana......	110.00
116	Isabela de Sagua to Cruces...	Cuban Central Ry. Ltd.....	49.31
117	Altamisal to Macagua..........	Cárdenas and Júcaro Ry....	20.20
118	Empalme to Güines..............	United Rys. of Havana......	25.88
119	Matanzas to Colón..............	Matanzas Ry....................	70.00
120	Máximo Gómez to Itabo......	Cárdenas and Júcaro Ry....	13.62
121	Júcaro to Morón..................	Júcaro and S. Fernando Ry.	42.30
122	Navajas to Murga.......	Matanzas Ry....................	30.00
123	Nuevitas to Puerto Príncipe.	Puerto Príncipe and Nuevitas Ry...........................	45.63
124	Ranchuelo to San Juan de las Yeras..............	Cuban Central Rys. Ltd....	5.00
125	Tunas de Zaza to Sancti Spíritus......................................	Tunas and S. Spíritus Ry...	24.47
126	Santiago de Cuba to S. Luis	Sabanilla and Marota Ry..	20.63
127	Sagua la Grande to Caguaguas..................................	Cuban Central Ry. Ltd......	9.69
128	Santiago de Cuba to Firmeza	Juragua Iron Co...............	19.00
129	Sitiecito to Camajuaní..........	Cuban Central Ry. Ltd......	36.18
130	Caimanera to Jamaica..........	Guantánamo Ry........... ...	29.00
131	Cristo to Songo....................	Sabanilla and Maroto Ry..	6.25
		Total.......................	1,092.01

WAGON-TRANSFER SERVICE.

Number of routes, 3.
Length of routes, miles, 14.64.
Miles traveled per annum, 24,430.
Rate of annual cost, $4,950.00.
Cost per mile, $338.11.
Cost per mile traveled, 20.27 cents.

This service shows no change except a small increase in pay, $260.00 over last year.

Last August an attempt was made to let the wagon service at Santiago by contract, but under the advertisement for bids, the prices asked were so high it was concluded to continue the service as before, by using the equipment belonging to the department. A very good regulation wagon was already in use, and by purchasing a pair of horses and set of harness and employing a driver, the service has been conducted very satisfactorily.

The cost of this service is as follows:

Route No. 901.	Havana.........	$ 3,750.00	per annum.
,, ,, 902.	Cienfuegos......	600.00	do
,, ,, 903.	Matanzas.......	600.00	do
Total		$ 4,950.00	

MAIL-MESSENGER SERVICE.

Number of routes, 7.
Length, miles, 2.66.
Annual cost, $1,040.00.
Cost per mile, $390.98.
Annual travel, miles, 3,837.40.
Cost per mile traveled, 27.1 cents.

This service has only been classed and managed as such since the beginning of this fiscal year. It was determined to treat it as such at those places where the person who should become mail messenger was not needed as an employee of the office served. The experiment has not proved a success by any means, as the proposals received were usually too high in price for the work required. Therefore, no encouragement has been given to setting it aside as an individual service. It is admitted that it could be conducted better if the prices named were not beyond reason in most cases.

RAILWAY MAIL SERVICE.

The railway mail service shows few changes from that reported a year ago. It is believed that the efficiency of the clerks has very much improved, and the interest taken by most of them is highly commendable.

The bureau has been able to give more attention to the minor details of the service during the past year. The men have been instructed in and shown more of the correct methods of performing their work. Special attention has been given to distribution. An important factor in this instruction, and one that has been urged to a great extent, has been the checking of errors.

During the year there have been three R. P. O. lines discontinued. They were short runs that actually needed no clerks The railways were induced to permit their own employees to handle the made up mails. There has been no occasion to regret taking our employees off, as the service has been rendered satisfactorily.

The most notable improvement in equipment has been on the Havana, Batabanó and Santiago R. P. O. on the Menéndez line. That company has constructed on all its steamers an office with suitable fixtures for distributing mail, with a sleeping apartment for the clerk, also a storage room for made up mail, all conveniently located for handling the large quantity of mail passing over the line.

It has been impossible to put railway postal service on the northern coast. The steamboat company, which practically has a monopoly of that business, cannot be induced to build the apartments, nor carry the clerks.

The following statement gives a general idea of the railway mail service in operation at the close of the past fiscal year:

RAILWAY MAIL SERVICE.

Number of lines, 27.
Number of clerks, 43.
Miles of railway mail service, 1,931.06.
Annual mileage of clerks, 1,131,159.37.
Total pay of clerks, $20,724.00.
Average pay per clerk, $481.96 per annum.

SUMMARY OF RAILWAY MAIL SERVICE.

Number of railway lines, 23.
Clerks on railway lines, 38.
Number of steamboat lines, 4.
Clerks on steamboat lines, 5.
Miles of service on railways, 1,153.52.
Annual travel on railways, 1,003,045.27.
Miles of service on steamships, 777.54.
Annual travel on steamships, 128,114.10.
Total mileage, 1,931.06.
Total annual travel, 1,131,159.37.

CLASSIFIED LIST OF SALARIES OF RAILWAY POSTAL CLERKS.

8	clerks at...	$600.00	$ 4,800.00
21	,,	500.00	10,500.00
1		480.00	480.00
2		420.00	840.00
7		400.00	2,800.00
1		384.00	384.00
1		360.00	360.00
1		320.00	320.00
1		240.00	240.00
Total.. 43			$20,724.00

Average pay per clerk.. .... $ 481.96

CASE EXAMINATIONS OF RAILWAY POSTAL CLERKS.

The case examinations indicate a small increase in percentage. Reported last year 83.08 per cent, this year 89.72, an increase of 6.64 per cent.

Number of examinations, 29.
Total number of cards handled, 8,544.
Number correct, 7,665.
Percentage correct, 89 72.

As stated already the checking of errors in the distribution of mails has been given special attention during the past year, and great pressure has been brought to bear, not only upon the railway postal clerks, but upon the postoffices as well. However, it is conceded that the statistics gathered should not be relied upon as giving sufficient data to indicate the percentage of missent mail. Therefore no estimate is presented. The calculations made proved unworthy to be credited as statistical. The records kept are given.

ERRORS IN DISTRIBUTION.

	Total.	*R. P. O.*	*Postoffices.*
Pieces of ordinary mail	4,657	360	4,297
Missent letter packages	69	10	59
Missent sacks of papers	9	5	4
Mislabeled letter packages	19	0	19
Mislabeled sacks of papers	4	2	2
Missent pouches	1	1	0
Missent registered packages	2	2	0
Missent registered pouches	3	3	0

The mail distributed in transit by railway postal clerks is 4 per cent more than that reported last year. This estimate is made upon the number of packages reported, and cannot indicate satisfactorily the increase in the mail in the island. Nearly every package is picked up by the clerks on the road, probably the same number of packages every day of each year, and there is no way of telling if the packages contain more letters this year than last The registered mail, however, handled by the R. M. S. clerks shows an increase of 25 per cent, and the report of this class of mail is quite reliable, as each registered piece is counted.

The following table shows the amount of work in distribution performed by each line, together with the number of trips made:

MAIL WORKED BY R. P. O. LINES.

No. of Clerks.	No. of Trips.	R. P. O. LINE.	Packages letters.	Sacks Papers.	Reg'd Packages.	Reg'd Pouches.	No. case.	Inner R Sacks.
1	730	Caibarién, Camajuaní and Placetas	18,141	907	1,051	....	1	1
1	730	Caibarién and Placetas	11,470	154	2,031	1		
3	1,569	Cárdenas and Santa Clara	45,891	4,146	14,307	3,691	174	22
1	730	Cárdenas and Yaguaramas	38,297	1,467	3,717			
1	376	Cartagena and Rodas	1,706	192	194	1		
1	443	Cienfuegos and Congojas	1,583	435	144			
2	1,460	Cienfuegos and Santa Clara	17,740	1,473	2,924	2	7	
1	324	Gibara and Holguín	493	1	2,197		4	
4	1,458	Havana and Alacranes	50,686	2,325	9,498		9	
2	1,454	Havana and Guanajay	26,865	1,759	3,696		9	
4	1,455	Havana and Jovellanos	48,339	2,728	12,549	5,056	174	18
1	1,946	Havana and Marianao	13,360	1,116	346	....	1	980
3	1,460	Havana and Pinar del Río	24,785	1,639	6,779	738	43	
2	730	Isabela and Caibarién	26,817	2,770	7,223	728	....	2
2	1,460	Isabela and Cienfuegos	35,304	2,370	10,151	2,212	26	7
1	649	Júcaro and Morón	4,744	1,094	608	275	2	
1	730	Macagua and Altamisal	5,072	669	1,474	3	1	
1	1,226	Madruga, Empalme and Güines	5,373	371	648	1	3	
1	730	Matanzas and Colón	28,944	1,805	3,839			
1	486	Máximo Gómez and Itabo	2,675	240	167			
1	730	Navajas and Murga	6,829	564	1,292			
1	528	Nuevitas and Puerto Príncipe	534	....	1,611	267	3	1
1	417	Sancti Spíritus and Tunas	2,387	....	2,250			
1	492	San Felipe and Batabanó	3,076	295	487			
2	828	Santiago and San Luis	9,414	1092	2,541			
40	23,141	Total Ry. Lines	430,525	29,612	91,724	12,965	457	1,031
2	105	Havana, Batabanó and Santiago	11,201	5,519	5,703	489	29	19
1	512	Manzanillo and Niquero	1,737	16	511			
1	730	Cienfuegos and Rodas	10,702	477	1,527	....	1	
1	190	Cienfuegos and Tunas	....	....	2,899			
5	1,537	Total S. S. Lines	23,640	6,012	10,640	489	30	19
45	24,678	Total all lines	454,165	35,624	102,364	13,454	487	1,050

NOTE:—San Felipe and Batabanó R. P. O. was discontinued Nov. 1st, 1900.
Máximo Gómez and Itabo R. P. O. was discontinued March 1st, 1900.

There have been constructed during the past year on railway trains and steamboats nine apartments for distributing the mails, making in all now in use thirty-six. On some of the lines the apartments have been moved from the 2d-class cars to the baggage cars, where they are of more service. This is true of all those on the Cuban Central Railway. The other leading roads have agreed to build them in the baggage cars in all cases hereafter, and when their present equipment goes in for repairs they are to be moved.

The envelopes ordinarily in use in this country are quite wide. For this reason there has been adopted as standard size for letter boxes 5½ inches wide by 4½ inches high.

The following table gives the list of the railway postoffice lines now in service, the number of clerks assigned to each, the length of each line, the annual travel, and the number and dimensions of the mail apartment:

STATEMENT OF RAILWAY POSTAL LINES.

DESIGNATION OF LINE.	LENGTH MILES.	NO. CLERKS.	ANNUAL TRAVEL.	MAIL APARTMENTS. NO.	LENGTH.	WIDTH.
Caibarién, Camajuaní and Placetas	32.93	1	24,038.90	1	7 ft.	3 ft. 6 in.
Caibarién and Placetas	22.31	1	16,286.30	1	6 ft. 2 in.	4 ft.
Cárdenas and Santa Clara	105.53	3	91,224.39	1	5 ft.	4 ft. 6 in.
				1	6 ft. 6 in.	5 ft. 6 in.
				1	8 ft. 2 in.	5 ft. 8 in.
Cárdenas and Yaguaramas	71.16	1	51,946.80	1	5 ft.	4 ft. 6 in.
Cartagena and Rodas	20.00	1	7,520.00	......	......	......
Cienfuegos and Congojas	24.38	1	10,800.34	1	6 ft. 6 in.	2 ft. 6 in.
Cienfuegos and Santa Clara	42.81	2	62,502.60	1	8 ft. 3 in.	3 ft.
Gibara and Holguín	20.00	1	6,480.00	1	4 ft.	7 ft.
Havana and Alacranes	81.20	4	118,389.60	1	6 ft.	6 ft.
				2	5 ft.	5 ft.
				2	6 ft.	5 ft.
Havana and Guanajay	35.63	2	51,806.02	1	4 ft. 9 in.	2 ft. 6 in.
Havana and Jovellanos	88.70	4	104,154.75	1	6 ft. 4 in.	5 ft. 6 in.
				2	6 ft.	5 ft. 4 in.
				1	4 ft. 9 in.	4 ft. 9 in.
Havana and Marianao	10.00	1	19,460.00	......	......	......
Havana and Pinar del Río	110.00	3	112,690.10	1	10 ft.	2 ft.
				1	10 ft.	2 ft.
				1	7 ft. 11 in.	2 ft. 11 in.
Isabela and Caibarién	69.29	2	50,581.70	1	9 ft.	4 ft.
Isabela and Cienfuegos	68.37	2	64,999.40	1	7 ft.	3 ft. 2 in.
				1	8 ft. 2 in.	4 ft.
Júcaro and Morón	42.30	1	27,452.70	......	......	......
Macagua and Altamisal	20.20	1	14,746.00	1	5 ft. 6 in.	5 ft.
Madruga, Empalme and Güines	25.88	1	31,728.88	1	6 ft.	3 ft.

STATEMENT OF RAILWAY POSTAL LINES.—(CONTINUED.)

DESIGNATION OF LINE.	LENGTH MILES.	NO. CLERKS.	ANNUAL TRAVEL.	MAIL APARTMENTS. NO.	LENGTH.	WIDTH.
Matanzas and Colón	70.00	1	51,100.00	1	8 ft.	2 ft. 11 in.
Navajas and Murga	65.86	1	29,953.32	1	8 ft.	2 ft. 11 in.
Nuevitas and Puerto Príncipe	45.63	1	24,092.64	1		
Sancti Spíritus and Tunas	24.47	1	10,203.99	1	4 ft.	2 ft. 6 in.
Santiago and San Luis	20.63	2	17,081.64	1	6 ft. 10 in.	2 ft. 10 in.
Havana, Batabanó and Santiago by rail	36.24		3,805.20			
Total by rail	1,153.52	38	1,003,045.27	32		
Havana, Batabanó and Santiago by steamer	614 46	2	64,518.30	1	*8 ft. 6 in.	6 ft. 5 in.
				1	*10 ft. 5 in.	7 ft. 11 in.
				1	*10 ft.	6 ft. 11 in.
Manzanillo and Niquero	51.00	1	26,112.00		A desk is used by the clerk for his work.	
Cienfuegos and Rodas	30.00	1	21,900.00	1	4 ft. 6 in.	4 ft. 6 in.
Cienfuegos and Tunas	82.08	1	15,583.80		The clerk is also purser of the steamer.	
Total by steamer	777.54	5	128,114 10	4		
	1,153.52	38	1,003,045.27	32		
	777.54	5	128,114.10	4		
Total of all service	1,931.06	43	1,131,159.37	36		

*Each steamer has also a mail storage room of the same dimensions.

Again during the past year a record has been kept of all accidents to railway trains and steamboats carrying mail, which is herewith given.

1900.

July 24. A strike of the firemen on the United Rys. of Havana began on July 24th and lasted through July 26th.

Havana and Alacranes R. P. O. Trains Nos. 1 and 14 ran regularly during the time of the strike. Trains Nos. 6 and 11 did not run on the 24th, 25th and 26th. All trains resumed service on July 27th.

Havana and Jovellanos R. P. O. Trains Nos. 5 and 10 ran regularly. July 24th, train No. 2 arrived at Havana from Jovellanos, but train No. 9 did not go out. On July 25th and 26th trains Nos. 9 and 10 failed to run. All trains resumed service July 27th.

Havana and Guanajay R. P. O. Train No. 4 was permitted to run after leaving Guanajay 5 hours late July 24th. At Ciénaga a party of strikers boarded the train and required all passengers to leave it. They attempted to make the R. P. C. leave it also, but he opposed them with the result he arrived in Havana with the mail all right. July 25th trains Nos. 4 and 13 did not run, trains Nos. 7 and 8 did. July 26th train No. 4 only failed to run. July 27th all trains resumed service.

Madruga, Empalme and Güines R. P. O. All trains ran during the time of the strike with some delay.

Sept. 6th. Macagua and Altamisal R. P. O. The train from Macagua for Altamisal ran off the track between Banaguises and Altamisal, which necessitated making transfer to another train, arriving at Altamisal 2 hours and 33 minutes late. There was no damage done to either the clerk or the mail.

Oct. 6th. Havana and Alacranes R. P. O. Train No. 14 was wrecked at Melena del Sur. There was no damage done. Arrived at Havana 4 hours and 35 minutes late.

Nov. 3rd. Havana and Alacranes R. P. O. Train No. 1 was wrecked at Unión de Reyes causing delay of 1 hour and 24 minutes. No damage was done.

Nov. 7th. Isabela and Caibarién R. P. O. The tender of the engine on train No. 1. jumped the track between Sitiecito and Sitio Grande. Delayed 2 hours and 28 minutes. No damage was done.

Nov. 27th. Isabela and Caibarién R. P. O. Train No. 9 got off the track near Taguayabón, thereby causing a transfer to another train. The clerk and mail car uninjured. Delayed 4 hours.

Dec. 5th. Havana and Pinar del Río R. P. O. Train No. 5 going into Gabriel station, the side track switch having been left open through mistake, the engine jumped the track, and had to wait for another engine from Havana. Arrived at Artemisa 3 hours and 5 minutes late. There was no damage except to the engine.

Dec. 13th. Havana and Alacranes R. P. O. Train No. 11 had a collision at Unión de Reyes with the yard engine. The apartment mail car No. 4 was injured. No mail was lost or damaged, clerk unhurt. Train arrived at Alacranes.

1901.

Jan. 16th. Madruga, Empalme and Güines R. P. O. The engine of train No. 21 got off the track at Robles station. Delay 3 hours and 45 minutes. No damage.

Jan. 22d. Macagua and Altamisal R. P. O. Train No. 8 was wrecked at kilometer No. 31 between Macagua and San José de los Ramos. The car in which the mail apartment is located was overturned, slightly damaging the mail. The clerk was unhurt.

Jan. 31st. Isabela and Caibarién R. P. O. Train No. 10 was wrecked at 9.00 A. M. between Encrucijada and Mata. There was no damage done. A transfer was made to another train sent out from Calabazar, arriving at Isabela about 2 hours late.

Feb. 4th. Cienfuegos and Congojas R. P. O. Train No. 14 made up of two passenger coaches and fourteen empty freight cars, between Palmira and Arriete, the rail gave out and the engine left the track, derailing the first six freight cars, two of which were completely demolished. There were no casualties except a severe shock was received by one of the passengers. The R. P. C. succeeded in reaching Arriete with the mail, returning to Cienfuegos by means of horseback to Palmira and from there via the Isabela and Cienfuegos R. P. O. Regular travel was resumed the next day.

Feb. 4th. A strike of the employees of the Cárdenas and Júcaro R. R. Feb. 4th to 10th, inclusive, was inaugurated. The strikers caused the abandonment of trains Nos. 3 and 6, Cárdenas and Santa Clara R. P. O. which ran only between Cárdenas and Jovellanos, during the whole period of the strike. the clerk performing service on trains Nos. 1 and 2. Trains Nos. 1 and 2 were permitted to run without interruption on February 4th. During the remainder of the strike, however, only an engine and mail car was permitted to run. The railway postal lines on other branches of the system, Cárdenas and Yaguaramas, Macagua and Altamisal, Máximo Gómez and Itabo, were not materially affected.

March 22. Macagua and Altamisal R. P. O. The train from Macagua to Altamisal was wrecked between kilometer 19 and 20, caused by the rail giving out. No damage was done. The train went throuh to Cárdenas, arriving too late to make connection for Havana.

March 22. Havana and Guanajay R. P. O. train No. 7 ran off the track at Rincón. Delayed 1 hour and 37 minutes. There was no damage.

NUMBER OF ERRORS MADE BY VARIOUS POST OFFICES IN CUBA IN DISTRIBUTION AND DISPATCH OF MAIL FROM THEIR RESPECTIVE OFFICES, FROM JULY 1ST, 1900, TO JUNE 30TH, 1901.

POST OFFICE.	Missent pieces of Mail.	Missent Pckgs Letters.	POST OFFICE.	Missent Pieces of Mail.	Missent Pckgs Letters.
Aguacate	3		Manzanillo	117	2
Artemisa	7		Marianao	82	1
Aguada del Cura	4		Matanzas	141	1
Baiṅoa	3		Mayarí	15	
Baracoa	11		Nuevitas	35	2
Batabanó	39		Palos	6	
Bayamo	9		Pinar del Río	37	
Bejucal	4		Placetas	12	
Caibarién	25	1	Puerto Padre	26	
Cárdenas	128	2	Puerto Príncipe	87	
Cartagena	4		Remedios	9	
Ciego de Avila	63		Rincón	7	1
Cifuentes	4		Rodas	18	
Cienfuegos	323	10	Sagua la Grande	117	
Caimanera	32		San Antonio de los Baños	6	
Columbia Barracks	107	2	Sancti Spíritus	58	
Dimas	5		Santa Clara	45	1
Gibara	44	6	Santiago	362	4
Guanabacoa	7		Santo Domingo	6	
Guanajay	36		Santiago de las Vegas	6	
Guantánamo	267		Trinidad	33	
Guara	6		Tunas de Zaza	7	
Güines	55		Santa Cruz del Sur	27	
Havana	1718	39	Sagua de Tánamo	26	
Holguín	8		Vieja Bermeja	5	
Jamaica	10		Yaguajay	8	
Júcaro	56	1			

Very respectfully,

M. H. BUNN,

Chief, Bureau of Transportation.

HON. M. C. FOSNES,

Director-General.

REPORT

OF THE

BUREAU OF STAMPS AND SUPPLIES.

DEPARTMENT OF POSTS.

DEPARTMENT OF POSTS OF CUBA

BUREAU OF STAMPS AND SUPPLIES.

Havana, July 30, 1901.

SIR:

I have the honor to submit the following report for the fiscal year ending June 30, 1901. The subjects within the jurisdiction of this bureau may be treated under two heads:

First: Stamps, stamped envelopes, postal cards, newspaper wrappers and penalty envelopes.

Second: All other postoffice supplies furnished by the department of posts to postmasters.

All stamps, stamped envelopes, postal cards and newspaper wrappers are ordered for the Cuban postal service through, and by the courtesy of, the Honorable Postmaster-General of the United States, thereby enabling the department of posts to obtain them at a nominal cost, and insuring a prompt and safe delivery. The denominations of stamps in use and printed especially for the Cuban postal service, are one-cent, two-cent, three-cent, five-cent, ten-cent, and ten-cent special-delivery. Also one-, two- and five-cent number five envelopes, and two- and five-cent number eight envelopes, and one- and two-cent number twelve newspaper wrappers. United States postage-due stamps of the denominations of one, two, five and ten cents are in use, being over-printed for the Cuban postal service, as are also one- and two-cent United States postal cards.

The following statement shows the values of stamps, stamped envelopes, postal cards and wrappers on hand July 1st, 1900, the value of stamped supplies received each month, the value of issues for each month upon requisitions from postmasters, and balance on hand June 30th, 1901.

(STATEMENT NO. 1.)

The following statement shows the sales of all kinds of stamps, stamped envelopes, postal cards and newspaper wrappers for each month for the same period.

(STATEMENT NO. 2.)

The decrease in sales of ordinary five-cent stamps on and after April 1st, 1901, is doubtless due largely to the change in the postal rates between the United States and Cuba. Previous to April 1st the letter rate was five cents for each half-ounce and fraction thereof, and after that date it was reduced to two cents per ounce and fraction thereof, causing a much lighter demand for five-cent stamps. This change of rate, no doubt, limited the necessity of using so many postage-due stamps on mail matter dispatched from the United States on the two-cent rate, causing a portion of the postage to be collected at this end by the use of postage-due stamps.

There is a noticeable increase in the demand for No. 5 two-cent envelopes and one-cent postal cards; the convenience of them is apparently being realized more and more each month.

REMITTANCES.

All remittances of money arising from the sales of stamps, stamped envelopes, postal cards and newspaper wrappers by the postmasters of the island, are sent direct to the Treasurer of Cuba. No money from any source is received by this bureau, nor has been since June 30, 1900.

Postoffices on the island are divided into two classes in relation to obtaining their supplies of stamps, stamped paper, etc., known as bonded and unbonded offices. Bonded offices mail their requisitions, unaccompanied by funds, directly to the department of posts, bureau of stamps and supplies, and remit to the Treasurer at the close of each month the entire amount of postal funds on hand, accompanying such remittance with a statement showing the exact financial condition of the office at the close of the month.

Unbonded offices make requisitions upon the department of posts for what stamps they require from time to time, forwarding the requisition through the Treasurer of the island, accompanied by funds sufficient to cover the cost of the supplies ordered. Upon receipt of this requisition and money by the Treasurer, he signs the voucher attached thereto acknowledging receipt of the money, and forwards the requisition to the department of posts, bureau of stamps and supplies, whereupon the requisition is immediately filled and forwarded directly to the postmaster, by registered mail.

All postmasters are required to return a receipt to the Auditor for Cuba and to the department of posts, for all stamped paper sent them.

PENALTY ENVELOPES.

The privilege of using penalty envelopes extended by military order No. 108, to various civil officers of the island, is taken advantage of quite freely, as will be seen from the following statement showing the quantity of each size of envelopes prepared and furnished by the department of posts:

No. 7,	*No. 10,*	*No. 11,*	*No. 14,*
92,550	270,000	57,000	10,000

The envelopes are ordered upon a requisition mailed directly to the Treasurer of Cuba, accompanied by an amount of money sufficient to pay for them. The Treasurer certifies this requisition to the department of posts in the same manner as requisitions for stamps from unbonded postmasters, when the envelopes are prepared and forwarded by registered mail directly to the officer for whom they are intended. All penalty envelopes are furnished at cost prices to the department.

The contract for furnishing penalty envelopes is let by competitive bids, the lowest successful bidder furnishing the quantity required of each size for the fiscal year.

The printing of all forms and books is let in a similar manner, except that the lots required are smaller and bids called for as the stock becomes depleted.

SPECIAL-REQUEST ENVELOPES.

Special request envelopes are ordered by the postmasters in the same manner as other stamped supplies. Upon a requisition reaching this bureau it is sent to the Honorable Postmaster General of the United States, for execution, and upon receipt of the envelopes from Washington by this department they are forwarded directly to the postmaster ordering them, by registered mail.

An entirely new system of forms, statements, requisitions, etc., was formulated and adopted July 1st, 1900, which has proved a great safeguard against errors, as well as to add a much better record than was obtained by those in use previously.

OTHER SUPPLIES.

The supplies used by postmasters in their regular dispatch of business are forwarded from this bureau upon requisitions made by the postmasters, and consist chiefly of the following articles: statements, printed blanks and blank books, street-letter boxes and keys, mail bags, locks and keys, steel and rubber stamps, cancelling pads, and numerous other small articles used in the postal service.

By the courtesy of the Honorable Postmaster-General of the United States, extending the privilege to the department of posts, we are enabled to obtain at the same price many supplies from the contractors who furnish the United States postal service, the Honorable Postmaster-General causing a list of contractors to be furnished with the contract prices of various articles printed thereon.

The following statement shows the amount of money expended by the department of posts for supplies for the past fiscal year, and the nature of same:

Stationery and printing	$ 9,230.16
Postmarking and rubber stamps	306.94
Street-letter boxes	433.00
Mail wagons	500.00
Mail bags	133.43
Furniture	196.05
Building and repairs	879.26
Miscellaneous	256.66
Total	$11,937.50

I would state for your further information that since the organization of the department of posts equipment as follows, no report of which, I believe, has heretofore been made, has been furnished offices:

ARTICLE.	Quantity.
Letter-box keys, "XX" series	310
Letter-box locks, "XX" series	730
Letter-box keys, "HH" series	100
Letter-box locks, "HH" series	250
Through register locks	50
Through register keys	25
International through register locks	5
International through register keys	1
Star mail locks	1,500
Star mail keys	400
Ordinary pouches, No. 3	300
,, ,, ,, 2	300
,, ,, 4	150
,, ,, ,, 5	150
,, ,, ,, 3 class B	100
Saddle bags, all leather, No. 3	50
Combination saddle bags, No. 1	25
,, ,, ,, No. 2	75
Ordinary pouches, oblong bottom, No. 3	100
Sacks, for 2nd, 3rd and 4th class matter	2,000
Canvas sacks for foreign mail, No. 1	50
,, ,, ,, ,, 2	25
,, ,, ,, ,, 3	25
Through register pouches, ,, 1	9
,, ,, ,, ,, 2	32
,, ,, ,, ,, 3	33
Regular foreign mail sacks ,, 1	1,000
,, ,, ,, ,, 0	900

The street-letter boxes in use on the island are of the same size and pattern as those in the postal service of the United States, and are lettered "U. S. Mail."

Very respectfully,

GEORGE W. MARSHALL,

Chief, Bureau of Stamps and Supplies.

MR. M. C. FOSNES,

Director General.

STATEMENT SHOWING STAMPS AND STAMPED ENVELOPES RECEIVED AND ISSUED BY THE BUREAU OF STAMPS AND SUPPLIES, FOR THE FISCAL YEAR OF 1900–1901.

	Receipts.	Issues.
On hand July 1st, 1900	$ 176,596.36	
July	50,000.00	$ 31,789.32
August		25,328.11
September	57,237.50	28,054.83
,, transferred from stock Acct. to damaged stock account		31.93
October	40,053.00	38,552.60
November	21,074.50	24,006.13
December	40,063.60	34,847.39
January, 1901	2,173.30	33,177.12
February	10.60	32,306.23
March	76,117.50	37,187.42
,, transferred from stock account to damaged stock account		.15
March, over stock, accumulated	34	
April	2,373,00	28,613.56
May	190.80	21,257.70
June	40,021.20	21,306.21
,, transferred from stock account to damaged stock account		21.20
June, balance		149,431.80
	$ 505,911.70	$ 505,911.70

REPORT

OF THE

MONEY-ORDER AND REGISTRY BUREAU

FOR THE

FISCAL YEAR ENDED JUNE 30, 1901.

DEPARTMENT OF POSTS OF CUBA.

MONEY-ORDER AND REGISTRY BUREAU.

Havana, September 23, 1901.

SIR:

I have the honor to submit the following report of the operations of the money-order and registry bureau during the fiscal year ended June 30, 1901.

MONEY-ORDER REPORT.

Number of money orders issued at money-order offices in Cuba by quarters:

	Number.	*Amount.*
Quarter ended September 30, 1900	19,401	$ 679,462.92
" " December 31, 1900	21,369	646,271.50
" " March 30, 1901	20,967	623,045.11
" " June 30, 1901	21,370	618,741.71
Total	83,107	$2,567,521.24

Number of domestic money orders paid, by quarters:

	Number.	*Amount.*
Quarter ended September 30, 1900	10,718	$ 443,672.43
" " December 31, 1900	11,511	404,396.77
" " March 30, 1901	12,071	430,860.57
" " June 30, 1901	11,991	409,417.78
Total	46,291	$1,688,347.55

International money orders issued in cuba and payable in the United States, per exchange lists of the Havana postoffice:

QUARTER ENDED SEPTEMBER 30, 1900.

No. of List.	Date of List.	Number of Orders.	Amount of Orders.
1	July 7, 1900	900	$ 26,501.33
2	,, 14, 1900	800	24,698.00
3	,, 21, 1900	700	21,140.77
4	,, 28, 1900	400	11,961.43
5	Aug. 4, 1900	700	22,160.39
6	,, 11, 1900	800	22,780.23
7	,, 18, 1900	650	19,956.68
8	,, 25, 1900	550	14,549.82
9	Sept. 1, 1900	600	21,037.60
10	,, 8, 1900	800	21,145.75
11	,, 15, 1900	700	20,263.71
12	,, 22, 1900	600	16,894.47
13	,, 29, 1900	650	25,470.93
	Total	8,850	$268,561.11

QUARTER ENDED DECEMBER 31, 1900.

No. of List.	Date of List.	Number of Orders.	Amount of Orders.
14	Oct. 6, 1900	650	$ 19,956.40
15	,, 13, 1900	700	19,167.72
16	,, 20, 1900	700	17,095.83
17	,, 27, 1900	500	11,350.99
18	Nov. 3, 1900	750	20,870.86
19	,, 10, 1900	700	16,344.87
20	,, 17, 1900	700	18,084.90
21	,, 24, 1900	650	14,961.75
22	Dec. 1, 1900	600	13,752.57
23	,, 8, 1900	906	23,228.10
24	,, 15, 1900	961	18,945.44
25	,, 22, 1900	1,007	22,779.56
26	,, 31, 1900	797	18,878,50
	Total	9,621	$235,417.49

QUARTER ENDED MARCH 31, 1901.

No. of List.	Date of List.	Number of Orders.	Amount of Orders
27	Jan. 12, 1901	1,129	$ 28,711.01
28	,, 19, 1901	742	15,333.29
29	,, 26, 1901	658	12,940.22
30	Feb. 2, 1901	700	16,844.90
31	,, 9, 1901	700	15,281.23
32	,, 16, 1901	703	15,656.13
33	,, 23, 1901	664	14,691.41
34	Mar. 2, 1901	765	17,946.38
35	,, 9, 1901	664	13,731.14
36	,, 16, 1901	851	17,131.95
37	,, 23, 1901	559	10,452.16
38	,, 30, 1901	661	16,603.91
	Total	8,796	$195,323.73

QUARTER ENDED JUNE 30, 1901.

No. of List.	Date of List.	Number of orders.	Amount of orders.
39	April 6, 1901	716	$ 17,969.27
40	,, 13, 1901	811	14,945.40
41	,, 20, 1901	595	12,265.02
42	,, 27, 1901	554	10,820.71
43	May 4, 1901	811	21,000.00
44	,, 11, 1901	753	16,070.02
45	,, 18, 1901	780	16,639.60
46	,, 25, 1901	606	15,164.97
47	June 1, 1901	550	13,998.94
48	,, 8, 1901	779	17,927.24
49	,, 15, 1901	899	22,151.51
50	,, 22, 1901	652	14,208.45
51	,, 29, 1901	771	19,045.98
	Totals.	9,277	$212,207.11
	Grand totals....................	36,544	$911,509.44

Number of international money orders paid by quarters:

	NO. PAID.	AMT. PAID.
Quarter ended Sept. 30, 1900........	1,269	$ 28,078.48
,, ,, December 31, 1900	1,309	32,770.91
,, ,, March 31, 1901......... ...	1,363	39,650.15
,, ,, June 30, 1901...	1,519	50.068.14
Total .:.	5,460	$ 150,567.68

Number of Cuban international money orders repaid, by quarters:

	NO. PAID.	AMT. PAID.
Quarter ended September 30, 1900.......	71	$ 1,668.07
,, ,, December 31, 1900........	101	2,002.77
,, ,, March 31, 1901...........	82	1,727.20
,, ,, June 30, 1901..............	90	1,914.08
Total.......	344	$ 7,312.12

Number of United States money orders returned for repayment purposes, by quarters:

	NUMBER.	AMOUNT.
Quarter ended September 30, 1900.......	5	$ 38.50
,, ,, December 31, 1900.......	17	264.75
,, ,, March 31, 1901..... .	19	426.25
,, ,, June 30, 1901.......	28	776.50
Total....................	69	$ 1,506.00

Number of international money orders payable in Porto Rico, as certified by the Havana exchange office, by quarters:

	NUMBER.	AMOUNT.
Quarter ended September 30, 1900	46	$ 641.28
,, ,, December 31, 1900	55	766.54
,, ,, March 31, 1901	43	662.78
,, ,, June 30, 1901	96	1,986.43
Total	240	$ 4,057.03

Number of money orders issued in Porto Rico on Cuba, as shown by the exchange lists of the San Juan exchange office, by quarters:

Quarter ended September 30, 1900	42	$ 1,324.33
,, ,, December 31, 1900	56	2,960.37
,, ,, March 31, 1901	56	3,279.27
,, ,, June 30, 1901	59	2,133.68
Total	213	$ 9,697.65

Number of money orders issued in Cuba on Porto Rico, repaid, by quarters:

Quarter ended September 30, 1900	1	$ 25.00
,, ,, December 31, 1900		00.00
,, ,, March 31, 1901	3	53.50
,, ,, June 30, 1901	4	92.50
Total	8	$ 170.50

Number of money orders issued in Porto Rico on Cuba, advices returned for repayment rurposes, by quarters:

Quarter ended September 30, 1900		$ 00.00
,, ,, December 31, 1900		00.00
,, ,, March 31, 1901	1	20.00
,, ,, June 30, 1901	2	1.75
Total	3	$ 21.75

Duplicate money orders issued during the fiscal year ended June 30, 1901:

Domestic	188
International	183
Total	371

Money order offices and stations in operation:

	Stations.	Offices.
September 30, 1900	11	79
December 31, 1900	11	85
March 31, 1901	10	94
June 30, 1901	10	94

Fees for money orders issued in Cuba during fiscal year ended June 30, 1901, by quarters:

	AMOUNT.
Quarter ended September 30, 1900.....	$ 3,362.22
,, ,, December 31, 1900.....	3,345.65
,, ,, March 31, 1901.....	3,203.64
,, ,, June 30, 1901.....	3,232.50
Total...............	$ 13,144.01

During the fiscal year ended June 30, 1901, money-order funds were transmitted to the credit of the Postmaster-General of the United States, on money-order account, amounting to $756, 318.11, effected without cost for exchange to the Government.

In concluding this report your attention is specially called to the several causes of the marked decrease in the money-order business during the fiscal year ended June 30, 1901, as compared with the fiscal year 1900.

The orders which went into effect during the fiscal year 1900 limiting the sale of foreign money orders on the island of Cuba to five by one remitter to one payee, the increasing of the rate of fees on international money orders from thirty to fifty cents on each $100.00, and the accepting of United States currency only in payment for money orders drawn on the United States and Porto Rico, have remained in effect during the fiscal year 1901. As a result, the money-order system has not been used to the same extent at any time during the year by banking and large commercial houses as a means of exchange with the United States, as was the case during the first two quarters of the fiscal year 1900. The international orders issued have been, therefore, generally for small amounts. The number of American soldiers, American employees of the Government in Cuba, and Americans transacting business in Cuba, has been much smaller during the past fiscal year than previously. This has also greatly affected the money-order business between Cuba and the United States; particularly noticeable has this been the case in those towns where troops have been stationed. In some cases after their removal the money-order business with the United States has amounted to almost nothing. When it is taken into consideration that the majority of the merchants in all Cuban towns are Spaniards whose foreign business is transacted almost exclusively with Spain, the effect which the

American people in Cuba have on the money-order business with the United States is not singular.

Previous to July 1, 1900, insular funds were transmitted by means of the money-order system. When you consider the fact that the majority of the more important offices in Cuba were transacting domestic money-order business of this nature amounting in money orders received and paid at such offices from $30,000.00 to $60,000.00 monthly, the effect of the following order on the domestic money-order business in Cuba can be readily seen:

No. 246.

HEADQUARTERS DIVISION OF CUBA,

Havana, June 22, 1900.

The Military Governor of Cuba directs the publication of the following order:

I. Beginning July 1, 1900, the transmission by post-office money-orders of Insular Funds in amounts exceeding $300.00 will be discontinued, and the funds will be sent by registered mail.

II. In sending money by registered mail, the person sending it must properly secure it in a strong package or packages, the contents being counted and each package properly sealed in the presence of a witness whose signature, with that of the sender, must appear on each package. A person receiving such funds by registered mail, will open and count the same in the presence of the postmaster, taking care to so open the package as not to deface the seal, and should a shortage be found, the receiving postmaster will at once notify the forwarding postmaster and the post-office department of Havana.

III. All orders or instructions in force which conflict with the above are hereby revoked.

(Signed) J. B. HICKEY,
Assistant Adjutant-General.

Notwithstanding the decrease of the money-order business due to the causes as above cited, it is gratifying to know, however, that the money-order offices which, owing to their situation, have not been affected by said causes, have shown on the whole a steady growth in the money-order business transacted, and this may be safely said in connection with the use of the money-order system by the Cuban people for transmitting small amounts of money and for business purposes in general at all money-order offices.

DEPARTMENT OF POSTS OF CUBA,

MONEY-ORDER AND REGISTRY BUREAU.

September 23, 1901.

REGISTRY REPORT.

THROUGH REGISTERED-POUCH EXCHANGES.

During the fiscal year ended June 30, 1901, two additional through registered-pouch exchanges were established, which are given in the following list.

Between Matanzas and Havana, established April 13, 1899; exchange twice daily and once on Sunday.

Between Cienfuegos and Havana, established April 14, 1899; exchange daily.

Between Santiago and Havana, established March 2, 1899; exchange weekly.

Between Cárdenas and Havana, established June 1, 1899; exchange daily.

Between Pinar del Río and Havana, established August 14, 1899; exchange daily.

Between Santa Clara and Havana, established September 22, 1899; exchange daily.

Between Caibarién and Havana, established October 16, 1899; exchange daily.

Between Sagua la Grande and Havana, established April 1, 1900; exchange daily.

Between Columbia Barracks and Havana, established February 13, 1901; exchange from Columbia Barracks to Havana, daily except Sunday; from Havana to Columbia Barracks, daily except Monday.

Between Cienfuegos and Júcaro, established May 13, 1901; exchange weekly.

INNER REGISTERED-SACK EXCHANGES.

Between Marianao and Havana, established January 13, 1899; exchange daily.

Between Puerto Principe and Havana, established April 11, 1899; exchange irregular.

Between Gibara and Havana, established August 8, 1899; exchange irregular.

Between Nuevitas and Havana, established August 8, 1899; exchange irregular.

FOREIGN EXCHANGES OF REGISTERED MAIL,

The following exchanges are made with the Havana postoffice:

International through registered-pouch exchanges with New York, Jacksonville and Port Tampa. Dispatches made Monday, Wednesday and Friday of each week.

Sealed tie-sack exchanges with:

Via New York: Dispatches made Monday, Wednesday and Friday of each week....	Irun..	Spain.
	Madrid.......	Spain.
	Ver-Cologne....	Germany.
	London...........	England.
	Paris..	France.
	Ponce..........	Porto Rico.
	San Juan......	Porto Rico.

Sealed tie-sack exchanges with:

Direct: Dispatches made irregularly twice monthly	Madrid. Cádiz. Coruña. Santander.	Spain.

Sealed tie-sack exchanges with:

Direct: Dispatches made irregularly, five to seven times monthly	Mexico. Vera Cruz. Progreso.	Mexico.

Sealed tie-sack exchanges with:

Direct: Dispatches made twice monthly	San Juan. Ponce.	Porto Rico.

Sealed tie-sack exchanges with:

Dispatches direct monthly Dispatches, via New York, three times weekly	Columbia. Pto. Cabello. Guiara. Barranquilla. Colón. Cartagena. Puerto Limón. St. Thomas. Sto. Domingo.

Sealed tie-sack exchanges with:

Dispatch made three times weekly............. Key West.

The following exchanges are made with the Santiago postoffice:

International through registered-pouch exchanges with New York and Jacksonville, dispatch made from Santiago Monday of each week, established October 24, 1900.

REGISTRY STATISTICS.

Statistics of the registry business transacted at all postoffices during the fiscal year ended June 30, 1901, are given in the following statement:

Letters for foreign destination registered	76,117
Parcels " " " "	7,090
Domestic letters registered	64,170
" parcels "	7,697
Total paid registration	155,074
Pieces of mail matter registered free	31,444
Total registrations, paid and free	186,518

Statistics showing the registry business transacted each quarter during the fiscal year ended June 30, 1901:

QUARTER ENDED SEPTEMBER 30, 1900.

Domestic letters	12,774
Domestic parcels	1,312
Foreign letters	16,203
Foreign parcels	1,369
Official matter	7,201
Total	38,859

QUARTER ENDED DECEMBER 31, 1900.

Domestic letters	15,669
Domestic parcels	1,628
Foreign letters	17,937
Foreign parcels	1,444
Official matter	7,947
Total	44,625
	38,859
	83,484

QUARTER ENDED MARCH 31, 1901.

Domestic letters	16,947
Domestic parcels	1,940
Foreign letters	22,521
Foreign parcels	2,278
Official matter	7,797
Total	51,483

QUARTER ENDED JUNE 30, 1901.

Domestic letters	18,780
Domestic parcels	2,817
Foreign letters	19,456
Foreign parcels	1,999
Official matter	8,499
Total	51,551
	51,483
	103,034

Order No. 7 went into effect on and after April 1, 1901, whereby the fee for registration was reduced from 10 cents to 8 cents.

Total by quarters of mail matter registered with fee paid:

September	30, 1900	31,658	$ 3,165.80
December	31, 1900	36,678	3,667.80
March	31, 1901	43,686	4,368.60
June	30, 1901	43,052	3,[illegible]4.16
		155,074	$ 14,646.36

Increase over fiscal year ended June 30, 1900, of 27,360 paid registered articles, and $1,874.96 revenue derived from fees.

Very respectfully,

C. L. MARINE,
Chief, Money-Order and Registry Bureau.

MR. M. C. FOSNES,
Director-General.

REPORT

OF THE

DISBURSING OFFICER,

DEPARTMENT OF POSTS.

July 25, 1901.

SIR:

In the matter of a report for the year ending June 30, 1901, I have the honor to enclose herewith itemized statements of the business done by this office during that period.

My accounts have been inspected twice during the year. To include January 29, 1901, by Major R. H. Rolfe, Inspector-General, U. S. V.; and to include May 6, 1901, by Major B. K. Roberts, Artillery Corps, U. S. A., Acting Inspector-General. Colonel G. H. Burton, Inspector-General, has just completed an inspection to include to-day.

Very respectfully,

GEO. R. BUCHANAN,
Disbursing Officer,
Department of Posts of Cuba

MR. M. C. FOSNER,
Director-General.

RECEIPTS AND DISBURSEMENTS: JULY, 1900.

	ON ACCOUNT OF.	Fiscal year 1899.	Fiscal year 1900.	Fiscal year 1901.	TOTALS.
	Receipts:				
July 18	Allotment		$23,622.17	$39,637.12	$ 65,259.29
July 21	Allotment	$ 508.87	29,058.48		29,567.35
	Total	$ 508.87	$52,680.65	$39,637.12	$ 92,826.64
	Disbursements:				
	Salaries:				
	Dept. of posts		$ 263.73	$ 5,857.31	$ 6,121.04
	Clerks in postoffices		4,563.55	5,776.37	10,339.92
	Postmasters		11,112.35	303 26	11,415.61
	Ry. postal clerks		1,559.39	640.22	2,199.61
	Letter carriers		3,646.12	3,158.92	6,805.04
	Printing and stationery		1,343.43	30.00	1,373.43
	Rent		177.50		177.50
	Light		477.84		477.84
	Per diem		352.00		352.00
	Mail transportation		2,180.83		2,180.83
	Building and repairs		68.00		68.00
	Star routes		3,214.61		3,214.61
	Mail messengers		717.79		717.79
	Miscellaneous		226.49	394.06	620.55
	Total disbursed		$29,903.63	$16,160.14	$ 46,063.77
July 31	Balance to August account	$ 508.87	22,777.02	23,476.98	46,762.87
	Total	$ 508.87	$52,680.65	$39,637.12	$ 92,826.64

RECEIPTS AND DISBURSEMENTS:

AUGUST, 1900.

	ON ACCOUNT OF.	Fiscal year 1899.	Fiscal year 1900.	Fiscal year 1901.	TOTALS.
	Receipts:				
August 1	Balance from July	$ 508.87	$22,777.02	$23,476.98	$ 48,762.87
August 9	Allotment		2,649.77		2,649.77
August 18	Allotment			43,642.73	43,642.73
	Total	$ 508.87	$25,426.79	$67,119.71	$ 93,055.37
	Disbursements:				
	Salaries: Department of posts		$ 914.82	$ 6,810.79	$ 7,725.61
	Clerks in postoffices		203.41	9,575.54	9,778.95
	Postmasters	$ 25.00	1,049.85	9,783.65	10,858.50
	Ry. postal clerks		75.09	2,129.60	2,204.69
	Letter carriers		289.59	6,528.85	6,818.44
	Printing and stationery		1,697.11	553.04	2,250.15
	Furniture		83.00	15.00	98.00
	Rent		2,071.79	399.24	2,471.03
	Light		295.64	297.81	593.45
	Per diem		572.00	584.00	1,156.00
	Bond premiums		1,038.86		1,038.86
	Equipment		50.63		50.63
	Newspapers		3.00	7.50	10.50
	Mail transportation		7,208.56	2,340.07	9,548.63
	Mail bags		746.65	38.76	785.41
	Letter scales		279.59		279.59
	Postmarking and rubber stamps		69.40	18.25	87.65
	Letterboxes		422.50		422.50
	Transportation		32.80	62.00	94.80
	Building and repairs		126.19	122.60	248.79
	Star routes		299.03	2,083.73	2,382.76
	Mail messengers		5.05	637.91	642.96
	Miscellaneous		1,079.15	821.20	1,900.35
	Total disbursed	$ 25.00	$18,613.71	$42,809.54	$ 61,448.25
August 31	Balance to September account	483.87	6,813.08	24,310.17	31,607.12
	Total	$ 508.87	$25,426.79	$67,119.71	$ 93,055.37

RECEIPTS AND DISBURSEMENTS: SEPTEMBER, 1900.

	ON ACCOUNT OF.	Fiscal year 1899.	Fiscal year 1900.	Fiscal year 1901.	TOTALS.
	Receipts:				
September 1	Balance from August	$ 483.87	6,813.08	$24,310.17	$31,607.12
September 18	Allotment	5,245.24	6,788.13	40,319.17	52,352.54
September 18	Allotment			237.00	237.00
	Total	$ 5,729.11	$13,601.21	$64,866.34	$84,196.66
	Disbursements:				
	Salaries: Dept. of posts		$ 131.87	$ 5,933.75	$ 6,065.62
	Clerks in postoffices		2,31	6,705.10	6,707.41
	Postmasters	24.72	665.24	4,661.08	5,351.04
	Ry. postal clerks			1,305.30	1,305.30
	Letter carriers	23.74	3.06	4,279.88	4,306.68
	Printing and stationery	91 71	303.32	1,019.93	1,414.96
	Telegraph and cable		76.25		76.25
	Furniture			8.50	8.50
	Rent	30.00	432.74	621.41	1,084.15
	Light		40.00	317.51	357.51
	Per diem		228.00	652.00	880.00
	Equipment			235.00	235.00
	Newspapers		19.00		19.00
	Mail transportation		12.00	2,564.16	2,576.16
	Mail bags			1,052.04	1,052.04
	Transportation		22.45	3.06	25.51
	Postmarking and rubber stamps			67.05	67.05
	Letterboxes			13.40	13.40
	Building and repairs		164.50	107.88	272.38
	Star routes		100.00	1,978.65	2,078.65
	Mail Messengers			210.23	210.23
	Miscellaneous		721.58	904 99	1,626.57
	Total disbursed	$ 170.17	$ 2,922.32	$32,640.92	$35,733.41
September 30	Balance to October account	5,558.94	$10,678.89	$32,225.42	$48,463.25
	Total	$ 5,729.11	$13,601.21	$64,866.34	$84,196.66

RECEIPTS AND DISBURSEMENTS: OCTOBER, 1900.

	ON ACCOUNT OF.	Fiscal year 1899.	Fiscal year 1900.	Fiscal year 1901.	TOTALS.
	Receipts:				
October 1	Balance from September	$ 5,558.94	$ 10,678.89	$ 32,225.42	$ 48,463.25
October 15	Allotment		490.44	39,339.66	39,830.10
	Total	$ 5,558.94	$ 11,169.33	$ 71,565.08	$ 88,293.35
	Disbursements:				
	Salaries:				
	Dept. of posts		$	$ 7,372.40	$ 7,372.40
	Clerks in post-offices			7,822.82	7,822.82
	Postmasters		114.86	7,456.70	7,571.56
	Ry. postal clerks			1,796.85	1,796.85
	Letter carriers		54.29	5,515.41	5,569.70
	Telegraph and cable		16.87		16.87
	Printing and stationery		22.25	854.88	877.13
	Furniture		25.00	32.50	57.50
	Rent		80.00	773.47	853.47
	Light		25.60	343.22	368.82
	Per diem			548.00	548.00
	Mail transportation		2,674.00	3,638.66	6,312.66
	Postmarking and rubber stamps		67.25	27.79	95.04
	Transportation			30.00	30.00
	Safes		75.28		75.28
	Building and repairs			121.34	121.34
	Star routes		58.18	2,126.63	2,184.81
	Mail messengers			437.86	437.86
	Miscellaneous		62.19	982.60	1,044.79
	Total disbursed		$ 3,275.77	$39,881.13	$ 43,156.90
October 31	Balance to November account	5,558.94	7,893.56	31,683.95	45,136.45
	Total	$ 5,558.94	$ 11,169.33	$ 71,565.08	$ 88,293 35

RECEIPTS AND DISBURSEMENTS: NOVEMBER, 1900.

	ON ACCOUNT OF.	Fiscal year 1899.	Fiscal year 1900.	Fiscal year 1901.	TOTALS.
	Receipts:				
November 1	Balance from October	$ 5,558.94	$ 7,893.56	$31,683.95	$ 45,136.45
November 30	Allotment		177.46		177.46
November 30	Allotment		2,012.46	37,079.07	39,091.53
	Total	$ 5,558.94	$10,083.48	$68,763.02	$ 84,405.44
	Disbursements:				
	Salaries.				
	Department of posts			$ 6,075.69	$ 6,075.69
	Clerks in postoffices			6,516.09	6,516.09
	Postmasters		$ 35.26	7,043.20	7,078.46
	Ry. postal clerks			1,679.70	1,679.70
	Letter carriers			4,979.28	4,979.28
	Printing and stationery			460.54	460.54
	Furniture		15.81	4.00	19.81
	Rent		208.16	886.80	1,094.96
	Light			403.87	403.87
	Per diem			532.00	532.00
	Newspapers		121.85		121.85
	Mail transportation			2,902.29	2,902.29
	Postmarking and rubber stamps			22.86	22.86
	Safes		9.00	3.00	12.00
	Transportation			8.42	8.42
	Building and repairs		10.04	52.00	62.04
	Star-routes			2,099.79	2,099.79
	Mail messengers		2.53	300.46	302.99
	Miscellaneous		145.24	861.92	1,007.16
	Total disbursed		$ 547.89	$34,831.91	$ 35,379.80
November 30	Balance to December account	$ 5,558.94	9,535.59	33,931.11	49,025.64
	Total	$ 5,558.94	$10,083.48	$68,763.02	$ 84,405.44

RECEIPTS AND DISBURSEMENTS. DECEMBER, 1900.

	ON ACCOUNT OF:	Fiscal year 1899.	Fiscal year 1900.	Fiscal year 1901.	TOTALS.
	Receipts:				
December 1	Balance from November	$ 5,558.94	$ 9,535.59	$33,931.11	$ 49,025.64
December 26	Allotment		2,070.75	38,070.18	40,140.93
	Total	$ 5,558.94	$11,606.34	$72,001.29	$ 89,166.57
	Disbursements:				
	Salaries:				
	Department of posts			$ 6,705.81	$ 6,705.81
	Clerks in postoffices		2.69	7,121.04	7,123.73
	Postmasters		12.36	6,771.34	6,783.70
	Ry. postal clerks			1,674 68	1,674.68
	Letter carriers			4,986.88	4,986.88
	Printing and stationery			825.19	825.19
	Furniture			72.70	72.70
	Rent		99.00	604.56	703.56
	Light		31.20	396.95	428.15
	Per diem			468.00	468.00
	Bond premiums		117.85		117.85
	Equipment			42 00	42.00
	Mail transportation		1,910.00	2,852.95	4,762.95
	Postmarking and rubber stamps		3 15	76.77	79.92
	Safes		2,050.48	35.99	2,086.45
	Building and repairs			91.84	91.84
	Star-routes			2,330.91	2,330.91
	Mail messengers		5.34	338.93	344.27
	Miscellaneous		41.53	871.09	912.62
	Total disbursed		$ 4,273.58	$ 36,267.63	$ 40,541.21
December 31	Balance to January account	$ 5,558.94	7,332.76	35,733.66	48,625.36
	Total	$ 5,558.94	$11,606.34	$72,001.29	$ 89,166.57

RECEIPTS AND DISBURSEMENTS: JANUARY, 1901.

	ON ACCOUNT OF.	Fiscal year 1899.	Fiscal year 1900.	Fiscal year 1901.	TOTALS.
	Receipts:				
January 1	Balance from December	$ 5,558.94	$ 7,332.76	$35,733.66	$48,625.36
January 29	Allotment		39.69	36,303.35	36,343.04
January 31	Allotment		5,163.12	5,163.12	10,326.24
	Total	$ 5,558.94	$12,535.57	$77,200.13	$95,294.64
	Disbursements:				
	Salaries:				
	Dept. of posts			$ 6,297.48	$ 6,297.48
	Clerks in postoffices		$ 28.02	7,436.04	7,464.06
	Postmasters		18.28	7,617.60	7,635.88
	Ry postal clerks			1,836.06	1,836.06
	Letter carriers			5,464.04	5,464.04
	Telegraph and cable	$ 261.95			261.96
	Printing and stationery			550.41	550.41
	Furniture			12.50	12.50
	Rent			874.22	874.22
	Light		4.00	461 89	465.89
	Per diem			524.00	524.00
	Equipment			7.00	7.00
	Mail transportation	5.169.37	10,332.52	8,178.11	23,680,00
	Postmarking and rubber stamps			30.00	30.00
	Safes			33.63	33.63
	Building and repairs			80.48	80.48
	Star-routes			2,059.39	3,059.39
	Mail messengers			405.86	405.86
	Miscellaneous			751,27	751.27
	Total disbursed	$ 5,431.33	$10 382.82	$42,619.98	$58,434.13
January 31	Balance to February account	127.61	2,152.75	34,580.15	36,860 51
	Total	$ 5,558.94	$12,535.57	$77,200.13	$95,294.64

RECEIPTS AND DISBURSEMENTS: FEBRUARY, 1901.

	ON ACCOUNT OF.	Fiscal year 1899.	Fiscal year 1900.	Fiscal year 1901.	TOTALS.
	Receipts:				
February 1	Balance from January	$ 127.61	$ 2,152.75	$34,580.15	$ 36,860.51
February 21	Allotment			670.00	670.00
February 28	Allotment	16.92	32.70	36,377.08	36,426.70
	Total	$ 144.53	$ 2,185.45	$71,627.23	$ 73,957.21
	Disbursements:				
	Salaries:				
	Department of posts			$ 6,333.07	$ 6,333.07
	Clerks in postoffices			6,690.27	6,690.27
	Postmasters		$ 35.44	7,943.31	7,978.75
	Ry. postal clerks			1,783.25	1,783.25
	Letter carriers			5,099.88	5,099.88
	Printing and stationery			3.64	3.64
	Furniture			15.50	15.50
	Rent			405.94	405.94
	Light			439.06	439.06
	Per diem			796.00	796.00
	Bond premiums			670.00	670.00
	Mail transportation	$ 14.66	29.32	3,954.41	3,998.39
	Postmarking and rubber stamps			10.36	10.36
	Safes			11.00	11.00
	Transportation			33 53	33.53
	Building and repairs			73.30	73.30
	Star-routes			2,295.42	2,295.42
	Mail messengers			421.57	421.57
	Miscellaneous		5.00	781.28	786.28
	Total disbursed	$ 14.66	$ 69.76	$37,760.79	$37,845.21
February 28	Balance to March account	129.87	2,115.69	33 866.44	36,112.00
	Total	$ 144.53	$ 2,185.45	$71,627.23	$ 73,957.31

RECEIPTS AND DISBURSEMENTS: MARCH, 1901.

	ON ACCOUNT OF.	Fiscal year 1899.	Fiscal year 1900.	Fiscal year 1901.	TOTALS.
	Receipts:				
March 1	Balance from February	$ 129.87	$ 2,115.69	$33,866.44	$ 36,112.00
March 29	Allotment		283.97	33,335.08	33,819.05
	Total	$ 129.87	$ 2,399.66	$67,401.52	$ 69,931.05
	Disbursements:				
	Salaries:				
	Department of post s		$ 10.38	$ 6,287.62	$ 6,298.00
	Clerks in postoffices			5,911.25	5,911.25
	Postmasters		57.44	6,454.14	6,511.58
	Ry. postal clerks			1,608.32	1,608.32
	Letter carriers			4,351.06	4,351.06
	Printing and stationery			1,798 64	1,798.64
	Telegraph and cable	$ 16.92	22.32		39.24
	Furniture			[illegible]	64.00
	Rent			170.08	170.08
	Light			56.98	56.98
	Per diem			580.00	580.00
	Bond premiums		200.00		200.00
	Mail transportation			4,844.69	[illegible]44.69
	Postmarking and rubber stamps			91.83	91.83
	Bldg and repairs			80.83	80.83
	Star-routes			2,318.27	2,318.27
	Mail messengers		3.96	231.32	235.28
	Miscellaneous		18.00	669.52	627.52
	Total disbursed	$ 16.92	$ 312.10	$35,458.55	$ 35,787,57
March 31	Balance to April account	112.95	2,087.56	31,942.97	34,143.48
	Total	$ 129.87	$ 2,399.66	$67,401.52	$ 69,931.05

RECEIPTS AND DISBURSEMENTS: APRIL, 1901.

	ON ACCOUNT OF	Fiscal year 1899.	Fiscal year 1900.	Fiscal year 1901.	TOTALS.
	Receipts:				
April 1	Balance from March	$ 112.95	$ 2,087.55	$31,942.97	$ 34,143.48
April 22	Allotment	100.01	126.23	38,589.25	38,815.47
	Total	$ 212.96	$ 2,213.79	$70,532.22	$ 72,958.97
	Disbursements:				
	Salaries:				
	Dept. of posts			$ 5,393 46	$ 5,393.46
	Clerks in postoffices			6,067.24	6,067.24
	Postmasters		$ 105.16	7,507.87	7,613.03
	Ry. postal clerks			1,759.12	1,759.12
	Letter carriers			5,227.67	5,227.67
	Printing and stationery			753.29	753.29
	Furniture			37 00	37.00
	Rent			406.09	406.09
	Light			770.81	770.81
	Per diem			712.00	712.00
	Bond premiums			480.00	480.00
	Mail transportation		6.26	5,129.10	5,135.36
	Postmarking and rubber stamps			129.87	129.87
	Safes			11.00	11.00
	Building and repairs			63.93	63.93
	Star-routes			2,397.67	2,397.67
	Mail messengers			381.21	381.21
	Miscellaneous			707.14	707.14
	Total disbursed		$ 111.42	$37,934.47	$ 38,045.89
April 30	Balance to May account	$ 212.96	2,102.37	32,597.75	34,913.08
	Total	$ 212.96	$ 2,213.79	$70,532.22	$ 72,958.97

RECEIPTS AND DISBURSEMENTS: MAY, 1901.

	ON ACCOUNT OF.	Fiscal year 1899.	Fiscal year 1900.	Fiscal year 1901.	TOTALS.
	Receipts:				
May 1	Balance from April	$ 212.96	$ 2,102.37	$32,597.75	$34,913.08
May 18	Allotment		60.41	35,462.64	35,523.05
	Total	2 212.96	$ 2,162.78	$68,060.39	$70 436.13
	Disbursements:				
	Salaries:				
	Dept. of posts			$ 5,159.27	$ 5,159.27
	Clerks in postofficers			6,547.03	6,547.03
	Postmasters			7,553.94	7,553.94
	Ry. postal clerks			1,811.50	1,811.50
	Letter carriers			5,397.00	5,397.00
	Printing and stationery			956.69	956.69
	Furniture			6.50	6.50
	Rent			741 33	741.33
	Light			392.23	392.23
	Per diem			696.00	696 00
	Mail transportation	$ 112.75	$ 278.25	4,486.84	4,877.84
	Mail bags			218.22	218.22
	Postmarking and rubber stamps			25.00	25.00
	Building and repairs			96.26	96.26
	Transportation			13.25	13.25
	Star-routes			2,348.84	2,338.84
	Mail messengers			462.39	462.39
	Miscellaneous		21.07	960.60	981.67
	Total disbursed	$ 112.75	$ 299.32	$37,872.89	$38,284.96
May 31	Balance to June account	100.21	1,863.46	30,187.50	32,151.17
	Total	$ 212.96	$ 2,162.78	$68,060.39	$70,436.13

78

	ON ACCOUNT OF:	Fiscal year 1899.	Fiscal year 1900.	Fiscal year 1901.	TOTALS.
	Receipts:				
June 1	Balance from May	$ 100.21	$ 1,863.46	$30,187.50	$ 32,151.17
June 7	Allotment	547.92	1,670.18	1,538.03	3,756.19
June 29	Allotment		60.40	35,462.65	35,523.05
	Total	$ 648.13	$ 3,594.04	$67,188.24	$ 71,430.41
	Disbursements:				
	Salaries:				
	Department of posts			$ 5,041.51	$ 5,041.51
	Clerks in postoffices			5,940.88	5,940.88
	Postmasters		$ 10.05	7,201.72	7,211.77
	Ry. postal clerks			1,685.11	1,685.11
	Letter carriers			5,002.63	5,002.63
	Printing and stationery			778.39	778.39
	Furniture			12.50	12.50
	Rent			509.00	509.00
	Light			294.06	294.06
	Per diem			616.00	616.00
	Bond premiums			200.00	200.00
	Equipment			8.13	8.13
	Mail transportation	$ 547.92	1,670.18	3,837.59	6,055.69
	Postmarking and rubber stamps			55.11	55.11
	Building and repairs			103.11	103.11
	Transportation			15.00	15.00
	Star-routes			2,351.22	2,351.22
	Mail messengers			375.24	375.24
	Miscellaneous			766.62	766.62
	Total disbursed	$ 547.92	$ 1,680.23	$34,793.82	$ 37,021.97
June 29	Transferred to the Treasurer of Cuba	100.21	1,763.69	8,193.17	10,057.07
June 30	Balance to July account		150.12	24,201.25	24,351.37
	Total	$ 648.13	$ 3,594.04	$67,188.24	$ 71,430.41

ON ACCOUNT OF.	Fiscal year 1900.	Fiscal year 1901.	TOTALS.
Salaries:			
Department of posts		$ 441.65	$ 441.65
Clerks in postoffices		1,636.27	1,636.27
Postmasters		7,055.47	7,055.47
Ry. postal clerks		1,026.91	1,026.91
Letter carriers		1,906.88	1,906.88
Printing and stationery		502.91	502.91
Rent		717.33	717.33
Light		209.13	209.13
Per diem		332.00	332.00
Equipment		124.00	124.00
Mail transportation		4,887.97	4,887.97
Bonds	100.00		100.00
Postmarking and rubber stamps		42.02	42 02
Building and repairs		35.56	35.56
Mail wagons		500.00	500.00
Star-routes		2,351.22	2,351.22
Mail messengers		438.72	438.72
Miscellaneous	20.81	198.08	218.89
Total disbursed	$ 120.81	$22,406.12	$ 22,526.93
Balance	29.31	1,795.13	1,824.44
Total	150.12	24,201.25	$ 24,351.37

STATEMENT OF AMOUNTS RETURNED TO THE TREASURER OF CUBA,

JUNE 29, 1901.

General Head: Finance.

Sub-Head: Postal Service.

Pertaining to:

FISCAL YEAR 1899.

Allotted for:

Salaries postmasters	$ .01	
Telegraph and cable	1.60	
Printing and stationery	98.60	$ 100.21

Pertaining to:

FISCAL YEAR 1900.

Allotted for:

Salaries clerks in postoffices	$ 39.01	
Salaries railway postal clerks	148.05	
Salaries letter carriers	3.37	
Salaries mail messengers	.83	
Mail transportation	71.64	
Star-route contracts	447.40	
Telegraph and cable	1.53	
Printing and stationery	672.58	
Furniture	175.65	
Rent	25.00	
Light	91.14	
Postmarking and rubber stamps	30.35	
Safes	34.79	
Transportation	8.62	
Building and repairs	8.93	
Exchange	5.00	$ 1,763.69

Pertaining to:

FISCAL YEAR 1901.

Allotted for:

Salaries department of posts	$ 2,472.82	
Salaries clerks in postoffices	835.19	
Salaries railway postal clerks	121.17	
Salaries letter carriers	508.51	
Telegraph and cable	100.00	
Furniture	104.30	$ 4,141.99
Carried forward		$ 6,005.89

Brouhgt forward.........	....	$ 6,005.89
Rent	373.06	
Light	151.03	
Per diem......	272.00	
Newspapers......................	197.50	
Mail transportation........	1,521.69	
Mail bags..............................	108.02	
Letter balances and scales...... ..	100.00	
Letterboxes.....	486.60	
Safes..........	62.71	
Transportation........	134.74	
Star-routes..............	293.83	
Exchange......................... ...	150.00	
Bonds...	200.00	$ 4,051.18
Total...........	....	$ 10,057.07

FISCAL YEAR 1899.

	...RY.	MARCH.	APRIL.	MAY.	JUNE.	TOTAL.
Salaries:						
Post...	......	....	....	....	....	$ 49.72
Lett...	......	....	....	....	....	23.74
Printing ...	......	....	....	....	....	91.71
Rent	......	....	....	....	....	30.00
Telegrap...	......	$ 16.92	....	....	....	278.88
Mail tra...	.66	....	....	$ 112.75	$ 547.92	5,844.70
	.66	$ 16 92	....	$ 112.75	$ 547.92	$ 6,318.75

OF CUBA.

FISCAL YEAR 1900.

	Y.	March.	April.	May.	June.	1901 July on account F. Y. 1901.	
Salaries:							
Dept o		$ 10.38					$ 1,
Clerks							4,
Postm	4	57.44	$ 105.16		$ 10.05		13,
Ry. po							1,
Letter							3,
Telegraph		22.32					
Printing a							3,
Furniture							
Rent							3,
Light							
Per diem							1,
Bonds		200.00				$ 100.00	1,
Equipmen							
Newspape							
Mail trans	32		$ 6.26	$ 278.25	1,670.18		26,
Mail bags							
Letter sca							
Postmarki							
Letter box							
Safes							2,
Transport							
Building a							
Star-route							3,
Mail messe		3.96					
Miscellane	00	18.00		21.07		20.81	2,
	76	$ 312.10	$ 111.42	$ 299.32	$ 1,680.23	$ 120.81	

FISCA

	MARCH.	APRIL.	MAY.	J
Salaries:				
Depart	6,287.62	$ 5,393.46	$ 5,159.27	$ 5,
Clerks	5,911.25	6,067.24	6,547.03	5,
Postm	6,454.14	7,507.87	7,553.94	7,
Ry. po	1,608.32	1,759.12	1,811.50	1,
Letter	4,351.06	5,227.67	5,397.00	5,
Printing	1,798.64	753.29	956.69	
Furniture	64 00	37.00	6.50	
Rent..	170.08	406.09	741.33	
Light......	56.98	770.81	392.23	
Per diem..	580.00	712.00	696.00	
Bonds.....	....	480.00	....	
Equipmen	....	....	....	
Newspape	....	....	....	....
Mail tran	4,844.69	5,129.10	4,486.84	3,8
Mail bags	....	....	218.22	....
Postmark	91 83	129.87	25.00	
Letter bo	....	....	....	....
Safes......	....	11.00	....	....
Transpor	....	....	13.25	
Building	80.83	63.93	96.26	
Mail wag	....	....	....	....
Star-rout	2,318.27	2,397.67	2,348.84	2,3
Mail mes	231.32	381.21	462.39	
Miscellan	609.52	707.14	960.60	
	5,458.55	$37,934.47	$37 872.89	$34,7

RECAPITULATION.

		Fiscal year 1899.	Fiscal year 1900.	Fiscal year 1901.	TOTALS.
	[illegible]ipts:				
July 18	Allotment		$ 23,622.17	$ 39,637.12	$ 62, [illegible]9.29
July 21	Allotment	$ 508.87	29,058.48		29,567.35
August 9	Allotment		2,649.77		2,649.77
August 18	Allotment			43,642.73	43, [illegible]2.73
September 18	Allotment	5,245.24	6,788.13	40,319.17	52, [illegible]2.54
September 18	Allotment			237.00	237.00
October 15	Allotment		490.44	39,339.66	39, [illegible]0.10
[illegible]ber 30	All[illegible]		177.46		177.[illegible]6
November 30	Allotment		2,012.46	37,079.07	39, [illegible]1.53
[illegible]ber 26	Allotment		2,070.75	38,070.18	40,140.93
January 29	Allotment		39.69	36,303.35	36,343.04
January 31	Allotment		5,163.12	5,163.12	10, [illegible]6.24
February 21	All[illegible]ment			670.00	670.00
February 28	Allotment	16.92	32.70	36,377.08	36, [illegible]6.70
March 9	Allotment		283.97	33,535.08	33,819.05
[illegible]ril 22	Allotment	100.01	126.23	38,589.25	38,815.49
May 18	Allotment		60.41	35,462.64	35, [illegible]3.05
June 7	Allotment	547.92	1,670.18	1,538.09	3,756.19
June 29	Allotment		60.40	35,462.65	35,523.05
	Total	$ 6,418.96	$ 74,306.36	$461,426.19	$542,151.51
	Disbursements:				
	Itemized sheet 1	$ 6,318.75			$ 6,318.75
	Itemized sheet 2		$ 72.513.36		72,513.36
	Itemized sheet 3			$451,437.89	451,437.89
	Returned to the Treasurer of Cuba	100.21	1,763.69	8,193.17	10,057.07
	Balance		29.31	1,795.13	1,824.44
	Total	$ 6,418.96	$ 74,306.36	$461,426.19	$542,151.51

GEO. R. BUCHANAN,
Disbursing Officer,
Department of Posts of Cuba.

REPORT

OF THE

BUREAU OF SPECIAL AGENTS

DEPARTMENT OF POSTS.

DEPARTMENT OF POSTS OF CUBA.

BUREAU OF SPECIAL AGENTS.

Havana, Cuba, August 8, 1901.

SIR:

I have the honor to invite your attention to the following statement of the operations of this bureau for the fiscal year ended June 30, 1901:

As to the extent, variety, and importance of duties performed by the special agents' force, it may be stated that they relate to the examination of accounts, investigation into the character and conduct of all classes of employees, locations and removals of postoffices, leases of premises for postoffice purposes and detailed inquiry into all classes of complaints pertaining to postal matters. The special agents also submit recommendations for the extension and improvement of the postal system, and instruct employees in the laws, regulations, and usages of the service.

In order that a complete record may be kept, every complaint received in the bureau is jacketed, and, for the sake of convenience, divided into classes as follows:

"A." Complaints relating to the domestic registered matter.

"B." Complaints relating to the domestic ordinary mail.

"C." Inspection of postoffices and miscellaneous complaints affecting the employees, highway robberies of the mail, robberies of postoffices, violations of postal laws, and other special depredations.

"F." Complaints affecting mail matter dispatched to and received from foreign countries.

The total number of complaints of all classes received during the last fiscal year aggregated 4,320 and the total number disposed of 4,821.

The fact that the number of cases closed exceeds the total number of complaints received during the same period is accounted for by reason that there were pending at the close of the previous year 1,253 cases. Special attention is called to the fact that the aggregate of complaints remaining on hand at the close of the fiscal year is greatly diminished, and this notwithstanding the corps of special agents and clerks is about one-half what it was the previous year. This indicates that the bureau is not only keeping pace with the growth of the department, but that it is gradually bringing the work more closely up to date, thus rendering a more efficient and satisfactory service. In presenting this review little more will be done than to produce a summary of the work accomplished during the past twelve months. To review all of the statistical data *in extenso* would require more space than can be given to the subject.

The work of inspection covered all departments of the postal service, in every postoffice, station, railway, steamboat and star-route conveyance and the department itself. It was designed to instruct postmasters, their assistants, and railway postal clerks in the intelligent conduct of the business, and to give them a better understanding of the details, for the greater number of them had been employed in the service for a year or more and had obtained a knowledge of principles. Especially did it aim to give the postmasters a firm grasp of the theory and practice of the money-order and registry systems; of the method of keeping and rendering accounts, and of an understanding of the important services they perform in the world of business.

All money-order postoffices have been inspected twice and many of them several times. Frequency of inspection is not only for the protection of the department, but also in the interest of the patrons of the postoffices, in that postmasters may be properly instructed as to their duties, so far as they relate to their obligation to the general public in the way of giving the very best service possible.

Especial precaution was taken to insure that postmasters rendered weekly money-order statements and monthly returns on postal account.

One of the questions which engaged the attention of the bureau early in the year, and which the growing necessity of the case demanded, was increased space, compartments for the safe keeping of registered mail and distributing cases, on railroads and steamboats. These improvements were made on some of the railway and steamship postoffices and have resulted in speedier separations, and fewer mistakes on the part of postal clerks have occurred.

A bureau book of account was opened during the past year. In it is kept a record of all collections made by the special agents and the disposition thereof. The total amount of money collected by the special agents for the fiscal year aggregates $2,447.50, which represents balances due from postmasters, and penalties for violating the postal laws and regulations.

Mistakes do occur, of course, dishonest persons sometimes get into the postal service, but these are the exception. The effort for the past year has been to correct errors, and weed out delinquent employees. The decreased number of complaints against the postal service and those employed in it, as compared with the previous year, is evidence sufficient of itself to show improvement and, besides, we have a greater number of arrests, an increased number of convictions, and more money recovered to add to this record of credit. I believe that the above is a proper statement of the facts, and that the bureau of special agents is one of the most efficient divisions of the department of posts.

"A" CASES, OR CASES RELATING TO THE DOMESTIC REGISTERED MAIL.

All complaints received referring to depredations upon or irregularities in the registered mail are included in tables Nos. 1 and 2. Of the 140 complaints which have been received and jacketed, only 16 necessitated the personal investigation of a special agent. The complaint in the 124 other cases investigated was satisfactorily closed by correspondence. Of the 15 complaints remaining on hand from the previous year, 7 were assigned to and investigated by special agents, while 8 were closed by correspondence. It will be observed, therefore, that complaints of the domestic registered mail are very few, and only a small percentage of them require personal investigation.

The alleged amount of money and articles of value involved in the 140 complaints received aggregated $1,882.83. Of this amount, $1,705.69 was recovered and paid through this bureau, and $57.14 was traced and delivered through the mails. $100.00 is still under investigation, leaving $20.00 as the actual loss sustained.

Seven cases which were referred to special agents in previous years were reopened and closed during the fiscal year just ended. Of these actual loss occurred in five, amounting to $2,843.47, while in two complaints it was discovered that no loss had been sustained.

It has occurred to me that a comparative showing of the work done by the bureau since its organization on February 14, 1899, might be of interest. Attention is therefore invited to the following tables:

TABLE No. 1.—"A" CASES.

FISCAL YEAR.	Complaints.	Cases investigated.	O. K.	Recovered.	Alleged Loss.	Outstanding.
1899.—4½ mos.	26	19	19			7
1900	61	53	48	$ 6.00	$ 2,843.47	8
1901	140	137	135	1,705.69	20.00	3
TOTAL	227	209	202	$ 1,711.69	$ 2,863.47	18

TABLE No. 2.

SHOWING THE NUMBER OF "A" CASES TREATED DURING THE FISCAL YEAR ENDED JUNE 30, 1901.

		MADE UP AND REOPENED.			CLOSED.			
		Reg.	Reop.	Total.	Reg.	Reop.	Total.	On hand
On hand July 1, 1900	15	140	1	156	137	1	138	18
Investigated by special agents					23	1	24	
Closed in the office by correspondence					114		114	

"B." CASES, CASES AFFECTING THE DOMESTIC ORDINARY MAIL.

The great bulk of the matter annually deposited for transmission through the mails belongs to the ordinary or unregistered mail, and notwithstanding the greater security provided by the registry system, the public persists in employing the ordinary mail as a medium for remitting money and the despatch of articles of value.

It is a natural consequence of this that the greater portions of depredations are committed on this character of mail. The postal employee lacking in integrity, though not bold enough to tamper with registered matter, may venture to rifle ordinary packages, and notwithstanding the fact that detection of depredations upon this character of mail is, as a rule, more difficult, it is scarcely less certain than in the case of registered matter.

Every effort possible is made by special agents to justify the almost unlimited confidence evinced by the public in the reliability of the ordinary mail; and it is a subject of congratulation that the percentage of losses in this class of matter is so small, when we consider the extent of the service and the magnitude of the mail handled. The experience of the past year proves that most of the complaints filed for investigation are chargeable to the patrons of the service on account of improper or incomplete address, or failure to give any address whatever and other errors.

Of the 297 complaints received, 67 were investigated by special agents, and 215 were closed by correspondence. The total alleged value involved in the 297 complaints received amounted to $8,267.84, of which $8,057.18 was recovered to the addressees or senders, $38.00 is still under investigation, and $172.66 is the total unaccounted for. Of the 20 cases on hand July 1, 1900, sixteen were investigated by special agents and four closed by correspondence. A comparative statement of the work done in this class of cases during the last twenty-eight and one-half months is subjoined:

TABLE No. 3.

FISCAL YEAR.	Complaints.	Investigated.	O. K.	No. Dis.	Amount involved.	Alleged Loss.	Cases Outstanding.
1899 (4½ mos)...	26	13	9	4	$ 1.00	1.00	13
1900....................	247	240	155	85	499.99	39.16	20
1901....................	297	301	110	191	8,267.84	172.66	16
Total......	570	554	274	280	....	....	....

TABLE No. 4.

SHOWING THE NUMBER OF "B" CASES TREATED DURING THE FISCAL YEAR ENDED JUNE 30TH, 1901.

Cases on hand July 1, 1900......	20	Old cases closed	20	Cases on hand:	
„ made up during the year	297	New „ „	281	New...........	16
„ reopened........................	2	Repn'd cases „	1	Reopened....	1
Total..................	319	Total...........	302	Total......	17

"C." CASES, OR MISCELLANEOUS COMPLAINTS AND INQUIRIES AFFECTING THE EMPLOYEES OR BUSINESS OF THE POSTAL SERVICE.

A reference to exhibits "A" and "B" below will show the number and character of this class of cases received, and referred to the special agents for investigation during the fiscal year ended June 30, 1901. It will be seen that the number of complaints received during the twelve months aggregated 1,155; of these 154 were special cases made up in the field by the special agents; 138 were received from the bureau of appointments, salaries and allowances; 30 from the bureau of stamps and supplies; 67 from the bureau of transportation; 7 from the money-order and registry bureau; and the remaining 759 cases were made up in this bureau.

At the beginning of the fiscal year there were 593 cases brought forward from the previous year. Of these 298 were made up on inspection of postoffices. Add to this (593) the 1,001 cases made up in the office; 154 special cases; and 161 cases reopened, and we have 1,909 cases to be accounted for. Of this total, 1,767 were closed, leaving 142 cases on hand July 1, 1901.

The amount of money collected by special agents in this class of cases during the twelve months aggregated $694.01, divided as follows: Balance due on postal account, $260.36; payment upon forged checks and warrants, $125.00; balance due on money-order account, $13.33; postmaster subletting portion of postoffice premises, $75.00; overpayment of salary, $42.87; balance due on money-order remittance, $19.30; balance due on key deposit, $6.11; rifling registered letter, $4.00; embezzlement, $148.04.

Exhibit "A," showing the number of cases made up on the various provinces during the fiscal year ended June 30, 1901:

Department of posts		109
Havana	province	225
Pinar del Río	,,	135
Matanzas	,,	168
Santa Clara	,,	295
Puerto Príncipe	,,	38
Santiago de Cuba	,,	185
	Total	1,155

Exhibit "B," showing the nature and character of the cases made up during the fiscal year ended June 30, 1901:

Leases and new quarters for P. O. premises	13
Discontinuing postoffices	2
Combining P. O. and telegraph offices	8
General inspection of postoffices	130
General inspection of R. P. O's. and star routes	49
Establishing star routes and mail-messenger service	18
Establishing postoffices and postal stations	29
Establishing the money-order business at postoffices	7
Carried forward	256

Brouhht forward	256
Readjusting the postal accounts of postmasters	34
Investigating expenditures and disbuisements	97
Readjusting salaries of postmasters and other employees	12
Appointment of postmasters and postal clerks	86
Furnishing supplies	30
Investigating complaiuts against postmasters, etc	35
Violation of postal code, section 14	1
" " " " " 35	291
" " " " " 39	1
" " " " " 40	1
" " " " " 44	1
" " " " " 52	6
" " " " " 60	1
" " " " " 11-12-14	2
Investigation of miscellaneous complaints	301
Total	1,155

TABLE No. 5.

SHOWING THE NUMBER OF "C" CASES MADE UP DURING THE LAST TWENTY-EIGHT AND ONE-HALF MONTHS.

	Complaints.	Cases investigated.	Cases outstanding.
1899 4½ months	992	688	304
1900	2,224	1,935	593
1901	1,155	1,623	125
	4,371	4.246	125

TABLE No. 6.

SHOWING THE NUMBER OF "C" CASES TREATED DURING THE FISCAL YEAR ENDED JUNE 30, 1901.

On hand July 1, 1900	593	
Made up during the year	1,001	
Cases reopened	161	
Special cases received	154	1,909
Cases closed during the year		1,767
Cases on hand July 1, 1901		142

CLASS OF "F" CASES.

Inquiries and complaints relating to international mail matter forwarded to and received from foreign countries and in transit across the island of Cuba to a foreign country are designated "F" cases. For the most part these cases are simply inquiries relative to the delivery of foreign matter, which necessarily requires considerable correspondence. A glance at the tables will show what a small percentage requires personal investigation by a special agent. During the year there were 2,728 "F" cases made up, of which 2,282 related to registered matter, 442 to the ordinary mail, and 4 were of a miscellaneous nature. To the 2,728 cases made up, there should be added 533 registered and 92 ordinary cases brought forward from the previous year. In the 625 cases just referred to, 496 registered cases were closed without loss; the loss in 5 was charged to the depredations of a clerk and in 3 registered cases no information was obtainable, the facts relating thereto dating prior to the American occupation; leaving 29 registered cases of the year 1900 still under investigation. Of the 92 ordinary cases no loss was sustained in 25, and in 66 the loss could not be located, leaving 1 ordinary case still under investigation. Of the 2,282 registered cases received during the past year, 1,893 were closed, the loss in 37 cases being charged to the depredations of one clerk; 116 ordinary cases were closed without loss, and in 153 cases the loss could not be located. Of the 3,354 cases treated during the year 2,761 cases were closed, leaving 593 on hand at the close of the year. The total loss reported amounted to $7,365.62, divided in $4,728.33 registered and $2,637.29 ordinary. Of the $4,728.33 loss reported in registered cases $2,298.50 was investigated; of which $1,904.50 was recovered to the addressees, $373 was charged to the depredations of one clerk, and the loss of $21.00 could not be located. Of the $2,637.29 loss reported in ordinary cases, $1,822.29 was investigated, resulting in the recovery to the addressees of $1,016.82, and $805.47 not located. There is still under investigation $2,429.83 loss reported in registered cases, and $815 in ordinary cases.

The following comparative statement shows the number of cases treated since February 14, 1899:

TABLE No. 7.

	MADE UP.	CLOSED.	ON HAND.
1899. 4½ months	858	319	539
1900.	2,536	2,450	625
1901.	2,728	2,760	593

TABLE No. 8.

SHOWING THE NUMBER OF "F" CASES TREATED DURING THE FISCAL YEAR ENDED JUNE 30, 1901.

On hand July 1, 1900	625		
Made up and reopened	2,729		
Total	3,354		3,354
Closed by special agents		53	
Closed in the office by correspondence		2,708	
Total		2,761	2,761
Balance on hand July 1, 1901			593

TABLE No. 9.

SHOWING THE TOTAL NUMBER OF CASES OF ALL CLASSES TREATED DURING THE FISCAL YEAR ENDED JUNE 30, 1901.

	A.	B.	C.	F.	TOTAL.
On hand July 1, 1900......	15	20	593	625	1,253
Made up..........................	140	297	1,001	2,728	4,166
Reopened.........................	1	2	161	1	165
Special reports................	....	....	154	....	154
Total............	156	319	1,909	3,354	5,738
Cases disposed of...........	138	302	1,767	2,761	4,878
Cases on hand...............	18	17	142	593	770

COLLECTIONS.

During the year the bureau through its special agents and the office collected and disbursed $2,454.60. Of this amount $7.10 was brought forward from the previous year. The collections were balances due on postal account, $277.30; balance due on money-order account, $375.88; money obtained from forged checks and warrants, $152.49; rifling registered mails, $45.20; postmaster subletting postoffice premises, $75.00; over payment of salary, $42.87; balance due on money-order remittance, $19.30; embezzlement, $1,448.04; loss of registered letter, $5.00; found loose in mails, $0.31; balance due on key-deposit account, $6.11.

DISBURSEMENTS.

To the Postmaster of Havana, Cuba.........	$ 1,814.47
,, ,, Treasurer of the Island of Cuba......	318.85
,, ,, Senders of registered letters...........	160.20
,, ,, Owners of P. O. premises.............	50.00
,, ,, Owner of forged warrants......	42.49
,, ,, Sender of M. O. remittance....	19.30
,, ,, P. M. San Juan, Porto Rico...........	42.87
,, ,, P. M. Pinar del Rio...............	6.11
,, ,, Chief of the bureau of dead letters...	0.31
Total...	$ 2,454.60

In addition to the above it may be proper to state that there were other complaints filed involving losses amounting to $12,741.33, which were traced to their destinations by this bureau and restored to their proper owners; it having been discovered that there were no real losses, the delays being, in most cases, due to improper address, or to the failure of the addressees to promptly acknowledge receipt.

ARRESTS FOR OFFENSES AGAINST THE POSTAL LAWS.

Exhibit "C."

The number of cases pending in the courts at the close of the fiscal year ended June 30, 1900, was ten (10), charged as follows:

four (4) for conspiracy to defraud the Government; one (1) for embezzlement and misappropriation of postal funds; five (5) for removal and re-use of cancelled stamps.

During the year ended June 30, 1901, twenty-eight (28) arrests were made, charged as follows: Conspiracy to defraud the Government, one (1); embezzlement and misappropriation of postal funds, four (4); rifling, two (2); conveying mail over post-roads by private express, one (1); removal and re-use of cancelled stamps, twenty (20).

The employment of the persons thus arrested during the past year and those whose trial was pending may be given as follows: Heads of department or office, four (4); clerks, four (4); star-route contractors, one (1); and civilians, twenty-nine (29).

Eight cases were brought to trial, resulting in six (6) convictions and two being acquitted. One defendant died pending trial; and five were released by the order of the Governor-General promulgated January 16, 1900, and twenty-four (24) cases are pending in the Audiencias of the provinces of Havana, Santa Clara and Santiago de Cuba.

The foregoing covers the workings of this bureau during the last fiscal year, and is submitted for your information.

Very respectfully,

F. M. Hamilton,

Acting Chief Special Agent.

Mr. M. C. Fosnes,

Director-General.

REPORT

OF THE

BUREAU OF TRANSLATION.

DEPARTMENT OF POSTS.

DEPARTMENT OF POSTS OF CUBA

BUREAU OF TRANSLATION.

Havana, July 20, 1901.

During the past year the work of this bureau has somewhat diminished in volume. This is no doubt due to the noticeable improvement in the manner in which the postmasters and other employees attend to their several duties in the service, and a consequent avoidance of frequent instructions involving considerable correspondence. Owing to this fact two translators and two typewriters (also translators) are now doing all the work allotted to the bureau, it having become possible to dispense with the services of five translators during the year.

A record of the work done in this office was started in the month of October, 1900, by order of the director-general. This record is kept in a book in the shape of a daily entry, and summarized at the end of each month, which gives the following showing:

NUMBER OF TRANSLATIONS.

1900.	Incoming letters.	Outgoing letters.	Miscellaneous documents.
Oct. 31	681	693	79
Nov. 30	625	696	45
Dec. 31	755	687	28
1901.			
Jan. 31	677	767	46
Feb. 28	695	697	74
Mar. 31	525	693	45
Apr. 30	510	807	81
May. 31	629	637	92
Jun. 30	576	605	46
	5,673	6,282	536

It is thus seen that the total of 12,491 translations were made from October 1st, 1900, up to June 30th, 1901, which shows a monthly average of 1,388 documents translated during the nine months covered by the report.

It is a matter of justice to the bureau to explain in connection with the number of miscellaneous items which have been translated, that many of them were of great length. These were depositions and statements made in relation to the investigation of the department, with which the public is more or less acquainted. These papers oftentimes covered twenty-five or thirty pages of legal cap size, and as they were for the use of the court the utmost care had to be exercised in making a translation which conveyed the exact meaning of the original. After the translations were made a most careful revision of the work was necessary in order that the highest perfection possible might be obtained.

I am glad to be able to state that as the clerks in the bureau have become better acquainted with the work of the department and have learned thoroughly the meaning of the technical words and phrases in a service heretofore unknown to them, they have been able to make much more rapid translations and all have noticeably increased in efficiency.

The work has kept the present force busy, but the methods employed are such that time is not wasted, and there is rarely an overcrowded condition existing. In this, as in all offices, there are times when the work is slack, but there are other times when the force of clerks have all they can do, and do the kind of work that is required.

I desire to make acknowledgment of the efficiency of the force; and also, in closing, to express my gratitude for courteous treatment by all in the department.

Very respectfully,

R. VENCE,

Chief, Bureau of Translation.

MR. M. C. FOSNES,

Director-General

REPORT

OF THE

DEAD-LETTER BUREAU.

DEPARTMENT OF POSTS.

DEPARTMENT OF POSTS OF CUBA

REPORT OF THE DEAD-LETTER BUREAU.

I have the honor to submit a report, showing the volume of business transacted by this bureau from July 1st, 1900, to June 30th, 1901.

CLASSIFICATION OF MAIL MATTER RECEIVED IN THE DEAD-LETTER BUREAU DURING THE FISCAL YEAR FROM JULY 1ST, 1900, TO JUNE 30TH, 1901.

Ordinary unclaimed letters		39,147
,, ,, letters returned from foreign countries		10,605
Ordinary unclaimed held for postage		7,005
,, ,, blank matter		55
,, misdirected		416
,, refused letters		1,528
,, unclaimed miscellaneous		192
Unclaimed registered letters and parcels, (Domestic)	276	
Unclaimed reg. letters and parcels returned from foreign countries	379	655
PARCELS.		
Unmailable	308	
Unclaimed	200	508
Unclaimed domestic matter		23,755
ORIGINATING IN FOREIGN COUNTRIES.		
Ordinary letters	34,017	
Parcels and printed matter	55,620	
Registered articles	2,387	92,024
Total		175,890

DISPOSITION OF MAIL MATTER UNOPENED (DOMESTIC).

Card and request matter returned to sender.	3,553	
Registered letters and parcels	452	4,005
Carried forward		4,005

FOREIGN MATTER.

Brought forward	....	4,005
Returned to countries of origin	79,563	
Delivered to applicants	361	
Waste paper	12,100	92,024
Total unopened	....	96,029

CLASSIFICATION OF MAIL MATTER OPENED.

Ordinary unclaimed letters	35,594
Unclaimed letters returned from foreign countries	10,605
Refused matter	1,528
Misdirected matter	416
Held for postage	7,005
Miscellaneous letters	192
Parcels	508
Unclaimed domestic printed matter	23,755
Registered letters	203
	79,806

DISPOSITION OF MAIL MATTER OPENED.

Delivered:

Letters containing money	60	
,, ,, money orders and drafts	61	
,, miscellaneous matter	69	
,, postage stamps	9	
,, photographs	55	
,, manuscripts	17	
,, ,, correspondence	2,559	
,, ,, property	188	
Parcels	219	3,237

OPENED AND FILED.

Letters containing money	2	
,, ,, money orders and drafts	67	
,, miscellaneous papers	212	
,, postage stamps	30	
,, photographs	185	
,, manuscripts	23	
,, ,, correspondence	00	
,, ,, property	144	
Parcels	36	
Registered	165	864
Carried forward	....	100,130

Brought forward		100,130

OPENED AND AWAITING EVIDENCE OF DELIVERY.

Letters containing money orders and drafts	1	
Letters containing miscellaneous papers	3	
Letters containing postage stamps	4	
Letters containing photographs	1	
Letters containing manuscripts	3	
Letters containing property	2	
Registered letters	38	52

DESTROYED.

Domestic printed matter (waste paper)	23,755	
Ordinary letters and circulars without inclosures which could not be returned to writers	51,953	75,708
Grand total	....	175,890

RECAPITULATION SHOWING AMOUNT OF MATTER HANDLED RECEIVED.

Domestic original dead matter	....	83,866
Foreign dead matter	....	92,024
Total domestic and foreign	....	175,890

DISPOSITION.

Domestic:		
Delivered	7,242	
Filed	864	
Awaiting evidence of delivery	52	
Destroyed	75,708	83,866
Foreign:		
Returned to countries of origin	79,563	
Delivered to applicants	361	
Waste paper	12,100	92.024
Grand total	....	175,890

MATTER RETURNED FROM FOREIGN COUNTRIES.

Classified as follows:		
Registered articles	379	
Ordinary letters, including postal cards	10,605	
Parcels and printed matter	1,219	12,203

Of the 655 unclaimed registered letters and parcels of domestic origin received there were:		
Delivered to addresses or restored to senders	452	
Filed to discover ownership	103	655

VALUE OF INCLOSURES IN MAIL MATTER OPENED.

Description:	*Number.*	*Value.*
Letters containing money returned to owners	20	47.51
Letters containing money delivered to Acting P. M., Havana	40	114.04
Letters containing money filed in dead-letter bureau	2	1.06
Total	62	162.61

PARCELS FILED IN DEAD-LETTER BUREAU.

Addressed	182	
Unaddressed	71	253

STATEMENT SHOWING NUMBER OF PIECES OF DEAD MAIL MATTER TREATED IN THE DEAD-LETTER BUREAU, FROM JULY 1ST TO JUNE 30TH, 1901.

Received:

Domestic mailable letters	51,280

DOMESTIC UNMAILABLE.

Held for postage	7,005
Blank matter	55
Misdirected	416
Unclaimed miscellaneous	192
Domestic third and fourth-class matter	24,263

FOREIGN MATTER.

Letters	34,017
Parcels and printed matter	55,620

REGISTERED MATTER.

Domestic	655
Foreign	2,387
Total	175,890

DISPOSITION.

	Delivered.	
	Unopened.	*Opened.*
Domestic mailable letters	3,553	47,727
DOMESTIC UNMAILABLE LETTERS.		
Held for postage	....	7,005
Blank matter	....	55
Misdirected	....	416
Unclaimed miscellaneous	....	192
REGISTERED LETTERS.		
Domestic letters	650	5
Foreign letters	2,387	....
Domestic third-and fourth-class matter	....	24,263
FOREIGN MATTER.		
Ordinary letters	34.017	....
Printed matter	55,620	....
Total	96,227	79,663
Grand total	....	175,890

Table showing class and number of undelivered matter returned to, and received from foreign countries.

	RETURNED.				RECEIVED.			
	Reg.	Ord.	Pkg.	Total.	Reg.	Ord.	Pkg.	Total.
Argentine Rep.	34	202	90	326		255	1	256
Austria Hungary	11	84	124	219				
Bahamas		46	1	47		20		20
Barbadoes	2	16	20	38				
Belgium	9	49	185	243			1	1
Bermudas		9		9				
Brazil	8	42	2	52				
British Guiana		9		9				
British Honduras		8		8		1		1
British India	5	4		9				
Canada	7	238	59	304	3	47	1	51
Chile	11	31	6	48				
Colombia	13	40	31	84				
Costa Rica	1	44	4	49		6		6
Danish West Indies	1	16		17				
Denmark	1	10		11				
Dominica, W. I.	1	1		2				
Ecuador	1	19		20		3		3
Egypt	1	6		7				
France	105	680	8,613	9,398		165	54	219
French West Indies	5	16		21			2	2
Germany	44	529	1,970	2,543				
Gibraltar	6	11		17		2	2	4
Great Britain	25	414	1,815	2,254	5	169	8	182
Greece		6		6				
Granada, W. I.		3		3				
Guatemala	1	14	1	16		4		4
Hawaii								
Hayti	8	10		18		7		7
Honduras Rep.	2	2		4	3	7		10
Hong Kong	2	16		18				
Italy	70	296	271	637		5		5
Jamaica, W. I.	6	347	2	355	9	174	2	185
Japan		5		5				
Java, Neth. Indies	2			2				
Malta		1		1				
Mexico	114	942	375	1,431	66	953	419	1,438
Monserrat		1		1				
Netherlands	2	22	35	59				
Nether. W. I.	1	10		11		4		4
Nevis		5		5				
Nicaragua	2	10		12				
Norway	5	33	4	42				
Paraguay		2		2				
Peru	3	22	8	33	1	2		3
Philippines	3	51		54		60	3	63
Portugal	6	41		47				
Porto Rico	34	363	3	400	10	132		142
Russia	7	15	2	24				
St. Kitts, W. I.	1	14		15				
St. Lucia, W. I.		5		5				
St. Vincent, W. I.		3		3				
Salvador Rep.		1	2	3	2	2		4
Carried forward.								

TABLE SHOWING CLASS AND NUMBER OF UNDELIVERED MATTER RETURNED TO, AND RECEIVED FROM FOREIGN COUNTRIES.—(CONTINUED.)

	RETURNED.				RECEIVED.			
	Reg.	Ord.	Pkg.	Total.	Reg.	Ord.	Pkg.	Total.
Brought forward.	....	....	....	....	....	....	....	....
Dominican Rep.........	15	170	2	187	18	178	22	218
Spain.................... ...	1,465	12,114	6,492	20,071	95	1,593	453	2,141
Straits Settlements..	1	....	....	1	....	....	....	....
Sweden.....................	4	14	....	18	....	....	....	....
Switzerland..............	15	34	24	73	....	....	....	....
Trinidad, W. I..........	....	19	1	20	....	8	....	8
Turkey.................. ..	6	38	....	44	....	....	....	....
Turks Islands...........	....	1	....	1	....	....	....	....
Uruguay...................	6	30	5	41	....	....	....	....
Venezuela.................	25	115	8	148	7	....	....	7
Victoria	1	3	....	4	....	....	....	....
United States...........	256	16,420	23,332	40,008	160	6,808	251	7,219
Total......	2,354	33,722	43 487	79,563	379	10,605	1,219	12,203

STATEMENT SHOWING DEAD MATTER OF FOREIGN ORIGIN RECEIVED AND DISPOSED OF FROM JULY 1st TO JUNE 30th, 1901.

RECEIVED.		DISPOSITION.	
Class.		*Class.*	
REGISTERED ARTICLES.		REGISTERED ARTICLES.	
Registered letters..	2,387	Returned to country of origin	2,354
Ordinary letters..........	34,017	Delivered to addressee..	33
Parcels and printed matter	55,620	Ordinary letters returned to countries of origin......	33,722
		Delivered to addressee..	295
		Parcels and printed matter returned to countries of origin....	43,487
		Delivered to addressee..	33
		Waste paper...............	12,100
Total...........	92,024	Total....	92,024

Respectfully submitted,

ALFREDO ARTEAGA,
Chief Dead-Letter Bureau.

MR. M. C. FOSNES,
Director General.

IMFORME

DEL

DEPARTAMENTO DE CORREOS DE CUBA,

CORRESPONDIENTE AL EJERCICIO VENCIDO EN

30 DE JUNIO DE 1901.

DEPARTAMENTO DE CORREOS DE CUBA,

DIRECCION GENERAL,

Habana, Agosto 23 de 1901.

SEÑOR:

Tengo el honor de presentar á Vd. el informe anual de este departamento comprendiendo en detalle los asuntos de sus diversos Negociados, así como los de carácter general, y referente á la administración y dirección de este importante ramo del servicio público en la Isla de Cuba.

Cumpliendo instrucciones sometí á Vd., con fecha doce de Febrero de 1901, un informe que abarca el primer semestre del año económico, el cual informe era complementario del mío para el año económico de 1900. El presente ha sido hecho para abarcar el año todo que termina el 30 de Junio de 1901, dado que la naturaleza del trabajo del departamento es tal, que para formarse una idea cabal del servicio, es necesario incluir los doce meses completos, tomando el año económico por unidad.

Esto, necesariamente, hará extenso el informe semestral en su parte estadística, demostrándose en el presente compendio cuales son los asuntos despachados durante todo el año.

Es innecesario extenderse sobre adversas circunstancias bajo las cuales empezó el año económico del Departamento de correos; basta con lamentarse de que tanto del tiempo y de la energía que debió heberse dedicado á trabajos reconstructivos de administración, en un curso normal de asuntos ha sido absorbido por una investigación retroactiva en sus numerosas y complicadas fases, incluyendo los procedimientos iniciados en los Tribunales y que han surgido de los mismos. A pesar de esta pesada y constante carga, que aún nos agobia, tengo el gusto de poder informar que, durante el año, el servicio postal ha sido mejorado en todas sus ramas, el interés de los empleados ha aumentado, habiendo demostrado notable adelanto en su trabajo; las rentas han correspondido á las esperanzas del departamento; los gastos han sido considerablemente disminuidos, y el sistema postal de la Isla ha sido firmemente restablecido sobre una base que, fundadamente, debemos creer resultará ser duradera, y de beneficios crecientes, en el transcurso del año, para el pueblo que está tan vitalmente interesado en tener el mejor sistema que las condiciones permitan.

Tener un buen servicio, ha sido el primordial propósito fijo de la Administración; después el reducir los gastos á un mínimum prudencial, ó invertir económicamente los ingresos, teniendo en cuenta el tiempo en que el servicio postal de Cuba pueda sostenerse por sí mismo. La realización de esta política impuso la necesidad de disminuir los gastos pero, por supuesto, no se tuvo la intención de causar daño alguno individual en ningún caso. Ha continuado la política de retirar á los americanos tan rápidamente como ha sido posible, sin perjudicar al servicio, y colocar á los cubanos permanentemente en los destinos vacantes. Estoy satisfecho con el resultado de la aplicación práctica de esta política, y me alegro poder informar que los empleados cubanos, por regla general, han mostrado aptitud para el trabajo, y plausible celo en el cumplimiento de sus deberes, patentizando ser eficaces y fieles en alentador grado. Esta política ha dado por resultado el que todos los Administradores de Correos han cesado en el ejercicio de sus funciones, siendo americanos, en toda la Isla, excepción hecha del de Santiago de Cuba. Las peculiares condiciones que existen en dicha Isla no han aconsejado realizar allí hasta hoy ningún cambio. En la Habana, la oficina la mas grande é importante de Cuba, el Coronel Charles Hernández ha sido colocado como Administrador interino. Esta medida se adoptó el 1º de Mayo de 1901 al ser llamado á los Estados Unidos el Inspector de Correos Sr. J. R. Harrison que ha desempeñado el puesto como administrador interino casi durante un año. Ha demostrado especial aptitud en la administración de la oficina, ha disminuido constantemente los empleados y reducido los gastos, esforzándose en colocar dicha oficina á la misma altura que cualquier otra de igual categoría en los Estados Unidos. El Coronel Hernández ha sido inspirado por el mismo deseo, y al mismo tiempo que ha sostenido un servicio eficaz y satisfactorio ha realizado mayores economías, habiendo reducido los gastos á una suma inferior á $100,000 anuales, fin que se ha tenido constantemente á la vista.

En las oficinas departamentales, no ha sido posible retirar á los americanos en número tan crecido como en las Administraciones. Necesariamente, bajo las actuales condiciones, los asuntos del departamento, en sus relaciones con el Gobernador Militar de la Isla y con la Administración de Washington, han sido despachados en inglés. La correspondencia con todos los empleados de correos de la Isla es llevada en su propio idioma, haciéndoseles sentir, de todo modo practicable, que son parte del servicio y que están personalmente interesados en su desenvolvimiento y adelanto permanente.

Como se ha dicho antes, el gran fin del departamento ha sido reducir los gastos, aumentar los ingresos, y al mismo tiempo mejorar el servicio. Habiéndose hecho esfuerzos para disminuir los gastos, los resultados de mayor importancia obtenidos en este sentido lo han sido en el concepto de sueldos. Después de la gran rebaja de gastos de esta naturaleza hecha por mi anterior predecesor, el Honorable Joseph L. Bristow, Cuarto Administrador General de Correos, el total de sueldos el 30 de Junio de 1900 era de $385,679. El 30 de Junio de 1901, los sueldos ascendían á $514,773, con una disminución durante el año económico de $70,906. Es oportuno consignar que actualmente se intentan realizar cambios, que ya están resueltos prácticamente, en virtud de los cuales se obtendrá una disminución mayor de cerca de $5,500. Esto demostrará que existe una reducción en los sueldos, desde Junio 30 de 1900, de $76.000 en números redondos. Con el fin de patentizar donde se han hecho estas reducciones, el siguiente cuadro es de valor:

GASTO ANUAL POR SUELDOS.

	Junio 30, 1900.	*Junio 30, 1901.*
Departamento de Correos	$ 89,420	$ 58,280
Administradores	89,400	90,302
Oficiales en Administraciones....	109,234	75,110
Carteros.........	70,310	61,514
Mensajeros, porteros, etc..... ...	8,215	8,843
Empleados de correos en ferrocarriles......................	19,100	20,724
Total.........	$ 385,679	314,773
Disminución........		70,906

Se observará que de esta reducción, $31,000, han sido practicamente rebajados á los empleados del departamento de correos en la Habana. Los sueldos de los Administradores se aumentaron en cerca de $1,000, los de los oficiales en correos fueron disminuidos en $34.000 en números redondos, los de los carteros en $9.000, y los de los empleados de correos en ferrocarriles aumentados en en $1.000. Emprendióse un arreglo de los sueldos de los Administradores sobre la base de ventas y cancelaaiones tan aproximadamente como puede ser aplicado dicho plan á un servicio tan nuevo como lo es el presente sistema. Existían desigualdades en estos sueldos, según los asuntos que había que despachar en las distintas oficinas. Se han hecho muchos arreglos, y al paso que se hicieron algunas reducciones debido á que se retiraron Administradores americanos en ejercicio, el efecto general ha sido un aumento en los sueldos de los Administradores cubanos. La considerable reducción en los sueldos de los empleados en las oficinas de Correos ocurrió, en su mayor parte, en la Habana, aún cuando el personal de las oficinas ha sido disminuído en harmonía con el buen servicio.

La disminución de los sueldos de los carteros fué ocasionada por haber cesado la repartición libre en muchas de las oficinas más pequeñas de la Isla. El aumento en los sueldos de los emleados postales de ferrocarriles es debido á ascensos merecidos; y para hacer frente á los asuntos que van aumentando al despacho de la del departamento en lo que se refiere al despacho de la correspondencia en la Isla.

Debido al efecto del sistema de las cuentas, descrito más detalladamente en mi último informe, efectos sellados se suministran por el Administrador General de Correos de los Estados Unidos, cargándose los mismos al Director General de Correos. Inmediatamente pasa á manos del Jefe del Negociado de sellos y suministros, empleado con fianza, que expide los recibos para el Director General, siendo entonces responsable de lo recibido. Estos efectos son suministrados á los Administradores prévio pedidos. A los Administradores con fianza les son remitidos los efectos á crédito, existiendo un márgen seguro entre el límite de la suma del crédito y la de la fianza. Los efectos sellados son suministrados á los Administradores sin fianza en virtud de certificado del Tesorero de la Isla haciéndose constar que el Administrador ha depositado en sus manos la cantidad de dinero necesaria para pagar la suma de efectos especificados en el pedido. No sobrecargaré este informe más con los detalles de la intervención de estas cuentas y el sistema vigente por el cual el Interventor de la Isla está informado de todos los asuntos existentes entre el Departamento y los Administradores. Esto fué ligeramente tratado en el Informe semestral, y basta decir que dicho sistema opera satisfactoriamente. Durante el año económico se recibieron de manos del Administrador General las siguientes cantidades de papel sellado, remitidas á los Administradores.

MES.		INGRESOS.	ENTREGAS.
Julio,	1900..............	$ 50,000.00	$ 31,789.32
Agosto,	,, ...	....	25,328.11
Septiembre	,, ...	57,237.50	28,054.83
Octubre	,, ...	40,053.00	38,552.60
Noviembre	,, ...	21,074.50	24,006.13
Diciembre	,, ...	40.063.60	34,847.39
Enero	1901	2,173.30	33,177.12
Febrero	,, ...	10.60	32,306.23
Marzo	,, ...	76,117.50	37,187.42
Abril	,, ...	2,373.00	28,613.56
Mayo	,, ...	190.80	21,257.70
Junio	,, ...	40,021.20	21,306 21
Total	....	$ 329,315.00	$ 336,426.62

Hubo una emisión mayor de papel sellado que el recibido, pero la suma existente el 30 de Junio de 1900 fué mucho mayor que la que había el 30 de Junio de 1901.

La existencia promedia mensual de papel sellado fué de $29,702.21 durante el año económico, y el promedio diario lo fué $976.51. Esto demuestra una ligera disminución de las existencias promedias mensuales y diarias de los primeros seis meses del año. Pero tal disminución explícase fácilmente, por la reducción á bases interiores de los tipos postales entre Cuba y los Estados Unidos, que se hizo efectiva el 1º de Abril de 1901. La tabla siguiente demuestra cuales han sido las ventajas mensuales de sellos y papel sellado durante los primeros nueve meses del año cuando los tipos postales extranjeros estaban vigentes entre Cuba y los Estados Unidos, y separadamente por los últimos tres meses, de acuerdo con la reducción de tipos postales.

MESES.		INGRESOS.
Julio de	1900	$ 427,905.57
Agosto,	,,	28,043.79
Septiembre,	,,	25,496.28
Octubre,	,,	28,327.95
Noviembre,	,,	27,304.81
Diciembre,	,,	31,666.35
Enero,	1901	31,900.87
Febrero,	,,	29,582.62
Marzo,	,,	31,640.79
Total		$ 261,869.03
Promedio mensual		29,096.56
Promedio diario		955.73

Durante los meses de Abril, Mayo y Junio, después que comenzaron á regir las tarifas interiores, los ingresos fueron como sigue:

Abril,	1901	$ 26,845.15
Mayo,	,,	27,016.97
Junio,	,,	25,056.97
Total		$ 78,919.09
Promedio mensual		26,306.36
Promedio diario		67.24

La diferencia diaria media de $88.49 es equivalente á un total anual de $32,298,85. Pero los tres últimos meses corresponden á la época de los pocos negocios, y es justo dar por sentado que la pérdida anual de ingresos debido á esta causa es de $30,000, haciendo un cálculo aproximado. Y es de esperar que el consiguiente aumento de los asuntos portales compensará esta pérdida en el curso de este ano.

INGRESOS.

La siguiente tabla demuestra cuáles son en su totalidad los ingresos postales, provenientes de todas fuentes, durante el año económico que terminó el 30 de Junio de 1901:

MES.		Ventas de sellos.	Rentas de apartados.	Giros postales por trimestres.	Conceptos diversos.	TOTAL.
Julio,	1900	$ 27,905.57	$ 3,065.00	....	$ .81	$ 30,971.38
Agosto,	,,	28,043.79	67.10	$ 3,362.22	.80	28,173.04
Septiembre,	,,	25,496.28	3,073.50	....	1.44	28,927.04
Octubre,	,,	28,327.95	116.87	....	1.68	31,403.13
Noviembre,	,,	27,304.81	101.30	$ 3,345.65	3.30	27,424.98
Diciembre,	,,	31,666.35	3,188.50	....	1.81	35,115.11
Enero,	1901	31,900.87	93.07	....	32.56	35,121.93
Febrero,	,,	29,582.62	112.96	3,203.64	11.33	29,687.02
Marzo,	,,	31,640.79	3,220.50	....	17.20	34,974.59
Abril,	,,	26,846.15	132.42	....	10.61	30,076.26
Mayo,	,,	27,016.97	159.30	3,232.50	135.58	27,284.96
Junio,	,,	25,056.97	....	....	26.29	28,475.06
Total		$340,788.12	$13,458.97	$13,144.01	$ 243.40	$367,634.50

Ingresos totales bajo todos conceptos	$367,634.50
Ingresos medio mensuales	30,636.20
Promedio de ingresos diarios	1,007.21

GASTOS.

En el informe del Oficial Pagador del departamento, se encontrarán detallados los gastos del año económico. De dicho informe doy aqui los siguientes totales mensuales:

MES.		GASTOS. Año económico de 1901.
Julio,	1900	$ 16,160.14
Agosto,	,,	42,809.54
Septiembre,	,,	32,640.92
Octubre,	,,	39,881.13
Noviembre,	,,	34,831.91
Diciembre,	,,	36,267.63
Enero,	1901	42,619.98
Febrero,	,,	37,760.79
Marzo,	,,	35,458.55
Abril,	,,	37,934.47
Mayo,	,,	37,872.89
Junio,	,,	34,793.82
Julio,	,,	22,406.12
Total		$ 451,437.89

Esta tabla demuestra cuales son los gastos actuales del Departamento durante el año económico que abarca este Informe, en tanto en cuanto son conocidos hasta Julio 31 de 1901. La cantidad de $22,406.12 desembolsada en Julio de este año. tal como se demuestra en la tabla, era por gastos hechos antes del primero de Julio, y ha sido preciso incluirlos para demostrar cuáles son los gastos totales del año económico.

El total de los ingresos y de los gastos durante el año económico es como sigue:

Ingresos	$ 367,634.50
Gastos	451,437.89
Déficit	83,803.39

NOMBRAMIENTOS Y FIANZAS.

El Director General está facultado para hacer nombramientos para el servicio postal, y para realizar todos los cambios necesarios, pero en harmonía con una orden del Administrador General, los nombramientos son certificados al Gobernador Militar para su conocimiento y aprobación. El 30 de Junio, existían 300 oficinas de correos en funciones en la Isla, 31 de las cuales son de entregas grátis. Durante el año estableciéronse 19 oficinas, y 14 fueron suprimidas. Al terminar el año económico, existían 720 empleados en todas las ramas del servicio postal. De estos, 300 eran Administradores 266 empleados en oficinas postales, 43 empleados en el departamento de Correos, 43 dependientes postales de ferrocarriles y 74 contratistas para la entrega de correspondencia (star route contractors) y mensajeros. De los 726 empleados, 686 son cubanos y 40 americanos. Durante el año, concediéronse créditos para fines diversos en 191 oficinas, por $8,154.63. Los créditos anuales de 26 oficinas llegan á $7,967.15. En 84 oficinas los créditos concedidos fueron suprimidos, sumando $5,101.75.

En materia de fianzas, el Departamento se ha esforzado continuamente durante el año para hacer comprender á los Administradores que no han prestado fianza la importancia de prestarla, y á todos los Administradores con fianza las ventajas de las personales que son como á manera de índice de su reputación en la sociedad. El primero de Julio de 1900 existían 209 empleados con fianza, sobre cuales fianzas las responsabilidades que pesaban sumaron en conjunto $521,000.

Durante el año, 254 empleados dieron fianza, las penalidades sobre las cuales llegaron á la suma de $425,900, y se cancelaron las fianzas de 197 empleados en que las penalidades llegaron á la suma de $457,500. Sin embargo, esto no quiere decir que las nuevas fianzas representan nuevos nombramientos, porque muchas fianzas de corporaciones fueron canceladas, y los mismos empleados prestaron las personales. Las fianzas en vigor el 30 de Junio de 1901, eran de 266, y las penalidades sumaban en conjunto $489,400.

Entre estas están incluidas otras dos fianzas, una por $45.000, que comprende á los empleados del servicio postal de ferrocarriles, y la otra que comprende á los de la oficina de correos de la Habana, que suman $67.000.

TRANSPORTACION.

Se llama especialmente la atención al informe de la oficina de Transportación que tiene á su cargo el arrendamiento de contratos para llevar la correspondencia, incluyendo los de ferrocarriles, vapores y contratistas. Existen en la Isla 118 vías de comunicaciones de todas clases en uso con un número total de 5.563.30 millas utilizadas con un costo anual de $77,478. A este gasto para la transportación de la correspondencia es preciso añadir los sueldos de los empleados postales en los ferrocarriles, que suman $20,724 durante el año económico, haciendo un gasto total para el servicio interior de $98,202.00.

La suma amillarada contra Cuba, según el Reglamento de la Unión Postal Universal por el transporte de su correspondencia y por las administraciones extranjeras, llamadas "tránsito marítimo de correspondencias, tránsito territorial y tránsito territorial extraordinario" es de $12,299.15 anuales. Esta suma, añadida á la de la transportación interior, hacen $110,501.15 que representa el gasto del departamento de transportación de correspondencia. Estos gastos han sido algún tanto aumentados por el hecho de que la Compañía de vapores de la línea de Ward exige ahora que se le pague por llevar la correspondencia cubana á los Estados Unidos y á Méjico, siendo así que hasta ahora no se hacían dichos pagos. En efecto, se ha exigido el pago y hecho durante el año económico de este informe por servicios pasados de esta naturaleza desde que empezó la ocupación americana en Cuba.

Pequeño ha sido el cambio hecho en las vías de comunicación durante el año económico. El servicio ha adelantado puesto que los empleados de correos y otros funcionarios del mismo se han familiarizado con los métodos actuales de tratar con la correspondencia. Creo que se le está dando á la Isla el mejor servicio posible dadas las presentes condiciones.

AGENTES ESPECIALES.

Puesto que el servicio postal de la Isla hase establecido en condiciones más normales, y los Administradores y empleados se han familiarizado más con su trabajo, no ha sido tan necesario hacer frequentes investigaciones de las officinas postales, y las quejas han disminuído. Esto ha hecho posible el reducir aún más el nómero de agentes especiales del ramo, y consiguientemente los empleados de correos. El Jefe en funciones de los agentes especiales es un Inspector de Correos de los Estados Unidos destinado á prestar sus servicios aquí, Además hay tres individuos empleados en la oficina y cuatro agentes fuera de ella. Con estos, créese posible llevar debidamente este importante trabajo. Han existido muy pocos casos de graves infracciones de la ley durante el año, y estos han sido tratados con tal prontitud y tan completamente que las lecciones han sido saludables.

Los agentes especiales hicieron durante el año una investigación muy completa de todas las oficinas de la Isla, y en relación con ese trabajo instruyeron á los Administradores de sus deberes, habiendo fortalecido el servicio bajo muchos aspectos en alto grado.

Una de las cosas más embarazosas en relación con el servicio todo ha sido el persistente esfuerzo de muchos para usar sellos cancelados en el franqueo de las cartas. Algunos parecen haber hecho esto pos ignorancia, pero en la gran mayoría de los casos la transgresión de la ley parece haber sido á sabiendas y voluntariamente. Han existido numerosas causas, y algunas condenas y multas impuestas. La pena que señala el Código Postal de la Isla es tan severa, que ha sido materia difícil en muchos casos conseguir la condena, y se ha recomendado que el Código sea modificado.

Sin embargo, el arresto de los culpables y el llevarlos á la presencia judicial donde han sido severamente amonestados ha producido un efecto limitativo y saludable que tiende á reducir tales delitos en la localidad determinada en que se hicieron los arrestos. Este delito ha hecho conocer á los funcionarios algunos ardides peculiares del pueblo y una deplorable falta de integridad en las cosas pequeñas entre las clases desgraciadamente ignorantes. El informe mas detallado del Jefe de agentes especiales demostrará cual es el número y la naquraleza de los casos de que se ha tratado durante el año, y la disposición dictada en los terminados.

EL SISTEMA DE CERTIFICADOS.

Tengo el gusto de informar que las constancias referentes á este servicio demuestran un aumento muy decidido en el empleo del sistema de certificados para el despacho de materia postal valiosa, tanto interiores como extranjeras. Ha existido un aumento de medios durante el año, y el público hase aprovechado de los seguros métodos disponibles para despachar materias valiosas, siendo el resultado que el sistema ha obtenido creciente patrocinio, habiendo naturalmente aumentado los asuntos. Durante el año 76,117 cartas y 7,000 paquetes para paises extranjeros fueron despachados en correspondencia certificada, y 64,170 cartas y 7,697 paquetes lo fueron por correspondencia del país, por los cuales se pagaron derechos, que dan una suma total de 155,074 objetos de correspondencia despachados, dando por resultado ganancia para el servicio. Existieron 31,444 objetos de correspondiencia que fueron certificados grátis. El número total de todos los objetos despachados fué de 186,518. El número total de cartas certificadas y de paquetes certificados que pagaron derechos durante el año, demuestra un aumento de 27,360 sobre el del año económico de 1900, con un aumento en las rentas que suma $1,874.96. El servicio debe ser congratulado por el resultado obtenido, y por la confianza del público en el servicio, confianza que vá en aumento.

GIROS POSTALES.

El negocio de giros postales realizado en la Isla durante el año es menor en la cantidad del dinero manejado del que lo fué en el año anterior. Esto no significa que ha existido una disminución en los negocios entre la clase de personas para las que el sistema fué originariamente establecido. El servicio de los giros postales no es un negocio de banca, sino un medio general de remisiones de sumas mas pequeñas de dinero, como una conveniencia para el público en general. Antes, los empleados del Gobierno al trasmitir fondos de una provincia á otra, ó de la Habana á otros puntos de la Isla donde tenían que hacerse desembolsos de importancia, emplearon el sistema de los giros postales. Esta práctica fué abolida en virtud de ordenes oficiales, limitándose la suma que podía ser remitida por empleados. Se publicó también una orden por el Administrador General de Correos de los Estados Unidos, durante el año económico de 1900, con arreglo á la cual el número de órdenes que podían ser expedidas para un comprador para un pagador en la misma oficina en los Estados Unidos era limitada, y continuó vigente durante el último año económico; todo lo cual redujo considerablemente el negocio comparándolo con el año económico de 1900, y tendió á reducirlo á un campo normal y legítimo.

Seáme permitido decir que el negocio de los giros postales de Cuba durante el año económico de 1901 fué manejado de acuerdo con las líneas tenidas en cuenta por la orden creando el servicio, es decir; para el beneficio del público en general al transmitir pequeñas sumas de dinero, segura y prontamente.

El número total de giros postales, tanto de la Isla como extranjeros, expedidos por los Administradores de Cuba durante el año, fué de 83,107, que representan en conjunto $2.567,521.24. El número total de órdenes certificadas sobre los Estados Unidos por conducto de la Bolsa en Tampa fué de 36,544, que representan una suma de $911,509.44. El número de órdenes interiores pagadas en la Isla, fué de 46,291 y el número de las internacionales pagadas fué de 5,469, representando respectivamente $1.668,347.55 y $150,657.68 ó un total de 51,751 órdenes, y de $1.838,915.25 en totalidad. El número de órdenes internacionales expedidas, pagaderas en Puerto Rico, según certificación de la lista de la Bolsa de la Habana, fué de 240 y la suma $4,057.03. El número expedido en Puerto Rico certificadas sobre Cuba por la lista de la Bolsa de San Juan, fué de 213, representando la suma de $9,697.95. El número de oficinas de giros postales en operación el 30 de Junio de 1901, fué de 94, y el de las estaciones que realizan el negocio de giros postales, fué de 10.

Los derechos recaudados en el negocio de los giros postales sumó $13,144.01.

La cuestión de transmitir balances debidos á los Estados Unidos, ha sido cuestión embarazosa. El negocio de los giros postales internacionales que hoy opera constantemente, produce balances en favor de los Estados Unidos en la cuenta de los giros postales. Cómo remitir estos fondos ha sido la cuestión.

Afortunadamente ha sucedido que pagadores del Ejército y el Comisario General han necesitado á veces sumas considerables de dinero y he dado mis cheques oficiales sobre la Subtesorería en Nueva York que han sido remitidas al Administrador General de Correos pagaderas á su orden. Este ha resultado ser un método seguro de transferir los fondos, y no originaba gasto alguno.

Durante el año se trasmitió al Administrador General la suma de $56,318.11 á cuenta de los fondos de los giros postales debidos á los Estados Unidos.

CARTAS NO RECLAMADAS.

En el Negociado de cartas no reclamadas recibiéronse durante el año económico 175,890 cartas no reclamadas, cartas devueltas de paises extranjeros, detenidas por falta de franqueo, mal dirigidas, rechazadas y por cualquier otro motivo no entregables. Como es bien sabido, toda carta ó paquete que por cualquier motivo no puede ser expeditada por los funcionarios del correo va al Negociado de cartas no reclamadas, donde se hacen esfuerzos para entregar la misma. Si esto no es posible, la correspondencia extranjera es devuelta al país de su orígen y la correspondencia de la Isla es abierta y devuelta al escritor si puede averiguarse el nombre. Los métodos de esta rama del servicio son tan bien conocidos, que referencias más ámplias á la misma es innecesaria. Devolvieróuse como no entregables durante el año 16,420 correspondencias á los Estados Unidos, y 12,114 á España. Estas representan la mayor proporción de correspondencia devuelta á los paises extranjeros, aun cuando correspondencia nc entregable fué devuelta á sesenta y cinco administraciones extranjeras.

Este compendio ha sido hecho con urgencia, y no puede ser tan minucioso como fuera de desear, sin embargo me atrevo á creer que demuestra una condicion satisfactoria y progresiva del servicio Postal cubano. E información más detallada podrá encontrarse en los informes que siguen de los diversos Negociados de que se compone el departamento de correos.

Respetuosamente,

(Firmado:) M. C. Fosnes,

Director-General.

Brig. Gen. Leonard Wood,

Gobernador Militar,

Habana, Cuba.

INFORME

DEL

NEGOCIADO DE PERSONAL, HABERES Y CONSIGNACIONES,

DEPARTAMENTO DE CORREOS.

DEPARTAMENTO DE CORREOS DE CUBA.

JUNTA DE NOMBRAMIENTOS.

Habana, Julio 30 de 1901.

SEÑOR:

Tengo el honor de acompañar adjunto el informe del movimiento de este Negociado de Personal, correspondiente al año económico vencido en 30 de Junio de 1901.

Atentamente de usted,

El Jéfe de Negociado de Personal,

ALBERTO J. HUNTER.

RELACIÓN DE LAS OFICINAS POSTALES EXISTENTES.

PROVINCIA.	NUMERO.
Habana	62
Matánzas	50
Pinar del Río	40
Puerto Príncipe	10
Santa Clara	93
Santiago	45
Total	300

Forman parte de esta relación treinta y una carterías servidas por ciento diez y siete carteros.

Oficinas postales de servicio en 30 de Junio de 1900			295
Oficinas postales establecidas desde 1º de Julio, 1900, hasta 31 de Diciembre, 1900		5	
Oficinas postales establecidas desde Enero 1º, 1901, hasta Junio 30, 1901		14	
Total de las existentes de Julio 1º, 1900, á Junio 30, 1901		19	
Oficinas postales suprimidas de Julio 1º, 1900 á Diciembre 31, 1900	6		
Oficinas postales suprimidas de Enero 1º, 1901, á Junio 30, 1901	8		
Total de las suprimidas de Julio 1º, 1900, á Junio 30, 1901		14	
Aumento de Julio 1º, 1900, á Junio 30, 1901			5
Oficinas postales de servicios en 30 de Junio, 1901			300

RELACIÓN DE LOS EMPLEADOS EN EL SERVICIO.

Empleo.	*Cubanos.*	*Americanos.*	*TOTAL.*
Administradores	298	2	300
Empleados subalternos.	253	13	266
En la Jefafura	18	25	43
En los ferrocarriles	43	....	43
Total	612	40	652

Administradores, subalternos y empleados de la Jetura	652
Agregando el número de empleados que obran por contrata, se obtiene el siguiente resultado:	
Contratistas para la conducción de correspondencia	64
Mensajeros de distribución y traslación de correspondencia	10
Total de empleados	726

ALTAS Y BAJAS EN EL SERVICIO.

	Altas.		*Bajas.*	
Julio 1º á Diciembre 31, 1900:				
Empleados de la Jefatura Central.	16		24	
Administradores	63		64	
Demás empleados	43		76	
Total		122		164
Julio 1º á Junio 30, 1901:				
Empleados de la Jefatura Central.	3		20	
Administradores	74		68	
Demás empleados	53		69	
Total		130		157
Total en Julio 1º, 1900, á Junio 30, 1901		252		321

GASTO ANUAL POR EL CONCEPTO DE HABERES.

En Junio 30, 1901.

Oficina Central de Correos	$	58,280
Administradores.		90,302
Oficiales de las administraciones		75,110
Carteros		61,514
Mensajeros, conserjes, etc.		8,843
Oficiales en los trenes ferroviarios		20,724
Total	$	314,773

CONSIGNACIONES.

Conceptos varios.

	NUMERO.	CANTIDAD.
Julio 1º á Decembre 31, 1900.............	89	$ 3,281.96
Enero 1º á June 30, 1901..	102	4,872.67
Total	191	$ 8,154.53

Consignaciones de presupuesto.

NUMERO DE OFICINAS.	CANTIDAD.
26	$ 7,967.15

CONSIGNACIONES DE PRESUPUESTOS SUPRIMIDAS.

	NUMERO DE OFICINAS.	CANTIDAD.
De Julio 1º á Diciembre 31, 1900...	57	$ 3,380.50
De Enero 1º á Junio 30, 1901	27	1,721.25
Total....................	84	$ 5,101.75

FIANZAS.

Fianzas vigentes en 30 de Junio 1900.				
Oficiales del Centro....................	19	$ 75,000		
Administradores propietarios é interinos	81	255,000		
Empleados de las oficinas...........	91	170,000		
Administradores auxiliares..........	18	21,000		
Total.....			209	$521,000
Fianzas constituidas de Julio 1º á Diciembre 31 de 1900.				
Oficiales del Centro...........	5	$ 25,000		
Administradores propietarios é interinos	91	108,700		
Empleados de las oficinas.	29	73,000		
Total.........			125	206,700
			334	727,700

Fianzas canceladas de Julio 1º á Diciembre 31 de 1900. (Incluyendo fianzas personales anuladas.

Oficiales del Centro....................	10	$ 36,000		
Administradores propietarios, é interinos	27	75,600		
Empleados de las oficinas............	30	98,500		
Administradpres auxiliares...........	13	13,000		
Total..			80	223,100
			254	504,600

Fianzas vigentes en Diciembre 31, 1900:

Oficiales del Centro......................	14	$ 64,000		
Administradores propietarios é interinos	145	288,100		
Empleados de las oficinas.............	90	144,500		
Administradores auxiliares..........	5	8,000		
Total..			254	$ 504,600

Fianzas constituídas de Enero 1º, á Junio 30, 1901.

Oficiales del Centro....................	2	$ 21,000		
Administradores propietarios é interinos	73	135,200		
Empleados de las oficinas............	53	61,000		
Administradores auxiliares..........	1	2,000		
Total..			129	$ 219,200
			383	$ 723,800

Fianzas canceladas de Enero 1º, á Junio 30, 1901: (Incluyendo las fianzas anuladas).

Oficiales del Centro.....................	9	$ 40,000		
Administradores propietarios é interinos..................................	43	116,400		
Empleados de las oficinas............	61	71,000		
Administradores auxiliares..........	4	7,000		
Total..			117	$ 234,400
Total de fianzas vigentes en Junio 30, 1901...			266	$ 489,400

RESUMEN.

Fianzas colectivas vigentes en Junio 30, 1900			209	$ 521,000
Fianzas colectivas constituidas de Julio 1º 1900 á Junio 30 1901	125	$ 284,300		
Fianzas colectivas canceladas de Julio 1º 1900, á Junio 30 1901	180	446,600		
Disminución de fianzas colectivas de Julio 1º 1900, á Junio 30 1901			55	162,300
Fianzas colectivas existentes en Junio 30 1900			154	$ 358,700
*Fianzas personales:				
Fianzas personales hechas efectivas de Julio 1º 1900, á Junio 30 1901	129	$ 141,600		
Fianzas personales anuladas de Julio 1º 1900, á Junio 30 1901	17	10,900		
Anmento de fianzas personales de Julio 1º 1900, á Junio 30 1901			112	130,700
Total de fianzas vigentes en Junio 30 de 1900			266	$ 489,400

De las 112 fianzas personales existentes en Junio 30 1901; 36 garantizan á los Administradores de oficinas de giros postales.

*No se hicieron efectivas fianzas personales con anterioridad á Julio 1º 1900.

INFORMES DE LOS AGENTES ESPECIALES.

Conformes y diligenciados de Julio 1º, á Diciembre 31, 1900	275
Conformes y diligenciados de Enero 1º á Junio 30, 1901	124
Total	399

EXPEDIENTES PASADOS AL NEGOCIADO DE LOS AGENTES ESPECIALES PARA CURSARLOS Y EMITIR INFORMES SOBRE LOS MISMOS.

De Julio 1º á Diciembre 31, 1900	113
De Enero 1º á Junio 30, 1901	73
Total	186

SOLICITUDES DE INGRESO EN EL SERVICIO.

	CUBANO.	AMERICANO.	TOTAL.
De Julio 1º á Diciembre 31, 1900	176	18	194
De Enero 1º á Junio 30, 1901	113	9	122
Total	289	27	316

INFORME

DEL

NEGOCIADO DE CONDUCCION

DE LA

CORRESPONDENCIA.

DEPARTAMENTO DE CORREOS.

DEPARTAMENTO DE CORREOS DE CUBA.

NEGOCIADO DE CONDUCCIÓN DE LA CORREPONDENCIA.

Habana, Julio 30 de 1901.

Sr. M. C. Fosnes,

Director General de Correos.

SEÑOR:

Tengo el honor de acompañar un informe estadístico y algunas explicaciones, con referencia á los asuntos del servicio postal de Cuba, que dependen de este Negociado, durante el ejercicio vencido en 30 de Junio de 1901.

De Vd. atentamente,

M. H. BUNN,

Jefe del Negociado de Conducción de la Correspondencia.

Desde el 30 de Junio de 1900 á la fecha, en poco se han alterado los elementos de conducción de los correos cubanos. Hay un aumento de 9 nuevas vías postales; pero 7 son vías servidas por mensajeros postales, servicio de que hasta ahora no conocía este Negociado. De consiguiente, con relación al mismo del año pasado, solo resulta un aumento de dos vías. Las únicas alteraciones de importancia resultan en el servicio de conducción por contrata en el interior. El servicio por buques de vapor y ferrocarriles materialmente se conserva en el mismo estado.

Se han abierto ocho vías por contrata, cinco se han suprimido y dos han pasado á barcos de vapor. No obstante, de la relación resulta un aumento de solo una vía por contrata sobre el pasado año. Las dos observaciones que anteceden han de tomarse como relacionadas entre sí.

El siguiente estado es una relación general del servicio que directamente comprende al Negociado de conducción de correspondencia.

SERVICIO GENERAL DE CONDUCCION.

	Número.	EXTENSION.	COSTO ANUAL.
Vias interiores por contrata..	64	1,366,74 millas	$ 27,634.00
Vias por buques de vapor....	13	3,087.25 ,,	38,610.00
Vias por ferrocarriles	31	1,092.01 ,,	5,244.00
Vias por carros auxiliares. ..	3	14.64 ,,	4,950.00
Vias por mensajeros postales	7	2.66 ,,	1,040.00
Total de vias............	118	5,563.30 millas	$ 77,478.00
Lineas postales por ferrocarril	27	1,931.06 ,,	
Empleados postales en ferrocarril	43	....	$ 20,724.00
Total del servicio interior del país			$ 98,202.00
Servicio postal extranjero..................................			$ 12,299.15
Total al año.........			$ 110,501.15

Así pues, el costo de la conducción de la correspondencia de Cuba y los haberes de los empleados necesarios para su distribución como corresponde cuando va de tránsito importa al año $110,501.15.

A continuación va el cuadro demostrativo del costo anual de la conducción de la correspondencia por las diferentes vías de que dispone la Jefatura y el detalle de la proporción.

RESUMEN DE TODAS LAS CLASES DE VÍAS POSTALES.

Número de vías, 118.
Extensión de todas las vías, 5,563.30 millas.
Gasto anual, $77,478.00
Número de millas recorridas al año, 1.776,122.
Importe del gasto por milla lineal, $13.93.
Importe del gasto por milla recorrida, $4.36.

Comparando el servicio actual con el de 30 de Junio del año pasado resulta lo siguiente:

Aumento del número de vías, 9.
Disminución en su longitud, 54.25.
Aumento en el costo anual, $16,237.00.
Aumento de millas recorridas al año, 139,826.
Aumento del costo por milla recorrida, .66 de centavo.
Aumento del costo por milla lineal, $3.04.

Es de observarse que la extensión total de todas las vías ha disminuido en 54.25 millas al paso que el gasto total ha aumentado en $16,237.00 al año. Esto se explica de la manera siguiente. Las distancias consignadas en el pasado año han sido rectificadas en cnanto fué posible. La rectificación fué causa de rebaja en las millas consignadas, lo que basta para explicar la disminución advertida.

Es sabido que en el pasado año había varias líneas de vapores, que ahora reciben una buena gratificación anual, figurando en el servicio sin incurrir en gastos. El crecido tanto por ciento de aumento en el costo anual y la proporción del costo por milla, queda así explicado.

CONTRATAS.

La forma de contratar la correspondencia se ha simplificado mucho en el año pasado. Se ha podido apreciar mejor esta forma y los postores han presentado sus proposiciones debidamente, llevándose á cabo las contratas con poca dificultad y para el servicio por contrata hubo muchas licitaciones.

Para el servicio por barcos de vapor este año no se pusieron anuncios, por parecer un gasto innecesario. Se hiciron conciertos con las Compañías por cartas y entrevistas, después de lo cual se pusieron las fianzas y se llevaron á cabo las contratas. La licitación por parte de las Compañías de vapores no es de mayor importancia en las mismas vías, y todas las líneas se ocupan en conducir la correspondencia. De consiguiente sería supérfluo anunciar este servicio.

A continuación va una relación de las contratas clasificadas que para este servicio se llevaron á cabo durante el pasado año económico:

CONTRATAS CELEBRADAS.

Por vapores	13
Por conducción de las valijas en el interior	47
Por traslación en carros	1
Por servicio ferroviario	2
Total	63

Los convenios para la conducción de correspondencia por contrata en el interior, en las provincias de la Habana y Matanzas terminaron en 30 de Junio y algunas de las otras Provincias, sumando entre todas 22 contratas. Estas se anunciaron debidamente y continuaron prorrogando el servicio en 1º de Julio. El importe de las contratas anteriores fuè de $8,794.00 al año y de las nuevas al comenzar el 1º de Julio de 1901, $7689.00 al año, lo que da una rebaja de $1,105 00. Cabe bien decir sin embargo, que la mayor parte de este importe fué debido á la disminución del servicio entre Ciego de Avila y Puerto Príncipe, que antes se llevaba como si fueran dos vías, dos veces á semana, reduciéndolo á una sola vez y combinándolo en una sola via. Como esta reducción del servicio montó efectivamante á $900.00 al año, la rebaja del costo de idéntico servicio comparado con el de anteriores contratas fué de $205.

MULTAS.

Las siguientes multas fueron impuestas á los contratistas por faltas en el servicio contratado, por irregularidades y omisiones:

Multas á los contratistas de vapores...	$390.68 en	17 casos.
Multas á contratistas conductores..	81.48 ,,	41 ,,
Multas á contratistas, servicio de carros.....	5.00 ,,	3 ,,
Multas á mensageros postales	2.50 ,,	2 ,,
Total	$479.66	63 casos.

No es tan grande el servicio para que muchas irregularidades no lleguen á conocimiento del Negociado antes de denunciárselas, y presupuestas las circunstancias atenuantes que concurren, muchas veces no se imponen multas, á no ser que resulte positivamente que no se den esplicaciones suficientes. Por esta razón se da cuenta de pocas condonaciones.

CONDONACIONES DE MULTAS.

Contratistas de vapores................	Condonadas	$ 4.25	1 vez.
Contratistas conductores................	,,	2.72	2 ,,
Contratistas de carros	,,	....	
Mensajeros postales..........	,,	....	
Total.......		$6.97	3 veces.

Al inspeccionar el servicio por buques de vapor, se tiene en cuenta el hecho de que casi todos los buques que llevan correspondencia, navegan en alta mar. Así pues, es necesario proceder con lenidad al exijirles la observancia del plazo reglamentario. En realidad, pocas multas se han impuesto en este concepto. Las multas á los contratistas por vapores han sido más bien por haber reducido el número de sus expediciones á causa del mal tiempo que no permitiera salir con toda seguridad.

Tratándose de las vías interiores por contrata, se han impuesto las multas por razones varias, la mayor parte de las veces por faltas á la disciplina.

Es de creerse que los conductores por estas vías del servicio merecen se les recomiende por su empeño en llevar la correspondencia dentro del tiempo reglamentario. En ciertas épocas del año son extraordinarias sus fatigas. En un momento, cualquier camino bueno se pone casi intransitable, á causa de las lluvias que caen en este país. El arroyo que parece más inofensivo se convierte de repente en torrente peligroso. Algunos de los casos citados demuestran que los conductores de estas vías por contrata desafían los elementos, cuando bien podrían sin compromiso esperar ocasión más propicia para que no se les acusara la demora. Sabiéndose el celo con que proceden, viene la tendencia á dar crédito á los motivos de demora que alegan cuando participan haberse encontrado con arroyos crecidos y caminos intransitables. Complace reconocer de esta manera el empeño y el celo que se notan en los conductores de la correspondencia por contrata en el interior de la Isla.

CORRESPONDENCIA EXTRANJERA.

La tercera parte de la materia postal que se despacha en Cuba va dirigida al extranjero. El servicio postal extranjero, de consiguiente, no es de mucho menos importancia que el servicio interior.

Una gran parte de la correspondencia extranjera sale para los Estados Unidos. Aquel país sostiene una línea de vapores de Tampa, Florida, á la Habana, que no sólo trae la correspondencia á Cuba, sino que la lleva á los Estados Unidos en los viajes de retorno. Por lo que nos toca cuanto á sostener la comunicación, se ha efectuado un contrato con otra línea para llevar y traer la correspondencia entre la Habana y Miami. Ambas líneas han concertado un buen servicio cuatro veces á la semana en dichas dos direcciones. También hay comunicación postal entre New York y la Habana, bisemanalmente.

Aprovéchase también estas vías para despachar la correspondencia para Europa y demás países con escala en New York.

Hay despacho directo para España los días 15 y 20 de cada mes, comunicación establecida por España, partiendo de la Habana, y de allí se recibe correspondencia tres veces al mes. El servicio de la correspondencia española, sin embargo, parte de España por la vía de la Habana, para Méjico y las repúblicas de Colombia y Venezuela, permitiendo que se despachen las expediciones en la Habana para los mencionados países. También Francia sostiene su servicio desde el puerto de Santander, vía St. Nazaire, á la Habana y Veracruz, una vez al mes en ambas direcciones. El servicio en Cuba utiliza ambas vías.

Además hay una vez al mes cambio de correspondencia entre la Habana y México conducida por la Compañía de vapores correos entre New York y la Habana.

Como antes se ha dicho, Cuba tiene una vasta correspondencia con el extranjero, y en mucho depende de los medios que proporcionan los demás países para que aquella llegue á su destino. Desde luego que estos medios se pagan con arreglo á las prescripciones del Código Postal universal. También se paga por las expediciones directas al extranjero con sujeción á las mismas prescripciones, á la línea de vapores correos entre New York y la Habana. Este pago comprende las expediciones para la misma línea que van á Méjico y New York.

RELACIÓN DEL IMPORTE DE GASTOS AL AÑO POR EL DESPACHO DEL CORREO EXTRANJERO.

Importe de lo devengado con sujeción á la Unión Postal, á países extranjeros. Vía marítima......	$	5,119.90
Por tierra..		5,473.69
Total..........................	$	10,593.59
Importe pagado por expediciones directas á países extranjeros..		1,705.56
	$	12,299.15

Correspondencia despachada para países extranjeros, por la cual se pagó á razón de 44 centavos la libra por cartas y tarjetas postales, y 4½ cts. por libra de otro material.

Cartas y tarjetas postales, 3,008.20 libras...........	$	1,323.00
Demás materiales, 8,448.12 libras.....................		381.96
Total.....	$	1,705.56

Además de la cantidad de $1,705.56 pagada á la Compañía de vapores correos entre New York y Cuba por servicios prestados dentro del ejercicio, la compañía exigió al Departamento la liquidación total por los servicios prestados desde Enero 1º de 1899 en que empezó la ocupación de Cuba por las fuerzas americanas. Se hizo la liquidación sobre la base expresada, por conducción de 3.794.52 libras de cartas y targetas postales, y 12.189.30 libras de otros materiales, montante á $2,218 10, durante el período de Enero 1º de 1899 á Junio 30 de 1900.

Hay comunicación establecida con las islas de Santo Domingo y Puerto Rico, dos veces al mes, por la línea de Herrera, que recibirá compensación con arreglo á la Unión Postal Universal, en lo adelante. No hay medios de comunicación para un servicio regular entre Cuba y la Isla de Jamaica, pero suele haber cambio de correspondencia entre Santiago de Cuba y Puerto Antonio en Jamaica.

PORMENOR DEL SERVICIO.

SERVICIO INTERIOR, CONDUCCION POR CONTRATA.

Número de vías, 64.
Millas lineales de la vía 1,366.74.
Recorrido anual, millas, 378,260.
Gasto anual, $27,634.00.
Promedio de expediciones semanales, 4.25.
Costo por milla lineal, $20.22.
Costo por milla de recorrido, $7.31 centavos.

COMPARACIÓN CON JUNIO 3 DE 1900.

Aumento en el número de vías, 1.
Disminución en millas lineales de vía, 16.76.
Aumento de costo anual, $3,635.00.
Aumento de recorrido anual, 56,557.
Aumento de costo por millas lineales, $2.87.
Disminución de costo por milla de recorido, .19 de centavo.
Aumento del promedio de expediciones, por semana, .75.

POR PROVINCIAS.

PROVINCIAS.	Núm. de vías.	Millas.	Costo anual.	Costo por milla.	Recorrido anual	Costo por milla recorrida.
Habana	9	104.87	$ 3154.00	$ 30.07	54,470	5.79 Cents.
Pinar del Río	15	252.87	6,925.00	27.38	92,833	7.45 „
Matanzas	4	30	940.00	31.33	10,400	9
Santa Clara	19	295	6,615.00	22.42	119,704	5.52 „
Puerto Príncipe	4	212	3,280.00	15.47	36,608	8.96 „
Santiago	13	472	6,720.00	14.40	64,245	10.46 „
Total	64	1,366.74	$27,634.00	$ 20.22	378,260	7.31 Cents.

ALTAS, BAJAS Y CAMBIOS DURANTE EL EJERCICIO.

Nº de nuevas vías establecidas		8	
Nº de vías suprimidas	5		
Pasadas á servicio por vapor	2		
Alta efectiva		1	vía.
Aumento de millas lineales, nuevas vías		192	millas
Millas lineales suprimidas	68		
Disminución por cambio, modificación y rectificación de distancias	140.76		
Baja efectiva		16.76	millas
Aumento de costo por adopción de nuevas vías		$2,554.00	
Aumento por costo de nuevos contratos al vencer los anteriores		1,136.00	
Por aumento de servicio en las vías		605.00	
Disminución por supresión de vías	$660.00		
Alza efectiva de costo		$3,635.00	

SERVICIO ESPECIAL.

Existen nueve administraciones con servicio especial, á cinco de las cuales corresponde que los administradores conduzcan la correspondencia á la base de donde se surten, y sus haberes son así sobreentendidos. En dos de ellas ferrocarriles particulares llevan la correspondencia y en las otras dos se valen de medios extraordinarios, pero sin gastos para el Departamento.

SERVICIO INTERIOR POR CONTRATA VIGENTE EN JULIO 1º, 1901.

Número de vías, 66.
Extensión de las vías, millas 1,462.74.
Proporción de costo al año, $27,513.00.
Aumento de número de vías, 2.
Aumento de millas lineales, 96.
Disminución de costo anual, $121.00.

Se han establecido tres nuevas vías y empezó el servicio en Julio último. El número de vías, sin embargo, arroja solo un aumento de dos vías. Esto se explica con el hecho de que para empezar en 1º de Julio se concentraron dos líneas en una.

Los contratos celebrados conforme á la última convocatoria para empezar en 1º de Julio, como se consigna bajo el rubro de "Contratas" arroja una disminución en el costo anual, de $1,105.00. El costo de las tres nuevas vías $984.00 al año. Hay, pues, una disminución efectiva de $121.00 en el costo anual del servicio, á contar desde el 1º de Julio de 1901.

SERVICIO POR VAPORES.

El servicio por vapor como se realiza en la actualidad, es en efecto el mismo del año anterior. Todos los vapores que hacen el servicio en torno de la Isla, que es conveniente utilizar, se ocupan en conducir la correspondencia. Bien sabido es que hasta el 30 de Junio de 1900, existían algunas líneas, que este año han percibido gran parte del devengo de este capítulo, condujeron la correspondencia sin retribución. Por esta razón, un cuadro comparativo sobre la base del costo por milla lineal de extensión ó recorrido carecería de importancia. Los cuadros que se acompañan, son por tanto, una sencilla exposición del servicio normal.

SERVICIO POR VAPORES.

Número de vías, 13.
Extensión de las vías, 3,087.25 millas.
Costo anual, $38,610.00.
Costo por milla lineal, $12.51.
Recorrido anual, 327,505 millas.
Costo por milla de recorrido, $11.78.

COMPARACIÓN CON EL SERVICIO EN OPERACIÓN EN 30 DE JUNIO DE 1900.

Aumento del número de vías, 1.
Disminución en longitud de las vías, 44.
Aumento de costo por año, $11,302.00.
Disminución de viaje, en millas, 11,950.

SERVICIO POR VAPORES.

EN OPERACION DESDE JULIO 1º DE 1900 A JUNIO 30 DE 1901.

Via Núm.	TERMINOS.	CONTRATISTA.	Pago anual.	Longitud en millas.	Viajes por semana.
1	Habana á Santiago	Sobrinos de Herrera	$ 12,000.00	840.	3 al mes.
2	Batabanó á Santiago	Menéndez y Cª	9,000.00	614.46	1 á la semana.
3	Batabanó á Nueva Gerona	Angel G. Ceballos	600.00	92.	1 á la semana.
4	Santiago á Caimanera	Gallego-Messa y Cª	1,000.00	45.	2 á la semana.
5	Habana á Nuevitas	Alonso, Jauma y Cª	300.00	409.	1 á la semana.
6	Cienfuegos á Tunas de Zaza	José Castro Monje	300.00	82.08	2 á la semana.
7	Habana á La Fé	A. del Collado y Cª	1,200.00	227.49	4 al mes.
10	Cienfuegos á Rodas	Boullón y Cª	360.00	30.	7 á la semana.
11	Batabanó á Manzanillo	Alonso Jauma y Cª	200.00	425.22	2 al mes.
12	Mayarí á Puerto de Mayarí	Carlota Grau	600.00	15.	1 á la semana.
13	Manzanillo á Niquero	José Muñoz	1,200.00	51.	7 á la semana.
14	Miami, Florida, á Habana, Cuba	Pen. y Occ. S. S. Cª	11,700.00	242.	1 á la semana.
15	Cienfuegos á Belmonte	E. Atkins y Cª	150.00	14.	2 á la semana.
			$ 36,610.00	3087.25	

En el 1º de Julio, cesó el servicio de la Compañía de Vapores Peninsular y Occidental, y esto explica la disminución de una via, y 242 millas, en el estado siguiente:

SERVICIO DE VAPORES SUMINISTRADO DESDE JULIO 1º, 1901.

Número de vías, 12.
Longitud de las vías en millas, 2,845.25.
Razón del costo por año, $26,910.00.

COMPARACION CON JUNIO 30, 1901.

Disminución de número de vías, 1.
Disminución de número de millas, 242.
Disminución del costo, $11,700.00.

SERVICIO POR FERROCARRIL.

Número de vías por ferrocarril, 31.
Extensión de vías por ferrocarril, 1,092.80.
Recorrido anual. Millas, 942,089.80.
Importe del pago anual, $5,244.00.

Este servicio efectivamente no ha cambiado durante el año anterior.

La rectificación de un error en el cálculo de las distancias arroja una alza pequeña en las millas lineales expresadas, 3.85 millas.

El estado actual de los ferrocarriles de Cuba que llevan correspondencia, es bien conocido y no se necesita repetirlo. De las 1,092 millas de carrileras que hay en la isla, solamente 188.88 millas se subvencionan por llevar la correspondencia, ó sea el 17 por 100.

Los ferrocarriles Unidos de la Habana perciben $32.00 por milla por 143.25 millas, $4,584.00 al año (229.20 kilómetros á $20.00 por kilómetro.)

Esta compañía tiene 261 millas de extensión. Hay sin embargo 117.25 millas por las que no se le subvenciona, exigiendo el R. D. de 10 de Diciembre de 1858 que lleve la correspondencia.

El ferrocarril de Puerto Príncipe y Nuevitas no está obligado por la concesión á llevar la correspondencia gratis. A esta Compañía se le pagan al año $14.46 la milla por llevar la correspondencia en toda la línea, 45.63 millas, $660.00, 73 kilómetros á $9.04 por kilómetro.

Las vías por ferrocarril en explotación son las siguientes:

Vias por ferrocarril en explotación en 30 de Junio, 1901.

Via No.	EXTREMOS DE LA VIA.	NOMBRE DE LOS FERROCARRILES.	Millas lineales.
101	San Felipe á Batabanó	F. C. Unidos de la Habana.	9.38
102	Caibarién á Placetas	Cuban Central Ry. Ltd	32.93
103	Caibarién á Placetas	Cuban Central Ry. Ltd	22.31
104	Cárdenas á Esperanza	F. C. de Cárdenas y Júcaro.	96.47
105	Cárdenas á Yaguaramas	F. C. de Cárdenas y Júcaro.	71.16
106	Rodas á Cartagena	F. C. de Rodas, Turquino y Cartagena	20.00
107	Cienfuegos á Santa Clara	Cuban Central Ry. Ltd	42.81
108	Palmira á Congojas	Cuban Central Ry. Ltd	15.63
109	Gibara á Holguín	F. C. de Gibara y Holguín.	20.00
110	Habana á Alacranes	F. C. Unidos de la Habana.	81.20
111	Regla á Guanabacoa	" " " " " "	3.00
112	Rincón á Guanajay	" " " " " "	21.26
113	Habana á Jovellanos	" " " " " "	88.70
114	Habana á Marianao	F. C. de Marianao	10.00
115	Habana á Pinar del Río	F. C. del Oeste	110.00
116	Isabel de Sagua á Cruces	Cuban Central Ry. Ltd	49.31
117	Altamisal á Macagua	F. C. de Cárdenas y Júcaro.	20.20
118	Empalme á Güines	F. U. de la Habana	25.88
119	Matanzas á Colón	F. C. de Matanzas	70.00
120	Máximo Gómez á Itabo	F. C. de Cárdenas y Júcaro.	13.62
121	Júcaro á Morón	F. C. de Júcaro y San Fernando	42.30
122	Navajas á Murga	F. C. de Matanzas	30.00
123	Nuevitas á Puerto Príncipe.	F. C. de Puerto Príncipe y Nuevitas	45.63
124	Ranchuelo á San Juan de las Yeras	Cuban Central Ry. Lt	5.00
125	Tunas de Zaza á S. Spíritus.	F. C. de Tunas y S. Spíritus.	24.47
126	Santiago de Cuba á San Luis	F. C. de Sabanilla y Maroto.	20.63
127	Sagua la Grande á Caguaguas	Cuban Central Ry. Ltd	9.69
128	Santiago de Cuba á Firmeza.	Juragua Iron Co	19.00
129	Sitiecito á Camajuaní	Cuban Central Ry. Ltd	36.18
130	Caimanera á Jamaica	F. C. de Guantánamo	29.00
131	Cristo á Songo	F. C. de Sabanilla y Maroto	6.25
		Total	1,092.01

SERVICIO DE CARROS AUXILIARES.

Número de vías, 3.
Extensión de las vías, millas 14.64.
Millas de recorrido anual, 24,430.
Costo anual, $4,950.00.
Costo por milla, $338.11.
Costo por milla de recorrido, 20.27 cents.

Este servicio no acusa cambio excepto un alza de $260.00 sobre el pasado año.

En el pasado Agosto se intentó establecer el servicio de carros por contrata en Santiago, pero al anunciar la subasta, los precios que pidieron fueron tan alzados, que se optó por seguir como hasta entonces utilizando los medios conque contaba el Departamento. Estaba utilizándose un buen carro de reglamento, y con la compra de un par de caballos y los arreos, y colocando un carrero, el servicio ha resultado satisfactorio.

El costo de este servicio es el siguiente:

Vía Nº 901.	Habana.....	$ 3,750.00	al año.
,, ,, 902.	Cienfuegos.........	600.00	id.
,, ,, 903.	Matanzas	600.00	id.
	Total.....	$ 4,950.00	

SERVICIO DE MENSAJEROS POSTALES.

Número de vías, 7.
Extensión, millas 2.66.
Costo anual, $1,040.00.
Costo por milla, $390.98.
Recorrido anual, millas, 3,837.40.
Costo por recorrido de milla, 27.1 cents

Se ha introducido este servicio y conducido como tal, á partir de los comienzos del ejercicio. Se dispuso llevarlo en esta forma en los lugares en que el individuo que había de ser mensajero no se necesitaba como empleado de la oficina á que servía. El ensayo no ha dado resultado en absoluto, puesto que las proposiciones presentadas generalmente eran demasiado alzadas con relación al servicio. Por tanto, no se ha procurado desecharla como servicio particular. Es de admitirse como cierto que podría llevársele mejor si los precios mencionados no fueran exagerados las más de las veces.

SERVICIO POSTAL POR FERROCARRIL.

El servicio postal por ferrocarril acusa pocos cambios del año pasado á la fecha. Es de creer que la aptitud de los empleados ha obtenido gran progreso y el celo que muchos despliegan es merecedor de elogios.

El negociado ha podido atender mejor á los pequeños detalles del servicio durante el pasado año. Se ha dado instrucción á los empleados y se les han enseñado los métodos de ejecución del servicio. Se ha puesto especial cuidado en la distribución. Un importante factor en esta enseñanza y que se ha exigido con ahinco, fué la rectificación de los errores.

Durante el año se suprimieron tres líneas postales por ferrocarril. Eran tramos cortos que no necesitaban servidores. Se consiguió de los ferrocarriles que permitieran á sus mismos empleados entenderse en el manejo de las valijas. No ha habido motivo para arrepentirse de la separación de los nuestros, pues el servicio se ha atendido cumplidamente.

Donde más se ha adelantado en habilitación material de oficinas ha sido en las de la Posta de la Habana, Batabanó y Santiago, línea de Menéndez. Esta Compañía ha construido en todos sus vapores una oficina con apartados á propósito para distribuir la correspondencia, con dormitorio para el empleado, también un cuarto depósito para la correspondencia arreglada, todo convenientemente colocado para atender á la voluminosa correspondencia que pasa por esa línea.

Ha sido imposible instalar un servicio postal por ferrocarril en la costa Norte. La Compañía de vapores que efectivamente ha monopolizado el negocio, no hay forma de que les destine lugares separados ni lleve á los empleados. El siguiente estado dá una idea general del servicio postal por ferrocarril, existente al cerrar el ejercicio pasado.

SERVICIO POSTAL POR FERROCARRIL.

Número de líneas, 27.
Número de empleados, 43.
Millas de ferrocarril, 1,931.06,
Recorrido en millas por los empleados, 1.131,159.37.
Total haber de empleados, $20,724.00
Promedio del haber del empleado, $481.96 por año.

RESUMEN DEL SERVICIO POR FERROCARRIL.

Número de líneas ferroviarias, 23.
Empleados en las líneas, 38.
Número de líneas de vapores, 4.
Empleados en las líneas de vapores, 5.
Millas de servicio en ferrocarril, 1,153.52.
Recorrido anual en ferrocarril, 1.003,045.27.
Millas de servicio en vapores, 777.54.
Recorrido anual en vapores, 128,114.10.
Total de millas lineales, 1,931.06.
Total de recorrido anual, 1.131,159.37.

RELACIÓN CLASIFICADA DE HABERES DE EMPLEADOS POSTALES EN FERROCARRILES.

8	empleados....	$600.00	$ 4,800.00
21	,,	500.00	10,500.00
1		480.00	480.00
2		420.00	840.00
7		400.00	2,800.00
1		384.00	384.00
1		360.00	360.00
1		320.00	320.00
1		240.00	240.00
Total.. 43			$ 20,724.00

Promedio de haber del empleado. $ 481.96

EXPEDIENTES FORMADOS Á EMPLEADOS DE CORREOS EN FERROCARRILES.

La formación de expedientes dá por resultado un pequeño aumento proporcional. Informe del pasado año 83.08 por ciento: este año, un aumento de 6.64 por ciento.

Número de expedientes, 29.
Número total, movimiento de targetas, 8,544.
Número en que no hubo error, 7,665.
Tanto por ciento en que hubo error, 89.72.

Como ya se ha dicho, la rectificación de errores en la distribución de la correspondencia, ha merecido especial atención durante el año pasado y mucho se ha exigido no solo á los empleados en los ferrocarriles, sino á las Administraciones. Sin embargo, es de convenirse en que los datos estadísticos allegados no han de aceptarse en absoluto como demostrativos de la proporción de correspondencia mal dirijida. De consiguiente, no se expone el cálculo. El que se hizo, no mereció los honores de cálculo estadístico. Se acompañan los datos de referencia.

ERRORES DE DISTRIBUCIÓN.

	Total.	Empleados en ferrocarril	Oficinas de Correos.
Material correo ordinario	4,657	360	4,297
Cartas mal dirigidas	69	10	59
Sacos de impresos mal dirigidos	9	5	4
Paquetes de cartas mal rotulados	19	0	19
Sacos de impresos mal rotulados	4	2	2
Valijas mal dirigidas	1	1	0
Paquetes certificados mal dirigidos	2	2	0
Valijas certificadas mal dirigidas	3	3	0

La correspondencia distribuida en el tránsito por los empleados de correos en los ferrocarriles es un 4% más que la de que se dió cuenta el año pasado. Este cálculo se basa en el número de bultos de que se dió cuenta y no puede indicar satisfactoriamente el aumento en la correspondencia de la Isla. Casi todos los bultos son recojidos en el camino por los empleados todos los días, y no hay manera de averiguar si los bultos contienen más cartas que el año anterior. La correspondencia certificada, sin embargo, de que se encargó el servicio postal en los ferrocarriles, presenta un aumento de 25 por 100 y el informe acerca de esta clase de correspondencia resulta fehaciente, puesto que se revisan uno á uno los certificados.

El siguiente cuadro es una exposición de la suma de trabajo llevado á cabo en todas las líneas, juntamente con el número de viajes.

CORRESPONDENCIA DESPACHADA POR OFICINAS POSTALES EN FERROCARRILES.

Número del empleado.	Número de viajes.	LINEAS DE VIAS POSTALES POR FERROCARRILES.	Paquetes de cartas.	Sacos de impresos.	Paquetes certificados.	Valijas certificadas.	Número del expediente.	Sacos del interior por F. C.
1	730	Caibarién, Camajuaní y Placetas	18,141	907	1,051	....	1	1
1	730	Caibarién y Placetas	11,470	154	2,031	1		
3	1,569	Cárdenas y Santa Clara	45,891	4,146	14,307	3,681	174	22
1	730	Cárdenas y Yaguaramas	38,297	1,467	3,717			
1	376	Cartagena y Rodas	1,706	192	194	1		
1	443	Cienfuegos y Congojas	1,583	435	144			
2	1,460	Cienfuegos y Santa Clara	17,740	1,473	2,924	2	7	
1	324	Gibara y Holguín	493	1	2,197		4	
4	1,458	Habana y Alacranes	50,686	2,325	9,498		9	
2	1,454	Habana y Guanajay	26,865	1,759	3,696		9	
4	1,455	Habana y Jovellanos	48,339	2,728	12,549	5,056	174	18
1	1,946	Habana y Marianao	13,360	1,116	346	....	1	980
3	1,460	Habana y Pinar del Río	24,785	1,639	6,779	738	43	
2	730	Isabela y Caibarién	26,817	2,770	7,223	728	....	2
2	1,460	Isabela y Cienfuegos	35,304	2,370	10,151	2,212	26	7
1	649	Júcaro y Morón	4,744	1,094	608	275	2	
1	730	Macagua y Altamisal	5,072	669	1,474	3	1	
1	1,226	Mádan, Empalme y Güines	5,373	371	648	1	3	
1	730	Matanzas y Colón	28,944	1,805	3,839			
1	486	Máximo Gómez é Itabo	2,675	240	167			
1	730	Navajas y Murga	6,829	564	1,292			
1	528	Nuevitas y Puerto Príncipe	534	....	1,611	267	3	1
1	417	Sancti Spíritus y Túnas	2,387	....	2,250			
1	492	San Felipe y Batabanó	3,076	295	487			
2	828	Santiago y San Luis	9,414	1,092	2,541			
40	23,141	Total de líneas ferroviarias	430,525	29,612	91,724	12,965	457	1,031
2	105	Habana, Batabanó y Santiago	11,201	5,519	5,703	489	29	19
1	512	Manzanillo y Niquero	1,737	16	511			
1	730	Cienfuegos y Rodas	10,702	477	1,527		1	
1	190	Cienfuegos y Túnas	....	....	2,899			
5	1,537	Total de líneas de vapores	23,640	6,012	10,640	489	30	19
45	24,678	Total de todas las líneas	454,165	35,624	102,364	13,454	487	1,050

ADVERTENCIA:—Se suprimió la oficina postal en el Ferrocarril de San Felipe y Batabanó, en 1º de Noviembre de 1900.
Se suprimió la oficina postal en el Ferrocarril de Máximo Gómez á Itabo, en 1º de Marzo de 1901.

Se han construido durante el pasado año en trenes de ferrocarril y vapores nueve departamentos para distribuir la correspondencia, utilizándose por todo en la actualidad treinta y seis. En algunas lineas estos departamentos se han pasado del coche de 2ª clase al de equipages, donde son más útiles. Esto resulta así en el "Cuban Central Railway." Las demás líneas principales han convenido en ponerlos en los carros de equipajes en adelante, y cuando el material rodante tenga que ir al taller de reparaciones se les muda.

Comunmente los sobres que en el pais se usan son muy anchos. Por este motivo, se han adoptado por regla general buzones de 5½ pulgadas de ancho por 4½ de alto.

El siguiente estado presenta la relación de las lineas postales por ferrocarriles que hacen actualmente el servicio, el número de empleados destinados á cada vía, la extensión de cada una, el recorrido anual, y el número y las dimensiones de las casetas ó departamentos para distribuir la correspondencia.

ESTADO DE LINEAS POSTALES POR FERROCARRIL.

DENOMINACION DE LA LINEA.	MILLAS LINEALES	NUM. DE EMPLEADOS.	RECORRIDO ANUAL.	CASETAS DE CORREOS. NO.	LONGITUD.	ANCHURA.
Caibarién, Camajuaní y Placetas	32.93	1	24,038.90	1	7 piés	3 piés 6 pulg.
Caibarién y Placetas	22.31	1	16,286.30	1	6 piés 2 pulg	4 piés.
Cárdenas y Santa Clara	105.53	3	91,224.39	1	5 piés	4 piés 6 pulg.
				1	6 piés 6 pulg	5 piés 6 pulg.
				1	8 piés 2 pulg	5 piés 8 pulg.
Cárdenas y Yaguaramas	71.16	1	51,946.80	1	5 piés	4 piés 6 pulg.
Cartagena y Rodas	20.00	1	7,520.00	...	...	...
Cienfuegos y Congojas	24.38	1	10,800.34	1	6 piés 6 pulg	2 piés 6 pulg.
Cienfuegos y Santa Clara	42.81	2	62,502.60	1	8 piés 3 pulg	3 piés.
Gibara y Holguín	20.00	1	6,480.09	1	4 piés	7 piés.
Habana y Alacranes	81.20	4	118,389.60	1	6 piés	6 piés.
				2	5 piés	5 piés.
				2	6 piés	5 piés.
Habana y Guanajay	35.63	2	51,806.02	1	4 piés 9 pulg	2 piés 6 pulg.
Habana y Jovellanos	88.70	4	104,154.75	1	6 piés 4 pulg	5 piés 6 pulg.
				2	6 piés	5 piés 4 pulg.
				1	4 piés 9 pulg	4 piés 9 pulg.
Habana y Marianao	10.00	1	19,460.02	...	...	...
Habana y Pinar del Río	110.00	3	112,690.10	1	10 piés	2 piés.
				1	10 piés	2 piés.
				1	7 piés 11 pulg	2 piés 11 pulg.
Isabela y Caibarién	69.29	2	50,581.70	1	9 piés	4 piés.
Isabela y Cienfuegos	68.37	2	64,999.40	1	7 piés	3 piés 2 pulg.
				1	8 piés 2 pulg	4 piés.
Júcaro y Morón	42.30	1	27,452.70	...	...	...
Macagua y Altamisal	20.20	1	14,746.00	1	5 piés 6 pulg	5 piés.
Madruga, Empalme y Güines	25.88	1	31,728.88	1	6 piés	3 piés.

ESTADO DE LINEAS POSTALES POR FERROCARRIL.—(CONTINUACIÓN).

DENOMINACION DE LA LINEA.	MILLAS LINEALES	N.º DE EMPLEADOS.	RECORRIDO ANUAL.	CASETAS DE CORREOS. NO.	LONGITUD.	ANCHURA.
Matanzas y Colón	70.00	1	51,100.00	1	8 piés	2 piés 11 pulg.
Navajas y Murga	65.86	1	29,953.32	1	8 piés	2 id. 11 id.
Nuevitas y Puerto Príncipe	45.63	1	24,092.64	1	......	......
Sancti-Spíritus y Tunas	24.47	1	10,203.99	1	4 piés	2 id. 6 id.
Santiago y San Luis	20.63	2	17,081.64	1	6 piés 10 pulg	2 id. 10 id.
Habana, Batabanó y Stgo. por ferrocaril	36.24	......	3,805.20	......		
Total por ferrocarril	1,153.52	38	1,003,045.27	32		
Habana, Batabanó y Stgo. por vapor	614.46	2	64,518.30	1	* 8 piés 6 pulg	6 id. 5 pulg.
	......	......	......	1	*10 piés 5 pulg	7 id. 11 id.
	......	......	......	1	*10 piés	6 id. 11 id.
Manzanillo y Niquero	51.00	1	26,112.00	......	El empleado usa una carpeta para su	
Cienfuegos y Rodas	30.00	1	21,900.00	1	trabajo 4 piés, 6 pulg	4 id. 6 id.
Cienfuegos y Tunas	82.08	1	15,583 80		El empleado es el sobrecargo del vapor.	
Total por vapores	777.54	5	128,114.10	4		
	1,153.52	38	1,003,045.27	32		
	777,54	5	128,114.10	4		
Total del servicio	1,931.06	43	1,131,159.36			

*Cada vapor tiene también un cuarto para depósito de correspondencia de las mismas dimensiones.

Además, durante el ejercicio se ha llevado cuenta de todos los accidentes en los trenes de ferrocarril conductores de correspondencia, según estado que se acompaña:

1900.

Julio 24. Hubo una huelga de fogoneros en los Ferrocarriles Unidos de la Habana, que empezó el 24 de Julio y duró hasta el 26.

Las oficinas de correos en el ferrocarril entre la Habana y Alacranes, en los trenes núms. 6 y 11 no operaron el 24, 25 y 26.

Las oficinas de correos en el ferrocarril entre la Habana y Jovellanos, por los trenes núms. 5 y 10 anduvieron con regularidad. El 24 de Julio el tren núm. 2 llegó á la Habana de Jovellanos, pero el tren núm. 9 y el 10 dejaron de andar. Todos los trenes reanudaron el servicio el 27 de Julio.

En la línea de correos por ferrocarril entre la Habana y Guanajay, se dejó salir el tren núm. 4 de Guanajay el 24 de Julio con 5 horas de retraso. En la Ciénaga una partida de huelguistas abordó el tren haciendo salir á los pasajeros. Intentaron también hacer salir al empleado de correos, pero éste se negó, resultando que llegó á la Habana sin novedad. El 25 de Julio los trenes núms. 4 y 13 no salieron, los de los núms. 7 y 8 sí. El 26 de Julio sólo el tren núm. 4 dejó de salir. El 27 de Julio todos los trenes reanudaron el servicio.

La oficina de correos en el ferrocarril entre Madruga, Empalme y Güines, funcionó durante toda la huelga aunque con alguna demora.

Oficina de correos en el ferrocarril entre la Macagua y el Artemisal: El tren de la Macagua al Artemisal, descarriló entre Banagüises y Artemisal, lo que hizo necesario un trasbordo, llegando al Artemisal con 2 horas y 33 minutos de demora. No tuvo novedad el empleado ni la correspondencia.

Octubre 6. Oficina de correos en el ferrocarril entre la Habana y Alacranes. El tren número 14 se salió de la vía en Melena del Sur. No hubo novedad. Llegó á la Habana con 4 horas y 35 minutos de demora.

Noviembre 3. Oficina de correos en el ferrocarril entre Habana y Alacranes. El tren número 1 descarriló en la Unión de Reyes ocasionando la demora de 1 hora y 24 minutos. Sin novedad.

Noviembre 7. Oficina de correos en el ferrocarril entre la Isabela y Caibarién. El alijo de la máquina en el tren número 1 descarriló entre Sitiesito y Sitio Grande. Demora, 2 horas, 20 minutos; sin novedad.

Noviembre 27. Servicio de correos en el ferrocarril entre la Isabela y Caibarién. El tren número 9 descarriló cerca de Taguayabón, ocasionando un trasbordo. El conductor y carro de la correspondencia, sin novedad. Demora 4 horas.

Diciembre 5. Oficina de correos en el ferrocarril entre la Habana y Pinar del Río. El tren número 5 de viaje para el paradero de Gabriel, por estar abierto el "chucho" debido á una equivocación, la máquina salió de la vía y tuvo que esperar otra máquina de la Habana. Llegó á Artemisa con 3 horas 5 minutos de demora. No hubo novedad, exceptuando en la locomotora.

Diciembre 13. Oficina de Correos en el ferrocarril entre la Habana y Alacranes. El tren número 11 chocó en Unión de Reyes con la locomotora del batey. El coche de la correspondencia sufió averías. La correspondencia no tuvo novedad, tampoco el empleado. El tren llegó á Alacranes.

Enero 16. Oficina de Correos en el ferrocarril entre Madruga, Empalme y Güines. La locomotora del tren número 21, descarriló en el paradero de Robles. Demora, 3 horas 45 minutos; sin novedad.

Enero 22. Oficina de Correos en el ferrocarril entre Macagua y Artemisal. El tren número 8 descarriló en el kilómetro 31, entre Macagua y San José de los Ramos. El coche en donde está la caseta de la correspondencia se volcó, con poco daño á la correspondencia. El empleado salió sin novedad.

Enero 31. Oficina de correos en el ferrocarril entre la Isabela y Caibarién. El tren número 10 descarriló á las 9 A. M. entre la Encrucijada y Mata. No hubo averías. Se hizo un trasbordo á otro tren que vino del Calabazar, llegando á la Isabela con 2 horas de retraso.

Febrero 4. Oficina de correos en el ferrocarril entre Cienfuegos y Congojas. El tren número 14, compuesto de 2 coches de pasajeros y 14 carros de carga vacíos, entre Palmira y Arriete, falló la carrilera y la locomotora descarriló, desviando los primeros seis carros de carga, dos de los cuales quedaron completamente destrozados. No hubo accidentes personales exceptuando la conmoción que recibió uno de los pasajeros. La oficina de correos del ferrocarril logró llegar á Arriete con la correspondencia, volviendo á Cienfuegos; á lomo hasta Palmira y de allí por la oficina de correos en el ferrocarril entre la Isabela y Cienfuegos. Se restableció el viaje normal al día siguiente.

Febrero 4. Una huelga de los empleados de Cárdenas y Júcaro ocurrió entre el 4 y 10 de Febrero inclusive. Los huelguistas obligaron á abandonar los trenes 3 y 6, entre Cárdenas y Santa Clara que sólo anduvieron entre Cárdenas y Jovellanos mientras duró la huelga, haciendo el servicio el oficial de correos en los trenes núms. 1 y 2. A éstos se les permitió andar sin interrupción el día 4 de Febrero. Durante el resto de la huelga, no obstante, solo se permitió andar una locomotora y el carro de la correspondencia. Las líneas postales por ferrocarriles y otros ramales del servicio, Cárdenas y Yaguaramas, Macagua y Artemisal, Máximo Gómez é Itabo, no sufrieron materialmente.

Marzo 22. Oficina de correos por ferrocarril entre Macagua y Artemisal. El tren de la Macagua al Artemisal descarriló entre los kilómetros 19 y 20 por haber fallado la carrilera. No hubo averías. El tren pasó para Cárdenas, llegando tarde para la combinación con la Habana.

Marzo 22. Oficina de correos por ferrocarril entre la Habana y Guanajay. El tren número 7 descarriló en el Rincón. Demorado 1 hora 37 minutos. No hubo novedad.

ERRORES COMETIDOS EN VARIAS OFICINAS DE CORREOS DE CUBA, EN LA DISTRIBUCION Y DESPACHO DE LA CORRESPONDENCIA SALIDA DE LAS MISMAS, DESDE JULIO 1º, 1900 Á JUNIO 30, 1901.

OFICINAS DE CORREOS.	Materia postal mal dirigida.	Paquetes cartas mal dirigidos.	OFICINAS DE CORREOS.	Materia postal mal dirigida.	Paquetes cartas mal dirigidos.
Aguacate	3		Manzanillo	117	2
Artemisa	7		Marianao	82	1
Aguada del Cura	4		Matanzas	141	1
Bainca	3		Mayarí	15	
Baracoa	11		Nuevitas	35	2
Batabanó	39		Palos	6	
Bayamo	9		Pinar del Río	37	
Bejucal	4		Placetas	12	
Caibarién	25	1	Puerto Padre	26	
Cárdenas	128	2	Puerto Príncipe	87	
Cartagena	4		Remedios	9	
Ciego de Avila	63		Rincón	7	1
Cifuentes	4		Rodas	18	
Cienfuegos	323	10	Sagua la Grande	117	
Caimanera	32		San Antonio de los Ba-		
Columbia Barracks	107	2	ños	6	
Dimas	5		Sancti Spíritus	58	
Gibara	44	6	Santa Clara	45	1
Guanabacoa	7		Santiago	362	4
Guanajay	36		Santo Domingo	6	
Guantánamo	267		Santiago de las Vegas	6	
Guara	6		Trinidad	33	
Güines	55		Tunas de Zaza	7	
Habana	1718	39	Santa Cruz del Sur	27	
Holguín	8		Sagua de Tánamo	26	
Jamaica	10		Vieja Bermeja	5	
Júcaro	56	1	Jaguajay	8	

De Vd. respetuosamente,

M. H. BUNN,

Jefe del Negociado de Conducción de Correspondencia.

INFORME

DEL

NEGOCIADO DE SELLOS Y MATERIALES.

DEPARTAMENTO DE CORREOS.

DEPARTAMENTO DE CORREOS DE CUBA,

NEGOCIADO DE SELLOS Y MATERIALES.

Habana, Julio 30 de 1901.

SEÑOR:

Tengo el honor de presentar el siguiente informe correspondiente al ejercicio vencido en Junio 30 de 1901. Los asuntos que competen á este negociado pueden dividirse en dos capítulos.

Primero: Los sellos, sobres timbrados, tarjetas postales, fajas de periódicos y sobres oficiales.

Segundo: Todos los demás artículos que facilita el Departamento de Correos á los Administradores.

Todos los sellos, sobres timbrados, tarjetas postales y fajas de periódicos destinados al servicio general, son facilitados por la deferencia del Sr. Administrador general de Correos de los Estados Unidos, proporcionando su obtención al Departamento de Correos mediante un costo nominal y proporcionando prontitud y seguridad en su entrega. La denominación de los sellos corrientes, especialmente impresos para el servicio de Cuba corresponde á los de un centavo, dos centavos, tres centavos, cinco centavos, diez centavos y los de diez centavos reparto especial. También los sobres de uno, dos y cinco centavos, y de dos y cinco centavos sobres número ocho y uno y dos centavos fajas número doce para periódicos. Se utilizan sellos postales de los Estados Unidos por alcance de uno, dos, cinco y diez centavos, que se reimprimen para el servicio postal de Cuba como se hace también con las tarjetas postales de los Estados Unidos de uno y dos centavos.

El siguiente estado demuestra el valor de los sellos, sobres timbrados, tarjetas y fajas postales existentes en 1º de Julio de 1900, el valor del material timbrado recibido por meses, el valor de lo expedido por meses á petición de los Administradores y la existencia en 30 de Junio de 1901.

ESTADO Nº 1.

El siguiente estado demuestra las ventas de todas clases de sellos, sobre timbrados, targetas postales y fajas de periódicos verificadas en cada mes durante el mismo período.

ESTADO Nº 2.

La disminución de la venta de los sellos comunes de cinco centavos desde el 1º de Abril de 1901, inclusive, se debe sin duda en gran parte al cambio del valor del franqueo entre los Estados Unidos y Cuba. Antes del 1º de Abril el valor del franqueo de cartas, era de 5 cts. por cada media onza ó fracción, y después de esa fecha se redujo á dos centavos por onza y fracción de la misma, produciéndose así menos pedidos de sellos de cinco centavos. Esta alteración de precio, sin duda, hizo decrecer la necesidad de usar tantos sellos postales pagaderos por correspondencia despachada con arreglo al franqueo de dos centavos, haciendo que una parte del franqueo se cobre aquí mediante el franqueo de sellos postales de alcance.

Hay un notable aumento en los pedidos del número 5, sobres de dos centavos y targetas postales de un centavo, de la conveniencia de lo cual se dá cuenta más y más cada mes.

REMESAS.

Todas las remesas de dinero procedentes de ventas de sellos, sobres timbrados, targetas postales y fajas de periódicos que efectúan los Administradores de la isla, van directamente á la Tesorería General de Cuba. No ingresa en este negocio cantidad alguna por ningún concepto, ni ha ingresado ninguna desde el 30 de Junio de 1900.

Las Administraciones de Correos de la Isla están divididas en dos clases con relación á obtener los sellos, sobres timbrados, etcétera, conocidas como Administraciones afianzadas y no afianzadas. Las afianzadas envían por la posta sus pedidos, sin remesar dinero, directamente al Departamento de Correos, negociado de sellos y materiales, y remesan á la Tesorería al fin de cada mes el importe total de los fondos postales existentes, acompañando la remesa de un estado demostrativo del estado de fondos de la Administración al vencimiento del mes.

Las Administraciones no afianzadas hacen los pedidos al Departamento de Correos de los sellos que necesitan periódicamente haciendo el pedido por conducto de la Tesorería de la Isla, acompañado de la remesa de fondos suficiente para satisfacer el pedido. Al recibir este pedido y los fondos, la Tesorería autoriza el comprobante anexo, dando recibo de la cantidad y pasa el pedido al Departamento de Correos, negociado de sellos y materiales, con lo cual se satisface el pedido inmediatamente y se pasa al administrador, sin demora, en pliego certificado.

Todos los administradores están en el caso de dar recibo al Interventor general y al Departamento de Correos de todos los efectos timbrados que reciban.

SOBRES OFICIALES CONMINATORIOS.

La concesión para el uso de sobres oficiales conminatorios ampliada por la Orden Militar núm. 108, á distintos empleados civiles de la Isla, se ha prestado á abuso, como se verá de la siguiente relación demostrativa de la cantidad de sobres de todos tamaños, confeccionados y facilitados por el Departamento de Correos.

No. 7,	*No. 10,*	*No. 11,*	*No. 14,*
92,550	270,000	57,000	10,000

Se piden los sobres por solicitud dirijida por correo á la Tesorería General, acompañada de la cantidad de dinero suficiente para pagarlos. El Tesorero certifica este requisito al Departamento de Correos en la misma forma que para los pedidos de sellos de los Administradores no afianzados, al confeccionarlos y enviarlos en pliego certificado seguidamente al empleado á quien corresponde. Se dán los sobres oficiales conminatorios al costo que tienen en el Departamento.

La contrata para la provisión de sobres conminatorios se adjudica por concurso, al postor que lo haga por ménos precio, y es el proveedor para todo el ejercicio.

La impresión de todos los libros y modelos se realiza de la misma manera, exceptuando que el surtido necesario, es menor y se convoca á concurso, según se agota el surtido.

SOBRES DE ENCARGOS ESPECIALES.

Los sobres de encargos especiales son dispuestos por los Administradores en la misma forma que los demás efectos timbrados. Al llegar un pedido á este Negociado, se envía al Sr. Administrador General de los Estados Unidos para satisfacerlo y al recibir los sobres de Washington en el Departamento, se pasan inmediatamente al Administrador que los pidió, en pliego certificado.

Una forma completemente nueva de modelos, estados, pedidos, etc., se llevó á cabo y se adoptó en 1º de Julio de 1900, la cual ha resultado una garantía contra los errores, y lo ha dado mejor que las usadas anteriormente.

OTROS MATERIALES.

Los materiales que usan los administradores en su despacho normal de los asuntos, son expedidos por este Negociado á solicitud de los administradores, y constan, generalmente, de los siguientes efectos: Estados, hojas y libros en blanco, buzones en la vía pública y llaves, valijas, cerraduras con llave, sellos de acero y de goma, marchamos y demás numerosos efectos de uso constante en el servicio postal.

Gracias á la atención por parte del Administrador General de Correos de los Estados Unidos, haciendo concesiones al departamento de Correos, podemos obtener al mismo precio los materiales de manos de los contratistas que surten á los Estados Unidos en el servicio de Correos. El señor Administrador General ha hecho facilitar la relación de los contratistas con los precios estipulados de varios efectos estampados en los mismos.

La siguiente relación demuestra el importe gastado por el Departamento de Correos en materiales para el servicio del pasado año y la clase de los mismos:

Efectos de escritorio é impresos	$	9,230.16
Marchamos y contraseñas		306.94
Buzones en la vía pública		433.00
Carros de correspondencia		500.00
Sacos de correspondencia		133.43
Menage		196.05
Construcciones y reparaciones		879.26
Varios		256.66
Total	$	11,937.50

Para mayor claridad, cábeme exponer que desde la organización del Departamento de Correos, se ha dotado de los siguientes elementos á las Administraciones, sobre lo cual paréceme que no se había informado hasta ahora:

EFECTOS.	Cantidad.
Llaves para buzones, serie "XX"	310
Cerraduras para buzones, serie "XX"	730
Llaves para buzones, serie "HH"	100
Cerraduras para buzones, serie "HH"	250
Cerraduras de Registro	50
Llaves de Registros	25
Cerraduras de Registro Internacional	5
Llaves de cerraduras de Registro Internacional	1
Cerraduras para valijas interiores por contratas	1,500
Llaves para cerraduras de valijas interiores por contrata	400
Valijas ordinarias núm. 3	300
,, ,, ,, 2	300
,, 4	150
,, ,, ,, 5	150
,, ,, ,, 3 clase B	100
Alforjas de cuero núm. 3	50
,, ,, combinación ,, 1	25
,, ,, ,, ,, 2	75
Valijas ordinarias oblongas núm. 3	100
Sacos para material de la 2ª, 3ª y 4ª clase	2,000
Sacos de lona para correspondencia extranjera núm. 1	50
,, ,, ,, ,, ,, ,, ,, 2	25
,, ,, ,, ,, .. 3	25

Valijas registro núm. 1.	9
" " " 2.	32
" " " 3.	33
Sacos regulares para correspondencia extranjera núm. 1..	1,000
" " " " " " 0..	900

Los buzones en la vía pública que se usan en la isla son del mismo tamaño y modelo que los del servicio en los Estados Unidos y están rotulados "U. S. Mail."

Atentamente,

El Jefe del Negociado de sellos y materiales,
GEORGE W. MARSHALL.

Director General,
M. C. FOSNES.

RELACION DEMOSTRATIVA DE LOS SELLOS Y SOBRES TIMBRADOS RECIBIDOS Y EXPEDIDOS POR EL NEGOCIADO DE SELLOS Y MATERIAL GENERAL, DURANTE EL EJERCICIO DE 1900–1901.

	Recibidos.	Expedidos.
Existencia en Julio 1º de 1900....	$ 176,596.35	
Julio.	50,000.00	$ 31,789.32
Agosto.	....	25,328.11
Septiembre.	57,237.50	28,054.83
" Pasado de la cuenta de existencias á la de material averiado.	....	31.93
Octubre.	40,053.00	38,552.60
Noviembre.	21,074.50	24,006.13
Diciembre.	40,063.60	24,847.39
Enero, 1901.	2,173.30	33,177.12
Febrero.	10.60	32,306.23
Marzo.	76,117.50	37,187.42
" Pasado de la cuenta de existencias á la de material averiado.	....	.15
" Sobrante de las existencias acumuladas.	.34	
Abril.	2,373,00	28.613.56
Mayo.	190.80	21,257.70
Junio.	40,021.20	21,306.21
" Pasado de la cuenta de existencias á la de material averiado.	....	21.20
" Balance.	....	149,431.80
	$ 505,911.70	$ 505,911.70

…s clases expedidos.

	…rero.	Marzo.	Abril.	Mayo.	Junio.	TOTAL.
Sellos d…	…0,362	336,963	299,829	293,436	457,205	3,995,171
	…54,569	885,115	809,032	569.416	584,651	8,545.858
"	9,925	7,892	23,245	12,225	11,430	119,941
"	…74,542	196,598	74.590	100,208	103,696	1,807,153
"	…30,462	34,240	32,175	3,250	6,010	285,755
"	2.375	3,495	3.350	2,765	1,865	38,635
"	402	800	2,100	250	....	22,697
Sobres…	…15,403	33,425	43,100	28,800	17,550	318,886
"	2,002	2,550	1,250	1,600	150	24.385
"	101	850	....	....	....	3,158
"	1,901	4,100	3,300	1.075	2,000	34,297
"	…16,676	15,535	13,860	13,125	10,200	167,360
Tarjet…	1,696	2,650	600	....	....	18,505
"	601	1,000	3,000	250	2,500	13,506
Fajas …	601	....	1,000	....	50	7,031
"	4.531	6.122	2,550	2,300	3,475	58.535
Sellos …	…10.130	11,610	3,425	1,710	2,325	90,594
"	3.250	6,388	620	525	1,040	40,242
"	3,920	4,320	525	202	600	31,200
"						
	…306.23	$ 37,187.42	$ 28.613.56	$ 21,257.70	$ 21,306.21	$ 356,426.62

INFORME

DEL

NEGOCIADO DE GIROS Y CERTIFICADOS,

CORRESPONDIENTE AL AÑO FISCAL VENCIDO EN

30 DE JUNIO DE 1901.

DEPARTAMENTO DE CORREOS DE CUBA,

NEGOCIADO DE GIROS Y CERTIFICADOS.

Septiembre 23, 1901.

Sr. Director General de Correos,
Habana, Cuba.

SEÑOR:

Tengo el honor de acompañar el siguiente informe de las operaciones efectuadas en el Negociado de Giros y Certificados, durante el ejercicio vencido en 30 de Junio de 1901.

INFORME SOBRE GIROS.

Número de giros librados en las oficinas del ramo por trimestres:

	Número.	Importe.
Trimestre vencido en Sept. 30, 1900.....	19,401	$1.679,462.92
,, ,, ,, Dic. 31, 1900.....	21,369	646,271.50
,, ,, Marzo 30, 1901.....	20,967	623,045.11
,, ,, Junio 30, 1901.....	21,370	618,741.71
Total.......................	83,107	$2.567,521.24

Giros pagados por trimestre:

	Número	Importe
Trimestre vencido en Sept. 30, 1900......	10,718	$ 443,672.43
,, ,, ,, Dicb. 31, 1900......	11,511	404,396.77
,, ,, Mrz. 30, 1901..... ..	12,071	430,860.57
,, ,, Jun. 30, 1901......	11,991	409,417.78
Total..............	46,291	$1.688,347.55

Giros internacionales librados en Cuba y pagaderos en los Estados Unidos, conforme á las listas de cambios del correo de la Habana:

TRIMESTRE VENCIDO EN SEPTIEMBRE 30, 1900.

No. de la lista	Fecha de la lista.	Número del giro	Importe del giro.
1	Julio 7, 1900	900	$ 26,501.33
2	,, 14, 1900.........	800	24,698.00
3	,, 21, 1900	700	21,140.77
4	,, 28, 1900	400	11,961.43
5	Agosto 4, 1900........	700	22,160.39
6	,, 11, 1900..	800	22,780.23
7	,, 18, 1900.........	650	19,956.68
8	,, 25, 1900.........	550	14,549.82
9	Septiembre 1º, 1900	600	21,037.60
10	,, 8, 1900........	800	21,145.75
11	,, 15, 1900	700	20,263.71
12	,, 22, 1900.........	600	16,894.47
12	,, 29, 1900.........	650	25,470.93
	Total..................	8,850	$268,561.11

TRIMESTRE VENCIDO EN DICIEMBRE 31, 19 0.

No. de la lista	Fecha de la lista.	Número del giro.	Importe del giro.
14	Octubre 6, 1900	650	$ 19,956.40
15	,, 13, 1900	700	19,167.72
16	,, 20, 1900...........	700	17,095.83
17	,, 27, 1900........ ..	500	11,350.99
18	Noviembre 3, 1900	750	20,870.86
19	,, 10, 1900......	700	16,344.87
20	,, 17, 1900..	700	18,084.90
21	,, 24, 1900........ ..	650	14,961.75
22	Diciembre 1, 1900	600	13,752.57
23	,, 8, 1900........ ..	906	23,228.10
24	,, 15, 1900........ ..	961	18,945.44
25	,, 22, 1900	1,007	22,779.56
26	,, 31, 1900...........	797	18.878.50
	Total..................	9,621	$235,417.49

TRIMESTRE VENCIDO EN MARZO 30, 1901.

No. de la lista	Fecha de la lista.	Número del giro.	Importe del giro
27	Enero 12, 1901...........	1,129	$ 28,711.01
28	,, 19, 1901...........	742	15,333.28
29	,, 26, 1901...........	658	12,940.22
30	Febrero 2, 1901..	700	16,844.90
31	,, 9, 1901..	700	15,281,23
32	,, 16, 1901....... ...	703	15,656.13
33	,, 23, 1901...........	664	14,691.41
	Suma y sigue	....	....

No. de la lista	Fecha de la lista.		Número del giro.	Importe del giro.
		Suma anterior	....	....
34	Marzo	2, 1901	765	17,946.38
35	,,	9, 1901	664	13,731.14
36	,,	16, 1901	851	17,131.95
37	,,	23, 1901	559	10,452.16
38	,,	30, 1901	661	16,603.91
		Total	8,796	$195,323.73

No. de la lista	Fecha de la lista.		Número del giro.	Importe del giro.
39	Abril	6, 1901	716	$ 17,969.27
40	,,	13, 1901	811	14,945.40
41	,,	20, 1901	595	12,265.02
42	,,	27, 1901	554	10,820.71
43	Mayo	4, 1901	811	21,000.00
44	,,	11, 1901	753	16,070.02
45	,,	18, 1901	780	16,639.60
46	,,	25, 1901	606	15,164.97
47	Junio	1, 1901	550	13,998.94
48	,,	8, 1901	779	17,927.24
49	,,	15, 1901	899	22,151.51
50	,,	22, 1901	652	14,208.48
51	,,	29, 1901	771	19,045.98
		Total	9,277	$ 212,207.11
	Total general		36,544	$ 911,509.44

Número de giros internacionales pagados por trimestre:

	Numero pagado.	Importe pagado.
Trimestre vencido en Septiembre 30, 1900.	1,269	$ 28,078.48
,, ,, en Diciembre 31, 1900.	1,309	32,770.91
,, en Marzo 30, 1901.	1,363	39,650.15
,, en Junio 30, 1901.	1,519	50,068.14
Total	5,460	$ 150,567.68

Número de giros internacionales de Cuba reembolsados por trimestre:

	Numero pagado.	Importe pagado.
Trimestre vencido en Septiembre 30, 1900.	71	$ 1,668.07
,, ,, ,, Diciembre 31, 1900.	101	2,002.77
,, ,, Marzo 30, 1901.	82	1,727.20
,, ,, Junio 30, 1901.	90	1,914.08
Total	344	$ 7,312.12

Número de giros postales de los Estados Unidos devueltos para su reembolso, por. trimestre:

	NUMERO.	IMPORTE.
Trimestre vencido en Septiembre 30, 1900.	5	$ 38.50
,, ,, ,, Diciembre 31, 1900.	17	264.75
,, ,, Marzo 30, 1901.	19	426.25
,, ,, Junio 30, 1901.	28	776.50
Total....................	69	$ 1,506.00

Número de giros internacionales pagaderos en Puerto Rico, conforme á lo certificado por la Oficina de Cambios de la Habana, por trimestre:

	NUMERO.	IMPORTE.
Trimestre vencido en Septiembre 30, 1900.	46	$ 641.28
,, ,, ,, Diciembre 31, 1900.	55	766.54
,, ,, Marzo 30, 1901.	43	662.78
,, ,, Junio 30. 1901.	96	1,986,43
Total....................	240	$ 4,057.03

Número de giros librados en Puerto Rico sobre Cuba, conforme á las listas de cambio de la Oficina de Puerto Rico, por trimestre:

Trimestre vencido en Septiembre 30, 1900.	42	$ 1,324.33
,, ,, ,, Diciembre 31, 1900.	56	2,960.37
,, ,, Marzo 30, 1901.	56	3,279.27
,, ,, Junio 30, 1901.	59	2,133.68
Total....................	213	$ 9,697.65

Número de giros librados en Cuba sobre Puerto Rico, reembolzados por trimestre.

Trimestre vencido en Septiembre 30, 1900...	1	$ 25.00
,, ,, ,, Diciembre 31, 1900...	....	....
,, ,, ,, Marzo 30, 1901...	3	53.50
,, ,, ,, Junio 30, 1901...	4	92.00
Total......................	8	$ 170.50

Número de giros librados en Puerto Rico sobre Cuba. Avisos devueltos para reembolsos, por trimestre:

Trimestre vencido en Septiembre 30, 1900...	....	....
,, ,, ,, Diciembre 31, 1900 ..	....	....
,, ,, ,, Marzo 30, 1901...	1	$ 20.00
,, ,, ,, Junio 30, 1901...	2	1.75
Total	3	$ 21.75

Giros duplicados librados durante el ejercicio vencido en 30 de Junio de 1901:

Interiores	188
Internacionales...	183
Total	371

Oficinas de giro y estaciones establecidas en

	Oficinas.	Estaciones.
Septiembre 30, 1900...........	11	79
Diciembre 31, 1900...........	11	85
Marzo 30, 1901......	10	94
Junio 30, 1901...........	10	94

Gabelas devengadas por giros librados en Cuba durante el ejercicio vencido en 30 de Junio de 1901. Por trimestre.

			Importe.
Trimestre vencido en	Septiembre	30, 1900..	$ 3,362.22
,, ,, ,,	Diciembre	31, 1900..	3,345 65
,, ,,	Marzo	30, 1901..	3,203.64
,, ,,	Junio	30, 1901..	3,232.50
	Total.......		$ 13,144.01

Durante el ejercicio vencido en 30 de Junio de 1901 se pasaron al crédito del Administrador general de los Estados Unidos en la cuenta de giros, los fondos de los mismos que ascendieron á $756,318.11 que se llevaron á cabo sin costo de cambio para el Gobierno.

Al cerrar este informe es de llamarse especialmente la atención á las diversas causas de la notable disminución de los giros postales durante el ejercicio vencido en 30 de Junio, 1901, comparado con el de 1900.

Las órdenes que se pusieron en vigor durante el ejercicio de 1900, limitandó la venta de giros postales extranjeros sobre la Isla de Cuba á cinco por un remitente á un destinatario, el aumento de la gabela sobre giros internacionales de 30 á 50 centavos por 100 pesos, y la aceptación de la moneda corriente americana solamente en pago de giros sobre los Estados Unidos, y Puerto Rico, han continuado en vigor durante el año de 1901. El resultado ha sido que el sistema de giros no se ha adoptado tan extensamente en ninguna época durante el año por las empresas bancarias y comerciales como un medio de realizar el cambio con los Estados Unidos, como sucedía en el primer semestre del ejercicio de 1900. Los giros internacionales despachados, lo fueron por pequeñas cantidades. El número de soldados americanos, los americanos empleados en el Gobierno de Cuba y los que en Cuba tienen negocios, ha sido más reducido en el año último que en el anterior. Esto ha afectado grande-mente los giros entre Cuba y los Estados Unidos; lo que especialmente se ha notado en las poblaciones guarnecidas por las tropas. En algunos casos después de relevadas, los giros con los Estados Unidos casi no llegaron á nada. Cuando se piensa en que la mayoría de los comerciantes en todas las poblaciones cubanas son españoles, cuyos negocios son casi exclusivamente con España, el efecto de los americanos en Cuba sobre los giros con los Estados Unidos no tiene nada de particular.

Antes de Julio 1º 1900, se remesaban los fondos insulares valiéndose del sistema de los giros. Cuando uno toma en cuenta el hecho de que la mayoría de las oficinas más importantes de Cuba corría con las transacciones interiores de los giros de esta clase recibidos y pagados por las mismas en sumas de $30,000 á $60,000 mensualmente, se cae con facilidad en la cuenta del efecto producido por la orden relativa á giros interiores que se agrega á continuación:

Nº 246.

CUARTEL GENERAL DIVISION DE CUBA.

Habana, Junio 22, 1900.

El Gobernador General de Cuba ha tenido á bien disponer la publicación de la siguiente orden:

I. Desde el 1º de Julio de 1900, la remisión de fondos de la isla, cuando excedan de $300.00, dejará de hacerse por medio de giros postales, enviando dichos fondos por correo certificado.

II. Al enviar dinero por correo certificado, el remitente lo deberá asegurar en un fuerte paquete ó paquetes, contará el contenido y sellará debidamente cada paquete en presencia de un testigo, cuya firma junto con la del remitente deberá aparecer en cado paquete. La persona que reciba tales fondos en paquetes certificados los abrirá y contará el contenido ante el Administrador de Correos, teniendo cuidado de abrir el paquete de tal modo que el sello quede intacto, y si faltare dinero, el Administrador de Correos que haya recibido el paquete, pondrá el hecho en conocimiento del Administrador de Correos que lo haya remitido y del Departamento de Correos de la Habana.

III. Quedan por la presente derogadas todas las órdenes é instrucciones vigentes que contravengan lo arriba dispuesto.

El Comandante de Estado Mayor,

J. B. Hickey,

Ayudante General interino.

No obstante la disminución de los giros postales, debida á las causas arriba expresadas, es satisfactorio saber, que las oficinas de giros, debido á su situación, no han sufrido por dichas causas, en lo general han aumentado en cuanto á giros realizados, y esto puede asegurarse respecto á utilizar el sistema de giros el pueblo cubano para las pequeñas sumas y para otros negocios en general por medio de las oficinas de giros.

DEPARTAMENTO DE CORREOS DE CUBA,

NEGOCIADO DE GIROS Y CERTIFICADOS.

Septiembre 23, 1900.

INFORME SOBRE LOS CERTIFICADOS.

CAMBIO DE VALIJAS CERTIFICADAS.

Durante el ejercicio vencido en Junio 30, 1901, se establecieron dos cambios de valijas certificadas, como resulta de la siguiente relación:

Entre Matanzas y la Habana, establecido en Abril 13, 1899; cambio doce veces al día y una vez el domingo.

Entre Cienfuegos y la Habana, establecido en Abril 14, 1899; cambio diario.

Entre Santiago y la Habana, establecido en Marzo 2, 1899; cambio semanal.

Entre Cárdenas y la Habana, establecido en Junio 1º 1899; cambio diario.

Entre Pinar del Río y la Habana, establecido en Agosto 14, 1899; cambio diario.

Entre Santa Clara y la Habana, en Septiembre 22, 1899; cambio diario.

Entre Caibarién y la Habana, establecido en Octubre 16, 1899; cambio diario.

Entre Sagua la Grande y la Habana, establecidos en Abril 1, 1900; cambio diario.

Entre Barracas de Columbia y la Habana, establecido en Febrero 13, 1901, cambio; de las Barracas de Columbia á la Habana, diario, excepto el domingo; de la Habana á las Barracas de Columbia, diario excepto los lunes.

Entre Cienfuegos y Júcaro, establecido Mayo 13, 1901, cambio semanal.

CAMBIO INTERIOR DE VALIJAS CERTIFICADAS.

Entre Marianao y la Habana, establecido en Enero 13, 1899; cambio diario.

Entre Puerto Príncipe y la Habana, establecido en Abril 11, 1899; cambio irregular.

Entre Gibara y la Habana, establecido en Agosto 8, 1899; cambio irregular.

Entre Nuevitas y la Habana, establecido en Agosto 8, 1899; cambio irregular.

CAMBIOS CON EL EXTRANJERO DE CORRESPONDENCIA CERTIFICADA.

Los siguientes cambios se efectuaron en el Correo de la Habana:

Cambios de valijas certificadas internacionales con New York, Jacksonville y Port Tampa. Se despachan en lunes, miércoles y viernes de cada semana.

Valija sellada cambio:

Vía New York: Expediciones los lunes, miércoles y viernes de cada semana........	Irun .... Madrid.	España.
	Ver-Cologne ..	Alemania.
	Londres	Inglaterra.
	París............	Francia.
	Ponce......... San Juan.....	Puerto Rico.

Valija sellada, cambio:

Directo: Expediciones irregulares dos veces al mes...........	Madrid........ Cádiz. .... Coruña........ Santander...	España.

Valija sellada, cambio:

Directo: Expediciones irregulares de 5 á 7 veces al mes..................	Méjico .... Veracruz..... Progreso	Méjico.

Valija sellada, cambio:

Directo: Dos expediciones al mes.....	San Juan.... Ponce.........	Puerto Rico.

Valija sellada, cambio:

Expeciones directas mensuales.. .... Expediciones vía New York, tres á la semana.................	Colombia. Puerto Cabello. Guiara. Barranquilla. Colón. Cartagena. Puerto Limón. Santo Tomás. Santo Domingo.

Valija sellada, cambio:
Expediciones, tres á la semana .... Cayo Hueso.

Los siguientes cambios se efectúan con el Correo de Santiago de Cuba:

Valija internacional, cambio con New York y Jacksonville; expediciones de Santiago los lunes; establecida Octubre 24, 1900.

ESTADISTICA DE CERTIFICADOS.

La estadistica referente al movimiento de certificados to todas las oficinas de correos durante el ejercicio vencido en Junio 30. 1901, es como sigue:

Cartas certificadas para el extrangero......	76,117
Paquetes ,, ,, ,, ...	7,090
Cartas del interior certificadas....................	64,170
Paquetes ,, ,, ...	7,687
Pagado por importe de certificados.....................	155,074
Materia postal certificado gratis......................	31,444
Total de certificados, pagados y gratis.................	186,518

Estadística del movimiento de certificados por trimestre durante el ejercicio vencido en Junio 30, 1901:

TRIMESTRE VENCIDO EN SEPTIEMBRE 30, 1901.

Cartas, interior	12,774
Paquetes, interior	1,312
Cartas, extranjero	16,203
Paquetes, extranjero	1,369
Material oficial	7.201
Total	38,859

TRIMESTRE VENCIDO EN DICIEMBRE 31, 1900.

Cartas, interior	15,669
Paquetes, interior	1,628
Cartas, extranjero	17,937
Paquetes, extranjero	1,444
Material oficial	7,947
Total	44,625
	38,859
	83,484

TRIMESTRE VENCIDO EN MARZO 31, 1901.

Cartas, interior	16,947
Paquetes, interior	1,940
Cartas, extranjero	22,521
Paquetes, extranjero	2,278
Material oficial	7,997
Total	51,483

TRIMESTRE VENCIDO EN JUNIO 30, 1901.

Cartas, interior	18,780
Paquetes, interior	2,817
Cartas, extranjero	19,456
Paquetes, extranjero	1,999
Material oficial	8,499
Total	51,551
	51,483
	103,034

La Orden No. 7 empezó á regir desde 1º de Abril inclusive, por la cual el valor de los certificados se redujo de 10 centavos á 8 centavos.

Total por trimestre de la materia postal registrada pagado su valor:

Septiembre	30, 1900	31,658	$ 3,165.80
Diciembre	31, 1900	36,678	3,667.80
Marzo	31, 1901	43,686	4,368.60
Junio	30, 1901	43,052	3,444.16
		155,074	$ 14,646.36

Aumento sobre el ejercicio vencido en Junio 30, 1900, de 27,360 efectos certificados pagados y producto de su valor.

Atentamente,

El Jefe del Negociado de Giros y Certificados,

C. L. Marine,

INFORME

DE LA

OFICINA DE PAGOS.

DEPARTAMENTO DE CORREOS.

Habana, Julio 25, 1901.

Al Director General

del Departamento

SEÑOR:

En lo que respecta al informe correspondiente al año vencido en 30 de Junio de 1901, tengo el honor de acompañar adjuntas relaciones pormenorizadas de las operaciones de esta oficina durante dicho año.

Mis cuentas fueron examinadas dos veces durante el año. Comprendiendo el día 29 de Enero de 1901, por el Comandante R. H. Rolfe, Inspector General, y comprendiendo el día 6 de Mayo de 1901, por el comandante B. K. Roberts, de Artillería, Inspector General interino. El coronel G. H. Burton, Inspector General, acaba de completar una inspección en el día de hoy.

Atentamente,

El Oficial Pagador del Departamento

de Correos de Cuba,

W. H. BUCHANAN.

INGRESOS Y EGRESOS: **JULIO, 1900.**

	CONCEPTO.	Ejercicio 1899.	Ejercicio 1900.	Ejercicio 1901.	TOTAL.
	Ingresos:				
Julio 18	Consignación		$23,622.17	$39,637.12	$ 63,259.29
Julio 21	Consignación	$ 508.87	29,058.48		29,567.35
	Total	$ 508.87	$52,680.65	$39,637.12	$ 92,826.64
	Egresos:				
	Haberes:				
	Departamento de Correos		$ 263.73	$ 5,857.31	$ 6,121.04
	Empleados en las administraciones		4,563.55	5,776.37	10,339.92
	Administradores		11,112.35	303.26	11,415.61
	Oficiales de correos		1,559.39	640.22	2,199.61
	Carteros		3,646.12	3,158.92	6,805.04
	Impresos y efectos de escritorio		1,343.43	30.00	1,373.43
	Alquileres		177.50		177.50
	Alumbrado		477.84		477.84
	Dietas		352.00		352.00
	Conducción		2,180.83		2,180.83
	Construcciones y reparaciones		68.00		68.00
	Contratas vías interiores		3,214.61		3,214.61
	Mensajeros postales		717.79		717.79
	Varios conceptos		226.49	394.06	620.55
	Total de egresos		$29,903.63	$16,160.14	$ 46,063.77
Julio 31	Saldo á la cuenta de Agosto	$ 508.87	22,777.02	23,476.98	46,762.87
	Total	$ 508.87	$52,680.65	$39,637.12	$ 92,826.64

INGRESOS Y EGRESOS: AGOSTO, 1900.

	CONCEPTO.	Ejercicio 1899.	Ejercicio 1900.	Ejercicio 1901.	TOTAL.
	Ingresos:				
Agosto 1	Saldo de Julio	$ 508.87	$22,777.02	$23,476.98	$ 48,762.87
Agosto 9	Consignaciones		2,649.77		2,649.77
Agosto 18	Consignaciones			43,642.73	43,642.73
	Total	$ 508.87	$25,426.79	$67,119.71	$ 93,055.37
	Egresos:				
	Haberes: Departamento de correos		$ 914.82	$ 6,810.79	$ 7,725.61
	Empleados de las administraciones		203.41	9,575.54	9,778.95
	Administradores	$ 25.00	1,049.85	9,783.65	10,858.50
	Oficiales de correos		75.09	2,129.60	2,204.69
	Carteros		289.59	6,528.85	6.818.44
	Impresos y efectos de escritorio		1,697.11	553.04	2,250.15
	Menaje		83.00	15.00	98.00
	Alquileres		2,071.79	399.24	2,471.03
	Alumbrado		295.64	297.81	593.45
	Dietas		572.00	584.00	1,156.00
	Réditos de fianzas		1,038.86		1,038.86
	Material general		50.63		50.63
	Periódicos		3.00	7.50	10.50
	Conducción de la correspondencia		7,208.56	2,340.07	9,548.63
	Valijas		746.65	38.76	785.41
	Pesadores de cartas		279.59		279.59
	Marchamos y contraseñas		69.40	18.25	87.65
	Buzones		422.50		422.50
	Conducción		32.80	62.00	94.80
	Construcciones y reparaciones		126.19	122.60	248.79
	Contratas, vías interiores		299.03	2,083.73	2,382.76
	Mensajeros postales		5.05	637.91	642.96
	Varios conceptos		1,079.15	821.20	1,900.35
	Total egresos	$ 25.00	$18,613.71	$42,809.54	$ 61,448.25
Agosto 31	Saldo en la cuenta de Septiembre	483.87	6,813.08	24,310.17	31,607.12
	Total	$ 508.87	$25,426.79	$67,119.71	$ 93,055.37

INGRESOS Y EGRESOS: SEPTIEMBRE, 1900.

	CONCEPTO.	Ejercicio 1899.	Ejercicio 1900.	Ejercicio 1901.	TOTAL
	Ingresos:				
Septiembre 1	Saldo de Agosto	$ 483.87	6,813.08	$24,310.17	$31,607.12
Septiembre 18	Consignaciones	5,245.24	6,788.13	40,319.17	52,352.54
Septiembre 18	Consignaciones			237.00	237.00
	Total	$ 5,729.11	$13,601.21	$64,866.34	$84,196.66
	Egresos:				
	Haberes: Departamento de Correos		$ 131.87	$ 5,933.75	$ 6,065.62
	Empleados de las Administraciones		2.31	6,705.10	6,707.41
	Administradores	24.72	665.24	4,661.08	5,351.04
	Oficiales de Correos			1,305.30	1,305.30
	Carteros	23.74	3.06	4,279.88	4,306.68
	Impresos y efectos de escritorio	91 71	303.32	1,019.93	1,414.96
	Telégrafos y cable		76.25		76.25
	Menaje			8.50	8.50
	Alquileres	30.00	432.74	621.41	1,084.15
	Alumbrado		40.00	317.51	357.51
	Dietas		228.00	652 00	880.00
	Material general			235.00	235.00
	Periódicos		19.00		19.00
	Conducción de correspondencia		12.00	2,564.16	2,576.16
	Valijas			1,052.04	1,052.04
	Conducción		22.45	3.06	25.51
	Marchamos y contraseñas			67.05	67.05
	Buzones			13.40	13.40
	Construcciones y reparaciones		164.50	107.88	272.38
	Contrata vías interiores		100.00	1,978.65	2,078.65
	Mensajeros postales			210.23	210.23
	Conceptos varios		721.58	904.99	1,626.57
	Total egresos	$ 170.17	$ 2,922.32	$32,640.92	$35,733.41
Septiembre 30	Saldo en la cuenta de Octubre	5,558.94	$10,678.89	$32,225.42	$48,463.25
	Total	$ 5,729.11	$13,601.21	$64,866.34	$84,196.66

INGRESOS Y EGRESOS: OCTUBRE, 1900.

	CONCEPTO.	Ejercicio 1899.	Ejercicio 1900.	Ejercicio 1901.	TOTAL.
	Ingresos:				
Octubre 1	Saldo de Septiembre	$ 5,558.94	$ 10,678.89	$ 32,225.42	$ 48,463.25
Octubre 15	Consignación		490.44	39,339.66	39,830.10
	Total	$ 5,558.94	$ 11,169.33	$ 71,565.08	$ 88,293.35
	Egresos:				
	Haberes:				
	Departamento de correos		$	$ 7,372.40	$ 7,372.40
	Empleados en las Administraciones			7,822.82	7,822.82
	Administradores		114.86	7,456.70	7,571.56
	Oficiales de correos			1,796.85	1,796.85
	Carteros		54.29	5,515.41	5,569.70
	Telégrafo y cable		16.87		16.87
	Impresos y artículos de escritorio		22.25	854.88	877.13
	Menaje		25.00	32.50	57.50
	Alquileres		80.00	773.47	853.47
	Alumbrado		25.60	343.22	368.82
	Dietas			548.00	548.00
	Conducción de correspondencia		2,674.00	3,638.66	6,312.66
	Marchamos y contraseñas		67.25	27.79	95.04
	Conducción			30.00	30.00
	Cajas de caudales		75.28		75.28
	Construcciones y reparaciones			121.34	121.34
	Contrata vías interiores		58.18	2,126.63	2,184.81
	Mensajeros postales			437.86	437.86
	Conceptos varios		62.19	982.60	1,044.79
	Total de egresos		$ 3,275.77	$39,881.13	$ 43,156.90
Octubre 31	Saldo en la cuenta de Noviembre	5,558.94	7,893.56	31,683.95	45,136.45
	Total	$ 5,558.94	$ 11,169.33	$ 71,565.08	$ 88,293.35

INGRESOS Y EGRESOS: **NOVIEMBRE, 1900.**

	CONCEPTOS.	Ejercicio 1899.	Ejercicio 1900.	Ejercicio 1901.	TOTAL
	Ingresos:				
Noviembre 1	Saldo de Octubre	$ 5,558.94	$ 7,893.56	$31,683.95	$ 45,136.45
Noviembre 30	Consignaciones		177.46		177.46
Noviembre 30	Consignaciones		2,012.46	37,079.07	39,091.53
	Total	$ 5,558.94	$10,083.48	$68,763 02	$ 84,405.44
	Egresos:				
	Haberes.				
	Departamento de correos			$ 6,075.69	$ 6,075.69
	Empleados de las Administraciones			6,516.09	6,516.09
	Administradores		$ 35.26	7,043.20	7,078.46
	Oficiales de correos			1,679.70	1,679.70
	Carteros			4,979.28	4,979.28
	Impresos y efectos de escritorio			460.54	460.54
	Menaje		15.81	4.00	19.81
	Alquiler		208.16	886.80	1,094.96
	Alumbrado			403.87	403.87
	Dietas			532.00	532.00
	Periódicos		121.85		121.85
	Conducción de correspondencia			2,902.29	2,902.29
	Marchamos y contraseñas			22.86	22.86
	Cajas de caudales		9.00	3.00	12.00
	Conducción			8.42	8.42
	Construcciones y reparaciones		10.04	52.00	62.04
	Contrata vías interiores			2,099.79	2,099.79
	Mensajeros postales		2.53	300.46	302.99
	Conceptos varios		145.24	861.92	1,007.16
	Total egresos		$ 547.89	$34,831.91	$ 35,379.80
Noviembre 30	Saldo de la cuenta de Diciembre	$ 5,558.94	9,535.59	33,931.11	49,025.64
	Total	$ 5,558.94	$10,083.48	$68,763.02	$ 84,405.44

INGRESOS Y EGRESOS. DICIEMBRE, 1900.

	CONCEPTO:	Ejercicio 1899.	Ejercicio 1900.	Ejercicio 1901.	TOTAL.
	Ingresos:				
Diciembre 1	Saldo de Noviembre	$ 5,558.94	$ 9,535.59	$33,931.11	$ 49,025.64
Diciembre 26	Consignación		2,070.75	38,070.18	40,140.93
	Total	$ 5,558.94	$11,606.34	$72,001.29	$ 89,166.57
	Egresos:				
	Haberes:				
	Departamento de Correos			$ 6,705.81	$ 6,705.81
	Empleados de las Administraciones		2.69	7,121.04	7,123.73
	Administradores		12.36	6,771.34	6,783.70
	Oficiales de Correos			1,674 68	1,674.68
	Carteros			4,986.88	4,986.88
	Impresos y efectos de escritorio			825.19	825.19
	Menaje			72.70	72.70
	Alquiler		99.00	604.56	703.56
	Alumbrado		31.20	396.95	428.15
	Dietas			468 00	468.00
	Réditos de fianzas		117.85		117.85
	Material general			42 00	42.00
	Conducción de correspondencia		1,910.00	2,852.95	4,762.95
	Marchamos y contraseñas		3.15	76.77	79 92
	Cajas de caudales		2,050.48	35.99	2,086.45
	Construcciones y reparaciones			91.84	91.84
	Contrata vias interiores			2,330.91	2,330.91
	Mensajeros postales		5,34	338 93	344.27
	Varios conceptos		41.53	871.09	912.62
	Total egresos		$ 4,273.58	$ 36,267.63	$ 40,541.21
Diciembre 31	Saldo en la cuenta de Enero	$ 5,558.94	7,332.76	35,733.66	48,625 36
	Total	$ 5,558.94	$11,606.34	$72,001.29	$ 89,166.57

INGRESOS Y EGRESOS: **ENERO, 1901.**

	CONCEPTO.	Ejercicio 1899.	Ejercicio 1900.	Ejercicio 1901.	TOTAL.
	Ingresos:				
Enero 1	Saldo de Diciembre	$ 5,558.94	$ 7,332.76	$35,733.66	$48,625.36
Enero 29	Consignación		39.69	36,303.35	36,343.04
Enero 31	Consignación		5,163.12	5,163.12	10,326.24
	Total	$ 5,558.94	$12,535.57	$77,200.13	$95,294,64
	Egresos:				
	Haberes:				
	Departamento de Correos			$ 6,297.48	$ 6,297.48
	Empleados de las Administraciones		$ 28.02	7,436.04	7,464.06
	Administradores		18.28	7,617.60	7,635.88
	Oficiales de Correos			1,836.06	1,836 06
	Carteros			5,464.04	5,464.04
	Telégrafos y cable	$ 261.95			261.96
	Impresos y efectos de escritorio			550.41	550.41
	Menaje			12.50	12.50
	Alquiler			874.22	874.22
	Alumbrado		4.00	461 89	465.89
	Dietas			524.00	524.00
	Material general			7.00	7.00
	Conducción de correspondencia	5,169.37	10,332.52	8,178.11	23,680,00
	Marchamos y contraseñas			30.00	30.00
	Cajas de caudales			33.63	33.63
	Construcciones y reparaciones			80.48	80.48
	Contratas vías interiores			2,059.39	2,059.39
	Mensajeros postales			405.86	405.86
	Conceptos varios			751,27	751.27
	Total egresos	$ 5,431.33	$10 382.82	$42,619.98	$58,434.13
Enero 31	Saldo en la cuenta de Febrero	127.61	2,152.75	34,580.15	36,860.51
	Total	$ 5,558.94	$12,535.57	$77,200.13	$95,294.64

INGRESOS Y EGRESOS: FEBRERO, 1901.

	CONCEPTO.	Ejercicio 1899.	Ejercicio 1900.	Ejercicio 1901.	TOTAL.
	Ingresos:				
Febrero 1º	Saldo de Enero	$ 127.61	$ 2,152.75	$34,580.15	$ 36,860.51
Febrero 21	Consignación			670.00	670.00
Febrero 28	Consignación	16.92	32.70	36,377.08	36,426.70
	Total	$ 144.53	$ 2,185.45	$71,627.23	$ 73,957.21
	Egresos:				
	Haberes.				
	Departamento de Correos			$ 6,333.07	$ 6,333.07
	Empleados de las Administraciones			6,690.27	6,690.27
	Administradores		$ 35.44	7,943.31	7,978.75
	Oficiales de Correos			1,783.25	1,783.25
	Carteros			5,099.88	5,099.88
	Impresos y efectos de escritorio			3.64	3.64
	Menaje			15.50	15.50
	Alquiler			405.94	405.94
	Alumbrado			439.06	439.06
	Dietas			796.00	796.00
	Réditos de fianzas			670.00	670.00
	Conducción de correspondencia	$ 14.66	29.32	3,954.41	3,998.39
	Marchamos y contraseñas			10.36	10.36
	Cajas de caudales			11.00	11.00
	Conducción			33.53	33.53
	Construcciones y reparaciones			73.30	73.30
	Contratas, vías interiores			2,295.42	2,295.42
	Mensajeros postales			421.57	421.57
	Conceptos varios		5.00	781.28	786.28
	Total egresos	$ 14.66	$ 69.76	$37,760.79	$37,845.21
Febrero 28	Saldo en la cuenta de Marzo	129.87	2,115.69	33,866.44	36,112.00
	Total	$ 144.53	$ 2,185.45	$71,627.23	$ 73,957.31

INGRESOS Y EGRESOS: MARZO. 1901.

	CONCEPTO.	Ejercicio 1899.	Ejercicio 1900.	Ejercicio 1901.	TOTAL.
	Ingresos:				
Marzo 1	Saldo de Febrero	$ 129.87	$ 2,115.69	$33,866.44	$ 36,112.00
Marzo 29	Consignaciones		283.97	33,335.08	33,819.05
	Total	$ 129.87	$ 2,399.66	$67,401.52	$ 69,931.05
	Egresos:				
	Haberes:				
	Departamento de correos		$ 10.38	$ 6,287.62	$ 6,298.00
	Empleados en las administraciones			5,911.25	5,911.25
	Admistradores		57.44	6,454.14	6,511.58
	Oficiales de correos			1,608 32	1,608.32
	Carteros			4,351.06	4,351.06
	Impresos y efectos de escritorio			1,798.64	1,798.64
	Telégrafo y cable	$ 16.92	22.32		39.24
	Menaje			64.00	64.00
	Alquileres			170.08	170.08
	Alumbrado			56.98	56.98
	Dietas			580.00	580.00
	Réditos de fianzas		200.00		200.00
	Conducción de correspondencia			4,844.69	4,844.69
	Señas y contra señas			91.83	91.83
	Construcciones y reparaciones			80.83	80.83
	Contrata vías interiores			2,318.27	2,318.27
	Mensajeros postales		3.96	231.32	235.28
	Conceptos varios		18.00	609 52	627.52
	Total egresos	$ 16.92	$ 312.10	$35,458.55	$ 35,787,57
Marzo 31	Saldo en la cuenta de Abril	112.95	2,087.56	31,942.97	34,143.48
	Total	$ 129.87	$ 2,399.66	$67,401 52	$ 69,931.05

INGRESOS Y EGRESOS: ABRIL, 1901.

	CONCEPTO.	Ejercicio 1899.	Ejercicio 1900.	Ejercicio 1901.	TOTAL.
	Ingresos:				
Abril 1	Saldo de Marzo	$ 112.95	$ 2,087.56	$31,942.97	$ 34,143.48
Abril 22	Consignación	100.01	126.23	38,589.25	38,815.47
	Total	$ 212.96	$ 2,213.79	$70,532.22	$ 72,958.97
	Egresos:				
	Haberes:				
	Departamento de Correos			$ 5,393.46	$ 5,393.46
	Empleados de las Administraciones			6,067.24	6,067.24
	Administradores		$ 105.16	7,507.87	7,613.03
	Oficiales de Correos			1,759.12	1,759.12
	Carteros			5,227.67	5,227.67
	Impresos y efectos de escritorio			753.29	753.29
	Menaje			37.00	37.00
	Alquiler			406.09	406.09
	Alumbrado			770.81	770.81
	Dietas			712.00	712.00
	Réditos de fianzas			480.00	480.00
	Conducciones de correspondencia		6.26	5,129.10	5,135.36
	Marchamos y contraseñas			129.87	129.87
	Cajas de caudales			11.00	11.00
	Construcción y reparaciones			63.93	63.93
	Contrata vías interiores			2,397.67	2,397.67
	Mensajeros postales			381.21	381.21
	Conceptos varios			707.14	707.14
	Total egresos		$ 111.42	$37,934.47	$ 38,045.89
Abril 30	Saldo de la cuenta de Mayo	$ 212.96	2,102.37	32,597.75	34,913.08
	Total	$ 212.96	$ 2,213.79	$70,532.22	$ 72,958.97

INGRESOS Y EGRESOS: **MAYO, 1901.**

	CONCEPTO.	Ejercicio 1899.	Ejercicio 1900.	Ejercicio 1901.	TOTAL.
	Ingresos:				
Mayo 1.......	Saldo de Abril	$ 212.96	$ 2,102.37	$32,597.75	$34,913.08
Mayo 18.......	Consignación		60.41	35,462.64	35,523.05
	Total	2 212.96	$ 2,162.78	$68,060.39	$70 436.13
	Egresos:				
	Haberes:				
	Departamento de Correos			$ 5,159.27	$ 5,159.27
	Empleados de las Administraciones			6,547.03	6,347.03
	Administradores			7,553.94	7,553.94
	Oficiales de Correos			1,811.50	1,811.50
	Carteros			5,397.00	5,397.00
	Impresos y efectos de escritorio			956.69	956.69
	Menaje			6.50	6.50
	Alquiler			741 33	741.33
	Alumbrado			392.23	392.23
	Dietas			696.00	696.00
	Cond cción de correspondencia	$ 112.75	$ 278.25	4,486.84	4,877.84
	Valijas			218.22	218.22
	Marchamos y contraseñas			25.00	25.00
	Construcciones y reparaciones			96.26	96.26
	Conduccion			13.25	13.25
	Contrata vías interiores			2,348.84	2,338.84
	Mensajeros postales			462.39	462.39
	Conceptos varios		21.07	960.60	981.67
	Total de egresos	$ 112.75	$ 299.32	$37,872.89	$38,284.96
Mayo 31.......	Saldo en la cuenta de Junio	100.21	1,863.46	30,187.50	32,151.17
	Total	$ 212.96	$ 2,162.78	$68,060.39	$70,436.13

INGRESOS Y EGRESOS. JUNIO, 1901.

	CONCEPTO.	Ejercicio 1899.	Ejercicio 1900.	Ejercicio 1901.	TOTAL.
	Ingresos:				
Junio 1	Saldo de Mayo	$ 100.21	$ 1,863.46	$30,187.50	$ 32,151.17
Junio 7	Consignación	547.92	1,670.18	1,538.03	3,756.19
Junio 29	Consignación		60.40	35,462.65	35,523.05
	Total	$ 648.13	$ 3,594.04	$67,188.24	$ 71,430.41
	Egresos:				
	Haberes				
	Departamento de correos			$ 5,041.51	$ 5,041.51
	Empleados de las Administraciones			5,940.88	5,940.88
	Administradores		$ 10.05	7,201.72	7,211.77
	Oficiales de Correos			1,685.11	1,685.11
	Carteros			5,002.63	5,002.63
	Impresos y efectos de escritorio			778.39	778.39
	Menaje			12.50	12.50
	Alquiler			509.00	509.00
	Alumbrado			294.06	294.06
	Dietas			616.00	616.00
	Restos de fianzas			200.00	200.00
	Material general			8.13	8.13
	Correspondencia	$ 547.92	1,670.18	3,837.59	6,055.69
	Marchamos y contraseñas			55.11	55.11
	Construccoines y reparaciones			103.11	103.11
	Conducción de correspondencia			15.00	15.00
	Contratas vías interiores			2,351.22	2,351.22
	Mensajeros postales			375.24	375.24
	Conceptos varios			766.62	766.62
	Total de egresos	$ 547.92	$ 1,680.23	$34,793.82	$ 37,021.97
Junio 29	Transferencia á la Tesorería general	100.21	1,763.69	8,193.17	10,057.07
Junio 30	Saldo en la cuenta de Julio		150.12	24,201.25	24,351.37
	Total	$ 648.13	$ 3,594.04	$67,188.24	$ 71,430.41

CONCEPTO.	Ejercicio 1900.	Ejercicio 1901.	TOTAL.
Haberes:			
Departamento de Correos		$ 441.65	$ 441.65
Empleados en las Administraciones		1,636.27	1,636.27
Administradores		7,055.47	7,055.47
Oficiales de Correos en los ferrocarriles		1,026.91	1,026.91
Carteros		1,906.88	1,906.88
Impresos y efectos de escritorio		502.91	502.91
Alquileres		717.33	717.33
Alumbrado		209.13	209.13
Dietas		332.00	332.00
Material general		124.00	124.00
Conducción de correspondencia		4,887.97	4,887.97
Fianzas	100.00		100.00
Marchamos y contraseñas		42.02	42 02
Construcciones y reparaciones		35.56	35.56
Carros		500.00	500.00
Contrata vías interiores		2,351.22	2,351.22
Mensajeros postales		438.72	438.72
Conceptos varios	20.81	198.08	218.89
Total de egresos	$ 120.81	$22,406.12	$ 22,526.93
Saldo	29.31	1,795.13	1,824.44
Total	150.12	24,201.25	$ 24,351.37

RELACIÓN

DE LAS

CANTIDADES ENTREGADAS Á LA TESORERÍA GENERAL DE CUBA,

JUNIO 29, 1901.

Sección: Hacienda.

Capítulo: Correos.

Correspondiente al

EJERCICIO DE 1899.

Consignaciones:

Haberes de los Administradores	$ .01	
Telégrafos y cable..	1.60	
Impresos y efectos de escritorio..	98.60	$ 100.21

Correspondiente al

EJERCICIO DE 1900.

Consignaciones:

Haberes de oficiales de las Administraciones	$ 39.01	
Haberes de oficiales en los ferrocarriles	148.05	
Haberes de los carteros.............	3.37	
Haberes de los mensajeros postales	.83	
Conducción de correspondencia..	71.64	
Contrata de vías interiores	447.40	
Telégrafo y cable	1.53	
Impresos y efectos de escritorio ..	672.58	
Menaje.......	175.65	
Alquiler..............	25.00	
Alumbrado.......	91.14	
Marchamos y contraseñas	30.35	
Cajas de caudales.............	34.79	
Conducción..........................	8.62	
Construcciones y reparaciones....	8.93	
Cambios......	5.00	$ 1,763.69

Carried forward..........................	$ 1,863.90

Brought forward		$ 1,863.90
Correspondiente al		

EJERCICIO DE 1901.

Consignaciones:

Haberes del Departamento de correos......	$ 2,472.82	
Haberes de oficiales de las administraciones..................... ...	885.19	
Haberes de oficiales en los ferrocarriles.....	121.17	
Haberes de carteros.................	508.51	
Telégrafos y cable....	100.00	
Menaje............	104.30	
Alquiler	373.06	
Alumbrado..........	151.03	
Dietas...........	272.00	
Periódicos	197.50	
Conducción de correspondencia..	1,521.69	
Valijas..........	108.02	
Básculas y pesadores de cartas...	100.00	
Buzones.	486.60	
Cajas de caudales	62.71	
Conducción.	134.74	
Contrata de vías interiores.......	293.83	
Cambio....	150.00	
Fianzas.....	200.00	$ 8,193.17
Total	....	$ 10,057.07

EJERCICIO 1899.

	Febrero.	Marzo.	Abril.	Mayo.	Junio.	TOTAL.
Habe						
Ad	....	....	....	....	....	$ 49.72
C	....	....	....	....	....	23.74
Impre	....	....	....	....	....	91.71
Alquil	....	....	....	....	....	30.00
Telégr	....	$ 16.92	....	....	....	278.88
Condu	14.66	....	....	$ 112.75	$ 547.92	5,844.70
	14.66	$ 16 92	....	$ 112.75	$ 547.92	$ 6,318.75

EJERCICIO 1900.

...o.	Marzo.	Abril.	Mayo.	Junio.	Julio cuenta del ejercicio 1901.	TOTAL.
	$ 10.38					$ 1,320.80
						4,799.98
44	57.44	$ 105.16		$ 10.05		13,216.29
						1,634.48
						3,993.06
	22.32					115.44
						3,361.11
						123.81
						3,069.19
						874.28
						1,152.00
	200.00				$ 100.00	1,456.71
						50.63
						143.81
32		$ 6.26	$ 278.25	1,670.18		26,310.92
						746.65
						276.59
						139.80
						422.50
						2,134.74
						55.25
						368.73
						3,671.82
	3.96					734.37
00	18.00		21.07		20.81	2,341.06
76	$ 312.10	$ 111.42	$ 299.32	$ 1,680.23	$ 120 81	$72,513.36

0

Ma

6,
5,
6,
1,
4,
1,

4,

2

5

EJERCICIO DE 1901.

...Marzo.	Abril.	Mayo.	Junio.	Julio.—Cuenta del ejercicio de 1901.	Total.	Proporción del total de gastos por %.
6,287.62	$ 5,393.46	$ 5,159.27	$ 5,041.51	$ 441.65	$ 73,709.81	16.3
5,911.25	6,067.24	6,547.03	5,940.88	1,636.27	83,745.94	18.6
6,454.14	7,507.87	7,553.94	7,201.72	7,055.47	87,353.28	19.4
1,608.32	1,759.12	1,811.50	1,685.11	1,026.91	20,736.62	4.7
4,351.06	5,227.67	5,397.00	5,002.63	1,906.88	61,898.38	13.7
1,798.64	753.29	956.69	778.39	502.91	9,087.55	2.1
64.00	37.00	6.50	12.50	....	280.70	.1
170.08	406.09	741.33	509.00	717.33	7,109.47	1.6
56.98	770.81	392.23	294.06	209.13	4,383.52	.9
580.00	712.00	696.00	616.00	332.00	7,040.00	1.5
....	480.00	....	200.00	....	1,350.00	.3
....	....	....	8.13	124.00	416.13	.1
....	....	....	....	....	7.50	0.0
4,844.69	5,129.10	4,486.84	3,837.59	4,887.97	49,616.84	11.0
....	....	218.22	....	....	1,309.02	.3
91.83	129.87	25.00	55.11	42.02	596.91	.1
....	....	....	....	....	13.40	0.0
....	11.00	....	....	....	94.62	0.0
....	....	13.25	15.00	....	165.26	0.0
80.83	63.93	96.26	103.11	35.56	1,029.13	.2
....	....	....	....	500.00	500.00	.1
2,318.27	2,397.67	2,348.84	2,351.22	2,351.22	26,741.74	5.9
231.32	381.21	462.39	375.24	438.72	4,641.70	1.
609.52	707.14	960.60	766.62	198.08	9,610.37	2.1
5,458.55	$37,934.47	$37,872.89	$34,793.82	$22,406.12	$451,437.89	100.0

RESUMEN.

		Ejercicio de 1899.	Ejercicio de 1900.	Ejercicio de 1901.	TOTAL.
	Ingresos:				
Julio 18	Consignación		$ 23,622.17	$ 39,637.12	$ 62,259.29
Julio 21	Consignación	$ 508.87	29,058.48		29,567.35
Agosto 9	Consignación		2,649.77		2,649.77
Agosto 13	Consignación			43,642.73	43,642.73
Septiembre 18	Consignación	5,245.24	6,788.13	40,319 17	52,352.54
Septiembre 18	Consignación			237 00	237.00
Octubre 15	Consignación		490.44	39,339.66	39,830.10
Noviembre 30	Consignación		177.46		177.46
Noviembre 30	Consignación		2,012.46	37,079.07	39,091.53
Diciembre 26	Consignación		2,070.75	38,070.18	40,140.93
Enero 29	Consignación		39.69	36,303.35	36,343.04
Enero 31	Consignación		5,163.12	5,163.12	10,326.24
Febrero 21	Consignación			670.00	670.00
Febrero 28	Consignación	16.92	32.70	36,377.08	36 426.70
Marzo 29	Consignación		283.97	33,535.08	33,819 05
Abril 22	Consignación	100.01	126.23	38,589.25	38,815.49
Mayo 18	Consignación		60.41	35,462.64	35,523.05
Junio 7	Consignación	547.92	1,670.18	1,538.09	3,756.19
Junio 29	Consignación		60.40	35,462.65	35,523.05
	Total	$ 6,418.96	$ 74.306.36	$461.426.19	$542.151.51
	Egresos:				
	Relación circunstanciada número 1	$ 6,318.75			$ 6,318.75
	Relación circunstanciada número 2		$ 72,513.36		72,513.36
	Relación circunstanciada número 3			$451,437.89	451,437.89
	Entregado á la Tesorería General de Cuba	100.21	1,763.69	8,193.17	10,057.07
	Saldo		29.31	1,795.13	1,824.44
	Total	$ 6,418.96	$ 74.306.36	$461.426.19	$542,151.51

El Pagador del Departamento
de Correos de Cuba.
GEO. R. BUCHANAN.

INFORME

DEL

NEGOCIADO DE AGENTES ESPECIALES.

DEPARTAMENTO DE CORREOS.

DEPARTAMENTO DE CORREOS DE CUBA.

NEGOCIADO DE AGENTES ESPECIALES.

Habana, Cuba, Agosto 3 de 1901.

SEÑOR:

Tengo el honor de llamar su atención á la siguiente relación de los trabajos realizados por este negociado durante el ejercicio vencido en 30 de Junio de 1901.

En cuanto á la extensión, variedad é importancia de los deberes desempeñados por el Cuerpo de Agentes Especiales, puede decirse que se refieren al examen de cuentas, á la investigación del carácter y de la conducta de los empleados de todas clases, al establecimiento y mudanza de las Oficinas de Correos, al arrendamiento de edificios para las administraciones y á las investigaciones minuciosas de toda clase de quejas relativas á los asuntos postales. Los Agentes Especiales también hacen recomendaciones para la extensión y mejora del sistema postal é instruyen á los empleados en lo concerniente á las leyes, reglamentos y costumbres del servicio.

Para poder conservar una relación completa, cada queja recibida en el negociado se encasilla, y para mayor conveniencia se ha adoptado la clasificación siguiente:

"A" Quejas referentes á certificados de la Isla.

"B" Quejas referentes á correspondencia ordinaria de la Isla.

"C" Inspección de Administraciones de Correos, quejas diversas que afectan á los empleados, robos de correspondencia en despoblado, robos en las Administraciones de Correos, infracciones de leyes postales y demás actos criminales.

"F" Quejas relativas á la correspondencia remitida á paises extranjeros y recibida de los mismos.

El número total de quejas de todas clases recibidas durante el último ejercicio fué de 4,320 y el número total de las quejas que fueron despachadas 4,821.

El hecho de que el número de expedientes despachados es mayor que el número total de quejas recibidas durante el mismo período, resulta de haber quedado pendientes al fin del año anterior 1,253 expedientes, y se le llama la atención especialmente al hecho de que la cantidad de las quejas pendientes al fin de este ejercicio se ha disminuido mucho, á pesar de que el número de Agentes Especiales y de oficiales es como la mitad de lo que era el año anterior. Esto demuestra que el negociado no solamente sigue á la par del progreso del Departamento, sino que también se va poniendo gradualmente al día, prestando así más útiles y satisfactorios servicios.

Esta reseña vendrá á ser poco más que un resúmen de los trabajos efectuados durante el año pasado. Presentar datos estadísticos completos exigiría más espacio del que se puede dedicar al asunto.

La inspección abarca todos los ramos del servicio postal, en todas las Administraciones de Correos, carterías, ferrocarriles, vapores, rutas postales y hasta el mismo Centro. El propósito era instruir á los Administradores, á sus auxiliares y á los "Railway Postal Clerks en el desempeño inteligente de sus deberes y hacerles comprender más claramente los detalles, pues la mayor parte de ellos habían estado empleados en el servicio durante un año ó más y habían adquirido un conocimiento de los principios del ramo. Era propósito especial inculcar á los Administradores de Correos un conocimiento positivo de la teoría y práctica de los sistemas de Giros Postales y de Certificados; de la manera de llevar y rendir las cuentas y de la importancia de los servicios que rinden en el mundo de los negocios.

Todas las Oficinas de Giros postales han sido inspeccionadas dos veces y muchas de ellas varias veces. Las frecuentes inspecciones no solamente protegen al Departamento, sino que también son en interés del público, por las oportunidades que tienen los Administradores de Correos de recibir las instrucciones necesarias relativas á sus deberes, en lo que se refiere á sus obligaciones hácia el público en general para que presten el mejor servicio posible.

Se han adoptado medidas especiales para que los Administradores de Correos rindan estados semanales de Giros Postales y cuentas postales mensuales.

Una de las cosas que más llamaron la atención del Negociado á principios del año y que las necesidades crecientes del servicio exigían, fué ensanchar el lugar para la custodia de la correspondencia certificada y para los casilleros de distribución en los ferrocarriles y vapores. Estas mejoras fueron hechas en muchos de los ferrocarriles y vapores y dieron por resultado acelerar las operaciones y disminuir el número de errores por parte de los empleados de correos.

El año pasado se abrió en el negociado un libro de cuentas. En él se asienta toda la recaudación hecha por los Agentes Especiales y el destino que se dá á su importe. La suma total de las cantidades recaudadas por los Agentes Especiales durante el año asciende á $2,447.50 y representa el cobro de saldos adeudados y multas impuestas por infracción de las leyes y reglamentos postales.

Ocurren errores, naturalmente, y, á veces, personas que no son honradas entran en el Servicio de Correos, pero estas son excepciones. Ha habido empeño el año pasado en rectificar errores y en deshacerse de los empleados desleales. El menor número de quejas del Servicio Postal y contra los empleados, comparado con el del año anterior, es de por sí suficiente evidencia para demostrar la mejora del servicio. Además se ha hecho un menor número de detenciones, un mayor número de sentencias y se ha recuperado más dinero, todo lo cual hay que agregar á este favorable informe.

Creo que lo precedente es una exposición correcta de los hechos y que el Negociado de Agentes Especiales es una de las divisiones más eficaces del Departamento de Correos.

EXPEDIENTES "A" O CASOS RELATIVOS A LA CORRESPONDENCIA CERTIFICADA DE LA ISLA.

Todas las quejas recibidas referentes á abusos y á irregularidades en la correspondencia certificada están incluidas en las tablas números 1 y 2. De las 140 quejas que se recibieron y fueron encasilladas, solamente 16 de ellas necesitaron que un Agente Especial hiciera una investigación personal. Las otras 124 quejas investigadas fueron satisfactoriamente resueltas por correspondencia. De las 15 quejas pendientes del año anterior, 7 fueron trasladadas á Agentes Especiales é investigadas por ellos y las otras 8 fueron resueltas por correspondencia. Es de observarse, por consiguiente, que las quejas referentes á la correspondencia certificada de la Isla son muy contadas y solamente un número muy pequeño de ellas exige investigación.

La supuesta cantidad de dinero y las prendas de valor de que se dió parte en las 140 quejas recibidas, ascienden á $ 1,882.83. De esta cantidad, $1,705.69 fueron recuperados y pagados por medio de este Negociado y $57.14 fueron encontrados y entregados por correo. La suma de $100.00 está todavía sujeta á investigación, y la de $20.00 fué la única pérdida efectiva.

Siete casos que fueron trasladados á agentes especiales en años anteriores, fueron revisados y terminados en el año que acaba de expirar. De éstos 5 dieron pérdidas que ascendieron á $2,843.47, y en dos casos se ha averiguado que no hubo pérdida alguna.

Se me ha ocurrido que un cuadro comparativo de los trabajos realizados por el Negociado desde su organización en 14 de Febrero de 1899, pudiera ser útil.

Se llama la atención á los siguientes cuadros:

CUADRO Nº 1.

EXPEDIENTES "A"

Ejercicio.	Quejas.	Expedientes cursados.	Aprobados.	Recuperados.	Pérdida supuesta.	Pendientes.
1899, 4½ meses	26	19	19	....	....	7
1900................	61	53	48	$ 6.00	$2843.47	8
1901................	140	137	135	1705.69	20.00	3
Total.........	227	209	202	1,711.69	2863 47	18

CUADRO Nº 2.

DEMOSTRATIVO DEL NUMERO DE EXPEDIENTES "A" CURSADOS DURANTE EL EJERCICIO QUE TERMINÓ EN JUNIO 30 DE 1901.

	Iniciados y Revisados			Resueltos.			
	Corrientes.	Revisados.	Total.	Corrientes.	Revisados.	Total.	Pendientes.
Pedtes. en Julio 1º 1900, 15	140	1	156	137	1	138	18
Investigados por Agentes Especiales................				23	1	24	
Resueltos en el Negociado por correspondencia.				114	....	114	

EXPEDIENTES "B" Ó CASOS RELATIVOS Á LA CORRESPONDENCIA ORDINARIA DE LA ISLA.

La masa de la correspondencia que se deposita para ser trasmitida por correo pertenece á la clase ordinaria ó séase sin certificar, y sin embargo de la mayor seguridad que ofrece el Sistema de Certificación, el público persiste en emplear la correspondencia ordinaria como medio de remisión de dinero y prendas de valor.

La consecuencia natural es que la mayor parte de los abusos se comete en esta clase de correspondencia. Los empleados de correos, faltos de honradez, aunque no sean suficientemente atrevidos para tocar á la correspondencia certificada, suelen arriesgarse á robar la correspondencia ordinaria, y á pesar de que por lo general, es más difícil de descubrir abusos en esta clase de correspondencia, sin embargo la certeza de que sean descubiertos es apenas menor que en los casos de correspondencia certificada.

Los Agentes Especiales hacen todos los esfuerzos posibles para justificar la confianza ilimitada que muestra el público en la seguridad de la correspondencia ordinaria, y objeto de plácemes es que la proporción de pérdidas en esta clase de correspondencia sea tan reducida, si tenemos en cuenta la extensión del servicio y la magnitud de la correspondencia. La experiencia adquirida el año pasado demuestra que la mayor parte de las quejas recibidas son debidas al público que utiliza el Servicio de Correos, sea por incompletas ó erróneas direcciones ó sea por la falta de toda dirección ú otros errores.

De las 297 quejas recibidas, 67 se averiguaron por los Agentes Especiales y 215 se terminaron por correspondencia. El valor total presentado en las 297 quejas recibidas ascendía á $ 8,267.84 de los cuales $8,057.18 fueron recuperados y entregados á los remitentes ó destinatarios, $38.00 están pendientes de averiguaciones y $172.66 es la suma total de que no se ha podido dar cuenta.

De los 20 expedientes existentes en 1º de Julio de 1900, diez y seis fueron cursados por Agentes Especiales y cuatro terminaron por correspondencia. Se acompaña un estado comparativo de lo practicado en esta clase de expedientes durante los últimos veintiocho meses y medio.

CUADRO Nº 3.

EJERCICIO.	Quejas.	Cursados.	Aprobados.	No descubiertos	Suma interesada.	Supuesta pérdida.	Expedientes pendientes.
1899, 4½ meses..	26	13	9	4	$ 1.00	$ 1.00	13
1900	247	240	155	85	499.99	39.16	20
1901....................	297	301	110	191	8,267.84	172.66	16
Total.....	570	554	274	280	....	....	....

CUADRO Nº 4.

DEMOSTRATIVO DEL NUMERO DE EXPEDIENTES "B" CURSADOS DURANTE EL EJERCICIO TERMINADO EN 30 DE JUNIO DE 1901.

Expedientes pendientes en 1º de Julio de 1901.........	20	Expedientes antiguos terminados.	20	Expedientes pendientes nuevos.....	16
Expedientes iniciados durante el ejercicio............	297	Expedientes nuevos terminados..	281	Revisados...	1
Expedientes revisados	2	Expedientes revisados terminados..	1		
Total..................	319	Total..............	302	Total......	17

EXPEDIENTES "C" Ó QUEJAS Y AVERIGUACIODES DIVERSAS REFERENTES Á EMPLEADOS Ó Á LOS ASUNTOS DEL SERVICIO POSTAL.

Los siguientes justificantes "A" y "B" demostrarán el número y clase de estos expedientes recibidos durante el ejercicio vencido en 30 de Junio de 1901 y trasladados á los Agentes Especiales para su gestión. Se verá que el número de quejas recibidas durante los 12 meses, asciende á 1,155; de éstos 154 fueron casos especiales iniciados sobre el terreno por los Agentes Especiales; 138 fueron recibidos del negociado de nombramientos, sueldos y concesiones; 30 del negociado de sellos y materiales; 67 del negociado de trasporte; 7 del negociado de giros postales y certificados y los 759 restantes se iniciaron en este negociado.

Al principio del ejercicio quedaron 593 casos pendientes del año anterior. De éstos, 298 se iniciaron en las inspecciones hechas en las Administraciones de Correos. Agréguense á éstos 593 casos los 1,001 iniciados en esta Oficina; 154 casos especiales y 161 casos revisados y tenemos un total de 1,909 casos. De ese número se terminaron 1,767, dejando un saldo de 142 casos pendientes en 1º de Julio de 1901.

El montante del efectivo cobrado por los Agentes Especiales en esta clase de casos durante los 12 meses, asciende $694.01, divididos como sigue: Saldo pendiente de pago por cuenta postal, $260.36; pagos efectuados á cuenta de cheques y abonarés falsos, $125.00; saldo pendiente de pago por cuenta de Giros Postales, $13.33; por subarriendo de parte del edificio de correos al Administrador, $75.00; por demasía en el pago de sueldo, $42.80; saldo pendiente de pago en la remisión para Giros Postales, $19.30; saldo pendiente de pago por cuenta de depósitos de llaves, $6.11; robo de carta certificada, $4.00; malversación de caudales, $148.04.

Justificante "A" demostrativo de los expedientes iniciados en las diferentes provincias durante el ejercicio terminado en 30 de Junio de 1901:

Departamento de Correos....................	109
Provincia de la Habana.........................	225
,, ,, Pinar del Río......................	135
,, ,, Matanzas.......	168
,, ,, Santa Clara........	295
,, ,, Puerto Príncipe..............	38
,, ,, Santiago de Cuba	185
Total	1,155

Justificante "B" demostrativo de la naturaleza y clase de los casos iniciados durante el ejercicio terminado en 30 de Junio de 1901:

Arrendamientos y nuevos locales.....	13
Supresiones de Oficinas	2
Fusiones de Administraciones con Oficinas de Telégrafos.	8
Inspección General de Administraciones...........	130
Inspección General de "R. P. Os." y de Rutas Postales ..	49
Establecer Rutas Postales y servicio de mensajero de correos	18
Establecer Administraciones y Carterías...........	29
Establecer el Sistema de Giros Postales en las Administraciones	7
Rectificar las cuentas postales de los Administradores......	34
Revisar los gastos y desembolsos	97
Fijar los sueldos de los Administradores y otros empleados	12
Nombrar á los Administradores y otres empleados postales	86
Surtir materiales..	30
Averiguar quejas contra los Administradores, etc...........	35
Infracciones del Código Postal, Sección 14............	1
,, ,, ,, ,, ,, 35......	291
,, ,, ,, ,, 39	1
,, ,, ,, ,, 40.....................	1
,, ,, ,, ,, 44......	1
,, ,, ,, ,, 52	6
,, ,, ,, ,, ,, 60................ . .	1
,, ,, ,, ,, ,, 11, 12 y 14.........	2
Averiguaciones de quejas várias	301
Total.....................	1,155

CUADRO Nº 5.

DEMOSTRATIVO DEL NÚMERO DE EXPEDIENTES "C" INICIADOS DURANTE LOS ÚLTIMOS VEINTE Y OCHO MESES Y MEDIO.

	Quejas.	Expedientes cursados.	Expedientes pendientes.
1899 4½ meses	992	688	304
1900	2,224	1,935	593
1901	1,155	1,623	125
	4,371	4,246	125

CUADRO Nº 6.

DEMOSTRATIVO DEL NÚMERO DE EXPEDIENTES "C" CURSADOS DURANTE EL EJERCICIO TERMINADO EN 30 DE JUNIO DE 1901.

Pendientes en 1º de Julio de 1900	593	
Iniciados durante el año	1,001	
Revisados	161	
Especiales recibidos	154	1,909
Terminados durante el año	....	1,767
Pendientes en 1º de Julio de 1901	....	142

EXPEDIENTES DE LA CLASE "F."

Las investigaciones y quejas relativas á la correspondencia internacional recibida del extrangero y despachada al mismo y de tránsito por la Isla al extranjero están comprendidas en la letra "F." En su mayor parte estos expedientes son simples preguntas referentes á la entrega de material extrangero que necesariamente requieren extensa correspondencia. A la simple vista los cuadros mostrarán la pequeña proporción que exige la investigación personal de un Agente Especial. Durante el año se iniciaron 2,728 expedientes "F," de los cuales 2,282 se referían á certificados, 442 á correspondencia ordinaria y 4 á varios conceptos. A los 2,728 expedientes iniciados se deben agregar 533 expedientes de certificados y 92 de correspondencia ordinaria pendientes del año anterior. De estos 625 expedientes mencionados, 496 referentes á certificados se terminaron sin pérdidas; la pérdida en 5 de ellos fué cargada á los abusos de un empleado y en 3 de certificados no se pudieron conseguir los pormenores, pues los datos referentes al caso eran de fecha anterior á la ocupación americana; quedando 29 expedientes de certificados del año 1900 pendientes de investigación. De los 92 expedientes relativos á correspondencia ordinaria en 25 no hubo pérdida y en 66 la pérdida no se pudo localizar, quedando uno de correspondencia ordinaria en curso de investigación. De los 2,282 expedientes de certificados recibidos durante el año pasado, se terminaron 1,893, cargándose la pérdida en 37 de ellos á los abusos de un empleado; se terminaron 116 de correspondencia ordinaria sin haber pérdida y en 153 la pérdida no se pudo localizar. De los 3,354 expedientes cursados durante el año, se terminaron 2,761, dejando 593 pendientes al fin del año. La totalidad de la pérdida declarada ascendía á $7,365.62, divididos en $4,728.33 de certificados y $2,637.29 de correspondencia ordinaria. De la pérdida declarada de $4,728.33 en certificados se investigaron $2,298.50; de los cuales se recuperaron $1,904.50 que fueron entregados á los destinatarios, $373 se cargaron á los abusos de un empleado, y los $21.00 no se pudieron localizar. De la pérdida de $2,637.29 declarada, relativa á la correspondencia ordinaria. $1,822.29 fueron investigados, y de estos se recuperaron $1,016.82 que fueron entregados á los destinatarios, quedando $805.47 que no se pudieron localizar. Quedan todavía pendientes de investigacion $2,429.83, declarados en la correspondencia certificada y $815.00 en la ordinaria.

El siguiente cuadro comparativo demuestra el número de expedientes cursados desde el 14 de Febrero de 1899:

CUADRO N? 7.

	INICIADOS.	TERMINADOS.	PENDIENTES.
1899, 4½ meses	858	319	539
1900	2,536	2,450	625
1901	2,728	2,760	593

CUADRO No. 8.

DEMOSTRATIVO DEL NUMERO DE EXPEDIENTES "F" CURSADOS DURANTE EL EJERCICIO TERMINADO EN 30 DE JUNIO DE 1901.

Pendientes en Julio de 1900	625		
Iniciados y revisados	2,729		
Total	3,354	3,354	
Terminados por Agentes Especiales		53	
,, en la Oficina por correspondencia		2,708	
Total		2,761	2 761
Pendientes en Julio 1? de 1901		....	593

CUADRO No. 9.

DEMOSTRATIVO DEL NUMERO TOTAL DE EXPEDIENTES DE TODAS CLASES CURSADOS DURANTE EL EJERCICIO TERMINADO EN 30 DE JUNIO DE 1901.

	A.	B.	C.	F.	TOTAL.
Pendientes en 1? Julio de 1900	15	20	593	625	1,253
Iniciados	140	297	1,001	2,728	4,166
Revisados	1	2	161	1	165
Informes especiales	....	....	154	....	154
Total	156	319	1,909	3,354	5,738
Expedientes terminados	138	302	1,767	2,761	4 878
,, pendientes	18	17	142	593	770

RECAUDACIÓN.

Durante el año el Negociado por medio de sus Agentes Especiales y de la Oficina, recaudó y desembolsó $2,454.60. De esta suma, $7.10 quedaban pendientes del año anterior. Los cobros fueron saldos pendientes de cuentas postales $277.30; saldo pendiente de cuenta de Giros Postales $375.88; dinero recibido por cheques y abonarés falsos $152.49; robo de certificados $45.20; subarriendo del local de la Administración de Correos por el Administrador $75.00; exceso en el pago de sueldos $42.87; saldo pendiente en la remisión por cuenta de Giros Postales $19.30; malversación de caudales $1,448.04; pérdida de carta certificada $5.00; hallado suelto en la balija $0.31; saldo pendiente por cuenta de depósito de llaves $6.11.

DESEMBOLSOS.

Al Administrador de Correos de la Habana..........	$ 1,814.47
,, Tesorero de la Isla..................	318.85
Á los remitentes de certificados.........	160.20
,, ,, dueños de locales de Oficinas de Correos........	50.00
,, ,, ,, ,, abonarés falsos...............	42.49
Al remitente de Giro Postal............................ .	19.30
,, Administrador de Correos de San Juan de Puerto Rico........	42.87
Al Administrador de Correos de Pinar del Río......	6.11
Al Jefe de la Oficina de cartas muertas	0.31
Total.................	$ 2,454.60

Además de lo que precede puede ser admisible manifestar que se recibieron otras quejas relacionadas con pérdidas por valor de $12,741.33, cuyos paraderos fueron descubiertos por el Negociado y fueron devueltos á sus legítimos dueños; se descubrió que no había pérdida verdadera y que las demoras eran debidas, en su mayor parte, á la mala dirección, ó á la culpa de los destinatarios en no acusar recibo con prontitud.

DETENCIONES POR INFRACCIONES DE LAS LEYES POSTALES.

Justificante "C."

El número de casos pendientes ante los tribunales al fin del ejercicio terminado en 30 de Junio de 1900 era de diez (10) como sigue: 4 por intento de defraudar al gobierno; 1 por malversación de fondos postales; 5 por quitar y volver á usar sellos cancelados.

Durante el año terminado en 30 de Junio de 1901, se hicieron veintiocho detenciones como sigue: Intento de defraudar al Gobierno 1, malversación de caudales 4; robos 2; llevar correspondencia por vías postales por expreso particular 1; quitar y volver á usar sellos cancelados 20.

Las ocupaciones de las personas así detenidas durante el año pasado y las de las personas cuyas causas estaban pendientes son como sigue: Jefes de Departamentos ú Oficinas 4; Empleados 4; contratistas de rutas 1; paisanos 29.

Se celebraron 8 juicios en los cuales resultaron 6 sentenciados y dos absueltos. Uno de los procesados murió estando pendiente su causa; 5 fueron puestos en libertad por orden del Gobernador General promulgada en 16 de Enero de 1900, y 24 causas están pendientes en las Audiencias de las Provincias de la Habana, Santa Clara y Santiago de Cuba.

Lo que precede es una exposición de los trabajos realizados por este Negociado durante el último ejercicio, de lo que se da á usted cuenta para su conocimiento.

De usted atentamente,

F. M. Hamilton,

Jefe Interino de Agentes Especiales.

Sr. M. C. Fosnes,

Director General.

INFORME

DEL

NEGOCIADO DE TRADUCCIONES.

DEPARTAMENTO DE CORREOS.

Julio 20, 1901.

Sr. Director General de Correos,

Presente.

Durante el pasado ejercicio el cometido de este Negociado se redujo un tanto. Esto se debe sin duda al notable progreso de la forma en que los Administradores y demás empleados atienden á sus diversos deberes del servicio y á la consiguiente supresión de frecuentes instrucciones que aparejan voluminosa correspondencia. Debido á esto, dos traductores y dos manipuladores de máquinas (también traductores) desempeñan ahora todo el trabajo que toca al Negociado, habiéndose facilitado el prescindir de cinco traductores durante el año.

Una relación del trabajo realizado se empezó en el mes de Octubre de 1900, por orden del Director General. Esta relación se lleva en un libro á manera de diario de entrada y se resume á fin de mes, dando el siguiente resultado:

1900.	Cartas recibidas.	Cartas salidas.	Documentos varios.
Octubre 31	681	693	79
Noviembre 30	625	696	45
Diciembre 31	755	687	28
1901.			
Enero 31	677	767	46
Febrero 28	695	697	74
Marzo 31	525	693	45
Abril 30	510	807	81
Mayo 31	629	637	92
Junio 30	576	605	46
	5,673	6,282	536

Vése, pues, que el total de 12,491 traducciones comprende desde el 1º de Octubre de 1900, á Junio 30, 1901, lo cual da un promedio mensual de 1,388 documentos traducidos, en los nueve meses que el informe abarca.

Punto de justicia es para el negociado exponer, respecto del número de documentos varios que se han traducido, que muchos eran muy extensos. Eran declaraciones y asertos hechos con respecto á las investigaciones del departamento, de lo cual tiene el público más ó menos conocimiento. Estos documentos á menudo ocupaban 25 y 30 páginas del papel reglamentario, y como eran para los juzgados, había que poner en ello gran cuidado para que las traducciones fueran una exacta versión del original. Hecha la traducción se revisaba cuidadosamente como era preciso, para que saliera lo mejor posible.

Compláceme de poder decir que como los empleados del Negociado se han enterado mejor de la marcha del Departamento y han aprendido el significado verdadero de palabras y frases técnicas que antes no conocían, han logrado hacer traducciones más rápidas, y de una manera notable han progresado sus aptitudes.

Las tareas han ocupado á todo el personal, pero el método que se emplea no deja malgastar el tiempo, y casi no hay nadie de más. En ésta como en otras oficinas hay ocasiones que el trabajo es escaso, pero hay otras en que los empleados tienen tanto como pueden hacer, y hacen lo que se les manda.

Deseo hacer constar las aptitudes del personal, y también, antes de terminar, expresar mi agradecimiento al trato benévolo de todo el Departamento.

Atentamente,

El Jefe del Negociado de Traducciones,

R. Vence.

INFORME

DEL

NEGOCIADO DE CARTAS MUERTAS.

DEPARTAMENTO DE CORREOS.

DEPARTAMENTO DE CORREOS DE CUBA.

INFORME DEL NEGOCIADO DE CARTAS MUERTAS.

Tengo el honor de acompañar un informe que pone de manifiesto todos los trabajos realizados por este Negociado desde Julio 1º, 1900, á Junio 30 de 1901.

Atentamente,

El Jefe del Negociado de cartas muertas,

ALFREDO ARTEAGA.

CLASIFICACION DE LA MATERIA POSTAL RECIBIDA EN EL NEGOCIADO DE CARTAS MUERTAS EN EL EJERCICIO DE JULIO 1º DE 1900 Á JUNIO 29, 1901.

Servicio ordinario, cartas no reclamadas		33,147
,, ,, cartas devueltas del extranjero		10,605
Servicio ordinario, cartas detenidas por falta de franqueo		7,005
Servicio ordinario, material en blanco		55
,, mal dirigido		416
,, cartas rechazadas		1,528
,, varias no reclamadas		192
Cartas certificadas y paquetes no reclamados (interior)	276	
Cartas y paquetes devueltos del extranjero	379	655

PAQUETES.

Infranquebles	308	
No reclamado	200	508
Del interior no reclamado		23,755

PROCEDENTE DEL EXTRANJERO.

Cartas servicio ordinario	34,017	
Paquetes é impresos	55,620	
Objetos certificados	2,387	92,024
Total		175,890

PROCEDIMIENTO ADOPTADO CON LA CORRESPONDENCIA POSTAL NO ABIERTA.

Tarjetas y pedidos devueltos al remitente.	3,553	
Cartas certificadas y paquetes	452	4,005

DEL EXTRANJERO.

Devueltos al país de su orígen..............	79,563	
Entrégado á solicitantes	361	
Papel inútil	12,100	92,024
Total no abierto	....	96,029

CLASIFICACIÓN DE MATERIA POSTAL ABIERTA.

Cartas ordinarias no reclamadas..	35,594
Cartas no reclamadas devueltas del extranjero	10,605
Correspondencia rechazada.....................	1,528
Correspondencia mal dirijida	416
Detenidas por falta de franqueo.....	7,005
Cartas de distintas clases..............	192
Paquetes........	508
Correspondencia interior no reclamada....	23,755
Cartas certificadas	203
	79,806

DESPACHO DE LA CORRESPONDENCIA POSTAL ABIERTA.

Entregada:

Cartas con dinero.....	60	
Cartas con giros	61	
Cartas con diversos contenidos	69	
Cartas con sellos de correo......	9	
Cartas con fotografías..........................	55	
Cartas con manuscritos....	17	
Cartas con correspondeucia	2,559	
Cartas con objetos.......	188	
Paquetes.......	219	3,237

ABIERTAS Y ARCHIVADAS.

Cartas con dinero	2	
Cartas con giros postales y otros	67	
Cartas con diversos contenidos.........	212	
Cartas con sellos de correo.	30	
Cartas con fotografías	185	
Cartas con manuscritos	23	
Cartas con correspondencia	00	
Cartas con objetos	144	
Paquetes.........	36	
Certificadas	165	864
Carried forward..	....	100,130

Brought forward............	....	100,130

ABIERTAS Y EN ESPERA DE ENTREGA COMPROBADA.

Cartas con giros postales y letras de cambio	1	
Cartas con diversos contenidos..............	3	
Cartas con sellos de Correos.................	4	
Cartas con fotografía	1	
Cartas con manuscritos.....	3	
Cartas con objetos........................	2	
Cartas certificadas............	38	
		52

DESTRUIDA.

Impresos del interior (papel inútil).........	2,3755	
Cartas ordinarias y circulares sin contenido, que no pudo devolverse á los remitentes...........	51,953	75,708
Total.......	....	175,890

RESUMEN DEMOSTRATIVO DE CORRESPONDENCIA RECIBIDA.

Interior:	
Correspondencia no reclamada, interior.................	83,866
Extranjera no reclamada...	92,024
Total interior y extranjera...........	175,890

DESPACHO.

Interior:		
Entregada..	7,242	
Archivada...........	864	
En espera de entrega comprobada	52	
Destruida.........	75,708	83,866
Extranjera:		
Devuelta al país de orígen	79,563	
Entregada á solicitantes	361	
Papel inútil..	12,100	92,094
Total................	175,890	175,890

CORRESPONDENCIA DEVUELTA DEL EXTRANJERO.

Se clasifica de la manera siguiente:		
Objetos certificados	379	
Cartas ordinarias incluyendo tarjetas postales	10,605	
Paquetes é impresos	1,219	12,203
De las 655 cartas certificadas no reclamadas y paquetes del interior recibidos fueron:		
Entregadas á su dirección ó devueltas á los remitentes...........	452	
Guardadas en espera del interesado	103	655

VALOR DE CONTENIDOS EN LA CORRESPONDENCIR ABIERTA.

Pormenores:	Número.	Valor.
Cartas con dinero devuelto á sus dueños...	20	$ 47.51
Cartas con dinero entregado al Administrador de la Habana.........................	40	114.04
Cartas con dinero guardadas en el Negociado de correspondencia no reclamada.	2	1.06
Total..	62	$ 162,61

PAQUETES GUARDADOS EN EL NEGOCIADO DE CARTAS MUERTAS.

Con dirección..	182	
Sin dirección	71	253

RELACIÓN DEMOSTRATIVA DE CORRESPONDENCIA MUERTA

PASADA POR EL NEGOCIADO DESDE 1º DE JULIO

HASTA 29 DE JUNIO DE 1901.

Recibida:

Cartas del interior sujetas á franqueo....................	51,280

DEL INTERIOR INFRANQUEABLE.

Detenidas para franqueo......................................	7,005
Material en blanco...........................	55
Mal dirijidas..	416
Varias no reclamadas.......	192
Interior de tercera y cuarta clase	24,263

CORRESPONDENCIA EXTRANJERA.

Cartas.	34,017
Paquetes é impresos.....	55,620

CORRESPONDENCIA CERTIFICADA.

Interior	655
Extranjera......	2,387
Total......	175,890

DESPACHO.

	ENTREGADAS.	
	Sin abrir.	*Abiertas.*
Cartas del interior franqueables............	3,553	47,727

CARTAS DEL INTERIOR INFRANQUEABLES.

Detenidas para franqueo........................	....	7,005
Material en blanco................................	....	55
Mal dirijidas.......................................	....	416
Várias no reclamadas	....	192

CARTAS CERTIFICADAS.

Cartas del interior................................	650	5
Cartas extranjeras................................	2,387	....
Interior tercera y cuarta clase...............	....	24,263

CORRESPONDENCIA EXTRANJERA.

Cartas ordinarias..................................	34,017	....
Impresos...	55,620	....
Total......................	96,227	79,663
Total..............	....	175,890

Cuadro demostrativo de la clase y número de correspondencia detenida, devuelta y recibida del extranjero.

	DEVUELTA.				RECIBIDA.			
	Certificada.	Ordinario.	Paquetes.	Total.	Certificada.	Ordinaria.	Paquetes.	Total.
República Argentina	34	202	90	326	...	255	1	256
Austria Hungría	11	84	124	219	...	...	...	...
Bahamas	...	46	1	47	...	20	...	20
Barbadas	2	16	20	38	...	...	...	...
Bélgica	9	49	185	243	...	...	1	1
Bermudas	...	9	...	9	...	...	...	...
Brasil	8	42	2	52	...	...	...	...
Guayana británica	...	9	...	9	...	...	...	...
Honduras británica	...	8	...	8	...	1	...	1
India británica	5	4	...	9	...	...	...	...
Canadá	7	238	59	304	3	47	1	51
Chile	11	31	6	48	...	...	...	...
Colombia	13	40	31	84	...	...	...	...
Costa Rica	1	44	4	49	...	6	...	6
Islas Danesas	1	16	...	17	...	...	...	...
Dinamarca	1	10	...	11	...	...	...	...
Dominica Antillas	1	1	...	2	...	...	...	...
Ecuador	1	19	...	20	...	3	...	3
Egipto	1	6	...	7	...	...	...	...
Francia	105	680	8,613	9,398	...	165	54	219
Antillas francesas	5	16	...	21	...	...	2	2
Alemania	44	529	1,970	2,543	...	...	...	...
Gibraltar	6	11	...	17	...	2	2	4
Gran Bretaña	25	414	1,815	2,254	5	169	8	182
Grecia	...	6	...	6	...	...	...	...
Granada, antillas	...	3	...	3	...	...	...	...
Guatemala	1	14	1	16	...	4	...	4
Hawai	...	...	...	...	...	...	...	...
Haití	8	10	...	18	...	7	...	7
Repúb. de Honduras	2	2	...	4	3	7	...	10
Hong Kong	2	16	...	18	...	...	...	...
Italia	70	296	271	637	...	5	...	5
Jamaica	6	347	2	355	9	174	2	185
Japón	...	5	...	5	...	...	...	...
Java, india holandesa	2	...	...	2	...	...	...	...
Malta	...	1	...	1	...	...	...	...
México	114	942	375	1,431	66	953	419	1,438
Monserrate	...	1	...	1	...	...	...	...
Países Bajos	2	22	35	59	...	...	...	...
Antillas holandesas	1	10	...	11	...	4	...	4
Nevis	...	5	...	5	...	...	...	...
Nicaragua	2	10	...	12	...	...	...	...
Noruega	5	33	4	42	...	...	...	...
Paraguay	...	2	...	2	...	...	...	...
Perú	3	22	8	33	1	2	...	3
Filipinas	3	51	...	54	...	60	3	63
Portugal	6	41	...	47	...	...	...	...
Puerto Rico	34	363	3	400	10	132	...	142
Rusia	7	15	2	24	...	...	...	...
Isla San Cristobal	1	14	...	15	...	...	...	...
Santa Lucía	...	5	...	5	...	...	...	...
San Vicente	...	3	...	3	...	...	...	...
Rep. del Salvador	...	1	2	3	2	2	...	4
Al frente	570	28,958	29,864	60,616	280	8,587	726	9,593

Cuadro demostrativo de la clase y número de correspondencia detenida, devuelta y recibida del extranjero.—(CONTINUACION).

	DEVUELTA.				RECIBIDA.			
	Certificada.	Ordinaria.	Paquetes.	Total.	Certificada.	Ordinaria.	Paquetes.	Total.
Del frente....	570	28,958	29,864	60,616	280	8,587	726	9,593
Rep. Dominicana......	15	170	2	187	18	178	22	218
España......................	1,465	12,114	6,492	20,071	95	1,593	453	2,141
Factorías del Estrecho..	1	....	....	1				
Suecia........................	4	14	....	18				
Suiza..........................	15	34	24	73				
Trinidad Antillas.....	....	19	1	20	....	8	....	8
Turquía	6	38	....	44				
Islas turcas.............	....	1	....	1				
Uruguay....................	6	30	5	41				
Venezuela..................	25	115	8	148	7	....	....	7
Victoria......................	1	3	....	4				
Estados Unidos........	256	16,420	23,332	40,008	160	6,808	251	7,219
Total	2,354	33,722	43,487	79,563	379	10,605	1,219	12,203

RELACION DEMOSTRATIVA DE LA CORRESPONDENCIA MUERTA RECIBIDA DEL EXTRANJERO Y DESPACHADA DESDE JULIO 1º 1900 A JUNIO 29 1901.

RECIBIDA.		DESPACHO.	
Clase.		*Clase.*	
OBJETOS CERTIFICADOS.		OBJETOS CERTIFICADOS.	
Cartas certificadas	2,387	Devueltas á su orígen...	2,354
Cartas ordinarias..	34,017	Entregadas á su dirección	33
Paquetes é impresos...	55,620	Cartas ordinarias devueltas á su dirección.	33,722
		Entregadas á su dirección	295
		Paquetes é impresos devueltos á su orígen...	43.487
		Entregados á su direccréation	33
		Papel inútil......	12,100
Total...........	92,024	Total	92,024

Atentamente,

El Jefe del Negociado de cartas muertas.

ALFREDO ARTEAGA.

AL SR. M. C. FOSNES,

Director General de Correos.

Charles Hernandez,
Postmaster at Havana.

REPORT

OF

Mr. M. C. FOSNES,

DIRECTOR GENERAL OF POSTS,

FOR THE PERIOD OF SIX MONTHS ENDING

DECEMBER 31.

1901.

DEPARTMENT OF POSTS OF CUBA

OFFICE OF THE DIRECTOR GENERAL

Havana, April 5, 1902.

SIR:

I have the honor to submit the following report for the six months from July 1 to December 31, 1901:

During this period the ordinary business of the Department of Posts moved forward in an even course, unmarked by events of special note, but with gradual betterment of the service. Complaints were relatively few and unimportant, indicating general public satisfaction with the postal service of the island. The postal service touches directly all the people, and it is a business of detail, of a multitude of small detached transactions by many persons. It is typified by the 2-cent stamp, a small thing in itself, but the ultimate main basis of the postal revenues. In the nature of things, mischances do occur in the handling of mail, and all we can strive for is to reduce them to a minimum. From the dropping of a letter into the mail box until it reaches the person addressed, anywhere in Cuba, the United States, or the rest of the world, it must pass through many hands and be subjected to various processes, from postmarking to final delivery, in the regular course of transmission. Errors and obscurities in address must frequently be reckoned with, and not seldom investigation discloses that complaints are based on errors or circumstances outside the postal service. A familiar grievance is the non-receipt of *expected* letters, without any actual knowledge that the letters were ever mailed. It is the natural tendency to hold the postal service responsible for anything that may seem amiss with correspondence. One letter which goes astray or fails to appear as expected, excites more attention than a hundred properly received.

REVENUES.

The revenues of the Department maintain a remarkably close approximation to $1,000 per day. My report for the fiscal year ended June 30, 1901, could not definitely show the effect of the reduction to domestic basis of postage to the United States, then operative for only three months. It will appear from the subjoined comparison of receipts with the corresponding six months of 1900, that the drop in receipts from stamp sales has been reduced to a daily average of $4.76, equal to $1,737.40 per annum. It may fairly be assumed that this trifling difference of about ½ per cent has already been overtaken, and that now, just a year after the change occurred, the loss of revenue therefrom has been overcome. Such loss was estimated not to exceed $30,000 per annum in my report to the Postmaster-General recommending the change, submitted for your concurrence, and this estimate is thus proven to have been a very safe one. I quote the following from said report, dated March 9, 1901:

> This amount is less than half the economies in the service effected in the Department of Posts and Havana postoffice within the last nine months.... The decrease would immediately begin to correct itself, in the nature of things, by increasing the volume of mail matter.
>
> Last December, during my absence on account of sickness, the Military Governor, on his own initiative, recommended that domestic rates of postage be applied to Cuba. This was joined with another proposition for the establishment of a parcels post system between the two countries. The Military Governor, who controls the general budget of the island, has thus already faced the responsibility for the resultant drop in the postal revenues, which, however, we hope would be only temporary.

STATEMENT SHOWING TOTAL POSTAL RECEIPTS FROM ALL SOURCES DURING THE SIX MONTHS ENDED DECEMBER 31, 1901.

MONTH.	STAMP SALES.	BOX RENTS.	M. O. FEES (By Quarters).	MISCL.	TOTAL.
July.........1901	$ 27,286.21	$ 3,294.50	....	$ 93.44	$ 30,674.15
August "	27,105.17	61.80	....	17.05	27,184.02
September "	25,361.47	142.86	$ 3,312.66	10.62	28,827.61
October "	28,083.03	3,357.50	....	18.44	31,458.97
November "	27,355.79	163.74	....	19.71	27,539.24
December "	32,676.46	99.36	3,250.98	67.90	36,094 70
Total.....	$167,868.13	$ 7,119 76	$ 6,563.64	$ 227.16	$181,778.69

Total receipts from all sources..............................	$ 181,778.69
Average monthly receipts........	30,296.45
Average daily receipts......	987.92
Total receipts from stamp sales, July 1 to December 31, 1900........	168,744.75
Total receipts from stamp sales, July 1 to December 31, 1901.	167,868.13
Average monthly receipts from stamp sales, July 1 to December 31, 1900	28,124.12
Average monthly receipts from stamp sales, July 1 to December 31, 1901..	27,978.02
Average daily receipts from stamp sales, July 1 to December 31, 1900...	917.09
Average daily receipts from stamp sales, July 1 to December 31, 1901..	912.33

DISBURSEMENTS.

The attached report of the disbursing officer shows the expenses of the Department for the six months to have been $200,702.88, equal to $401,405·76 per annum. There will accrue for payment during the latter half of the fiscal year, however, transportation expenses, chiefly for foreign service, to an amount of about $16,000. The annual outlay has thus been brought well within a rate of $420,000, which is a reduction still of $34,284.95 over last fiscal year. The comparison stands as follows with the two previous fiscal years reported on by me. The report itself for the fiscal year 1900 explains the source and nature of the data from which the total was compiled. To such total is added here $7,830.65 of subsequent disbursements on account of that year.

Fiscal year ended June 30, 1900,	$606,328.34		
Fiscal year ended June 30, 1901,	454,274.95;	decrease	152.043.39
Fiscal year ended June 30, 1902, (estimated as above)...........	420,000.00;	,,	34,284.95

In my regular report for the fiscal year 1901, dated August 23, 1901, the expenditures were given as $451,437.89; but belated items straggled in afterwards and increased this amount to $454,284.95, the figure adopted in the foregoing comparison.

The expenditures still overrun the revenues by $56,000, about 13 per cent. However, to approach that near sustaining an independent postal establishment, such as we have, completely equipped in all parts, covering an area not very much less than the state of its Pennsylvania or the state of New York, on the postal revenues of a second or third-class American city, is something of an achievement. The city of Omaha, Neb., produces more postal revenues than the whole Island of Cuba, and the city of Des Moines, Iowa, nearly as much.

STAMPS AND STAMPED PAPER.

Of postage stamps and stamped paper there was received during the six months from the Postmaster-General a total of $170,638.30, and supplied to postmasters of the island on requisition, $174,421.98.

PERSONNEL, SALARIES, BONDS.

Of 718 persons borne on the payrolls of the Department at the close of the six-month period under review, including star-route contractors, 33 were Americans—4.6 per cent. Several resignations of American employees have occurred since, and the postal service is becoming more and more completely Cubanized as the time draws near for transfer of administration. The only remaining American acting postmaster is at Santiago de Cuba, and with this exception it may be said that the service outside of Havana is already wholly in the hands of Cubans.

Salaries of postmasters constitute the largest item of expenditure of the Department, about 22 per cent. The large economies effected within the last two years have left untouched the compensation of postmasters, as a whole, and indeed of other

Cuban employees. On the contrary, the aggregate of such compensation has advanced. The lesson hardest to teach has been the relation of a postmaster's salary to the business of his office. Under the old Spanish order of things graded officials of the general administration were assigned to the charge of postoffices, under fixed compensation, and they were transferrable from one place to another. The salary attached to the officer and not to the office, regardless of the amount of business transacted. Discrimination and inequality were the inevitable result, and the postmaster had no permanent identity of interest with the community he was serving. It has been difficult to wean the people away from the idea that an appointment necessarily implies a living salary, and to inculcate the contrary principle that the amount of business must govern the compensation, which means that keeping a small postoffice is an incident to some other main occupation.

The establishment of a business standard of compensation has met with its own difficulties. As in the United States, we regulate salaries at the larger offices by the amount of revenues, which for practical purposes means stamps sold, and at the smaller offices by the amount of stamps canceled. Normally, these are reliable measures of business. In Cuba, country merchants find it profitable to carry postage stamps as merchandise, buying them for American money and selling them at the retail price in Spanish money. Such stamps are frequently ordered from Havana by the merchants, or from some other of the larger towns, as part of general orders for goods, thus deranging the normal operation of supply and demand for postage within the community itself. This can only be cured effectively by a stable and uniform currency.

Another serious obstacle to uniformity of salary-scale and of accounts is the division of postmasters into bonded and unbonded. This we have sought steadily to overcome, and instructions are finally operative for every postmaster to furnish bond. This may result in the discontinuance of some small offices, where the postmasters have resigned rather than comply, but ultimately, we believe, some person will be found willing to serve on the regular conditions in every such place.

During the six months corporation bonds decreased in number from 154 to 133, and in total amount of penalties from $358,700 to $313,220; while personal bonds increased from 112, representing $130,700, to 130, representing $159,500. The bonds which are now being received, responsive to the general requirement, are mostly personal bonds. We expect to leave every postmaster in Cuba under bond on our retirement from the island. This will not only operate to the advantage of business, but impart stability and character to the service.

MONEY ORDERS.

July 1, 1901, there went into effect a new arrangement for the exchange of postal money orders with the United States, which was described as follows in the instructions to postmasters, dated June 18, 1901:

In harmony with the recent introduction between Cuba and the United States of the domestic rates of postage, this Department is able to announce a further step toward uniformity in their postal systems by a similar arrangement in respect to money-order exchanges.

The practical effect of this assimilation will be the extension to the United States of the domestic money-order service of Cuba on July 1, 1901, and the reciprocal extension to Cuba of the domestic money-order service of the United States. The scale of fees will be the same, and the methods of business substantially identical.

The ready and sure means of remittance planted at a hundred different points over the Island by a postal system shaped on American lines, facilitating business intercourse of all kinds among the citizens, may now on like terms and under like conditions be offered by Cuban postmasters to their patrons on a range of potentiality immensely enlarged. There are more than 32,000 money-order postoffices in the United States, not counting island dependencies, and the proposed alliance will make Cuba an integral part of the greatest postal money-order community in the world.

On and after July 1 the postmaster at any money-order postoffice in Cuba may draw orders directly on any money-order postoffice in the United States, the same as is now done by one postoffice on another within the island, and may receive and pay orders from any money order postoffice in the United States. In the term United States are included for this purpose Puerto Rico and Hawaii. Havana and Tampa will be abolished as exchange offices, also the exchange office of San Juan, Puerto Rico.

A notable increase marked the first six months of business under this convention, as will appear from the following comparison:

MONEY ORDERS ISSUED:

July 1 to Dec. 31, 1900, Number, 40,770; amount, $1.325.734.42
July 1 to Dec. 31, 1901, .. 51.622; ,, 1.577,245.62
Actual increase, 1901 over 1900, $251,511.20; percentage, .189.

MONEY ORDERS PAID:

July 1 to Dec. 31, 1900, Number, 25.177; amount, $ 923.591.98
July 1 to Dec. 31, 1901, .. 30.366; ,, 1,085,885.50
Actual increase, 1901 over 1900, $162,293.52; percentage, .176.

The audit compilation for 1900 does not separate the domestic and international business, hence the comparison must be made by gross totals. It will be observed that the number of orders, both issued and paid, has increased faster than the amounts, which goes to show that the postal money-order service is assuming in Cuba the normal function of a means for small remittances, as distinguished from commercial exchange. The average amount of orders issued is still much larger than the average in the United States, as follows:

Average amount of money orders, July 1 to Dec. 31, 1900.. $32.51.
Average amount of money orders, July 1 to Dec. 31, 1901.. 30.55.
Average amount of money orders, United States (computed from last annual report, 1901).................... 8.00.

During the six months Cuban money-orders were paid in the United States to an amount of $428,525.83, and there were paid in Cuba orders drawn in the United States to the amount of $85,480.88. The balance, which runs steadily against Cuba, must be liquidated by remittances of funds, which were made during the same period to a total of $421,591.40, without cost of exchange. The year closed with a balance of $51,800.79 in favor of Cuba, which amount to an advance payment on account. The safe and convenient means of remittance, through exchange of funds with army disbursing officers, will soon cease, but we continue to take advantage thereof while it lasts, and whatever over-payment to the United States results will soon be liquidated by the normal operation of money-order exchanges, the balance on which must continue to run against Cuba. This has the concurrence of the Post Office Department.

The postal money-order service in Cuba can reach its legitimate measure of usefulness and popularity only on the basis of one uniform circulating medium. Our present standard is American money, while Spanish coins of different and fluctuating values circulate commercially, and the process of conversion involves inconvenience and often loss to the remitter of money orders. The following recent letter from a Cuban postmaster illustrates how a diverse currency represses the growth and utility of the postal money-order service. This is the translation from Spanish:

"In Bulletin No. 8, just received, it is stated that the money-order system in Cuba is highly satisfactory, although many localities were slow to avail themselves of the benefits of the system.

"This was not the case with this town, which was the first to understand its advantages, as is proven by the sale of money orders in the statistics published by the Secretary of War at Washington in December, 1901, placing this office in the third class in this province, which, in proportion to its inhabitants and its wealth, should appear in the second class.

Since December to this date there has been a considerable falling off in the sale of money orders, and it was my duty to investigate the cause among the business community. The merchants told me: We have asked the Director General to establish the money-order business here, because we understand its advantages. He granted our request and we kept our word. But, in the present circumstances, we are the losers. Our accounts with the Havana business houses are carried on in Spanish gold; the centen its worth $4.78 in American gold, and when our remittances are turned into Spanish gold, at the market rate, we have a considerable loss. If the Department of Posts could find a way to do away with the loss, we would always make our remittances in money orders.

"If such thing could be done, all the business houses of the island would use the money-order system."

SPECIAL AGENTS.

The report of the chief special agent summarizes the operations of the inspection service of the Department. Upon this branch depends largely the maintenance of official discipline and the general tone and standard of service. The special agents instruct postmasters, inspect accounts, investigate complaints of all sorts, and in cases of grave irregularity bring delinquents to the attention of the criminal courts. 35 arrests and 25 convictions occurred during the six months for various postal offences, mostly of a minor nature, such as the re-use of canceled stamps. This inveterate evil has been greatly abated in consequence. It is not amiss to bear testimony here to the merit of the Cuban judiciary. The experience of this Department with the Cuban courts has been satisfactory, indeed, and by no means warrants the indiscriminate criticism sometimes heard, imputing to them inertia and inconclusiveness. The procedure may seem peculiar to one accustomed to a different system, but the essential aim is justice, and this aim is achieved with the average celerity and directness of like cases in the United States. Such at any rate is the experience of the Department of Posts.

This does not relate to the tentative jury system in the inferior Correctional Courts, our experience with which, as I have had occasion to report before, has been wholly bad.

At the time of rendering my last periodical report, that for the fiscal year 1901, it was confidently expected that the prosecutions based on the general frauds in the Department of Posts would be concluded and that burdensome case finally disposed of before the close of the calendar year. But the event disappointed such expectation. It is useless to rehearse the various causes and stages of delay. The Primary Court closed the "Sumario" on Sept. 30. This preliminary proceeding was open to the scrutiny and participation of the defence during the many months of its pendency. Nevertheless unpreparedness was finally claimed, and extension of time was granted the defence beyond the regulation maximum period, until the year expired with the trial still in the future. The continual inroads on the time of the Department by this case, in various ways, cannot be separated or measured in the sum total of salaries, but it represents no slight element of the same. As late as December, at the eleventh hour, I was called upon at instance of the defence for a mass of records which could have been secured as well any previous time during the year then closing. Such requisitions for testimony had to be given the right of way, and in responding thereto other work must be thrown aside. Much translation work was performed. Every scrap of record evidence called for was supplied so far as could be ransacked from the files of the Department.

Full statistical information may be found in the annexed reports of the several bureau chiefs of the Department. In general and in conclusion, the affairs of the Department are believed to be in a healthy condition, and established firmly on a basis of permanent success.

Very respectfully,

M. C. Fosnes,

Director-General.

The Military Governor,

Havana, Cuba

REPORT

OF THE

DISBURSING OFFICER

DEPARTMENT OF POSTS OF CUBA.

DEPARTMENT OF POSTS OF CUBA

DISBURSING OFFICE

Havana, March 12, 1902.

The Director General,

Department of Posts.

Sir:

In compliance with your instructions of the 8th inst., I have the honor to forward herewith statements of the disbursements made on account of the Postal Service of Cuba during the six months ended December 31, 1901.

To obtain the actual cost of the service during that period it would be necessary to add to the statement herewith the following payments made during the month of January, 1902, for services, material, etc., furnished during the month of December.

Salaries, Department of Posts	$ 599.98
,, Clerks in postoffices	1,161.30
,, Postmasters	6,136.41
,, Railway postal clerks	990.26
,, Letter Carriers	1,481.24
Printing and stationery	490.05
Rent of postoffices	587.00
Lighting postoffices	278.07
Per diem	372.00
Bond premiums	510.00
Mail transportation	3,095.54
Postmarking and rubber stamps	31.75
Building and repairs	49.73
Star route contractors	2,327.65
Mail messengers	234.58
Miscellaneous	1,668.91
	$ 20,014.47
Amount as shown by statement	$ 180,688.41
Actual expenditures on account of the six months	$ 200,702.88

Since August last this office has had charge of money order remittances made to the United States. They have been as follows:

August	$ 141,591.40
September	65,000.00
October	45,000.00
November	90,000.00
December	80,000.00
	$ 421,591.40

Very respectfully,

GEO. R. BUCHANAN,

Disbursing Officer,

Department of Posts of Cuba.

FISCAL YEAR 1900.

GENERAL HEAD, FINANCE.—SUB-HEAD, POSTAL SERVICE.

	July.	August.	September.	October.	TOTAL.
Receipts:					
Balance on hand as shown by last report	$ 29.31				$ 29.31
Received from the Treasurer of Cuba	32.00		$226.13		258.13
Total	$ 61.31		$226.13		$287.44
Disbursements:					
Salaries, postmasters			$ 30.18	$185.44	$215.62
Miscellaneous		$ 32.00		20.00	52.00
Deposited, Treasurer of Cuba		16.06		3,76	19.82
Total		$ 48.06	$ 30.18	$209.20	$287.44

FISCAL YEAR 1901.

GENERAL HEAD, FINANCE.—SUB-HEAD, POSTAL SERVICE.

	JULY.	AUGUST	SEPTEMBER.	OCTOBER.	NOVEMBER	DECEMBER.	TOTAL.
Receipts:							
Balance on hand, as shown by last report	$ 1,795.13						$ 1,795.13
Received from the Treasurer of Cuba			$ 2,008.13		$ 35.00		2,043.13
TOTAL	$ 1,795.13		$ 2,008 13		$ 35.00		$ 3,838.26
DISBURSEMENTS.—*Salaries:*							
Department of Posts		$ 124.27					$ 124.27
Postmasters	$ 16.60	102.67	$ 129.14		$ 54.93		303.34
Clerks in postoffices			31.11				31.11
Printing and stationery			181.32	$ 447.39			628.71
Rent of postoffices			48.00				48 00
Lighting postoffices		18.70			18.00		36.70
Per diem		116.00					116.00
Bond premiums	15.00						15.00
Mail transportation			917.47	45.00	50.00		1,012.47
Building and repairs		10.00	7.40				17.40
Postmarking stamps	15.57						15.57
Miscellaneous		6.50	151.27	31.07	35.00		223.84
TOTAL	$ 47.17	$ 378.14	$ 1,465.71	$ 523.46	$ 157.93		$ 2,572.41
Deposited, Treasurer of Cuba		1,030.02				$ 170.81	1,200.83
Balance to January account							65.02
	$ 47.17	$ 1,408.16	$ 1,465.71	$ 523.46	$ 157.93	$ 170.81	$ 3,838.26

FISCAL YEAR 1902.

GENERAL HEAD, FINANCE.—SUB HEAD, POSTAL SERVICE.

	JULY.	AUGUST.	SEPTEMBER.	OCTOBER.	NOVEMBER.	DECEMBER.	TOTAL.
Receipts:							
Treasurer of Cuba	$ 36,426.67	$ 36,154.79	$ 35,236.33	$ 34,806.33	$ 32,392.51	$ 32.330.30	$207,346.93
Total	$ 36,426.67	$ 36,154.79	$ 35,235.33	$ 34,806.33	$ 32,392,51	$ 32,330,30	$207,346.93
Disbursements:							
Salaries:							
Department of Posts	$ 4,258.20	$ 4,824.31	$ 4,103.76	$ 4,782.08	$ 4,681.55	$ 4,361.55	$ 27,011.45
Postmasters	291.66	7,221.53	7,507.65	7,356.05	7,647.07	8,354.77	38,378.73
Clerks in postoffices	4,447.55	5,796.50	5,703.48	5,563.50	6,202.82	6,373.15	34. 087.00
Railway postal clerks	699.92	1,715.16	1,698.33	1,656.96	1,814.07	1,726.84	9,311.28
Letter Carriers	3,283.15	5,173.80	5,192.09	5,111.61	4,927.67	5,219.76	28,908.08
Printing and stationery		369 80	332.54	1,222.73	833.19	907.20	3,665.46
Rent of postoffices		326.00	303.00	502.00	418.00	358.00	1,908.00
Lighting postoffices		330.41	207.75	192.35	227.32	214.36	1,172.19
Per diem		460.00	248.00	720.00	600.00	360.00	2,388.00
Bond premiums		260 00					260.00
Mail transportation		2,928.59	3,133.38	3,138.95	3,236.69	3,080.00	15,517.61
Postmarking and rubber stamps		41.12	12.25	17.31		14.02	84.70
Building and repairs	54.00	95.30	69.32	108.70	67.15	84.59	479.06
Star route contractors		2,284.65	2,360.81	2,297.88	2,385.98	2,842.65	11,671.97
Mail messengers		421.90	419.15	415.81	409.15	528.72	2,194.73
Equipment		20.00		27.50			47.50
Letter balances and scales				45 00			45.00
Street letter boxes				146.25			146.25
Mail wagons				16.00			16.00
Transportation					3.21		3.21
Miscellaneous	250.83	750.66	670.10	522 93	666.93	530.74	3,392.19
Total	$ 13,285.31	$ 33,019.73	$ 31,961.61	$ 33,844.61	$ 34,120 80	$ 34,456.35	$180,688.41
Deposited, Treasurer of Cuba		1,012.50	1,012.50			854.25	2,879.25
Balance to January account							23,779.27
	$ 13,286.31	$ 34.032.23	$ 32,974.11	$ 33,844.61	$ 34,120.80	$ 35,310.60	$207,346.93

RECAPITULATION.

	FISCAL YEAR 1900.	FISCAL YEAR 1901.	FISCAL YEAR 1902.	TOTAL.
Balances	$ 29.31	$ 1,795.13	....	$ 1.824.44
Received from Treasurer of Cuba	258.13	2,043 13	$ 207,346.93	209,648 19
TOTAL	$ 287.44	3,838.26	$ 207.346.93	$ 211,472 63
Disbursements	$ 267.62	$ 2.572.41	$ 180,688.41	$ 183,528.44
Deposited with Treasurer of Cuba	19.82	1,200.83	2.879.25	4,099.90
Balance to January account	....	65.02	23.779 27	23.844.29
TOTAL	$ 287.44	$ 3 838.26	$ 207.346.93	$ 211,472.63

REPORT

OF THE

BUREAU OF STAMPS AND SUPPLIES

DEPARTMENT OF POSTS OF CUBA.

DEPARTMENT OF POSTS OF CUBA

BUREAU OF STAMPS AND SUPPLIES

Havana, March 13, 1902.

Mr. M. C. Fosnes,
Director General,
Present.

SIR:

I have the honor to submit to you herewith a report of the transactions and the volume of business done through and by this bureau for the six months ending December 31, 1901, with a brief note regarding the property of the Department of Posts outside of stamped paper.

Statement "A" shows the denomination of each kind of stamped paper, and the quantity and value of the same issued by this bureau to the various postmasters of the island for the six months ending December 31, 1901.

Statement "B" is a condensed statement showing the value of the total amount on hand July 1, 1901, the total value issued, and the balance on hand December 31, 1901.

Statement "C" shows the quantity of each size of penalty envelopes issued for the same period, and the cost of same to the Department of Posts.

No accounting of office furniture, fixtures, etc., was made previous to December 31, 1901. Early in January, 1902, a complete return was made to the Auditor for Cuba of all insular property charged to the Department of Posts, most of which is out on the island in the postoffices. This report embraces public property purchased with insular funds since the inception of the Department of Posts of Cuba. Reports on the above property wherever it is located are in the files of this bureau and a regular property report filed with the Auditor for Cuba.

Very respectfully,

GEO. W. MARSHALL,

Chief, Bureau of Stamps and Supplies.

ths, from July 1, 1901, to December 31, 1901.

CARDS.	WRAPPERS.		POSTAGE DUE STAMPS.				VALUE.
2 cents.	1 cent.	2 cents.	1 cent.	2 cents.	5 cents.	10 cents	
125	1,100	500	2,550	2,550	1,000	500	$ 32,146.45
1,005	750	....	2,822	1,582	1,000	500	24,991.95
1,100	1,500	....	2,150	2,250	....	....	22,937.29
....	2,650	200	4,050	3,155	1,200	800	34,026.98
515	500	....	2,225	3,075	20	310	26,187.95
100	1,100	500	5,144	4,025	300	800	34,131.36
2,845	7,600	1,200	18,941	16,637	3,520	2,910	$174,421.98

STATEMENT "B"

STATEMENT OF THE VALUE OF STAMPED PAPER ON HAND, RECEIVED AND ISSUED FOR SIX MONTHS FROM JULY 1, 1901, TO DECEMBER 31, 1901.

	Dollars.	Cts.		Dollars.	Cts.
1.—To amount of postage stamps, stamped envelopes, newspaper wrappers and postal cards on hand July 1, 1901	149,431	80	A.—By amount of stamped paper sent to postmasters from July 1, 1901, to December 31, 1901	174,421	98
2.—To amount stamped paper received from the Director General of posts from July 1, 1901, to December 31, 1901	170,638	30	B.—By amount of stamped paper on hand December 31, 1901, as shown by actual count of stock	145,648	12
TOTAL	320.070	10	TOTAL	320,070	10

STATEMENT "C"

STATEMENT SHOWING QUANTITY AND COST OF PENALTY ENVELOPES ISSUED

FOR SIX MONTHS, FROM JULY 1 TO DECEMBER 31, 1901.

No. 7	34,783	$ 77.99
No. 10.....	202,392	605.15
No. 11	18,214	63.57
No. 14	1,500	5.85
Odd Sizes	20,125	97.85
Total	277,014	$ 850.41

REPORT

OF THE

BUREAU OF APPOINTMENTS AND TRANSPORTATION

DEPARTMENT OF POSTS OF CUBA.

DEPARTMENT OF POSTS OF CUBA

BUREAU OF APPOINTMENTS AND TRANSPORTATION

Havana, March 25, 1902.

The Director General,
Department of Posts of Cuba.

SIR:

I have the honor to submit herewith a report covering the operations of the Bureau of Appointments and Transportation, from July 1, up to and including December 31, 1901.

Very respectfully,

ALBERT J. XANTEN,
Chief Bureau of Appointments and Transportation.

NUMBER OF POSTOFFICES IN OPERATION.

PROVINCE.	Number.
Havana	62
Matanzas	51
Pinar del Río	41
Puerto Principe	12
Santa Clara	95
Santiago	41
Total	302

Of the number shown above 31 are free delivery offices, employing 113 letter carriers

Number of postoffices in operation June 30, 1901		300
Number of postoffices established	13	
Number of postoffices discontinued	11	2
Number of postoffices in operation December 31, 1901		302

NUMBER OF EMPLOYEES IN THE SERVICE.

	Cuban	American	Total
Postmasters	300	2	302
P. O. Employees	246	9	255
Dept. Employees	18	22	40
R. P. Clerks	42	......	42
Total	606	33	639

Postmasters, P. O. Employees. Dept. Employes, R. P. Clerks.	639
By adding the number of employees serving under contract, we obtain the following result:	
Star Route Contractors	67
Mail and Transfer messengers	12
Total of all employees December 31, 1901...	718

ADDITIONS TO AND SEPARATIONS FROM THE SERVICE.

July 1—Dec. 31, 1901.	*Additions.*	*Separations.*
Dept. Employees	1	4
Postmasters	39	37
Other Employees	33	45
Total	73	86

ANNUAL EXPENDITURE FOR SALARIES.

December 31, 1901.

Department of Posts	$ 56,260
Postmasters	89,855
Clerks in postoffices	73,710
Letter Carriers	57,690
Messengers, janitors, etc	7,838
Railway postal clerks	20,504
Total	$ 305,857

ALLOWANCES.

Miscellaneous Purposes.

No.	*Amount.*
60	$ 2,129.64

Stated Annual Allowances.

Offices.	*Amount.*
23	$ 8,030.95

Stated Annual Allowances Discontinued.

Offices.	*Amount.*
3	$ 394.20

Special Agents' reports considered and acted upon.... 58
Cases referred to Special Agents................ 146

BONDS.

Bonds in force June 30, 1901:

Department clerks.............	7	$ 45,000		
Postmasters......................	175	306,900		
P. O. employees	84	137,500	266	$ 489,400

Bonds issued.

Department clerks.....	1	$ 2,000		
Postmasters......................	39	59,700		
P. O. employees..........	21	52,000	61	$ 113,700
			327	$ 603,100

Bonds cancelled.

(Including Personal Bonds invalidated):

Department clerks............	.....	....		
Postmasters....................	33	$ 52,900		
P. O. employees.	31	77,500	64	$ 130,400
			263	$ 472,700

RECAPITULATION.

Corporation bonds in force June 30, 1901......			154	$ 358,700
Corporation bonds issued	25	$ 64,000		
Cancelled.	46	109,500	21	$ 45,500

Corporation bonds in effect December 31, 1901..........			....		133	$ 313,200
Personal bonds in force June 30, 1901 ......,........			112	$ 130,700		
Personal Bonds issued July 1, to December 31, 1901.......	36	$49,700				
Invalidated July 1 to Dec. 31, 1901...	18	$20,900	18	$ 28,800	130	$ 159,500
					263	$ 472,700

Of the 130 personal bonds in force December 31, 1901, 45 cover postmasters in Money Order Offices.

December 31, 1901.

TRANSPORTATION MAIL SERVICE IN GENERAL.

	No.	*Length.*	*Annual cost.*
Star routes..............................	67	1,469.74	$ 27,693.00
Steamboat routes.	12	2,845.25	26,910.00
Railroad routes	31	1,097.51	5,244.00
Wagon transfer routes.........	3	14.64	4,950.00
Mail messenger routes........	9	5.88	1,556.00
Total routes........	122	5,433.02	$ 66,353.00
Ry. postoffice lines	26	1,889.20	....
Ry. postal clerks	42	....	$ 20,504.00
Total for domestic service	.....	. ...	$ 86,857.00
Foreign mail service......	.....	....	$ 3,983.31
			$ 90,840.31

SUMMARY OF ALL CLASSES OF MAIL ROUTES.

Number of all routes, 122.
Length of all routes, 5,483.02 miles.
Annual rate of expenditure, $66,353.00.
Number of miles traveled per annum, 1,691,929.00.
Rate of cost per mile of length, $12.21.
Rate of cost per mile traveled, 3.922 cents.

COMPARISON WITH SERVICE IN OPERATION JUNE 30, 1901.

Increase in number of routes, 4.
Decrease in length of routes, 130.28 miles.
Decrease in annual rate of expenditure, $11,125.00.
Increase in miles traveled per annum, 7,066.
Decrease in rate of cost per mile traveled, .674 of a cent.
Decrease in cost per mile of length, 1.72 cents.

STAR ROUTE SERVICE.

Number of routes, 67.
Length of routes, miles, 1,469.74.
Annual travel, miles, 389,908.
Rate of annual expenditure, $27,693.00.
Average number of trips per week, 5.3.
Rate of cost per mile of length, $18.84.
Rate of cost per mile traveled, 7.1 cents.

COMPARISON WITH JUNE 30, 1901.

Increase in number of routes, 3.
Increase in length of routes, miles, 103.
Increase in annual cost, $59.00.
Increase in annual travel, miles, 11,648.
Decrease in cost per mile of length, $1 38.
Increase in average number of trips a week, .06 of a trip.
Decrease in cost of mile traveled, .21 of a cent.

BY PROVINCES.

PROVINCE.	Number of routes.	Miles.	Annual cost.	Cost per mile	Annual travel.	Cost per mile trav
Havana	9	110.87	$ 3,301	29.78	58,838	5 61 cts.
Pinar del Río	16	264.87	6,903	26.06	96,577	7.15 ,,
Matanzas	4	30.	966	32.20	10,400	9.289 ,,
Santa Clara	20	303.	6,953	22 95	122,200	5.69 ,,
Puerto Príncipe	5	290.	3,100	10 07	37,856	8.189 ,,
Santiago de Cuba	13	471.	6,470	13.74	64,037	10.103 ,,
Total	67	1469 74	$27,693	18.842	389,908	7,102 cts.

INCREASES, DECREASES AND CHANGES.

Number of new routes established............	4	
Number of routes discontinued (by merging route 5004 with route 5003.....	1	
A net increase of............	3 routes.	
Increased mileage, new routes.................	98	
Increased mileage, account additional service on old routes (No. 1009).	6	
	104 miles.	
Decreased mileage account rearrangement in route No. 6005.	1	
	103	
Cost of service June 30, 1901...........		$27,634
Decrease by new contracts on old routes...	$ 205	
Decrease by merging route number 5004 with 5003....	900	
Total decrease $1,105		1,105
		$26.529
Increased cost account new contracts..................		1.164
		$27,693

STAR ROUTE SERVICE PROVIDED FOR AFTER DECEMBER 31, 1901.

Number of routes, 67.
Length of routes, miles, 1,469.74.
Rate of cost per annum, $27,693.00.
Increase in number of routes, 3 over June 30, 1901.
Increase in mileage, 103 miles.
Increase in annual cost, $59.00.

STEAMBOAT SERVICE

Number of routes, 12.
Length of routes, miles, 2.845.25.
Cost per annum, $26,910.00
Cost per mile of length, $9 46.
Annual travel, 302,337.
Cost per mile traveled, 8.9 cents.

COMPARISON WITH SERVICE IN OPERATION JUNE 30, 1901.

Decrease in number of routes, 1.
,, in length of routes, miles, 242.
,, in cost per annum, $11,700.00.
,, in cost per mile of length, $3.05.
,, in annual travel, 25,168
,, in cost per mile traveled, $2.88.

COMPARISON WITH JUNE 30, 1901.

Decrease in number of routes, 1.
,, in mileage, 242.
,, in cost, $ 11,700.00.

ITEMIZED STEAMBOAT SERVICE.

Operative July 1, 1901, to December 31, 1901.

Route	TERMINI.	CONTRACTOR.	Annual pay $	Length miles.	Trips.
1	Havana to Santiago.	Sobrinos de Herrera.	12,000	840	3 a month.
2	Batabanó to Santiago	Menendez & Co.	9,000	614.46	1 a week.
3	Batabanó to Nueva Gerona	Angel C. Ceballos	600	92.	1 a week.
4	Santiago to Caimanera	Gallego, Mesa & Co.	1,000	45.	2 a week.
5	Havana to Nuevitas.	Alonso Jauma & Co.	300	409.	1 a week.
6	Cienfuegos to Tunas de Zaza	José Castro Monje	300	82.08	2 a week.
7	Havana to la Fé	A. del Collado	1,200	227.49	4 a month.
10	Cienfuegos to Rodas.	Boullón & Co	360	30.	7 a week.
11	Batabanó to Manzanillo	Alonso Jauma & Co	200	425.22	2 a month.
12	Mayarí to Port Mayarí	Carlota Grau	600	15.	1 a week.
13	Manzanillo to Niquero	José Muñiz	1,200	51.	7 a week.
15	Cienfuegos to Belmonte	E. Atkins & Co	150	14.	2 a week.
			26,910	2845.25	

RAILROAD SERVICE.

Number of railroad routes, 31.
Length of railroad routes, 1,097.51.
Annual travel, 980,852 miles.
Annual pay, $ 5,244.

COMPARISON WITH JUNE 30, 1901.

Decrease in number of routes, (128) 1.
Increase in number of routes, (132) 1.
Increase in mileage, 5.5 miles.
Increase in annual travel, 38,762.20 miles.
Annual pay.—No change.

WAGON TRANSFER SERVICE.

Number of routes, 3.
Length of routes, 14.64 miles.
Miles traveled per annum, 24,430.

Rate of annual cost, 4,950.
Cost per mile, 338.11.
Cost per mile traveled, 20.27 cents.
No change from service June 30, 1901.

MAIL MESSENGER SERVICE.

Number of routes, 9.
Length, miles, 5.88.
Annual cost, $1,556.00.
Cost per mile, 364.63.
Annual travel, 7,971.02.
Cost per mile traveled, 19.6 cents.

RAILWAY MAIL SERVICE.

Number of lines, 26.
Number of clerks, 42.
Miles railway mail service, 1,889.20.
Annual mileage of clerks, 1,139,140.51.
Total pay of clerks, $20,504.00.
Average pay for clerk, $488.19 per annum.

COMPARISON WITH JUNE 30, 1901.

Decrease number of lines, 1.
Decrease number of clerks, 1.
Decrease in miles of service, 41.86.
Increase in annual mileage of clerks, 7,981.14.
Increase total pay of clerks, 220.00
Increase in average pay per clerk, $6.23.

FINES.

Fines against steamboat contractors.........	$ 78.31
Fines against star route contractors.........	2.44

NOTE.—In addition to the fines of $78.31 against steamboat contractors a fine of $11.54 was imposed upon S. B. Route No. 3, Angel G. Ceballos, for failure to perform service November 23 to 27 inclusive, acc't S. S. "Nuevo Cubano," condemned, but no vouchers were ever presented for payment (although the contractor was requested to send same) for service performed during that month, and the fine stands against this contractor's credit for one month's pay.

STATEMENT OF THE RATE OF EXPENDITURES PER ANNUM FOR DISPATCHING FOREIGN MAIL.

Amount paid for direct dispatches to foreign countries ...... $ 3,983.31

Amount of mail dispatched to foreign countries for which payment was made at the rate of 44 cents per pound for letters and post-cards, and 4½ cents per pound for other matter.

Letters and post-cards.. 7,278.52 lbs. .... $ 3,202.55
Other matter.............. 17,350.01 " 780.76

$3,983.31

NOTE.—Amount due under the Universal Postal Regulations of foreign countries (for maritime and territorial transit) is not included in this report for the reason that statements of amounts due for the year ending December 31, 1901, were not received at the time of completion of report.

RAILWAY POSTOFFICE LINES IN OPERATION DECEMBER 31, 1901.

DESIGNATION OF LINE.	Length.	No. Clks.	Pay.	Annual travel.	Mail apts.
Caib. Cam. Placetas	32.93	1	$ 400	24,038.90	1
Caibarién and and Placetas	22.31	1	400	16,286.30	1
Cárdenas and Santa Clara	105.53	3	1,600	91,224.39	3
Cárdenas and Yaguaramas	71.16	1	500	51,946.80	1
Cienfuegos and Cartagena					
By boat 30 miles				21,900.00	
By rail 20 ,,	50.00		540	7,520.00	1
Cienfuegos and Santa Clara	42.81	2	1,000	62,502.60	1
Cienfuegos and Tunas, (by boat)	82.03	1	240	15,583.80	
Gibara and Holguín	20.00	1	384	6,480.00	1
Havana and Alacranes	81.20	4	2,000	118,389.60	5
Havana, Bat. and Santiago		2	1,200		3
By rail 36.24 miles	650.70			3,805.20	
By boat 614.46 ,,				64,518.80	
Havana and Guanajay	35.63	2	1,000	51,806.02	1
Havana and Jovellanos	88 70	4	2,200	104,154.75	4
Havana and Marianao	10.00	1	500	19,460 00	
Havana and Pinar del Río	110.00	3	1,500	112,690.10	3
Isabela and Caibarién	69.29	2	1,000	50,581.70	1
Isabela and Cienfuegos	68.37	2	1,000	64,999.40	2
Júcaro and Morón	42.30	1	400	27,452.70	
Macagua and Altamisal	20.20	1	400	14,746.00	1
Mad. Emp. and Güines	25.88	1	420	31,728.88	1
Manzanillo and Niquero (boat)	51.00	1	480	26,112.00	Desk.
Matanzas and Colón	70.00	1	600	51,100.00	1
Navajas and Murga	30.00	1	400	21,900.00	1
Nuevitas and Puerto Príncipe	45.63	1	400	24,092.64	1
Palmira and Rodas	18.36	1	420	26,834.80	1
Sancti-Spíritus and Tunas	24.47	1	500	10,203.99	1
Santiago and San Luis	20.63	2	1,020	17,081.64	1
Railway postoffices 26	1,889.20	42	$20.504	1,139,140.51	36

Total Railway Postoffices		26.
,, Miles		1,889.20
,, Railway postal clerks		42.
,, Pay to R. P. clerks	$	20,504.00
Annual travel on railways		1.011,026.41
,, ,, ,, steamboat		128,114.10
TOTAL	$	1.139,140.51

CLASSIFIED LIST OF SALARIES OF RAILWAY POSTAL CLERKS.

Number.	*Salary.*	*Total.*
8........................	$ 600.00	$ 4,800.00
1........................	540.00	540.00
20........................	500.00	10,000.00
1........................	480.00	480.00
3........................	420.00	1,260.00
7........................	400.00	2,800.00
1........................	384.00	384.00
1........................	240.00	240.00
42 Clerks....................	....	$ 20,504.00
Average pay for clerk	$ 488.19	

MAIL WORKED BY R. P. O. LINES JULY 1, 1901, UP TO DECEMBER 31, 1901.

Railway Postoffices.	Clerks.	Trips.	Pkgs. letters.	Sacks papers.	Reg. Pkgs.	Reg. Pchs.	Reg. Cases.	Inner Sacks.
Caibarien, Camarones and Placetas...............	1	368	4,308	339	695			
Caibarien and Placetas..	1	368	3,457	217	1,279			
Cárdenas and Sta. Clara.	3	736	16,660	1,357	8,241	1,828	81	4
Cárdenas and Yaguaramas..........................	1	368	10,493	604	2,276	....	1	1
Cienfuegos and Cartagena...........................	1	592	3,704	1,118	895			
Cienfuegos and Sta. Clara	2	736	7,146	851	1,816			
Cienfuegos and Tunas ...	1	76	....	....	1,402			
Gibara and Holguín.......	1	169	534	156	1,417			
Havana and Alacranes...	4	.736	22,008	1.168	5.881			
Hav Bat. and Santiago.	2	52	10.014	2.201	3,113	360	4	1
Havana and Jovellanos..	4	736	25,933	1,651	7.876	2,536	72	5
Havana and Guanajay...	2	736	14.563	667	2,302	....	3	1
Havana and Marianao...	1	1,000	4,267	461	281	....	......	684
Havana and Pinar del Rio............................	3	736	15,486	895	4,024	368	16	
Isabela and Caibarien....	2	368	6,737	1,061	4,259	368		
Isabela and Cienfuegos..	2	736	7,280	1,525	6,178	1,115	2	
Júcaro and Morón..........	1	436	2,265	686	1,270			
Macagua and Altamisal.	1	368	2,961	322	1,343			
Madruga, Empalme and Güines..........................	1	736	3,503	314	480			
Manzanillo and Niquero.	1	245	1,693	....	295			
Matanzas and Colón......	1	368	12,800	937	2,830			
Navajas and Murga.......	1	368	4,141	341	493			
Nuevitas and Pto. Príncipe..............................	1	262	229	46	1,279	133	7	
Palmira and Rodas........	1	480	3,113	480	154	....	2	
Scti. Spíritus and Tunas.	1	214	1,127	....	1,351			
Santiago and San Luis...	2	630	5,796	338	1,533	10	2	
	42	12,620	190,218	17,735	62,963	6,718	190	696

ERRORS IN DISTRIBUTION.

JULY 1 TO DECEMBER 31, 1901.

	Postoffice.	*R. P. Office.*	*Total.*
Pieces of ordinary mail.......	2,179	319	2,498
Missent letter packages.........	31	7	38
Mislabeled letter packages........	24	[illegible]	25
Missent sacks of papers.....	1		5
Mislabeled sacks of papers..............	10	....	10
Mislabeled pouch letters	[illegible]		[illegible]
Missent registered packages....			

REPORT

OF THE

MONEY-ORDER AND REGISTRY BUREAU

DEPARTMENT OF POSTS OF CUBA.

DEPARTMENT OF POSTS OF CUBA

MONEY ORDER AND REGISTRY BUREAU

Havana, April 1, 1902.

Director General of Posts of Cuba
Havana, Cuba.

Sir:

I have the honor to submit the following report of the money order and registry business transacted on the Island of Cuba during the six months ended December 31, 1901:

MONEY ORDER BUSINESS.

QUARTER ENDED SEPTEMBER 30, 1901.

	Number.	*Amount.*
Domestic money orders issued.	14,725	$ 524,580.39
Foreign ,, ,, ,, ...	10,101	288,432.22
Total	24,826	$ 813,012.61
Fees on domestic money orders issued.	....	$ 2,083.48
,, ,, foreign ,, ,, ,,	.. ..	1,229.18
Total........	....	$ 3,312.66

	Number.	*Amount.*
Domestic money orders paid	14,217	$ 518,113.31
Foreign ,, ,, ,, ...	1,394	42,158.67
Total	15,611	$ 560,271.98

	Number.	*Amount.*
Money orders repaid..	89	$ 2,341.71

QUARTER ENDED DECEMBER 31, 1901.

	Number.	*Amount.*
Domestic money orders issued.........	14,365	$ 481,498.46
Foreign ,, ,, ,, ...	12,431	282,734.55
Total.............	26,796	$ 764,233.01

Fees on domestic money orders issued	....	$	1,958.57
,, ,, foreign ,, ,, ,,	....		1,292.41
Total........		$	3,250.98

	Number.		Amount.
Domestic money orders paid	12,952	$	472,979.99
Foreign ,, ,, ,, ...	1,803		52,633.53
Total..................	14,755	$	525,613.52

	Number.		Amount.
Money orders repaid	107	$	2,349.40

FOR SIX MONTHS ENDED DECEMBER 31, 1901.

	Number.		Amount.
Domestic money orders issued.........	29,090	$	1,006,078.85
Foreign » » ».	22,532		571,166.77
Total	51,622	$	1,577,245.62
Fees on domestic money orders issued	....	$	4,042.05
» » foreign » » »	....		2,521.59
Total....................	....	$	6,563.64

	Number.		Amount.
Domestic money orders paid	27,169	$	991,113.30
Foreign » » »	3,197		94,772.20
Total..........	30,366	$	1,085,885.50

	Number.		Amount.
Money orders repaid......	196	$	4,691.11

REGISTRY BUSINESS.

QUARTER ENDED SEPTEMBER 30, 1901.

Number of domestic paid letters registered	20,691
» » » » parcels »	2,853
» » foreign » letters »	19,192
» » » » parcels »	2,115
Total number of paid registrations	44,851
Number of articles registered free.	6,544
Total number of articles registered, paid and free	51,395
Amount collected for registration fees......	$ 3,588.08

QUARTER ENDED DECEMBER 31, 1901.

Number of domestic paid letters registered	20,516.00
,, ,, ,, ,, parcels ,, ...	2,655 00
,, ,, foreign ,, letters ,, ...	19,901.00
,, ,, ,, ,, parcels ,, ...	3,678.00
Total number of paid registrations............	46,750.00
Number of articles registered free.......	11,285.00
Total number of articles registered paid and free $	58,035.00
Amount collected for registration fees......... $	3,740.00

FOR SIX MONTHS ENDED DECEMBER 31, 1901.

Number of domestic paid letters registered......	41,207.00
,, ,, ,, ,, parcels ,, ...	5,508.00
,, ,, foreign ,, letters ,, ...	39,093.00
,, ,, ,, ,, parcels ,, ...	5,793.00
Total number of paid registrations.....	91,601.00
Number of articles registered free.....	17,829.00
Total number of articles registered paid and free	109,430.00
Amount collected for registration fees......... $	7,328.08

Very respectfully,

C. L. Marine,

Chief, Money Order and Registry Bureau.

REPORT

OF THE

BUREAU OF SPECIAL AGENTS

DEPARTMENT OF POSTS OF CUBA.

DEPARTMENT OF POSTS OF CUBA

BUREAU OF SPECIAL AGENTS

Havana, March 17, 1902.

The Director-General,

Havana, Cuba.

SIR:

I have the honor to submit herewith a tabulated statement showing the work done by the Bureau of Special Agents for the six months ended December 31, 1901.

Very respectfully,

F. M. HAMILTON,

Chief Special Agent.

RECORD of cases treated during the six months ended December 31, 1901.

	CASES MADE UP AND REOPENED.										
	A.	B.			C.			F.			
	Regular.	Regular.	Reopened.	Total.	Regular.	Reopened.	Total.	Regular.	Reopened.	Total.	TOTAL.
Cases on hand July 1, 1901	18	16	1	17	125	17	142	593	....	593	770
Cases made up during six months	56	106	....	106	654	7	661	1,491	1	1,492	2,315
Total	74	122	1	123	779	24	803	2,084	1	2,085	3,085
Cases closed during six months	53	99	....	99	528	17	545	1,512	1	1,513	2,210
Of cases closed—by office	40½	70½	....	70½	13	12	25	1,465	....	1,465	1,601
„ „ „ —by Special Agents	12½	28½	....	28½	515	5	520	47	1	48	609
Cases on hand January 1, 1902	21	23	1	24	251	7	258	572	....	572	875

From Whom Collected.	American Currency.	Spanish Silver.
Shortage in the money-order account of postmasters	$ 323 95	
Shortage in the postal account of postmasters	130.79	
Illegal disposition of property of the department	20.00	
Foreign postal administration because of the wrong delivery of a registered letter.	4.60	
Rifling of registered mail	164.60	
Rifling of ordinary mail.	112.40	
Violation of Section 35 of the Postal Code.	150.00	
Violation of Section 49 of the Postal Code.	4.78	
Violation of Section 52 of the Postal Code.	35.09	
Fine imposed on driver of postal cart for failure to meet train	....	$ .25
Total amount collected	$ 946.21	$ .25

Disbursements.	American Currency.	Spanish Silver.
Deposited with the Treasurer of the Island (Fines and Postal Account)	$ 335.88	
Deposited with the postmaster at Havana (Money Order funds)	403.95	
Paid to the addressee of rifled registered letter	8.00	
Paid to the rightful payee of a forged money order	4.78	
Reimbursement to railway postal clerk for expense in conveying mail to railway station	....	$ .25
Total	$ 946.21	$ .25

ARRESTS.

Cases pending in Courts July 1, 1902	24	
Arrests during the six months ended December 31, 1901	38	62
Convictions secured	25	
Acquittals	12	37
Cases pending in Courts January 1, 1902.	...	25

TITLE OF "C" CASES INVESTIGATED AND CLOSED DURING THE SIX MONTHS ENDED DECEMBER 31, 1901.

Establishment of postoffices and postal stations.	14
Establishment of the money-order system in postoffices.	4
Appointment of postmasters.	18
Instruction of postmasters	38
Leases and removal of postoffices	2
Repairs, allowances and supplies for postoffices.	12
Readjustment of salaries and expenses in postoffices.	20
Inspection of postoffices	140
Readjustment of the accounts of postmasters	3
Miscellaneous matters.	21
Railway postoffices, star routes, and mail messenger service	13
Complaints against postmasters	17
Complaints against clerks and other employees in the service	6
Complaints against carriers	6
Alleged delay in the despatch of mail	6
Alleged tampering	11
Alleged loss	9
Miscellaneous complaints against the service	5
Alleged violation of section 8 of the postal code	1
" " " " 11 " " " "	1
" " " 12, 13, 14 " " " "	1
" " " 19 " " " "	4
" " " 23 " " " "	1
" " " 25 " " " "	1
" " " 27 " " " "	2
" " " 35 " " " "	174
" " " 41 " " " "	1
" " " 42 " " " "	1
" " " 45 " " " "	1
" " " 49 " " " "	1
" " " " 52 " " " "	6
" " " " 60 " " " "	3
Miscellaneous complaints against those not in the service	1
Burning of postoffice	1
TOTAL	545

REPORT

OF THE

DEAD-LETTER BUREAU

DEPARTMENT OF POSTS OF CUBA

Statement showing the receipt and disposition of all mail matter in the Dead Letter Bureau during the six months from July 1 to December 31, 1901.

RECEIVED.

Unregistered domestic unclaimed letters	23,393	
Unregistered domestic letters held for postage	2,146	
Unregistered domestic letters misdirected	31	
Unregistered domestic letters blank	11	
Unregistered domestic letters refused	2,086	
Unregistered printed matter unclaimed	13,606	
Unregistered domestic printed matter refused	252	
Unregistered domestic parcels unclaimed	74	41,599
Unregistered domestic letters returned from foreign countries	4,362	
Unregistered domestic articles and printed matter from foreign countries	394	4,756
Unregistered foreign unclaimed letters	15,251	
Unregistered refused letters (foreign)	728	
Unregistered foreign articles and printed matter	30,304	
Unregistered foreign printed matter refused	127	
Unregistered foreign unmailable letters	110	46,520
Registered domestic letters and parcels unclaimed	403	
Registered foreign letters and parcels unclaimed	1,344	1,747
Total	94,622	94,622

DISPOSITION.

Domestic matter.

Delivered to sender registered articles unopened	292	
Registered articles awaiting delivery by postmaster	84	
Delivered to sender ordinary letters unopened	3,156	3,532

Opened and delivered to sender.

Letters containing money orders	7	
Letters containing money	11	
Letters containing misc. matter	763	
Letters containing correspondence	10,663	
Printed matter	234	
Parcels	85	11,763

Opened and filed.

Letters containing money	8	
Letters opened and awaiting delivery by postmaster	109	
Letters opened containing miscellaneous matter	278	
Registered on file	96	
Unregistered parcels	26	517

Opened and destroyed.

Unsigned letters containing correspondence	16,408	
Printed matter (waste paper)	14,573	30,981

Foreign letters and parcels.

Registered letters and parcels sent to origin	1,296	
Registered letters and parcels delivered	48	
Unregistered letters sent to origin	15,825	
Unregistered articles delivered	310	
Unregistered articles and printed matter sent to origin	18,336	
Waste paper	12,049	47,864
Total	94,657	94,657

Letters containing money.

	Number.	Amount.
Filed in the Dead Letter Bureau	12	$ 5.72
Total	12	$ 5.72

Delivered to Mr. Chas. Hernandez, postmaster at Havana, all the money that was on file in the Dead Letter Bureau up to date, Nov. 29, 1901..	$	4.60
Delivered to Mr. Chas. Hernandez, postmaster at Havana, the money that was on deposit in the Bureau of Finance during March, 1900, from the Dead Letter Bureau, and has been returned to this Bureau on this date Nov. 29, 1901, by Mr. G. W. Marshall, Chief of Bureau of Stamps and Supplies.........		41.53
Total...............................	$	46.13

Respectfully submitted,

A. ARTEAGA.

Chief Dead Letter Bureau.

To the Director General of Posts,

Havana, Cuba.

REPORT

OF THE

BUREAU OF TRANSLATION

DEPARTMENT OF POSTS OF CUBA

DEPARTMENT OF POSTS OF CUBA

BUREAU OF TRANSLATION

Havana, March 29, 1902.

The Director General

Department of Posts of Cuba.

SIR:

Nothing of importance beyond the general routine have I to say in reference to this bureau, excepting that the work has somewhat diminished during the last six months compared with that of last year.

I shall therefore only give an abstract of the translations made from July 1, 1901, to December 31, 1901, inclusive, which is as follows:

NUMBER OF TRANSLATIONS.

1901.	Incoming Letters.	Outgoing Letters.	Miscellaneous.
July 31............	662	685	42
Aug. 31....................	484	587	58
Sept. 30.........	626	549	118
Oct. 31....................	601	617	53
Nov. 30.............	512	566	101
Dec. 31....	464	463	63
Total...........	3,349	3,467	435

Thus a total of 7,251 translations were made during the above mentioned period, a monthly average of 1,208, which compared with that of last year, viz., 1,388, shows a monthly decrease of 180 translations.

I must tender a word of praise in behalf of the force of this bureau, who have been constantly doing their best to render prompt and efficient work, and express once more my gratitude to all in the department for their kind treatment.

Respectfully,

R. VENCE,

Chief, Bureau of Translation.

INFORME

DE

Sr. M. C. FOSNES,

Director General de Correos.

COMPRENDIENDO EL SEMESTRE TERMINADO

EN DICIEMBRE 31

1901.

OFICINA DEL DIRECTOR GENERAL,

Habana, 5 de Abril de 1902.

SEÑOR:

Tengo el honor de presentar á Vd. el siguiente informe del semestre de 1º de Julio á 31 de Diciembre de 1901.

Durante dicho período las operaciones corrientes del Departapartamento de Correos han seguido su curso natural, sin acontecimientos notables que merezcan mención especial, si que con mejoramiento gradual del servicio. Han sido relativamente pocas las quejas y de ninguna importancia, lo que indica que el público en general está satisfecho con el servicio postal de la Isla. El servicio postal afecta directamente á todos, y es para algunas personas un negocio de detalle y de una infinidad de pequeñas operaciones. Está tipado por el sello de 2 centavos, una insignificancia en sí misma; pero es la base principal de las rentas postales. Como es natural suelen ocurrir peripecias en el manejo de la correspondencia, y todo lo que podemos hacer es luchar para reducirlas á un *mínimum.*

Desde que una carta es depositada en el buzón hasta que la recibe el destinatario, en cualquier punto de Cuba, los Estados Unidos ó el resto del mundo, tiene que pasar por muchas manos y ser sometida á varios procedimientos, desde que se le ponga el sello de la oficina hasta su entrega final, en el curso general de transmisión. Hay que contar á menudo con los errores é incomprensibilidad en las direcciones, y no pocas veces se averigua que las quejas se fundan en errores ó circunstancias ajenas al servicio postal. Un mal muy común es el de no recibir cartas que se esperan, sin saber si realmente esas han sido jamás depositadas. Hay una tendencia natural á hacer responsable al servicio postal de todo aquello que pareciese deficiente en la correspondencia. Una carta que se pierda ó no aparezca como se espera, despierta más la atención que cien debidamente recibidas.

INGRESOS.

Los ingresos del Departamento se sostienen de una manera notable á un aproximado de $1,000.00 al día. Mi informe del año fiscal que terminó en Junio 30 de 1901, no podía demostrar definitivamente el efecto de la reducción á la base de franqueo doméstico de los Estados Unidos, que entonces sólo estuvo en operación tres meses. Se verá en la adjunta comparación de los ingresos con los seis meses de 1900, que la baja de los ingresos procedentes de ventas de sellos se había reducido á un promedio diario de $4.76, ó sean $1,737.40 al año. Se puede muy bien asumir que esta diferencia insignificante de ½ p. % ha sido allanada, y que ahora, justamente, un año después de efectuado el cambio, se ha allanado la pérdida de ingresos por ese concepto.

En mi informe al Administrador General recomendando el cambio y sometiéndolo á su criterio, calculaba que dicha pérdida no excedería de $30,000 al año, y queda probado que ese cálculo era muy preciso.

Tomo lo siguiente de dicho informe fechado en 9 de Marzo de 1901:

"Esta cantidad es menos de la mitad de las economías en el servicio postal practicadas en el Departamento de Correos y en la Administración de Correos de la Habana en los últimos nueve meses. La disminución empezaría inmediatamente á corregirse, como es natural, aumentando el volumen de correspondencia.

"En el mes de Diciembre próximo pasado, durante mi ausencia por enfermedad, el Gobernador Militar, por su propia iniciativa, recomendó que se aplicase á Cuba los tipos de franqueo domésticos. Con esta iba unida otra proposición para el establecimiento de un sistema de fardos postales entre los dos países. El Gobernador Militar, que dispone sobre el presupuesto general de la Isla, ha hecho, pues, frente ya á la responsabilidad por la baja consiguiente en los ingresos postales, la que sin embargo, esperamos será solamente temporal."

ESTADO DEMOSTRATIVO DEL TOTAL DE INGRESOS POSTALES DE TODAS PROCEDENCIAS DURANTE EL SEMESTRE QUE TERMINÓ EL 31 DE DICIEMBRE DE 1901.

1901. Mes.	Sellos vendidos.	Alquiler de apartados.	Derechos de G. P. (por trimestre).	Miscelánea.	Total.
Julio	$ 27,286.21	$ 3,294.50		$ 93.44	$ 30,674.15
Agosto	27,105.17	61.80		17.05	27,184 02
Septiembre	25,361.47	142 86	$ 3,312.66	10.62	28,827.61
Octubre	28,083.03	3,357.50		18.44	31,458.97
Noviembre	27,355.79	163.74		19.71	27,539.24
Diciembre	32,676.46	99.36	3,250.98	67.90	36,094.70
Total	$167,868,13	$ 7,119.76	$ 6,563.64	$ 227.16	$181,778.69

Ingresos totales de todas procedencias	$ 181,778.69
Promedio de ingresos mensuales	30,296.45
Promedio de ingresos diarios	987.92
Ingresos totales de ventas de sellos, del 1 de Julio á 31 de Diciembre de 1900	168,744.75
Ingresos totales de ventas de sellos, del 1 de Julio al 31 de Diciembre de 1901	167,868.13
Promedio de ingresos mensuales de ventas de sellos del 1 de Julio á Diciembre 31 de 1900	28,124.12
Promedio de ingresos mensuales de ventas de sellos del 1 de Julio á Diciembre 31 de 1901	27,978 02
Promedio de ingresos diarios de ventas de sellos del 1 de Julio á 31 de Diciembre de 1900	917.09
Promedio de ingresos diarios de ventas de sellos del 1 de Julio á 31 de Diciembre de 1901	912.33

EGRESOS.

El adjunto estado del Habilitado demuestra que los gastos del Departamento durante el semestre ascendieron á $200,702,88, ó sean $401,405.76 al año. Se agregarán para su pago durante la última parte del semestre del año fiscal, los gastos de trasporte, principalmente del servicio extranjero, que ascenderá á unos $16,000.00. El egreso anual se ha traido, pues, dentro de un límite de $420,000, que representa una reducción de $34,284.95 más al último año fiscal. La comparación con los dos años fiscales anteriores de los cuales he presentado informe, es la siguiente. El informe mismo del año fiscal de 1900, esplica el orígen y la naturaleza de los datos por los cuales se ha resumido el total. A este total se agregan aquí $7,830.65 de desembolsos subsecuentes por cuenta del último año.

Año fiscal que terminó en 30 de Junio de 1900.. .. $ 606,328.34
Año fiscal que terminó en Junio 30 de 1901......... 454,284.95
Disminución ..... $ 152,043.39.
Año fiscal que terminó en 30 de Junio de 1902, (calculado como anteriormente se expresa)......... 420,000.00
Disminución...... $ 34,284.95.

En mi informe del año fiscal de 1901, fechado 23 de Agosto de 1901, los gastos se consignaron por la suma de $451,437.89, pero más tarde aparecieron partidas demoradas y aumentaron esta cantidad á $454,284.95, importe que se tomó en cuenta en la anterior comparación.

Los gastos aun exceden los ingresos en $56,000, ó sea poco más ó menos un 13 por ciento. Sin embargo, el aproximarse á casi sostener un establecimiento postal independiente, como el que tenemos, completamente provisto en todas sus partes, y cubriendo un area no mucho menor que el estado de Pensylvania ó el estado de New York, en los ingresos postales de una ciudad Americana de segunda ó tercera clase, es ya un buen éxito.

La ciudad de Omaha, Neb., produce más rentas postales que toda la Isla de Cuba, y la ciudad de Des Moines, Iowa, casi tanto.

SELLOS Y PAPEL TIMBRADO.

De estos se han recibido durante el semestre del Admor. General un total de $170,638.30, y se han suplido á los administradores de correos de la Isla en ejecución de sus pedidos $174 421.98.

PERSONAL, SUELDOS, FIANZAS.

De las 718 personas que figuraban en las nóminas del Departamento al finalizar el período semestral que se está examinando, incluso los contratistas de las rutas de postas 33 eran americanos, esto es, un 4.6 por ciento. Desde entonces varios empleados americanos han presentado su renuncia, y el servicio postal se va cubanizando más y más á medida que se acerca el tiempo del traspaso de administración. El único Administrador de Correos interino americano que queda está en Santiago de Cuba, y puede decirse que con esta excepción, el servicio fuera de la Habana está casi completamente en manos de los cubanos.

Los sueldos de los administradores de correos constituyen el mayor pormenor de los gastos del Departamento, como un 22 por ciento. Las grandes economías efectuadas en los dos últimos años no han afectado el sueldo de los administradores de correos, en general, como tampoco de los demás empleados cubanos. Al contrario, ha aumentado el total de dichos sueldos. Lo más difícil es hacerles comprender la relación que existe entre el sueldo del administrador de correos y las operaciones de su oficina. Bajo la antigua organización española, los empleados de rango de la administración general eran asignados al cargo de las administraciones de correos, con sueldo fijo, y transferibles de un punto á otro. El sueldo se asignaba al empleado y no á la administración, haciendo caso omiso de la importancia de las operaciones. Las distinciones y las desigualdades eran el resultado inevitable, y los administradores de correos no estaban en permanente igualdad de intereses con la comunidad que servían. Ha sido difícil desterrar de la gente la idea de que un nombramiento implica necesariamente un sueldo para vivir de él, é inculcarles el principio contrario de que el sueldo debe calcularse por la importancia de las operaciones, lo que quiere decir que el desempeño de una pequeña administración de correos es una adición á otra ocupación principal.

El establecimiento de sueldos fijos ha tropezado con sus propias dificultades. Como en los Estados Unidos reglamentamos los sueldos en las oficinas mayores por la cantidad de ingresos, que para los fines prácticos significa sellos vendidos, y en las oficinas menores por la cantidad de sellos inutilizados. Generalmente estas son medidas seguras de negocios. En Cuba los comerciantes del campo encuentran ventajosa la venta de sellos como mercancía, comprándolos por moneda Americana y vendiéndolos al precio de por menor en moneda española. Los comerciantes piden con frecuencia estos sellos á la Habana, ó á otras grandes poblaciones, como parte de su pedido general de mercancías, interrumpiendo así la operación normal de suministro y demanda de sellos dentro de la comunidad misma. Esto sólo podrá remediarse por medio de una moneda corriente estable y uniforme.

Otro obstáculo grave para la uniformidad de la escala de sueldos y de las cuentas es la división de administradores de correos que están bajo fianza y los que no lo están. Esto puede dar por resultado la supresión de algunas administraciones de correos pequeñas, en que los administradores antes han renunciado que cumplido, pero finalmente, creemos que alguna persona se encontrará que esté dispuesta á servir, en cada uno de esos puntos, bajo las condiciones generales.

Durante el semestre las fianzas de Compañías han disminuido

en número, de 154 á 133; y en importe total de $358,700 á $313.220, mientras que las fianzas personales aumentaron de 112 que representan $130,700 á 130, que representan $159,500. Las fianzas que se reciben ahora en cumplimiento á la exigencia general, son en su mayor parte fianzas personales. Esperamos dejar bajo fianza á todos los administradores de correos de Cuba al retirarnos de la Isla. Esto no solamente redundará en beneficio de las operaciones, sino que dará al servicio estabilidad y carácter.

GIROS POSTALES.

El dia 1º de Julio de 1901, se puso en vigor un nuevo arreglo para el cambio de giros postales con los Estados Unidos, que se explicó en las instrucciones de fecha 18 de Junio de 1901 á los administradores de correos, en los términos siguientes:

"En armonía con la reciente introducción de tipos domésticos de franqueo entre Cuba y los Estados Unidos, este Departamento puede anunciar un paso más hácia la uniformidad en sus sistemas postales por medio de un arreglo parecido respecto á los cambios de giros postales.

El efecto práctico de esta similitud será la extensión á los Estados Unidos del servicio de giros postales domésticos de Cuba en 1º de Julio de 1901, y la recíproca extensión á Cuba del servicio de giros postales domésticos de los Estados Unidos. La tarifa de derechos será la misma, y el método de las operaciones idéntico en esencia.

El modo pronto y seguro de hacer remesas, implantado en cien diferentes lugares de la Isla por medio de un sistema postal establecido en la forma del de los Estados Unidos, facilitando operaciones mercantiles de todas clases entre los ciudadanos, puede ser ofrecido ahora bajo las mismas condiciones por los administradores de correos cubanos á sus favorecedores, en una escala de potencialidad inmensamente ampliada. Hay más de 32,000 oficinas de correos de giros postales en los Estados Unidos, sin contar las dependencias insulares, y la propuesta alianza hará á Cuba una parte integrante de la comunidad de giros postales mayor del mundo.

Desde el 1º de Julio, el Administrador de cualquiera Administración de correos de giros postales de Cuba puede librar giros directamente sobre cualquiera administración de Correos en los Estados Unidos, lo mismo que hace ahora una Administración de Correos sobre otra dentro de la Isla, y puede recibir y pagar giros de cualquier Administración de Correos de giros postales en los Estados Unidos. En la palabra Estados Unidos están incluídos para este fin, Puerto Rico y Haway. La Habana y Tampa serán abolidas como oficinas de cambio, como también la oficina de cambio de San Juan, Puerto Rico."

Se ha observado un amento notable en los primeros seis meses de operaciones bajo esta convención, según se verá en la siguiente comparación:

GIROS POSTALES EXPEDIDOS:

Julio 1 á Dic. 31, 1900,	Núm. 40,770;	cantidad,	$1.325,734.42.
Julio 1 á Dic. 31, 1901,	,, 51,622;	,,	1.577,245.62.

Aumento verdadero en 1901 sobre 1900, $251,511.20; tanto por ciento, .189.

GIROS POSTALES PAGADOS:

Julio 1 á Dic. 31, 1900, Núm. 25,177; cantidad, $ 923,591.98.
Julio 1 á Dic. 31, 1901, „ 30,366; „ 1.085,885.50.

Aumento verdadero en 1901 sobre 1900, $162,293.52; tanto por ciento: .176.

El resumen del Interventor del año 1900 no distingue las operaciones domésticas de las internacionales, razón por la cual es preciso hacer la comparación con totales en conjunto. Se observará que el número de giros, tanto expedidos como pagados ha aumentado más rápidamente que las cantidades, lo que demuestra que el servicio de giros postales está asumiendo en Cuba la función normal de un medio para hacer pequeñas remesas, como se distingue del cambio comercial. El promedio del importe de giros expedidos es aun mayor que el promedio en los Estados Unidos, según se ve á continuación:

Promedio del importe de giros postales de Julio 1º á Diciembre 31 de 1900	$32.51
Promedio del importe de giros postales de Julio 1º á Diciembre 31 de 1901	30.55
Promedio del importe de giros postales en los Estados Unidos (tomado del último informe anual de 1901)	8.00

Durante los seis meses se pagaron en los Estados Unidos giros postales cubanos por valor de $428,525.83, y se pagaron en Cuba giros librados en los Estados Unidos por la suma de $85,480.88. El saldo que existe permanentemente contra Cuba tiene que ser liquidado por remesas de fondos, que se hicieron durante el mismo período ascendentes á un total de $421,591.40, sin costo de cambio. Al terminar el año quedaba pendiente un saldo de$51,800.79 á favor de Cuba, que representaba un pago adelantado en cuenta. La forma segura y conveniente de hacer remesas, por medio de cambio de fondos con los habilitados del ejército pronto cesará, pero continuamos valiendonos de ese medio mientras dure, y cualquier exceso de pago á los Estados Unidos que resultare será pronto liquidado por medio de la operación normal de cambio, de giros postales, cuyo saldo tiene que continuar pendiente contra Cuba. En esto está de acuerdo el Departamento de Correos.

El servicio de giros postales en Cuba solo puede alcanzar su límite legitimo de utilidad y popularidad con la base de un medio uniforme de circulación.

Nuestra actual moneda corriente es la americana, aunque circulan comercialmente monedas españolas de valores diversos y fluctuaciones, y el procedimiento de inversión encierra perjuicios y á menudo pérdidas al remitente de giros postales. La reciente carta de un administrador de Correos cubano da á conocer como una diversidad de moneda corriente restringe el desarrollo y utilidad del servicio de giros postales. Esta es copia de la carta original en español:

"El Boletín No. 8, que acabo de recibir, expresa que el Sistema Postal en la Isla de Cuba es halagador aunque en algunos puntos el público no se apresuró á sacar partido de las ventajas que le proporcionaba dicho sistema.

"Esto no reza con este punto, pues su comercio fué el primero que comprendió sus ventajas, como lo prueba la compra de giros, figurando esta localidad, según estadística por la Sección de asuntos insulares del Ministerio de la Guerra de Washington de Diciembre de 1901, en tercera clase en esta Provincia, y que en regla de proporción, por sus habitantes y riquezas le corresponde figurar en segnnda clase.

"Pero desde Diciembre á la fecha observo una baja muy respetable en la venta de Giros en esta Oficina, y mi deber era investigar en el comercio cual era la causa.

"Me dijeron los comerciantes: "Hemos pedido al Director General que nos estableciera la oficina postal porque comprendíamos sus ventajas. El Director otorgó nuestra petición y nosotros cumplimos nuestra palabra. Pero en las actuales circunstancias salimos muy perjudicados. Nuestras cuentas con el comercio de la Habana siguen siendo en Oro Español. El centén vale $4.78 Oro Americano, y el comerciante al hacer la inversión á Oro Español nos da, según cotización mercantil, una pérdida de bastante consideración. Si la administración hallare una forma que no tuvieramos esa depreciación, nosotros siempre haríamos nuestras operaciones por Giros Postales."

"Omito decirle á Vd. el parecer de los comerciantes cual sería la mejor forma para que desapareciera la causa y el comercio en general de la Isla se sirviera de Giros Postales, porque su ilustración no necesitaría de esos consejos."

AGENTES ESPECIALES.

El informe del Jefe de los Agentes Especiales resume las operaciones del servicio de inspección del Departamento. De este ramo depende en gran parte el sostenimiento de la disciplina oficial y de la marcha general y excelencia del servicio. Los agentes especiales instruyen á los administradores de correos, inspeccionan las cuentas, depuran las quejas de todas clases, y en los casos de grave irregularidad llevan á los delincuentes ante los Tribunales. Durante el semestre se llevaron á cabo 35 arrestos y 25 sentencias por varias ofensas postales, la mayor parte de naturaleza leve, como la utilización de sellos inutilizados. Este defecto inveterado ha sido corregido mucho de esa manera. No estaría de más hacer constar aquí el mérito de los jueces cubanos. La experiencia de este Departamento con los juzgados cubanos ha sido muy satisfactoria, en verdad, y de ninguna manera puede servir de testimonio la crítica distinta que á veces se oye, imputándoles inercia é indecisión. El procedimiento pudiera parecer irregular á uno que estuviera acostumbrado á otro sistema, pero el fin esencial es la justicia, y este fin se obtiene con la rapidez media y rectitud en semejantes casos en los Estados Unidos. Esta es, á toda costa la experiencia del Departamento de Correos.

Esto no se refiere al sistema del jurado de instrucción en los juzgados correccionales inferiores, de los cuales, como ya he tenido la oportunidad de informar anteriormente, ha sido enteramente mala nuestra experiencia.

Al presentar mi informe periódico del año fiscal de 1901, se confiaba en que los procesos basados en los fraudes generales en el Departamento de Correos, se concluirían y resolverían total-mente antes de finalizar el año, pero los acontecimientos han frustrado esas esperanzas. Sería inútilr epetir las diversas causas y períodos de demora. El Juzgado de Instrucción cerró el sumario el 30 de Setiembre. La causa preliminar fué abierta al escrutinio y participación de la defensa durante los muchos meses que ha estado pendiente. No obstante, se alegó, por último, falta de preparación y se le concedió extensión de tiempo á la defensa, más allá del período máximo reglamentario, hasta que terminó el año, dejando aún pendiente el juicio. Las continuas absorciones de tiempo al Departamento de Correos por la referida causa en diversas formas, no pueden especificarse ni apreciarse en la suma total de sueldos, pero representa alguna parte de la misma. Hasta el mes de Diciembre, á última hora, fuí llamado á instancias de la Defensa para producir una porción de constancias que muy bien podían haberse obtenido previamente durante el año que entonces concluía. Semejantes solicitudes de testimonios tenían que ser atendidas con preferencia, y al atenderlas se tenían que echar á un lado otros trabajos. Se hicieron muchos trabajos de traducción. Todo vestigio de evidencia que pedían, era suministrado hasta donde podía encontrarse en los archivos del Departamento.

Pueden encontrarse informes estadísticos completos en los adjuntos informes de los diferentes jefes de negociados del Departamento. En resumen, se crée que los asuntos del Departamento están en condiciones sanas, y firmemente establecidos sobre una base de buen éxito permanente.

Muy respetuosamente,

M. C. Fosnes.

Director General.

Al Gobernador Militar.

Habana, Cuba.

OFICINA DEL HABILITADO.

Habana 12 de Marzo de 1902.

Al Director General,

Departamento de Correos.

SEÑOR:

En cumplimiento con sus instrucciones del 8 de los corrientes, tengo el honor de remitirle adjunto estados sobre los desembolsos hechos por cuenta del Servicio Postal de Cuba durante los seis meses que finalizaron en Diciembre 31 de 1901.

Para obtener el costo verdadero del servicio durante el período antes mencionado, sería necesario agregar al adjunto estado los pagos siguientes verificados durante el mes de Enero de 1902, por servicios, material, etc., facilitados durante el mes de Diciembre.

Sueldos, Departamento de Correos	$	599.98
,, Empleados en oficinas de Correos		1,161.30
,, Administradores de Correos		6,136.41
,, Railway Postal clerks		990.26
,, Carteros		1,481.24
Imprenta y Efectos de Escritorio		490.05
Alquiler de oficinas de correos		587.00
Alumbrado de oficinas de correos		278.07
Dietas		372.00
Premios de fianzas		510.00
Trasporte de correspondencia		3,095.54
Cuños de oficina y gomígrafos		31.75
Construcciones y reparaciones		49.73
Contratistas de rutas de caballo		2,327.65
Mensajeros de correos		234.58
Misceláneas		1,668.91
	$	20,014.47
Cantidad que aparece en el estado		180,688.41
Gastos verdaderos por cuenta de los seis meses	$	200,702.88

Desde Agosto último esta oficina ha estado encargada de las remesas de giros postales hechos á los Estados Unidos, que se han verificado en la forma siguiente:

Agosto	$ 141,591.40
Septiembre	65,000.00
Octubre	45,000.00
Noviembre	90,000.00
Diciembre	80,000.00
	$ 421,591.40

Muy respetuosamente,

GEO R. BUCHANAN,

Habilitado del Departamento de Correos de Cuba.

AÑO FISCAL DE 1900.

PRIMERA PARTE, HACIENDA.—SEGUNDA PARTE, SERVICIO POSTAL.

	Julio.	Agosto.	Septiembre.	Octubre.	TOTAL.
Ingresos:					
Saldo existente en caja según el último informe	29.31				29.31
Recibido del Tesoro de Cuba	32.00		226.13		258.13
Total	61.31		226.13		287.44
Egresos:					
Sueldos de Administradores de Correos			30.18	185.44	215.62
Misceláneas		32.00		20.00	52 00
Depositado, Tesorero de Cuba		16.06		3.76	19 82
Total		48.06	30.18	209.20	287 44

AÑO FISCAL DE 1901.

PRIMERA PARTE, HACIENDA.—SEGUNDA PARTE, SERVICIO POSTAL.

	JULIO.	AGOSTO.	SEPTIEMBRE.	OCTUBRE.	NOVIEMBRE.	DICIEMBRE.	TOTAL.
Ingresos:							
Saldo en caja, según el último informe	$ 1,795.13						$ 1,795.13
Recibido del Tesorero de Cuba			$ 2,008.13		$ 35.00		2,043.13
Total	$ 1.795.13		$ 2,008.13		$ 35.00		$ 3,838.26
Egresos:							
Sueldos:							
Departamento de Correos		$ 124.27					$ 124.27
Administradores	$ 16.60	102.67	$ 129.14		$ 54.93		303.34
Empleados en Oficinas de Correos			31.11				31.11
Imprenta y efectos de escritorio			181.32	$ 447,39			628.71
Alquiler de oficinas de correos			48.00				48.00
Alumbrado de oficinas de correos		18.70			18.00		36.70
Dieta		116.00					116.00
Premios de fianzas	15.00						15.00
Transporte de correspondencia			917.47	45.00	50.00		1,012.47
Construcciones y reparaciones		10.00	7.40				17.40
Cuños de oficinas	15.57						15.57
Misceláneas		6.50	151.27	31,07	35.00		223.84
Total	$ 47.17	$ 378.14	$ 1,465.71	$ 523.46	$ 157.93		$ 2,572.41
Depositado, Tesorero de Cuba		$ 1,030.02				$ 170.81	1,200.83
Saldo á la cuenta de Enero							65.02
Total	$ 47.17	$ 1,408.16	$ 1,465.71	$ 523.46	$ 157.93	$ 170.81	$ 3,838.26

AÑO FISCAL DE 1902.

PARTE PRIMERA, HACIENDA.—PARTE SEGUNDA, SERVICIO POSTAL.

	JULIO.	AGOSTO.	SEPTIEMBRE.	OCTUBRE.	NOVIEMBRE.	DICIEMBRE.	TOTAL.
Ingresos:							
Tesorero de Cuba	$ 36,426.67	$ 36,154.79	$ 35,236.33	$ 34,806.33	$ 32,392.51	$ 32,330.30	$207,346.93
Total	$ 36,426.67	$ 36,154.79	$ 35,236.33	$ 34,806.33	$ 32,392.51	$ 32,330.30	$207,346.93
Egresos:							
Sueldos:							
Departamento de Correos	$ 4,258.20	$ 4,824,31	$ 4,103.76	$ 4,782.08	$ 4,681.55	$ 4,361.55	$ 27,011.45
Administradores de Correos	291.66	7,221.53	7,507.65	7,356.05	7,647.07	8,354.77	38,378.73
Empleados en oficinas de Correos	4,447.55	5,796.50	5,703,48	5,563.50	6,202.82	6,373.15	34,087.00
Railway Postal Clerks	699.92	1,715.16	1,698.33	1,656.96	1,814.07	1,726.84	9,311.28
Carteros	3,283.15	5,173.80	5,192.09	5,111.67	4,927.67	5,219.76	28,908.08
Imprenta y Efectos de Escritorio		369.80	332.54	1,222.73	833.19	907.20	3,665.46
Alquiler de oficinas de Correos		326.00	303.00	503.00	418.00	358.00	1,908.00
Alumbrado de oficinas de Correos		330.41	207.75	192.35	227.32	214.36	1,172.19
Dieta		460.00	248.00	720.00	600.00	360.00	2,388.00
Premios de fianzas		260.00					260.00
Transporte de correspondencia		2,928.59	3,133.38	3,138.95	3,236.69	3,080.00	15,517.61
Cuños de oficinas y gomígrafos		41.12	12.25	17.31		14.02	84.70
Construcciones y reparaciones	54.00	95 30	69.32	108.70	67.15	84.59	479.06
Contratistas de rutas de caballo		2,284.65	2,360.81	2,297.88	2,385.98	2,342.65	11,671.97
Mensajeros de Correos		421.90	419-15	415 81	409.15	528.72	2,194.73
Equipo		20.00		27.50			47.50
Balanzas de cartas y romanas				45.00			45.00
Buzones de calle				146.25			146.25
Carros pr.ª el trasporte de correspondencia				16.00			16.00
Trasporte					3.21		3.21
Miscélanea	250.83	750.66	670.10	522.93	666.93	530.74	3,392.19
Total	$ 13,285.31	$ 33,019.73	$ 31,961.61	$ 33,844.61	$ 34,120.80	$ 34,456.35	$180,688.41
Depositado, Tesorero de Cuba		1,012.50	1,012.50			854.25	2,879.25
Saldo á la cuenta de Enero							23,779.27
	$ 13,285.31	34,032.23	$ 32,974.11	$ 33,844.61	$ 34,120.80	$ 35,310.60	$207,346.93

RESUMEN.

	AÑO FISCAL 1900.	AÑO FISCAL 1901.	AÑO FISCAL 1902.	TOTAL.
Saldos	$ 29.31	$ 1,795.13	....	$ 1,824.44
Recibido del Tesorero de Cuba	258,13	2,043.13	$ 207,346,93	209,648.19
TOTAL	$ 287.44	$ 3,838.26	$ 207,346.93	$ 211,472.63
Egresos	$ 267.62	$ 2,572.41	$ 180,688.41	$ 183,528.44
Depositado en la Tesorería de Cuba	19.82	1,200.83	2,879.25	4,099.90
Saldo á cuenta de Enero	....	65.02	23,779.27	23,844.29
TOTAL	$ 287.44	$ 3,838.26	$ 207,346.93	$ 211,472.63

INFORME

DEL

NEGOCIADO DE SELLOS Y MATERIALES,

DEPARTAMENTO DE CORREOS DE CUBA.

DEPARTAMENTO DE CORREOS DE CUBA,

NEGOCIADO DE SELLOS Y MATERIALES.

Habana 18 de Marzo de 1902.

Sr. M. C. Fosnes,

Director General,

Departamento de Correos.

SR.

Tengo el honor de presentar á Vd. un informe de las operaciones y del conjunto de los negocios verificados por esta oficina y por medio de ella, que comprende el semestre que finalizó en 31 de Diciembre de 1901; acompañado de una breve nota acerca de la propiedad del Departamento de Correos, sin incluir el papel timbrado.

El estado A. demuestra las clases diversas de papel timbrado y la cantidad y valor del mismo suministrado por esta oficina á las diferentes administraciones de correos de la Isla durante el semestre que finalizó el 31 de Diciembre de 1901.

El estado B. es un resúmen que demuestra el valor de la cantidad total en existencia el 1º de Julio de 1901; el valor total suministrado y el saldo en existencia el 31 de Diciembre de 1901.

El estado C. demuestra la cantidad de sobres oficiales de todos tamaños suministrados durante el mismo período, y lo que por ellos ha abonado este Departamento.

No se ha dado cuenta del mobiliario, utensilios, etc., para oficinas, correspondientes á época anterior al 31 de Diciembre de 1901. A principios de Enero de 1902 se remitió un estado completo al Contador de Cuba de toda la propiedad insular cargada al Departamento de Correos, la mayor parte de la cual está esparcida en las distintas oficinas de correos de la Isla. Este informe comprende las propiedades públicas compradas con fondos insulares desde la inauguración del Departamento de Correos de Cuba. Los informes de las propiedades anteriores donde quiera que estas se encuentran están en los archivos de esta oficina y en los archivos del Contador de la Isla de Cuba existe un informe de propiedad corriente.

Respetuosamente,

GEO. W. MARSHALL,

Jefe del Negociado de Sellos y Materiales.

BA.

ERIALES.

semestre de Julio 1º al 31 de Diciembre de 1901.

	POSTALES.	Fajas para periódicos.		SELLOS DE TASA.				VALOR.
	2 cents.	1 cent.	2 cents	1 cent.	2 cents.	5 cents.	10 cents	
Jul	125	1,100	500	2,550	2,550	1,000	500	$ 32,146.45
Ag	1.005	750	....	2.822	1,582	1,000	500	24,991.95
Se	1,100	1.500	....	2,150	2,250	....	....	22,937.29
Oc	....	2,650	200	4.050	3,155	1,200	800	34,026.98
No	515	500	....	2,225	3,075	20	310	26,187.95
Di	100	1,100	500	5,144	4,025	300	800	34,131.36
	2,845	7,600	1,200	18,941	16,637	3,520	2,910	$174,421.98

ESTADO DEMOSTRATIVO DEL VALOR DE I

DEL 1º I

1.—Importe de sellos de correo, sobres sellad
envolturas de periódicos y tarjetas p
tales existentes el 1º de Julio de 1901..

2.—Importe de papeles sellados recibidos
Director General de correos desde el
Julio de 1901 hasta el 31 de Diciem
de 1901.........................

TOTAL.........................

ESTADO "B"

Estado demostrativo del valor de papeles sellados existentes, recibidos y expedidos durante el semestre del 1º de Julio de 1901 al 31 de Diciembre de 1901.

	Pesos.	Cts.		Pesos.	Cts.
1.—Importe de sellos de correo, sobres sellados, envolturas de periódicos y tarjetas postales existentes el 1º de Julio de 1901......	149,431	80	A.—Importe de papeles sellados remitidos á los administradores de correos desde el 1º de Julio de 1901 hasta el 31 de Diciembre de 1901......	174,421	98
2.—Importe de papeles sellados recibidos del Director General de correos desde el 1º Julio de 1901 hasta el 31 de Diciembre de 1901......	170,638	30	B.—Importe de papeles sellados existentes en 31 de Diciembre de 1901, demostrado por enumeración de los mismos......	145,648	12
Total......	320,070	10	Total......	320,070	10

ESTADO "C"

Estado demostrativo de la cantidad y costo de sobres oficiales suministrados durante el semestre desde julio 1º a 31 de diciembre de 1901.

No. 7..	34,783	$ 77.99
No. 10........	202,392	605.15
No. 11.....	18,214	63.57
No. 14	1,500	5.85
Tamaños irregulares......	20,125	97.85
Total..................	277,014	$ 850.41

INFORME

DEL

NEGOCIADO DE NOMBRAMIENTOS Y DE TRASPORTES,

DEPARTAMENTO DE CORREOS DE CUBA.

DEPARTAMENTO DE CORREOS DE CUBA,

NEGOCIADO DE NOMBRAMIENTOS Y DE TRASPORTES,

Habana, 25 de Marzo de 1902.

Sr. Director General de Correos de Cuba,

Departamento de Correos.

SEÑOR:

Tengo el honor de presentar el informe de las operaciones verificadas en el Negociado de Nombramientos y de Trasportes, desde el 1º de Julio de 1901 hasta el 31 de Diciembre del mismo año inclusive.

De Vd. atentamente,

ALBERT J. XANTEN,

Jefe del Negociado de Nombramientos y de Trasportes.

31 de Diciembre de 1901.

NUMERO DE ADMINISTRACIONES DE CORREOS QUE FUNCIONAN EN ESTA FECHA.

PROVINCIA.	NUMERO.
Habana	62
Matanzas	51
Pinar del Río	41
Puerto Príncipe	12
Santa Clara	95
Santiago de Cuba	41
TOTAL	302

Del número que antecede, 31 son Administraciones en que se presta el servicio de Libre Porteo y en las cuales se emplean 113 Carteros.

Número de Administraciones de Correos funcionando en 30 de Junio de 1901		300
Número de Administraciones de Correos esblecidas del 1º de Julio al 31 de Diciembre de 1901	13	

Número de Administraciones de Correos suprimidas desde el 1º de Julio hasta el 31 de Diciembre de 1901	11	2
Número de Administraciones de Correos funcionando en 31 de Diciembre de 1901........		302

NUMERO DE EMPLEADOS EN EL SERVICIO.

EMPLEADOS.	Cubanos.	Americanos.	TOTAL.
Administradores de Correos......	300	2	302
Empleados en las Administraciones de Correos..................	246	9	255
Empleados en la Dirección General	18	22	40
"R. P. Clerk"..............	42	....	42
Total	606	33	639

Administradores, empleados en las Administraciones, empleados en la Dirección General, "R. P. Clerks"...	639
Agregando el número de empleados que prestan servicio bajo contrato, obtenemos el resultado siguiente:	
Contratistas de Postas....................................	67
Mensajeros de Correos y de Traspasos.	12
Total general de empleados en 31 de Diciembre de 1901.	718

ALTAS Y BAJAS EN EL SERVICIO.

Del 1º de Julio al 31 de Diciembre de 1901.

	Altas.	*Bajas.*
Emplados en la Dirección General.............	1	4
Administradores de Correos............	39	37
Otros empleados	33	45
Total...........	73	86

GASTOS ANUALES POR CONCEPTO DE SUELDOS

31 de Diciembre de 1901.

Dirección General de Correos..............	$ 56,260
Administradores de Correos.........	89,855
Empleados en las Administraciones de Correos.........	73,710
Carteros	57,690
Mensajeros, Conserjes, etc	7,838
"Railway Postal Clerks"......	20,504
Total......	$ 305,857

CONCESIONES.—DIVERSOS CONCEPTOS.

1º de Julio al 31 de Diciembre de 1901.

Número.	*Cantidad.*
60	$ 2,129.64

CONCESIONES ANUALES ESTIPULADAS.

Oficinas.	*Cantidad.*
23	$ 8,030.95

CONCESIONES ANUALES ESTIPULADAS QUE SE HAN SUPRIMIDO.

Oficinas.	*Cantidad.*
3	$ 394.20

INSTANCIAS PARA PUESTOS EN EL SERVICIO.

Desde 1º de Julio hasta el 31 de Diciembre de 1901.

Cubanos........	67
Americanos.......	5
Total	72

Informes de Agentes Especiales tomados en cuenta é iniciados desde el 1º de Julio al 31 de Diciembre de 1901	58
Casos que se han trasladado á los Agentes Especiales desde el 1º de Julio al 31 de Diciembre de 1901.........	146

FIANZAS.

Fianzas vigentes en 30 de Enero de 1901:

Empleados de la Dirección General.......	7	$ 45,000		
Administradores de Correos.	175	306,900		
Empleados en las Administraciones de Correos........	84	137,500	266	$ 489,400

Fianzas emitidas desde el 1º de Julio al 31 de Diciembre de 1901:

Empleados de la Dirección General.....	1	$ 2,000		
Administradores de Correos.	39	59,700		
Empleados en las Administraciones de Correos........	21	52,000	61	$ 113,700
			327	$ 603,100

Fianzas canceladas desde el 1º de Julio al 31 de Diciembre de 1901. (Incluyendo fianzas personales caducadas):

Empleados de la Dirección General....	.....	....		
Administradores de Correos.	33	$ 52,900		
Empleados en las Administraciones de Correos........	31	77,500	64	$ 130,400
			263	$ 472,700

RESUMEN.

Fianzas vigentes en 30 de Junio y que han sido prestadasp or Compañías del giro........... ...					154	$ 358,700
Fianzas prestadas por Compañías del giro desde el 1º de Julio al 31 de Diciembre de 1901........			25	$ 64,000		
Canceladas			46	109,500	21	$ 45,500
Fianzas prestadas por Compañías del giro vigentes en 31 de Diciembre de 1901...			.....	....	133	$ 313,200
Fianzas personales vigentes en 30 de Junio de 1901. ..			112	$ 130,700		
Fianzas personales emitidas en 1º de Julio de 1901 hasta el 31 de Diciembre de 1901........................			36	49,700		
Caducadas del 1º de Julio al 31 de Diciembre de 1901......	18	$ 20,900	18	28,800	130	159,500
	...	....	.. ..	....	263	$ 472,700

De las 130 fianzas personales vigentes en 31 de Diciembre de 1901, 45 corresponden á Administradores de Correos en Oficinas de Giros Postales.

Diciembre 31 de 1901:

SERVICIO GENERAL DEL TRASPORTE DE LA CORRESPONDENCIA.

	No.	*Longitud*	*Costo anual.*
Postas	67	1469.74	$ 27,693.00
Rutas de vapores	12	2845.25	26,910.00
Rutas de ferrocarril.........	31	1097.51	5,244.00
Trasporte de correspondencia por carros	3	14.64	4,950.00

Trasporte por mensajeros de correspondencia	9	5.88	1,556.00
Total de rutas...... ..	122	5433.02	$ 66,353.00
Líneas de Oficinas de F. C............	26	1889.20	....
Conductores de Correos de F. C.....	42	....	20,504.00
Total del costo de Servicio Interior..			$ 86,857.00
Servicio de correspondencia extranjera..			3,983.31
			$ 90,840.31

RESUMEN DE TODAS LAS CLASES DE RUTAS POSTALES.

Número de todas las rutas, 122.
Longitud de todas las rutas, 5433.02 millas.
Costo anual de las mismas, $66,353.00.
Número de millas recorridas al año, 1,691,929.00 millas.
Costo por milla, $12.21.
Costo por milla recorrida, 3.922 centavos.

COMPARACION CON EL SERVICIO QUE FUNCIONABA

EN 30 DE JUNIO DE 1901.

Aumento en el número de rutas, 4.
Disminución en la longitud de las rutas, 130.28 millas.
Disminución en el costo anual, $11,125.00.
Aumento en millas recorridas al año, 7066. millas.
Disminución del costo por milla recorrida, .674 de un centavo.
Disminución en el costo por milla, 1.72 centavos.

SERVICIO DE POSTAS.

Número de rutas, 67.
Longitud de las rutas, 1469.74 millas.
Recorrido anual, 389,908 millas.
Costo anual, $27,693.00.
Promedio del número de viajes por semana, 5.3.
Costo por milla, 18.84.
Costo por milla recorrida, 7.1 centavos.

COMPARACION CON EL SERVICIO EN 30 DE JUNIO DE 1901.

Aumento en el número de rutas, 3.
Aumento en la longitud de las rutas, 103 millas.
Aumento en el costo anual, $59.00.
Aumento en el recorrido anual, 11,648 millas.
Disminución en el costo por milla, $1.38.
Aumento en el promedio de número de viajes por semana, .06 de un viaje.
Diminución en el costo por milla recorrida, .21 de centavo.

POR PROVINCIAS.

PROVINCIA.	Número de rutas.	Millas.	Costo anual.	Costo por milla.	Recorrido anual.	Costo por milla recorrida.
Habana	9	110.87	$ 3,301	29.78	58,838	5.61 cts.
Pinar del Río	16	264.87	6,903	26.06	96,577	7.15 ,,
Matanzas	4	30.	966	32.20	10,400	9.289 ,,
Santa Clara	20	303.	6,953	22.95	122,200	5.69 ,,
Puerto Príncipe	5	290.	3,100	10.07	37,856	8.189 ,,
Santiago de Cuba	13	471.	6,470	13.74	64,037	10.103 ,,
Total	67	1469.74	$ 27,693	18.842	389,908	7.102 cts.

AUMENTOS, DISMINUCIONES Y CAMBIOS.

Número de nuevas rutas establecidas	4	
Número de rutas suprimidas (por fusión de la 5004 con la 5003)	1	
Un aumento neto de	3 rutas.	
Aumento de recorrido, nuevas rutas	98 millas.	
Aumento de recorrido á consecuencia de servicio adicional en antiguas rutas, Nº 1009)	6	
	104 millas.	
Disminución en el recorrido á consecuencia de nuevos arreglos en la ruta Núm. 6005	1	
	103	
Costo del servicio en 30 de Junio de 1901		$27,634
Disminución por nuevos contratos en rutas antiguas	$ 205	
Disminución por haberse fusionado la ruta 5004 con la 5003	900	
Disminución total	$1,105	1,105
		$26,529
Aumento en el costo á consecuencia de nuevos contratos		1,164
		$27,693

ARREGLOS QUE SE HAN HECHO PARA EL SIGUIENTE SERVICIO DE POSTAS QUE SE PRESTABA DESPUÈS DEL 31 DE DICIEMBRE DE 1901.

Número de rutas, 67.
Longitud de las rutas, millas, 1,469.74.
Costo por año, $27,693.00.
Aumento en el número de rutas, 3 más de las que había en 30 de Junio de 1901.
Aumento en el recorrido, 103 millas.
Aumento en el costo anual, $59.00.

SERVICIO DE VAPORES.

Número de rutas, 12.
Longitud de las rutas, millas, 2,845.25.
Costo anual, $26,910.00.
Costo por milla, 9.46.
Recorrido anual, 302,337.
Costo por milla recorrida, 8.9 centavos.

COMPARACIÓN CON EL SERVICIO QUE FUNCIONABA EN 30 DE JUNIO DE 1901.

Disminución en el número de rutas, 1.
,, en la longitud de las rutas, millas, 242.
.. en el costo anual, $11,700.
en el costo por milla $3.05.
en el recorrido anual 25,168.
,, en el costo por milla recorrida, 2.88.

ARREGLO QUE SE HA HECHO PARA EL SIGUIENTE SERVICIO DE VAPORES QUE SE HA DE LLEVAR Á EFECTO DESPUÉS DEL 31 DE DICIEMBRE DE 1901.

Número de rutas, 12.
Longitud de las rutas, millas, 2,845.25-
Costo anual, 26,910.00.

COMPARACIÓN CON EL 30 DE JUNIO DE 1901.

Disminución en el número de rutas, 1.
,, en el recorrido, 242.
en el costo, $11,700.00.

PORMENORES DEL SERVICIO DE VAPORES.

Funcionando del 1º de Julio al 31 de Diciembre de 1901.

Ruta.	TERMINALES.	CONTRATISTAS.	Compensación anual.	Millas.	Viajes.
1	De la Habana á Stgo..	Sobrinos de Herrera..	12,000	840.00	3 al mes.
2	De Batabanó á Stgo...	Menéndez y Comp.....	9,000	614.46	1 por semana.
3	De Batabanó á Nueva Gerona....................	Angel G. Ceballos......	600	92.00	1 por semana.
4	De Stgo. á Caimanera.	Gallego, Mesa y Cop.	1,000	45.00	2 por semana.
5	De la Habana á Nuevitas..........................	Alonso, Jauma y Cop.	300	409.00	1 por semana.
6	De Cienfuegos á Tunas de Zaza....................	José Castro Monje.....	300	82.08	2 por semana.
7	De la Habana á la Fé..	A. del Collado...........	1,200	227.49	4 al mes.
10	De Cienfuegos á Rodas.	Boullón y Comp........	360	30.00	7 por semana.
11	De Batabanó á Manzanillo......................	Alonso, Jauma y Cop.	200	425.22	2 al mes.
12	De Mayarí á Pto. Mayarí.........................	Carlota Grau............	600	15.00	1 por semana.
13	De Manzanillo á Niquero.........................	José Muñiz................	1,200	51.00	7 por semana.
15	De Cienfuegos á Belmonte.......................	E. Atkins y Comp......	150	14.00	2 por semana.
			26,910	2845.25	

SERVICIO DE FERROCARRILES.

Número de Rutas de Ferrocarril, 31.
Longitud de las Rutas de Ferrocarril, 1,097.51
Recorrido Anual, 980,852 millas.
Costo Anual, $' ^44.

COMPARACI DEL SERVICIO EN 30 JUNIO DE 1901.

Disminución en el número de Rutas, (128) 1.
Aumento en el número de Rutas, (132) 1.
Aumento en el recorrido, 5.5 millas.
Aumento en el recorrido anual, 38,762.20 millas.
Costo Anual, no ha habido cambio.

SERVICIO DE TRASPORTE DE CORRESPONDENCIA POR CARROS.

Número de Rutas, 3.
Longitud de las Rutas, 14.64 millas.
Millas recorridas al año, 24,430.
Costo anual, $4,950.
Costo por milla, $338.11.
Costo por milla recorrida, 20.27 centavos.
En 30 de Junio de 1901 no hubo cambio en el servicio.

SERVICIO DE MENSAJERO DE CORREOS.

Número de Rutas, 9.
Longitud de las Rutas, millas, 5.88.
Costo anual, $1,556.
Costo por milla, 364.63.
Recorrido Anual, 7,971.02.
Costo por milla recorrida, 19.6 centavos.

COMPARACIÓN CON EL 30 DE JUNIO DE 1901.

Aumento en el número de Rutas, 2.
Aumento en el número de millas, 3.22.
Aumento en el Costo Anual, $516.00.
Disminución en el costo por milla, 26.35.
Aumento en el recorrido anual, millas, 4,133.62.
Disminución en el costo por milla recorrida, 7.5 centavos.

SERVICIO DE CORREOS POR FERROCARRIL.

Número de líneas, 26.
Número de conductores, 42.
Millas de extensión en el servicio de Correos de F. C. 1,889.20.
Recorrido anual de los conductores, 1,139,140.51.
Sueldo total de los conductores, $20,504.00.
Promedio del sueldo de los conductores, $488.19 al año.

CONPARACIÓN CON EL 30 DE JUNIO DE 1901.

Disminución en el número de líneas, 1.
Disminución en el número de conductores, 1.
Disminución en las millas del servicio, 41.86.
Aumento en el recorrido anual de los conductores, 7,981.14.
Aumento en el sueldo total de los conductores, $220.00.
Aumento en el promedio de los sueldos de los conductores, $6.23

MULTAS.

Multas á Contratistas de Vapores.............	$ 78.31
Multas á contratistas de postas...............	2.44

NOTA.—Además de las multas, ascendentes á $78.31 impuestas á los Contratistas de Vapores, también se impuso una multa de $11.54 á la Ruta de Vapores número 3, Contratista Angel G. Ceballos, por no haber prestado servicio desde el 23 al 27 de Noviembre inclusive, á consecuencia de haber sido declarado inútil (condenado) el vapor "Nuevo Cubano." Los comprobantes para el pago por los servicios correspondientes á ese mes no se han presentado (no obstante haberse rogado al contratista que los remitiese) y la multa citada queda cargada en la cuenta del contratista contra el sueldo del mes que se le adeuda.

ESTADO DE GASTOS ANUALES,

POR DESPACHOS DE LA CORRESPONDENCIA EXTRANJERA.

Cantidad pagada por despachos directos á paises extranjeros.......	$ 3,983.31
Cantidad de correspondencia despachada á paises extranjeros, cuyo pago se hizo á razón de 44 centavos por libra por las cartas y tarjetas postales, y á 4½ centavos por la libra de otros artículos.	
Cartas y tarjetas postales, 7,278.52 lbs.....	$ 3,202.55
Otros artículos, 17,350.01 ,, ...	780.76
	$ 3,983.31

NOTA.—La cantidad que se adeuda según las Reglas de la Unión Postal Universal á paises extranjeros (Por tránsito marítimo y territorial) no se ha incluido en este informe porque no se han recibido los estados de las cantidades que se deben correspondientes al año que terminó en 31 de Diciembre de 1901, en el momento de concluir el presente informe.

OFICINAS DE CORREOS DE FERROCARRIL QUE FUNCIONABAN EN 31 DE DICIEMBRE DE 1901.

Nombre de la Línea.	Longitud.	No. de conductores	Sueldo.	Recorrido anual.	Apartados para correspondencia
Caib. Cam. y Placetas....	32.93	1	$ 400	24,038.90	1
Caibarién y Placetas.......	22.31	1	400	16,286.30	1
Cárdenas y Santa Clara.	105.53	3	1,600	91,224.39	3
Cárdenas y Yaguaramas.	71.16	1	500	51,946.80	1
Cienfuegos y Cartagena,					
Por vapor 30 millas....	....	......	....	21,900.00	
Por ferrocarril 20 id...	50.00	......	540	7,520.00	1
Cienfuegos y Santa Clara.	42.81	2	1,000	62,502.60	1
Cienfuegos y Tunas, (por Vapor)................	82.08	1	240	15,583.80	
Gibara y Holguín	20.00	1	384	6,480.00	1
Habana y Alacranes.......	81.20	4	2,000	118,389.60	5
Habana, Batabanó y Santiago	....	2	1,200	....	3
Por F. C. 36.24 millas	....	......	....	3,805.20	
Por vapor 614.46 id....	650.70	......	....	64,518.30	
Habana y Guanajay.......	35.63	2	1,000	51,806.02	1
Habana y Jovellanos......	88.70	4	2,000	104,154.75	4
Habana y Marianao.......	10.00	1	500	19,460.00	
Habana y Pinar del Río..	110.00	3	1,500	112,690.10	3
Isabela y Caibarién.........	69.29	2	1,000	50,581.70	1
Isabela y Cienfuegos.......	68.37	2	1,000	64,999.40	2
Júcaro y Morón	42.30	1	400	27,452.70	
Macagua y Altamisal.....	20.20	1	400	14,746.00	1
Madruga, Empalme y Güines	25.88	1	420	31,728.88	1
Manzanillo y Niquero, Por vapor..................	51.00	1	480	26,112.00	escritorio
Matanzas y Colón	70.00	1	600	51,100.00	1
Navajas y Murga...........	30.00	1	400	21,900.00	1
Nuevitas y Pto. Príncipe	45.63	1	400	24,092.64	1
Palmira y Rodas............	18.36	1	420	26,834.80	1
Sancti-Spíritus y Tunas.	24.47	1	500	10,203.99	1
Santiago y San Luis.......	20.63	2	1,020	17,081.64	1
Oficinas, 26.	1,889.20	42	$ 20,504	1,139,140.51	36

Total de Oficinas de Ferrocarril...		26
Total de millas............................		1,889.20
Total de R. P. C...........................		42
Sueldo de los conductores............	$	20,504.00
Recorrido anual en ferrocarril.......		1.011,026.41
Id. id. en vapores		128,114.10
Total...............		1,139,140.51

CLASIFICACIONES

DE LOS SUELDOS DE LOS "RAILWAY POSTAL CLERKS."

Nº	Sueldo.	TOTAL.
8	$ 600.00	$ 4,800.00
1	540.00	540.00
20	500.00	10,000.00
1	480.00	480.00
3	420.00	1,260.00
7	400.00	2,800.00
1	384.00	384.00
1	240.00	240.00
42	....	$ 20,504.00

Promedio de sueldo por empleados, $488.19.

CORRESPOLDENCIA MANIPULADA EN LAS LINEAS R. P O. DEL 1º DE JULIO, AL 31 DE DICIEMBRE DE 1901.

LINEAS.	Conductores.	Viajes.	Paquetes de cartas.	Sacos de periódicos.	Paquetes certificados.	Balijas certificadas.	Cajas certificadas.	Sacos interiores.
Caibarién, Camarones y Placetas	1	368	4,308	339	695			
Caibarién y Placetas	1	368	3,457	217	1,279			
Cárdenas y Sta. Clara	3	736	16,660	1,357	8,241	1,828	81	4
Cárdenas y Yaguaramas	1	368	10,493	604	2,276	....	1	1
Cienfuegos y Cartagena	1	592	3,704	1,118	895			
Cienfuegos y Santa Clara	2	736	7,146	851	1,816			
Cienfuegos y Tunas	1	76	....	....	1,402			
Gibara y Holguín	1	169	534	156	1,417			
Habana y Alagranes	4	736	22,008	1,168	5,881			
Habana, Batabanó y Santiago	2	52	10,014	2,221	3,113	360	4	1
Habana y Jovellanos	4	736	25,933	1,651	7,876	2,536	72	5
Habana y Guanajay	2	736	14,563	667	2,302	....	3	1
Habana y Marianao	1	1,000	4,267	461	281	....	....	684
Habana y P. del Río	3	736	15,486	895	4,024	368	16	
Isabela y Caibarién	2	368	6,737	1,061	4,259	368		
Isabela y Cienfuegos	2	736	7,280	1,525	6,178	1,115	2	
Júcaro y Morón	1	436	2,265	686	1,270			
Macagua y Altamisal	1	368	2,961	322	1,343			
Madruga, Empalme y Güines	1	736	3,503	314	480			
Manzanillo y Niquero	1	245	1,693	....	295			
Matanzas y Colón	1	368	12,800	937	2,830			
Navajas y Murga	1	368	4,141	341	493			
Nuevitas y Pto. Príncipe	1	262	229	46	1,279	133	7	
Palmira y Rodas	1	480	3,113	480	154	....	2	
Sancti Spíritus y Tunas	1	214	1,127	....	1,351			
Santiago y San Luis	2	630	5,796	338	1,533	10	2	
Total	42	12,620	190,218	17,735	62,963	6,718	190	696

ERRORES EN LA DISTRIBUCION.

DEL 1º DE JULIO AL 31 DE DICIEMBRE DE 1901.

	Oficina.	*R.P.O.*	*Total.*
Piezas de correspondencia ordinaria ..	2,179	319	2,498
Paquetes de cartas mal encaminados...	31	7	38
Paquetes de cartas mal rotulados.... ..	24	1	25
Sacos de periódicos mal encaminados...	1	4	5
Sacos de periódicos mal rotulados......	10	....	10
Balijas de cartas mal rotuladas.........	1	....	....
Paquetes certificados mal encaminados.	1	....	....

INFORME

DEL

NEGOCIADO DE GIROS POSTALES Y DE CERTIFICADOS.

DEPARTAMENTO DE CORREOS DE CUBA.

DEPARTAMENTO DE CORREOS DE CUBA.

NEGOCIADO DE GIROS POSTALES Y DE CERTIFICADOS.

Habana 1º de Abril de 1902.

Hon. M. C. Fosnes,

Director General de Correos de Cuba,

Habana.

SEÑOR.

Tengo el honor de presentarle para su conocimiento el siguiente informe de las operaciones de Giros Postales y de Certificados verificadas en laIsla de Cuba durante los seis meses que terminaron en 31 de Diciembre de 1901:

SISTEMA DE GIROS POSTALES.

TRIMESTRE QUE TERMINÓ EL 30 DE SEPTIEMBRE DE 1901.

	Número.	*Importe.*
Giros Postales expedidos para la Isla.	14,725	$524,580.39
,, ,, ,, para el Extranjero	10,101	288,432.22
Total.........	24,826	$813,012.61

Derechos en los Giros expedidos para la Isla......	$ 2,083.48
,, ,, ,, ,, ,, para el Extranjero	1,229.18
Total.............. ...	$ 3,312.66

	Número.	*Importe.*
Giros para la Isla que se han pagado	14,217	$518,133.31
,, ,, el Extranjero ,, ,, ,, ,,	1,394	42,138.67
Total................	15,611	$560,271.98

	Número.	*Importe.*
Giros Postales que se han reembolsado	89	$ 2,341.71

TRIMESTRE QUE TERMINÓ EL 31 DE DICIEMBRE DE 1901.

	Número.	Importe.
Giros postales expedidos para la Isla.......	14,365	$ 481,498.46
,, ,, ,, para el extranjero....................	12,431	282,734.55
Total.............	26,796	$ 764,233.01
Derechos en los Giros expedidos para la Isla......		$ 1,958.57
Derechos en los Giros expedidos para el extranjero.		1,292.41
Total.........		$ 3,250.98

	Número.	Importe.
Giros para la Isla que se han pagado........	12,952	$ 472,979.99
Giros para el extranjero que se han pagado	1,803	52,633.53
Total	14,755	$ 525,613.52

	Número.	Importe.
Giros Postales que se han reembolsado.....	107	2,349.40

OPERACIONES DURANTE LOS SEIS MESES QUE TERMINARON EL 31 DE DICIEMBRE DE 1901.

	Número.	Importe.
Giros postales expedidos para la Isla........	29,090	$ 1.006,078.85
Giros postales expedidos para el Extranjero	22,532	571,166.77
Total.................	51,622	$ 1,577,245.62
Derechos en los Giros expedidos para la Isla..		$ 4,042.05
Derechos en los Giros expedidos para el extranjero..............		2.521.59
Total........		$ 6,563.64

	Número.	Importe.
Giros para la Isla que se han pagado......	27,169	$ 991,113.30
Giros para el extranjero que se han pagado.........	3,197	94,772.20
Total.........	30,366	$ 1,085,885.50

	Número.	Importe.
Giros postales que se han reembolsado.....	196	$ 4,691.11

SISTEMA DE CERTIFICADOS

TRIMESTRE QUE TERMINÓ EL 30 DE SEPTIEMBRE DE 1901.

Número de cartas que se han certificado para la Isla.....	20,691
,, ,, paquetes que se han certificado para la Isla..	2,853
,, ,, cartas que se han certificado para el extranjero............	19,192
Número de paquetes que se han certificado para el extranjero............	2,115
Número total de cartas que se han certificado abonando el derecho............	44,851
Número de artículos certificados grátis............	6,544
Total de artículos certificados........	51,395
Cantidad que se ha cobrado por derechos de certificación............	$ 3,588.08

TRIMESTRE QUE TERMINÓ EL 31 DE DICIEMBRE DE 1901.

Número de cartas que se han certificado para la Isla...	20,516
,, ,, paquetes ,, ,, ,, ,, ,, ,, ,, ...	2,655
,, ,, cartas ,, ,, ,, ,, para el Extranjero	19,901
,, ,, paquetes ,, ,, ,, ,, ,, ,, ,,	3,678
Número total de cartas que se han certificado abonando el derecho............	46,750
Número de artículos certificados grátis............	11,285
Total de artículos certificados	58,035
Cantidad que se ha cobrado por derechos de certificación	$3,740.00

OPERACIONES VERIFICADAS DURANTE LOS SEIS MESES QUE TERMINARON EL 31 DE DICIEMBRE DE 1901.

Número de cartas que se han certificado para la Isla...	41,207
,, ,, paquetes ,, ,, ,, ,, ,, ,, ,, ...	5,508
,, ,, cartas ,, ,, ,, ,, para el Extranjero	39,093
,, ,, paquetes ,, ,, ,, ,, ,, ,, ,,	5,793
Número total de artículos que se han certificado abonando el derecho............	91.601
Número de artículos certificados grátis	17,829
Total de artículos certificados........	109,430
Cantidad que se ha pagado por derechos de certificación..	$7,328,08

De Vd. con la mayor consideración,

C. L. Marine,

Jefe del Negociado de Giros Postales y Certificados.

INFORME

DE LA

OFICINA DE AGENTES ESPECIALES

DEL

DEPARTAMENTO DE CORREOS DE CUBA.

DEPARTAMENTO DE CORREOS DE CUBA.

OFICINA DE AGENTES ESPECIALES.

Marzo 17 de 1902.

Al Honorable Director General,

Habana, Cuba.

Señor:

Tengo el honor de someter á su consideración un estado demostrativo del trabajo hecho por la Oficina de Agentes Especiales por el semestre que terminó en Diciembre 31, de 1902.

Muy respetuosamente,

F. M. Hamilton,

Agente Especial en Jefe.

RELACION de casos tratados durante el semestre que terminó en Diciembre 31 de 1901.

	CASOS TERMINADOS Y REABIERTOS.										
	A	B			C			F			TOTAL.
	Regular.	Regular.	Reabierto.	Total.	Regular.	Reabierto.	Total.	Regular.	Reabierto.	Total.	
Casos pendientes, Julio 1, 1901	18	16	1	17	125	17	142	593	....	593	770
Casos formados durante el semestre	56	106	....	106	654	7	661	1,491	1	1,492	2,315
Total	74	122	1	123	779	24	803	2,084	1	2,085	3,085
Casos cerrados durante el semestre	53	99	....	99	528	17	545	1,512	1	1,513	2,210
De casos cerrados por Oficina	40	70	....	70	13	12	25	1,465	....	1,465	1,601
De casos cerrados por Agentes	12	28	....	28	515	5	520	47	1	48	609
Casos pendientes, Enero 1, 1902	21	23	1	24	251	7	258	572	....	572	875

COLECCIONES.

De quien colectados	*Monda Americana.*	*Plata Española.*
Déficit en cuenta de giros postales de Administradores	$ 323.95	
Déficit en la cuenta postal de los Administradores	130.79	
Disposición ilegal de propiedad del Departamento	20.00	
Administración postal extranjera por mala entrega de carta certificada	4.60	
Robo de la correspondencia certificada	164.60	
Robo de la correspondencia ordinaria	112.40	
Violación de la Sección 35 del Código Postal	150.00	
Violación de la Sección 49 del Código Postal	4.78	
Violación de la Sección 52 del Código Postal	35.09	
Multa impuesta al cochero del carro postal, por no llegar á tiempo á conectar con el tren		$ 00.25
Cantidad total colectada	$ 946.21	$ 00.25

Desembolsos.	*Moneda Americana.*	*Plata Española.*
Depositado con el Tesorero de la Isla (Multas y Cuenta Postal)	$ 335.88	
Depositado con el Administrador de Correos de la Habana por Fondos de Giros Postales	403.95	
Pagado al destinatario de carta certificada robada	8.00	
Pagado al pagadero legal de un giro postal falsificado	4.78	
Reembolsado á empleado Postal de Ferrocarril por gasto en conducción correo al paradero del Ferrocarril		$ 00.25
Total	$ 946.21	$ 00.25

ARRESTOS.

Casos pendientes en Tribunales en Julio 1º de 1902	24	
Arrestos durante el semestre terminado en Diciembre 31, 1901	38	
	—	62
Convicciones aseguradas	25	
Absoluciones	12	
	—	37
Casos pendientes en Tribunales en Enero 1, 1902		25

TITULOS DE CASOS "C" INVESTIGADOS Y CERRADOS DURANTE EL SEMESTRE QUE TERMINÓ EN DICIEMBRE 31, 1901.

Establecimiento de Administraciones y Estaciones Postales.	14
Establecimiento del Sistema de Giros Postales en Administraciones........	4
Nombramientos de Administradores de Correos	18
Instrucción de Administradores de Correos............	38
Contratos y traslados de Administraciones de Correos.......	2
Reparaciones, concesiones y material para Administraciones	12
Reajuste de sueldos y gastos en Administraciones...........	20
Inspección de Administraciones........	140
Reajuste de las cuentas de los Administradores	3
Materias misceláneas...	21
Servicios de Oficinas Postales de Ferrocarril, postas y de Mensageros de Correos	13
Quejas contra Administradores.................................. ..	17
Quejas contra Oficiales y otros empleados en el Servicio....	6
Quejas contra Carteros..........	6
Demoras alegadas en el despacho de correos.......	6
Violaciones alegadas.........	11
Pérdidas alegadas..	9
Quejas misceláneas contra el Servicio............................	5
Violación alegada de la Sección 8 del Código Postal.......	1
,, ,, ,, ,, ,, 11 ,, ,, ...	1
,, ,, ,, ,, ,, 12, 13, 14 ,, ,, ...	1
,, ,, ,, ,, ,, 19 ,, ,, ...	4
,, ,, ,, ,, ,, 23 ,, ,, ...	1
,, ,, ,, ,, ,, 25 ,, ,, ...	1
,, ,, ,, ,, ,, 27 ,, ,, ...	2
,, ,, ,, ,, ,, 35 ,, ,, ...	174
,, ,, ,, ,, ,, 41 ,, ,, ...	1
,, ,, ,, ,, ,, 42 ,, ,, ...	1
,, ,, ,, ,, ,, 45 ,, ,, ...	1
,, ,, ,, ,, ,, 49 ,, ,, ...	1
,, ,, ,, ,, ,, 52 ,, ,, ...	6
,, ,, ,, ,, ,, 60 ,, ,, ...	3
Quejas misceláneas contra personas que no están en el Servicio	1
Incendio en Administración de Correos..	1
	545

INFORME

DE LA

OFICINA DE CARTAS MUERTAS

DEL

DEPARTAMENTO DE CORREOS DE CUBA.

HABANA, CUBA.

ESTADO DEMOSTRATIVO DEL RECIBO Y DISPOSICION DE TODA LA MATERIA POSTAL EN LA OFICINA DE CARTAS MUERTAS, DURANTE LOS SEIS MESES TRANSCURRIDOS DE JULIO 1º, A DICIEMBRE 31 DE 1901.

"RECIBIDA."

Cartas ordinarias domésticas no reclamadas......	23,393	
Cartas ordinarias domésticas faltas de franqueo. .	2,146	
Cartas ordinarias domésticas mal dirigidas.........	31	
Cartas ordinarias domésticas en blanco....	11	
Cartas ordinarias domésticas rehusadas............	2,086	
Impresos ordinarios no reclamados	13,606	
Impresos ordinarios domésticos rehusados..........	252	
Paquetes ordinarios domésticos no reclamados....	74	41,599
Cartas ordinarias domésticas devueltas del Extrangero.....	4,362	
Artículos é impresos ordinarios domésticos Extrangero.....	394	4,756
Cartas ordinarias del Extrangero no reclamadas..	15,251	
Cartas ordinarias del Extrangero rehusadas.......	728	
Artículos é impresos ordinarios del Extrangero...	30,304	
Impresos extrangeros ordinarios rehusados........	127	
Cartas ordinarias prohibidas Extranjeras.........	110	46,520
Cartas certificadas y paquetes no reclamados domésticos.....	403	
Cartas certificadas y paquetes no reclamados del Extrangero.....	1,344	1,747
Total..	94,622	94,622

DISPOSICION.

Materia doméstica.

Entregado á espedidores artículos certificados sin abrir.....	292	
Artículos certificados en espera entrega por Administrador.....	84	
Cartas ordinarias entregadas á espedidores sin abrir.....	3,156	3,532

Abiertas y entregadas á espedidores.

Cartas conteniendo giros postales............	7	
Cartas conteniendo dinero	11	
Cartas conteniendo materia miscelanea............	763	
Cartas conteniendo correspondencia.................	10,663	
Impresos..	234	
Paquetes..	85	11,763

Abiertas y archivadas.

Cartas conteniendo dinero	8	
Cartas abiertas y en espera de entrega por el Administrador	109	
Cartas abiertas conteniendo materia miscelanea..	278	
Certificados en archivo	96	
Paquetes ordinarios	26	517

Abiertas y destruídas

Cartas sin firma conteniendo correspondencia	16,408	
Impresos papel de desecho	14,573	30,981

Cartas y paquetes extranjeros.

Cartas y paquetes certificados enviados á su orígen	1,296	
Cartas y paquetes certificados entregados	48	
Cartas ordinarias enviadas á su orígen	15,825	
Artículos ordinarios entregados	310	
Artículos é impresos ordinarios enviados á su orígen	18,336	
Papel de desecho	12,049	47,864
Total	94,657	94,657

Cartas conteniendo dinero.	Número.	Cantidad.
Archivadas en la Oficina de cartas muertas	12	$ 5.72
Total	12	$ 5.72

Entregado al Sr. Charles Hernández, Administrador de Correos de la Habana todo el dinero que estaba en archivo en la Oficina de Cartas Muertas hasta la fecha de Noviembre 29 de 1901	$	4.60
Entregado al Sr. Charles Hernández, Administrador de Correos de la Habana el dinero que estaba depositado en la Oficina de Finanza durante Marzo de 1900, procedente de la Oficina de Cartas Muertas, y que fué devuelto á esta Oficina en esta fecha Noviembre 29 de 1901, por el Sr. G. W. Marshall, Jefe de la Oficina de sellos y materiales	$	41.53
Total		46.13

Respetuosamente presentado.

A. Arteaga.

Jefe de la Oficina de Cartas Muertas.

Al Hon. M. C. Fosnes.

Director General de Correos. Habana, Cuba.

INFORME

DE LA

OFICINA DE TRADUCCIONES

DEL

DEPARTAMENTO DE CORREOS DE CUBA.

DEPARTAMENTO DE CORREOS DE CUBA.

Marzo 29 de 1902.

Al Honorable

Director General de Correos de Cuba.

SEÑOR:

Nada de importancia, fuera de la rutina general, tengo que informar referente á la marcha de esta Oficina, excepto que el trabajo ha disminuido algo durante el último semestre, comparado con el mismo del pasado año.

Daré, por tanto, sólo un extracto de las traducciones hechas de Julio 1º, 1901 á Diciembre 31, 1901 inclusive, que es como sigue:

NUMERO DE TRADUCCIONES.

1901.	Cartas de Entrada.	Cartas de Salida.	Misceláneas.
Julio 31............	662	685	42
Agosto 31..........	484	587	58
Septiembre 30......	626	549	118
Octubre 31.	601	617	53
Noviembre 30......	512	566	101
Diciembre 31.....	464	463	63
Total.........	3,349	3,467	435

Haciendo un total de 7,251 traducciones que fueron hechas durante el periodo antes mencionado, dando un promedio mensual de 1,208, el cual comparado con el del último año que fué de 1,388, arroja una disminución mensual de 180 traducciones:

Debo elogiar el celo del personal de esta Oficina, que ha venido constantemente haciendo los mayores esfuerzos en producir un trabajo pronto y eficiente, y expreso una vez más mi gratitud á todos en el Departamento por su benévolo trato.

Respetuosamente.

R. VENCE,

Jefe de la Oficina de Traducción.

Lightning Source UK Ltd.
Milton Keynes UK
UKHW02f1933060418
320655UK00009B/265/P

9 780331 706260